African Sexualities

〰

A READER

Through the voices of the peoples of Africa and the global South, Pambazuka Press and Pambazuka News disseminate analysis and debate on the struggle for freedom and justice.

Pambazuka Press – www.pambazukapress.org

A Pan-African publisher of progressive books and DVDs on Africa and the global South that aim to stimulate discussion, analysis and engagement. Our publications address issues of human rights, social justice, advocacy, the politics of aid, development and international finance, women's rights, emerging powers and activism. They are primarily written by well-known African academics and activists. Most books are also available as ebooks.

Pambazuka News – www.pambazuka.org

The award-winning and influential electronic weekly newsletter providing a platform for progressive Pan-African perspectives on politics, development and global affairs. With more than 2,500 contributors across the continent and a readership of more than 660,000, Pambazuka News has become the indispensable source of authentic voices of Africa's social analysts and activists.

Pambazuka Press and Pambazuka News are published by Fahamu (www.fahamu.org)

African Sexualities

A READER

Edited by Sylvia Tamale

Pambazuka Press
An imprint of Fahamu

Published 2011 by Pambazuka Press, an imprint of Fahamu
Cape Town, Dakar, Nairobi and Oxford
www.pambazukapress.org www.fahamu.org www.pambazuka.org

Fahamu, 2nd floor, 51 Cornmarket Street, Oxford OX1 3HA, UK
Fahamu Kenya, PO Box 47158, 00100 GPO, Nairobi, Kenya
Fahamu Senegal, 9 Cité Sonatel 2, POB 25021, Dakar-Fann, Dakar, Senegal
Fahamu South Africa, c/o 19 Nerina Crescent, Fish Hoek, 7975 Cape Town, South Africa

British Library Cataloguing in Publication Data
A catalogue record for this book is available from the British Library

ISBN: 978-0-85749-016-2 paperback
ISBN: 978-0-85749-017-9 ebook – pdf
ISBN: 978-0-85749-014-8 ebook – epub
ISBN: 978-0-85749-015-5 ebook – Kindle

Printed in Istanbul, Turkey by Mega Print

Contents

Acknowledgements

Developing this Reader was an incredibly enriching and joyous experience. But it would have been impossible to complete the amazing 'learning journey' that it has been without the support and dedication of many individuals and agencies.

The enthusiastic response from all over the continent to the call for materials that I put out in February 2009 was both overwhelming and humbling. The standard of most submitted materials was extremely high, but constraints related to space and scope prevented many from being included. I am also deeply grateful to the many individuals and publishers who granted me permission to reprint copyrighted works.

The task of editing this volume was rendered less daunting and more bearable thanks to the following individuals: Chi-Chi Undie, Karim Tartoussieh, Chimara-oke Izugbara, Alex Ezeh and Harriet Birungi who helped conceive the shape and framework of the Reader; Stella Nyanzi, was extremely generous with her voluminous bank of knowledge, words, time and insight. Her ability to think creatively lent passion to this project and encouraged us to resourcefully go beyond the conventional limits; Jane Bennett, for her tireless support, intellectual generosity and sharp, witty humour; J. Oloka-Onyango, for constantly asking the 'so what' questions and encouraging me to be innovative; George Mpanga, for his editing skills; Carla Sutherland for encouraging me to take a path less travelled and for her critical role in bringing to life my dream of a Reader on African Sexualities; and the professional translators who translated various documents from Arabic, French and Portuguese.

I must acknowledge the inspiration, motivation and courage that I received over the years from colleagues and friends at the African Gender Institute—University of Cape Town, Women's Law Centre—University of Zimbabwe and the Institute of African Studies at the University of Ghana. Amina Mama, Julie Stewart and Takyi-waa Manuh, who respectively headed these transformative institutions, are particularly appreciated. Makerere University granted me full sabbatical leave for the academic year 2009–10, allowing me sufficient time to pursue this project, while the Law, Gender and Sexuality Research Project at Makerere's Faculty of Law lent me the necessary institutional support. Without the generous financial support of the Ford Foundation this book would not have come to fruition. Supplementary funds from the Norwegian Agency for Development (NORAD) were much appreciated.

The editors and production handlers at Pambazuka Press received and nurtured this project with enthusiasm and total dedication. Special thanks go to Firoze Manji, Shereen Karmali, Andrea Meeson and Judith Charlton, who exhibited meticulous professionalism in reviewing and pruning the final product.

Last, but by no means least, I wish to thank all the scholars and activists around the continent who, against all odds, have kept the fires of freedom, dignity and change burning. I sincerely hope this book will play its own small part in sharpening the critical thinking of its readers and nudging along the broader African struggle for social transformation.

Sylvia Tamale
Kampala, January 2011

 # Introduction

Sylvia Tamale

If Sexuality were a human being and she made a grand entrance (*l'entrée grande*) into the African Union conference centre, the honourable delegates would stand up and bow in honour. But the acknowledgement of and respect for Sexuality would no doubt be tinged with overtones of parody and irony, even sadness, because although Sexuality might represent notions of pleasure and the continuity of humanity itself, the term conjures up discussions about sources of oppression and violence. In fact, once Sexuality got to the podium and opened her mouth, the multiple complexities associated with her presence would echo around the conference room.

The *Reader on African Sexualities* (hereafter referred to as the Reader) intends to translate these echoes into comprehensible notions and concepts, carefully examining their different wavelengths and the terms of their power and laying bare the theoretical, political and historical aspects of African sexualities. The term 'African sexualities' immediately provokes the questions: who/what is African? What is sexuality? Who determines what qualifies as African sexualities? Among other things, the Reader attempts to address these deeply complex questions through the lenses of history, feminism, law, sociology, anthropology, spirituality, poetry, fiction, life stories, rhetoric, song, art and public health. In this way the Reader offers a rare opportunity to theorise sexuality through various modes. The idea is to deconstruct, debunk, expose, contextualise and problematise concepts associated with African sexualities in order to avoid essentialism, stereotyping and othering.

The material in this Reader has been carefully selected to surface the complexities associated with what has been pandered as African and the issues surrounding sexuality that have been taken for granted. One of the main challenges for contributors to the Reader was to refuse to perpetuate colonial reification of 'African' as a homogenous entity. Hence, the title's reference to African sexualities is not because we are unaware of the richness and diversity of African peoples' heritage and experiences. Jane Bennett's essay in Chapter 6 addresses this issue at great length.

Any reference to the term 'African' in this volume is used advisedly to highlight those aspects of cultural ideology – the ethos of community, solidarity and *ubuntu*[1] – that are widely shared among the vast majority of people within the geographical entity baptised 'Africa' by the colonial map-makers. More importantly, the term is used politically to call attention to some of the commonalities and shared historical legacies inscribed in cultures and sexualities within the region by forces such as colonialism, capitalism, imperialism, globalisation and fundamentalism. Even as these commonalities are proposed, however, readers will find them challenged.

Although diverse forces interrupted the shape of sexualities on the continent – redefining notions of morality, for example, and 'freezing' them into social and political spaces through both penal codification and complex alliances with political and religious authority – differences among continental spaces meant that such interruptions had diverse effects. Such forces further attempted to standardise global ideas about African sexualities, often erasing questions of diversities and complexities of sexual relations. As the material in Part 1 reveals, however, colonial methods of researching, theorising and engaging in sexualities in Africa left indelible and significant imprints on people's sexual lives.

This, however, is not to suggest that the continent became a hostage of its late colonial history. As the materials in this Reader clearly show, the continent is currently replete with vibrant movements, some seeking to reinforce sexual hegemonic powers and others challenging, subverting and resisting imposed modes of identity, morality and behaviour patterns. Some of the subversions have deep roots – Parts 2 and 3, titled 'Sexuality, power and politics' and 'Mapping sexual representations and practices of identity', respectively, offer expansions of these issues and excavate the political origins and social consequences of the politics of sexualities in Africa.

We speak of sexualities in the plural in recognition of the complex structures within which sexuality is constructed and in recognition of its pluralist articulations. The notion of a homogeneous, unchanging sexuality for all Africans is out of touch not only with the realities of lives, experiences, identities and relationships but also with current activism and scholarship. Ideas about and experiences of African sexualities are shaped and defined by issues such as colonialism, globalisation, patriarchy, gender, class, religion, age, law and culture. Because these phenomena are at play elsewhere in the world, and because of the various historical links that connect Africa to the rest of humankind, some theoretical and conceptual approaches that have informed sexualities studies elsewhere have relevance to the way writers think through questions of African sexualities.

Sexualities are often thought of as closely related to one of the most critical of biological processes, namely reproduction. But contemporary scholarship understands sexualities as socially constructed, in profound and troubling engagement with the biological, and therefore as heavily influenced by, and implicated within, social, cultural, political and economic forces. The study of sexualities therefore offers unending lessons about pleasure, creativity, subversion, violence, oppression and living. Attempts to define the term sexuality often end in frustration, and become in themselves exercises about writers' own orientations, prioritisations and passions. As Oliver Phillips reminds us:

> Sexuality can be defined by referring to a wide range of anatomical acts and physical behaviour involving one, two or more people. We can relate it to emotional expressions of love, intimacy and desire that can take an infinite variety of forms. Or it can be implicated in the reproduction of social structures and markers through rules and regulations that permit or prohibit specific relations and/or acts. In the end, it emerges that these definitions are far from exhaustive. None of them are adequate on their own but that when considered all

together they reflect the multiple ways that sexuality is manifest and impacts on our lives, and that above all; these definitions all consistently involve relations of power. (Phillips 2011: 285)

It is this question of power to which the materials in this Reader return time and again.

As a continent, Africa has made significant progress in creating the space at policy level for discussion of sexual and reproductive health and rights. Since the International Conference on Population and Development held in Cairo, Egypt in 1994, the African Union has adopted the Protocol on the Rights of Women in Africa (Maputo Protocol),[2] the Plan of Action on Sexual and Reproductive Health and Rights (Maputo Plan of Action),[3] and the Campaign on Accelerated Reduction of Maternal Mortality in Africa (CARMMA).[4] These continent-wide efforts have boosted the possibility of creating national policies on a wide variety of issues including gender-based violence, access to reproductive healthcare and a focus on sexualities education, among others.

Although these policies are numerous, missing are the theoretical and practical sparks to ignite the commitment required from both state and non-state actors to implement them. Moreover, studies have revealed the direct link between the delivery of sexual and reproductive health services and sustainable development (UN Millenium Project 2006). Part 5 of this volume addresses the latter, with the opening essay by Beth Maina Ahlberg and Asli Kulane clearly framing the link between sexual and reproductive rights and issues of development.

The law turns sexualities into a space through which instruments of state control and dominance can be deployed. For example, the criminal legal system in most African states attempts to regulate how, when and with whom we can have consensual sex. The offences of prostitution, abortion and adultery clearly curtail both women's and men's sexual autonomy (although as the Reader material suggests, it is women's autonomy that is most severely under threat), and the criminalisation of homosexuality affects both men and women who do not conform to the dominant ideology of heterosexuality. The material in Part 6, titled 'Sex and masculinities', demonstrates this very well.

Western scholars have thus far conducted the bulk of studies on sexualities and a big chunk of what has been published on the African continent emanates from South Africa.[5] This phenomenon has more to do with geopolitical power differentials than academic superiority. The dominance of Western theories and perspectives on sexuality studies and the fact that the main languages of academia are colonial have serious implications for rapidly growing sexualities scholarship on the continent. African feminists and other change agents are well aware of the dangers associated with the uncritical application of Western theories to non-Western contexts (Adomako Ampofo and Arnfred 2010). They constantly struggle to overcome the limitations and encumbrances that come with creating and disseminating cultural-specific knowledge in a foreign colonial language. They understand the capacity of language to confer power through naming and conveying meaning and nuance to sexuality concepts. Concepts such as silence, restraint, choice, gay, lesbian, coming out and drag queen, for example, all carry specific social meanings steeped in Western ideology and traditions.

It is worth reiterating the point made earlier: as researchers and theorists of sexualities we must always take great care not to fall into the homogenising trap. One of the salient points made by various authors in this volume is to avoid homogenising and essentialising people's sexualities (whether Africans, Europeans, Asians, Middle Eastern or Hispanics).

Although many writers often hold romanticised notions of pre-colonial African sexualities as having been unrestricted and unbridled, the facts are quite different. As in all social organisations, African societies historically involved the organisation of gender, sexuality and reproduction – the diverse shapes, fluidities, the visible and invisible, the spiritual and the political and economic dynamics of those societies – which resulted in certain restraints.

For instance, almost all societies on the continent would have treated sexual interaction with a child or between parent and offspring as abominations. Part 8 is titled 'Sexuality, spirituality and the supernatural', and provides a glimpse of some of the complexities that pervade African sexualities in light of traditional beliefs and practices.

In the context of a resurgence of cultural, religious and economic fundamentalist movements, feminists and gender activists on the continent have forged global alliances in the struggle for women's bodily integrity and sexual autonomy. After all, patterns of control seen in sexual and gender-based violence, marital rape, sex trafficking, teenage pregnancies, women's sexual pleasure and so forth bear no national, religious or cultural stamp. But as feminists across the continents increase their global political activism for women's reproductive health and sexual rights, so do they have to account more carefully for the differentials in culture and history.

So, although it is important to pay attention to the intersections among nations regarding gender inequality, it is crucial that the strategies employed by African feminists be informed by the lived experiences of women and men on the continent and the specificities of what they hold as their culture, taking into account that there is not always agreement among people in the same locale about the nuances and meanings of culture. Part 7, titled 'Who's having sex and who's not?', surfaces some of the most common stereotypes and prejudices about sexualities and the lived experiences of marginal groups in our societies.

Debates on sexual inequality represent the most fundamental challenge to struggles for global democracy. One of the biggest challenges of our times is how to confront the complexities of intersecting oppressions so that people identified as sexual minorities, for example sex workers, lesbians, gays, transgendered, intersexed, rape survivors and people living with HIV/AIDS, are able to stand with full status on the same podium such as those representing groups fighting dictatorships, corruption, social injustice, insecurity, discrimination against women, or people with disabilities. There are of course sexual minorities within each of these groups and often implicit among groups are concerns about sexualities. Until we close the gap between different voices demanding justice and equality, embracing the infinite possibilities of our sexual, social, economic and political beings, the African renaissance or the transformation that we are striving for will forever remain a mirage.

One important way of closing these gaps is by raising awareness through formal and informal education on sexualities. Part 9, titled 'Pedagogical approaches', demonstrates how this can be done in creative and effective ways.

How to use this Reader

The key objective of this Reader is to amplify the voices of Africans on the topic of sexualities. This is achieved through a critical mapping and unmapping of African sexualities.

The process of mapping is meant to inform readers about the plurality and complexities of African sexualities, including desires, practices, presentations, fantasies, identities, taboos, abuses, violations, stigmas, transgressions and sanctions. At the same time, it poses questions that challenge the reader to interrogate assumptions and hegemonic sexuality discourses, thereby unmapping the intricate and complex terrain of African sexualities. How is sexuality linked to gender and subordination? What is the 'Africanness' in sexualities? How has history shaped African sexualities? What explicit and implicit diversities exist within sexuality?

The Reader exposes the hidden or subtle lines that link the various aspects of our lives and sexualities. Such exposure facilitates our understanding of the negative and positive factors associated with the complex phenomenon of sexuality, including how it is instrumentalised, commodified and politicised, as well as its reproductive, pleasurable and empowering aspects.

Generally speaking, by the time we grow into adults many of us have done a great deal of learning, most of it rote (uncritical). Mechanical learning (cram, cram, cram, drill, drill, drill) is the norm for most of us as we move along the conveyor belt of examinations in post-colonial African education systems. The informal cultural systems of education that largely emphasise children's unquestioning obedience to adults do not help either. Both formal and informal education in the main promote learning in dualisms and absolute truths, such as right and wrong, good and bad, moral and immoral, inclusion and exclusion and male and female. These do little to foster reflective and critical thinking.

The end result is that our learning processes grossly neglect to instruct us in the important concept of unlearning. Without this skill, it is extremely difficult for us to think critically and to question unjust frameworks or challenge the established order. Most of us passively absorb the assumptions and perspectives of the dominant view and many of us have a visceral negative reaction to the concept of sexuality. Unlearning literally requires us to discard our old eyes and acquire a new set with which to see the world. It requires us to jettison assumptions and prejudices that are so deep-seated and internalised that they have become normal and appear to be natural.

The critical process of transformative learning requires us to apply our intellect, unlearn deeply entrenched behaviour patterns and beliefs and relearn new ones. It requires us to acquire the vital skills to critically analyse internalised oppression and complicity with patriarchy and capitalism. It further requires us to step out of our familiar comfort zones and enter the world of discomfort and anxiety associated with change. Such processes, which call for a reorganisation of the old, are always fraught with difficulty, disequilibrium and stress.

This Reader on African Sexualities calls on us to do exactly that. It challenges us to confront issues that society has clothed in taboos, inhibitions and silences, to unclothe them, quiz them and give them voice. It certainly requires us to unlearn

5

and relearn many things that we take for granted about sexualities and may well leave us confused, shocked, offended, embarrassed, scared and even a little excited. Many of us, for instance, will be baffled by the fact that issues of sexuality and desire, which are viewed as apolitical and private, are in fact steeped in politics and power relations. But such realisations are part of transformational learning and are reflections of our intellectual and political growth and our personal development.

To get maximum benefit from this Reader we need to pry our minds open to fresh ideas, absorb new knowledge and apply our intellect, knowledge and experience to develop a critical analysis of the issue at hand. Opening our minds means to accept differences, to see the world through the eyes of others, to open our ears to diverse viewpoints and to venture beyond our familiar horizons. To appreciate the Reader we have to tap deep into our inner resources of respect, empathy, tolerance, self-reflexivity and courage. We have to let our minds drift beyond the box, to see with our hands, hear with our skin and taste with our mind's eye.

The Reader is divided into nine thematic parts, each containing essays that introduce the reader to the main concepts as well as key issues and debates in the area, thus providing a solid framework for analysis, review of knowledge and transformative action. There is an inevitable overlap of issues across the parts, which serves as a constant reminder of the intertwining nature of sexualities in every aspect of our lives and the web-like political effects. The structured divisions are forced for conceptual neatness and reading convenience more than anything else. In addition to the essays, the Reader unconventionally carries a wide variety of genres including poetry, fiction, life stories, songs and diary entries. The range of writings is meant not only to connect readers to everyday, real-life sexual experiences, but also to stimulate creative, interesting and critical thinking about the inter-linkages between sexuality, power, rights, (under)development and various structures of inequality.

At the end of each thematic part, the reader will find a set of questions that acts as a guide for a systematic and critical approach to the key issues. Though this Reader attempts to use accessible language, analyses of African sexualities inevitably involve the use of complex and unfamiliar terms and concepts. For this reason, we have included a glossary at the end of book.

A final note concerns the authorship of the material. Almost all of the authors can be described as African writers, if the term African is understood as a geopolitical space. All of them can be termed African in the sense that the passion driving their research and writing comes from engagement with the idea that serious global knowledge creation requires that the lives, experiences, ideas and imagination of people throughout the continent be considered critically important.

The diversity of the authors defies categorisation: they are men, women, sex workers, intersexed and transgendered; they speak many languages and write, here, in English; they live in 16 of Africa's 54 countries and in the diaspora; they have experienced multiple African realities; they live their own sexualities across diverse possibilities of desire, attraction, family creation, political activism and identity. When working with this Reader, it is also important to recognise that many of the authors represented here are prolific and previously published writers in addition to a crop of fresh and exciting new scholarship.

Notes

1. The African philosophy of *ubuntu* (humaneness) refers to understanding diversity and the belief in a universal bond and sharing (Ramose 1999). Justice Yvonne Mokgoro of the South African Constitutional Court elaborated this difficult-to-translate concept:
   > In its most fundamental sense it translates as personhood and 'morality'. Metaphorically … [it describes] the significance of group solidarity on survival issues so central to the survival of communities. While it envelopes the key values of group solidarity, compassion, respect, human dignity, conformity to basic norms and collective unity, in its fundamental sense it denotes humanity and morality. Its spirit emphasizes a respect for human dignity, marking a shift from confrontation to conciliation. (Quoted in Sachs 2009: 106–107)
2. Adopted in 2003 and brought into force in 2005, the Maputo Protocol addresses the health and reproductive rights of African women in Article 14.
3. The Maputo Plan of Action was adopted in 2007 as a strategy to implement the continental policy framework for sexual and reproductive health and rights.
4. Launched in 2009, CARMMA was meant to speed up the process of implementing the Maputo Plan of Action.
5. These facts are clearly reflected by the dominance of Western theories as well as the over-representation of South African scholarship in this volume.

References

Adomako Ampofo, A. and Arnfred, S. (eds) (2010) *African Feminist Politics of Knowledge: Tensions, Challenges, Possibilities*, Uppsala, The Nordic Africa Institute

Phillips, Oliver (2011) 'Teaching sexuality and law in southern Africa: locating historical narratives and adopting appropriate conceptual frameworks', in Tsanga, A. and Stewart, J. (eds) *Women and Law: Innovative Approaches to Teaching, Research and Analysis*, Harare, Weaver Press

Ramose, M. (1999) *African Philosophy through Ubuntu*, Harare, Mond Books

Sachs, Albie (2009) *The Strange Alchemy of Life and Law*, London, Oxford University Press

United Nations Millennium Project (2006) *Public Choices, Private Decisions: Sexual and Reproductive Health and the Millennium Development Goals*, New York, UN Millenium Project

Part 1
Research, theory and methods

1

Researching and theorising sexualities in Africa[1]

Sylvia Tamale

Introduction

Researching human sexuality without looking at gender is like cooking pepper soup without pepper – it might look like pepper soup but one sip will make it clear that an essential ingredient in this Nigerian speciality is missing. The hot, tantalising taste that makes it real and only detectable by the sensitive tongue and palate is absent. In the same way, without a gendered analysis, the 'dish' of sexuality research simply cannot rise to the occasion. It is flat, empty and morose.

Sexuality and gender go hand in hand; both are creatures of culture and society, and both play a central and crucial role in maintaining power relations in our societies. They give each other shape and any scientific enquiry of the former immediately invokes the latter. Hence, gender provides the critical analytical lens through which any data on sexuality must logically be interpreted. Things that impact gender relations, for instance history, class, age, religion, race, ethnicity, culture, locality and disability, also influence the sexual lives of men and women. In other words, sexuality is deeply embedded in the meanings and interpretations of gender systems.

This truism, now taken for granted by African feminist scholars of sexuality, is by no means universal. Many researchers still view sexuality within the narrow spectrum of the sex act, and never investigate the extraneous factors that impact and shape our multifarious sexualities.

Several scholars caution against oversimplifying and essentialising the practice and discourse of sexualities in Africa, urging us to read their multiple and contextual meanings (Oinas and Arnfred 2009; Mama 2007; Helle-Valle 2004). Reference to sexuality in the plural does not simply point to the diverse forms of orientation, identity or status. It is a political call to conceptualise sexuality outside the normative social orders and frameworks that view it through binary oppositions and simplistic labels. In other words, thinking in terms of multiple sexualities is crucial to disperse the essentialism embedded in so much sexuality research.

The various dimensions of sexuality include sexual knowledge, beliefs, values, attitudes and behaviours, as well as procreation, sexual orientation, and personal and interpersonal sexual relations. Sexuality touches a wide range of other issues including pleasure, the human body, dress, self-esteem, gender identity, power and violence. It is an all-encompassing phenomenon that involves the human psyche, emotions, physical sensations, communication, creativity and ethics.

Given that sexuality is a deeply complex phenomenon, studies around it must be specialised to reflect its nuances, and its contextual and multilevelled nature. Because the topic of sexualities is often wrapped in silences, taboos and privacies, researchers need to hone distinctive techniques and methods that unearth invisible, silenced and repressed knowledge. Furthermore, because in Africa many acts associated with sexualities are criminalised or highly stigmatised, analysts need to tread the territory with care and sensitivity. Most importantly, researchers need to recognise that there is no uniform or monolithic way of experiencing sexualities within one culture or community, or even among individuals. Therefore, commencing from the premise of multiple sexualities provides a useful analytical tool for any study examining this subject matter.

It is also crucial to note that gender as a research variable is not a substitute for sex and cannot be taken for granted based on common sense knowledge about men and women. Nor can we make homogenised assumptions about African sexualities based on other intersecting factors, such as race, ethnicity, socio-economic status, age, religion and so forth. Almost every day we hear sexual stereotypes about individuals and groups of people. These, unfortunately, find their way into study projects, research designs and, ultimately, theory. Examples of such stereotypes include:

- Human beings engage in sex for reproductive purposes only.
- She is disabled and therefore has no sexual desire.
- He is a man and therefore desires only female sexual partners.
- He is a 45-year-old bachelor and therefore must be gay.
- She is menopausal and therefore asexual.
- She wears a religious veil and is therefore sexually submissive.
- She is wearing a dress and high heels and is therefore biologically a woman.
- He is openly gay and therefore his life is exclusively defined by the sex act.
- He is her father and therefore cannot have sex with his daughter.
- Sex workers are nymphomaniacs who cannot survive without sex.
- They are in a childless marriage and therefore she must be barren.
- Her hymen is intact and therefore she's a virgin.
- She is a feminist and is therefore sexually frustrated.
- Sexual activity that does not involve a penis or penetration is not real sex.
- Men naturally have more sexual libido than women.
- Black men have larger penises than white men.

The list goes on and on.

Another important point to note for knowledge production on African sexualities is the issue of language. The fact that the language of Western colonialists has dominated sexuality discourses means that the shape and construction of the meanings and definitions of related concepts necessarily reflect realities and experiences outside Africa. Foucault (1976) instructed us decades ago that it is through language and narratives that knowledge (and hence power) is produced. This poses serious limitations to researchers of African sexualities, who have to collect data in local languages and present their findings in the foreign language of the academy. Inevitably, rich cultural connotations and ambiguities (multiple meanings) are lost in translation.

A good example is the different meanings attached to the concept of silence. Though in the dominant Western tradition voice is valorised and silence constructed as a total blank, in many African cultures silence can be as powerful and as empowering as speech. For instance, studies have shown that there is a legitimate silence surrounding the sexualities of some African women, one that is ambiguous and not able to be engaged (Tamale 2005).

In this chapter, I retrace the key historical developments in researching and theorising sexualities in Africa. This helps us understand the present, the continuities and the changes. A historical analysis further illuminates some enduring assumptions and beliefs that underlie many of the studies and theories about African sexualities. Later, I discuss some pertinent issues about researching sexualities in an ethical, balanced and sensitive fashion. I conclude by looking at future prospects of researching sexualities in Africa.

Researching sexualities in Africa: a historical trajectory

Perhaps a good place to begin is to ask the question: why do we engage in research at all? There are probably as many answers to this question as there are types of researcher: a university lecturer might do it as a licence to academic titles and promotion; a policymaker does it to support and monitor policies; a company does it to improve its product and marketing, and so forth. But the primary and most important reason for conducting research is to create knowledge and explain physical and social phenomena.

So, for example, a sexuality-related research study would seek to increase our knowledge about numerous issues, including: how human beings relate sexually; what influences people's choices of whom they have sex with, how and when; how sexuality influences relationships, laws and policies; how sexualities are reflected in social norms, identities and attitudes; how intimate relationships are regulated and controlled; what causes sexually-transmitted diseases, and so forth. Sexuality theories are created through the research process that creates knowledge and provides explanations relating to various aspects of sexuality. How, where and by whom the data was collected are all critical in determining the usefulness and validity of such theories.

Nowhere were assumptions regarding the 'knower', the 'known' and the 'knowable' taken more for granted than in sexuality research conducted on colonised populations such as those found in Africa. In *Decolonising Methodologies*, Linda Tuhiwai Smith writes from the vantage point of a colonised indigenous Australian:

> The term 'research' is inextricably linked to European imperialism and colonialism. The word itself, 'research', is probably one of the dirtiest words in the

> indigenous world's vocabulary. When mentioned in many indigenous con-
> texts, it stirs up silence, it conjures up bad memories, it raises a smile that is
> knowing and distrustful. (Smith 1991: 1)

Generally speaking, research in the colonial context was conducted along a traditional hierarchy of power between the researcher and the researched. It was
almost always assumed that the researchers were all-knowing individuals and the
researched, naive 'subjects'. It was further presumed that only the former could
create legitimate, scholarly knowledge, usually through written reports and publications. There was often little or no acknowledgement of the role the researched
played in the process.

Examining these methodological and epistemological issues is extremely important to determine the legitimacy of the knowledge that has been constructed about
African sexualities. Thanks to methodologies such as Marxism, post-colonial theory,
feminist theory and post-structuralism, such hierarchical frameworks in research
have been challenged and deconstructed.

As in all research, studies on sexualities have been motivated by ideological,
political and/or social agendas. In Africa, the majority of these studies have been
programmatically and/or donor-driven (Arnfred 2004; Undie and Benaya 2006).
The hypotheses, research questions, research methods and analysis techniques are
heavily influenced by these agendas. I demonstrate this by further framing the discussion so that it more or less follows the historical sequence that has informed
sexuality research on the continent. Each sub-theme addresses the overall objective of the research, the players, the target audience and the methods, funders and
agendas involved.

Sexuality and the colonising project

A great deal of rich information about African sexualities lies in ancient histories
that live through griots, *ighyuwas, imbongies, jelis, igawens, guewels*[2] and other orators
around the continent. Historical accounts of African sexualities are alive in folklore,
traditional songs, dance, folk art, body markings, clothing, jewellery, names and
naming systems. Yet these systems of knowledge are denigrated in the theoretical
and normative domains of mainstream research. In fact they have been 'reclassified
as oral traditions rather than histories' (Smith 1999: 33).

Perhaps the earliest written records of studies on African sexualities were those
archived from colonial explorers and missionaries who traversed the continent in
the latter half of the 19th century.[3] During this period of imperial expansion and
colonisation, African bodies and sexualities became focal points for justifying and
legitimising the fundamental objectives of colonialism: to civilise the barbarian and
savage natives of the 'dark continent' (McClintock 1995; Young 1995). These colonial expeditions were financed by the imperial governments of Britain, Germany,
France, Portugal, Spain and Italy and private companies, such as the Imperial
British East Africa Company.

Texts from 19th century reports authored by white explorers and missionaries reveal a clear pattern of the ethnocentric and racist construction of African sexualities. Western imperialist caricatures of African sexualities were part of a wider design to colonise and exploit the black race. Narratives equated black sexuality with primitiveness. Not only were African sexualities depicted as primitive, exotic and bordering on nymphomania (Geshekter 1995; Mama 1996; Magubane 2001; Osha 2004), but also it was perceived as immoral, bestial and lascivious. Africans were caricatured as having lustful dispositions. Their sexualities were read directly into their physical attributes; these attributes were believed to reflect the (im)morality of Africans (Gilman 1985; Commons 1993). The imperialists executed this mission through force, brutality, paternalism, arrogance, insensitivity and humiliation.

The bodies of African women especially worked to buttress and apologise for the colonial project (Commons 1993). They were fundamental to the consolidation of the imperialist empire. Juxtaposed with the imported and highly conservative sexual norms of Europe, the sexualities of Africans, which were relatively unrestrained, posed huge challenges to the Victorian minds of the early explorers.[4] Indeed, Victorian women were expected to mute their sexuality and be sexually frigid (Wolf 1991). Their dress, behaviour and mores were geared to erasing any hint of sexuality. Women who acted otherwise would immediately be branded prostitutes or courtesans (Rees 1977).

African women's sexualities, however, were characterised as the antithesis of European mores of sex and beauty and were labelled primitive. The 1860s travel memoirs of English explorer Sir Richard Burton, for example, described the women that he encountered in the kingdom of Dahomey (present day Benin) as 'hideous' and 'taken in adultery or too shrewish to live with their husbands'. He described their physical appearance as male-like: 'muscular development of the frame … femininity could be detected only by the bosom' (quoted in Blair 2010: 98). Other myths and stereotypes of African female sexualities included that: 'African women could give birth without pain'; 'Negro women menstruated in greater quantity'; 'Negro women had long and pendulous breasts as an inherited physical trait' (Curtin 1964: 229).

Clearly, the depictions by Europeans of African women as insatiable, amoral, barbaric beings said more about the fears, fantasies and preoccupations with sexuality of the former than anything else. Leah Commons says of Western fixation with African women's sexualities:

> Rather than being a characteristic of African cultures, sexual obsession was a reflection of the repressed sexuality of the British. By describing the African as a lascivious beast, the Victorians could distance themselves from the 'savage', while indulging in forbidden fantasies. More importantly, by laying the blame for lust on women alone, colonisers made themselves blameless for their own sexual relations with African women. (Commons 1993: 4)

Many Western anthropologists who followed the explorers in the early 20th century picked up from where the latter stopped and continued (mis)representing African sexualities as exotic and backward. Indeed, several scholars have carefully studied and critiqued historical documents and scholarship that are deeply flawed in their presentations of African sexualities, portrayed in racist, patronising and morally normative ways (Owusu 1978; Lyons and Lyons 2004; Epprecht 2006, 2010).

Religion, especially Christianity and Islam, stressed the impurity and inherent sin associated with women's bodies (Goodson 1991). Through religion and its proselytising activities, Africans were encouraged to reject their previous beliefs and values and to adopt the 'civilised ways' of the whites. With these new developments came the emphasis on covering and hiding body parts.[5] Indeed, one of the most effective methods of controlling African women's sexuality has been through the regulation of their dress codes. Perhaps the most notorious post-colonial cases on the continent in this regard were the draconian laws on women's dressing sanctioned by dictators Kamuzu Banda of Malawi and Idi Amin of Uganda.[6] A new script, steeped in the Victorian moralistic, antisexual and body-shame edicts, was inscribed on the bodies of African women and with it an elaborate system of control.

The instrumentalisation of sexuality through the nib of statutory, customary and religious law is closely related to women's oppression and gender constructions. Unfortunately, the colonial legacies of African sexualities linger today and we see them in contemporary accounts and theories, as the ensuing discussion will show (see also Magubane 2001).

Medicalised sexuality and reproductive health

The baseline of sexuality research in the field of public health in Africa lies in the colonial medicalisation of African sexuality and a simultaneous reduction of its purpose to reproduction (Vaughan 1991; Musisi 2002). The positivist approach that treats people as objects and is preoccupied with reductionist representations of complex processes dominates studies in this area. The 'scientific' prejudices about women's bodies and their reproductive role that had been witnessed in Europe during the period of enlightenment was imported to Africa. The seminal works of philosophers such as Thomas Kuhn (1962), who analysed the history of science, and Michel Foucault (1976), who articulated the use of the body as a medium of social control and the socialisation of reproduction, were significant in unveiling the role of science and sexuality in constructing and perpetuating social power relations.

The main focuses of public health researchers during the colonial era were disease, pregnancy prevention and curbing sexual excesses and perversions. The narrow approach meant that the research by biomedicals, epidemiologists and demographers ignored (and still does in the main) sexual wellness and issues of eroticism and desire, leading to limited theoretical framings of African sexualities (Undie and Benaya 2006).

In the late 1960s and early 1970s there was panic about population explosion, spearheaded by demographers in the global North and focused particularly on developing countries (Ehrlich 1968; Hardin 1968). Researchers flocked to the continent to study the sexual behaviours of Africans in relation to fertility. Images of oversexed, promiscuous, less moral and less intelligent Africans were never far from the minds of demographers and other researchers interested in studies of fertility control.

Unfortunately, some African researchers bought into the imperialist overpopulation discourse and in the process reinforced racist ideologies and stereotypes. Indeed, this was a period in which great numbers of the African intelligentsia had not decolonised their minds to explore new frontiers of knowledge production. The process of consciousness decolonisation involves critical thinking, unpacking common sense knowledge and a radical reconceptualisation of dominant ideologies (Mamdani 1972; Kibirige 1997).

With the global onslaught of HIV/AIDS and Africa as its epicentre, more researchers from the North flocked to the continent in a bid to find ways of curbing its spread, and in the process engendered a profound re-medicalisation of African sexualities. Policies had to be formulated, national frameworks established, advocacy programmes drawn up and sexuality theories revisited and reconceptualised. The bulk of these were quantitative and epidemiological, largely ignoring the qualitative socio-economic aspects of the epidemic. The World Health Organisation (WHO), bilateral partners, international NGOs, pharmaceutical corporations and Western medical and health professionals competed with each other to tackle this uncharted territory. Their different agendas informed the strategies and meanings that they attached to the epidemic.

The dominant discourses reinforced the epidemiology and stigma of HIV/AIDS (Treichler 1999). The colonial stereotyped images of a specific African sexuality – insatiable, alien and deviant – to this day inform Western discourses in this area of research. Dilger observes:

> [A]part from rampant fantasies about prostitution and the red-light districts stretching from Nairobi to Johannesburg and Dakar, the European/North American discourse on sexuality and AIDS in Africa has been fed by images of an enforced, exotic and often violent sexuality said to prevail on the continent: polygyny, female genital mutilation, and especially the (gang) rapes of women and babies in South Africa have made sexual violence and child rape the main issues for international media reports on AIDS in Africa. (Dilger 2008: 125)

An excellent example of the essentialist approach, the totalising perspective and colonising representations adopted in research on African sexualities is the oft-cited study undertaken by demographers John Caldwell, Pat Caldwell and Pat Quiggin (1989). Their study, which sought to analyse the social context of AIDS in sub-Saharan Africa, developed a theory that African sexuality (an essentialist singularity for Caldwell et al) is inherently permissive, concluding that such immorality in the sexual behaviour of Africans spells doom in the context of the HIV/AIDS pandemic on the continent. Both the conceptual framework and conclusions of the Caldwell study have been subjects of a polemic, stirring up great controversy and criticism in contemporary sexuality scholarship (see Le Blanc et al 1991; Ahlberg 1994; Savage and Tchombe 1994; Heald 1999; Arnfred 2004). Nevertheless, their work made abundantly clear the weaknesses in colonial approaches to research on African sexualities and symbolised a watershed moment for reconstructing theory on the subject matter (Undie and Benaya 2006).

Research in the area of reproductive health on the continent has a long and chequered history. Because reproduction was viewed as the role par excellence for women in heteropatriarchal societies, it became the primary definer of their sexuality. The earliest studies followed the biomedical model, focusing on maternal and child health and divorced from the gendered aspects of epidemiology, access, decision making and health management systems.

The driving force behind most of these studies was to curb the high fertility rates that were typical of 'traditional' African families and to forge policies that would reduce these rates and put Africa on the road to modernity. Reproductive health was viewed within the confines of the heterosexual family and women similarly reduced to their conventional mothering roles.

The overriding theory developed from this research established a causal link between overpopulation and underdevelopment. The essay on reproductive health and sexual rights by Ahlberg and Kulane in Part 5 elaborates how quantitative research methods, such as KAP (knowledge, attitude and practice) surveys associated with the biomedical model, resulted in skewed findings, suspect theories and faulty policies about African women's reproductive health and sexuality.

During the 1990s, reproductive health in sub-Saharan Africa became a subject of particular interest to development partners, who directed significant funds to set up research centres and institutes, many of which continued to apply the biomedical model. These new entities were to complement old-school non-governmental organisations, such as the International Planned Parenthood Federation Africa Region. The African Population and Health Research Centre set up in 1995 in Nairobi, Kenya and the Africa Regional Sexuality Resource Centre established in Lagos, Nigeria in 2003 were only two examples. The fact that the activities of the latter organisation focused on Africa's most populous countries (Egypt, Kenya, Nigeria and South Africa) spoke volumes about its primary mandate, suggesting that population control was on its agenda. It must nevertheless be noted that, despite the shortcomings associated with donor-driven initiatives such as these, some African scholars and researchers working within these institutions have reinterpreted and reinvigorated their mandates and goals to shift primary attention to the critical needs of the local communities.

Another important aspect of research relating to medicalised sexualities in capitalist conditions reveals the desire of outsiders to explore and discover traditional herbs and plants related to sexuality. Often herbal formulas that are part of the traditional knowledge nurtured by generations of indigenous populations are appropriated, patented and licensed in Western countries for their exclusive enrichment. Many African communities, for example, have keen historical knowledge of local herbs that enhance sexual desire in males and females as well as those that cure erectile dysfunctions (Tamale 2005; Wane 2000).

Multinational pharmaceutical and agrichemical companies, keen to exploit such indigenous knowledge, are the key funders of research in the fields of ethnopharmacology and ethnomedicine. Publications such as the *Journal of Ethnopharmacology* share information on indigenous people's use of plants, fungi, animals, micro-organisms and minerals and their biological and pharmacological effects. The phenomenal success and profitability of drugs such as Viagra are the direct outcome of such exploitative ventures.

Sexual cultures and violence

Beginning with the first contact with African communities, researchers from the global North maintained a voyeuristic, ethnopornographic obsession with what they perceived as exotic (read perverse) African sexual cultures. In the same way that the early European explorers, funded by their imperialist states, laid claim to a plethora of geographical and natural resources on the African continent, they set out with equal zeal to explore and study the sexual artefacts and traditions of Africans. African cultures and sexualities were always framed as different, less urbane and inferior to those of the West. This othering process was, and still is, important in justifying racist and imperialist policies.[7]

The standard approach was to view these sexual cultures as primitive, bizarre and dangerous and apply a knee-jerk reflex to 'fix' them. 'Africanists' from various departments of social anthropology and cultural history in North America and Western Europe took particular interest in African cultural practices related to polygyny, circumcision, levirate, sexual cleansing rituals, dry sex and so forth (Raum 1939). The studies were typically juxtaposed with idealised Judaeo-Christian standards of sexuality and clearly reflected in the insensitive clichés used to define various practices such as widow inheritance, wife purchase, wife exchange and the ubiquitous bride price.

The late 1970s and 1980s saw a flurry of research activity on sexual violence with a special spotlight on female circumcision or female genital mutilation (FGM). The graphic depictions of this maimed African sexuality, published by the American journalist Fran Hosken (1980), set the stage for fervent action by Western researchers. In particular, the circumcision of African women became an obsession of social anthropologists and women's rights advocates from the global North. The inordinate attention that women's rights advocates from the North paid to this issue was reminiscent of the imperialist, colonial project. They flocked to the continent with the zeal of missionaries to save African women from this barbaric practice (Oloka-Onyango and Tamale 1995). Such zeal is evident in this passage taken from an early volume of the influential American feminist journal, *Signs*:

> Fran Hosken has … proposed a human rights/health action initiative to organise technical and financial assistance for African women's organisations requesting such support and to establish international cooperation and joint actions with women in the West. Anyone interested in further information should write to Fran Hosken, 187 Grant Street, Lexington, Massachusetts. (Copies of The Hosken Report are available from the same address). Fran Hosken's work is extremely important in bringing the issue of female genital mutilation to public attention. It would be useful if her book, suitably edited, could be republished by a commercial press and widely distributed. (Fee 1980: 809)

The bulk of approaches to the subject matter are culturally insensitive, focus narrowly on the negative aspects of female circumcision and completely overlook the multifaceted nature of the practice and the meanings attached to the rituals associated with it (Nnaemeka 2005). Although African feminists do not condone the negative aspects of the practice, they take strong exception to the imperialist, racist and dehumanising infantilisation of African women.

The destructive approaches to this cultural practice perpetuated '... staples of the canon of racist clichés about Africa, particularly ideas about barbarity, perpetual female victimhood, and the refusal of enlightenment and modernity' (Kaler 2009: 178–9). Indeed, the latest manifestation of such approaches can be seen in the attempts by a US-based organisation called Clitoraid to collect money (since 2006), under the banner of its racist 'Adopt a Clitoris' campaign[8] and purportedly for surgically restoring the clitorises of African women who have undergone FGM.

Same-sex relationships within African communities also attracted the attention of early anthropologists. The tendency was to uncritically apply standard Western research indicators and assumptions, which often resulted in skewed results. When anthropologist Jane Kendall (1998) arrived in Lesotho in the early 1990s searching for lesbian woman, she had a rude awakening: she encountered Basotho women who engaged in erotic woman-to-woman relationships, but these were not analogous to lesbianism or homosexuality as known in North America or Western Europe. Kendall had to put aside the theoretical and empirical assumptions about same-sex erotics that she had been exposed to in her native United States and be instructed in the novel concepts and meanings of the woman-to-woman (*batsoalle*) relationships of the Basotho (see also Gay 1985; Herdt 1987; Gatter 2000; Dankwa 2009).

There is a growing body of research on the continent pertaining to sexual citizenship and identity politics (Morgan and Wieringa 2005; Morgan, Marais and Wellbeloved 2009). Today, more nuanced research on the topic of female circumcision explores the multifarious dimensions associated with the practice, including the spiritual (Dellenborg 2004), identity politics (Dellenborg 2004) and even desire (Diallo 2004). There is an inevitable overlap between tradition, religion (especially Christianity and Islam) and the law in most studies of sexual cultures on the continent. But most of what is understood as culture in contemporary Africa is largely a product of constructions and reinterpretations by former colonial authorities in collaboration with African male patriarchs (Women and Law in Southern Africa 2000; Mama 2007). The tendency is to commence from the premise that views culture as being hostile to women, an antithesis to their rights. Researchers and theorists speak of rights as if they are culture-less at best or, at worst, born of a superior culture.

Moreover, culture is interpreted narrowly and grouped with custom or tradition on the assumption that these are natural and unchangeable (Bigge and von Briesen 2000). Mainstream feminist scholarship within and outside Africa, for example, largely tends to view culture in negative terms and to consider it an impediment to effective legal reform (McFadden 1999; Wanyeki 2003; Tripp 2004). Although this indictment is not totally unfounded, such beliefs have the effect of obscuring the potential that culture may hold as a tool for emancipation (Whitehead and Tsikata 2003; Tamale 2008a). In fact, culture is a double-edged sword that can be wielded creatively and resourcefully to enhance women's access to sexual justice.

Response to HIV/AIDS in the globalised world

Panic about HIV/AIDS was sparked in the 1990s, when it became apparent that in Africa the virus was spreading with unprecedented speed and in populations other than those considered high risk. As earlier observed, public health professionals and medical anthropologists descended on the sub-Saharan areas of the continent, ostensibly to work at finding preventive measures, but in reality resurrecting the colonising project through research that again focused on the sexual practices and behaviours of African men and women in the hopes that cultural and behavioural change would curb the spread of the virus.

Noting how 'the AIDS-in-Africa discourse in most scholarly journals and books and in policy documents has been uncritical of its assumptions and sources', Eileen Stillwaggon (2003: 809–810) laments the wasted decade of AIDS research that has failed to get to the bottom of the complexities of AIDS, especially among poor communities.

Hence, HIV provided the opportunity for a resurgence of the colonial mode of studying sexuality in Africa – racist, moralistic, paternalistic and steeped in liberal thinking (see Caldwell et al 1989; Deniaud et al 1991; Macdonald 1996; Gresenguet et al 1997). In the words of Gausset:

> Like the first studies of African sexuality, it was once again the 'exotic, tradi-tional, irrational and immoral practices' that were the focus of the research. If the pattern of AIDS epidemics was different in Africa than in Europe, the explanation obviously had to be the difference between African and European culture and sexualities ... Early researchers were looking for things to blame, and identified African cultural practices as culprits. The logical consequence of this was to fight against African cultures and sexualities. (Gausset 2001: 511)

The discourse of 'risky cultural practices' was so intimately bound to the theories and explanations that had emerged on the continent that it became a main resource for public health advocates and policy-makers. One outcome was that African gov-ernments were encouraged to integrate the pandemic into their criminal justice sys-tems. So criminal law began to be applied to cases in which a person transmitted or exposed others to HIV infection through risky practices. It was hoped that these HIV-specific laws would curb sexual immorality and reduce incidents of sexual violence against women. Model legislation, such as that developed in N'Djamena, Chad, was also enacted in Benin, Guinea, Guinea Bissau, Mali, Niger, Sierra Leone and Togo (Canadian HIV/AIDS Legal Network 2007). Other countries, such as Lesotho, Zimbabwe, Swaziland and Uganda have reinforced their existing sexual offences legislation to address the problem.

But the criminal approach to the pandemic has come under heavy criticism from human rights defenders, who view it as a violation of human rights. It is further condemned for its decontextualised and ahistoric approach to African sexualities. To date, there has been no convincing evidence to show that criminal prosecution has reduced the spread of HIV in Africa. Instead, it has enhanced stigma, increased women's vulnerability to the disease and circumvented the fundamental challenges of eradicating HIV from the continent (UNAIDS 2008). The International Planned Parenthood Federation (IPPF) is convinced that the 'criminal law is a blunt instrument for HIV prevention'.[9] After two decades of muddled approaches to HIV prevention in Africa with minimal success, researchers are beginning to revisit their methods and theories (Epprecht 2009; Kippax 2010). It has become evident that the insensitive approaches that call for the elimination of cultural and sexual practices will not yield significant results.

The key is not to fight people's cultures and identities but rather to raise their awareness of practising the safe exchange of body fluids, including blood, semen, vaginal secretions and breast milk. Studies have shown that cultures are flexible enough to adapt to new threats, such as those posed by HIV (Nyanzi et al 2009; Gausset 2001). Furthermore, raising public awareness about the gender and human rights aspects of sexuality and HIV/AIDS would yield better results in addressing AIDS risk than the 'social vaccine' approach that emphasises behavioural change.[10]

It is important for researchers to be aware of the vulnerabilities to HIV in the context of debilitating poverty and social disenfranchisement. This fact points to the syndemic[11] nature of the epidemic with significant effects on the sexualities of African communities. It means that HIV cannot be compartmentalised as a disease outside the context of sexual health and rights, gender and class. In order to honour the lives of Africans affected by HIV, scholars must adopt an integrated, comprehensive approach to researching, theorising and combating the disease.

Another important aspect of HIV/AIDS research (and research on sexuality generally) is that it has been engulfed in the ever-growing commodification of sexual health. The insatiable drive for profits and power has penetrated the 'sexuality industry' in alarming ways. HIV/AIDS has become a multibillion-dollar money spinner for national and international bureaucrats and pharmaceutical companies. Moreover, technological advances in communication and distribution have facilitated the unprecedented spread of information, allowing the exotic and subjective interpretations of African sexualities by Western (mainly US) scholars to be taken to a whole new level.

In the process of researching material for this essay, for example, I entered the words 'black lesbian rape' on the Google search engine and was shocked to find that almost 90 per cent of the 473,000 results were sites advertising or otherwise promoting pornographic videos and other racist, misogynist material.[12] On the Google Scholar search engine, the same phrase yielded zero results. This, in my opinion, was a good indication of a dangerous trend of research on sexuality in the globalised, capitalist, patriarchal world.

Rewriting and rerighting African sexualities

By the 1990s it had become apparent that the prevailing research agendas and methods related to sexuality in Africa – mostly drawn from biomedical science and public health policy – remained blind to its important pluralities. Very little funding was available for sexuality research in Africa, beyond the issues of disease, reproduction and violence. Non-clinical aspects of men's and women's sexualities were largely ignored by mainstream researchers, who continued to objectify Africans, and the age-old legacies of medicalised and exoticised sexuality were far from being broken (Oinas and Arnfred 2009).

As the concept of gender was overlooked when exploring sexuality, its nuanced pluralities and meanings within different communities were missed. Moreover, most researchers and scholars shied away from this taboo area of study, focusing only on what are considered safe topics, such as reproductive health and violence. Conspicuously missing from the mainstream sexuality research repertoire prior to the 1990s were studies on positive aspects of African sexualities, such as pleasure, eroticism and desire. But after the United Nations International Conference on Population and Development held in Cairo in 1994, activists were determined to reconceptualise sexuality as a human rights issue. The language of sexual rights made its debut on the international human rights stage in the Cairo meeting rooms and it has received increasing recognition ever since.

As part of the struggle for self-determination, Linda Tuhiwai Smith urged indigenous peoples who were colonised through imperialism to 'rewrite' and 'reright' their position in history, to 'tell our own stories, write our own versions, in our own ways, for our own purposes' (1999: 28). At the turn of the century African feminists heeded this call with unprecedented activism. Anxious to deepen our own understanding of the link between women's sexualities and their subordinate status in society, the African Gender Institute (AGI) at the University of Cape Town, in collaboration with the Institute of African Studies (IAS) at the University of Ghana, organised in 2003 a pan-African workshop on mapping African sexualities. This initiative inspired several case studies undertaken by a network of African intellectuals that deliberately pursued anti-imperialist ethics in exploring this largely uncharted territory (Mama 2007).[13] Several of these case studies were published in special issues of the journal, *Feminist Africa* (Arnfred 2009).[14]

Several other feminist institutions, networks and scholars on the continent embraced sexuality research in new ways. For example, the South African feminist journal, *Agenda*, which had been around for almost 20 years, began publishing themed editions relating specifically to sexuality issues.[15] The pan-African network, AMANITARE, which focuses on sexual and reproductive health and the rights of women, was formed in 2000 with an objective to support research and publication.[16] There was a deliberate move to break the traditional mould of analysing sexuality through the biomedical and public health frameworks. Not only did these studies and publications emanate from social science and the humanities, but they also analysed human sexualities in a holistic fashion, including its pleasurable and empowering aspects (see Baylies and Bujra 2000; McFadden 2003; Arnfred 2004; Khamasi and Maina-Chinkuyu 2005; Bennett 2005; Morgan and Wieringa 2005; Amadiume 2006; Maticka-Tyndale et al 2007; Tamale 2007; Gould and Fick 2008).

One of the first publications to seriously challenge Eurocentric approaches to African sexualities was *Rethinking Sexualities in Africa*, an anthology edited by Signe Arnfred (2004). The essays in that book reflected upon and synthesised African sexualities in ways that scholarship in this field had never done before. Most of the material was concerned with feminist research methods and analyses, foregrounding women's agency and pleasure.

Another important network involved in researching, theorising and publishing on the subject of African sexualities is Women Living Under Muslim Laws (WLUML). Although this solidarity network embraces all 'women whose lives are shaped, conditioned or governed by laws and customs said to derive from Islam',[17] African feminists have been actively involved in its work. For example, the Nigerian women's rights organisation, BAOBAB has received international recognition for its work in promoting women's rights through research, reinterpretation and theorising Muslim jurisprudence, criticising negative constructions and practices (done under the name of Islam) and discriminatory sharia criminal law, such as *zina* (extramarital sex) (Imam 2000; BAOBAB 2003).

Such blossoming scholarship has very clearly sought to embed an African socio-cultural and political imprint (in all its diversity) on the discourses about human sexuality, hitherto dominated by perspectives from the global North. The aim has been to create knowledge that would facilitate innovative and transformative social change. Concepts of sexual pleasure, the erotic and desire have begun to be unveiled in sophisticated studies, such as those exploring the ingenious, subtle messages embedded in local *kanga* cloth that Tanzanian women wrap loosely around their waists (Moyer and Mbelwa 2003); or the celebration of the power of the vagina among the Nigerian Igbo (Nzegwu 2006); or the indigenous sexual initiation institution of Ssenga among the Baganda of Uganda (Tamale 2005).[18]

Despite sex and sexuality having been at the core of most historical disputes within the Christian church – with one faction seeking sexual liberties against the wishes of a more conservative faction – the conceptualisation of sexuality within the framework of human rights has dogged Eurocentric scholars and researchers for a very long time. Thus, for example, one of the reasons the Protestant Church broke off from the Roman Catholic Church was because the latter was too rigid in its policy on issues such as clerical celibacy and allowing the clergy to marry. Also, there have long been divergent views on divorce, abortion and homosexuality.

But the close link between what is termed a universal human rights corpus and Western liberal democracy has diminished voices other than those of the West, and differing concepts of sexualities have remained largely buried in the cultural practices of various non-Western communities. The concept of sexual rights, for instance, is not alien to many African and Islamic communities. Take the example of a wife in many pre-colonial African cultures who was (and still is) guaranteed the right to sexual pleasure; or the fact that sexual violence within marriage was frowned upon; or that denial of such formal rights constituted a clear ground for divorce in these traditions (Awusabo-Asare et al 1993; Pereira 2003; Tamale 2008a). Perhaps had historians and sociology researchers not shied away from studying African sexualities in more open ways, they would have discovered that the controversial foundations of sexual rights have their roots in African traditional values.

Indeed, the conceptualisation of sexual rights within a liberal democratic framework is fraught with tensions and contradictions. Alice Miller and others have articulated the paradoxes that burden the context of rights when it comes to sexuality (Miller and Vance 2004). One cannot simultaneously use the language of sexual rights to police harm, such as rape or homophobia, and to demand privacy in the defence of the sexual pleasure of consenting adults. The contradictions can be seen further in the awkwardness of claiming the rights of people to sell/make images of sexual activity and simultaneously claim that people should be protected from sexual objectification.

Conducting ethical, sensitive research on African sexualities

I have noted that there have been a number of studies conducted on African sexualities that are sensitive to the complexities of the subject matter. In this section I delve into more detail of what it takes to conduct an ethical and sensitive study in the field of sexuality, providing as many examples as I can from existing studies that have been conducted in Africa.

As stated earlier in this essay, the primary purposes of conducting research are to create knowledge and to explain physical and social phenomena. It has also been pointed out that the bulk of the body of knowledge and published scholarship in the field of sexuality emanates from the global North. What does this portend for researchers of African sexualities? Does it mean that we reject *in toto* the validity of foreign-grown theories of sexuality as being inappropriate and irrelevant to our contexts? I think not.

Though it is extremely important to develop our home-grown theories of African sexualities and to always be keenly aware of the dangers of uncritically using theories that are constructed from the global North to explain African societies, the latter cannot be completely ignored, for three reasons. First, many of the contemporary codes of sexual morality and most of the laws pertaining to sex contained in the statute books of post-colonial countries are rooted in the history and tradition of the former colonising European nations. To a certain extent this means that Western theoretical perspectives define the underlying rationale and practice of the legal regime governing sexualities in Africa. Moreover, as Bibi Bakare-Yusuf usefully reminds us:

> For millennia, Africa has been part of Europe, as Europe has been part of Africa, and out of this relation, a whole series of borrowed traditions from both sides has been and continues to be brewed and fermented. To deny this intercultural exchange and reject all theoretical imports from Europe is to violate the order of knowledge and simultaneously disregard the (continued) contribution of various Africans to European cultural and intellectual history, and vice-versa. (Bakare-Yusuf 2003: 140)

Second, if we were to totally jettison Western concepts and theoretical frameworks, we would spend considerable resources reinventing the wheel – an unnecessary enterprise. There is a lot of sense in using existing theoretical bases as a starting point and then correcting/revising them in light of the contextual evidence collected in current studies.[19] Existing theoretical frameworks, such as Foucault's conceptualisation of sexuality in terms of power relations (Foucault 1976) or Judith Butler's implicit theory of heteronormativity and her views on the subversive potential in gender performativity (Butler 1990) or Gayle Rubin's concept of sexual hierarchy (Rubin 1984), can be extremely useful in analysing sexualities in Africa, as long as this is done with the continental specificities in mind and a view to improve upon them.

A simple illustration of the point can be made using Rubin's (1984) model of sexual hierarchy. Rubin shows how American society classifies sexual behaviour into a sexual value system in which good, normal, natural and privileged sexuality (located in what she refers to as the 'charmed circle' of sex) must be 'heterosexual, married, monogamous, procreative, non-commercial, in pairs, in a relationship, same generation, in private, bodies only and vanilla'. Those that conform to this ideology enjoy privileges and concrete material benefits from society. Outside the 'charmed circle' and on the 'outer limits' is 'bad, abnormal, unnatural and damned sexuality'. Characteristics of the latter include 'homosexual, unmarried, promiscuous, non-procreative, commercial, alone or in groups, casual, cross-generational, in public, pornography, with manufactured objects and sadomachistic'. Those that engage in sexual relations outside the charmed circle face legal and social sanctions as well as maltreatment (Rubin 1984: 281).

Most of the elements in Rubin's hierarchical model resonate with the experiences in many African societies. However, there are certain elements that clearly differ. For instance, polygyny would replace monogamy in the charmed circle of most African societies. In the same vein, cross-generational sex in the sex value systems of many African societies would move from the outer limits to the inner circle as this is relatively acceptable (albeit privileging sexual relations between older men and young women and not vice versa). Rubin's stratification could further be criticised for its failure to show how some individuals who seem to fit into the ideology of the 'charmed circle' might simultaneously suffer discrimination through, for example, exempting marital rape from criminal sanction.

The third reason why Western theories can be relevant and useful to African contexts is that gendered sexualities, whether in the West or in Africa, are primarily based on similar predictions, namely labour, authority and performance (Bennett 2000). In other words, the hierarchical constructions of sexuality in either context are linked by the force of gender to labour, authority and performance against the backdrop of capitalism and patriarchy (in their multiple variants). Hence there is an underlying resonance between the respective structures of Western and African societies that compels us not to completely reject or dismantle Western theoretical scaffoldings because they provide some useful tools for researchers to reflect upon and to develop insights concerning African sexualities. Having said that, because of certain ideologies and practices unique to the continent, theorising African sexualities would differ from Western sexualities in nuanced specificities (Helle-Valle 2004). For example, one cannot ignore those aspects of cultural ideology that are widely shared among Africans, such as community, solidarity and the ethos of *ubuntu* (humaneness),[20] just as one must pay attention to the common historical legacies inscribed in cultures within Africa by forces such as colonialism, capitalism, imperialism and globalisation. Take the self-identifying terms gay, lesbian and transgendered that have emerged from Western societies. These differ quite markedly from the descriptors for some same-sex relations found on the continent (e.g. *batsoalle* woman-to-woman relationships in Lesotho – see Kendall 1998). The identity politics that underpin these Western notions do not necessarily apply in African contexts (Amadiume 1987; Kendall 1998; Tamale 2003; Oyewumi 2005).

In the same vein, it would be foolhardy for anyone theorising women's sexualities to ignore the machinations of Africa's 'structurally adjusted' economies and the attendant 'feminisation of poverty' when analysing women's involvement in commercial sex work and the heightened prevalence of HIV/AIDS. It is also necessary to make the philosophical link between institutionalised and state-inspired homophobia and Africa's autocratic and dictatorial regimes.[21] By constantly attacking homosexuals, attention is conveniently diverted from the pressing issues that ensure that the population suffers.

An increasing trend in the area of research generally are the 'strings' that come tied to huge research funds offered by various donors and/or development partners. For example, many research funding applications will only be approved and disbursed to projects that promote North–South collaboration.[22] So, a research institution in the global North must partner with one located in the global South, supposedly to facilitate the cross-pollination of ideas and enhance the project's knowledge base.

Inevitably, such forced collaborations are imbued with historical legacies of inequality and prejudice. The tendency is for the Northern partner to dominate, control and exploit the Southern counterparts. Notably, the bulk of such studies are focused on the south, with few cases of African researchers heading north to investigate European and North American sexualities.

So, when conducting collaborative research projects, it is extremely important to be reflexive and sensitive to any possible inequalities (Tamale 2008b). This by no means suggests that researchers from the global North studying African sexualities should constantly walk on egg shells with imagined sensitivities or that they should wallow in feelings of guilt and contrition. Rather, researchers should develop a keen awareness of all the historical objectifications and derogations in research experiences on the continent. Elina Oinas and Signe Arnfred, for instance, recommend that Nordic researchers of African sexualities view the process as 'a breaking of silences and hesitance and the application of a reflective approach when studying sexualities in Africa, in addition to a call for scrutiny of actual practices and politics, including the politics of research and writing' (Oinas and Arnfred 2009: 150).

The researcher obviously has a lot of power in that she or he represents and creates knowledge and understanding about the researched subject matter. The process of acquiring information is crucial because it determines the depth and quality of knowledge. When it comes to sexuality, the level of knowledge received during research might be influenced by a number of challenges and sensitivities that relate to issues of process, presentation and politics. Table 1.1 elaborates some of the interrelated ways that these issues might affect data collected in sexuality research.

Sexuality researchers must take seriously such methodological and epistemological issues. There are several publications that speak to these issues with useful tips on how to handle tricky situations (see Gune and Manuel's article in Part 1 of this book; see also Adomako Ampofo and Arnfred 2010).

Table 1.1: Methodological issues to consider in sexuality research

Process	Presentation	Politics
Sex is a taboo subject, therefore it is difficult to get people to talk and engage because of coyness, discomfort, stigma	The way participants relate to researcher's age, sex, gender, sexuality, status, personal presentation, religion	Unequal relationship between researcher and researched
Developing rapport with research participants: participants might feel threatened to relate or put down something so private/ personal	Language: it might be impossible to translate words or nuanced meanings that do not exist in the research language	How does the researcher facilitate the voices of the participants and make the research relevant to them?
Personal beliefs, values, prejudices of researcher and researched	Veracity: how does the researcher know that the participant is being honest and not embellishing a story or experience? How can they test for accuracy of memory?	Issues of confidentiality
The study might force a participant to remember things they wish to forget, which makes the research process traumatic and deeply hurtful for them	The topic might be too complex. The participant might genuinely ask themselves: 'Where do I start? There is no narrative, no language to convey the experience. No linear way to tell the story. It is too layered'	Private issues moving into the public realm
The experience might be too deep and embarrassing for the participant. It might invoke shame, denial, intimidation, tension or anger		The sensitivity of the topic might make it difficult to get people to participate because of internal sensibilities, such as people's spirituality and external sensibilities, such as breaking the law
The participant might hesitate to divulge information because they loathe being pitied or fear damaging their bodily integrity		Hopelessness of the situation, whereby the researcher is not in a position to do anything to help a desperate participant
The research is likely to engage the researcher in difficult and unpredictable ways		

The complexity of the subject matter means that the process of designing a research project on sexuality is by no means a linear exercise. Rather it is a circuitous, undulating process. This means that there is nothing straightforward about the research; there are no holy cows, and the twists and turns are numerous. As the researcher plans, implements and reflects upon the study, each decision might produce implications that require revisiting earlier decisions. This calls for maximum flexibility and minimum bias on the part of the researcher.

A good sexuality research project does not view methodology as a mere appendage of issues of epistemology or 'a way of carrying out an enquiry'. Rather, methodology itself is conceptualised as a political process, a 'space' in which complex issues of context, voice, ethics and ideological depth are played out (Bennett 2008: 1). It is part and parcel of theory-building and transformative change.

I have a firm conviction that feminist methods of research are best suited for research on sexuality (see also Reinharz 1992; Nagar and Geiger 2007; Adomako Ampofo and Arnfred 2010). This is because they consciously attempt to:

* Foreground the experiences of participants, as well as the meanings and interpretations that they attach to these experiences. This is important to allow for linkages between real life experiences and the phenomena under study. The researcher gets to appreciate the research issues within the framework of their lived experiences and life situations
* Excavate complex and abstract qualitative phenomena that are unquantifiable, such as emotions, feelings and other sensitive issues critical in sexuality research
* Not objectify participants and avoid hierarchical representations of knowledge about their lived experiences. This allows considerable space for the actual voices of participants to be part of the knowledge creation process in the final report or publication
* Work within a human rights framework, providing contexts that begin with a consideration of the constitutional and legal context in which sexuality issues are played out.

It would be foolhardy to study HIV/AIDS, for example, without paying attention to gender and the political economy within which sexualities in Africa operate (Mbilinyi 2010). *Politics of the Womb*, the work of Lynn Thomas (2003), which analyses the linkage between women's reproductive capacities and patriarchal state interests in Kenya, is an example of an excellent multidisciplinary and sensitive case study of African sexualities. Her careful attention to gender, class, generation and race using ethnographic, oral, legal and archival sources forcefully exposes the complex ways that colonial and post-colonial powers controlled female sexual initiation (excision), abortion, childbirth and premarital pregnancies. Thomas's research clearly shows how women's bodies constitute an important site of political struggle in Africa and their connections to the political economies of the state.

Conclusion and future prospects

Researchers in the field of sexuality must remember that the concepts of sexuality and gender, as normatively used, both denote power and dominance. It is therefore useful to speak of gendered sexualities and/or sexualised genders. Such an approach allows for in-depth analyses of the intersections of the ideological and historical systems that underpin each concept, which is an important factor in knowledge production.

The historical trajectory of research on African sexualities began from a place where colonial and imperial interests, biases and agendas defined their parameters in damaging ways. Conceptualised within a tripartite framework of morals, reproduction and dysfunction, the sexualities of Africans were largely constructed as immoral, lascivious and primitive. Although that legacy has endured over generations, it has been subjected to serious challenge in recent years. The biomedical and Western researcher is gradually being replaced with the multidisciplinary, home-based researcher who embraces holistic and grounded approaches.

As it has emerged that sexuality examined exclusively through the lens of natural science leads to problematic theoretical and methodological concerns, scholarship has turned an important conceptual corner. Today, a comprehensive understanding of African sexualities means that the researcher must observe through several lenses that take in history, politics, economics, art, law, philosophy, literature and sociology. The study of sexualities cannot be abstracted from power and particular interests. It is a dialectical, circuitous process that allows for back-and-forth movement and empathetic understanding, and recognises the fusion between sexualities and various structures of power.

Though researchers will find that African sexualities differ in many ways from those outside the continent, a fresh and open approach might reveal that there are more intra-continental differences in practices and norms of sexualities than there are variations across continents. After all, we cannot underestimate the global effects of neocolonialism, organised religion and globalisation on contemporary sexualities around the world. Not only do othering systems lead to oversimplified theories, but also they lead to discrimination and xenophobic attitudes.

There is considerable virgin ground for researching and theorising African sexualities. There is a great deal still that scholarship has to address. The prospects and possibilities for researching sexualities on the continent have greatly expanded thanks to the internet. One of the biggest challenges for African researchers is how to apply and draw from theories that emerged from studies conducted elsewhere in a way that simultaneously gives serious consideration to the specificities of African contexts within which various sexualities operate.

In other words, theoretical globetrotting for the African researcher must inevitably be enriched and rejuvenated by the historical and cultural realities of the studied communities. Researching and theorising sexualities beyond the tired polemics of violence, disease and reproduction and exploring their layered complexities beyond heterosexual normativity and moral boundaries will lead to fresh conceptual insights and paradigm shifts. It will illuminate the limitless and diffuse capacities that the human body, as well as the mind, heart and soul, have for eroticism and pleasure.

Furthermore, repositioning both the geographical and conceptual locations of what is African will avoid the slippery terrain of the essence of who and what is African. Collecting further quantitative and rich textual ethnographic empirical data that is not only interdisciplinary but also transdisciplinary is a must. This is the way to embark on a more complex theoretical journey through the constructs and issues that deepen our understanding of African sexualities.

Notes

1. I wish to thank Jane Bennett, who was my primary source of inspiration for writing this chapter, for her generosity in reading the first draft and providing valuable comments.
2. These are different names of traditional story tellers/entertainers from various parts of Africa.

3. There is archaeological evidence to prove that written traditions existed in ancient Africa e.g., in Timbuktu, Ethiopia and Egypt. However, such records are too under-researched to provide a useful academic resource. The 54 countries in Africa were at one time or another colonised by a European imperial power (Britain, France, Germany, Belgium and Portugal), with the exceptions of Liberia and Ethiopia. Liberia was created in the 1820s as a nation for freed slaves from the United States of America, and Ethiopia repulsed attempts by the Italians to colonise it in 1896. However, the Italians occupied Ethiopia briefly between 1936 and 1941.

4. This generalised example by no means signifies a homogenised African or European sexuality.

5. This can clearly be seen in religious garb, such as veils, burkas, jilbabs, habits and other wide, ankle-length, full-sleeved loose dresses.

6. The Malawian Decency in Dress Act of 1973 and Uganda's decree of 1972 imposed strict dress codes for women during the reign of these two African autocrats. In both cases women were prohibited from wearing shorts, mini-skirts, hot pants, slacks or low-necked garments. The Ugandan decree gave precise definitions and hemline lengths of what was legally acceptable. For example, it prohibited hemlines that rose '5.08 centimetres above the upper edge of the patella' (knee cap) – see section 1 (ee) of the Penal Code Act (Amendment) Decrees of 1972, 1973 and 1974.

7. Kathryn (aka Limakatso) Kendall's (1997) treatment of the Musotho woman, Mpho 'M'atsepo Nthunya in *Singing Away the Hunger: The Autobiography of an African Woman*, for example, is in many ways more imperialist than the gaze that she criticises.

8. See www.clitoraid.com. African feminists have challenged and condemned the work of Clitoraid in an online petition at www.thepetitionsite.com/1/ feministschallengingclitoraid, accessed 9 July 2010.

9. See the IPPF news release, 'Criminalisation of HIV transmission and exposure" available at www.ippf.org/en/News/Press-releases/Criminalization+of+HIV+transmission+and+ex posure.htm, accessed 27 October 2010.

10. During the 15th International AIDS Conference held on 11–16 July 2004 in Bangkok, Ugandan President Yoweri Museveni reiterated his strong belief in the abstinence approach, arguing that without a medical vaccine in sight what his poor African country needed was the 'social vaccine' of behavioural change (Akkara 2004).

11. The term 'syndemic' was coined in the early 1990s by anthropologist Merrill Singer to describe the mutually reinforcing nature of health crises with harsh and inequitable living conditions. That is, 'Two or more afflictions, interacting synergistically, contributing to excess burden of disease in a population' (Milstein 2004: 1). Also see www.cdc.gov/syndemics/encyclopedia.htm, accessed 28 October 2010.

12. Google search conducted 5 July 2010.

13. Another offshoot of this initiative was the establishment in 2006 of the Law, Gender and Sexuality Research Project at Uganda's Makerere University Faculty of Law.

14. See *Feminist Africa* 5 (2006), 6 (2006) and 11 (2008). The journal is available online at www. feministafrica.org.

15. For instance, see 'African feminisms: sexuality in Africa', *Agenda* 62 (2004); 'African feminisms: body image', *Agenda* 63 (2005); 'Homosexuality', *Agenda* 67 (2006); 'Rape', *Agenda* 74 (2007). Also see Volume 15(1) (2009) of the *East African Journal of Peace and Human Rights*, which is a special issue on gender, law and sexuality.

16. Named after the ancient Nubian Queen Amanitare, the AMANITARE partnership invokes a legacy of African women's leadership and agency (Horn 2003).

17. The current coordinator of this international network is a Senegalese feminist, Fatou Sow.

18. These were welcome additions to the few indigenous publications by scholars such as Patricia McFadden (1992).

19. The exception would be studies that adopt the grounded theory methodology.

20. For a detailed explanation of the African philosophy of *ubuntu* see note 1 of the Introduction.

21. Being aware that legalised homophobia in Africa was a direct import by colonial powers.

22. Another example of conditions that are increasingly being tied to research funding is the requirement for a gendered analysis of the research problem. Although this condition might seem laudable at face value, in fact many times it translates into a pro forma and abusive application of the gender concept, doing more harm than good to knowledge production. For instance, by essentialising the term gender and/or using it in a descriptive fashion or as shorthand for 'women and men', its analytical and conceptual value is watered down; it becomes depoliticised and ahistorical.

References

Adomako Ampofo, A. and Arnfred, S. (eds) (2010) *African Feminist Politics of Knowledge: Tensions, Challenges, Possibilities*, Uppsala, The Nordic Africa Institute

Ahlberg, Beth Maina (1994) 'Is there a distinct African sexuality? A critical response to Caldwell', *Africa* 64(2): 220–240

Akkara, A. (2004) 'The "Social Vaccine"', Catholic Education Research Centre (CERC), http://www.catholiceducation.org/articles/sexuality/se0104.html, accessed 20 April 2010

Amadiume, I. (1987) *Male Daughters, Female Husbands: Gender and Sex in an African Society*, London, Zed Books

—— (2006) 'Sexuality, African religio-cultural traditions and modernity: expanding the lens', CODESRIA Bulletin 1&2: 26-28

An-Na'im, Adbdullahi (1990) 'Problems of universal cultural legitimacy for human rights', in Adbullahi, A. and Deng, F. (eds) *Human Rights in Africa: Cross-cultural Perspectives*, Washington DC, Brookings Institution Press

Arnfred, S. (ed) (2004) *Rethinking Sexualities in Africa*, Uppsala, The Nordic Africa Institute

—— (2009) 'African feminists on sexualities', *Canadian Journal of African Studies* 43(1): 151–159

Awusabo-Asare K., Anarfi, J. and Agyeman, D. (1993) 'Women's control over their sexuality and the spread of STDs and HIV/AIDS in Ghana', *Health Transition Review* 3: 69–83 (supplementary issue)

Bakare-Yusuf, Bibi (2003), 'Yorubas don't do gender: a critical review of Oyeronke Oyewumi's "The invention of women: making an African sense of western gender discourses"', *African Identities* 1(1): 121-142

BAOBAB (2003) 'BAOBAB for women's human rights and sharia implementation in Nigeria: the journey so far', Lagos, BAOBAB for Women's Human Rights

Baylies, C. and Bujra, J. (eds) (2000) *AIDS, Sexuality and Gender in Africa: Collective Strategies and Struggles in Tanzania and Zambia*, New York, Routledge

Bennett, Jane (2000) 'Thinking sexualities', Cape Town, African Gender Institute Newsletter 7

—— (ed) (2005) *Killing the Virus with Stones? Research on the Implementation of Policies against Sexual Harassment in Southern African Higher Education*, Cape Town, African Gender Institute

—— (2008) 'Editorial: Researching for life: paradigms and power', *Feminist Africa* 11: 1–12 http://www.feministafrica.org/uploads/File/Issue%2011/11_3_Editorial.pdf, accessed 25 June 2010

Bigge, D.M. and von Briesen, A. (2000) 'Conflict in the Zimbabwean courts: women's rights and indigenous self-determination in *Magaya v. Magaya*', *Harvard Human Rights Journal* 13: 289–313

Blair, Cynthia (2010) *I've Got to Make my Livin': Black Women's Sex Work in Turn-of-the-Century Chicago*, Chicago, University of Chicago Press

Butler, Judith (1990) *Gender Trouble: Feminism and the Subversion of Identity*, London, Routledge

Caldwell, J., Caldwell, P. and Quiggin, P. (1989) 'The social context of AIDS in sub-Saharan Africa', *Population and Development Review* 15 (2): 185–234

Canadian HIV/AIDS Legal Network (2007) 'A human rights analysis of the N'Djamena model legislation on AIDS and HIV-specific legislation in Benin, Guinea, Guinea-Bissau, Mali, Niger, Sierra Leone and Togo', http://www.aidslaw.ca/publications/publicationsdocEN.php?ref=967, accessed 25 June 2010

Commons, L. (1993–94) 'Savage Sexuality: Images of the African woman in Victorian literature', *Latitudes* 3, http://ssmu.mcgill.ca/journals/latitudes/3vsex.htm, accessed 10 May 2010

Curtin, P. (1964) *The Image of Africa: British Ideas and Action 1780–1850*, Madison, University of Wisconsin Press

Dankwa, Serena (2009) '"It's a silent trade": female same-sex intimacies in post-colonial Ghana', *Nordic Journal of Feminist and Gender Research* 17(3): 19–205

Dellenborg, Liselott (2004) 'A reflection on the cultural meanings of female circumcision: experiences from fieldwork in Asamance, southern Senegal', in Arnfred, S. (ed) *Rethinking Sexualities in Africa*, 79–96 Uppsala, The Nordic Africa Institute

Deniaud, Francois, Livrozet, Jean-Michel and Rey, Jean-Loup (1991) 'Point de vue sur les liens unissant VIH et pratiques rituells en Afrique tropicale', *Cahiers Sante* 1: 327–33

Diallo, A. (2004) 'Paradoxes of female sexuality in Mali: on the practices of Magnonmaka and Bolokoli-kela', in Arnfred, S. (ed) *Rethinking Sexualities in Africa*, 173–194, Uppsala, The Nordic Africa Institute

Dilger, H. (2008) 'African sexualities revisited: gender, social relations and culture in the context of globalisation and AIDS in Tanzania', in Pope, C., White, R.T. and Malow, R. (eds) *HIV/AIDS: Global Frontiers in Prevention/Intervention*, New York, Routledge

Epprecht, Marc (2006) '"Bisexuality" and the politics of normal in African ethnography', *Anthropologica* 48: 187–201

—— (2009) 'New Perspectives on Sexualities in Africa: introduction', *Canadian Journal of African Studies* 43(1): 1–7

—— (2010) 'The making of "African sexuality": early sources, current debates', *History Compass* 8(8): 768–79

Ehrlich, P. (1968) *The Population Bomb*, New York, Ballantine

Fee, Elizabeth (1980) 'Review of The Hosken Report: Genital and Sexual Mutilation of Females by Fran P. Hosken', *Signs: Journal of Women in Culture and Society*, 5(4): 807–809

Foucault, Michel (1976 [1998]) *The History of Sexuality, Volume 1: The Will of Knowledge*, London, Penguin

Gatter, Phillip (2000) 'Global theories and sexuality', paper presented at the IDS Queering Development Research Seminar Series, University of Sussex. http://www.ids.ac.uk/go/.../-queering-development-seminar-series-2000–2001

Gausset, Quentin (2001) 'AIDS and cultural practices in Africa: the case of the Tonga (Zambia)', *Social Science and Medicine* 52: 509–518

Gay, Judith (1985) 'Mummies and babies and friends and lovers in Lesotho', *Journal of Homosexuality* 2(3 and 4): 97–116

Geshekter, Charles (1995) 'Outbreak? AIDS, Africa and the medicalisation of poverty', *Transitions* 5(3): 4–14

Gilman, S. (1985) 'Black bodies, white bodies: toward an iconography of female sexuality in late nineteenth century art, medicine and literature', in Gates, H.L. (ed) *Race, Writing and Difference*, Chicago, University of Chicago Press

Goodson, A. (1991) *Therapy, Nudity and Joy*, Los Angeles, Elysium Growth Press

Gould, C. and Fick, N. (2008) *Selling Sex in Cape Town: Sex Work and Human Trafficking in a South African City*, Pretoria, Institute for Security Studies

Gresenguet, G., Kreiss J.K., Chapko M.K. and Weiss N.S. (1997) 'HIV infection and vaginal douching in Central Africa', *AIDS* 11: 101–6

Gune, Emídio and Manuel, Sandra (2007), 'Doing research on sexuality in Africa: ethical dilemmas and the positioning of the researcher', *OSSREA Bulletin*, http://www.ossrea.net/publications/newsletter/jun07/article8.htm, accessed 10 March 2010

Hardin, Garrett (1968) 'The tragedy of the commons', *Science* 162: 1243–48

Heald, Suzette (1999) 'The power of sex: reflections on the Caldwells' "African Sexuality" thesis', in Heald, S. (ed) *Manhood and Morality: Sex, Violence and Ritual in Gisu Society*, New York, Routledge

Helle-Valle, Jo (2004) 'Understanding sexuality in Africa: diversity and contextualised dividuality', in Arnfred, S. (ed) *Rethinking Sexualities in Africa*, Uppsala, The Nordic Africa Institute: 195–207

Herdt, G. (1987) *The Sambia: Ritual and Gender in New Guinea*, New York, Holt, Rinehart and Winston

Horn, Jessica (2003) 'AMANITARE and African women's sexual and reproductive health and rights', *Feminist Africa* 2: 73–9

Hosken, F. (1980) *The Hosken Report: Genital and Sexual Mutilation of Females*, Lexington, MA, Women's International Network News

Imam, Aisha (2000) 'The Muslim religious right ("fundamentalists") and sexuality', in Ilkkaracan, P. (ed) *Women and Sexuality in Muslim Societies*, Istanbul, Women for Women's Human Rights (WWHR) and Kadmin Insan Haklari Projesi (KIHP)

Kaler, Amy (2009) 'African perspectives on female circumcision', *Canadian Journal of African Studies* 43(1): 178–183.

Kendall, Kathryn (aka Limakatso) (ed) (1997) *Singing Away the Hunger: The Autobiography of an African Woman*, Bloomington, Indiana University Press

— (1998) 'When a woman loves a woman in Lesotho', in Murray, S. and Roscoe, W. (eds), *Boy-Wives and Female Husbands: Studies in African Homosexualities*, New York, Palgrave

Khamasi, J. and Maina-Chinkuyu, S. (eds) (2005) *Sexuality: An African Perspective, The Politics of Self and Cultural Beliefs*, Nairobi, Moi University Press

Kibirige, Joachim (1997) 'Population growth, poverty and growth', *Social Science & Medicine* 45(2): 247–259

Kippax, Susan (2010), 'It's not as simple as ABC', in Aggleton, Peter and Parker, Richard (eds) *Routledge Handbook of Sexuality, Health and Rights*, London, Routledge

Kuhn, T. (1962) *The Structure of Scientific Revolutions*, Chicago, University of Chicago Press

Le Blanc, Marie, Meintel, Deirdre and Piché, Victor (1991) 'The African sexual system: comment on Caldwell et al', *Population and Development Review* 17(3): 497–505

Lyons, Andrew and Lyons, Harriet (2004) *Irregular Connections: a History of Anthropology and Sexuality*, Lincoln and London, University of Nebraska Press

Macdonald, David (1996) 'Notes on the socio-economic and cultural factors influencing the transmission of HIV in Botswana', *Social Science and Medicine* 42(9): 1325–33

Magubane, Zine (2001) 'Which bodies matter? Feminism, postructuralism, race, and the curious theoretical odyssey of the "Hottentot Venus"', *Gender and Society* 15(6): 816–34

Mama, Amina (1996) 'Women's studies and studies of women in Africa during the 1990s', *CODESRIA Working Paper Series* 5/96

— (2007) 'Is it ethical to study Africa? Preliminary thoughts on scholarship and freedom', *African Studies Review* 50(1): 1–26

Mamdani, M. (1972) *The Myth of Population Control: Family, Caste and Class in an Indian Village*, New York, Monthly Review Press

Maticka-Tyndale, E., Tiemoko, R. and Makinwa-Adebusoye, P. (eds) (2007) *Human Sexuality in Africa: Beyond Reproduction*, Johannesburg, Fanele

Mbilinyi, Marjorie (2010) 'The linkages between resources, policy, gender and HIV/AIDS: a conceptual note', in Kitunga, D. and Mbilinyi, M. (eds) *A Transformative Feminist Analysis of HIV and AIDS*, Dar es Salaam, Tanzania Gender Networking Programme (TGNP)

McClintock, A. (1995) *Imperial Leather: Race, Gender and Sexuality in the Colonial Conquest*, New York and London, Routledge

McFadden, Patricia (1992) 'Sex, sexuality and the problems of AIDS in Africa', in Meena, R. (ed) *Gender in Southern Africa: Conceptual and Theoretical Issues*, Harare, Sapes Books

— (ed) (1999) *Reflections on Gender Issues in Africa*, Harare, Sapes Books

— (2003) 'Sexual pleasure as feminist choice', *Feminist Africa* 2: 50–60

Miller, Alice and Vance, Carol (2004) 'Sexuality, human rights and health', *Health and Human Rights* 7(2): 5–15

Milstein, B. (2004) 'Syndemic' in Mathison, S. (ed) *Encyclopedia of Evaluation*, Thousand Oaks, CA, Sage Publications

Morgan, R., Marais, C. and Wellbeloved, J. (eds) (2009) *Trans: Transgender Life Stories from South Africa*, Johannesburg, Jacana

Morgan, R. and Wieringa, S. (2005) *Tommy Boys, Lesbian Men and Ancestral Wives: Female Same-Sex Practices in Africa*, Johannesburg, Jacana

Moyer, Eileen and Mbelwa, Derrick (2003) 'Secret pleasures: imagining sexuality on the Swahili coast', paper presented at the 4th Conference of the International Association for the Study of Sexuality, Culture and Society (IASSCS), Johannesburg

Muller, Jean-Claude (1972), 'Ritual marriage, symbolic fatherhood and initiation among the Rukuba, Plateau-Benue State, Nigeria', *Man* 7(2): 283–295

Musisi, N. (2002), 'The politics of perception or perception as politics? Colonial and missionary representations of Baganda women, 1900–1945', in Allman J., Geiger S. and Musisi, N. (eds) *Women in African Colonial Histories*, Bloomington, Indiana University Press

Mutua, M. (2002) *Human Rights: A Political and Cultural Critique*, Philadelphia, University of Pennsylvania Press

Nagar, R. and Geiger, S. (2007) 'Reflexivity and positionality in feminist fieldwork revisited', in Tickell A., Sheppard E., Peck J. and Barnes, T. (eds) *Politics and Practice in Economic Geography*, London, Sage, http://www.tc.umn.edu/~nagar/documents/NagarandGeigerfinaldraftReflexivityandPositionalityinFeministFieldworkjan07.pdf, accessed 10 July 2010

Nnaemeka, O. (ed) (2005) *Female Circumcision and the Politics of Knowledge: African Women in Imperialist Discourses*, Westport, CT, Praeger Publishers

Nyanzi, Stella, Emodu-Walakira, Margaret and Sewaniko, Wilberforce (2009) 'The widow, the will and widow-inheritance in Kampala: revisiting victimisation arguments', *Canadian Journal of African Studies* 43(1): 12–33

Nzegwu, Nkiru (2006) 'African sexuality', in *Sex from Plato to Paglia: A Philosophical Encyclopedia Volume 1*, 38–45 Westport, CT, Greenwood Press

Oinas, Elina and Arnfred, Signe (2009) 'Introduction: sex and politics – case Africa', *Nordic Journal of Feminist and Gender Research* 17(3): 149–157

Oloka-Onyango, J. and Tamale, Sylvia (1995) '"The personal is political" or why women's rights are indeed human rights: an African perspective on international feminism', *Human Rights Quarterly* 17(4): 691–731

Osha, Sanya (2004) 'A postcolonial scene: on girls' sexuality', paper presented at the 2nd Understanding Human Sexuality Seminar Series, Africa Sexuality Resource Centre, Lagos

Owusu, Maxwell (1978) 'Ethnography of Africa: the usefulness of the useless', *American Anthropologist* 80(2): 310–34

Oyewumi, Oyeronke (2005) 'Visualizing the body: western theories and African subjects', in Oyeronke, O. (ed) *African Gender Studies: A Reader*, New York, Palgrave Macmillan

Pereira, Charmaine (2003) 'Where angels fear to tread? Some thoughts on Patricia McFadden's "Sexual pleasure as feminist choice"', *Feminist Africa* 2: 61–65

Raum, Otto (1939), 'Female initiation among the Chaga', *American Anthropologist* 41(4): 554–565

Rees, B. (1977) *The Victorian Lady*, London, Gordon and Cremonesi

Reinharz, Shulamit (1992) *Feminist Methods in Social Research*, New York, Oxford University Press

Rubin, Gayle (1984), 'Thinking sex: notes for a radical theory on the politics of sexuality', in Vance, C., *Pleasure and Danger: Exploring Female Sexuality*, London, Routledge and Kegan Paul, 267–319

Savage, Olayinka and Tchombe, Therese (1994) 'Anthropological perspectives on sexual behaviour in Africa', *Annual Review of Sex Research* 5: 50–72

Smith, Tuhiwai Linda (1999) *Decolonising Methodologies: Research and Indigenous Peoples*, London, Zed Books

Stillwaggon, Eileen (2003) 'Racial metaphors: interpreting sex and AIDS in Africa', *Development and Change* 34(5): 809–832

Tamale, Sylvia (2005), 'Eroticism, sensuality and "women's secrets" among the Baganda: a critical analysis', *Feminist Africa* 5: 9–36, http://www.feministafrica.org/uploads/File/Issue%205/FA5_feature_article_1.pdf, accessed 21 June 2010

—— (ed) (2007) *Homosexuality: Perspectives from Uganda*, Kampala, Sexual Minorities Uganda (SMUG)

—— (2008a) 'The right to culture and the culture of rights: a critical perspective on women's sexual rights in Africa', *Feminist Legal Studies* 16: 47–69

—— (2008b) 'Review of *Tommy Boys, Lesbian Men and Ancestral Wives: Female Same-Sex Practices in Africa*', *Feminist Africa* 11: 135–138 http://www.feministafrica.org/uploads/File/Issue%2011/11_13_Review%201.pdf, accessed 25 May 2010

Thomas, L. (2003) *Politics of the Womb: Women, Reproduction, and the State in Kenya*, Berkeley, University of California Press

Treichler, P. (1999) *How to Have a Theory in an Epidemic: Cultural Chronicles of AIDS*, Durham, Duke University Press

Tripp, Aili (2004) 'Women's movements, customary law, and land rights in Africa: the case of Uganda', *African Studies Quarterly* 7(4): 1–19

UNAIDS (2008) *Policy Brief: Criminalisation of HIV Transmission*, accessed 27 October 2010

Undie, Chi-Chi and Benaya, Kwabe (2006) 'The state of knowledge on sexuality in sub-Saharan Africa: a synthesis of literature', *Jenda: A Journal of Culture and African Women Studies* 8, http://www.jendajournal.com/issue8/undie-benaya.html, accessed 17 March 2010

Vaughan, M. (1991) *Curing Their Ills: Colonial Power and African Illness*, Stanford, CA, Stanford University Press

Wane, Njoki (2000) 'Indigenous knowledge: lessons from the elders, a Kenyan case study', in Dei, G., Hall, B. and Rosenberg, G. (eds) *Indigenous Knowledge in Global Context: Multiple Readings of Our World*, Toronto, University of Toronto Press

Wanyeki, M. (ed) (2003) *Women and Land in Africa: Culture, Religion and Realising Women's Rights*, London, Zed Books

Whitehead, Ann and Tsikata, Dzodzi (2003) 'Policy discourses on women's land rights in sub-Saharan Africa: the implications of the re-turn to the customary', *Journal of Agrarian Change* 3 (1 & 2): 67–112

Wolf, N. (1991) *The Beauty Myth: How Images of Beauty are Used Against Women*, New York, William Morrow and Company

Women and Law in Southern Africa (WLSA) (2000) *In the Shadow of the Law: Women and Justice Delivery in Zimbabwe*, Harare, WLSA Research and Educational Trust

Young, R. (1995) *Colonial Desire: Hybridity in Theory, Culture and Race*, London, Routledge

2

Doing research on sexuality in Africa: ethical dilemmas and the positioning of the researcher[1]

Emídio Gune and Sandra Manuel

The process of knowledge production involves a series of steps and is influenced by several factors, which impact upon the end result of the research in various ways. When the topic of research is sexuality such conditions and influences become surrounded by a greater number of implications, some with far-reaching consequences. Not only is this because sexuality is generally regarded as a sensitive topic, if not a taboo, but also because it is a topic that poses difficult questions that the researcher must resolve if the success of the project is not to be jeopardised.

This chapter reflects on key epistemological conversations and debates on doing research on sexuality in Africa. We are both anthropologists who have conducted research on young people's sexuality in urban areas of Mozambique.

One of us, Emídio Gune, focused his interest on exploring the socio-cultural construction of sexual scripts for sexual acts in the capital, Maputo. The other, Sandra Manuel, worked first on the perceptions and routines of condom use and later explored the practices, meanings and narratives of sex among youth in the same city. The fact that one of us is a male and the other a female generated interesting nuances in the experiences and results we were able to produce. Being part of graduate studies at the University of Cape Town (UCT), the studies followed strict ethical protocols.

Whose ethics exactly?

After the selection of the research theme, our next challenge was to convince the Department of Social Anthropology that the proposal complied with ethical guidelines. The guidelines to be followed combined, *inter alia*, the UCT code of ethics for research on human subjects; the ethical guidelines and principles of conduct for anthropologists issued by Anthropology Southern Africa (ASA 2005) and the statement on ethics by the American Anthropological Association (AAA 1971).

Given that ethical considerations may decide whether or not a project is approved, they are key to the process of obtaining permission to conduct research. The university's ethics committee has the last word on whether students may proceed with the research and consequently with their graduate programme. So, in this case, we were aware that researching sexuality and other sexual matters or issues would be a challenge, because 'anything having to do with sex causes a great many people to feel embarrassed' (Kelley and Byrne in Frith 2000: 281) mostly because 'sexual practices always involve some degree of privacy, and the ethical implications of their scientific study and of the publication of findings are myriad' (David 1987: 4).

Therefore, in committing to the various ethical guidelines, we made clear we would not abuse the power inequity that could emerge as a result of the research encounters, such as during interviews (Scheurich 1997; ASA 2005). Also, we needed to avoid overriding the social and cultural values of the participants, and guard against undue intrusion into their intimate and sexual lives or other related subjects.

From the start we were clear that the participants who agreed to participate in the study would be treated as subjects and not objects. This was especially the case if the participants were selected from among previous studies.[2] We would obtain oral informed consent from the participants who had agreed to take part in the previous studies. Also, only after the participants were made aware of the research objectives and methodologies, volunteered to take part and were assured of their anonymity (for protection from exposure after obtaining their consent) would the study proceed. We would inform the participants and remind them that they were free to ask anything of interest, to choose not to answer specific questions, to discontinue the interview or to withdraw at any time with no risks to confidentiality. We would also let them know that the study was being conducted for academic purposes at the Department of Social Anthropology at UCT and that the research results would be widely available once published in academic journals or presented in seminars and conferences.

Doing research 'at home' posed challenges to us, because it required us to unpack and question our assumptions of normality. An inspiring strategy to deal with such a challenge was the one adopted by Mkhwanazi (2005). In his research 'at home' he was confronted, especially when conducting focus group discussions, with 'people who thought that men menstruated' (2005: 115).[3] To deal with such a challenge he decided to share with the study participants his points of view about the issues in a reflexive way, without imposing his standpoint, having been warned by Das (1989) about the need to share sensitive information.

We were also alerted to the challenge that 'while a strict adherence to the code of ethics might protect one's research participants, who or what protects the anthropologist in the field?' (Becker et al 2005: 126). We both felt that, because we were doing ethnography 'at home', the need for protection was not an issue; we were comfortable in the setting and were familiar with the relevant support networks. Finally, and inspired by Spiegel (2005: 135), we were cautioned that in the event that we encountered a situation that raised serious ethical concerns we should follow an ethic of care. Such an ethic would include getting in touch with supervisors or other lecturers from the department for guidance, advice and support.

After submission and approval of our proposals, we were each confronted with a new reality: there was a clear realisation that we would be using a code of ethics produced and informed by a cultural order different from the one practised in the social and cultural context where the study would be developed. By proceeding in such a manner, would we not be ignoring the fact that 'anthropologists don't study villages (tribes, towns, neighbourhoods...), but they study in villages?' (Geertz 1973: 22). Specifically, by using the approved UCT code of ethics we were bound to override the participants' own ethics when they were different from the approved professional research.

This dynamic raised a number of questions: what was the ethical thing to do? Because researchers are socioculturally informed, rather than culturally free, where would our own ethics be placed in this context? How were we to manage the coexistence of diverse ethics without contradicting the principles of their discipline and simultaneously learning about and capturing, by description or otherwise, the diversity of human life? Was the solution to give less weight to the ethics of the study's participants and more weight to the approved ethical considerations, or vice versa? If we chose to act in the approved manner, would we not be going back to Geertz's (1973) utopia, presenting only the natives' point of view in a context in which we were also natives living in the cosmopolitan and heterogeneous 'village' that is Maputo?

One of the possible ways to get around this dilemma was to consider Spiegel's (2005) ethics of care. In Spiegel's view, it is important to 'protect the participants, the researcher and protect anthropology'. But how should the researchers interact with participants? Should they strictly follow the approved ethical considerations or learn and adopt the codes of ethics produced and reproduced in Maputo, including those informing the researchers themselves? Which ethics would inform the formulation of ethically appropriate questions? How should the researchers guide their work in such a way as to avoid being intrusive or overriding the sociocultural values of the participants?

Clearly, the main challenge was how to reconcile the various ethical codes of the discipline, of the participants and of the researchers themselves without sacrificing any of them. And because the aim of the research was to produce a thesis, how could this exercise not be exploitative – be seen as using participants as a means to an end?

The dilemmas highlighted played a role in the development of the research study for both of us. Gune noted that many times while conducting focus groups discussions, interviews, informal conversations and observation, he perceived the interaction with participants in the field as 'violent', albeit not in a physical way. His ears refused to 'accept' some words which when uttered invoked a strange reaction in him, and even today he does not feel comfortable writing about them. At times, his eyes refused to see the images on television when sex-related pictures were displayed, even if they were familiar to him. He realised how wrong he had been in minimising the warning of Becker et al (2005) about the need to ensure that researchers themselves are always protected.

In this regard Gune was heavily influenced by the conflict of dealing with what people were saying on the one hand, and his expectation about what should be acceptable under the UCT code of ethics that he subscribed to, on the other. He was concerned that when it came to writing his dissertation he would not be able to adequately reflect what he experienced. He knew that any further ethical adjustment by the supervisor would detract from the lessons and sexual scripts provided by his Maputo context and which he shared with participants.

Should his data be considered pornographic or not? Was it appropriate to write about certain things and not others? If he accepted exactly what participants shared with him would this be regarded as overriding their sociocultural values? And what if he refused to use them in his thesis? Would this not also serve to reduce the perceptions and cosmologies that informed their sexualities to fit the approved ethical considerations?

Similarly, Manuel was confronted with challenging dilemmas centred on the subtle distinction between writing sexuality and writing pornography.[4] The discussions from the focus group and interviews provided graphically descriptive narrations of sexual acts and practices that, unlike Gune, she enthusiastically transcribed and discussed in her paper in order to give a 'thick description' of the target group. However, discussions with the supervisor and reading of the ASA (2005) and AAA (1971) ethics flagged her to the possibility of going against academic writing standards. Indeed one of the pieces of advice from the supervisor was not to write in a way that creates sexual arousal.

Here, she identified one of the greatest contradictions in studying sexuality. Sex and its dynamics, in the dominant discourse, are most often eroticised and sensualised. In the Mozambican and South African context, speaking publicly about sexuality and sex is rare. The advent of debates and awareness campaigns about HIV/AIDS has propelled the discourse about sex and sexuality into the public arena. Yet much of the discussion remains mechanical, lacking profound descriptions of its ways and means, almost as if sexuality without HIV is not relevant.

When Manuel used ethnography to deeply explore youth sexuality, the details were profound and meticulous. Most definitely, those details were able to create sexual arousal in contexts in which public reference to sex is a taboo. How should we proceed then? What can be said or not said regarding the vivid descriptions people provided of their own practices? Is it not the aim of the discipline of anthropology to deeply explore meanings and practices in order to understand or explain people's behaviour? How could the 'rich description' of sexuality then be a problem?

For researchers working in Africa, the excuse for not writing the details in the exact way they were narrated has been associated with the need to discontinue the colonial tendency to construct Africans and African sexualities as exotic. As Arnfred (2004: 7) points out, African sexuality is often constructed as different from the European or Western and portrayed as deviant. Indeed, many Western views and discourses still automatically blame HIV in Africa on the 'promiscuous and undisciplined sexual life of savages'. Although such concern is valid for the African context, bearing in mind the historical constructions of the sexualities of Africans, some questions about the aims of the discipline of anthropology can be raised:

- How do we write about the knowledge provided by informants when they can be read in various ways, including those that see only promiscuity in African sexualities?
- Should we filter the information given? Shouldn't the emphasis be on critically accessing the perspectives that read African sexualities as promiscuous and not necessarily on restraining local narrations for fear that they would promote such destructive perspectives?

- With regards to the writing of sexuality that creates sexual arousal, would it not be crucial to engage cultural relativism and read sexuality in the context of where it was produced?
- How can we write a rich description of sexuality (sexual practices in this case), guaranteeing that such information will not create arousal?
- Is self-censorship ethical because it protects the people and the discipline?

All indications are that old prejudices die hard and will not necessarily be put to rest by ethically sanitised ethnography.

Even researchers are sexual beings

Kulick and Willson (1995) illuminated some of the dilemmas faced by researchers working on sexuality in *Taboo: Sex, Identity and Erotic Subjectivity in Anthropological Fieldwork,* a rare exploration of the sexual lives of anthropologists and one that exposed the ambiguity of doing fieldwork and doing anthropology. On the one hand anthropologists are tasked with writing about close contacts with native populations, documenting social rituals, such as eating, sleeping, farming, hunting and fishing, and yet on the other hand there is considerable silence in anthropological narratives about the sexualities of anthropologists themselves.

By keeping the researcher's sexuality muted, anthropological discourse perpetuates the dubious image of the asexual scientist/ethnographer and the assumption that the fieldwork experience follows the professional code of ethics to the letter.

Kulick (1995) revealed the hitherto whispered-about homosexual and heterosexual fieldwork experiences that emerged as research results which, according to the very restrictive codes of ethics, were about things that were not supposed to have occurred. His critique also revealed the issue of heterogeneity in dealing with ethical principles, because he was proposing an anthropology that stressed the sexual experiences of the anthropologist as opposed to other codes that recommend the muting of the researcher's sexuality, at least when in the field. So were we to follow Kulick's approach or stick to the approved UCT code of ethics?

As the data collection proceeded, the sociocultural proximity of the words, pictures and films involved in the study allowed Gune to get closer to the local cosmologies of sex and related issues in the context of Maputo, allowing for the steady improvement of his data-collection technique. However, sometimes what he considered appropriate differed from, and even clashed with, what some of the participants considered correct, or vice versa. Gune, ultimately, was nativised in the heterogenous 'village'.

According to the AAA briefing paper (2000) (about consideration of the ethical implications of sexual relationships between anthropologists and members of a study population), the anthropological fieldworker must be aware of the actual or perceived difference in economic and social power between the researcher and the population studied. In many field situations, the anthropologist is an exotic 'other', whose presence might be disruptive to the local cultural group and who is often perceived to be from a world of wealth and power.

Rather than a context in which the ethnographer holds power over powerless participants, we found that in the Maputo context we were taking part in encounters in which power shifted continuously from participants to us, and back again. That fact led us to incorporate new elements, perceptions and even practices related to sex issues, because the participants were not immune to the practices or narratives or to the exotic perceptions that they shared with or even taught us. The AAA paper goes on to warn that:

> Humans are sexual animals, and the possibility exists that the researcher may be placed in an ethical dilemma should a sexual relationship develop in a field situation. It is equally important to the anthropologist to be aware of the health implications of such a relationship to the researcher as well as the population under study. (AAA 2000)

Although this concern is legitimate, its relevance in the context of fieldwork could be questioned: is awareness of health implications not a must in any context and any kind of relationship, be it in the field at home or abroad? Does the advice and ethical code apply only to anthropologists abroad and not, say, on campus as well?

Being a young heterosexual male, Gune was not immune to the glances and the 'provocative' and sensual dress of some of the women participants. Were they dressed in such a way only to impress him or was that their usual dress code? Was he treating female participants only as participants or also as women? During the fieldwork, was his sexuality suspended and only reactivated when he left the field and was reviewing his field notes in his tent or hut?[5] He was sexually active while in the field, which helped him understand differences and similarities in sexual scripts provided by other participants, as well as to make sense of the dynamics shaping them. However, his sexual interaction or involvement was not part of the study and he had no consent from his steady partner to engage as such.

Manuel, as a young woman researching and studying sexuality, noticed that the topic itself was loaded with all manner of prejudice. Within her networks of friends and acquaintances, the perception of her choice of study was generally linked to the idea of sexual availability. In the Maputo context, a 'decent' woman, in the public arena, is seen to be a heterosexual, subservient, docile, fragile and domesticated female. Women are required to hide their sexual desires and needs, and to wait for men to initiate and propose any romantic or sexual relationship. Manuel's choice to conduct her research project on sexuality created among most men and women she encountered the perception that she was different from their view of the 'decent' woman. The consequence was the widespread idea that she was sexually available and an 'easy catch'. That assumption was not limited to the field. A number of her male respondents viewed her this way outside the research setting.

Although in most cases Manuel felt disgusted by the constructed view of a woman studying sexuality in Maputo, during her fieldwork she also manipulated the stigma to get more in-depth information, mostly from male informants. By playing the role of a sexually liberated woman, Manuel allowed participants to talk more openly about their views and practices of sex than they ever could with a 'decent' woman. Although this strategy was very useful, even necessary, Manuel was aware that the ethical code emphasised the need to maintain her security and integrity in the field. However, if all research (whether on sexuality or not) were to strictly follow the guidelines and avoid dangerous or sexually charged situations, much of the process of gathering information would be impossible.

It is common that people open up only after developing a more profound rapport (Spradley 1979). This, however, has its risks. The codes of ethics appear to imply that during fieldwork the researcher should maintain a professional distance from the informants, and should not get aroused or be shocked or shy over what is being said. This only works if the researcher can block his/her emotions and only reactivate them after leaving the field. Is this feasible?

In Gune's experience, when he was not responding to women's advances they mocked him, calling him *matreco*,[6] especially those he considered 'loose' girls, but including some of the other study participants. Conversely, Gune and the other male participants joked and teased each other about girls who did not respond to their greetings or advances. Following local sexual scripts, the person who makes an advance is free to mock when it fails, but according to whose ethics should it fall to check if this constitutes sexual harassment? Should it be according to the participants' ethics, which sometimes coincided with those of the researcher? Or should it be according to the approved codes of ethics, themselves products of a different sociocultural context?

In respect of dissemination strategies, we were committed to discussing with all participants how to utilise the data once it had been analysed. Discussions would also include the best way to write up the study's results and an explanation of dissemination strategies. Finally, we agreed to distribute copies of the studies to the participants as a way of sharing knowledge. But when Gune presented the raw findings and the very preliminary analysis to participants in his group, two contentious issues emerged: should he use participants' real names or pseudonyms in his writing? And should he distribute copies of his report to them?

The 12 participants debated these issues vociferously and four of them insisted that their names be used in the final dissertation. One participant argued that:

> People should know that we are modern people with no problems talking about sex and related matters, since sex is something that we do regularly in our lives ... (E)verything we shared with you, through the last month, all our trips around the city, in bars, car riding at the beach, barbecue sessions, meetings in Rua Araújo,[7] avenues and other forbidden[8] spaces, it was all true. Why then should I hide myself? I assume my attitudes and no one forced my participation in this study, nor to share what I shared. That is why I see no problem in displaying my name.

Another one stated that:

> I want my full name displayed in the dissertation, and whenever you present papers at conferences you should use the examples that I provided. If you do so, people all around the world will know that I do exist and I have a say regarding sex and related issues.

Other participants, however, demanded anonymity, arguing:

> You should not forget that people used to see us together, and if our names are displayed they will find a link between the study and us. I promise you that if my wife reads the study results, as you suggest we each should hold one copy, she will catch me and I will be in trouble … divorce for sure. Since she is my wife she will easily spot me in the study.

> My husband should not even dream about the details that I provided … And you see I have been talking about sex-related things that we do and worse … things that I have done with other guys but never with him … tell me it's a joke and you will not display my name.

> When I decided to participate in the study it was because I found it really interesting. I shared things that I never did before, even with my female friends. You know, it was therapeutic and some of the things that we discussed I had never thought about. You do not have the right to expose my name. Think about my parents, think about how they will react when they read explicit details about my sexual life (that they have never imagined) being available worldwide and followed by my name…

> As for me, it's not negotiable. I just don't want my name exposed and that is final.

> I have nothing to prove to anyone, but since I am not a sex professional and I am not advertising sexual services or favours, why would you want to expose my name?

In a context in which, according to Spiegel (2005), researchers should consider an ethic of care to protect participants, the participants themselves were arguing about their right to be heard and recognised or to remain anonymous. It was not possible to satisfy both groups. The compromise solution was to impose our ethics and exclude all the names. However, this was clearly prejudicial to the ethics of some participants. By imposing his professional code on everyone, Gune was exercising his power privilege. Simultaneously, he was following his own ethics to protect marriages, steady relationships and parents' sensibilities – for him more important than giving a few of his research participants due recognition or protecting his profession and himself.

Conclusion

We survived the discursive narratives on sex (after the initial discomfort and the 'shock' of diversity) and the prospect of entering too deeply into 'dangerous' territory. We adjusted to the situation, learning about sex and related issues through speaking and sharing experiences with people not too close to us. Our respective projects resulted in us learning not only about the sexuality of the participants, but also about our own.

This discussion highlights a number of questions and the need to negotiate ethics in the context of the fieldwork location, rather than to strictly follow professional ethics derived from different sociocultural perspectives. It suggests that anthropology is about expanding the understanding of the diversity of human behaviour, rather than forcing diversity to comply with a particular way of thinking about being human.

We were caught in a complex web of codes of ethics. Though all rooted in the same professional scientific academy, in themselves these were nevertheless diverse. Furthermore, the ethics of the participants of the study and of the fieldwork location were heterogeneous and complex. A third dimension was our own ethics, which contradicted completely or in part one or all codes of ethics.

In all research situations ethics are shifting and changing. Researchers learn about diverse dimensions of sexuality in a dialectical process in which sometimes they hide participants' voices, the research context, the codes of ethics or even their own ethics.

Moreover, there are times when researchers wish to share moments with the study participants and even make them co-authors of the research findings, only to confront whether anonymity is more important than recognition. The scenarios discussed in this essay exposed some ambiguities arising from conflicts emerging in the presence of participants' heterogeneous ethics, researcher ethics and professional codes of ethics. It is clear that there remains much to learn about how to balance these competing priorities without overriding sociocultural values contained in the different ethical perspectives.

Notes

1. An earlier version of this article was published in the *OSSREA Bulletin* 4(2), June 2007. Reprinted with permission.
2. See Manuel (2005 and 2008) and Paulo (2004).
3. Mozambican-Sowetan playwright Richard Nwamba's radio play *Menstruating Men*, a critique of South African xenophobia, was inspired by the reaction of South African mineworkers to some of their Mozambican counterparts when seen in the communal ablution blocks to be urinating blood because they were suffering from bilharzia. Apparently the South Africans mocked the Mozambicans, calling them menstruating men.
4. There is, of course, an element of the pornographic in all ethnography. That is why it is easier to capture the 'sexual life of savages' à la Malinowski (1929) and not of the average fellow citizen. Even when one refrains from reporting on sexualities, prying into people's sacred rituals and studying their lives under a microscope is not only intrusive but also very colonial. The best anthropologists are callous people when observed from an African perspective.
5. Located on the first floor of a three-storey building in Malhangalene, an area of Maputo.
6. Meaning someone considered backward, out of their context, and who does not know how to fit in with the fashion.
7. Araújo Street, the former name of a downtown Maputo street known for its night clubs and sex workers.
8. Places where sex and related issues are less restricted.

References

American Anthropological Association (AAA) (1971) *Statements on Ethics: Principles of Professional Responsibility*, http://www.aaanet.org/stmts/ethstmnt.htm, accessed 9 March 2006

—— (2000) 'Briefing paper for consideration of the ethical implications of sexual relationships between anthropologists and members of a study population', AAA Committee on Ethics, prepared by Joe Watkins

Anthropology Southern Africa (ASA) (2005) 'Ethical Guidelines and Principles of Conduct for Anthropologists', *Anthropology Southern Africa*, 28(3&4): 142–143

Arnfred, S. (2004) 'Rethinking sexualities in Africa: Introduction', in Arnfred, S. (ed) *Re-thinking Sexualities in Africa*, Uppsala, The Nordic African Institute, 7–29

Becker, H., Boonzaier, E. and Owen, J. (2005) 'Fieldwork in shared spaces: Positionality, power and ethics of citizen anthropologists in Southern Africa', *Anthropology Southern Africa* 28(3 & 4): 123–132

Das, V. (1989) 'Public good, ethics, and everyday life: Beyond the boundaries of bioethics', *Daedalus* 118 (4): 99–133

Frith, H. (2000) 'Focusing on sex: Using focus groups in sex research', *Sexualities* 3(3): 275–297

Geertz, C. (1973) *Interpretation of Cultures*, New York, Basic Books

Kulick, D. (1995) 'Introduction', in Kulick, D. and Willson, M. (eds) *Taboo: Sex, Identity and Erotic Subjectivity in Anthropological Fieldwork*, London and New York, Routledge, 1–28

Malinowski, B. (1929) *The Sexual Life of Savages in North-Western Melanesia*, New York, Halcyon House

Manuel, S. (2005) 'Obstacles to condom use among secondary school students in Maputo city, Mozambique', *Culture, Health and Sexuality* 7(3): 293–302

—— (2008) *Love and Desire: Concepts, Narratives and Practices of Sex among Youths in Maputo City*, Dakar, CODESRIA

Mkhwanazi, N. (2005) 'Reflections on the ethical dilemmas that arise for anthropologists conducting fieldwork on the provision of sexuality education in South Africa', *Anthropology Southern Africa* 28(3 & 4): 115–22

Paulo, M. (2004) 'Fertility, sexuality and HIV/AIDS prevention campaigns in Mafalala barrio, Maputo, Mozambique', M.Soc.Sc thesis, University of Cape Town

Scheurich, J.J. (1997), 'A post-modernist critique of research interviewing', in Scheurich, J.J., *Research Methods in the Postmodern*, London, The Falmer Press, 61–79.

Spiegel, A. (2005), 'From exposé to care: preliminary thoughts about shifting the ethical concerns of South African social anthropology', *Anthropology Southern Africa* 28(3 & 4): 133–41

Spradley, J.P. (1979) *The Ethnographic Interview*, New York, Rinehart & Winston

University of Cape Town Code of Ethics (2005) http://web.uct.ac.za/depts/socialanth/dev/ethics/ethics.htm, accessed 9 March 2006

3

From minuscule biomedical models to sexuality's depths[1]

Stella Nyanzi

Nearly three decades of prevention interventions against HIV/AIDS have yielded little effect, with the few success stories heralded universally as potential blueprints in best-practice dossiers. Unprotected sex is still the most common mode of HIV transmission. Unintended or teenage pregnancies, sexually transmitted infections, including HIV/AIDS, sexual abuse, and violence and discrimination remain major public-health challenges, despite targeted strategies of redress.

So what is missing in available sexual health programmes, policies and activism? Why are they not as effective as they promise to be? What is wrong with these interventions? One possibility is foundational: interventions are premised on limited working definitions of sexuality as a concept (Boyce et al 2006). The production of knowledge on sexuality in the era of AIDS is a field rich in social actors – from diverse institutions and disciplines to political motivations and funding agencies. But biomedicine maintains the hegemony over what knowledge is valued and thereby implemented as policy and practice (Caceres 2000).

Before the advent of HIV/AIDS, human sexuality research was mainly the terrain of biomedicine, including physiology, psychology, psychiatry and epidemiology (Parker et al 2000). Sexuality was perceived in terms of deviance, disease and abnormality and in need of correction, control, punishment and cures. Early sexuality scholars reproduced the theoretical and methodological commitments of biomedical research. Statistics and quantitative methods dominated their inquiry. The onslaught of knowledge, attitude, behaviour and practice surveys to understand the dynamics of sexual behaviour responsible for transmitting HIV portrays the persistence of this trend in knowledge generation.

This positivist approach is good for measurements, such as how much, how often or how many, but not for exploring meanings, for example, how and why things occur. Despite the advantages of such an approach, including quantification, representativeness and generalisability, there are problems of the over-simplification of complex, nuanced and ambivalent concepts like sexuality. Straightforward questions such as 'Are you gay?' (Caceres 1996) or 'Are you married?' (Nyanzi et al 2004), which might elicit simple answers in Western society, are unanswerable in other contexts.

Conflicting systems of classification, fluid contextual connotations, ambivalent expressions, differences between self-definition and labelling by others and shifting meanings are salient issues within sexuality that challenge generalisations and bounded concepts with restricted definitions that focus on sexual behaviour, identities, practices and so on. In response to the crisis within sexuality, how do we measure shifting contexts? Where does sexuality start and end?

Limitations of the positivist approach to sexuality emphasise the urgency for alternatives, which yields a complementary role for social constructionists, including anthropologists and sociologists (Vance 1991). In qualitative models, they can explore the wider meanings embedded within sexuality to generate more context-specific conceptualisations that violate rigid, blueprint definitions.

Preventive interventions against HIV/AIDS reignited the overt medicalisation of sexuality, such that the sexual self became restricted by intricate ties to the body, to bodily functions of coitus and reproduction, and to illness and health. Responding to the crisis in sexuality, sexual health programmes focused on disease, pregnancy and death (Dixon-Mueller 1993). Sexual health has thus been subsumed under the rubric of reproductive health, although much of sexuality has no bearing on reproduction (Miller 2000). Since human sexuality is rife with contestation, politics and enactments of control and power (Weeks 1985), and because biomedicine has developed as a principal instrument of that control, is it safe for meaningful interventions to maintain this ancient premise? If they do, what is the opportunity cost for relevance, effectiveness and appropriateness?

Rather than conceptualising sexuality as merely situated in the body and bodily functions, consideration of the range of meanings that individuals and groups attach to it is critical (Jackson and Scott 1997). Such a nuanced definition should embrace, among others: desire, the erotic, emotions, sensuality, fantasy, intimacy, commitment, power, relationship, negotiation, exploration, exploitation, expression, trust, personhood, belonging, identity, pleasure, entertainment, consumption, obligation, transaction, dependence, work, income, resistance, abuse, masculine entitlement, feminine propriety, respectability, spirituality, custom and ritual. These factors touch on gender, race, class, citizenship, community and religion.

The hallmark of sexuality is its complexity – its multiple meanings, sensations and connections (Vance 1992). Therefore HIV prevention interventions that target sexuality must of necessity embrace its inherent ambivalence and depth of scope to be effective. Interventions driven, designed and implemented by the participation of targeted communities have warranted some success because of local input into conceptualisations, process and outcome.

Notes

1. Reprinted with permission from Elsevier (*The Lancet*, 2006, 368 (9550): 1851–2).

References

Boyce, P., Huong Soo, L., Jenkins, C. et al (2006) 'Putting sexuality (back) into HIV/AIDS: issues, theory and practice', Toronto, XVI International AIDS Conference, 13–18 August

Caceres, C.F. (1996) 'Male bisexuality in Peru and the prevention of AIDS' in Aggleton, P. (ed) *Bisexualities and AIDS: International Perspectives*, London, Taylor & Francis: 136–47

—— (2000) 'The production of knowledge on sexuality in the AIDS era: some issues, opportunities and challenges' in Parker R., Barbosa, R.M. and Aggleton, P. (eds) *Framing the Sexual Subject: The Politics of Gender, Sexuality and Power,* Berkeley, University of California Press: 241–59

Dixon-Mueller, R. (1993) 'The sexuality connection in reproductive health', *Studies in Family Planning* 24: 269–82

Jackson, S. and Scott S. (1997) 'Gut reactions to matters of the heart: reflections on rationality, irrationality and sexuality', *Sociological Review* 45(4): 551–75

Miller, A.M. (2000) 'Sexual but not reproductive: exploring the junction and disjunction of sexual and reproductive rights', *Health Hum Rights* 4: 69–109

Nyanzi, S., Nyanzi, B., Kalina, B. and Pool, R. (2004) 'Mobility, sexual networks and exchange among Bodaboda men in southwest Uganda', *Cult Health Sex* 6: 239–54

Parker, R., Barbosa, R.M. and Aggleton, P. (eds) (2000) *Framing the Sexual Subject: The Politics of Gender, Sexuality and Power,* Berkeley, University of California Press

Vance, C.S. (ed) (1991) 'Anthropology rediscovers sexuality: a theoretical comment', *Social Science and Medicine* 33: 875–84

—— (1992) *Pleasure and Danger: Exploring Female Sexuality,* London, Pandora Press

Weeks, J. (1985) *Sexuality and Its Discontents: Meanings, Myths and Modern Sexualities,* London, Routledge

4

TRACKS: researching sexualities walking abOUT the city of Johannesburg[1]

Zethu Matebeni

Space is integral to many gay[2] people's lives. Where and how you are located as a gay, lesbian or trans person determines how you will be perceived in that particular space and your experience of the space and place. At the same time, that space might be reconfigured by the presence of gay, lesbian or trans people's visibility in it. When spaces are not conducive to gay, lesbian or trans people, they have to move to spaces that are either safer or gay friendly or conducive to a gay lifestyle. This move suggests that many gay people spend some part of their lives in transition, moving from one place to another or looking for safer and more conducive areas, zones or landscapes.

This brief chapter looks at this form of transition, the move from one space to another through walking. In writing this chapter I was concerned with the meanings arising from tracking people's routes as they 'walk about' urban spaces. The urban landscape with which I am concerned is the city of Johannesburg, a dynamic and cosmopolitan African metropolis (Mbembe and Nuttall 2004). Here I am concerned with walking about urban spaces, which has both the potential of creating new landscapes and repositioning the way gay people are positioned and occupy particular spaces.

The chapter starts off with an extract from a well-known black lesbian in Johannesburg, South Africa. Her experiences as she occupies the different spaces show the different ways in which black lesbians in particular experience space in Johannesburg. It is important to note that the experiences of black gay people in South Africa differ to some extent from those of white gay people. Johannesburg as a space also differs quite significantly from other urban spaces in South Africa. It is a city that has a long history of gay and lesbian activism and involvement, having hosted the first gay and lesbian pride in Africa, and has a number of visible spaces and landmarks celebrating and commemorating the lives and contributions of gay and lesbian people in the city.

From that exploration of spaces and efforts to focus on the importance of space in relation to sexual identity, the chapter considers the importance of focusing on the concept of walking about the city, both as a form of exploring landscapes and also as a way of negotiating gay identity in relation to space.

Focusing on Johannesburg, Bev Palesa Ditsie, a Soweto-born black lesbian activist and film-maker, recounts her experiences in her township after she appeared on national television at the first gay and lesbian pride march in 1990 in downtown Johannesburg (Ditsie and Neuman 2001 and Ditsie 2006: 19-20; NoneOnRecord n.d.). Pride is an important event for many lesbian, gay, trans and intersex people because it is where they can visibly show themselves as well as occupy space by 'walking about' the city. Pride has become a popular event and form of activism in Johannesburg and it has recently been extended to Soweto and KwaThema, two of the city's townships.

In the following extract, Bev Ditsie shares what she experienced in her community after publicly identifying herself as lesbian. Although this was an opportune moment for gay and lesbian organising in Johannesburg and the country as a whole, it presented difficulties for Ditsie and her family because threats from people in her community loomed. She was unable to be a lesbian in her own neighbourhood and, whenever noticed, men believed she should be 'put right' by being shown that she was a woman or removed altogether from the black neighbourhood. Threats of sexual assault and violence were directed towards her.

After insisting to the mainly white organisers of the pride march that she be allowed to speak and represent black lesbian and gay people, this is what Ditsie experienced:

> So I made a speech. Those cameras around me didn't mean anything, until it hit the news. Wow! Church groups, parent's groups, school groups, and teacher's groups, you name it. Everywhere there was a whole petition to get me killed, to get people like me. It's like, 'We understand when it's these white people, we understand it's a very white thing to be doing, so, we understand. But when YOU stand up and tell us it's all South African, oh – well you're starting to insult people's sensibilities and you are shaking their moral ground, and you are shaking their own firm beliefs!'
>
> It was a frightening time; you know the threats to the family, threats to my mother, threats to my grandmother and my sister, guys coming around my house wanting to teach me I'm a woman. That was something I did not expect, like I could not walk to the shops without hearing at least one person or some car passing by (making a hooting sound) asking, 'Is that her?' saying, 'Bitch, we're going to get you, you're a woman, you faggot!' Every time I heard noises outside I kept thinking, am I being attacked? People would threaten and say to me, 'We're coming for you!' That actually got my parents totally and completely supporting me because the implications were if they do not support me, then who is? So my grandma became my rock…
>
> I was sitting in my room when I heard voices outside calling my name. I ran into the lounge and my granny opened the door and told me to hide. About twenty angry men were surrounding our house demanding I come with them so that they could teach me a lesson. They wanted to rape me. The worst thing is that they threatened to take my grandma if I didn't come with them. My grandmother stood at the door and said, 'Come in, but one of you will die with me…'

> So, I was escorted for about two weeks after the pride march. My mom
> would put on her converse, she'd put on her jeans and she'd say, 'We need to
> go there – let's walk.' I was scared, all the time. So, ja, I just pushed so hard,
> and I stuck out like a sore thumb and said, 'Ok, all right, look – I'm right here,
> I ain't moving, I ain't budging!' (Ditsie 2006: 19–20)

This extract offers a compelling starting point for an exploration of sexuality in relation to space, particularly in the city of Johannesburg. Not only does it highlight the
common notions of associating homosexuality with whiteness, but it also shows the
distinguishable ways in which sexual identity is/is not negotiated spatially.

At a lesbian and gay pride march in the inner city of Johannesburg, Ditsie had
made iconic history by talking openly as a black lesbian. Less than 20km from the
inner city, in the township of Soweto, presenting as a lesbian challenged societal
norms. These are the continuities/discontinuities and contradictions with which this
chapter is interested. Sometimes they are blatant, other times hidden. It is the complexity and dynamism of Johannesburg as a space that evokes these, but also how
identities shift and reconfigure such a space.

Ditsie's experiences are neither unique nor isolated. Twenty years later many
black lesbian, bisexual and transgendered people in South Africa still experience
marginalisation in their daily lives in the many cities, townships and rural areas.
In a recent exhibition project of the Gay and Lesbian Memory in Action (GALA),[3]
Jo'burg TRACKS: Sexuality in the city, curated by Mark Gevisser and myself, and
designed by Clive van den Berg, the story of Johannesburg through the lives of eight
lesbian, gay and transgender people living in the city is mapped. Using extraordinary archive, artefacts and photographs depicting the lives and experiences of the
eight participants, we track their journeys as they enter and traverse the streets,
private homes, social spaces and landscapes of Johannesburg.

The participants include a 75-year-old married Zulu man, Edgar Dlamini, living
a 'hidden' gay life; a gay Burundian man, Kaze Emile,[4] forced to flee from his country to South Africa after he was sentenced to death when found with another man;
and Vanya Maseko, a 24-year-old transsexual model. These participants' experiences
show the deep interconnections between space and sexuality in South Africa.

Jo'burg TRACKS builds on an earlier attempt to excavate, document and popularise the history and lives of gay and lesbian people in Johannesburg developed by
GALA through a walking 'queer tour' of Johannesburg. Here again, the concept of
'walking about' the city is evoked. The tour offers unique insight into the history of
lesbian and gay cultural identity in Johannesburg. Through a very extensive mapping process, the tour captures all of gay Johannesburg's famous landmarks, such
as the Harrison Reef Hotel in Hillbrow (a notorious area in the inner city), the oldest
gay bar and home to the first gay and lesbian church for black people; Forest Town,
an affluent northern suburb where a gay party was raided by police in 1966, leading to the implementation of harsh measures aimed at stamping out homosexuality;
Simon Nkoli Corner in Hillbrow, dedicated to the memory of the gay anti-apartheid
and AIDS activist, who was tried for treason; Constitutional Hill, a former prison
and now the home of South Africa's constitutional court and of two lesbian and gay
organisations; and the Soweto homes and spaces of gay and lesbian activists (Reid

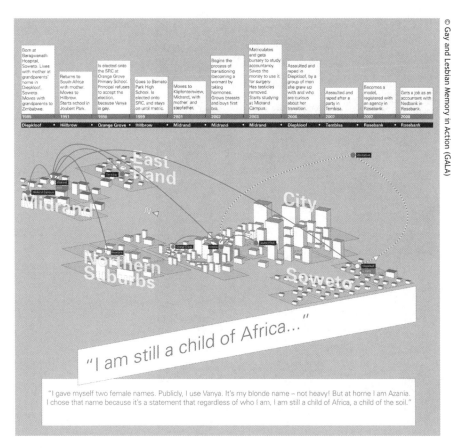

and Alberton 1999). Through this tour, it becomes evident that South Africa's social and political landscape is deeply entwined with sexuality and sexual identity.

Although the numerous historic 'queer' spaces might intimate the ease with which gay and lesbian identity is located within Johannesburg, researching sexuality in Johannesburg proves the contrary. Such research in the city is bound with complexities and contradictions. Ditsie alludes to these in the earlier extract, and I explore them further in the following section.

Walking abOUT the city

Much of the research on sexuality and space often looks at particular spaces, such as clubs, bars or neighbourhoods, with only a few focusing on the concept of walking the streets of the city or an urban context (Adler and Brenner 1992; Bell and Valentine 1995; Lewin and Leap 1996 and 2009). The general theme emanating from most studies on sexual identity and space suggests a consideration of time and space management of lesbian identities in particular. It is almost impossible to escape this theme, even in a place such as Johannesburg. This theme becomes evident in many people's narratives, including in the opening extract.

53

Vanya in Rosebank mall.

Researching sexuality through 'walking about' the city provides an opportune moment to be acquainted with the city's streets and its public and private spaces. The idea of 'walking about' the city captures the feel of the city as well as repositions the walker in that particular space, because the walker is visibly 'out'. For a black lesbian in Johannesburg, the city presents itself as both a place of danger and pleasure. It is dangerous because one is 'read' as lesbian or gay, through clothing, style, stance and other forms. This potential to be read can pose challenges and threatens many in South Africa who are still uncomfortable with gay identity. Walking about also entails having to continuously 'come out' or be 'outed' as one occupies the city. The pleasure is an ironic realisation of being looked at and being consumed as a lesbian or gay person. It is also the pleasure of walking through and occupying other spaces that are safer and conducive to gay life.

Shay MacLaren, a 79-year-old white lesbian who grew up in Johannesburg and was one of the participants in *Jo'burg TRACKS*, states this when talking about her experience of walking about downtown Johannesburg in the 1950s: 'Walking down Eloff Street in a pair of trousers and short hair, I might as well have been topless! The crowds actually parted like the Red Sea' (Gevisser and Matebeni 2008).

MacLaren's experience shows the very visible way in which the lesbian body is read through dress and style. In her time, it was odd for a woman to be seen in trousers and with short hair, and this immediately identified her as gay. More than half a century later, in the same streets of Johannesburg, gay people share similar experiences.

One participant, Nestar, a 22-year-old lesbian soccer player I have met and walked with through the streets of Johannesburg's inner city and the townships, shares her experiences as she travels between home and the inner city or while walking with her girlfriend:

> When I'm walking with my girlfriend in the streets I have to pretend that we are friends. When guys approach me I must pretend that I'm a femme girl, knowing very well that I'm not like that. I'm used to being greeted with 'hola' [township slang for hello]. I can't hold my girlfriend in public. I can't dress the way I want to in public because when people see me dressed like this they're going to insult me and beat me, or even rape me, so I'm afraid of those things, you see …When I have to go home I'm always in a hurry because I leave the city late and I still have to go and catch a taxi. When I get to the taxi I have to behave lady-like and soften my voice when I'm greeted. I have to think of my safety first because sometimes these guys greet you just to provoke you and to see what kind of person you are.[5]

While on the shoot for *Jo'burg TRACKS*, Vanya constantly felt both the pleasure and danger of being consumed in the streets and shopping malls of the city. As a transsexual model (read female), in her tight jeans, high-heeled shoes, long hair and feminine body, she walks and occupies the streets and public spaces as an exoticised and desired figure. This is challenged when men, in particular, find out that she is transsexual. These experiences have left Vanya with physical and emotional scars, and a survivor of rape and other hate crimes.

These experiences of everyday walking about the city suggest that Johannesburg as a space is an interesting site for work on sexual identities. Like other cities in Africa, as a research site it is yet to be uncovered. An interesting array of themes emanate from conducting research in such a site. However, the research process requires more sophisticated, adaptable and unconventional methods that allow researchers to traverse sexualised terrains that simultaneously present pleasure and danger. Researching sexualities requires this complex consideration of the sexualised landscape. It is not limited to reading urban spaces in relation to how sexual identities are managed, but also about exploring the ways in which sexual identities reconfigure existing spaces and landscapes.

The meanings of such interplay between sexual identity and space are yet to be realised. Only then can we capture the work done by Ditsie and other gay people's stance and positions when expressing, 'I'm right here, I ain't moving, I ain't budging'. This is the methodology that should preoccupy the researcher on African sexualities.

Notes

1. I am grateful to Ariane Vuckovic for her critical eye and engagement with the text. I would also like to thank Priscilla de Gasparis and Susan van Zyl for their invaluable comments on the initial draft of this paper. The Humanities Graduate Centre at the

University of the Witwatersrand generously offered a writing retreat while I was drafting the initial extended paper.
2. Gay here is used to refer collectively to lesbians, gay men and trans identified people. In other cases, when positioned next to men, it is used to refer particularly to gay men.
3. When GALA was established in 1997, it was known as the Gay and Lesbian Archives. In 2006 its name was changed to Gay and Lesbian Memory in Action.
4. Both these participants used pseudonyms because they cannot reveal their true identities.
5. Interview with Nestar, 23 April 2009.

References

Adler, Sy and Brenner, Johanna (1992) 'Gender and space: lesbians and gay men in the City', *International Journal of Urban and Regional Research* 16(1): 24–34

Bell, David and Valentine, Gill (eds) (1995) *Mapping Desire: Geographies of Sexualities,* London, Routledge

Ditsie, Bev Palesa (2006) 'Today we are making history', in de Waal, S. and Manion, A. (eds) *Pride: Protest and Celebration,* Johannesburg, Jacana Media, 19–20

Ditsie, Bev and Neuman, Nicky (Dirs) (2001) *Simon and I,* DVD, South Africa, See Thru Media/Steps for the Future

Gevisser, Mark (2008) 'Affairs of the heart', *Mail & Guardian,* 30 May, http://www.mg.co.za/article/2008-05-30-affairs-of-the-heart, accessed 26 August 2009

Gevisser, Mark and Matebeni Zethu (2008) '*Jo'burg TRACKS: Sexuality in the city* (art exhibition)', Johannesburg, Gay and Lesbian Memory in Action

Lewin, E. and Leap, W.L. (1996) *Out in the Field: Reflections of Lesbian and Gay Anthropologists,* Urbana and Chicago, University of Illinois Press: 212–235

—— (eds) (2009) *Out in Public: Reinventing Lesbian/Gay Anthropology in a Globalising World,* United Kingdom, Wiley Blackwell

Mbembe, Achille and Nuttall, Sarah (2004) 'Writing the world from an African metropolis' *Public Culture* 16(3): 347–72

NoneOnRecord (n.d.) 'Stories of Queer Africa. Interviews: Bev Ditsie', http://noneonrecord.com/blog/?page_id=25, accessed 18 March 2010

Reid, Graeme and Alberton, Paulo (directors) (1999) *Josi: the Queer Tour,* Johannesburg, The Gay and Lesbian Archives of South Africa (GALA)

5

Dialoguing culture and sex: reflections from the field

Amy S. Tsanga

Introduction

Hands-on supervision of masters students in their field research has, in my experience, emerged as a significant way of gaining insights into lived realities in order to develop theoretical constructs on problematic arenas for African women.[1] Part of helping students to be aware of the realities of doing women's law research (Stang Dahl 1997; Bentzon et al 1998) involves actually visiting them in the field and observing and participating, albeit briefly, in their data-gathering process. In this chapter, I utilise my hands-on observations from being in the field, listening in and supervising a student in Kenya who was researching sexual practices among the Luo community, to ask critical questions on representations of culture.[2] In essence, the cultural practices that were being explored and that involved sex related to a range of situations, including:

- The planting of crops: the belief is that when the rains start, before a couple can proceed with planting they must have sex.
- When a child is born: it is believed that the husband must have sex with the mother of the child before he can have sex with any of her co-wives, otherwise no more children will be born to that woman.
- When a husband dies: the widow must be cleansed sexually before she can be 'inherited'.
- In the case of a son or daughter getting married: the parents are expected to have sex a night before or on the day of the marriage.
- When a home has been constructed: before it can be occupied, the husband is supposed to have sex with his wife in the house.

The way that Kenyan Luo culture in particular shapes attitudes towards sex was a key aspect of the study I was supervising. The student herself was a Luo woman and therefore largely an insider looking at her own culture through feminist lenses. As the supervisor, I was particularly interested in ensuring that the student was alive to the dynamics that were at play in the field as she gathered her information:

who, for instance, speaks for whom on these cultural practices? What forces are at play in shaping whether or not these cultures are practised? What are the gendered dimensions in terms of perceptions of these cultural practices? Are they prevalent in today's society? Which ones are dying and why? Also to the extent that women are breaking away from these cultural practices, what are the motivating forces? To the extent that they are not, what are the constraints?

Culture in its wider sense has a rich, diverse and fluid meaning (Giles and Middleton 2008: 6–30). An aspect of culture is the focus on the way of life of a particular group. Within this context, it is the lives of ordinary men and women that provide critical insights into the nature of that culture. By hearing their views, the power relations that shape that culture also emerge. In relation to women, culture as a way of life is often narrowly interpreted, particularly by those with power, primarily to serve their own interests. It is for such reasons that African feminists often argue that culture is one of the arenas that present obstacles for women. Understanding the nature of hierarchies and discrimination is therefore key.

Given the centrality of human rights ideals as contained in both international and regional instruments, I am also always interested when supervising students in understanding how these lived realities measure up to the various ideals on a given topic. Thus, in relation to culture, for example, among the standards that I consciously bear in mind are the right of women to live 'in a positive cultural context and to participate at all levels in the determination of cultural policies'; the right to dignity; and the right to life, bodily integrity and security of the person, which incorporates the right to be protected from violence from public and private sources.[3] Also critical is the need for the state to:

> [M]odify the social and cultural patterns of conduct of men and women, with a view to achieving the elimination of prejudices and customary and all other practices which are based on the idea of the superiority or inferiority of either of the sexes or on stereotyped roles for men and women.[4]

In illustrating and unpacking how and why such issues call for attention, I relied on my observations of the dynamics at play while sitting in on four different interviews with:

- Angela,[5] a Luo woman and social development officer in the Ministry of Gender
- Peter, a 57-year-old Luo man and a senior civil servant
- A focus group of urban-based Luo men
- A focus group of urban-based Luo women.

Unearthing individual as opposed to social identities

The first interview I sat in on was with Angela. As will be illustrated, it introduced at the outset the need to be conscious of the distinction between individual and social identities, especially as regards cultural practices (Hewitt 2000). Though belonging to a specific ethnic and cultural group, she appeared to have formed an identity and perspective on issues involving sexual cultural practices that were not in tandem with what is understood to be the culture of the wider social group. The interview also raised the need to explore further the forces that were shaping such individual identity among Luos. Could it be a cocktail of factors, such as education, professional skills, religion, modernity or interaction with other cultures, or sheer rebellion? It also brought to the fore the need to explore more deeply whether social identities based on common beliefs, ideas and belonging to a common group, often so strongly used to perpetuate culture, are indeed as strong as they are often made out to be. But perhaps more importantly the interview also brought out the dangers of preconceived assumptions on the part of any researcher regarding workplace positioning and gender activism. On what basis, for instance, do we select key respondents? In this case, the student selection had been based on the interviewee being a Luo woman and hence the assumption that she was affected by these practices, but also because she was involved in gender issues at a fairly high level. Yet, in reality, neither of these positions turned her into the envisaged key informant.

I had expected to hear an in-depth analysis of these cultural sexual practices and especially any role that she saw for the Ministry of Gender, in dealing with those cultural practices that might be problematic for women. Yet what was most striking was the distancing of herself from these issues as critical concerns.

Asked about the cultural practices among the Luo that involve sex, Angela explained that she had heard of them while growing up and she essentially reiterated the practices that are outlined above. I was struck by her emphasis on the hearsay nature of the source of her knowledge, for it immediately suggested to me that, though she was a Luo woman, she had not followed these cultural practices. Asked specifically on the practice of having sex before you occupy a new home, she was forthright in her judgement:

> To me it does not make sense. The practice has no value to add. I have heard of these cultures being spoken about on the radio and I also heard about them growing up. Whether they are practised or not depends on your husband. If he is for the practices then it is very difficult not to comply.[6]

Interestingly, Angela's emphasis was on the power of the man to determine compliance, and not the power of the woman to refuse to comply, thus pointing to the pervasiveness of patriarchal control in such matters.

The significance of personal interviews is that you can also observe the interviewees' reactions – their level of engagement and interest in the topic and whether it strikes a nerve or not. In this instance, though what Angela had to say for the duration of the conversation had its merits, her detachment was palpable. In fact her change of demeanour was evident once the topic sunk in. She had the air of a hostile witness and it was easy to see that she would have labelled the interview a 'waste of time'. The conversation shifted to why people continue with some of these practices. Her answer was swift:

> In African culture you have two choices really. You either comply or you agree to disagree. There are people who just carry on what other people do. They

don't really understand what they are doing. They are doing it for compliance and also fear is instilled in them. A woman may fear losing her husband if she does not follow culture or she may fear that something will happen or she may be very dependent on her husband. Something that you do out of fear cannot be with your consent. It is just compliance. Therefore both men and women may follow these cultural practices but out of fear. To me all these cultural practices involving sex do not make sense.

From the above one gets a picture of the forces that might be at play in influencing choices and behaviour, such as fear of loss, of being ostracised and of bad omens. Angela observed the inherent dangers for women of having sex as part of the ritual of widow cleansing and inheritance. Probed on the role of the state to change harmful cultural practices, she saw little hope for change: 'These things are private. The state cannot come to your bedroom. It is one thing to have laws and quite another to enforce them.'

On the issue of couples having sex before planting, Angela's view was that it interfered with planning one's activities freely because her understanding was that, if in a polygynous union, the man had to do the rounds first before any planting could take place.[7] Her final remark before glancing suggestively at her watch was that culture had been tempered by religion and that it was difficult to know what people thought: 'Some people do these things privately. People don't want to expose their private lives.'

I could not help thinking that perhaps this was the real reason for Angela's visible detachment; that we were prying and othering and how dare we? This was understandable at some level because, indeed, we have our own sex lives to get on with, but at another level I had assumed that, given the nature of her job, she would have welcomed such dialogue.

There were several issues in particular that stood out for detailed exploration from what she said. The first was the extent to which people still carry on these sex-related cultural practices – understanding lived practices as opposed to what is merely said to be the culture – and whether women are particularly bound by these practices in today's society? The second issue was the extent to which living outside a culture might influence a person's view of their culture. A third issue introduced for further exploration was the influence of religion in shaping beliefs and attitudes towards certain cultural practices.

As we walked to the next interview I raised the possibility of the rural/urban divide with my student. 'Whether rural or urban, culture follows you,' she told me. This is indeed the case, as I later found out when we dialogued with a group of women about their lived experiences.

The passing on of culture: understanding the role of ethnicity-based social identities

The next interviewee was Peter, a 57-year-old Luo man.[8] I regarded this interview particularly as an important illustration of how members of an ethnic and cultural group, Luos in this case, pass on their culture. Although Peter readily confessed to having lived outside the Luo community for the greater part of his professional life, he nonetheless still felt able and willing as a man born into Luo culture to speak and pass on the knowledge of this culture. By so doing he was clearly playing a role in its perpetuation through representation.

It struck me as important how information on cultural practices often comes from people who are members of a group, yet have spent their lives largely outside that group. Understanding the implications of this from the perspective of the alternative forces that shape lived realities is vital, especially in the case of women. To what extent do those who fall into this category actually act on the cultural practices that they are aware of? How have interactions with other cultures influenced Luo culture on sexual cultural practices?

From a women's law perspective, men's views are important because they help to give insights into how men shape, influence and see issues that fundamentally affect women's lives. Peter was jovial and most willing to be interviewed. In my position as an African woman from another country (Zimbabwe), I have found throughout my journeys an openness generally and a welcoming spirit to me as a fellow African. But there might also be a tendency to want to over-impress, especially on the part of men.

Peter has worked as a civil servant throughout the country. His first statement said more than he realised. He said he would tell us about Luo culture as far as he could recall it because, in reality, for most of his working life he had lived outside Luo areas and had been mixing with other cultures. Which version of customary law were we therefore going to be presented with? Living Luo culture or some idealised version? What did it tell us about those who often speak so strongly of their cultural practices? What indeed is the impact of interaction with other cultures?

Peter insisted on starting with an overview of the Luo tribe before delving into their cultural practices involving sex. Of significance was the role of marriage among the Luos and the tremendous importance that they attach to this institution. He explained:

> If you have no wife you will not be respected. You must be able to run a home. There cannot even be a small job for you in the clan if you have no wife. That is the significance of marriage. You may be a drunk but if you have a wife you are respected. If you are not married you are like a pendulum swinging. At age 24 or 25 for men, the expectation these days is that they should get married. For girls it may be younger. We Luos generally do not marry our age mates. We believe that women are more mature and so we tend to marry women who are five to 10 years younger. We respect marriage and see it as a way of enhancing the family. Grandchildren top it all.

He further emphasised that a Luo man was supposed to take care of his wife and not the other way round. He was expected to build her a house, feed her and her children. Women were not supposed to take care of a man. Equally important was that marriages are arranged traditionally so as to ensure that you marry into a good family. While acknowledging that this has now been modified, he thought it was important.

When we turned to the cultural practices among the Luo that involve sex, I was keen to find out which ones Peter thought were still prevalent. He cited having sex before moving into a new house as important although he thought people under 30 might now be ignoring some of these practices. When I questioned why the practice was deemed necessary, he explained:

> The belief was that if you enter the house with another woman, some bad omen would come out of it. A girlfriend would bring bad omen into the house. The idea is to honour your wife so that nothing is done without her knowledge. People believe that a man cannot become rich without a wife.

This explanation had doubtlessly been influenced by the need to project Luo culture in a good light, given my request for a rationale behind the culture. I was curious if a man could bring another woman into the house thereafter. Peter explained that tradition said that if you brought someone else you did not enter with her into the main bedroom, although he conceded that men tended to ignore this. He saw this cultural practice as having evolved out of the need to instil good behaviour and to foster respect for the wife because, as he pointed out, there was no empirical evidence that showed that one would suffer misfortune. If a man had more than one wife then the eldest wife took precedence in all rituals.

Peter was also emphatic that Luo men were generally not monogamous: 'In the opinion of a Luo man, one wife cannot satisfy him. Every woman knows that when she is away, there is a woman helping her husband. Luo women tend to allow their men's "outings".' I wondered what Luo women themselves would say to this statement, because it seemed to point to a tendency to justify behaviour especially where it was deemed problematic.

In regards to having sex to usher in the planting season Peter explained that planting was a symbol of procreation and prosperity. Planting was associated with hope so when rain fell you crowned it all with sex:

> It was a kind of opening and welcoming ceremony and you could also plant a child in the woman in the process. You would call him Okomo meaning a child conceived when people are planting and if it is a girl you would call her Akomo. Even when harvesting you can beckon a woman.

Peter said that in the case that there was more than one wife, the sexual ceremony for planting was done with the first wife. His understanding was that you planted first and celebrated the day after you planted. He however conceded that nowadays, because of urbanisation, people have no farms so the practice might not be as prevalent. Peter spoke glowingly of the practice in which parents are expected to have sex when their child is getting married, as part of the celebration. He narrated his own lived experience in this regard:

> When our second son was wedding we were able to harmonise Christianity with tradition. The night before or the night after, parents are supposed to have sex although it can also be done symbolically by touching the woman's private parts. Such practices are very harmless as they are done in the spirit of celebration. Sex is associated in this instance with joy and abundance.

Sex, he explained is also used as a means of reconciliation in Luo culture: 'If you are my wife and I have slapped you in the afternoon, we should reconcile. The fact that I slapped you is neither here nor there.'

The cultural practice that Peter regarded as particularly problematic for women was that of widow cleansing, after a husband dies. He saw it as a problem not in terms of the violation of the woman's body but rather in relation to the spread of HIV/AIDS. The cleansing is done by an outsider to the clan called a *jakowiny*, who sexually cleanses the widow before she can be 'inherited'. Peter painted the following picture of the *jakowiny*:

> I would describe him as professional woman inheritor; not very normal but not very mad either – someone with a minus in his mental capacity. We believe that death was caused by the devil, caused by *richo* (sin). People did not believe that you just died from nothing. Because of a lot of spirits hovering around, some rituals had to be carried out to chase away the evil spirit. On the day the *jakowiny* comes to do the cleansing, some rituals would be carried out. He would be given a lot of drink so that by the time he sleeps with the woman he is very drunk. The spirit would then go into the *jakowiny*. Once the *jakowiny* has done his bit, that is cleansing, the real inheritor of the woman, called the *Ter*, then comes along.

I quizzed him about the logic of sex in this instance and he told me that he thought it was because for that moment the *jakowiny* married the woman and the temporary marriage had to be consummated. He also stressed that it was bad luck and a definite curse for a woman to die without being 'inherited'. Where such an eventuality takes place, then she had to be 'inherited' in death. A man is put in a room with the corpse and he symbolically touches her private parts or pretends to sleep with her. I asked further if there was an equivalent procedure when it was a woman who had died? In this case, Peter explained, it would be enough if he merely dreamt that he had had sex with his former wife.

Peter's overview was interesting for dialoguing sex and culture at several levels. Are there differences between idealised versions of cultural practices and living cultural practices? Are there good and bad practices? Can we talk about some as being less harmful to women? What views do women hold on these practices? In what ways do these practices treat women as 'others'? Clearly, because the nature of the dialogue was largely premised on my seeking to understand the nature as well as the rationale of these practices, motives were provided that largely put the cultural practices in a good light, especially from a male perspective. Whether they are all seen as such by those who are on the receiving end, namely women, is really at the heart of the matter.

Justifying culture through the power of hearsay and causality: focus group discussion with Luo men

The next dialogue was with a group of six Luo men. They included Mac, a lawyer; John, a retired bank manager; Bill, a development consultant; Eddie, an advocate; Philemon, a head teacher; and Chris, a retiree who joined the group a little later. Apart from John and Chris, who were retired, the rest were younger men between the ages of 35 and 45.

The conversation began with one of the men pointing out that all Luo cultures revolved around sex. We were told that sex in Luo culture brought order to society and that it was primarily food and sex that must satisfy cultural taboos. What I found interesting were the examples the men gave of the consequences that would follow if these cultural rituals were not observed, especially in cases in which the husband had died. None of the narratives were from personal experience, but had been told to the participants by other people. For example, Mac told the story:

> A man died, I am told, and left his son and widow. The widow refused to be inherited. One day one of the sons came home late. He ate with his mom and thereafter she said he could stay over. He was discovered dead in his mother's house because it was taboo for him to spend a night there without rituals having been followed. The spirit of the dead is very strong.

About having sex with a woman after she gave birth, the group's explanation was that if this did not happen the fear was that it would bring bad luck to the child. It was seen as clearing the way for the child. Bill shared this story:

> There was a case recently of a woman who was single and gave birth. She went to Nairobi and met a lover and had sex with him. Her child fell sick. She took the child to hospital but he did not get better. She shared with her sister what she had done in Nairobi. The child was then given a herbal antidote and survived.

Someone married a woman who was pregnant. He slept with the woman first after she gave birth. She has not given birth to another child since.

I was somewhat puzzled that the women would have had any trouble, since strictly speaking they were no longer with the fathers of the children. It did not make sense that a woman who had since married should go back to fulfil a sexual act with the father of her child. The hearsay nature of the stories also made them somewhat weak but the men were insistent, despite my protest about the admissibility of this evidence, that there was indeed a link between what they said ensued and their culture having been ignored. They were, however, willing to concede that it was a man's world and that they were the ones who made the rules regarding sex. As Eddie, the advocate, emphasised:

> Irrespective of where a woman comes from she must conform to the culture that she is married to. In fact a woman should simply obey her husband.

In respect of planting, the men explained that the cultural practice of sex before planting was to bless the seed so that the yield would be very high. They reported that sex prior to widow 'inheritance' could be symbolic in cases in which it was not possible for the widow to have sex, for example because of advanced age. But they were keen to emphasise that all acts of inheritance in Luo culture involving sex were otherwise actual. Eddie the advocate, the most vocal among the men, triumphantly outlined his understanding of the *jakowiny*:

> Where we cannot get a person from among ourselves to play this role, one comes from another clan.[9] He can be bribed or we get him drunk so he can perform the act. We know him as a *jakowiny* but he may not know. Our intent is that the cleansing ritual must be performed so if we need to drug him, so be it! What we want to know is that he has done the act. We will know by looking at the face of the woman who has had sex. Her skin texture is different. It is shiny.

The men appeared unwilling to view the issue as one of rights or of the violation of a woman's body. Mac, the lawyer, explained thus: 'When someone is practising culture, they do not see it as a violation. They see it as cultural fulfilment.' Again I sensed a strong use of justifications in this dialogue, particularly aimed at placing the culture in good light. Cultural defensiveness is in fact one of the strongest challenges that feminists on the continent encounter in seeking to democratise this arena.

In the case in which a man had lost a wife, the group explained that he could stay as long as he wanted without having sex, but that essentially when he dreamt of having sex with his wife then he was free to marry again. People would know when a man had dreamt when they saw him looking for another wife.

At this point, Chris, an older man, joined the group. I had observed that it was the younger members of the group who spoke the most and who were somewhat intransigent in their cultural positions. I was keen to hear Chris's opinions, particularly how he viewed these cultural practices in light of women's rights. His standpoint was markedly different from the dominant views that had thus far been expressed:

> Sometimes we have to change and be modernised. We have to listen to the opinion of the woman. If you are talking about the past, then perhaps there was not as much protection for women. Today, because women know their rights, we are bending to listen. Some cultures are no longer guiding Luos today. We have to pick only those that lead us somewhere and discard those

that don't. For example, forcing a widow to be inherited should no longer happen. The choice should entirely be left to the woman. When we move with modernity, some cultures are no longer useful. For example, when you go to plant, you jump on a woman; when you bring maize from the fields, you jump on a woman. This is not serving any purpose. In reality these cultural practices are no longer being practised in many homes and people suffer no consequences.

Ultimately, what emerged overall from this dialogue, particularly the younger members of the group, was a notable tendency to be overzealous about culture. It was almost as if they were on a crusade to protect their privileged position in the face of what they perceived to be an onslaught of women's rights. Perhaps they feared that they had more to lose from women's equality than members of the older generation, who seemed to be more alive to the flux in human viewpoints.

Clearly the issue of who speaks for whom was more poignant within this group. As we prepared to meet a group of Luo women the following day, I emphasised to my student the importance of letting the women tell stories about their actual experiences with any of these cultural practices, to enable her to get an actual sense of how they are applied in women's contemporary lives.

Resistance and rebellion: what are the contributory factors for women?

While it is important to understand culture from the perspective of those who belong to it, it is also crucial to understand how it is actually practised. As such, a group discussion took place with seven women. These included Tamara, a sales person with an insurance firm; Martha, a banker turned businesswoman; Mary, a revenue officer; Janet, a lawyer; and three other women, Alicia, Terri and Jane.

The common denominator among the women was that they were Luo. The discussion began at a general level. Mary emphasised that Luo culture did not come into practice until you faced a situation. While you might have your own views about the practices and think that they are not right, a situation might then arise where you are hit by reality. Tamara, on the other hand, said that although most of them were now Christians, women were still confronted by traditions when they went to rural areas, to bury loved ones, for example. She stated that women were warned of the repercussions, mainly for their children, if they did not follow tradition.

Janet said that, though she agreed that this was often the case, there were women who had gone against these traditions, and she was one of them. Her view was that the fear was mainly psychological. She shared her lived experience:

> I lost my husband in 2000. When he died I told the women who had come to mourn with me that I am not supposed to sweep the house until after he has been buried. I looked at the issue hygienically and how it would affect me. I swept the house. We buried him after one week. Also, I am not supposed to

mix with people or go to someone's house because I am supposed to have stigma. I was also told that I was not supposed to cook and eat with the children. I thought about it and how they would feel. We agreed as a family that we would not follow these traditions. Also a man is not supposed to sleep in the house unless he has inherited you. My son continued to sleep in his bedroom.

What riled me most was that I was expected to go and look for some funny character (a *jakowiny*) from the market place to cleanse me. In the olden days, I understand you were supposed to run naked on the day this ceremony was to take place. I declared publicly at the funeral that I would not do this ritual involving the *jakowiny*. It came out in the press. Reporters followed me. After the funeral a number of people were sent to coach me on the tradition. My husband's cousin was trying to court me and I did not want. For me Christianity is what helped me. If you want to go against tradition, then it is a war you have to fight. I have made sure that my wishes are known to the priest that when I die I want Christianity to be followed. I have told my son what I want and he has to be prepared to fight the war.

Janet's experience is of a woman who is part of the culture but at the same time is willing to find ways to negotiate around those aspects that do not suit her (An' Naim, 1994; Armstrong, 1998; Maboreke, 2000). From a feminist perspective, her story was especially significant in illustrating that women have agency. Women can take a stand, instead of simply reproducing culture; they can step out of the box and shape an alternative reality, rather than simply conforming.

Comprehending the tools that women like Janet have used for resistance and rebellion makes for a richer understanding of the concept of power and change. Is the fact that she is a lawyer a factor that contributed to the action that she took? Has her high level of education influenced the way she views her options? Do the perspectives of the middle class vary from those of the lower class?

While acknowledging Janet's ability to say no to tradition, Mary said that it depended on the capacity of the woman. Where a man was the sole breadwinner, a woman might think that she needed the assistance of the husband's family to survive and therefore agree to the cultural sexual practices that go with being 'inherited'. In Mary's view, the financial position of the woman was important, as well as what the woman stood for.

The conversation veered to the abuse that women faced at the hands of men who might be more interested in being financially looked after by a woman through wife 'inheritance'. They discussed the dangers of having sex with a man that you did not know, not just with regard to the issue of the woman controlling her own body, but also in light of HIV/AIDS. They also believed that a person who consented to be a *jakowiny* probably agreed to do so with more than one woman.

They discussed the fear that kept women bound to some of these traditions. Alicia was concerned that most of the women in this group were urban dwellers and she thought that women in the rural areas would most certainly see these practices differently. For them, she said, these practices might be good and proper. Tamara shared a story of her sister's experience:

> My sister's husband died in 2000 and she refused to be inherited. When she died, the husband's family looked for a *jakowiny*. They looked until they found one. He was expected to have sex with the corpse and they were old people to confirm that this had taken place. They said that they were doing it for the sake of the children. It was not like he pretended to have sex. It was done physically and practically.

She also lamented the treatment of single women, because if a woman dies without a husband she cannot be brought back to the homestead. 'You are buried far off, outside. They will even build a funny structure because they cannot bring you back to the compound.'

Alicia also shared a story of what happened when her mother died:

> We lost mummy in 1991. She was a Christian. There was concern among the relatives before the funeral that the reason we were not married was because my mom had not followed the inheritance rituals when my father died. We were going to bury her in the village. As we approached the homestead, we noticed that a structure had been built and heard that a *jakowiny* had been found for my mother. My brother did a u-turn to drive back to town with the body. They were throwing stones and *pangas* at us.
>
> We reported to the police and the body was kept in a local church. Just as we were about to bury her in town we received a court order that she could not be buried in Nakuru. The case went on for a month. My mom stayed in the mortuary for a month. The magistrate then gave a court order that she should be buried in the village but without the tradition. We were given police with guns. People thought it was a joke. They tried to snatch the coffin. The police told them they would shoot. We buried her and came back to Nakuru straight away.

Janet spoke of the empowerment of women and the need to educate girls from an early age. Alicia thought that having financial independence was very important for women and Mary added that the state, though it had a duty to do away with harmful cultural practices, was not the right player when it came to culture. Her view was that change must come from the people because they would not simply let government have its way. The only way was to empower girls and to learn from those who had defied tradition. Janet agreed that the law might play a secondary role in such cases, making it law on paper only, and argued that 'people have to know that what is happening to them is wrong, but they should also be able to run'.

Terri, a younger woman, said that you could only run away from tradition if you were old. As far as she was concerned, there were many families who did not practice Christianity so you could always depend on religion to avoid tradition. In such cases she said that they would force you to get a *jakowiny*. She argued that you could also get a good brother-in-law. She said that she saw the process as good for the children because the future of children was important to keep in mind. Janet insisted that the interplay between education, financial independence and Christianity was powerful for women to draw on to fight cultural practices that they did not want to follow.

Terri told her story to illustrate her reasoning:

> My husband died in 2005. His family is forcing me to be inherited so that the children can move forward. If I can get a brother-in-law to inherit me then I will be cleansed. At the moment there is a brother-in-law who would be the final inheritor. He is an assistant chief. He is married to two wives.

When asked about HIV she said she and the *jakowiny* would go for tests. The other women told her that with a *jakowiny* you had to have sex without a condom. She believed that because she had not been cleansed she had bad luck. The other women were curious to know more about Terri. She had primary school education and sold curios. She said that her family members were insisting that she go through with the ceremony. Although at first she was not ready, she thinks she is now. Janet was curious to know how Terri felt about her situation, especially since she was supporting herself. Terri emphasised the fear she had for her children.

My view, after listening to this dialogue, was that Terri was an example of a woman who had made calculations about what she would gain (or thought she would gain) by complying with the cultural demands and what she would lose by not complying. For her, security and her children's future were of paramount importance and so adherence to a cultural practice, however abominable in the eyes of others, became necessary and desirable.

Also, by rationalising thus, Terri absolved herself of responsibility for any ultimate decision that she might take. Her hands were tied, so to speak. As far as she was concerned, she was not to blame for her powerlessness in this matter. Yet it was also noticeable that this opportunity for her to talk to other women, who had experienced similar problems, seemed to boost her awareness of alternative possibilities as well as her self-esteem. This was vital in understanding the process of empowerment as being founded on knowledge in the first instance, then use of that knowledge and action to change one's reality.[10] Was her powerlessness then ultimately due to lack of self-confidence and her perception of self? I thought about what her story taught us about where we should be putting our efforts as we talk about empowering women.

Jane also shared her story:

> I find this discussion very interesting. Where I was married, we were three wives. I was the third wife. However, we did not get on well. When the *jakowiny* came, he wanted to cleanse us at the same time. I said I was a Christian and that my mother was also saved. People said that I should not use this reason as I have children. I realised that tradition was too strong for me and I ran away and came to Nakuru. It has been difficult for me. I have not been able to go home (to the village) because I fear that they will force me to be inherited. Also I did not want to share another husband with my co-wives since we had not gotten on when we had shared a husband before. But I have learnt a lot from listening to other women here and I know I can build my own house. All my children are presently healthy and going to school. I have a man right now in my life.

The women also shared their views when asked about the other Luo cultural practices that involve sex. Jane stated:

> On sex as a prelude to planting, well … it may not be bad if having sex is something that you do all the time with your husband. There is also nothing wrong with having sex when your children get married. What is bad is the expectation that women should have sex with a total stranger.

On sex after the birth of a child, one of them explained that, because in the past many men were polygynous they wanted to be released as soon as possible to go and have sex with the other wives, because they were not allowed to have sex with others before having it with the wife who had given birth.

What I found key about this dialogue with the women is how they claimed their space and shared their experiences openly with each other in ways that I was convinced would not have been the same if there had been men in the group. The dynamics speak volumes about strategising for the empowerment of women, in terms of what works best. I was most struck by the way Terri acknowledged a shift in her thinking as a result of the interaction.

For a researcher who is also seeking to understand how women engage with concepts of empowerment and liberation, it was also notable how women tended to frame their actions with the family in mind as opposed to their own individuality.

Conclusion

I concluded my interactions with the student by highlighting what I thought were some of the issues that called for her attention as she continued her research. Although the interviews at this point had given useful insights into the cultural practices that involved sex from the viewpoint of men and women, I saw opportunities for taking these dialogues further, as part of building grounded theory.[11]

For example, given that one of the issues that emerged from women in particular was that these cultural practices were even more likely to still be strongly practised in rural areas as compared to urban areas, especially when it came to planting, harvesting, widow cleansing and house construction, there was a need for the student to explore if this was indeed the case by going to the rural areas that are inhabited predominantly by Luo people.

In the context of her research I also thought it was important for her to pay particular attention to the forces that appeared to be contributing to change in women's lives in the rural areas or that seemed to keep women bound to it. I further asked her to remain vigilant to the intricate ways that women continued to refuse to consent to cultural practices that they did not agree with. The exploration of sex also had to be kept in a broader perspective. At one level the student was exploring the use of sex as a physical act in cultural rituals, but at another level she was exploring how being male or female impacted how one was affected by culture and the rules that applied to each by virtue of their sex.

The interviews with men in an urban setting tended to show how they could manipulate culture to suit themselves, often resorting to justifications as a way of perpetuating culture. I also thought it important to get the views of men and women separately, particularly in light of the dynamics observed in the interviews. From a human rights perspective it also seemed prudent for the student to dialogue on the kind of rights that people saw as being violated and the action that they thought should be taken. The question of where the state and other players come in, if at all, was also vital to explore. The student also would need to capture more fully the dynamics of her data-gathering process because these too could tell their own particular story.

Notes

1. The Southern and Eastern African Regional Centre for Women's Law at the University of Zimbabwe offers a masters programme to students from southern and eastern Africa in the specialist subject of women's law, a discipline that essentially seeks to analyse women's lived realities in understanding the law. In partial fulfilment of this masters programme, students are required to undertake grounded research (see note 11 below) in their own countries on a topic of their choice. They receive hands-on supervision from their lecturers as part of guiding them in the process.
2. The title of her research study was, 'Sex, consent and power: a case study of sex-related cultural practices among the Luo community of Kenya'. The supervision described in this chapter took place in November 2009 and covered events for that period only.
3. See article 17(1) and (2), articles 3 and 4, Protocol to the African Charter on the Rights of Women.
4. See Article 5 (a) of CEDAW.
5. All the names used in this article are fictitious in order to protect the privacy of the interviewees.
6. All the quotes used in this chapter are from interviewees as captured by me as a listener.
7. Something I learnt is that a cultural practice can be reported in various contexts by the different people who adhere to the culture.
8. The student had previously interviewed Peter but thought it was important for me to hear his version of the practices as a Luo man.
9. There was contradiction here because Peter had told me that the *jakowiny* was always an outsider. The reality seems to be dependent on who is telling the story.
10. For a general discussion of this concept of women and empowerment, see Schuler and Kadigamar (1992: 21–71).
11. Grounded theory is a research process which uses lived realities as its point of departure to examine norms and practices. In turn, what is unearthed from lived realities or starting from below (a grounded approach) is used to explore new directions and sources of data, with the aim of developing a sound theoretical basis for what is being researched.

References

An' Naim, Abdullahi (1994) 'State responsibility under international human rights law to change religious and customary laws', in Cook, R. (ed) *Human Rights of Women: National and International Perspectives*, University of Pennsylvania Press

Armstrong, Alice (1998) *Culture and choice: lessons for survivors of gender violence in Zimbabwe*, Harare Violence against Women in Zimbabwe Research Project

Bentzon, A., Hellum., A., Sewart, J., Ncube, W. and Torben Agersnap, A. (1998) *Pursuing Grounded Theory in Law: South North Experiences in Developing Women's Law*, Oslo, Tano Aschehoug and Harare, Mond Books

Giles, J. and Middleton, T. (2008) *Studying Culture: A Practical Introduction*, Oxford, Blackwell Publishing

Hewitt, J.P. (2000) *Self and Society: A Symbolic Interactionist Social Psychology*, Massachusetts, Allyn and Bacon

Maboreke, M. (2000) 'Understanding law in Zimbabwe', in Stewart, A. (ed) *Gender, Law and Social Justice*, London, Blackstone Press

Schuler, M. and Kadigamar, S. (1992) *Legal Literacy: A Tool for Women's Empowerment*, New York, UNIFEM

Stang Dahl, T. (1987) *An Introduction to Feminist Jurisprudence*, Oslo, Norwegian University Press

Questions for reflection

1.

What does the concept of sexuality encompass and why does this Reader refer to it in the plural?

2.

When analysing sexualities, how does a researcher avoid essentialising various categories, such as African, women, men, homosexuals, prostitutes?

3.

How does research on sexuality differ from other studies? What important factors must be taken into account when studying sexuality?

4.

Does the term sexuality carry the same meaning for men and women in Africa? How does gender shape sexualities? What other factors influence sexualities in Africa?

5.

Cultural anthropology has come under attack for its racist and ethnocentric approaches. How does this augur for research on African sexualities? Are the inherent problems with such approaches able to be overcome or solved? If so, how and under what circumstances?

6.

What is the danger of uncritically applying Western theories and concepts of sexuality to African contexts and experiences?

7.

What are the merits of employing a feminist approach, rather than a purely biological approach, to the study and analysis of sexuality? To help answer this question, draw three columns. In the first, list the key issues a biological approach to sexuality would focus on. In the second column, list the key issues that a feminist approach would emphasise and in the third column name the themes and concepts that sexuality links up with.

Part 2
Sexuality, power and politics

6

Subversion and resistance: activist initiatives

Jane Bennett

I adore the night. It reveals the many different shades of blackness. Shy midnight blues exude thoughtfulness and nobility. Sensual purples invite gentle probing from fingertips, much like bruises. Pitch black, as solid as the heart, grows into a mass of increasing impenetrability, like my father's retreats into liquor, jazz and memories…

I was proud, strong, intelligent, assertive, and funny. A natural leader, I had my own definitive ideas on feminism. These came to life in a picture I drew in crayon of a woman in a business suit juggling a pot, a baby, a briefcase and the planet. She was inspired by my mother. I won contests for my writing long before I would claim it as my life's passion.

I had black friends, white friends and I spoke freely about race, politics and my firm belief that the school's gym teacher was sexist.

I was magic.

Lebo Mashile - from A Tangled Web of Rainbows, 2009

Introduction

The past decade saw an increasing emphasis in African feminist scholarship, research and activism grounded in the importance of understanding sexualities and gender. Several key publications raised questions about the politics of gender and sexualities. From 2006, the African Regional Sexuality Resource Centre has produced (in both digital and print format) a magazine titled *Sexuality in Africa*, and there are many local, popular publications, such as *Straight Talk* in Uganda, for example, that enjoy wide circulation and address issues of sexuality, reproductive health and rights. Book-length projects, such as Signe Arnfred's *Rethinking Sexualities in Africa*, have been developed through workshop and conference processes, and several high-profile intellectual forums have been organised around the themes of sexuality, gender and political democracy.

Despite this, Africa has frequently found itself positioned within international reporting on issues of gender, reproductive rights and sexualities as predominantly hostile to any discussion of sexual and reproductive rights. In June 2000, for example, debate around the wording of the declaration on women's rights to be issued as the Beijing+5 Platform for Action polarised, in print, developing and developed countries: 'sexual rights activists from the West were also said to be blaming developing countries for "holding up the document"' (*New York Times* 2000); Nigerian and Ugandan ministers were reported as being disconcerted at the thought of lesbian presence in their countries; and Africa was represented beyond its borders mainly as a conservative block of voices expressing dismay at the notion of women's rights to reproductive freedom and disgusted objection to the idea that gay and lesbian people have civic and human rights.

More recently, global reports of debates about customary tradition (female genital mutilation in Kenya and virginity testing in South Africa), sharia interpretations of appropriate sexuality (in Nigeria and Sudan), and legal relationships to homosexuality and intersexuality (South Africa) have tended to represent African voices as conservative, narrowly religious, and opposed to radical engagement with issues of gender and sexuality.

It is certainly true that some prominent African leaders have denounced homosexualities in ways that seem to offer carte blanche to violent homophobia. It is also true that debates around the meaning of cultural practices concerning sexuality have been vigorous within African feminisms for decades: though some renounce practices such as virginity testing, female genital cutting or polygyny, others locate these practices within a cultural/post-colonial matrix too complex for simple censure. Where new state policies have made access to the termination of pregnancy easier in a few contexts, legislation has been qualified by deep, often religious concern about the ethics of abortion. Since 2001, the effects of the Mexico City policy[1] have strengthened conservative approaches to women's reproductive choice, and have had a powerful effect on overarching discourses concerning gender and sexual respectability.

A profile of African-based reluctance to explore issues of sexualities as part of debates concerning democracy, justice and equity can be mapped. However (and critically), such a profile operates in constant and dynamic engagement with feminist activism and advocacy, within different African contexts, in which conservative drives toward the repression of sexual rights, especially for women, are challenged.

The Women's Manifesto, launched by Ghanaian women in September 2004, for example, included within its broad-based concerns with issues of economic and political under-representation demands designed to address women's sexual vulnerability to HIV, to domestic and marital violence and to certain traditional practices. In November 2008, a public march through Cape Town – and grounded in the work of the South African One-in-Nine Project – demanded 'hands off women's bodies'. Indeed, across the continent, the need to combat the transmission of HIV, to curtail sexual violence and to ensure that women and girls have access to education, healthcare and political rights as basic conditions of democracy has increasingly placed issues of sexuality at the forefront of theoretical and activist engagement with the state.

The terms on which sexuality becomes foregrounded as political terrain remain contested. It is, for example, easier to insert conceptions of sexuality into frameworks of health than it is to discuss sexualities as sources of empowerment; constraint and management are often more audible as political approaches to sexuality than exploration or alliance-building across diverse sexual constituencies. Nonetheless, African-based debate on theoretical and activist engagement with local and continental struggles to understand the links between sexualities, gender and socio-economic space is vigorous, nuanced and valuable.[2]

In the end, of course, simple comparisons between the approaches of developed and developing countries (or continents) to sexual and reproductive rights are probably unhelpful. Given the intimacy with which sexual practices, norms, struggles and rebellions are woven into the material realities of living, people in any context (especially those characterised by rapidly changing political economies, multiculturalism and exposure to mass media systems) can be expected to engage in vigorous – even vicious – debates and dissension around the meaning of sexual bodies and sexual citizens. Perhaps the most interesting questions about activism in African contexts are not those framed (partially) through comparative dialogue with the West, but those that emerge from the issues facing men and women engaged in the work of strengthening continental access to material, political and spiritual empowerment. These issues at their core involve questions of sexualities and gender.

This chapter seeks to introduce readers to some of the most significant areas in which questions of sexualities and gender have galvanised activism on the continent during the past three decades. A brief historical framework is offered to orient the reader to the 21st-century context that the chapter discusses. The essay then explores what we mean when we use terms such as resistance and activism, and goes on to profile five different areas in which African-based challenges to the entrenched political, cultural and legal norms that regulate gender injustice are rooted. The objective of the essay is not to offer any comprehensive panorama of the genres of gender and sexualities activism on the continent, but more to offer the reader a sense of the dynamism and colour of the social, cultural and political African-based struggles for gender justice that take sexualities seriously.

A word of caution

Before the essay continues, a word of caution about language. The term Africa has a fraught history. There is debate even about the origins of the name for the continent,[3] and it is difficult to find histories of Africa that are not, in fact, histories focused on a relationship of colonialism (of different shapes and processes) between parts of the continent and other parts of the globe: the Roman Empire; liaisons between East and North Africa and the Middle East; the movement of Islam across Africa from the 16th century to the 20th century; the engagements with European powers; and current conversations between Africa contexts, China, the United States and a global economic order.

Critical to recognise is that it is impossible to speak of Africa as a generalisation without erasing complexity, nuance and difference. The continent is vast, and its civilisations, peoples, languages and histories are extremely rich. In a chapter such as this one, whose objective explicitly embraces the idea of a panorama – an overview of critical moments of political and social activism – the term Africa will be used sometimes to describe connections between African-based organisations, people and/or initiatives, but in every case we will try to avoid gross homogenisation.

In a very real way, there is no such thing as Africa, except as such a space is highlighted and debated in opposition to the discourses that stereotype the continent as undeveloped, its peoples as incapable of self-governance or poor and its cultures as primitive. Such discourses abound, even in the 21st century, and when we seek to understand questions of African-based activism in the area of gender and sexualities it is important to try to do so in a way that respects the depth and complexity of the political, social and historical realities of the continent. This chapter will introduce some of the most interesting activisms of the past few decades in order to understand them fully. But it is also vital to discover more about the contextual stories and histories invoked by what this chapter suggests.

Starting points

Deep history and sexualities

Historiographers teach us that the representation of time past is no more or less than a retrospective projection of contemporary anxieties: where we begin the history, in time, speaks only to the myths of human evolution; what and whom we include address hegemonic notions of progress; experiences that come into representation as history reflect current theologies concerning good and evil; and there is no easy translation between cause (economic interests, political forces, religious zeal) and effect (one man shackled to the bottom of a ship; one woman starving in a concentration camp). For those concerned with the exploration of sexualities in African contexts, two broad recognitions need to guide our thinking.

The first is that what can be understood (remembered) of the diverse paradigms, activities and performances that comprised sexual being within the lives of our ancestors is minimal. Though language, certain forms of art and the writings of colonial anthropologists and administrators hint – through varied lenses – at the possibilities, the dominant reality is that the histories of colonialism involved such extensive movement, warfare, deprivation and loss that it is rarely possible to say with certainty, for example, 'my ancestors have always practiced *ukumetsha*'[4] or 'women in my culture were never expected to initiate or enjoy sex'. Such things are said, but the source of the conviction informing them is often dubious.

Cultural formations on the continent, through the immense turbulence of the 16th to 19th centuries (the displacement, death and destruction of many different peoples previously living in semi-collectivity), do not have easily legible deep histories of sexuality that can connect contemporary African-based people to a pre-18th century ancestry.[5] The point is not that there is no deep African history of sexualities and gender; more that such histories are very hard to access for most contemporary writers and activists.

Second, the histories that are accessible tend to be profoundly engaged with the forces of European colonialism. These complex and diverse colonialisms – patches of a mere, say, 400 years at the most and in some countries, such as Zimbabwe, arguably only a century – are as nothing in comparison to the dozens of decades replete with social activity, civilisation and transformations that preceded. Furthermore, in many parts of the continent (Saharan Africa, much of North Africa, the Sudan, what is now northern Nigeria, Niger and Mali), Arab and Islamic influences were woven into African histories for many centuries prior to the disastrous 1884 Berlin Conference, which laid the foundation for 20th-century continental cartographies.

When exploring issues of sexuality, however, it is still important to note the effect of European colonialisms – including the effect of Christianity – on the citizens of the territories conquered and administered between the late 19th and the mid-20th centuries. Ideas about the appropriate conduct of heterosexuality, the perversion of homosexual behaviour, the formation of the family, the 'sexual' body,[6] and the regulation of sexual interaction between colonised and coloniser, which grew more severe across time and context, became deeply embedded in the lives of people whose children would become citizens of different African countries in the 21st century.

Discussion of sexuality in the current period has to proceed in the knowledge that deep histories of narrative on the norms of sexual culture are obscure, and simultaneously, that what can be gleaned from work on the norms wrapped into African approaches to sexuality through Christianity and colonial administrative practices suggest the dominance of European and Christian colonial values: no polygamy, no public displays of seduction or desire, no sexual liaisons outside of sanctioned marriage, no same-sex sexual play, no such thing as clean sexuality and the erasure of sexual power for people gendered as women. These ideas were more dominant in some colonial spaces than others but undoubtedly influenced various current contexts on the continent.

Specific country contexts

To illustrate what it means to take the specific contexts of African countries seriously, let us look very briefly at two and explore how their recent political and economic history organises questions of gender and sexualities.

South Africa lies at the tip of the African continent and is infamous for having instituted a very particular race-based approach to questions of governance after 1948. Known as apartheid, it categorised peoples by race – a practice whose roots lie in much earlier colonial practices – and used the classification to control labour, access to land, housing, education and social status. Kopano Ratele (2001) opens a discussion of the links between legislation enacted under apartheid and issues of sexuality by saying, 'it is commonplace that apartheid tried to govern most aspects of people's lives within the borders of South Africa. It is increasingly accepted that the policy was also targeted at regulating, directing, and shaping the most intimate parts of the lives of its subjects.'

Ratele's discussion moves into a compelling exploration of the connection between apartheid interests in racialisation (the construction of the body, as confined, through 'family genes' and arbitrary notions of hierarchy, to a biologically appropriate destiny within human liaison) and sexuality. Ratele highlights the way in which apartheid state machineries sought to organise possibilities for human interrelationship in a way that included the intensive and explicit regulation of sexual lives.

This was done in several ways. There were laws, built on pre-1948 legislation, which were explicitly dedicated to the prohibition of mixed-race sexual activity, reinforced by both the massive legal machinery dedicated to racial classification itself and laws, such as the Reservation of Separate Amenities Act (1953), which reserved public spaces, such as parks, beaches, sections of road or pavements, public toilets, waiting rooms, bus stations and benches, for the exclusive use of a particular race group.

Apartheid legislation also had extensive, even incalculable, effects on sexuality through its focus on the racial organisation of labour, housing and education and through the insistence that Africans were not legal citizens of South Africa, but of one of the ten Bantustans (homelands) – the reservation-like, mostly rural lands, dotted throughout the country proper. Migrant labour forced millions of men away from their wives for most of the year, the commodification of sex around and within male-dominated labour compounds (and elsewhere) expanded, urbanisation (a constant process of legal and physical civil war between the state and those seeking to live in zones to which they were not 'legally' entitled) created racially segregated city spaces in which sexual cultures flourished independently of one another.

The effect of apartheid legislation on the sexuality of South Africans was, then, powerful. What needs to be included here, however, is the fact that resistance to apartheid also influenced constructions of masculinity, womanhood, and notions of what constituted appropriate and liberating relationships to sexual experience. 'Struggle' masculinities encouraged young men's overt and visible heterosexuality in the name of commitment to the overthrow of the regime; the processes of political organisation (both within and outside the country's borders) involved high levels of mobility, communication and sometimes interracial connections. The distance between those actively engaged in struggle activities and their families was consciously created as part of struggle ideology. So thinking about South African sexualities in 2010 demands a clear recognition of apartheid's frameworks for human identity and of what it took to begin to dismantle these.

Post-1994, the politics of gender and sexualities in South Africa have been volatile and often at the heart of debates on what the new nation means for its people. On the one hand, there has been a great deal of legal reform, encompassing four different forms of marriage (including same-sex unions and the right to polygynous marriages under customary law), the right to the termination of pregnancy, new legislation around sexual and domestic abuse and new access to treatment and care for people living with HIV and AIDS. On the other hand, gender-based violence remains prevalent, and includes attacks against very young children and babies; homophobia is rife and growing; and strong debates rage about gendered and sexual norms.

A profile of Nigeria offers a very different picture. The history of contemporary Nigeria includes a centuries-long engagement with Arab and Islamic influence, and the ways in which Islam became embedded into continental life across North Africa and parts of central Africa from the 11th century. This is a narrative in itself, raising questions about the integration of Arab and African peoples, experiences and ideas. Where questions of gender and sexuality are concerned, clearly understanding Islam and the changes in Islamic thought and practice over centuries of life on African soil is essential.

When the British took control of parts of West Africa under the name Nigeria as a British protectorate in 1900, this colonial administration was building a relationship to empire on the back of centuries of the histories of different kingdoms and empires in the region, among them the Igbo, Yoruba, Hausa, the Efik – the Calabar Kingdom – and other civilisations. Sixty years of indirect British rule influenced the fragile shape of the new Nigeria, especially as far as issues of language, Christianity and education were concerned. But the stamp of British colonialism did not influence the ensuing politics of sexuality and gender as much as the deep hostilities and tensions between the different civilisations now tethered together within the imposed borders of one country.

It has been these tensions, fuelled by the oil industry, that more than any others have structured debate about the meaning of masculinity and femininity, the meaning of sexuality. Though Nollywood movies and television soaps are openly interested in sexual liaisons outside marriage and the drama of new possibilities for sexual pleasure and romance, Nigeria's 36 states are largely conservative in their approach to sexuality, hostile to alternative gender and sexual identities, interested in preserving marriage as the route to social stability and wary of adventurous young women. Though gender equality is visible at the level of some political activity and activism around gender-based violence and child sexual abuse, and women's political independence is strong in the south of Nigeria, in the north, where provinces are governed by sharia law, ideas about gender equality are largely structured through popular and religious ideas about the separation of women's and men's spheres of political and sexual power. These differences strongly influence the possibilities for activism and resistance.

Thinking historically, contextually and creatively

The preceding brief contrast of South Africa and Nigeria vividly illustrates the naivety of the idea that there are easy routes to debates about African realities or African contexts. Good scholarship always demands that an in-depth understanding of a particular environment is attempted before sweeping generalisations are made. This is particularly important when working with Africa-oriented discussions, because as a continent, a collective of peoples, and within the world's imagery, Africa has all too often been homogenised. It would take another chapter to unpack the implications of this, but perhaps one iconic narrative makes clear the difficulties of discussing questions of African sexualities in the 21st century.

The outline of Saartjie (Sarah) Baartman's narrative is well known (see Desiree Lewis's discussion in Chapter 19): she was taken from the tip of the Cape (from what is now the city of Cape Town) to Europe in 1807, and exhibited in London and elsewhere as a wonder of bodily form, a sexual spectacle because of the shape of her buttocks. After her death in Paris, her genitals were removed as curiosities and these parts of her body were not returned to South Africa until 2006. Numerous historians, including Abrahams (2000), have considered the way in which this story illustrates the British colonial fascination with African beings as sexual exoticisms.

There is a library of work on the ways in which African-located peoples, cultural traditions, landscapes and even animals evoke a special sexuality (think of the meaning of the title of Spike Lee's *Jungle Fever,* or the use of leopards and wild cats in the commodification of dark-skinned models, such as Alec Wek, as 'wild'). Anthropology has a long history of describing and explaining societies through perceived relation to gender and sexualities. The diverse forms of ideology informing European colonial mindsets took gender and sexualities very seriously as dangerous spaces – spaces in which colonising women were vulnerable to sexual violence by local men, and where the civilisations encountered as native were described as full of sexual perversion and immorality.

We are therefore faced with two important challenges in this chapter. The first is the need to reject any ready acceptance of the term African when exploring a specific context of the politics of gender and sexuality. In other words, one African context is not interchangeable with another. The second is the need to take African contexts seriously without reading them as other, without imagining that such contexts illuminate realities that are in any way exotic, and without rehearsing the long and familiar discourse of African marginalisation.

Both these challenges are tricky. They demand an ethical eye and a heart ready to acknowledge two seemingly contradictory imperatives. The first is to take the activism, scholarship, and writing of African-based people very seriously, seeking to understand as much as possible about continental histories, politics, languages and cultures. The second is about giving this attention without re-colonisation, without the hope that something African can be easily known or grasped from within a text but with the conviction that reading against the grain of historical discourses, which have presented African sexualities as parts of corrupt or underdeveloped civilisations, is critical to any engagement with questions of gender and sexualities. Understanding conversations about activism and resistances therefore demands a sense of creativity, which is provided in the following sections to introduce a range of zones in which such initiatives can be mapped.

Understanding activism

During the past century there have been thousands of political energies moving within the continent, engaged in struggles about sovereignty, land, livelihood and identities. When it comes to thinking about sexualities, once it is understood that they are embedded and powerful within all forms of social organisation and engagement, it is possible to argue that any initiative seeking to gather for itself strength, popularity and power would by definition include issues of gender and sexualities.

Thus, for example, we could argue that the liberation army that brought Ugandan President Yoweri Museveni to power in 1986 involved questions of sexualities, or that the huge trade union movements of the 1970s and 1980s in South

Africa had implications for how sexualities were understood as part of a worker-driven agenda for change. Indeed, the way the guerrilla underground armies were formed in Uganda between 1980 and 1986 involved the politics of gender and sexualities, offering women the opportunity to fight as operatives and at the same time supporting the heterosexual prerogatives of male leaders in overt and covert ways (Byanyima 1992). And certainly the South African trade union movement took subversive positions on issues of sexualities and gender – the movement was in fact the first organised African constituency in which women workers publicly insisted on an end to sexual harassment (Baskin 1991).

It is not that any one form of patriarchy can be targeted – there are myriad shapes through which elite masculinities come to control the terms of livelihood for others (who include other men), and much contextual conflict and negotiation among these diverse shapes. What matters for understanding the activisms introduced in the following sections is that they are grounded in an approach to action that seeks to transform gendered inequalities and injustices (of many kinds), and in so doing highlight the role played by sexualities in locking femininities and masculinities together into conservative scripts of interdependence, tension and structural violence and in creating the terrain from which it is possible to imagine new ways of being. There is a long history of such activism, and whether one names the diverse threads of voice, movement, organisation and policy work as feminist, or not, has a great deal to do with the local and strategic politics of a particular time and place.

This chapter is not going to rehearse debates about feminisms in African contexts; suffice to say that though the term feminist has, at times, carried overtones of western women's dominance over the expression of African-based discourses on injustice (and hence been roundly rejected), many contemporary struggles about gender justice on the continent embrace the term feminist. The term has become embedded in a very rich and complex network of initiatives, individuals, organisations and ideas, perhaps best illuminated by the debates of the past three African Feminist Forums.[7] It is true that there is no homogeneous women's movement, linking all convictions about the need for gender justice as part of the fight for Africa-focused self-determination and economic/political strength, but the following sections of this chapter profile activist initiatives whose roots in an understanding of patriarchies as key forms of political domination are solidly articulated.

The question of which issues become relevant to a profile of activisms that take gender injustices and sexualities seriously is an interesting one. When we understand that constructions of gender include contextually grounded predictions about people's sexual identities, orientations, knowledge, behaviours, beliefs and practices – and that though these predictions can be (and are) often resisted they remain powerful forces within the construction of normal sexuality – it is clear that many areas of everyday life might nourish seeds of sexual exploitation or injustice.

Where a child, for example, is gendered as a girl and this leads automatically to the expectation that she will become a wife or a mother, it is possible to envisage the need for activist initiatives to ensure her right to independence, education, reproductive health, sexual choice, political autonomy and so on. Where a child is gendered as a boy, this might readily lead to the expectation of his visible heterosexual prowess; again, it is possible to imagine activisms that protect his right to freedom from violation should he choose non-heterosexuality or that offer him the right to treatment in the face of sexually transmitted diseases.

Though on the face of it certain issues, such as vulnerability to HIV or the terror of a community's homophobia, might appear to regulate the dynamics of gender to the sidelines, any in-depth understanding of such issues will reveal not simply the interweaving of gender and sexualities, but the relevance of many other social forces: class, age, ethnicity, religion, race or ability. These forces are often singled out by those critically operative in the construction of political and social powers. But of course there are others, such as lineage, language, the shape of the family, political status, rural/urban linkages and seropositivity, and it takes a context to be able to engage usefully with ideas about the operation of gender dynamics.

Historically, in the 20th century, the issues that have most galvanised the activism that understands the power of sexualities in the construction of injustices include those engaged with reproductive rights (fighting for access to reproductive health, choice and decision-making); those targeting 'harmful traditional practices', especially female genital cutting; those addressing gender-based violence in myriad ways (from legal reform to creating safe spaces for abused women and children); those arising out of the HIV/AIDS epidemic; and those fighting against the criminalisation, stigmatisation and abuse of people who live outside the borders of conventional contextual heteronormativities.

What this means is that we are working with a very broad canvas of activisms. It is possible to describe these in terms of the different ideas by which they are driven. Legal reform work, for example, is usually driven by the conviction that it is possible to make critical changes in the lives of women by reorganising the laws governing what already constitutes justice, while movement-building is often rooted in the idea that only organised collectives of individuals dedicated to the complete transformation of class-based state structures can hope to introduce new meaning for gender and labour into society.

It also is possible to describe different forms of activism in terms of country-specific possibilities. What is possible in war-torn Sudan, for example, looks very different from what is possible in a more politically stable space, such as Botswana. And perhaps it would be sensible to imagine activisms as shaped by the issues being confronted – an initiative that tackles trafficking of women across borders, for example, does not look very much like the one that is concerned with the transmission of HIV within a specific community.

In the end, an introductory chapter on subversions and activisms would probably best respond to two key questions, rather than attempt a sketch of what is, in fact, a vast compendium of histories, voices, ideas and experiences. The first question is about the continent's voices: where are those speaking the subversion and the resistance and what are their ideas, passions and convictions? The second question then becomes one about change: which subversions and resistances have carried resonance and where can we see examples of major transformation in the politics of gender and sexualities on the continent?

Question One

Where are those speaking the subversion and the resistance and what are their ideas, passions and convictions?

In *Memoirs of a Woman Doctor*, the Egyptian author Nawal El Saadawi writes of a young woman doctor's encounters with medical science during her studies as the only woman in her class. The misogyny and the experiences of illness, cruelty and early death suffered by the women patients she encounters create for the character a feminist lens in which men are no longer (as her mother suggests) 'gods', but their views are part of systematic patriarchal abuse. She suggests that the women suffer from 'tyrannical femininity', a relation to the body that imprisons and mutilates their bodies and perverts their common sense and spirit.

El Saadawi's character is a fictional version of herself, and the book offers a radical critique of the politics of gender, religion, poverty and embodiment in mid-20th century Egypt. It is for her later works (especially *The Hidden Face of Eve*) and for her political activism – on several occasions, Egyptian authorities have threatened to retract her citizenship – that she is best known. But *Memoirs of a Woman Doctor* is one of the first 20th-century texts to concentrate on issues of gender injustice in ways that focus on the political nature of the body itself as sexual and reproductive.

A second voice to consider is that of Awa Thiam. Senegalese by birth, Thiam's *La Parole aux Negresses* is a feminist tour de force (and very poorly known both within the continent's feminist archive and beyond). The work presents itself as a mix of ethnography, narrative, theory and interview, working with a loose methodology in which Thiam interviews West African men and women about their lives, seeking to draw out stories of gendered sexual injustice and ideas about what the politics of gender mean to daily living. Though Thiam is well aware of the significance of political and economic realities, her dominant interest is in the gendered deconstruction of the everyday, in which questions of marriage, sexual desire and rejection, violence within intimate relationships and beauty are explored as political spaces in themselves.

Thiam works with four different themes: female genital cutting, polygamy, domestic violence and skin whitening. She locates all four themes in the construction of 1968 femininities and womanhood within West Africa, and was the first African-based feminist of the 20th century to link practices of skin-whitening (a colonial, racialist influence) to the kind of internal colonialism that can allow domestic violence, for example, to flourish. This is an interesting position, and one that places Thiam as theoretically and methodologically subversive – a woman in the late 1960s naming herself as a radical feminist and calling upon others (women and men) to include the private zones of family and culture as political spaces of gendered and sexual hierarchy.

The main point here is that there is a decades-long history on the continent of written, oral and performance activism on the question of sexuality. It would be naive to even attempt a short summary of the voices that can be found across the range of writing and performance. Some voices, such as those of Tsitsi Dangaremba of Zimbabwe or Chimamanda Adichie of Nigeria, are well known. Lesser known, but equally powerful, are the voices of Elizabeth Khaxas of the organisation Sister Namibia, Catherine Ngugi of Kenya, Ruth Ochieng of Uganda and Pumla Gqola of South Africa.

In the 21st century, of course, such voices – indeed some of the most vibrant of sexualities in African contexts – can be found in the online environment. Issues of bandwidth and access to constant electricity have an effect on the use of internet space in African countries, but the internet is nonetheless a powerful networking and news-building resource. Even the Facebook sites of LGBTI activists in different African countries, for example, include cross-country connections and material that goes far beyond enquiries about 'what is on your mind'.

APC-Africa Women has recently conducted research on the ways in which Africa-based activisms are drawing on social networking tools and other internet spaces to create connections, share news and strengthen solidarity. The research suggests that, as in other parts of the world, the online terrain offers access to subversive voices in interesting ways. The dangers of this are well known – Facebook, for instance, is a very public space and questions of the control of electricity and bandwidth demand attention. Yet, currently, Africa-based activists with access to the internet are finding myriad ways of debating ideas and spearheading action through internet connectivity.[8]

This is a critical form of voice in the 21st century. The point of this section is to alert readers to the fact that theories of activism (the analysis of contexts in which the politics of gender and sexualities form vectors of oppression, embedded as they always are in diverse economic and social realities) have been explored in African contexts for many decades. There are trenchant debates here and no hegemonic argument.[9] It is important to realise, however, that there is a plethora of resistance theory concerning the politics of sexuality and gender and generated by Africa-based activists and writers, and that understanding African sexualities requires in-depth negotiation with some of them (Mba 1982; Tamale 1996; Zeleza 1997b; Kalipeni and Zeleza 1999; Rukundwa and Van Aarde 2007).

Question Two

Which subversions and resistances have carried resonance and where can we see examples of major transformation in the politics of gender and sexualities on the continent?

Ngaitana!

Tiyambe Zeleza, the Malawian historiographer, writes on the ways that dominant versions of African history choke both women's lives and the meaning of gender dynamics and that it is critical to approach an understanding of continental experiences through a version of 'reading against the grain' or battling reading (Zeleza 1997a: 145). This approach to the discovery of what was he explores as a route toward both redressing the absence of people gendered as women, in different contexts, and more importantly re-imagining the process of making history itself. In this way, the processes of gendering are seen as vital energies influencing the options, opportunities, coercions and changes among people; uncovering the meaning of masculinity in the formation of historical change and events becomes just as important as uncovering the agency, presence and experiences of women.

In April 1956, the Njuri Ncheke (official local council of male elders) in Meru (a northeastern district of Kenya, far from Nairobi) banned clitoridectomy and in the three years that followed, 2,400 girls and women were charged in local courts (with colonial powers of administration) for defying the ban and circumcising themselves (*Ngaitana*). Female circumcision has long been a topic of controversy and polarised debates – from the 1920s on, it was argued by feminists in the British House of Commons that the practice was backward and of danger to the health of mothers and infants (Thomas 2005: 99).

The act of self-circumcision has to be seen as a radical move of subversion, one in which more than 2,000 young women were willing to risk imprisonment in colonial police stations. Understanding the movement, however, requires that we see the defiance of the girls and women both in the context of anti-colonial resistance and of negotiating the power of men and women within the Meru community.

Lynn Thomas (1997), in her article about the *Ngaitana* response, takes us back to earlier attempts by missionaries and colonial administrators to ban clitoridectomy, and to earlier defiance. But between the 1920s (when the Kikuyu Central Association opposed the Protestant missions' approach) and 1956 (when the Njuri Ncheke banned the practice), the forms of colonial administration were changing and some Kikuyu men became embedded in the daily administration of colonial rule. The decision of the 1956 Njuri Ncheke to cooperate with the colonial perspective was deeply influenced by the political instability of the time and the desire of some men to retain their colonial-granted powers after independence.

The significance of initiation ceremonies for girls was deep – it involved the transformation of girls to women (and to be a woman meant to be marriageable). The ceremonies formed part of the complex organisation of authority for older women and mothers (those with power to circumcise and elected by women's councils) and were integrated into social systems in which gender, age and transitions of sexuality and identity were critical forces within political space.

The *Ngaitana* time is remembered as one in which ceremonies were driven underground, stripped of attendant teachings and reduced to the secret practice of excision; many young men supported the women's and girls' defiance; some (men and women) refused to accept as legitimate women those who had circumcised themselves; and the colonial administrators were taken by surprise. Not only was the ban understood locally as an affront, but also as a challenge to the women's councils. It therefore caused rebellion among some young women, men – especially those in the Mau Mau movement, where young men were committed to fighting for liberation from colonial administration – and among some older women, and gained the approval of others including Kikuyu men on local councils, missionary-educated men, men associated with the church and some headmen.

The overarching point of the story is that no moment of subversion or resistance against norms experienced as oppressive within the continent can be read simply. At first glance, the notion of self-circumcision as a courageous and political act might appear bizarre. Currently, there is a very rich body of Africa-located research and activism, which sees women's and girls' circumcision as something that cannot be supported in any terms. Yet, the *Ngaitana* struggle is embedded in a particular moment of colonial oppression in Kenya, one in which rebellion on the part of young girls and women demanded that their rights to authority, power and status be claimed on their own terms. Such rights were articulated at a time when the growing paramilitary movement against the colonialists was strengthening, and signalled resistance to many elders, including the Njuri Ncheke, the colonial administrators and missionaries and the older women who held power over the initiation.

What this tells us is that it is not possible to read women's resistances in African contexts as ever monoaxial – as a strike against patriarchy alone or a strike against military rule alone. The history of resistance to diverse forms of patriarchy in the 20th century has always been embedded in local and regional stories of the resistances of the continent itself against colonial and neo-colonial economic and political policies, ideologies and systems.

Gender, sexuality and the post-colonial state

To understand 20th-century activisms, it is important to explore what kinds of reg-endered processes took place after flag independence. There are diverse historical trajectories of different African nations, but perhaps we can approach the idea of the post-colonial state by outlining a number of questions that facilitate analysis and comparison across nations.

The first question is what kind of colonialism existed prior to flag independence? British, French, Belgian and Portuguese colonialisms conquered different geographical swathes of the continent, leaving varying legacies in their wake. Second, there is the question of what happened after flag independence. This leads to a number of more specific questions: what kind of state was in place – military, civilian, monarchical? What kinds of societies existed – traditional, modern? What kinds of men were in power and what kinds were in opposition? What were women's relations to the state – resistant, autonomous, aligned (as in women's wings affiliated to political parties)? Finally, there is the question of the roles that global forces – such as the international financial institutions, the United Nations Decade for Women and the Beijing Platform for Action, as well as religious revivalism – have played in particular national contexts. All these questions highlight the different forces impinging on the forms of masculinity, femininity and sexualities found in any given national context.

It is also critical to note the significance of the structural adjustment programmes that have influenced the shape and ideologies of many post-colonial states. Though on the one hand, motherhood became part of much nationalist rhetoric in the new state, changing economic times brought with them changing male identities. Andrea Cornwall (2003), in the context that she explored of Ado-Odo (in Nigeria), suggests ideals of masculinity were shifting away from the notion of 'man as controller or provider'. Instead, masculinity in certain instances was becoming reconfigured in ways that shunned authority and control, and notions of love and care were gaining ascendance. Elsewhere, the linkages between love and money were the focus of attention, as in the reading by Richard Ssewakiryanga, 'No romance without finance', which explores the social power of money and the material power of love in intimate relations among students at Makerere University, pointing to the fluidity of gender in economies of dress and exchange where students are struggling through poverties created by structural adjustment policies.

In a number of African contexts, unlike in the global North, issues of women's rights were taken up in ways that did not partition political rights from organising around violence against women or the assertion of sexual freedom. In part this had to do with the fact that many post-colonial states embarked on legislation reform around issues of gender equality. Pushed by the criteria of both the World Bank and the International Monetary Fund for loans and, differently, by growing feminist and gender activism, the experiences of being gendered in ways that deprived women of access to land, rights, education and safety propelled legal activism.

This can be seen, for example, in the history of an organisation such as Women's Law in Southern Africa (WLSA), which lobbied in seven countries in southern Africa (excluding South Africa) for changes to the legal status of women. Non-governmental organisations simultaneously began to work holistically on issues connecting gender, sexuality, violence and the right to a public voice (Sister Namibia is an example of an organisation that works in an integrated manner on all these issues). The question of sexual rights or freedom, and what this meant, relied upon a feminist analysis of women's bodies, processes of gendering as well as sexual and political liaisons. At the same time, the priorities for struggle were shaped by considerations of differences among women in their levels of education, religious affiliation and notions of morality (Nyeck et al 2009).

The consideration of the post-colonial state also needs to take up certain other issues – questions of war and militarisation, questions of development, and questions of globalisation form part of what can be explored as critical dimensions of understanding the contemporary politics of gender and sexualities.

Gender, sexuality and development

The dominant approaches to gender and development between the 1970s and 1990s ignored the issue of sexuality almost completely. Whether theorists drew on the approaches of women in development, women and development or gender and development (WID, WAD and GAD respectively), women were seen primarily through the economic lenses that positioned them either as outside production (and needing to be recognised as being inside), central to production (in the household and beyond) and/or part of heterosexual dyads and family networks.

As Beth Maina-Ahlberg and Asli Kulane clearly articulate in Chapter 36, reproductive health has long been a development concern, but even so, the focus has been on women as mothers rather than as people whose sexuality includes fertility and the issue of control and choice over reproduction. Access to contraception in some contexts has radically changed women's relationship to the meanings of reproduction, but there are also countries (such as apartheid South Africa) in which forced sterilisation and government-sponsored programmes to inject contraceptives into poor women have formed part of state strategies for population control. In addition, of course, there are many cultural and religious contexts in which contraception is frowned upon. In 2010, for example, feminists in Malawi and Kenya were battling for the regularisation (legalisation) of abortion in contexts in which the leading cause of death in women of child-bearing age is illegal/unsafe abortion.

From the late 1990s, issues of sexuality moved more centrally onto the development stage, propelled by three main forces. First, the need to combat the transmission of HIV radically altered the face of development discourses, forcing conversations about women's access to microcredit schemes or improving girls' access to education to recognise the dynamics of sexuality at play at every level of society. The politics of development was forced to engage proactively with the meaning of constraints and controls over women's sexualities, the meaning of transactional sex in the management of poverty and the impact of multiple and concurrent sexual partnerships. At the same time, national and international discourses on sexual health and rights, spurred by the 1994 population conference in Cairo, encouraged debate about the salience of sexuality in thinking through issues of access to reproductive health, challenges around sexual violence and the meaning of non-heterosexual desire and relationships.

Alongside literature on the politics of gender and sexuality around HIV transmission has emerged literature on new sexual cultures and options, which arise as a result of globalisation, and the ways in which transnational mobilities can create new zones of sexual norms, for men and women. Sandra Manuel's book, *Love and Desire: Concepts, Narratives and Practices of Sex among Youth in Maputo City*, about youth sexual cultures in Maputo, is an excellent example of research which began from an interest in HIV transmission among youth and grew into a fascinating study of emerging norms around gendered and heterosexual sexual interactions in an urban environment that encourages pleasure, multiple partnership and a rejection of traditional values (Manuel 2008). This is an exciting arena in which to conduct research and one in which teaching – where students are open to discussion – could allow for the exploration of the emergence of new interactions between gender and sexuality in rapidly changing worlds.

A final theme here might be one that explores in-depth the concept of transactional sex. Often linked with issues of economic migration and the negotiation of poverty, forced or consensual transactional sex is part of a world in which sex as a commodity offers both opportunities and dangers. Trafficking remains a reality throughout the world, and is especially prevalent in southern Africa, across the borders of Zambia, Zimbabwe, Mozambique and Malawi, into South Africa. Africans are also trafficked beyond the continent, according to Mapode, an NGO working on issues of at-risk youth in Zambia, and sex tourism is part of tourist activity in places as far apart as Senegal and Zanzibar or Mombasa.[10]

Gender, sexualities and contemporary culture

It is difficult to even begin to define culture without foregrounding the link between gender processes and their implications for how sexualities are shaped. What is critical to note is that the dominant discourse on African cultures has a tendency to describe engagements with gender and sexuality in negative terms, and in terms that relegate the notion of transforming genders, through engagement with sexual potential and ideologies, to a timeless zone called 'tradition'. This zone then becomes separated from contemporary experiences, collectively identified as 'modernity'.

As Sylvia Tamale (2008) suggests, this is a naive and unhelpful discursive move, and can make the discussion of what is meant by culture, and how this entails sexually oriented embodiment of many kinds, fraught with difficulty. On the one hand, there are debates about the relationship between religious or customary 'cultures' and practices identified as harmful to the health, dignity and/or sexual well-being of women. On the other hand, as Tamale's work points out, the culture/modernity divide obscures the ways in which contemporary opportunities meld with what is valued about, for example, sexual initiation practices for women (or for men), and ignore the realities of multiple and simultaneous engagements with different gendered and sexual norms. Rather than rehearse material on female genital mutilation, virginity testing, polygyny, or widow inheritance (important as these practices are in the debates on gender, sexuality and culture), it is useful to integrate consideration of contemporary cultural vehicles into discussions of activism.

This means taking the media seriously, especially print advertisements, television dramas and popular music. Where the internet is available, and students have access to cellphone technology (such as MixIt), other opportunities to discuss culture are created. It is these forms of representation about norms, desirability, respectability and status that shape gender and its engagement with sexualities much more dynamically than is often acknowledged.

It is critical to engage culture as living social energy, policed and empowered by different interests (especially economic ones), and simultaneously rebelled against and rejected through the adoption of alternative norms. There is vibrant activism at this level, throughout the continent, through ICT-driven NGOs such as APC-Africa, or WomensNet, and challenges to media to include issues of gender, sexuality and the erotic and political power of women, through blogs, Facebook pages, websites designed to bring information on African LGBTI issues to the continent and myriad engagement with publishing, media critique and performance.

It is impossible to ignore, within this theme, the prevalence of violence against women, which seeks to abuse, humiliate and damage, through the use of force called sexual because the tools deployed involve the parts of the body conventionally thought of as sexual, and which carry deep and powerful meanings around sexuality. This is violence perpetrated by people gendered as men (who use it against other men, and also against children). Though many men would not dream of using such violence, it remains the case that masculinities tend to tolerate the potential for such violence within their shape. In many contexts, this potential becomes realised in such destructive ways that it is hard to imagine masculinities without imagining a predilection for sexual violence as culturally justified. This is certainly the case in conflict zones, in prisons and in many African countries.

In other contexts, such as in parts of Nigeria or Ghana, such masculine aggression might concentrate on controlling women's dress (see Bibi Bakare-Yusuf's essay in Chapter 8), or on public threats of punishment should women's independence seem to be contravening norms. These are generalisations, based on research on sexual harassment within tertiary educational settings in Nigeria, but they gesture toward institutional and urban cultures in which sexual violence against women is tolerated, and in some settings even encouraged discursively and by other means.

Gender-based violence

One of the most proactive and engaged areas of feminist and women's activism in African contexts involves gender-based violence. There are diverse layers of this activism: legal advocacy and reform; the establishment of organisations offering support, resources and education; the establishment of shelters for abused women and children; educational campaigns; movement building; trainings for police and judicial officers; provision of medical resources; marches and demonstrations; research on the links between gender-based violence and many other issues, such as poverty, HIV/AIDS and conflict. Across the continent, this activism forms one of the richest resources of experience on what it means to tackle patriarchies and social and economic injustice, and on how to describe and analyse daily realities of brutality, state indifference and community-based tolerances for particular forms of abuse, usually targeted at women and girls.

Despite this, we find that there is relatively little space in most readings on gender and development or gender and society for in-depth exploration of the histories and theorisation of gender-based violence. Even in educational curricula of psychology, social work or the law, it is difficult to find concentrated attention on the multiplicity of questions that arise when gender-based violence is taken seriously as a critical zone of African feminist thought and work.

The politics of identifying perpetrators of gender-based violence as unequivocally male are complex. On the one hand it is true that the perpetrators' gender does, with overwhelming regularity, differ critically from the gender of their victims. On the other hand, identifying perpetrators solely by their gender is an inadequate route to a full explanation of the myriad behaviours that can be called gender-based violence, and cannot explain the facts that women are differently vulnerable to gender-based violence and men are in diverse relationships to its perpetuation. Furthermore, in many countries men experience sexual assault in various contexts: in sexually abusive homes, in gang warfare, in prisons and at the hands of abusive male authority figures.

The term gender-based violence is perhaps most useful to remind us that the different forms of violence we are concerned with arise primarily through the dynamics of being gendered. In one light, the rape of a woman in the workplace, the school teacher's sexual coercion of a girl student and a wife's hand held on a hot-plate by her husband look like very different acts of violence. The institutional contexts are different, the damage caused differs, the relationship between the victim and the assailant differs, and ways of addressing the situation legally and therapeutically differ.

What the assaults have in common is the fuel of gender relations. Noting this takes us beyond an analysis that says women are vulnerable to men. It suggests that both women and men are vulnerable to the way dominant norms of gender relation, within their contexts, are working. Within a country such as South Africa, where gender-based violence is high, men are as likely to become blunt assailants of women (and, often, of men) as women are to become victims of sexual abuse, domestic battery, economic abuse and incest. Clearly, those who actively assault retain responsibility for their violence – that is a matter of principle and law. But the challenge is to untangle both victim and perpetrator from the terrible interlock of violence, no matter how shocking the perpetration or how resonant the victimhood/ survivorship.

It is safe to say that African-located research and activism have shown that gender-based violence exists in every community, in millions of households, in every form of institution, within all public spaces – in short wherever people interact. Despite the inevitable difficulties of counting assaults, it is widely accepted that gender-based violence in African contexts is high. Because of this and because of the many different shapes particular incidents of gender-based violence can take, understanding context becomes very important to developing strategies to combat it.

In addition to the realities of gender-based violence, there are currently three themes that could dominate any analysis. The first of these is the prevalence of poverty. Although it would be absurd to suggest that poverty causes gender-based violence, it is true that poverty creates an environment of vulnerability for women in which escape from violence is much more difficult than it is in better-resourced environments. Poverty is also characterised by poor access to education, health services and NGO outreach, and this might contribute to the normalisation of gender roles in which legitimacy for gender-based violence is increased.

This by no means suggests that gender-based violence in well-resourced environments does not occur – it certainly does. The majority of Africa's women, however, live in poverty, and thus it is important to take poverty as a condition in which gender-based violence might be impossible to escape, when it occurs, and where the challenges of subsistence might overcome the need to tackle sexual and/or domestic violence, so that survivors choose the personal violence against themselves and/or their sons and daughters over starvation and indigence.

The second theme involves familiarity with violence. In many post-democracy settings, the legacies of institutionalised violence remain in the treatment of many prisoners and illegal migrants, and in the acceptance of violence as a legitimate and immediate means of settling disputes. The combination of escalating unemployment, more permeable boundaries between countries and between neighbourhoods, the depletion of police resources, heightened ethnic and/or religious tensions and the lack of effective and inspirational engagement of youth into political movements has facilitated violence within criminal activities and the experience of violent interaction as a modus vivendi for many.

Emerging democratisation and the flow of conflict and wars is a third theme. On the one hand, much of the legislation that held colonial cultures in place has been formally dismantled and new policies aimed at the redress of poverty and national democracies have been initiated. On the other hand, in the midst of newly accessible television images of middle-class wealth and national rhetoric about rights, freedom and redress, many constituencies continue to endure enormous hardships. The tension between ideological – and some legal – commitment to change and the tenacity of old inequities contributes to the difficult negotiation of day-to-day reality for Africans. The shape of this shifts radically from one country to the next, but tensions about gender, identity and the meaning of citizenship haunt African contexts in ways which frequently spark intense violence of many kinds.

A final issue concerns the meaning of gender itself. It has been argued that gender as a socio-political category which organises power between and among men and women is an exceptionally violent force in itself. Human beings are forced to access identity through becoming gendered (usually first at birth, and then as a life-long process of direct and indirect initiation), and research on the lives of transgendered people suggests that this process is not benign, and limits the potential of all human beings through the proscription of roles, norms and options for life. This is a very important idea, suggesting that, like racialisation under colonialism or ethnicisation as a route to political power under many current political regimes, becoming gendered can be seen as violence itself, creating powerful and painful divisions between human beings as a condition for their survival (Butler, 2004).

The most important achievement in the area of gender-based violence on the continent has perhaps been an ideological shift of momentous significance: up until 40 years ago in many African contexts, very dangerous discourses of two kinds erased the rights of sexually abused women and girls. One discourse claimed that defilement or violation of a woman or girl was predominantly an assault on her family and needed to be dealt with as such – often by marrying the survivor to her abuser (this remains current thought in some contexts, but has been, by 2010, powerfully challenged) (Fried 2003; Moshenberg 2009).

The other discourse, fuelled by colonial notions of 'the black savage' (Pape 2006), who was projected as aggressively and rampantly sexually violent toward colonial women, was that only women with colonial ancestry or high status could be abused in a way that demanded redress. Both these notions have been attacked, during decades of feminist work, and though their legacies remain, Awa Thiam's call to African feminists to tackle gender-based violence achieved a dramatic shift in our notions of what it means to be raped, sexually abused as a child, sexually harassed, abducted, beaten by partners or coerced into brutal and exploitative sex.

New genders, new sexualities

The strategies employed for political activism through the mobilisation of women shift dramatically in different historical, social, economic and cultural contexts. Some analyses of such shifts privilege identity politics as a key resource in understanding differences, tensions and alliances, so that religious or racial identities, for example, become central to the theorisation of particular activist agendas or initiatives. Others are more interested in the contextual confluence of economic and political realities through which people gendered as women find themselves deprived of access to power, material resources and/or political representation. In the past several years, there have been vibrant, critical discussions on the nature, shape and direction of women's movement organising, and in African contexts, and much of this has included – or even prioritised – questions of sexualities.

There are four overarching debates that have circled continually in intellectual writing on women's movements, activist organisation at several levels and within numerous forums – workshops, conferences, world social forum tents, small rooms and patches of shade in which planning, arguing and celebrations have been undertaken.

The first debate concerns the meaning of the state. During the past four decades, considerable energy has been vested in the struggle to hold post-flag democracy states accountable to ideals of gender equality within political representation, state-based budget processes and the delivery of resources and services. In terms of sexuality activism that has taken gender seriously, this has meant intensive focus on issues of legal reform around gender-based violence and on issues of reproductive health service delivery, or access to treatment and care for people living with HIV and AIDS. However, where states themselves are corrupt, fragmented, in rapid transition or organised through military rule, there has been debate about the value of this work and its vulnerability to being co-opted by interests far from feminist.

This debate is interlinked with a second: the meaning of the interaction between the global North and diverse initiatives concerned with women's human rights, South-based feminisms and gender-alert social justice. As Aili Tripp (2004) suggests: 'the term transnational feminism is sometimes used as shorthand for western involvement in and influence on feminist movements globally', and although this shorthand expresses only one dynamic of transnational feminist organising, it is the dynamic that provokes difficult questions concerning integrity, sustainability, control and long-term strategy.

A third debate concerns the fact that from the time of the International Conference on Population and Development in Cairo in 1994 (and in some contexts, earlier), concerns long animating women's organising – access to reproductive health and freedom from gender-based violence – became embedded in new articulations, which linked ideas about sexual health and rights to language addressing reproduction. The link between gender, culture and sexuality has been intricate and so deeply naturalised within discourses of nationalism, the family and indeed being human that women's organising through recognition of sexuality as a political force has been challenging (see Deborah Posel's discussion in Chapter 9).

The fourth debate concerns the very existence of a women's movement (Essof 2005). In an era in which the policies of the World Trade Organisation, the US war on Iraq and the increasing gaps between the world's wealthy and its poor belie notions of progress or democracy, there has been a powerful escalation of political protest demanding alternatives. The place of gender justice within these protests, alongside the seeming intransigence of local gender oppressions, has led to serious reflection, analysis and a desire for new beginnings and new strategies.

Some voices have approached current political and economic contexts of complex gender injustices with renewed vigour, theoretical analysis that seeks to engage a wide array of local and transnational activists and strategy that encompasses the streets and the screen. The One-in-Nine Campaign is a young South African organisation that fits into this category, and speaking more widely across the continent. The African Feminist Forums have sought to bring energy to the meaning of challenging not simply the 'old' – neo-capitalism, the ongoing and shifting forms of colonialism that seek to drain African contexts of resources, weak and corrupt governance and violence – but also continually engaging 'the new': the demand for bodily integrity, the quest for alternative worlds of transaction and exchange and the need to create new alliances in the fight against sexual surveillance as a political weapon.

It is also within research that it is possible to witness activist engagement. The African Regional Centre for Sexuality Resources, in addition to its magazine, offers leadership trainings and seminars and supports research. The internet itself is a major terrain of activism around the rights of LGBTI people – the Association of Progressive Communicators women's projects have included initiatives such as 'Take Back the Tech!', feminist technology exchanges and the promotion of digital storytelling as a form of activism around issues of gender and sexuality.

Conclusion

In the end, gender and sexualities activism should probably be imagined archaeo-logically. As we suggested earlier through citing the work of Thiam and El Saadawi, it was one of the oldest areas of African feminist activism in the 20th century, in which the politics of sexuality was examined as part of hierarchised relations of gender and the strategic focus often concerned women's rights to independent adulthood, to freedom from sexual violence and to education beyond their repro-ductive roles.

At the same time, however, new challenges have arisen, partly as a result of changing material conditions and partly as a result of deeper feminist vision. Thus, the need to centralise the politics of gender within debates on the transmission of HIV emerged as a feminist imperative during the 1990s. And the need to take on board issues of gender-based violence within war took on an activist life of its own after the Rwandan genocide, and continues to be an area of innovative and extraordinary work. The work of Isis-WICCE in Kampala, of Femmes Solidarité (FAS) in West Africa and of Breaking the Silence in Namibia attests to this.

The question of sexual orientation toward people of one's own sex/gender was raised in the mid-1990s but not until recently have the politics of state, religious and popular homophobia appeared so powerfully on activist agendas. The meaning of transgender experiences and lives has come to illuminate questions about bodies, identities, gender, solidarities and political activism and this in turn has galvanised new thinking and activism. All in all, contemporary work around gender and sexualities in diverse African contexts constitutes a continued and dynamic subversion of all Afro-pessimist predictions about the continent's place in global understandings of what it means to fight for one's life and the lives of others.

Notes

1. The Mexico City policy sought to control the terms on which the USA funded reproductive and sexual rights by proscribing aid to organisations that were in any way associated with women's right to the termination of pregnancy.
2. See, for example, the debate between Charmaine Pereira and Patricia McFadden (2003) in *Feminist Africa* 2: 50–65.
3. Some say that the name comes from the term *Afer*, used to describe a number of northern African peoples in the Roman era, and which gave rise to the province under Roman control being known as the 'Africa Province'. Leo Africanus, the 16th century Moroccan adventurer, suggested that the Greek word *apherike* (meaning without cold and terror) was also involved in the name for the continent.

4. A sexual game between young people (men and women, men and men) in southern Africa in which the penis is inserted between the thighs for pleasure. Also referred to as 'thigh sex'.

5. As a generalisation, this of course can be challenged: the Timbuktu manuscripts, in Mali, offer access to pre-18th century worlds in astonishing ways. So do the multiple historiographies that are possible through archaeology, especially the study of civilisations visible through the contemporary 'ruins' of their architecture, such as the Rozvi Empire's Great Zimbabwe, in what is now south-east Zimbabwe; the cultural study of the manuscripts that detailed the intimate and widespread Arab engagement with African terrains from the 11th century; and linguistic work, such as that of Oyeronke Oyewumi with the Yoruba, mythology, genealogies and so on.

6. It was the British colonial gaze that sexualised women's breasts, for example.

7. The African Feminist Forum (AFF) is a biennial conference that brings together African feminist activists to deliberate on issues of key concern to the movement (see www.africanfeministforum.com). The first AFF was held in Accra, Ghana in 2006, the second in Kampala, Uganda in 2008 and the third in Dakar, Senegal in 2010.

8. See www.apcafricawomen.org, accessed 14 January 2011.

9. See www.mask.org.za; www.genderdynamix.org; http://adventuresfrom.com (all accessed 20 May 2009).

10. See Mapode's website at www.mapode.freewebpages.org.

References

Abrahams, Yvette (2000) 'Colonialism, dysfunction and dysjuncture: the historiography of Sarah Baartman', PhD dissertation, Cape Town, University of Cape Town

Baskin, Jeremy (1991) *Striking Back: a History of COSATU*, Johannesburg, Ravan

Butler, Judith (2004) *Undoing Gender*, New York, NY, Routledge

Byanyima, Karagwa (1992) 'Women in political struggle in Uganda', in Bystydzienski, Jill (ed), *Women Transforming Politics: Worldwide Strategies for Empowerment*, Bloomington, Indiana University Press

Cornwall, Andrea (2003) 'To be a man is more than a day's work: shifting ideals of masculinity in Ado-Odo, southwestern Nigeria', in Lindsey, Lisa and Miescher, Stephan (eds) *Men and Masculinities in Modern Africa*, Portsmouth, NH, Heinemann

El Saadawi, Nawal (1957 [1973]) *Memoirs of a Woman Doctor*, London, Wiley and Son

Essof, Shereen (2005) 'She-murenga: challenges, opportunities and setbacks of the women's movement in Zimbabwe', *Feminist Africa* 4: 29–45

Fried, Susana (2003) 'Violence against women', *Health and Human Rights* 6(2): 88–111

Kalipeni, Ezekiel and Zeleza, Tiyambe (eds) (1999) *Sacred Spaces and Public Quarrels: African Cultural and Economic Landscapes*, Asmara, African World

Manuel, Sandra (2008) *Love and Desire: Concepts, Narratives and Practices of Sex among Youth in Maputo City*, Dakar, Council for the Development of Economic and Social Research in Africa (CODESRIA)

Mba, Nina (1982) *Nigerian Women Mobilized: Women's Political Activity in Southern Nigeria, 1900–1965*, Berkeley, Institute of International Studies, University of California, Berkeley

Moshenberg, Daniel (ed) (2009) 'Sexual and gender-based violence in Africa', *ACAS Bulletin*, 83, accessed 7 March 2010.

New York Times (2000) 27 June, p. A37

Nyeck, S., Moreau, A., Gueboguo, C. and Azuah, U. (eds) (2009) 'Intersectionality and sexuality in Africa: a critical assessment of women's experiences', *Outliers: A Collection of Essays and Creative Work on Sexuality in Africa*, 2, IRN, accessed 30 November 2010

Pape, John (1990) 'Black and white: The perils of sex in colonial Zimbabwe', *Southern African Studies* 16(4)

Ratele, Kopano (2001) 'The sexualisation of apartheid', unpublished PhD thesis, Cape Town, University of the Western Cape

Rukundwa, Lazare and Van Aarde, Andries (2007) 'The formation of postcolonial theory', *HTS Theological Studies* 63(3): 1171–94

Tamale, Sylvia (1996) 'Taking the beast by its horns: formal resistance to women's oppression in Africa', *African Development,* 21(4): 5- 21

—— (2008) 'The right to culture and the culture of rights: a critical perspective on women's sexual rights in Africa', *Feminist Legal Studies* 16: 47–69

Thiam, Awa (1978) *La Parole aux Negresses* (Black Women, Speak Out!) Paris, Denoël/Gonthier

Thomas, Lynn (1997) 'Ngaitana! (I will circumcise myself!): the gender and generational politics of the 1956 ban on clitoridectomy in Meru, Kenya', in Hunt, N.R., Liu, T. and Quataert, J. (eds) *Gendered Colonialisms in African History*, Oxford, Blackwell

—— (2005) *Politics of the Womb: Women, Reproduction, and the State in Kenya,* Kampala, Fountain Publishers

Tripp, Aili (2005) 'Regional networking as transnational feminism: African experiences', *Feminist Africa* 4: 46–63

Zeleza, Tiyambe (1997a) 'Gender biases in African historiography', in Imam, A., Mama, A. and Sow, F. (eds) *Engendering African Social Sciences*, Dakar, Council for the Development of Economic and Social Research in Africa

—— (1997b) 'Visions of freedom and democracy in postcolonial African literature,' *Women's Studies Quarterly* 25(3/4): 10–34

7

The 'perils' of sex and the panics of race: the dangers of interracial sex in colonial Southern Rhodesia[1]

Oliver Phillips

What peril? Why panic?

Between 1910 and 1920 there were a number of episodes of collective panic among the white communities of Johannesburg, Bulawayo and Salisbury (Harare) (Pape 1990; McCulloch 2000). These were manifestations of social anxieties serious enough to bring about rampaging lynch mobs, whose dispensing of violent retribution was fuelled by newspaper campaigns and strident rhetoric from politicians, church leaders and other influential social figures. These panics about sex and race were identified as social problems threatening the fundamental moral fibre and social order of colonial society, and they resulted in legislation aimed directly at restoring the sexual and social distance that was necessary for the survival of racial hierarchies in the colonial order.

Reading accounts of these critical espisodes of social anxiety today invariably produces a sense of astonishment at the almost surreal simplicity of the crude politics of race and desire that underlie them. But detailed analysis by scholars, such as McCulloch (2000), reveals a jostling for access to power and the positioning of gender and race in the nascent structures of colonial society far more complex than can be effectively reflected here.

The principle aim of this chapter, then, is to offer a broad account of the great fears, fantasies and forces that so characterised sexual relations between white settlers and colonised black subjects in the early years of Southern Rhodesia. These striking dynamics vividly illustrate the powerful under-currents that framed relations of sex, race and gender in the process of colonisation. Readers might like to consider the extent to which the legacy of these highly charged moments of panic in the then newly established settler society is remarkably manifest in the furore around sex that so often erupts in post-colonial relations today.

The quickest introduction to the issues is provided by the opening paragraphs of an internal British South African Police (BSAP) report titled 'Black and white peril', written in 1915 by Superintendent Brundell of the Bulawayo Criminal Investigation Department (CID):

> It is necessary to define and differentiate between 'Black Peril,' and by this I mean the following:
>
> (1) The actual commission of the crime of Rape on White females.
>
> (2) Assault with intent to commit Rape on White females.
>
> (3) Indecent assaults, acts or overtures, or molesting white females for the purpose of exciting or satisfying bestial desires.
>
> and 'White Peril' which I may classify as follows:-
>
> (A) White females who prostitute themselves with natives for the purpose of monetary gain....
>
> (B) The indiscreet and careless attitude adopted by white females in their personal relations with their native male servants which undoubtedly leads to undue familiarity bordering on licence to which many actual attempts to commit sexual crime must be attributed.
>
> (C) 'Nymphomania'. A well known condition which takes the form of hysterical curiosity in sexual matters, in many cases due to inherent temperamental qualities of the individual, although in some instances when the condition is not inherent the climatic effect on the human produces the same form of temporary hysteria.

The document makes extraordinary reading as, through vivid reference to the behaviour of particular white women, Brundell articulates all the fears and anxieties that white Rhodesian settlers cultivated in relation to interracial sex and the resulting possibilities of miscegenation.

White communities in colonial Southern Rhodesia, South Africa and other regional states rooted definitions of black peril in what was perceived to be the inevitable desire of black men for white women, but it is worth noting that there was no such consensus about what constituted white peril. In Southern Rhodesia, white peril was represented as the danger presented by white women who consorted with black men, so that the notion of peril was consistently fixed around the relationship between white women and black men. Whereas, in many other southern African countries, such as Zambia (Hansen 1989) and some parts of South Africa (Pape 1990), the gender dimensions were not so fixed because white peril was taken to refer to white men who consorted with black women. The implications of this distinction will become clear during the course of this chapter, which will work with the former definition because it is so focused on Brundell's report and its immediate context.

Those white women who were thought to initiate, encourage or accept the advances of black men were either discreetly removed or hospitalised or, in more serious cases, were subject to imprisonment. A woman's class might well have determined her sanction, because colonial wives accused of transgressing the boundaries of appropriate racial distance did not suffer the same fate as the white prostitutes who accepted black clients – the latter were subjected to the public humiliation of being tarred and feathered. This entailed stripping the woman naked in public, pouring hot tar over her body, then rolling her in feathers which would stick to the tar, before parading her 'tarred and feathered' down the streets and then chasing her out of town.

The severest treatment, though, was undoubtedly reserved for the black men often spuriously accused of propositioning, flirting, raping, seducing or being seduced by white women. A number of black men were hanged during the 1910–20 episodes, both with and without official sanction, as marauding mobs lynched those men the courts found reason not to. Prudent reticence on the part of colonial authorities simply inspired ferocious acts of vigilantism by settlers, as attempts from London to overturn obviously unsafe convictions of black men for rape of white women (which carried the death sentence) were fiercely resisted by settlers. Due process was frequently overridden and attempts by colonial authorities to moderate the fearful zeal of settler populations simply fuelled the settlers' unilateral desire for independence. These episodes therefore carried all the hallmarks of symbolisation, distortion, exaggeration and amplification that give moral panics such galvanising significance and can certainly be seen to reflect the dynamics that Gayle Rubin highlights in her analysis of 'sex panics',[2] including the enactment of new laws:

> Because sexuality in Western societies is so mystified, the wars over it are often fought at oblique angles, aimed at phony targets, conducted with misplaced passions, and are highly, intensely symbolic. Sexual activities often function as signifiers for personal and social apprehensions to which they have no intrinsic connection. During a moral panic, such fears attach to some unfortunate sexual activity or population. The media become ablaze with indignation, the public behaves like a rabid mob, the police are activated, and the state enacts new laws and regulations. When the furore has passed, some innocent erotic group has been decimated and the state has extended its power into new areas of erotic behaviour. (Rubin 2000: 171)

The laws of sex and race: producing subjectivity and objectification

The fearful anxieties about interracial sex that necessitated Brundell's CID report, led to the passing of the Immorality and Indecency Suppression Ordinance in 1916, which expressly forbade any sexual activity (or even inactive voyeurism) between black men and white women. The previous Immorality Suppression Ordinance of 1903 had been restricted to specifically prohibiting full sexual intercourse. It stated that 'any white woman or girl who shall voluntarily have illicit sexual intercourse with any native shall upon conviction thereof be liable to imprisonment with or without hard labour for a period not exceeding two years' (Section 1 of the Immorality Suppression Ordinance (No. 9) of 1903).

Similarly, Section 3 of the 1903 Ordinance made a black man party to consensual sex with a white woman liable to imprisonment with hard labour for a maximum period of five years. It also prescribed a maximum sentence of five years (and 25 lashes if the offender was a male) for anyone who procured a white girl or woman to have sexual intercourse with a black man. But following the Brundell report and the anxieties out of which it arose, the law of 1916 did not limit itself to sexual intercourse:

> Any white woman or girl who by words, writing, signs, or any other form of suggestion, entices, incites, solicits, or importunes any native to have illicit sexual intercourse with her or to commit any act of indecency with or upon her shall be guilty of an offence, and upon conviction shall be liable to imprisonment with or without hard labour for a period not exceeding one year. (Section 1: Immorality Suppression Ordinance of 1916)

> Any native who ... commits, attempts to commit, or is party to the commission of any act of indecency towards any white woman or girl shall be guilty of an offence and liable upon conviction to a period not exceeding two years and to receive corporal punishment not exceeding fifteen lashes or strokes with a cane. (Section 3: Immorality Suppression Ordinance of 1916)

The 1916 law was clearly much more broadly framed than the 1903 ordinance in order to include all possibilities of enticement, incitement or suggestion, but more importantly it relied on the unrestrictive notion of 'any act of indecency' in addition to sexual intercourse. It is also here that the extraordinary detail of settlers' fears and the precision of their fantastic anxieties become clear, as reference is made to:

> the raising or opening of any window, blind, or screen of any room, or the trap door, or flap of any privy, for the purpose of observing any woman, or girl who may be in such a room in a nude or semi-nude state, or maybe using such privy for the necessary purposes of nature. (Section 4, Immorality Suppression Ordinance of 1916)[3]

In relation to this concern with the voyeurism of black men, it is remarkable that in the 19th century the naked bodies of black men and women were displayed in public exhibitions in European cities, with a focus explicitly centred on the genitalia (Gilman 1985: 85). While these exhibitions clearly appealed to the lascivious curiosities of 'civilised' Europeans, this officially sanctioned pattern of voyeurism reflected a clear attribution of subjectivity and objectification. For Europeans to gaze studiously at the labia of black women was rationalised as educational and represented as the scientific study of the atavistic anatomy of 'primitive' people. In other words, black women became the object of study for white subjects, thereby reinforcing black women's absence of subjectivity. Whereas, for a black man to gaze upon the sexual anatomy or even upon the body of a white woman in a naturalist or intimate setting was seen to reverse the ordained positioning of subject-objectification because it implicitly objectified white women, allowing and reinforcing the subjectivity of black men.

This presented a clear problem, because it threw into question the naturalness of a colonial social order in which whiteness occupied the terrain of subjectivity. But ironically, in articulating this law white legislators implicitly constructed a white woman as an object of desire for black men and therefore they inadvertently colluded in the fetishisation of a white woman as an object of desire.

Thus, to protect the dignified subjectivity of white women, the definition of an 'act of indecency' was left as completely discretionary for the court to infer. We are left in no doubt that any act of voyeurism was against the law and the clearest definition given for an act of indecency was 'the ordinary acceptance of the term' (Section 4, Immorality Suppression Ordinance of 1916). This was precisely in accordance with the notions of peril that Brundell described and that resulted in his locating danger in the broader concept of desire, rather than just in penetration. The dangers of desire contributed a symbolic level, which magnified the more pedestrian anxieties of miscegenation and eugenics into the running panics around sexual peril.

Where they are differently contrived for different genders, attempts to regulate desire and sexual behaviour are ultimately attempts to regulate gender. In this case they were laden with such constructions of power that sex and race would be conflated into law differently for men and women. This might explain why black women and white men were so invisible in Brundell's report, in the legislation passed in 1916 and in the most vociferous sexual panics that arose. The 1903 legislation provided the possibility of the death penalty for any black man found guilty of the rape or attempted rape of a white woman, but there was no equivalent punishment for the rape of black women. This legislation was enacted directly as a result of the rising panic among the white settlers about the perils of sex between white women and black men, though the reverse relationship was never a source of such panic. *(white) men can do whatever they damn well want to*

Intersections of race and gender: determined trajectories of desire

For the first two years after the arrival of the settlers no white women were allowed in the colony – indeed the first white woman to land among the settlers arrived disguised as a man.[4] In 1911, women only made up 34 per cent of the settler population, and it took a further 10 years for that to grow to 44 per cent – such demography giving Salisbury the boarding-house culture of a miner's frontier society with an 'abnormal' number of prostitutes (Phimister 1988: 100). Those prostitutes astute enough to make their services available to a market of black as well as white clients were seen as the source of great threat (white peril) to all white women and to 'civilisation' in general. Indeed, just prior to the legislation of 1903, a prostitute named Louisa Newman was tarred and feathered in downtown Bulawayo for not discriminating in the clients she accepted; her colour-blindness had led her to be labelled responsible for 'a number of black peril cases which occurred at this period' (Pape 1990: 703).

There was never such a strong reaction to white men who took either willing or unwilling black women as common-law wives, mistresses, or lovers. The Native Affairs Department regulations of 1898 prohibited native commissioners from keeping African wives, and 'public disapproval acted as a powerful and openly expressed deterrent' (Jeater 1993: 90). But Pape refers to the relative acceptance of

the children born from the marriage of native commissioner Scott of Melsetter to a
black woman in the early 1900s:

> Scott died sometime before 1910 but left his wife and children a farm. However,
> according to a daughter of Scott's wife, the white community acknowledged
> the so-called coloured children as legitimate. Scott's brother even went so far
> as to try to take them away from their mother so that he could look after
> them. A few years later, when Scott's wife had a child by a black man, she was
> arrested 'for producing a black man's children when she had been a white
> man's wife'. (Pape 1990: 712)

This makes clear black women's lack of subjectivity, because Scott's wife was seen as
just that, the passive receptacle of her husband's status. She was seen as incapable
of passing on to her own (half-white) children any real social subjectivity and was
depicted either as the wife of another, or as the mother of another's children. It was
perhaps this very lack of subjectivity that allowed black women to be taken into
relationships with white men, whose subjectivity was seen as unquestionable.

Interestingly, Hansen (1989) describes how such concubinage was readily
accepted in the early days of colonial Northern Rhodesia (Zambia),[5] but that
increasing settlement required that white men should not display their black lovers
in public and should keep them veiled from the eyes of 'metropolitan prudery'
(Hansen 1989: 94). The most official attention focused on white men and black
women in Southern Rhodesia appears to have been in that same year of desperate
concern about interracial sex – 1916 – when the CID was asked to compile strictly
confidential reports on all white men known to be having regular sexual relations
with black women. By 1920, the CID had found that the 'number of Europeans
who are reported to live or habitually have sexual intercourse with native females
between 1916 and 30 June 1920 is 77' (Pape 1990: 711).

Pape goes on to describe incidents in which it is clear that the colonial authorities
declined to prosecute white men known to be forcing their attentions on black women
(Pape 1990: 710–13), whereas for the 15-year period 1899–1914, Brundell reports only
24 cases in which white women were known to have had consensual intercourse with
black men (Brundell 1915: 33) and these elicited far more concern. Jeater relates these
different reactions directly to the gendered relations of social power:

> Women were perceived as appendages to men and derived their social sta-
> tus from them. A man's status was independent of his choice of female com-
> panion, and was defined primarily by his background and economic class.
> However, a woman who became publicly associated with a man lost her sta-
> tus and took on that of the man.
>
> This happened because men took precedence over women in assuming the
> role of the household head, that is, the person who represented the household
> in the public sphere. This meant that in any liaison between a white woman
> and a black man, the woman 'lowered' herself to the social level of the African.
> (Jeater 1993: 92)

The validity of Jeater's analysis is persuasive and can be extended to incorporate a metaphysical status. For at a more symbolic level, white women, far more than men, were seen as the embodiment of civilisation. This had the result of burdening them with the responsibility of bearing the standards of civilisation, and so civilised women were obliged to collude in their own restriction. Hansen notes that:

> such 'incorporated wives' whose ascribed social character was a function of their husband's occupation and culture, had a role beyond wifehood. They helped to define the local standards of white civilisation. These standards were assumed to set educational examples for African men servants who laboured under white women's supervision within colonial households, and to be of great help to African women. White women's work, in other words, revolved around day-to-day reproduction of labour, and social reproduction of a racially divided and class structured colonial society. (Hansen 1989: 56)

Although women had not been permitted to join the settlement for the first two years of its existence because conditions were not considered suitable, on arrival they were lauded most vociferously in instances in which they displayed a delicacy thought to be quite contrary to the 'savage brutality of untamed lands' (Boggie 1938: 37–43). Thus, the horror of black peril was not only based on a white woman's personal loss of status, but also was compounded by the sense that white civilisation had somehow been polluted. This was a pollution based on the arrogant belief that the penetration of white civilisation (embodied in the refined femininity of a man's most precious possession – his wife) must be highly desirable to the primitive native who, it was assumed, would inevitably wish to appropriate such virtuous civilisation.

The strength of this assumption in Southern Rhodesia was made explicit in correspondence between the commissioner of police and the attorney general concerning the drafting of the 1916 Immorality and Indecency Suppression Ordinance. The commissioner wrote to the attorney general suggesting that Section 3 of the ordinance, prohibiting any 'native' from 'any act of indecency' with 'any white woman or girl', should be amended to 'afford protection to other females, i.e. Japanese, Chinese, Indians, Coloured and Natives' (Commissioner of Police, Official Correspondence 1916, N.A.Z. S1227/1). The attorney general's reply is clear:

> [T]he whole idea is the protection of the European community. I do not think we should go further than this at present. The same danger is not to be apprehended from indecent acts between natives and the classes now mentioned ← yikes. as from similar acts between natives and white women. I think we had better retain the present wording. (Attorney General, Official Correspondence 24 March 1916, N.A.Z. S1227/1)

acknowledges power of colonized!

Physical intimacy between white women and black men was perceived as symbolic of the yielding of civilisation to barbarism. It was the realisation of the threat of degeneracy that exists for any person undertaking to civilise the uncivilised: the danger that instead of civilising the other, the other corrupts the qualities of the civilised. Influence flows in the wrong direction, power relations are subverted, ideological assumptions of righteousness and the natural order of things are challenged; subjectivity is decentred and objectified; civilisation finds its justification, and therefore its existence, under threat.

In the minds of colonial men, white women epitomised all that was felt to be refined, fair and loving in civilisation, and so bore its most delicate and vulnerable qualities. Embodying both motherhood and pleasure, they signified all that was desirable in a culture worthy of protection from necessarily covetous rivals. The arrogance of imperialism dictated that civilisation was more than desirable to the native, it was irresistible and necessary, but native culture contained the potential to contribute degeneracy to the metropolitan culture.

White women's race lent them a contingent subjectivity. As women, they had none, but as white members of the colonising class, it was necessary to recognise a subjectivity that could subordinate black men. This subjectivity, whose contingency made it fragile and whose fragility made it even more valuable, could only exist through the objectification and subordination of an other. Penetration by the other would decentre this subjectivity, and in the colonial order of things sex between a black man and a white woman would undo her fragile and contingent status and confer increased subjectivity on the black man.

> Society's power to define the other was articulated through an explanatory model of human pathology. But all this distancing reflected only the deep-seated anxiety stemming from the consciousness that power (including the power to stigmatise) could be lost, leaving its erstwhile possessor in danger of becoming the other. This anxiety affected biologists and physicians, as well as other members of society. The magic of any overarching explanatory model, such as degeneracy, disguised but did not eliminate the potential loss of power. The only buffer that science could provide against the anxiety that remained because of this inherent flaw – the fear of oneself being labelled as degenerate – was to create categories that were absolutely self-contained. (Gilman 1985: 214–15)

Law was similarly deployed to create a buffer against the collective colonialist dread that emerged from the nightmare of interracial sex and degeneracy; for white fears about sexual desire manifested in enough panic to produce legislation that strictly enforced the boundaries between self-contained categories of race. The trajectories of desire between these categories were seen as reflecting what was imagined to be the inclination of nature; so that the civilised subject (white woman) was represented as patently desirable and the primitive black woman, who lacked subjectivity and epitomised the other, was represented as undesirable and unworthy of protection. Anxiety would have been considerably compounded by the myths of a rampant and voracious sexuality, which black men were supposed to possess; a sexuality 'labelled as perverse because it was seen as retrogressive' (Gilman 1985: 213). The Cartesian rationality of 18th century enlightenment was paramount here in the ready contrasting of 'desire and reason, native instinct and white self-discipline, native lust and white civility, native sensuality and white morality, subversive unproductive sexuality and productive patriotic sex' (Stoler 1995: 179).

Intersections of race and gender: white men's (in)visibility

Nowhere in either Brundell's report, or in the subsequent immorality ordinance, were white men mentioned. The invisibility of the white man reflected his status as the occupier of the central, determining role; the subject who described and defined others, but steadfastly refused to turn the narrative upon himself; the narrator who directed and censured the actions of the others, and whose discursive power was such that the Western masculine perspective becames the sole, but unreflexive, subjectivity universalised as the norm. *be cause he controls everything anyway*

The reference point from which the discourse of black and white peril emanated was that of the white man. The notion of civilisation was the hallmark of white male society, and it was the white man who detected threat and erected defence networks. All the various inhabitants of colonial society (regardless of sex, class, race or desires) were represented through the voice of the white man and his interests were generalised to be the interests of all. Thence derived his invisibility.

But he is visible; his presence pervades the whole of this arena. He can be detected through his censure of the others. The panics, the prohibitions, the legitimations, the definitions that he propounds and the techniques he employs to direct the others, speak more tellingly of him than of those he seeks to control. By analysing his narrative, we make the concealed narrator visible. For instance, analysis of Brundell's report tells us more about Brundell as a white colonial male police officer than it tells us about the subjects of his reports:

> Further, I think it must be admitted that the extraordinarily careless attitude permitted to themselves by white women in this country in their domestic arrangements has had not a little to do with many attempts at criminal offences chargeable to persons who are human males notwithstanding their colour. Another point which must not be overlooked is the employment of native males in shops and for domestic purposes, such men being apart from women of their own colour and tribe. It cannot humanely be expected that for months and in some cases years, such human beings can remain continent.
> (Brundell 1915: 56)

This was the only point in the whole of his report at which Brundell mentioned black women, and even then it was only in relation to how the women serve the men about whom he was actually writing. Not yet incorporated into the wage-labour economy, African women were forced to remain in the rural areas (Sender and Smith 1986: 54–6); alienated from 'civilisation', they were of marginal interest and incidental value to the colonial authorities. Their worth lay in their peripheral existence, quietly reproducing the workforce conveniently far from the centre of production. Their lack of involvement limited their visibility and apparent worth and this invisibility was derived from their supposed lack of subjectivity.

Dangerous white women: prostitutes, careless innocents and nymphomaniacs

So, how did white women come to be seen as perilous and precisely what did this peril consist of? Who manifested peril? Black peril clearly consisted of all black men, who Brundell intimated were barely human – 'bestial practices', 'human males notwithstanding their colour' (1915: 56) – and who, he reiterates, found it difficult to resist temptation, especially that of a white woman. Brundell's report explicitly categorises those white women who formed the source of white peril as being of three different types: prostitutes, careless innocents and 'nymphomaniacs' (1956: 1).

Definitions of prostitution were often coextensive with definitions of degeneracy (Gilman 1985: 94–108), and were not constrained to the exchange of sex for money. Maggie Sumner's research on prostitution in Victorian England makes clear that the label prostitute applied as a censorious representation of deviant women rather than being restricted to a specific commercial practice (Sumner 1980 [1990]: 32). She suggests that though the police patrolled prostitution as a way of earning a living, the prostitute was the embodiment of three Victorian discourses: '(1) a fallen woman; (2) a fallen worker; and (3) a dangerous citizen' (Sumner 1980 [1990]: 33).

And thus it was that Brundell portrayed as beyond redemption those prostitutes who 'cohabit with natives' (Brundell 1915: 25). He constantly represented them as 'fallen women', noting that their immorality was 'too impossible to describe' (Brundell 1915: 28). Sometimes he referred almost explicitly to the notion of 'fallen worker' as he attributed a prostitute's acceptance of black clients to 'her age and unprepossessing appearance' (Brundell 1915: 31).

Most significantly though, Sumner's third category of 'dangerous citizen' preoccupied the fears of settlers intent on producing a society reflective of their racist conception of civilisation. On a number of occasions mobs of settlers tarred and feathered particular prostitutes in an effort to contain the danger that they represented (Brundell 1915: 28). The women concerned were subsequently deported from the colony. For it was to these prostitutes who accepted black clients 'attributed the responsibility for a number of Black Peril cases which occurred at this period' (Brundell 1915: 27). By refusing to turn away black clients, they sold the inviolability of white women and so were held responsible for the rape of white women by black men.

Considered similarly perilous was the behaviour of white women who were not prostitutes but willingly indulged in sexual intercourse with black men: 'The white women implicated apparently not having any other view than the illicit satisfaction of sexual desire due to unbalanced curiosity and hysterical wish to experience comparative sexual relationship' (Brundell 1915: 43). Lacking a commercial explanation, Brundell is obliged to describe these women as 'unbalanced' and 'hysterical', as he cannot conceive or allow the possibility that they may be acting of their own wilful volition, as white women fulfilling their mutual desires with black men. This, it seems, is so out of balance with the natural order that it is inconceivable to Brundell.

By labelling these women as mad, and such behaviour as beyond reason, Brundell succeeded not only in conjuring up an explanation for their behaviour which refused their challenge to his ideology of 'natural order', but also he managed to censure their behaviour both medically and legally. For white women to have consensual sex with black men was not only presented as wrong, but also insane and so degenerate. Brundell's contention was that it was against the law, contrary to scientific and medical knowledge of what constituted normal desire, and therefore it was unnatural and implicitly degenerate. The magnitude of the offence was multiplied with each new legal, moral and medical barrier crossed.

Slightly less culpable, but just as perilous was how Brundell portrayed 'the indiscretion and carelessness of women in their relations with male natives' (Brundell 1915: 37). This third category of perilous women consisted mainly of women who did not take what Brundell considered to be sufficient cautionary measures against being seen in an intimate setting by their servants, or allowing too familiar a relationship to develop between them:

> No. 3. 1913
>
> ... an unmarried European woman by her careless and familiar attitude to the native house servant undoubtedly led the boy to think that his mistress had a more than general interest in him. She admitted that she had been in the habit of correcting his writings for him and would go to his room in the morning to call him when she was only attired in her nightdress. Although there is nothing to show that she was anything more than careless and indiscreet she certainly raised great objection to the boy being deported, and could not see that it was a precautionary measure necessary for her protection as well as the safeguarding of any other white females whom he might come into contact with.
>
> No. 4. 1914
>
> In this instance ... a white woman the wife of a well known professional man in the Territory was in the habit while she was naked in her bath of calling in her male native boy aged 17 'to pour water over her'. Further remarks would appear to be unnecessary. (Brundell 1915: 39–40)

If these were not women who had already 'fallen', they were women whose inability to overcome their own naivety demanded that they be protected from themselves. Their naivety and carelessness was seen to endanger not only themselves, but also all white women. Such carelessness was therefore tantamount to culpability. The implication was that sensible women did not need to be reminded about such questions of propriety – care should always be taken because danger was always present.

In this way the notion of white peril operated as a censure on the behaviour of most women. Prostitutes and other women who exercised an independent control over their sexuality were blatantly censured according to their overtly deviant behaviour (thus the reference to 'nymphomaniacs'). But by suggesting that all women needed to be constantly on guard for their own sakes, for the sakes of all other white women and for the sake of the entire colonial structure, men succeeded in instilling in women such fear or conscience that they disciplined themselves for what was presented as the collective good.

The notions of black and white peril had the effect of controlling the movement, dress, manners, habits, sociability and independence of all white women, not just those who were already noted as deviant and a threat to hegemonic conceptions of order, nature and morality. The implication was that all white women had the potential to endanger themselves and the fragile foundations of civilisation in Africa, just through a moment of carelessness or indiscretion. They didn't need to be 'hysterical' to 'be considered contributory to or inducive of criminal sexual assault by coloured persons' (Brundell 1915: 55), making them accomplices in the downfall of civilisation.

Wherein black women presented no threat, on account of the confluence of race and gender that deprived them of subjecthood, black men were obvious threats because they were men and so had subjectivity tempered by race. White women's subjectivity was vulnerable to the debilitations of either immorality, or hysteria, or just plain carelessness – perilous conditions, which in turn delivered the perilous menace of black men. This vulnerability made them potential, if unwitting, threats to colonial hegemony. The contradictory status of being both 'desired objects' and 'unruly desiring subjects' (Stoler 1995: 41) reflected the contingency of their subjectivity and the relativity of their autonomy.

Although white men could be immoral and careless (though 'hysteria' was said to be a medical affliction exclusive to women),[6] and their 'taking' of a black woman would be seen as reprehensible, it did not pose so direct and immediate a threat to the natural order as sex between a black man and a white woman. This has as much to do with sexist assumptions of a woman's status being determined by the man/ men with whom she consorts, as with heterosexist notions of women's submissive virtue and men's rampant virility and with racist ideas of the innate superiority of white people. What it represents most of all, though, is the subjectivity of white men. For at the time they were the law-makers and controlled the mechanisms of censure.

There was much pressure from white Rhodesian women to place similar racial restrictions on the sexual practices of white men, but never to any avail and never resulting in similar panics. In 1921, more than half the white adult women in Southern Rhodesia signed a petition calling for the criminalisation of the cohabitation of black women and white men, and thereafter passionate campaigns to this end were conducted by the Rhodesian Women's League, the Women's Christian Temperance Union and the Women's Federation of Southern Rhodesia, though none were successful (Pape 1990: 715; Jeater 1993: 160). Similarly, there were calls from African chiefs and headmen campaigning around the Native Adultery Punishment Ordinance for the law to protect their women from being abused or seduced by white men, which also came to nought (Pape 1990: 716–17; Jeater 1993: 153). Neither black men nor white women had the discursive power to mobilise the resources necessary to engender sex panic.

Conclusion

The whole phenomenon of black and white peril was therefore not only concerned with the protection of white civilisation from the pollution of miscegenation, but also it was preoccupied with the extreme punishment of black men who were suspected of the rape of white women (black peril) and the prevention of consensual sex between the two (white peril).[7] It is clearly significant that the settler authorities were not content to prevent these acts through recourse to already existing laws around rape, and by simply prohibiting interracial sex. It was necessary to coin specific terms denoting these as particular phenomena invested with graphically described dangers, and it was only possible to do this through the popular mobilisation of fear and anxiety that occurred through the particular episodes of panic that took place between 1910 and 1920.

It was necessary to do this in order to signify that the danger lay specifically between *white women* and *black men*. In a world in which subjectivity was not just male but also white, they each constituted the different halves of the subordinated other. These parallel contingencies meant that neither was a stable marker of superordination or subordination – whereas the subjectivity of white men and the objectification of black women appeared immutable – but that the subjectivity of one was dependent on the subordination of the other. This contesting but mutual status meant that their closeness was invested with all the fears and anxieties produced around white male subjectivity's 'other' and the mechanism for bringing this about was panic.

In formulating these definitions of black and white peril, Brundell recognised explicitly the demographic and symbolic importance of the control of sexual relations. Gender and race were the two primary modalities through which the law was able to intervene in the intimate relationships of subjects, thereby reproducing the structure of a hierarchy ultimately predicated on their intersection. The colonial authorities reinforced the powers of African chiefs and headmen over African women, specifically to manufacture a level of consensus that ensured their cooperation.[8] This was a hegemonic alliance built around the treatment of women (white and black) as possessions to be coveted or protected by men.

At the same time, racial difference and social distance were safeguarded through the patrolling of white women. That white men remained outside much of this regulation was testimony to their ascendant position in the hegemonic order. With this distribution of social powers, the boundaries of sex and race in the new colony were established within a legal framework, setting precedents, reproducing a racially contoured discourse and fixing the patterns of a gender-bound partiality.

Notes

1. A similar, extended version of this essay appears in Oliver Phillips (forthcoming 2011) *Sexuality and the Politics of Rights in Post-Colonial Southern Africa: The Legacy of Venus*, London, Monstrosa, Routledge-Cavendish. Reprinted with permission.
2. Symbolisation, distortion, exaggeration and amplification are the key elements of a moral panic as first articulated by Stan Cohen in his seminal 1972 book on the subject, *Folk Devils and Moral Panics*. See also S. Hall et al *Policing the Crisis: Mugging, the State, and Law and Order*. But Jeffrey Weeks (1981: 14–15) and Gayle Rubin (1984) highlight the

frequency with which 'moral panics' take on a specifically sexual focus, in their analysis of 'sex panics'.

3. This is a good example of how the colonial law did not necessarily invent any new activities, but certainly invented new prohibitions by setting up new rules and hence newly fetishised old activities. For example, this law served as an invitation for curious African men to wonder what it was that made white women so deserving of special attention, most particularly when in the privy. This is evidenced by the fact that African custom forbade the observance of someone in the process of urinating or defecating, because having samples of another's urine and faeces gave one the ability (with the help of a spirit medium) to bring misfortune on them. Within a few months of the new law, the first arrests of men looking through the flap of a privy at a white woman, however inadvertently, took place (Jeater 1993: 191; McCulloch 2000: 20).

4. In 1891, 'Billy' arrived in the company of the Count de la Panouse. Later to become the Vicomtesse de la Panouse, Billy's real name was Fanny and she was described as having the fiercely tenacious temperament of all frontiers people while still maintaining a 'delicate' femininity (Boggie 1938: 37–43; Tanser 1965: 45). Boggie also points out that the first European woman settler to arrive in Canada in 1806 was similarly disguised as a man (W.J. Healy, *The Women of Red River,* quoted in Boggie 1938: 42).

5. In a letter to the South African high commissioner in October 1910, the acting administrator of north-eastern Rhodesia defends monogamous and 'decently veiled' concubinage for colonial officals in remote areas, on the following practical grounds: 'a) health; b) learning the native language; c) learning native "ideas and modes of thought"; d) receiving early warning of crime or rebellion; e) material comfort and antidote to loneliness; f) it is not degrading to the women; g) it may enhance the status of the official in the eyes of the natives. It at least saves him from the contempt of many among them and from the suspicion of the worst moral state they are apt to impute to a man living by himself' (Hansen 1989: 95).

6. 'Hysteria was given its present meaning by Renaissance doctors, who explained women's diseases with a theory that the womb became detached from its place and wandered about inside the body causing uncontrolled behaviour' (Barbara G. Walker (1983) in C. Kramerae et al (1985: 202). Apparently, the wandering womb theory can be traced even further back as classicists believe that medical practicioners in ancient Greece subscribed to it (Dr J. Walters, personal comment).

7. The term white peril was used in South Africa to describe white men's sexual desire for black women, and Pape uses the term in this way; but it is clear from his report that Inspector Brundell and the Rhodesian (male) authorities saw white peril as white women's desire for black men.

8. The clearest example of this was the promulgation of the Native Adultery Punishment Ordinance of 1916, which criminalised adultery with African women. This legislation was passed after considerable pressure from African men fearful of what they considered a diminution of control over their wives, in a social context increasingly fragmented by the economic and political changes brought by colonisation, and a political context in which colonial authorities had superseded traditional authorities, with attempts to regulate African marriages and provide some limited measures to ensure the consent of African women. For more on this see Jeater (1990) and Phillips (2006).

References

Boggie, J.M. (ed) (1938) *Experiences of Rhodesia's Pioneer Women,* Harare, University of Zimbabwe Library

Brundell, J.C. (1915) 'Black and white peril' CID, BSAP, Bulawayo, National Archives of Zimbabwe S1227/1

Cohen, S. (1972) *Folk Devils and Moral Panics,* London, McGibbon and Kee Ltd

Gilman, S.L. (1985) *Difference and Pathology: Stereotypes of Sexuality, Race and Madness,* Ithaca, Cornell University Press

Hall, S., Critcher, C., Jefferson, T., Clark, J. and Roberts, B. (1978) *Policing the Crisis: Mugging, the State, and Law and Order,* London, MacMillan

Hansen, Karen T. (1989) *Distant Companions: Servants and Employers in Zambia 1900–1985,* London, Cornell University Press

Jeater, D. (1993) *Marriage, Perversion and Power: The Construction of Moral Discourse in Southern Rhodesia 1894–1930,* Oxford, Clarendon Press

Kramarae, C., Treichler, P. and Russo, A. (eds) (1985) *A Feminist Dictionary,* London, Rivers Oram Press

McCullough, J. (2000) *Black Peril, White Virtue: Sexual Crime in Southern Rhodesia, 1902–1935,* Bloomington, Indiana University Press

Pape, J. (1990) 'Black and white peril: the "perils of sex" in colonial Zimbabwe', *Journal of Southern African Studies* 16(4): 669–720

Phillips, O. (2006) 'Gender, justice and human rights in post-colonial Zimbabwe and South Africa', in Heidensohn, F. (ed) *Gender and Justice: New Concepts and Approaches,* Collumpton, Willan Publishing

Phimister, I. (1988) *An Economic and Social History of Zimbabwe 1890–1848: Capital Accumulation and Class Struggle,* London, Longman

Rubin, G. (1984) 'Thinking sex: notes for a radical theory of the politics of sexuality', in Vance, C.S. *Pleasure and Danger: Exploring Female Sexuality,* London, Routledge and Kegan Paul. Also reprinted in Parker, R. and Aggleton, P. (eds) (2000) *Culture, Society and Sexuality: A Reader* (2nd edn) London, Routledge

Sender, J. and Smith, S. (1986) *The Development of Capitalism in Africa,* London, Methuen

Stoler, A.L. (1995) *Race and the Education of Desire: Foucault's History of Sexuality and the Colonial Order of Things,* London, Duke University Press

Sumner, C. (ed) (1990) *Censure, Politics and Criminal Justice,* Milton Keynes, Open University Press

Tanser, G.H. (1965) *A Scantling of Time,* Salisbury (publisher unknown, but a copy is available in the University of Zimbabwe Library)

Weeks, J. (1981) *Sex, Politics, and Society: The Regulation of Sexuality since 1800,* New York, Longman

8

Nudity and morality: legislating women's bodies and dress in Nigeria[1]

Bibi Bakare-Yusuf

In recent years, women's fashion or sartorial practices have become the site for pernicious policing and debates about social and moral decay in Africa generally and Nigeria in particular. This has resulted in calls for intervention and the imposition of sanctions within Nigeria's higher education institutions by religious organisations, as well as by media and government agencies. Some universities have banned the wearing of trousers, the bearing of mid-riffs, spaghetti tops and any item of clothing that reveals female flesh. Young women's fashion choices are seen not only as a distraction to male students, but as a provocation of male lecturers. The argument is that revealing attire has made sexual violation and harassment a marked feature of university life in Nigeria and therefore the only way to curb this is to impose a strict dress code on female students.

Similarly, toward the end of 2007, when the general overseer (GO) Adeboye of the Redeemed Christian Church of God (RCCG), the largest Pentecostal church in the country, decided to address the issue of moral laxity and social corruption among his congregation, it was at women's clothing that he directed his condemnation. Adeboye banned the wearing of revealing clothes and trousers for his female church members. The GO's proscription coincided with the arrest by Lagos state police of women wearing trousers and skimpy clothes, which they claimed was aimed at discouraging vice in the city, especially among sex workers, who allegedly harboured criminals.[2] Most of the women were arrested on allegations of either 'indecent dressing' or 'wandering', a term from a law that was repealed more than two decades ago.[3] After a wave of public outcry against the police, the state governor and the chief of police went on record to deny authorising the arrest of women.

The call to ban and criminalise women's sartorial choices received legislative support in January 2008, when Senator Eme Ufot Ekaette, the chairperson of the senate committee on women and youth affairs, presented a bill for a second hearing to the senate against public nudity and sexual intimidation. The ostensible aim of the bill was to reduce the increasing sexual intimidation and immorality that women's fashion choices help to generate. Although the bill has gone through several readings in the national assembly (Nigeria's parliament), it has not been passed into law.

But the widespread denunciation of women's sartorial choices raises interesting questions about normative attitudes towards women, morality, sex and sexuality, the state and the economy. It also raises the question about the gendered subtexts that make it possible to draw a causal link between the previously unrelated issues of sexual intimidation, indecent exposure and women's fashion in order to talk about contemporary social tensions and morality.

Focusing on the textual analysis of the proposed bill, I argue that in order to make her case, the senator collapses various distinct issues into a confused and spuriously unified account. First, she assumes that there is a causal relationship between nudity and sexuality. Second, women's sartorial agency is assumed to always be directed at men and is held to be an invitation to an erotic encounter that might often lead to unwanted consequences. Women must therefore be disciplined and protected from any potential masculine sexual terror that acts under provocation. Finally, the senator assumes that the judicial system must be based on a religiously grounded morality, which can be universalised regardless of differences.

What is important to note is that the debate about women's exposed flesh and perceived immorality is less about the personal choices of women, and more about how young women's bodies have become the site onto which many social insecurities and existential anxieties are projected: women's sexuality and agency in urban space (Little 1973; Wilson 1985; Ivaska 2004); the proliferation of new information technologies, images and the semiotics of fashion (Hebidge 1979; Barthes 1985); increasing economic and social inequalities; and public morality and private vices. Because women's bodies are the trope for the articulation of these anxieties, they also become the site for both the attempted resolution and restitution of them. Although the bill states that the law will be applied to men, women are its target and its central subject – both to be protected and criminalised at once.

The bill: public nudity and sexual offences

In this section, I perform a critical reading of two texts: first the bill titled 'A Bill for an Act to prohibit and punish public nudity, sexual intimidation and other related offences in Nigeria' (2007); and second, Senator Ekaette's written defence of the bill to the senate in February 2008. In the bill, public nudity is defined as a 'state of indecent dressing which expose in the public or in the open the breast, belly, waist and lap of a female above the age of 14 years, as well as any part of the body from two inches below the shoulders downwards to the knee' (Nigeria 2007: 1). For men, indecent dressing is classified as any exposure of the male aged 14 years and above from the 'waist to the knee'.

In a textual defence of the bill, the senator points out that 'indecent dressing' has reached such epidemic proportions that 'even the most disciplined clergyman could have his/her conscience polluted by acts of indecent dressing or public nudity in every place in our society' (Nigeria 2007: 2). She adds that clergymen are not the only ones under threat – young men and women whose 'hearts and thought' are polluted and seduced by such lewd images are 'forced to battle with reflections of obscenity in their mind' (Nigeria 2007: 2).[4]

The bill defines sexual intimidation in terms of:

> a) Any action or circumstances which amount to demand for sexual inter-
> course with either a male or a female under any guise, as a condition for

passing examination, securing employment, business patronage, obtaining any favour in any form whatsoever …

b) The exposure of any private part of the human body … by any person whatsoever by form of indecent dressing or any form … which is capable of sexually seducing the other person to demand or request for sexual intercourse in exchange for any favour in any form ….

c) Acts of deprivation, withholding, replacing and or short-changing of entitlements, privileges, rights, benefits, examination or test marks/scores, and any other form of disposition capable of coercing any person to submit to sexual intercourse for the purpose of receiving reprieve thereto. (Nigeria 2007: 1–2)

The subsequent sections of the bill go on to define punishments, which include a prison sentence of three months for public nudity and three years for sexual intimidation. The remainder of the bill deals with enforcement (by the police), jurisdiction (by both magistrate and high courts), legal obligations (placed upon the heads of educational institutions) and details on the right of appeal. The bill ends with a short section (16) on the 'Roles of religious bodies and public agencies'. For the purposes of the analysis to come, it is worthwhile to quote this section in full:

The roles of religious bodies in moral rejuvenation of our country is by this Act hereby guaranteed:

a) The Ministries of Information, Cultures and National Orientation shall develop policies and programmes for the integration of religious bodies in the reformation of the society for moral uprightness;

b) religious bodies shall be encouraged in teaching moral uprightness to its adherents. (Nigeria 2007: 6)

In the short presentation defending the bill to the senate, the senator makes two key points to justify the urgent need for legislative intervention. First, she points to the collapse in morals in society and suggests that God is the touchstone for moral and spiritual rebirth. In her opening paragraph, she writes:

Over the years, I have watched helplessly as our society degenerate from a community of people with very high values, morals, self-esteem/respect, dignity of the human person, upright family values/upbringing, etc. to a state of near-madness, collapse of moral values, tolerance of immorality and all forms of decadence of social ethics which uphold the dignity of the human person. I am happy that now, GOD has given me the golden opportunity to steer the partnership with you, Distinguished Senators, on the project for the RESTORATION OF HUMAN DIGNITY. [caps in original text] (Ekaette 2008: 1)

The senator buttresses the pivotal significance she accords to God in the presentation of her bill by making reference to the 1999 constitution statement that we the people resolve 'to live in unity and harmony as one indivisible and indissoluble Sovereign Nation UNDER GOD' [caps in original text]. For the senator, the danger of not legislating against public lewdness would result in the complete annihilation of 'our age-long values of very high morals, [and] we would be forced to all wear iron jeans trousers with padlocked belts to avoid being raped or sexually assaulted. God forbid!' (Ekaette 2008: 2).

Second, by way of comparative analysis, the senator states that careful examination of the Nigerian laws and penal codes shows the absence of a 'prohibition or punishment for the social crime such as public nudity, public lewdness or nakedness' (Ekaette 2008: 3).[5] Such omission in the law makes it possible for people to 'decide to go naked in the name of fashion'. This prompted her research into legal precedence elsewhere. It will be instructive in our later analysis to note the criteria she uses here:

> In my desperation to find a redress for these moral decadence, I was forced to examine the laws of various *advanced democracies* of the world and other *highly religious nations*. The laws of the United States of America, the Great Britain, Canada, Saudi Arabia, Iran, Israel, Germany, India, China etc. [emphasis mine] (Ekaette 2008: 2)

Having provided a brief summary of the key points made in both the text of the bill and the senator's presentation of it to the legislative body, it is now time to unpack and offer some critical analysis of its key claims.

Law and morality

For the senator, individual moral permissiveness is a sign of a collective social degradation that must be remedied through legislative intervention. The first point to note is the use of God in the senator's text and how she aligns God with morality. This appeal to morality proffered both by God and the law means that it is possible to regulate and discipline an individual's liberty in order to prevent immoral behaviour. Such legal moralism rests on two assumptions.

First, she assumes that there is a moral consensus in Nigeria that can be reached. In a society that divides into Muslims, Christians and followers of traditional indigenous religions, layered onto a patchwork of several hundred ethnic groups, it is difficult to imagine how any kind of moral consensus can be reached, whether it originates from a specific religious framework, ethnic derivation or perhaps from within a more secular, universalist context, especially in the case of dress and other perceived moral transgressions. We know that, even within the same religious community, a shared moral consensus is difficult because this is always fractured by ethnicity, geography and generational and other differences (Uwais 2008). Indeed, another senator from across the Atlantic knew very well that he could not impose faith-based morality on a pluralistic society, such as the USA. Barack Obama argued:

> [T]he religiously motivated translate their concerns into universal, rather than religion-specific values. It requires that their proposals be subject to argument, and amenable to reason. I may be opposed to abortion for religious reasons, but if I seek to pass a law banning the practice, I cannot simply point

> to the teachings of my church or evoke God's will. I have to explain why abor-
> tion violates some principle that is accessible to people of all faiths, including
> those with no faith at all. (Mansfield 2008: 89–90)

The fact that religion and state are not separated in the 1999 constitution of Nigeria, thus halting the development of a modern secular state, does not preclude or abne-gate the reality of the country's socio-ethnic complexity and the rural–urban matrix with its myriad conceptions of dress and nudity, morality and immorality. It is hard to imagine that any religious prescription, specifically in relation to dress and adornment, can be universalised across this complex patchwork of beliefs without considerable resistance and contestation on the basis of local cultures and practices in the emerging context of global semiotic flows and exchange.

For example, though some Nigerian pentecostal groups attempt to restrict the wearing of trousers for women because of a fear of blurred gender boundaries announced and reproduced by dress, among Muslims the wearing of trousers by women fits into the doctrinal code to cover the flesh. Such diverse positions about a single item of clothing contest the senator's claim that 'all our religions forbid public lewdness, public nudity or public nakedness' (Ekaette 2008: 4). This statement, in the face of the examples just provided, shows that in a plural society such as Nigeria, the senator's desire for a unified legal moral position is already doomed and unworkable.

Second, the senator assumes that the social fabric and judicial system of a society must be grounded in a universally shared morality that can be adhered to across time and space. This pre-secular presumption takes the law to be the codification of religious and cultural custom into abstract principle. It does not occur to the senator that the law could be grounded in a secular principle of human rights or ethics that does not require an underlying moral consensus across social difference. Many legal theorists would agree that the use of morality in criminal law has no traction in a modern legal system, let alone in a plural society such as Nigeria. Yet, the senator continues to view the law through a religious and cultural lens and regards the semi-nudity of rural African women as harking back to a pre-historic era that has no place in a modernising Africa.

It is interesting in this regard to note that the comparator benchmark countries that the senator mentions to support her legal moralism are 'advanced democracies', such as Germany, the USA and Britain and 'other highly religious nations' such as Saudi Arabia and Iran. What all these countries have in common, according to the senator, are laws prohibiting and punishing public nudity and lewdness. The contradiction between open societies, such as Germany where nudity is legal, and Saudi Arabia, where there is a strict standard that requires women to be covered in the burka or the hijab remains unresolved in her text. She does not see the chasm of difference between public lewdness and indecent exposure legislation in secular advanced democratic nations and its equivalent in theocratic nations, precisely because she does not make a distinction between theological and secular conceptions of the law and morality.

Moreover, the senator conveniently misunderstands the content of the laws sur-rounding public lewdness and indecent exposure in advanced democracies. These laws, variously referred to as 'public nudity', 'public indecency' or 'indecent expo-sure' are quite specific and generally refer to crimes involving the exposure of an adult's (usually male) genitalia with the aim of causing affront or alarm.[6] This may also include masturbation and sexual intercourse in a public place. Public nudity laws tend to be much less concerned with moral censure and more focused on cur-tailing offence to the general public. Moreover, these laws make no reference to types or patterns of dress.

Now, even if a moral consensus can be reached about women's dress codes, it is not clear that society should be able to punish perceived misconduct simply because most people disapprove of it or believe that it is offensive. In this bill, there is an assumption that beyond own private morals, judicial moral principles are required to guide the conduct of the citizen, who would otherwise be immune from moral and social censure.

For the senator, it is both right and necessary to insist on some moral conformity and to legally enforce that conformity in a country such as Nigeria, which we are told is fast losing its moral compass. She writes: 'society must use the law to preserve morality in the same way it uses it to safeguard anything else if it is essential to its existence' (2008: 5). The law becomes part of the disciplinary regime that will not only produce a regulated, civilised subject (Elias 1969; Foucault 1978), but subjects who can represent and 'safeguard' the interest of the nation (Allman 2004; Moorman 2004) as opposed to those bent on perpetuating the stone-age position of their naked ancestors.

Culture, nudity and sexuality

Arguments against indecent dressing in African contexts often cite Western influ-ence as the source of all moral degeneration. In this vein, Senator Ekaette makes frequent appeals, in both her presentation to the senate and in a follow-up live radio debate on the BBC World Service,[7] to the moral conservatism of Nigerian culture. Given this, it is significant that the proposed bill makes an exception to 'sports, festi-vals, theatre/stage acting and swimming exercises' (Nigeria 2007: 3), as moments in which nudity is legally permissible and is de-eroticised. If certain forms of naked-ness or state of undress were an abiding feature of Nigerian festivals and tradition, why then would the bill propose a waiver in this area?

The obvious underlying point here is that the senator is well aware that to this day and outside of the large cities partial nudity is commonplace in Nigeria, as is attire that exposes the body in ways that contravene the definitions of the proposed bill. What the text of the bill unwittingly reveals is a repressed indigeneity. Historically and even now, minimal clothing or exposure of the torso is a common feature among a diverse group of Nigerians, especially in the rural areas where most Nigerians still live.

If the bill was passed, would we then not have to force large communities of Nigerians to readjust their sociocultural perspective to one that eroticises or sexualises states of nudity or semi-nudity, which were previously normatively neutral? By eroticising the naked body, does the senator not participate in both real and symbolic dismembering of the female body? In a context in which commodification is commonplace, by measuring areas of the female body parts that can be legislated upon, is she not reducing women's bodies to a collection of sexual organs perpetually ready for sexual appropriation?

By drawing a causal relationship between nudity and sexuality and attempting to legislate against its occurrence in order to preserve a pristine Nigerian cultural and moral universe, the senator betrays her ignorance about the way in which Nigerian society is overlaid with what we can call the globalisation of signifiers. Nigeria is not immune to global cultural flows of images, vocabulary, sartorial practices, language, memes and concepts. Although only a fraction of Nigerians have access in their homes to satellite television, the images of scantily-clad women on MTV or Channel O are well known and well circulated. There is strong liquidity between youth culture formation in Nigeria and hip-hop subcultures and mainstream cultures in North America and Europe. One sees this transference in both locally produced music videos in which women in different states of (un)dress are displayed and consumed as part of the commodity fetishism of late capitalism, as well as in the popularity in Nigeria of black American rappers.

More importantly, with increased urban migration, education and an influx of global fashion styles and imageries, young women use fashion to signal their non-conformity to restrictive rules about hegemonic norms of femininity even as they resubscribe to it (McRobbie 1994, 1999). This globalisation of signifiers intensifies and confuses the question of social development. In other words, the question of whether Nigeria should position itself as a modern society with the goal of becoming an 'advanced democracy', or whether Nigeria should benchmark itself against 'highly religious' societies, remains moot in the analysed texts. From a religious perspective on the law and the heterosexual subtext of the bill, this swirl of eroticised signifiers through dress is quickly constructed as an attack from a degenerate occidental outside, against which a more conservative, highly fictionalised African cultural heritage is framed, even as the terms of the bill repress it.

More significant still is the collapsing of nudity with sexuality. The unclothed body, which in many Nigerian cultures was previously read in a non-sexual way, is now overburdened with sexual meaning and anxiety that acts as a prelude to sexual intercourse. This new meaning is part of a pattern of 'culturally and historically shifting ideas about shame' (Hansen 2004: 168) inherited from the two colonising religions – Islam and Christianity. In both these Abrahamic religions, especially in its Judaeo-Christian guise, the female body is often viewed as the seat of sin, moral corruption and a 'source of distraction from Godly thoughts' (Entwistle 2000: 84).

From the tales of the First Testament through to the letters of St. Paul, women have been associated with temptations of the flesh and decoration. This is part of what Elizabeth Spelman (1990) has referred to as the somaphobic impulse at the heart of Western philosophy and Christian teaching. In this teaching, the body must be 'mortified and chastised into submission' (Entwistle 2000: 84) for the sake of the soul. The unclothed body is thus regarded as 'inseparable from sex and sexuality and has hence been located adjacent to the indecent, the obscene and the immoral' (Cover 2003: 55).

Within this obscenity discourse, nudity or the partially clothed female body is seen as part of a libidinal opportunity that threatens to unleash an unrestrained sexual energy into the world. This unbridled erotic force must be condemned and contained through disciplinary institutions, such as the family, law, religion, educational institutions and community organisations. Just like the primordial heterosexual couple – Adam and Eve – nudity signals a fall from grace, an invitation to illicit desire and yearning which should inspire shame and disgust in the fallen, who is always a woman (Tseelon 1997).

According to Efrat Tseelon, the discourse of modesty and chastity in dress is one of the ways in which Christianity tries to link women's bodies with sexuality in order to better control it. In the view of the moralists, by shamelessly flaunting their bodies young women show their disregard for the body's sacredness, which should be for the intimate gaze of their husbands, and their refusal to carry the moral burden of Eve's guilt. The fear therefore is that since semi-clothed women are unwilling to be morally burdened, they must be protected against themselves because their partial nudity 'might give off unintended sexual signals' (Duits and Van Zoonen 2006: 107), which they cannot control and might lead to unintended consequences.

For the senator, there are several consequences of public exposure: promiscuity and violation, and desire and penalty (rape and intimidation). The unclothed female body therefore becomes a site for both seduction and an invitation for violating experiences, especially when this body moves around in urban public space (Hansen 2004). This is because normatively, the naked female body is only meant for the private male gaze, an expectation that fits into a broader discourse about the sexualisation (Dworkin 1981) and compulsory heterosexualisation (Rich 1983) of women's bodies and the anxiety about women's erotic agency.

The moment the naked body moves from the private arena and is displayed in the public realm, it becomes marked as sexual and exposed to social conventions of policing and disciplinary apparatus. This 'ignores the fact that sexuality is not an essential feature of bodily display and dress, but the effect of the reaction of others' (Duits and Van Zoonen 2006: 108). From the senator's perspective, what is important is less the agency and opinion of the wearer, but the reaction of others who are forced to confront the public display of youthful female flesh. It is precisely because the Judaeo-Christian subtext of the bill associates women with the body, sexuality, decoration and morality that the senator privileges the perspective of the different publics (law, church, institutions, media) over the agency of women. The very fact that both the senator/moralist and the wearer of the clothes or the semi-naked women can encode their actions with multiple meanings shows the malleability and mutability of dress.

While I would not want to deny the possibility of latent eroticism or arousal that the body and dress might generate, I would rather argue that this is always a potentiality in any given context, including being fully clothed. The injunction to cover up assumes that veiling or being fully clothed will eliminate erotic desire and prevent or minimise sexual misdemeanour. Indeed, the senator alluded to this in her BBC interview when she said that covered women are unlikely to be raped.

Through the work of feminist and gender activists the world over, we know that being clothed or unclothed does not prevent sexual intimidation or violation. In fact, it is possible to argue that the very act of clothing and covering can actually open up the possibility for more erotic imaginings. Because the closeness of clothing to the body involves an interplay between concealment and exposure, we can never know in advance what will cause arousal. In saying this, I do not intend to draw any correlations between cause and effect. Rather, I contend that being dressed or partially undressed does not automatically expose the wearer to or protect them from inappropriate and unwanted sexual advances. The fact that unwanted sexual advances and violations are always read as imminent is part of a structured patriarchal system, which assumes that female sexuality is always for and available to the male gaze and open to manipulation and violation.

Heterosexuality and the economy of signs

In closing, I want to point to what I think of as the three interrelated surface aspects of the senator's argument that I take to be symptomatic of an underlying logic that is at the core of her desire to sanction dress codes for Nigerian women.

First, the senator assumes that women's sole motivation in dressing is to please, impress and attract men as well as to stimulate male sexual desire. By suggesting a causal relationship between women's dress, sexuality and the potential for violation, the bill treats women's bodies as sex objects to be made available for the male gaze. Women's dress is part of the arena of patriarchal surveillance, control, power and meaning. Women who dress modestly do so in order to be viewed as modest by men and avoid being harassed, raped and beaten up. Conversely, women who expose their flesh are, under this logic, considered to be indecent harlots who dress to give off sexual messages with the inevitable consequence of provoking or awakening an irresistible sexual urge in men.

Senator Ekaette and other moralists therefore assume that female sexuality cannot be conceptualised or lived outside its capacity to cause arousal in men (Rich 1983). The image of the scantily dressed female is therefore directed at and displayed for the consuming male spectator, who has the privilege of looking and possessing the objectified female (Berger 1972).

Second, once women's sartorial choice has been invested with sexual meaning in this way, it appears to be a matter of logic that regulation and self-regulation should follow, in order to protect women from the inevitable masculine terror that is automatically provoked by the revelation of female flesh. In so doing, both texts and the senator's media commentaries tacitly reassert the normative power of heterosexuality as the only legally, theologically and culturally legitimate form: that women's dress is directed at men and should be regulated by men. The possibility of women dressing for themselves or being directed at other forms of sexuality is erased in the assumption of the normativeness of heterosexual desire.

Yet, the image of heterosexual desire offered here is one of potential threat and an instrument of perennially abusive power relations, from which women must be protected as well as conform to. Here, we see why the senator considers the relationship between revealing clothing and sexual harassment to be automatic (as they are contiguously placed in the actual bill): women are sexually harassed, or sexually harass, only when they wear provocative clothing.

As already noted above, it is therefore no surprise to hear, in the debate on the proposed bill on the BBC radio programme, that the senator concedes (with no supporting evidence) that almost all women in Nigeria who have been raped must have provoked the attack, and were 'asking for it' by making the choice to wear what they were wearing. Women are therefore held not only responsible for their own comportment, but also taken to be responsible for the sexual responses of men (Entwistle 2000). The senator's simple prescription for women to avoid either harassing or being harassed by men is for them to dress with decency and for this to be within the ambit of legislative decree.

What is absent from her texts is any sense in which male desire itself should be circumscribed, or that men should be held to account (either morally or within the law) for their desires in specific circumstances. In other words, women's desire for sartorial expression and women's sexuality must at all times be controlled and protected from the violating male gaze, whereas male desire itself must be allowed its untrammelled course. Herein, we see the ontological violence of internalised patriarchal logic, whereby women's agency and modes of identity are subordinated to male desire and male control, without any trace of reciprocal delimitation.

Third, the bill fails to place Nigerian women's vulnerability in the context of social and economic inequality, instead masking the brutal reality of scant options within a moralistic discourse. We should be clear that the proposed bill has a clear target in mind: young women on campuses and in the workplace. At the very moment when many young women are experimenting, exploring and playing around with a multiplicity of identities through expressions in dress and corporeal styling, the person responsible for speaking on women's behalf in the senate is pushing for a restrictive definition of acceptable femininity and feminine comportment to be brought under the law. The pains the bill takes to define education institutions and leaders of such institutions, as well as the senator's defence of the bill to the senate, in which she mentions female banking staff, leave no room for ambiguity. Young women in Nigerian universities and banks are taken to be reducing their bodies into transactional value.

What the attempt to police women's dress shows is the critic's inability to engage with the realities that contest the economic vulnerability and existential insecurity of women and the greater pressure poverty places upon them. Because of the economic disadvantage of most women in African societies, and their limited ability to participate in decision-making structures and the creation of symbolic capital (Bourdieu 1986), most women become more dependent on their bodies and sexual relations with men ranging from legal marriage to literal prostitution (Gallop 2001: 32–3). It is therefore important that the question of the 'indecent dressing' and transactional sex among young women in Nigeria should be placed squarely in the context of the economic and social inequality that forces women to enter varying forms of coercive relationships, rather than trying to restrict women's agency and mobility by resorting to moralistic arguments.

It is a fact that each year hundreds of thousands of students graduate to face a society in which there are simply not enough jobs to absorb them. Part of the dynamic of a patriarchal society, such as Nigeria, is to ensure that there is less competition for jobs by reducing the chances for women to build careers. Young women are therefore encouraged at an early age to marry and reproduce; they are also deterred from entering competition with men on the corporate ladder through myriad subtle and unsubtle prejudices and tacit barriers to entry.

The consequence of this is that though both young male and female graduates are placed under severe pressure in their search for work, it is female graduates who face the most extreme pressure in circumstances where there is a tacit expectation that they present their youthful bodies for commodification and sexualisation.[8] The picture is the same at universities (Bennett 2004). Research has shown that the key opportunities for sexual abuse of female students lie at two stages: in the struggle to get accommodation on campus, and during and after the exam period.[9] In both cases, men act as gatekeepers, requesting sexual favours in order to assure results (a room on campus and successful exam scores).

Similar accounts can be given of women in the workplace itself. In each case (women as students, as graduates, in the workplace), we see women positioned as economically vulnerable and dependent on the sanction of men. It is in the context of this social pressure that we see processes by which the flesh is commodified and objectified in Nigeria. With few options available, many women are forced to face one of three alternatives: destitution, dependency upon the favours of men or to offer their bodies for transaction through the various forms of prostitution available to them. Women who choose the latter two options are pushed down a transactional path, whereby their bodies are valued in monetary terms by clients who pose as either Uncle figures (known popularly as *Aristos*), or more simply as prostitutes through hotel night clubs or on-the-street modes of pick up.

It is in this context that Senator Ekaette's proposed bill about sexual intimidation should be properly framed. Rather than a sign of moral degeneracy, the transactional use of the body by young female students, graduates and women in the workplace is a response to huge social strain and inequality in Nigeria, whereby competition for jobs, and ultimately, financial stability, requires and almost demands the commodification of female flesh.

The three points raised in the senator's various texts and pronouncements – a heterosexual over-determination of the reasons why women dress the way they do; an emphasis on regulation and control of women's dress; and the refusal to recognise the economic context within which Nigerian women's vulnerability is situated – point to a deeper underlying model that shapes the senator's thinking and the structure of the bill itself. What is at work is a patriarchal model of heterosexuality, where women's relations with men are taken to be determined and controlled solely by men. Women can either be virgins, mothers or whores in this scenario. Any other model of explanation, for instance the idea of women dressing as a form of agency outside of a male regulatory framework, is nullified.

The possibility that young women might relate to their body and sexuality in a non-abusive or non-violating way is utterly masked by the senator's moralistic stance and logic of victimhood. The possibility that women's sartorial choices could also be a site of conscious erotic play that is not channelled towards men is completely elided and replaced by a fearful model of heterosexuality, within which women's comportment must at all times be contained.

In this sense, it is interesting to appreciate more clearly how women, as the embodiment of economic vulnerability and dependency within a normatively heterosexist, masculinist framework such as Nigeria, are subsequently blamed as the source of moral degeneracy. It might seem doubly cruel that women under conditions of extreme social strain are pressured to commodify their own bodies and then blamed as the source of provocation. It is also interesting to witness such extreme heteronormativeness issuing forth from a woman. The most insidious forms of power in society operate through the silent internalisation of its strictures by the victims themselves: the *ressentiment* of the oppressed, as Nietzsche might have put it.[10]

Notes

1. First published in 2009 in the *East African Journal of Peace and Human Rights* 15(1). Reprinted with permission.
2. See the Lagos state police press release about the connection between sex workers and criminals, http://fiyanda.blogspot.com/2007/08/police-press-release-on-indecent.html, accessed 19 January 2009.
3. The defunct omnibus law against 'wandering' was repealed in 1989. It targeted, among others, 'loose' women who were thought to be prostitutes or 'sluts'. It was imported in the penal codes of many former British colonies with variants of the following text: 'Every person found wandering in or upon or near any premises or in any road or highway or any place adjacent thereto or in any public place at such time and under such circumstances as to lead to the conclusion that such person is there for an illegal or disorderly purpose.'
4. Similar arguments have been made elsewhere on the continent. For example, in September 2008 the Ugandan minister of ethics and integrity proposed the banning of miniskirts on the basis that they distract motorists and cause road accidents. He was quoted in the *Daily Monitor* (Tumusiime-Kabwende 2008) as saying that a woman wearing a miniskirt 'can cause an accident because some of our people are weak mentally'.
5. The Nigerian criminal and penal codes already have clauses about indecent acts and sexual offences (see sections 214–22, 252–53, 351–60 of the criminal code and section 285 of the penal code). Because there are already provisions (however inadequate) within the legal system, we can only conclude that (1) the senator has not really explored existing provisions; (2) she is not interested in modifying or strengthening the existing codes so that they will be more favourable to women; and (3) she is more concerned with instituting a dress code where it was previously absent and by doing so criminalising women's expressive agency.
6 Commonly referred to as 'flashing', this exhibitionist phenomenon usually involves a male opening his fly and in a 'flash' exposing his genitalia to an unsuspecting individual (typically female).
7. *Africa Have Your Say* (2008) BBC World Service, 12 February.
8. It is a common practice in the banking sector to put new attractive female graduates in the marketing section and as new recruits send them into the field, provided with condoms and encouragement to do 'whatever' is necessary to bring in the account. One way to acquire new accounts is for the women to use their bodies and revealing dress becomes an entry point for this. It is therefore possible to say that the senator is responding to the outward manifestation of a complex social process, whereby women are forced to use their bodies to perform certain roles. Yet in her response to the banking industry's use of women's bodies to grow their business, the senator fails to outline the economic vulnerability of women.
9. See Pereira (n.d.).
10. Friedrich Nietzsche in his book, *On The Genealogy of Morals* (1969), uses the French word for resentment to explain the emotion felt by the oppressed, an imaginary revenge meted out by those who are too powerless to do anything effective to their oppressors.

References

Allman, Jean (2004) '"Let your fashion be in line with our Ghanaian costume": nation, gender, and the politics of clothing in Nkrumah's Ghana', in Allman, J. (ed) *Fashioning Africa: Power and the Politics of Dress*, Bloomington and Indianapolis, Indiana University Press

Barthes, Roland (1985) *The Fashion System*, London, Cape

Bennet, Jane (2004) 'Exploration of a gap: strategising gender equity in African universities', *Feminist Africa* 1, African Gender Institute e-journal, http://www.feministafrica.org, accessed 7 January 2009

Berger, J. (1972) *Ways of Seeing*, London, British Broadcasting Corporation and Penguin Books

Bourdieu, Pierre (1986) Distinction: A Social Critique of the Judgement of Taste, London, Routledge

Cover, Rob (2003) 'The naked subject: nudity, context and sexualisation in contemporary culture', *Body and Society* 9(3): 53–72

Duits, Linda and van Zoonen, Liesbet (2006) 'Headscarves and porno-chic: disciplining girls' bodies in the European multicultural society', *European Journal of Women's Studies* 13(2): 103–17

Dworkin, Andrea (1981) *Pornography: Men Possessing Women*, New York, Perigee

Ekaette, Senator E.U. (2008) 'Lead debate on the bill for an act to prohibit and punish public nudity, sexual intimidation and other related offences in Nigeria', Abuja, National Assembly

Elias, Norbert (1969) *The Civilising Process: The History of Manners* Vol. 1, Oxford, Blackwell

Entwistle, Joan (2000) *The Fashioned Body: Fashion, Dress and Modern Social Theory*, Cambridge, Polity Press

Foucault, Michel (1978) *The History of Sexuality: An Introduction*, Harmondsworth, Penguin

Gallop, Jane (2001) 'Feminist accused of sexual harassment (excerpt)', in Bronfen, Elisabeth and Kavka, Misha (eds) *Feminist Consequences: Theory For The New Century*, New York, Columbia University Press

Hansen, K.T. (2004) 'Dressing dangerously: miniskirts, gender relations and sexuality in Zambia', in Allman, J. (ed) *Fashioning Africa: Power and the Politics of Dress*, Bloomington and Indianapolis, Indiana University Press

Hebidge, Dick (1979) *Subculture: The Meaning of Style*, London, Methuen

Ivaska, A.M. (2004) '"Anti-mini militants meet modern Misses": urban style, gender and the politics of "national culture" in 1960s Dar es Salaam' in Allman, J. (ed) *Fashioning Africa: Power and the Politics of Dress*, Bloomington and Indianapolis, Indiana University Press

Little, Kenneth (1973) *African Women in Town: An Aspect of Africa's Social Revolution*, London, Cambridge Press

Mansfield, Stephen (2008) *The Faith of Barack Obama*, Nashville, Thomas Nelson

McRobbie, Angela (1994) *Post-Modernism and Popular Culture*, London, Routledge

—— (1999) *In the Culture Society: Art, Fashion and Popular Music*, London, Routledge

Moorman, Marissa (2004) 'Putting on Pano and dancing like our grandparents: nation and dress in late colonial Luanda', in Allman, J. (ed) *Fashioning Africa: Power and the Politics of Dress*, Bloomington and Indianapolis, Indiana University Press

Nietzsche, Friedrich (1969) *On The Genealogy of Morals*, tr. Walter Kaufmann, New York, Vintage

Nigeria (2007) 'Senate bill for an act to prohibit and punish public nudity, sexual intimidation and other related offences in Nigeria', Abuja, National Assembly Press

Pereira, Charmaine (n.d.) 'Bibliography on sexuality', http://www.gwsafrica.org/teaching/charmaine's%20essay.html, accessed 24 November 2008

Rich, Adrienne (1972) 'Compulsory heterosexuality and lesbian existence', in Berger, J. *Ways of Seeing*, London, British Broadcasting Corporation and Penguin Books

Spelman, Elizabeth (1990) *Inessential Woman: Problems of Exclusion in Feminist Thought*, London, Women's Press

Tseelon, E. (1997) *Masque of Femininity*, London, Sage

Tumusiime-Kabwende, Deo (2008) 'Mini skirts banned, Buturo fighting a losing battle?', *Daily Monitor,* 23 September, 11

Uwais, Maryam (2008) 'Feminism and transforming lives: fundamentalism and Muslim women', paper presented at the First Nigerian Feminist Forum, Abuja, 24–27 January

Wilson, Elizabeth (1985) *Adorned in Dreams: Fashion and Modernity*, London, Virago

9

'Getting the nation talking about sex': reflections on the politics of sexuality and nation-building in post-apartheid South Africa[1]

Deborah Posel

This chapter is a preliminary attempt to demonstrate and make sense of the intense politicisation of sex and sexuality in South Africa since 1994. The first part begins to consider 'how sex is put into discourse', as Michel Foucault (1979: 11) puts it, and how this discursive constitution of sexuality has been informed by wider dimensions of the post-apartheid social order. Again, Foucault's questions are pertinent: 'why is sex so widely discussed and what is said? What are the effects of power generated by what is said?' (Foucault 1979: 11). The focus in this paper, however, is limited to open conversations about sex and sexuality in a range of public media.[2]

Drawing on this discussion, the second part proposes a reading of the notorious so-called HIV/AIDs controversy, which came to summarise the presidency of Thabo Mbeki in many national and international circles and which generated more division, conflict, uncertainty and anguish within the polity than any other issue since the inauguration of the post-apartheid state. I argue that this controversy – although immediately concerned with questions of science and drugs – was also a struggle over the discursive constitution of sexuality, in a form that dramatised some of the ways in which struggles over the manner of sexuality are enmeshed in the politics of nationalism, and the inflections of race, class and generation within it.

The discursive constitution of sexuality post-apartheid

At a time when many other parts of the world were sites of increasingly (albeit unevenly) liberal, experimental sexual practice, the apartheid regime subjected sex and sexuality to particularly heavy censorship and repressive policing, which actively excluded the kinds of public sex talk that marked the growth of consumer capitalism, particularly in the West in the latter half of the 20th century (Sontag 1988; Hennessy 2000: 99; Altman 2001: 52–8). Particularly obsessive in its determination to prohibit sex across racial boundaries, and driven by typically colonial anxieties about rapacious black sexuality, the apartheid state accumulated an extensive armoury of regulations and prohibitions to control the practice and transaction of sex, its public representations and performance. Within these political and legislative strictures, sex within the domestic domain was deemed a private matter, with no sense of the contradiction entailed.

So, sexual violence (particularly within the home) was typically not a site of political concern, unless the perpetrator was black and the victim white, in which case the public outrage was virulent. Sex across the black–white racial divide was forbidden and miscegenation intensely stigmatised. Reinforced by laws that criminalised homosexuality, a deep-seated and widespread homophobia deterred the open expression or assertion of sexualities deemed transgressive. Legislation prohibited any media from explicit depictions of sex or avowedly sexual conversation. Pornography was wholly banned and the public display of eroticised nude bodies (particularly male) was unthinkable.

This draconian policing of sexuality was absolutely fundamental to the apartheid project. Inherent in the call for white supremacy was a zealous drive to preserve the 'purity' of the white 'race', by preventing the sexual sullying of the white body. Powerful imagery of the black mass and the ever-immanent threat of its overwhelming the far smaller numbers of whites (*oorstroming*) fanned fears of black overpopulation and the imperative of controlling black fertility. Nor was the sense of sexual menace confined to the predatory black mass. Sexual malignancy was assumed to be lurking within the body of the white nation too, in the form of the communistic left wing – its politics a symptom of its sexual permissiveness and moral depravity. So, stringent censorship and a regime of moral prohibition were seen as critical weapons in efforts to expurgate the threat of white dissidence and preserve the rigours of a 'civilised' way of life.

Particularly given these extremities of the apartheid era, the changes post-1994 have been remarkably dramatic and swift, although by no means either wholesale or uncontested. Issues of sexuality have a newfound prominence, but not in ways that indicate widespread comfort or acceptance of these changes. And the anxieties, denials and stigmas that persist in the midst of new and unprecedented declarations of sexuality – often provoked directly by them – contribute directly to the new sites and intensities of the politicisation of sexuality.

Post-1994, sexuality has become the site of right, in a number of ways and with enormously profound consequences. In terms of the discourse of South Africa's democratic politics, the regulation of sexuality is now first and foremost a matter of the allocation of rights (on the part of citizens) and responsibilities (on the part of fellow citizens as well as the state) – rather than the subject of contending and shifting moral positions associated with particular party political programmes. These rights and obligations have been firmly and resolutely fixed according to impeccably liberal democratic norms, enshrined in a constitution and championed by a constitutional court. There is stability and authority attached to these new rights, which (in theory) render them unassailable in the face of religious or other moral claims to authority.[3]

The new Bill of Rights (formally enacted in the new constitution in 1996) affirmed rights to freedom of expression (with liberal provisos of the prevention of moral harm as a limiting factor), which paved the way for a radical revision of the country's censorship laws, including the legalising of adult pornography. Sexual preference likewise became a matter of right. And the right to gender equality (as an ingredient of the right to equality more generally), along with the right to 'freedom and security of the person' (including the right to 'be free from all forms of violence from either public or private sources'),[4] have redefined the issue of sexual violence as an avowedly public matter – a violation of constitutionally entrenched rights – in relation to which the state has undertaken a new set of obligations to its citizenry, and women and children in particular. These include the creation of dedicated helplines, special police units to deal with rape and the promise of more effective legislation to combat sexual violence.[5]

The first noteworthy feature of the politics of sexuality post-1994, therefore, is the extent to which sexuality has been thrust into public prominence, in ways that would have been absolutely unthinkable and intolerable during the apartheid years. There is now an abundant circulation of movies, magazines and pornography, previously considered taboo. As is the case in most other liberal democracies, sex scenes in films and television have become de rigueur, even during 'family hour'; sex shops and strip clubs abound, particularly in the suburbs; and the pornography industry is said to be booming.

The point is perhaps most graphically made by singling out a few instances of sexual representation and display, which demonstrate the starkness of the transition inaugurated in 1994. In each case, the sexuality newly on display is male – always more of a shock to those accustomed to old prohibitions than the heightened visibility of female sexuality. The 1999 annual Johannesburg Gay and Lesbian Pride Parade, the first of which had taken place in 1995, took to the streets of Johannesburg city centre led by a group of openly gay police officers, members of the South African Gay and Lesbian Policing Network. As Mark Gevisser (2000: 112) writes, 'it takes your breath away when you remember how central the role of the police force was to apartheid repression, and how brutally it policed sexuality too'.

A second instance has a more heterosexual setting. As part of a national AIDS education campaign, thousands of students have witnessed demonstrations of how to use a condom. As though this were now simply an issue of technique, the workshop convenors solemnly unrolled condoms onto black dildos, thousands of which were imported into the country for the purpose. The breach of erstwhile apartheid prohibitions was dramatic, not only because the dildos were black. Similarly remarkable, by way of historical rupture, was the advertising campaign mounted by Pfizer pharmaceuticals during 2002 and aired on a 'serious' morning news programme with a largely middle-class listenership. In an effort to bring the problem of male impotence 'into the open', male listeners were exhorted to 'try saying "I took my erection for coffee this morning"'.

It is not simply the newfound visibility of sex and sexuality that marks the post-apartheid landscape. The proliferation of public images, representations and modes of sex talk has been patterned, producing a series of discrete discursive nodes, each nested in and shaped in particular ways by recent global economic positionings, national processes of class and status formation (particularly the emergence of new black elites), the acceleration of the AIDS epidemic, as well as the strategies and powers of new social movements.

Each of these discursive nodes is fluid and in some respects ill-formed, as is to be expected from newly emergent strands of public representation and conversation. Still, there are now multiple public sites, activated by intersecting pressures and interests, for more open, explicit and graphic sex talk and sexual display. And the ways in which sexuality is discursively constituted varies between these sites, producing different and often discordant – yet interconnected – grammars of speech and silence. The following discussion briefly explores each of these discursive nodes in turn, and then considers their aggregate effects.

With the formal abolition of apartheid, along with the neoliberal predilections of the new ANC-led government, South Africans have new opportunities to participate in global economic networks of production, distribution and trade. The material underpinnings of sexual liberalisation are therefore strengthening all the time. Sex sells and the circuits of sale are global, as are the images that sell (Sontag 1988; Hennessy 2000; Altman 2001). So, with the lifting of old barriers on these sites of massive profit, South Africans can now partake fully in global trends toward increasing sexual explicitness in mainstream media, along with the proliferation of ever more hardcore pornography. And the versions of sexuality being exhibited in South African settings increasingly invoke global images of 'cool' alongside more local registers.

The cultural logic of late capitalism – particularly its valorisation of the pleasures of consumption – articulates closely with national trajectories of class and status formation, particularly in respect of younger generations and their burgeoning elites. Here, the urge to consume has become the fulcrum of intersecting political interests, economic imperatives, cultural aspirations and notions of selfhood. And particularly among black youth growing up in metropolitan centres, consumption is closely coupled with sex, making for the overt sexualisation of style, status and power.

For large numbers of young women, sex is often the indispensable vehicle for consumption. In the midst of powerful hankerings for designer labels, cellphones and access to smart cars as the conditions of social status and style, transacting sex for immediate payment, for more regular financial support (in the case of an ongoing relationship) or directly for the goods themselves, is often the condition of their acquisition (Ashforth 1999: 51; Selikow et al 2002; Hunter 2002: 51).[6] Sex is also the object of consumption, in a genre of popular culture that eroticises possession and accumulation as icons of sexual prowess and libido. For young men with aspirations to macho status, an expensive car and flashy, designer clothing have become signifiers of their sexual bravado as men 'in control', with the power to command multiple sexual partners (Selikow et al 2002; Ashforth 1999: 51).[7] For young women intent on establishing their social standing by 'driving on the left side' of these hip young men, *borgwa* (bourgeois) dress and accessories have become a statement of sexual capital as much as social style (Selikow et al 2002: 8).

Sex is consumed, at the same time as consumption is sexualised – in ways that mark the engagement of popular culture in South Africa with more global cultural repertoires of sex. But in the South African case, these meanings are over-determined by the local history of political struggle. In the aftermath of political liberation, and in the midst of the widespread demobilisation of political movements, sex has become a sphere – perhaps even pre-eminently the sphere – within which newfound freedoms are vigorously asserted. Popular magazines targeting the aspirant black elite, and advertising campaigns aimed at black consumers, craft the message that blackness – and the newfound freedom to be and assert a stylish blackness – is sexy and consumption is replete with desire. For black youth – particularly women – asserting a sexualised 'freedom' might be as much a statement of the rupture between the apartheid and post-apartheid generations, as a symptom of the erosion of parental authority.[8] The combination is then a fecund celebration of the liberation from the manifold prohibitions of the past. From this standpoint, sex has been politicised, at the same time as liberation – political freedom – has become sexualised in an erotics of race, class and generation.

In this milieu, sexuality is boldly and openly on display. In part, this is vested in the body: assertively sexy ways of dressing and walking – for women, wearing tight clothing, short skirts, showing lots of cleavage, for example, and for men, choosing fashionable clothing styled to show off good physiques.[9] But it also manifests in new modes of sex talk: open any magazine with a largely young black readership and you are bound to find one or more articles on sex, typically an advice column, which prints a striking number of letters seeking help with problems of sexual performance, men's sexual infidelities, the place of sex in relationships and the manner of 'normal' sexuality, among others. As the editor of Y Magazine (2002: 12) put it, the magazine promises to deliver 'the best in youth culture', in which 'sex dialogues' are writ large. Much of this is relatively new – partly because of the recently expanding magazine business associated with the growth of a consuming black middle class, but also as a sign of the newly assertive prominence of sexuality as style on the cultural agenda of black youth.

Similarly high exposure to sexual matters can be discerned within older social strata of urban elites. Other magazines aimed at more middle-aged black consumers, such as True Love and even Drum (with a less affluent target market), are also replete with sex talk: how to improve sexual performance, how to become more sexually desirable, bringing the romance back into sex, the pros and cons of oral sex, as well as in raising concerns about the high incidence of sexual violence, rape and incest.

The proliferation of post-apartheid sex talk is not confined to these circles or registers, however. The acceleration of South Africa's HIV/AIDS epidemic, and the ways in which a host of NGOs have responded to it, have produced a very voluble but different genre of sex talk, in a remarkably wide range of public settings. Although evidence of the disease was undeniable during the 1980s, the issue of HIV/AIDS has been largely a post-apartheid problem.[10] The pace of the epidemic in South Africa has lagged about 15–20 years behind that of other parts of Africa. As late as 1990, the estimated prevalence of HIV infection in the country was less than 1 per cent. These figures grew dramatically more serious by the mid-1990s, reaching 22.8 per cent by 1998 (and as high as 32.5 per cent in some parts of the province of KwaZulu-Natal) (Marks 2002: 16).

In other words, during the apartheid era, the spread of disease within South Africa remained relatively slow; its acceleration occurred in the wake of the transition. In the midst of lingering silences from political leaders during Mandela's presidency (notably on the part of Mandela himself), followed by heated denials and controversies during Mbeki's presidency (to be discussed in more detail later), many NGOs have reacted with both vigour and concern. Extensive (although not necessarily successful) public health education campaigns have been mounted, with the priority of heightening public awareness about the transmission of the HI virus. And since this is largely sexual (at least according to mainstream science, which the NGO sector has endorsed), these campaigns have tried to bring the subject of sex out into the open and to stimulate a national conversation about sex, sexuality and the risks of contracting HIV. Many of them vigorous and well-funded, these initiatives have made full use of the spaces opened up by the country's democratic constitution, in their bid to 'get the nation talking about sex'.

The so-called HIV/AIDs controversy

Prompted by Mbeki's direct interventions in public debate about the nature and treatment of HIV/AIDS, the 'controversy' became a *sine qua non* of Mbeki's presidency, nationally and internationally, having generated more political heat than any other single issue. Mbeki's so-called denialism[11] produced accusations of bankrupt political leadership, along with international condemnation from a range of places and people.

A host of international and national leaders, analysts and observers repeatedly expressed their incredulity and disgust at Mbeki's actions, particularly in the face of the deepening crisis of the country's epidemic, worsening death rates and the seeming indifference of the then president to the plight of the infected. As then minister of health, the late Manto Tshabala-Msimang, admitted, 'even some of our friends say they don't understand what South Africa is doing' (*San Francisco Examiner* 2000).This issue is alleged to have brought the ANC closer to internal rupture than any other since 1994.

The controversy also provoked open collisions between national and provincial government,[12] and thrust the post-apartheid government into bruising and humiliating confrontations with the constitutional court. And it was this controversy that spawned the most vibrant and powerful social movement of post-apartheid era – the Treatment Action Campaign (TAC) – and animated the growth of many NGOs and lobbies alarmed at the positions taken by the state and concerned to intervene in one way or another. So what was the controversy about and why did it produce this order of politicisation?

There are many versions of the nub of this controversy, with various explanations given for Mbeki's positions and tactics – ranging from the prohibitive costs of providing anti-AIDS medication on a mass scale, along with the unmanageable burdens of care this would impose on the state health service, through to Mbeki's own sex life and sexuality. My aim here is not to attempt a complete explanation for the controversy or Mbeki's views and actions within it, nor to engage with the merits or otherwise of these other modes of argument; but rather, to assert what I see as a critically important element of the controversy – a necessary ingredient in its analysis, albeit insufficient to explain the controversy in its entirety.

The analysis is conducted largely on a discursive terrain – drawing solely on what seem to me extremely revealing speeches, discussions and public interventions by

Mbeki – in the conviction that there are critical facets of the controversy which can only be captured within the domain of its discourses. And the discursive domain is in turn fundamental within the wider politics of nationalism. 'The nation' is an imaginary construct; 'nation-building' is critically a discursive project.[13] Hence my interest in the wider implications of the discursive dimensions of the HIV/AIDS controversy.

From one vantage point, this was a public confrontation about drugs, pharmaceutical companies and the science that underpins current understandings and treatments of HIV and AIDS. This medico-technical rendition was certainly the terrain on which Mbeki chose to situate most of his interventions and assert his personal interest, presidential authority and right of veto. And many of his opponents – notably the TAC, Mbeki's principal adversary on this front – made strategic decisions to challenge him on exactly these terms. But, as the TAC well understood, the wider, more painful and powerful reaches of the debate concerned the manner of sexuality and its malcontents.[14]

Arguably, in the midst of the newly heightened visibility of sexuality and multiplication of sites and registers of sex talk (as discussed earlier in the chapter), Mbeki's position on AIDS was an assertive and angry intervention in the discursive constitution of sexuality and the contestations associated with it. By rhetorically uncoupling the debate about AIDS from an engagement with the manner of sexuality, he aligned himself with those who refused the invitation to 'talk sex' as offensive and irrelevant. These refusals, moreover, went to the heart of the country's ongoing nation-building project – surfacing repressed anxieties about race and the colonial sexualisation of race, as well as raising questions about the manner of national unity and the identity of the national subject. On this reading, it was a debate about sex, race and the fate of the nation.

Mbeki did not insist outright that sex is not a vector of AIDS. Indeed, on some occasions, his speeches reiterated the scientific orthodoxy that one of the challenges in confronting the epidemic was to promote practices of 'safe sex' – the use of condoms. Yet, his most insistent interventions in debating the nature of HIV/AIDS demonstrated a denial of the connection between HIV/AIDS and sex in two ways. The first was an argument by (tacit) exclusion. AIDS, he argued (in line with the 'dissident' position), is a syndrome of familiar diseases associated with poverty and malnutrition – and therefore, by implication, not sex. The second was an argument by (overt and angry) refusal, the structure of which was: if AIDS was sexually transmitted, then – given the scale of the problem – the consequences would be intolerable. This was the line of argument that underpinned three strident public moves made by Mbeki disputing the statistics of HIV prevalence, AIDS-related deaths and, more generally, concerns about sexual violence and promiscuity.

The first, and widely publicised, formed part of Mbeki's open correspondence with Tony Leon, then leader of the opposition Democratic Alliance, published in the national newspaper *The Sunday Times* (2000) – a dialogue that reiterated the by then familiar arguments about drugs and science, but in ways that brought the racial halo of contention unusually clearly into focus. In his opening salvo to Leon, Mbeki revealed his perception that the debate about AIDS was deeply racialised. The call to provide antiretroviral drugs to HIV-positive women, which included a plea to include women who had been raped, he declared had an offensive racist agenda, rooted in stereotypes about the rapacious and violent sexuality of black men:

> I imagine that all manufacturers of antiretroviral drugs pay great attention to the very false figures about the incidence of rape in our country, that are regularly peddled by those who seem so determined to project a negative image of our country. What makes this matter especially problematic is that there is a considerable number of people in our country who believe and are convinced that most black (African) men carry the HI virus ... The hysterical estimates of the incidence of HIV in our country and sub-Saharan Africa made by some international organisations, coupled with the earlier wild and insulting claims about the African and Haitian origins of HI, powerfully reinforce these dangerous and firmly entrenched prejudices. (*The Sunday Times* 2000)

From this standpoint, allegations about the scale of the epidemic and its sexual vectors – including rape – rested on racist renditions of black sexuality; to speak about the epidemic in sexual terms carried the accusation of racism. A similar attack on his opponents in the AIDS 'controversy' followed a month later. Responding to accusations by Leon in parliament that Mbeki had 'injected race into the debate about AIDS and rape', Mbeki used the annual Oliver Tambo memorial lecture in Johannesburg to respond. Without referring to Leon by name – calling him 'the white politician' – Mbeki accused Leon of being an 'arrogant racist' who 'spoke openly of his disdain and contempt for African solutions to the challenges that face the peoples of our continent' and who saw Africans as 'pagan, savage, superstitious and unscientific' (*Time Magazine* 2000).

The third came a year later, in a speech by Mbeki at the University of Fort Hare, in which he reiterated the idea that claims about the rampant scale of the AIDS epidemic in the country, and therefore desperate calls for urgent action on the part of the government – including the provision of antiretrovirals – rested on racist renditions of blackness and black sexuality in particular. After referring to medical schools where black people were 'reminded of their role as germ carriers', he continued:

> [T]hus does it happen that others who consider themselves our leaders take to the streets carrying their placards, to demand that because we are germ carriers, and human beings of a lower order that cannot subject its [sic] passions to reason, we must perforce adopt strange opinions, to save a depraved and diseased people from perishing from self-inflicted disease ... Convinced that we are but natural-born, promiscuous carriers of germs, unique in the world, they proclaim that our continent is doomed to an inevitable mortal end because of our unconquerable devotion to the sin of lust. (*Mail and Guardian* 2001)

The most recent argument along these lines was developed in a document with disputed authorship, but allegedly closely associated with Mbeki. 'Castro Hlongwane, caravans, cats, geese, foot and mouth and statistics: HIV/AIDS and the struggle for the humanisation of the African',[15] a long, rambling and vitriolic document, made a somewhat mysterious appearance in the public domain in April 2002, as an anonymous contribution to 'the controversy' about HIV/AIDS. One hundred-and-fourteen pages long, this document ranged erratically through the familiar landmarks of controversy: science and pseudo-science, toxicity of antiretrovirals and the conspiracy of Western pharmaceuticals. Up to page 88, the document was a pastiche of long quotes from a miscellany of scientific journals, delivered in a solemnly academic – if fragmented – style of assertion, at which point it erupted into a frenzied declamation of the scientific orthodoxy:

> Yes, we are sex crazy! Yes, we are diseased! Yes, we spread the deadly HI virus through our uncontrolled heterosexual sex! In this regard, yes we are different from the US and Western Europe! Yes, we, *the men,* [my emphasis] abuse women and the girl-child with gay abandon! Yes, among us rape is endemic because of our culture! Yes, we do believe that sleeping with young virgins will cure us of AIDS! Yes, as a result of all this, we are threatened with destruction by the HIV/AIDS pandemic! Yes, what we need, and cannot afford because we are poor, are condoms and anti-retroviral drugs! Help! (Anon. 2002)

Here again is the argument by exclusion: AIDS is not about sex, because the consequences would be intolerable – consequences, in particular, for the manner of male sexuality. In refusing the connection between AIDS and sex, Mbeki (and those who share his arguments) rhetorically refused to engage in any public argument about sexuality – male sexuality, in particular – and even more emphatically in any public scrutiny of the sexual practices of black men.

As suggested earlier, many of Mbeki's opponents engaged him on his own terms. Much of the debate was focused on questions of treatment and the merits, or otherwise, of orthodox scientific research on HIV/AIDS and against that of the 'dissidents'. But in more popular sites of debate and contestation, the issue of sexuality and the sexual transmission of HIV loomed large. In some instances, Mbeki's critique of Western science was interpreted – and often welcomed – as a refutation of the existence of the virus, and therefore an exoneration of calls to sexual discipline and safety.

Many health workers and NGO activists complained that their efforts to promote the use of condoms were undermined by the president's interventions. In other instances, Mbeki's position was publicly scorned, particularly for its refusal to confront the centrality of sex. As David Kupane, director of the Kupane Funeral Home in Soweto said in an interview on US television about the AIDS 'controversy' in South Africa: 'it's a waste of time, a waste of money. We all know the truth – everybody knows that the cause [of HIV] is sexual transmission' (*San Francisco Examiner* 2000).

Paradoxically, Mbeki's efforts to refute the sexual connection reasserted the salience of the issue. At the same time as engaging the issues about drugs and science/pseudoscience, AIDS activists, health educators, politicians, community leaders and many citizens phoning in to radio chat shows, writing letters to newspapers and magazines and participating in community organisations grew more resolute and insistent in publicising the sexual transmission of the virus, the dangers of unsafe sex and the enormity of the sexual problem. These efforts in turn intensified Mbeki's irritation at what he saw as the inappropriately catastrophic rendition of the scale and impact of the epidemic. Arguably, however, the sense of catastrophe – and the felt need to communicate a sense of alarm, urgency and national crisis – was borne, in part, of Mbeki's refusals and strenuous efforts to rebut them. It was, to this extent, a product of the controversy.

The notion of HIV/AIDS as a national catastrophe marked the point at which the controversy exceeded issues of sexuality, and reached more deeply into the politics of nation-building, such that the debate about HIV/AIDS became a reflection of the identity and values of the national subject, along with the moral character of the nation. This chapter thus far has interpreted Mbeki's denialism as an effort to police the discursive constitution of sexuality. It remains to argue that this exercise was in turn shaped by Mbeki's aspirations as champion of the nation-building project.

Sexualising the nation

Many scholars have posited a close connection between the imagining of the nation and renditions of the place and manner of sexuality (male and female), such that the idea of the nation is incompatible with the unruliness of sex. From this standpoint, the disciplining of sexual energies and the constitution of a productive, life-giving sexuality inheres in the idea of a stable, orderly and unified nation.[16] And this association is facilitated, at least in part, by the proliferation of familial and bodily metaphors for the nation.

Benedict Anderson (1983) has argued that the nation as an 'imagined community', is a cultural artefact, produced by 'the metonymic extension of "those we know"' (Herzfeld 1997: 5) to include a huge and anonymous population. Metaphors of the family, body and kinship provide the symbolic resources to produce this sense of familiarity and intimacy. Indeed, as Michael Herzfeld argues, 'perhaps people everywhere use the familiar building blocks of body, family and kinship in order to make sense of larger entities' (Herzfeld 1997: 5). A nation is like a closely knit, stable and nurturing family; a nation is like a healthy, growing, energetic and disciplined body.

This repertoire of images and metaphors – particularly those of the body and the family – in turn provides symbolic recipes for the healthy containment of sexuality within the community of the nation. Disciplining the body, and stabilising the family, are techniques for the production of a procreative and life-sustaining sexuality. If unruly, on the other hand, sex destabilises the family and corrupts the body. Within this symbolic schema, therefore, aspirations to nationhood are intimately linked to the productive disciplining of sexuality as a force of order rather than chaos, life rather than death.

The symbolic association of nationhood with order rather than chaos, life rather than death, with sexuality at the fulcrum, was at the heart of Mbeki's imagery of nation-building – with a particularly strong evocation of the forces of chaos and death that threaten to destroy the fledgling nation at the very vulnerable moment of its birth. Mbeki took on the mantle of nation-builder very explicitly and enthusiastically, with the imagery of the African Renaissance as the centrepiece of his rhetoric. Images of birth and new life constituted its symbolic core. 'The word "Renaissance"', he explained, 'means rebirth, renewal, springing up anew. Therefore, when we speak of the African Renaissance, we speak of the rebirth and renewal of our continent' (Mbeki 1999a). The new South African nation is drawn into a larger affirmation of a vigorous life-force replenishing the continent at large, adding moment and enormity to the significance of South Africa's rebirth.

Yet, this new lease on life was profoundly tenuous, threatened by ominously predatory forces of destruction that were not yet fully vanquished. Although Nelson Mandela had become an international moral paragon, signifier par excellence of the possibility of moral redemption, and Mbeki had been cast as the pragmatic, urbane arch-politician, it was Mbeki's rhetoric more than Mandela's which invoked the theme of redemption from a dark, oppressive and morally tainted past.[17]

All nationalisms – in the process of imagining community – render a version of the past replete with meaning and purpose; a teleology of struggle. Mbeki's African Renaissance discourse was no exception, but it was unusual in the extent of contamination and despair it attached to the idea of the past.

Whereas Mandela tended to give a triumphalist rendition of the colonial and apartheid eras as struggles for liberation marked by key moments of progress and success,[18] Mbeki (1997) painted a particularly bleak picture of a 'wretched' past, the landscape of which was Africa-wide. The humiliations of apartheid were evoked within a wider canvass of despair – 'the African nightmare … the march of African time' marked by the 'footprints of despair' and the 'footprints of misery' (Mbeki 1999b) – from colonialism through to the present. For, not only did Africa have to suffer the degradations and brutalisations of colonial oppression, but also post-colonial Africa betrayed the promise of liberation. When the colonial Gold Coast won independence as Ghana, Mbeki mused, 'the African giant was awakening. But it came to pass that the march of African time snatched away that promise. Very little seemed to remain along its path except the footprints of despair' (Mbeki 1999b).

The depth of the 'abyss' of the past made the rebirth of the present 'a miracle' (Mbeki 1997), 'an act of creation' of extraordinary – god-like – proportions. Speaking of the peaceful demise of apartheid, Mbeki intoned that:

> As Africans we are moved that the world concedes that miracles of this order
> can come out of Africa, an Africa which in the eyes of the same world is home
> to an unending spiral of anarchy and chaos, at whose unknown end is a dark
> pith of an utter, a complete and unfathomable human disaster. (Mbeki 1997)

Yet the enormity of the transformation also made the project fragile and vulnerable. In the case of the new South African nation, Mbeki (1997) spoke of it as 'an infant in swaddling clothes', which 'requires the most careful nurturing to ensure that its ethos, its institutions and its practices mature and take firm root'.[19] And in the case of the African Renaissance more widely: 'it is upon us. As we peer through the looking glass darkly, this may not be obvious. But it is upon us' (Mbeki 1997). In

Mbeki's texts, its reality needed continual assertion and proof, not only in the midst of Western disbelief, but because there were subversive forces – threats of destruction and death – *within*:

> The Janus Face, the Faustian dilemma, Oscar Wilde's *Picture of Dorian Gray*, the necessary coexistence of good and evil in our cultures, according to which each blessing is its own curse – let the dogs off the leash, there are things in the African bush! – are we not met here to challenge all this troubled imagery, much of which describes our real world! (Mbeki 1998)

In the first instance, this 'imagery' was 'troubled' for having been constructed and inflicted by the oppressor, the coloniser with racist intentions and sensibilities. Yet, in terms of Mbeki's text, there was also an element of the 'troubled imagery' which 'described our real world': Africa is not wholly safe within itself. The African Renaissance is an effort to vanquish these dualities: 'hopefully our actions will obviate the needs to maintain a pride of guard dogs against those in the world, including *our African selves* [my emphasis], who might be forced to advance against a human advance which for us might represent disempowerment, marginalisation and regression' (Mbeki 1998).

Africa – 'our African selves' – needs to transform, therefore, from within. Hence Mbeki's insistence that the African Renaissance was a struggle that required commitment and energy from a new type of person borne of moral regeneration, a person markedly different from:

> those in our cities and towns who have lost all hope and all self-worth, who have slid into a twilight world of drug and alcohol abuse, the continuous sexual and physical abuse of women and children, of purposeless wars fought with fists and boots, metal rods, knives and guns, everyday resulting in death and grievous bodily harm. (Mbeki 1999a)

It was the birth of new type of person that would finally and irrefutably overthrow the burden of the colonial stereotypes of the African and their lingering power within the African self.

Discursively, Mbeki's denialism in the HIV/AIDS controversy was an expression of his refusal to retrace 'the footprints of despair'. Recall his arguments by refusal: to concede the sexual transmission of HIV would be to revitalise the racist stereotypes of rampant and unruly sex ('the things in the African bush'). It would be tantamount to acknowledging the unruliness of sex, on a catastrophic scale – bringing back the 'black hordes … against which ferocious dogs must be kept on the leash' (Mbeki 1998) – once again 'snatching away the promise' of new life.

For not only did the catastrophic version of HIV/AIDS entail the reiteration of the colonial burden; if HIV was sexually transmitted, then sex itself would become the vector of death. To concede the scientific orthodoxy was to recognise that once HIV infiltrated the social body, it snuffed out the fragile promise of new life; if sex produced death, then the infant nation was stillborn. To concede that the real issue in respect of HIV/AIDS was sexual would have been to admit to other symbolic registers similarly disruptive of the effort to imagine the nation's renewal. The fatality of sex was anchored in the family itself – the crucible of the nation. It was the very intimacy of the home – mother, father and children – that had become contaminated.

In short, in terms of Mbeki's rhetoric of nation-building, to admit to the enormity of the epidemic would have been to reinstate the imagery of 'the abyss', 'the African nightmare' and the death, disintegration and contamination which Mbeki associated with it. Indeed, the imagery of sexuality that Mbeki associated with the orthodox rendition of HIV/AIDS is the spectre of the past: the colonial nightmare that imprisoned the black mind, enslaved the black body and degraded the pursuit of pleasure. It is exactly that which the African Renaissance has to vanquish: the demon within 'our African selves'.

Notes

1. An earlier version of this essay was published in 2004 under the title, 'Getting the nation talking about sex: reflections on the discursive constitution of sexuality in South Africa since 1994' in *Agenda*, 62: 53–63. Reprinted with permission.
2. There are – and always have been – multiple sites of conversation about sex and sexuality, some of which are more secretive, culturally bound and proscribed than others. Given the paper's focus on the recent politicisation of sexuality, the plethora of discourses is beyond the scope of its immediate concerns.
3. The extent to which the values espoused in the constitution coincide with, or are changing, popular attitudes on sexual issues is another question. There are some indications that a discourse of rights is sometimes invoked in popular debates and collisions on sexual matters – as much in order to dispute perceived excesses of freedom that have been conferred by the constitution (such as in men claiming that women have become so assertive in claiming their rights to equality that they have thereby undermined men's rights as fathers), as in defending newfound freedoms (such as in women dealing with sexual violence by exposing it and seeking police protection in the name of their constitutional right to safety). But the scope of these shifts has been limited by the well-established patriarchal 'common sense' of the old order.
4. The Constitution of the Republic of South Africa, Act no. 108 of 1996, chapter 2, para. 12c.
5. Again, the extent to which these obligations are effectively and/or seriously discharged in practice is another matter. NGOs dealing with rape victims continue to complain about the treatment meted out by police; a pitiful proportion of rape cases are successfully prosecuted and even then, sentencing of rapists is widely seen as inappropriately lenient – all of which speaks in other ways to the political and cultural contestations that surround the allocation of new sexual rights.
6. This research shows how young women make explicit and deliberate recourse to a range of sexual partners who meet particular material needs (for transport and rent, as well as for fashionable clothing and cellphones). These men, who are sometimes called *inkukhuyami* (the chicken) are to be plucked for their money rather than their love – and, in a different genre of classification, are coined the 'minister of finance', 'minister of transport' or 'my ATM'.
7. Drawing on research done in urban townships in and around Gauteng province, Selikow et al (2002) explain how male and female sexuality is being shaped by the urge to consume – for example, in the notion of the *ingaraga* (the macho man), who commands respect in part by virtue of his perceived control over women, particular flashy and fashionably dressed women, and who pursues multiple sexual partners, embracing the risks of HIV infection in the name of masculine bravado (*tata ma chance*).
8. Thanks to Nthabiseng Motsemme for this insight.
9. In its bid to reach youth with its messages about safe sex and the prevention of HIV infection in ways which explicitly mimic the imagery of popular youth culture, the

billboard campaigns of the sexual health NGO, loveLife, have used increasingly provocative and revealing bodily poses to represent a 'positive lifestyle', or 'loving life'.

10. South Africa borders on countries with some of the highest HIV infection rates in the world, such as Botswana and Zimbabwe. The first cases of HIV infection were recorded in these countries at roughly the same time as in the USA and Europe, in the mid-1980s. And their epidemics accelerated rapidly, with roughly equivalent timing (even if the scale of infection differed dramatically) during the 1990s.

11. Mbeki's position on HIV/AIDS has not always been clear; but in the main, he rejects the Western scientific orthodoxy, in terms of which AIDS is caused by HIV, which is in turn largely transmitted sexually. Mbeki sometimes disputes the existence of the virus, sometimes the cause of AIDS (as not caused by HIV in the manner claimed by scientists), and sometimes the cause of HIV (seeing this to lie primarily in conditions of poverty and malnutrition).

12. Mbhazima Shilowa, then premier of Gauteng province, announced that the provincial health service would provide antiretroviral therapy to pregnant women (in the wake of assurances from the president that it was government policy to permit provinces with adequate infrastructure and resources to do so), only to be publically rebuked by the minister of health.

13. Of course, there is more to the politics of nationalism than simply its discursive modalities.

14. Certainly for the TAC itself, its identity as a social movement is closely associated with its engagement with issues of sexuality. As Mark Heywood put it, the creation of the TAC had 'two triggers', both of which were saturated with the politics of sexuality: the death of Simon Nkoli, a black gay activist who died of AIDS, and the murder of Gugu Dlamini by her husband and others after she declared herself HIV positive – the case of 'men killing a woman whose pronouncement of her HIV status indicted them' (interview with author, Johannesburg, 22 August 2002). Although the collision with Mbeki over drugs and treatment issues once dominated the national profile of the TAC, the bulk of its routine activity across the country includes running workshops and discussions aimed at promoting awareness of, and also a capacity to live with, the virus, which as Heywood underlines inevitably raises the subject of sex. 'The people who support the TAC are people who talk about sex, in workshops.'

15. Castro Hlongwane was an African boy who had been barred from a caravan park because he was black.

16. A fuller discussion of this articulation would need to take account of the hedonistic impulse and aesthetic of pleasure which have inhered in the elaboration of modernity, particularly in the West, in terms of which the affirmation of sexuality is as integral to the self-expression of a modern nation as the disciplining of otherwise unruly sexual energies – all of which underscores even further the significance of the sexual domain within the imaginary realm of the nation.

17. Thanks to Mark Gevisser for a fascinating conversation on this point.

18. For example, in his address to the closing session of the 50th National Conference of the ANC, in Mafikeng on 20 December 1997, Mandela spoke of his 'time to hand over the baton' [hand over leadership of the ANC]: 'the time has come to hand over the baton in a relay that started more than 85 years ago in Mangaung; nay more, centuries ago when the warriors of Autshumanyo, Makhanda, Mzilikazi, Moshweshwe, Khama, Sekhukhuni, Lobatsibeni, Cethswayo, Nghunghunyane, Uithalder and Ramabulana laid down their lives to defend the dignity and integrity of their being as a people. In their mysterious ways, history and fate were about to dictate to us that we should walk the valley of death again and again before we reached the mountain-tops of the peoples' desires. And so the time has come to make way for a new generation, secure in the knowledge that despite our numerous mistakes, we sought to serve the cause of freedom; if we stumbled on occasion, the bruises sustained were the mark of the lessons that we had to learn to make our humble contribution to the birth of our nation.'

19. Republic of South Africa (1997), Debates of the National Assembly, 10 June, col. 3647.

References

Altman, D. (2001) *Global Sex*, Sydney and Aukland, Allen and Unwin

Anderson, B. (1983) *Imagined Communities: Reflections on the Origin and Spread of Nationalism*, London, Verso

Anon. (2002) 'Castro Hlongwane, caravans, cats, geese, foot and mouth and statistics: HIV/ AIDS and the struggle for the humanisation of the African', circulated at 51st Conference of the African National Congress, Stellenbosch, University of Stellenbosch, 16–20 December

Ashforth, Adam (1999) 'Weighing manhood in Soweto', *CODESRIA Bulletin*, 3 and 4, Dakar, CODESRIA

Foucault, M. (1979) *The History of Sexuality, Volume 1: An Introduction*, London, Penguin

Gevisser, Mark (2000) 'Mandela's stepchildren: homosexual identity in post-apartheid South Africa', in Drucker, P. (ed) *Different Rainbows*, London, Gay Mens' Press

Hennessy, R. (2000) *Profit and Pleasure: Sexual Identities in Late Capitalism*, New York and London, Routledge

Herzfeld, Michael (1997) *Cultural Intimacy: Social Poetics in the Nation-State*, New York and London, Routledge

Hunter, Mark (2002) 'The materiality of everyday sex: thinking beyond prostitution', *African Studies* 61(1): 99–120

Mail and Guardian (2001) 'Mbeki in bizarre AIDS outburst', 26 October

Marks, S. (2002) 'An epidemic waiting to happen', *African Studies* 61(1): 13–26

Mbeki, Thabo (1997) 'Address to the corporate council on Africa attracting capital to Africa summit', Virginia, USA, 19–22 April

—— (1998) 'Statement of the Deputy President Thabo Mbeki at the Africa Telecom '98 forum', Johannesburg, 4 May, http://www.doc.org.za/docs/speeches, accessed 5 March 2002

—— (1999a) speech given at the launch of the African Renaissance Institute, Gaborone, 11 October

—— (1999b) 'Statement at the memorial service for the late Mwalimu Julius Nyerere, Pretoria, 18 October

—— (1999c) 'Address at the opening of parliament', Cape Town, 25 June, http://www.anc. org.za, accessed 5 March 2002

San Francisco Examiner (2000) 'An epidemic of denial', 11 July, http://www.aegis.com/news/ sfe/2000, accessed 14 February 2011

Selikow, Terry-Ann, Zulu, Bheki and Cedras, Eugene (2002) 'The ingaragara, the regte and the cherry: HIV/AIDS and youth culture in contemporary townships', *Agenda* 53: 22–32

Sontag, Susan (1988) *AIDS as Metaphor,* New York, Farrar, Straus and Giroux

The Sunday Times (2000) 'Mbeki vs Leon: Dear Tony', 1 July

Time Magazine (2000) 'The legacy that won't die', 28 August

Y Magazine (2002) 'Editorial', April/May

10

Paradoxes of sex work and sexuality in modern-day Uganda[1]

Sylvia Tamale

Introduction

> What is Love?
> Love is something natural
> Love is a key to life
> Love is education
> Love is science
> Love is light
> Love is a gift of speaking in strange tongues
> Love is beyond human control
> Love is secret
> Love creates hope
> Love is history.
>
> [Graffiti on the wall of a brothel in Kisenyi]

The last thing I expected to find on the wall of a slum brothel in the research field was poetry. The experience of seeing and reading the poem reproduced above opened my eyes to the deeper reality of people's lives, beyond the rough of the wall. Those simple lines sent out a powerful message of a voiceless and marginalised subculture.[2]

Police swoops of prostitutes on Ugandan streets and various brothels are a relatively common occurrence (*The Monitor* 2006; *New Vision* 2009). Despite being outlawed, this form of subversive sexuality has boldly endured over time and space, shaped and reshaped by forces such as colonialism, racial and gender supremacy, capitalism and globalisation, compelling me to explore and analyse the link between sex work, gender and the law, and the nexus between labour, desire and female offending.[3] I sought to contribute to the sparse and insufficient scholarship regarding Ugandan women's sexuality generally and sex work in particular (see Bakwesigha 1982; Ssewakiryanga 2002).

Under Ugandan law, prostitution is illegal and has been penalised in criminal law. The legal regime is based on the belief that effective law enforcement and repression can and should reduce prostitution. Section 138 of the penal code defines a prostitute and prostitution: 'In this code "prostitute" means a person who, in public or elsewhere, regularly or habitually holds himself or herself out as available for sexual intercourse or other sexual gratification for monetary or other material gain and "prostitution" shall be construed accordingly.'

Clearly this definition limits culpability of the offence to the sellers of sex (the majority of whom are women) and not to the clients (mostly men). So, if a woman is found guilty of 'selling her sex' she is liable to a sentence of up to seven years, while the client that paid for her services walks away scot-free (Section 139, penal code). Furthermore, the dependants of a prostitute, such as her children or elderly parents, for example, may also be sentenced to seven years imprisonment for living 'wholly or in part on the earnings of prostitution' (Section 136(1), penal code).

It is important to reflect on the primary purpose of criminal law, for which three main functions have been advanced: first, to protect the public from harm (by forbidding conduct that may lead to harmful results); second, to respond to harmful acts committed by individuals (through punishment); and finally, through criminal punishment, to achieve the goals of deterrence, retribution, restraint, rehabilitation and restoration.

So, what harm does prostitution introduce in society? Proponents of criminalising prostitution argue that it poses a health hazard to society through the spread of sexually transmitted diseases, such as HIV/AIDS. They further argue that prostitution occasions physical and moral harm to the prostitute and that the trade promotes ancillary crimes, such as trade in illegal drugs. But there are indications from past studies in Uganda and elsewhere that reveal that the criminalisation of prostitution, in fact, does not prevent or control these harms. Instead it often creates or exacerbates them (Ssewakiryanga 2002).

The study[4] on which this essay is based clearly reveals that the continued criminalisation of adult sex work in Uganda is equivalent to a man pissing in the wind – futile, irrational and counterproductive. Its blanket prohibition appeals more to the hypocritical moral compass of the powerful policymakers than to the primary purpose of criminal law, which is to protect society from penal harm. Hence, the logic of the law is not necessarily the logic of the wider population. It flies in the face of justice and dignity, sound public health policy, the economic realities of women who engage in the trade and deep-seated human sexual needs.[5]

The sociocultural and legal regimes governing sex work are fraught with paradoxes and contradictions. The paradoxes present themselves variously through: the ambivalence of the sexed body, of the private and public spaces where sex is traded; the opposition between morality and economic survival; between religion and rights; and between virtue and deviance. They are also present in the illogicality of forbidden sexualities in the context of human pleasurable desires, the irreconcilability of class and status antagonisms, and the contradictions of poor and underdeveloped economies.

The findings further show that arguments located in Western radical feminist theory, which reduces sex work to the 'victimisation and objectification of women' and views its practice as inherently violent, are too far removed from the realities and complexities of grassroots women who engage in this trade.[6] A firm material base, nuanced with passion, anxiety, anger, joy, competition and obsession, shapes the dynamics of commercial sex in Uganda.[7] The victimisation, objectification and violence associated with sexual labour might be amplified by the fact of its criminalisation, but it is all part of the wider exploitative gender/power relations existing in Ugandan society. These are circumstances occasioned by male supremacy, capitalism, globalisation and other forces beyond women's control. The majority of women are forced to make livelihood decisions between only different bad alternatives. In other words, most African women 'choose' to do one exploitative job and not another. The choices range from domestic labour (as housewives or house maids) to factory work (for example, the AGOA girls, who work 14 to 18 hours daily in textile factories producing cotton goods for the US market).[8]

Sexuality as a discourse is the lens that enhances theoretical and conceptual clarity to the otherwise murky, seemingly incomprehensible aspects of social power and control over resources. Sexuality itself is a powerful resource in human relations (Lorde 1984). Like gender, race and class, sexuality is a system of power in which the socio-political structures of power define what is acceptable sexual behaviour for men and women in our societies. Women's sexuality is particularly interwoven with ideologies of reproduction and domesticity. The profession of sex work exemplifies the resourcefulness of the erotic, the contradictions, paradoxes and anomalies of our society, as well as the complexities of patriarchal capitalism.

When Ugandan ministers of finance, planning and economic development deliver the national annual budget and its background, there are two types of work that they never acknowledge as contributing to the country's economic growth: (1) women's domestic work; and (2) sex work. Mainstream economic analyses obscure the economic benefits and productive value of these two forms of caring. Criminalisation further pushes sex work into the hidden economy, thus increasing the vulnerability and marginalisation of the people who operate in that arena.

In this essay I present data from in-depth interviews and focus group discussions conducted in Kampala and Jinja, the two largest cities in Uganda.[9] The data unravels some of the hidden, complex issues regarding women's erotic sexuality, gender power imbalances and the control of women's bodies. I also explore the potential subversiveness intrinsic to the act of commercial sex.

Assessing the literature on sex work

There exists a vast and wide-ranging body of literature on the subject of sex work. Issues that have dominated scholarship and debate around the phenomenon of sex work vary across time, space and cultural tradition. A cursory review of the contemporary literature on the subject reveals the depth and breadth of complexities and controversies that surround this phenomenon. The discussions are entangled with concepts such as choice, violence, agency, labour, morality, identity, disease, commodification, exploitation, discrimination, immigration, colonialism, globalisation, pleasure, tourism and so forth.

My review of the literature is delineated by the scope of this study; it covers adult female sex work and is divided into three thematic subsections to reflect the main trends of the debates and discussions related to issues tackled in this study. First, I consider the theoretical scholarship that relates to sex work. Next, I summarise the trends and patterns that emerge from empirical studies on sex work around the world. Finally, I tackle the scholarship pertaining to issues of law, policy and human rights on the subject matter.

Theorising female prostitution: work or abuse?

The phenomenon of female prostitution has since the 1960s been a source of fierce controversy even among feminist thinkers.[10] The theoretical literature on prostitution is mostly grounded in feminist interpretations of gender and sexuality and can be divided into two major schools of thought. The first is that which views prostitution as part of the gender-based violence continuum and is vehemently opposed to it. They condemn it uncompromisingly, equating it to slavery and other forms of social oppression. Underlying such arguments is the belief that sex workers are vulnerable victims of systematic patriarchal exploitation.

The second school of thought perceives prostitution as legitimate labour and argues for its recognition as such. Supporters draw a distinction between voluntary adult sex work and forced prostitution or trafficking. Their view is that women engage in the trade as active agents of their destiny.

Scholars such as Gayle Rubin (1975), Andrea Dworkin (1981, 1993), Catharine MacKinnon (1987, 1993), Carole Pateman (1988), Christine Overall (1992) and Sheila Jeffreys (1997) belong to the first school of thought. They have argued strongly against prostitution, holding the position that it is a manifestation of the exploitation of women's vulnerability. They find sex work fundamentally objectionable because, for them, it involves women's subordination; by commercialising male access to female bodies, sex work institutionalises women's sexual subordination and com- modification. Rachel Harrison (1999) critiques such arguments by radical feminists, maintaining that they parallel and inadvertently reinforce the Victorian construc- tion of sex workers as sinful and immoral whores juxtaposed with the purity and chastity of the Madonna image. The whore image goes against societal gender roles set out for women as mothers, wives and homemakers, while the Madonna figure reinforces the ideology of domesticity for women.

Heidi Tinsman (1992) also compares those who treat sex work as uniquely exploitative to paternalists, who rush to protect female sexuality in the name of women. For Tinsman, '*sex* is central to the way in which *all* women are exploited in *all* types of work' (1992: 241) [emphasis mine]. Her point is that, like other women's work, sex work is simultaneously structured by a global capitalist market and by gender relations. Other Marxist feminists have also argued that the interconnected- ness between sex and capitalism means that it is impossible to distinguish women's subjugation in sex work from that of women in non-sex work employment (Kuhn and Wolpe 1978; Barrett 1980). Read together, the liberal and radical arguments sur- face the complexities and contradictions fraught in analyses of women's sexualities as sites of pleasure, desire, freedom of expression, violence, oppression and control.

Tinsman (1992) asks the pointed question: 'What is the difference between sex work and other forms of work performed by women that compels advocates to call for the abolition of the industry in the first case, but not in the second?' She argues:

> Many forms of non-sex work are extremely exploitative … Garment work-
> ers in Mexico are paid below-subsistence wages that leave them unable to
> provide appropriate nutrition or healthcare for themselves and their families
> … Yet advocates for these women believe that the state and organized labor
> must act to improve work conditions, raise wages, and give workers greater
> power within decision-making processes. They do not call for the abolition
> of these specific types of employment. Why do they do so in the case of sex
> work? (Tinsman 1992: 242)

Tinsman suggests that instead of calling for the elimination or criminalisation of sex work, anti-prostitution advocates should – like their labour counterparts – stress the need for greater empowerment within the sex industry.

Among the theorists who view prostitution as work that should be treated with the same rights and duties as any other work within the formal labour force are S.R. Bell (1994), Lisa Law (2000), Prabha Kotiswaran (2001) and Berta Harnández-Truyol and J. Larson (2006) (also see Gail Pheterson 1989). Harnández-Truyol and Larson argue that a proper scrutiny of prostitution within a human rights frame-work needs to be done within a labour paradigm: 'Prostitution can be analysed by applying internationally-embraced labour rights outside of the coercion/consent binary without denying women agency or moralistically condemning all commercial sex. A labour analysis permits deconstruction of the practice of prostitution and unearths its component elements' (Harnández-Truyol and Larson 2006: 391).

Viewing prostitution through the labour frame transcends all generations of rights, given the indivisibility and interdependence of economic and social rights with civil and political rights. Instead of focusing on the essential aspects of sex or the individuals engaged in sex work, the labour discourse allows for a political debate around what constitutes just and humane conditions of labour (Harnández-Truyol and Larson 2006: 395). Indeed, in 2001 the European Court of Human Rights recognised sex work as an 'economic activity' that deserves protection when pursued by a self-employed individual.[11]

Elsje Bonthuys and Carla Monteiro (2004: 673) also argue that prevailing dis-courses about male and female sexuality that view men as 'naturally sexually aggressive' and perceive women as people who 'do not enjoy sex for its own sake' stand at the root of the commodification of women's sexuality and the sexual dou-ble standards:

> Negotiating the contradictory norms of male and female sexuality is difficult
> for all women. On the one hand, the commercial environment and sexual
> norms in general tell us that all women's sexuality is for sale; yet, when women
> sell sex, they are socially stigmatized and legally persecuted. Labelling certain
> women as whores is fundamental to upholding the status of decent women or
> Madonnas, as sexually pure while obscuring the perception that all women's
> sexuality is for sale. (Bonthuys and Monteiro 2004: 674)

For these scholars, therefore, in light of societal construction of women's sexuality, it is normal that some women would sell their sexuality. They conclude that legal responses to prostitution are inadequate for dealing with the societal norms and ideals that underlie the practice. They call for a positive model of female sexuality that theorises it as 'a source of enjoyment in itself as opposed to a vehicle for gaining acceptance from men or maintaining relationships of economic and emotional dependence' (Bonthuys and Monteiro, 2004: 676).

Some non-Western scholars have criticised the uncritical analyses of sex work in their societies by Western scholars. For example, Nicola Tannenbaum (1999: 249) faults scholars who construct Thai sex work in Western middle-class moral terms – unitarian, degrading and restricted to women who are impoverished and legally, socially and religiously degraded by their inferior status. She argues that 'unlike Christianity which mandates celibacy for people who are not married, the Buddhist precepts do not' (Tannenbaum 1999: 250). She further criticises studies that assume Buddhism to be the entry point for all sociocultural analyses of Thai culture. Tannenbaum calls for all discourses on sex work to be ethnographically grounded. Another example is the Indian scholar, Prabha Kotiswaran (2001), who condemns essentialist formulations of Third World womanhood and urges both governments and scholars to listen to the stifled voices of sex workers. She strongly recommends full decriminalisation in addition to anti-discriminatory civil rights protection of sex workers.

The polarised theoretical debate on prostitution appears to be irreconcilable. However, analysing the phenomenon through a human rights framework provides a negotiable position that strengthens the legal interventions to protect women (and men) who engage in the trade.

Sex work: trends and patterns

Much of the research on sex work is devoted to exploring the reasons behind women's involvement in this work. Some explanations locate the determinants within the sex worker, such as the personal psychosocial, emphasising perceived instabilities in the women's personality (Maerov 1965; Potter et al 1999). Writers such as Deborah Posel (1993) have critiqued these deterministic explanations, arguing that reasons for individuals' entry into commercial sex lie within the wider and more complex socioeconomic contexts, such as global poverty and structural inequality (Posel 1993; Pauw and Brener 1997; Bernstein 1999). The underside of the global capitalist system is increasing poverty, unemployment, inequality, marginalisation and deprivation, with an apparent trend of driving more women into the sex trade (Anarfi 1998; Gangoli and Westmarland 2006).

In Uganda, some of the reasons attributed to women's entry into sex work include poverty, the disintegration of the traditional African family, domestic violence, orphaning, peer pressure, armed conflict, sexual violence and premarital pregnancies (Slum Aid Project 2002). Some studies have been devoted to attitudinal trends to reveal what various sectors of society think of sex work. Chanpen Saengtienchai et al (1999), for example, investigated the views of Thai married women regarding extramarital relationships with commercial sex workers and non-commercial sex partners of Thai men. They found that there is a pervasive acceptance of premarital commercial sex patronage for single Thai men and a tolerance of occasional commercial sex patronage for married men. However, non-commercial extramarital sex is condemned. In other words, married women in this society are inclined to choose commercial sex work patronage over non-commercial partners for their husbands, as the lesser of two evils.

In his fascinating study on Kampala sex workers, Richard Ssewakiryanga (2002) analyses the various ways that sex workers construct their identities in relation to societal structures of power and the material contexts. His findings indicate that age, education, space, ethnicity and sex are critical factors in the self-identities and discursive social identities of sex workers. Such constructions are fraught with contradictions and competing desires. For example, he found that while retaining a youthful look is vital for the marketability of sex workers, advanced age becomes a lucrative identity when clients seek 'experienced' women. Education (especially proficient articulation in the English language) allows sex workers to access different kinds of spaces as well as to mobilise different identities. Many times, sex workers have to negotiate different identities to fit different contexts. They even challenge state hegemonies through what Ssewakiryanga terms 'resistance identities' (Ssewakiryanga 2002: 15).

From the early 1990s behavioural research paradigms have emerged that link sex work and HIV/AIDS to the sex trade (Varga 1997; Poulsen et al 2000, Parker 2001; Kapiga et al 2002; UNAIDS 2006). Such studies portray sex workers as vectors of sexually transmitted diseases (STDs), particularly HIV/AIDS. The bulk of these studies identify sex workers among the so-called high-risk populations in the spread of HIV. The studies also reveal a pattern, which matches the emergence of HIV/AIDS with a corresponding increase in government surveillance of female commercial sex workers (Ministry of Health 2006). The overall effect of such literature is to increase the stigma attached to the trade, strengthening the justification and advocacy for outlawing the practice.

Notably, the bulk of studies on sex work in Uganda begin from the premise that it is a problem (Slum Aid Project 2002; Walakira 2004; Omondi 2006). They objectify women who engage in sex work, portraying them as hapless victims and denying them any form of agency. Such essentialist constructions reinforce the age-old Madonna/whore dichotomy dominant in Western feminist thought. They tie in very well with the broader construction of women as domestic, maternal beings and the global control of women's identity and sexuality. Studies across cultures seem to hold the consensus that acceptable female sexuality is that mediated through the framework of heterosexual marriage and procreation (Harrison 1999; Slum Aid Project 2002; Aderinto 2006; Omondi 2006). Sex work is therefore viewed as deviant and destabilising. The inevitable result of such analyses is an eternal attempt to reconstruct the sex worker through rehabilitative strategies.

Law, policy and human rights issues

One of the earliest published studies on the legal status of sex work is the 1957 British Report on Homosexual Offences and Prostitution, authored by the Wolfenden Committee. The oft-quoted report states that prostitution cannot be eradicated through the agency of criminal law.[12] Unfortunately, Ugandan judicial jurisprudence has not lent itself to any substantive discussion of prostitution or sex work.

One issue that various feminist scholars agree on, irrespective of their theoretical leaning, is that all criminal sanctions against females who offer services in the sex industry should be abolished (Bernstein 1999; Law 2000b; Aronson 2006). In other words, feminists are united in fighting the stigma and discrimination suffered by women who engage in the sex trade. There are three main legal regimes that govern sex work around the world: (1) total prohibition of all aspects of sex work (Uganda, see Tamale 2005; Namibia, see Legal Assistance Centre 2002); (2) legalised or regulated sex work (the Netherlands, see Vanwesenbeeck 1994; Australia, see Perkins et al 1994); and (3) decriminalisation of voluntary adult sex work (New Zealand, see Olowu 2006).

Total prohibition regimes take various forms. The majority of countries under this legal regime target sellers of sex, and only a few target buyers of sex. The contradictions and gender inequality associated with illegal sale of sex on the one hand and its legal purchase have received extensive discussion within contemporary feminist literature (Law 2000b; Legal Assistance Centre 2002). In 1999, Sweden introduced radical legislation that penalised only the buyers of sex (mostly men) and not the sellers (mostly women). Yvonne Svanström (2006) reports that this piece of legislation was promoted as a feminist law, meant to curb violence against women. She attributes this development to the increased number of female parliamentarians who were united in perceiving prostitution as exploitation of women. However, she cautions that the effect of the law has been watered down by the relatively light punishment meted out to the male offenders (comparable to that of a shoplifter) and the overall sympathies for the offenders exhibited by the patriarchal law enforcement agencies.

Legalised or regulated regimes do not primarily focus on the rights and welfare of female sex workers, but usually cater for the interests of male clients (the spread of STDs) and public decency aspects, such as zoning. Here, the state controls the conditions under which commercial sex operates (Gangoli and Westmarland 2006). The committee that monitors the implementation of the United Nations Convention on the Elimination of All Forms of Discrimination Against Women (CEDAW) interpreted 'voluntary prostitution' to fall within 'free choice of profession' under Article 11.1(c) of CEDAW, which upholds the 'right to free choice of profession and employment' (Hevener 1986). The committee is of the view that regulated sex work is the best option for protecting human rights and combating trafficking (Chan 2007).

In Senegal, the only African country in which prostitution is legal, the legal preoccupation since 1969 has been ensuring that sex workers are subjected to regular medical check-ups and that licensed workers operate discreetly, presumably not to offend public morality (Ndoye 1995; Homaifar and Wasik 2005).[13] Contrary to popular belief, which associates commercial sex trade with widespread HIV epidemics,

Senegal reports one of the lowest prevalence rates of HIV infection on the continent. In 2005 the country's prevalence rate stood at only 0.7 per cent (UNAIDS 2006) compared to 6.4 per cent in Uganda (Uganda AIDS Commission 2006: 4).

The so-called red light areas, legitimate in countries such as the Netherlands (Wonders and Michalowski 2001) and Germany (Dodillet 2004) are part of the effort to confine sex work to certain zones and limit the public nuisance that is associated with street prostitution. Many scholars have investigated the potential that legalised regimes hold for law enforcement agents abusing the regulations and extorting bribes from sex workers (Shaver 1985; D'Cunha 1991).

Several studies have characterised prostitution law as a patriarchal tool that reflects societal control and regulation of female sexuality. In her article, 'The regulation of prostitution: avoiding the morality traps', Frances Shaver (1994) argues that social and legal policies on prostitution that are based on sexual moralistic arguments (both overt and covert) are bound to fail.[14] She advocates for the evaluation of commercial sex that focuses not on the specificity of prostitution but on the specificity of women.

Very few countries around the world have adopted the liberal approach to sex work, allowing its unprohibited existence. The literature points to New Zealand as a rare case of nearly total decriminalisation of sex work (Olowu 2006). Decriminalised sex work in this country was enforced in June 2003 and therefore it is still too early to evaluate the effect of the legislation.

Some scholars locate sex work within the human rights framework, arguing that sex workers are human beings who deserve the same rights and dignity that are accorded to all people. The health and safety of women who engage in commercial sex work are questions of rights, in addition to the other rights such as life, free speech, education, housing, access to information and so forth (Kempadoo and Doezema 1998; Sex Workers Project 2003, 2005). Gendered analyses of prostitution law point to the double standards inherent in its provisions – those that treat women within the sex industry more harshly than men (Levick 1996).

Notably, mainstream human rights and women's rights movements around the world do not advocate for the rights of sex workers to ply their trade freely. Since the 1990s there has emerged a growing social movement by sex workers themselves advocating for their right to freely engage in commercial sex trade. Janet Wojcicki's (1999) study of the Sex Workers Advocacy and Education Taskforce (Sweat) in South Africa (see also Arnott 2006) and Valerie Jenness' (1990) research on Call Off Your Old Tired Ethics (Coyote) in the USA are two cases in point. In February 2009, a pan-African network of sex workers' organisations called African Sex Workers Alliance (Aswa) was formed with the objective of building a 'capacitated, coherent, sex-worker led movement defending the rights of sex workers across Africa'.[15]

Such organisations have challenged constructions of sex workers as 'fallen women' or 'hapless victims', insisting that sex work is a legitimate trade in which service providers deserve all the rights of any worker (Delascoste and Alexander 1987; Jenness 1990). At the international level, the International Committee for Prostitutes' Rights was established in 1985 with the agenda to ensure that sex workers enjoyed their full human rights. However, Kamala Kempadoo (1998) has noted the absence of third world sex workers from the international movement of sex workers.

Arguments that locate sex work within the aegis of morality/sin are intolerant of using the human rights framework as a basis for decriminalising it. In her book, *Politics of the Womb*, Lynn Thomas (2005) documents the anti-prostitution arguments that were advanced in the post-colonial Kenya parliament to strike down the affiliation law, which granted single women the right to claim child maintenance from the biological fathers of their children. And there is no shortage of efforts to rehabilitate sex workers and mainstream them into the formal labour force. Several NGOs and faith-based organisations around the world run programmes that attempt to 'reintegrate' sex workers into society (Soderlund 2005).

Advocates for sex workers' rights attempt to highlight the fact that legal prohibition of sex work does not eliminate the exploitation of women or male domination over women. It does not abrogate the commodification of female sexuality; neither does it propose viable alternatives for women who engage in the trade. Tinsman argues that 'prohibition attempts to eliminate a source of income without altering the economic realities that make sex-work a primary source of income for women all over the world' (Tinsman 1992: 243).

The historical evolution of sex work in Uganda

Sex work has not always been a criminal offence in Uganda. The customary law of crime, for example, did not penalise sex work. Two of the most distinctive customary law crimes in the area of sexuality included rape and adultery (Morris and Read 1966: 290–291). But married men were only penalised for the customary crime of adultery when it was committed with a married woman or a betrothed girl. Hence the exchange of material gain for sexual services was generally tolerated in pre-colonial Uganda. However, with the unprecedented rural–urban migration in the 1910s and 1920s, the growth of the city of Kampala and the attendant 'social explosion', sex work flourished (Southall and Gutkind 1957; Obbo 1980; Musisi 2001). In a bid to chastise and curb illicit sexual behaviour and commercialised sex, the colonial penal code of 1930 criminalised sex work. Hence the cultural landscape that had accorded spaces for non-procreative sexuality was changed by a stroke of the colonialist's pen.

Needless to say, the colonial law against prostitution was very much modelled on that of Britain at the time.[16] The dye of Victorian common law morality and Judaeo-Christian culture was firmly bound into all the sexual penal offences. All of them imposed female sexual monogamy and chastity. Similarly, in the Buganda kingdom, where the capital Kampala was located, the elite members of the Lukiiko (Buganda parliament) with their colonial education and missionary influence felt the need to curb what they perceived as moribund morality. Hence in 1941, the Buganda government enacted a separate legislation to prevent sex work in the royal capital. It criminalised sex work and prohibited 'an unmarried girl under twenty years of age to enter employment or engage in any kind of work which takes her away from the home of her parents or lawful guardians at night' (Gutkind 1963; Morris and Read 1966: 291) Many women were rounded up under this law and herded back to the rural areas (Gutkind 1963: 156).

The irrational double standards in regulating the sexualities of Ugandan women and men not only cast doubt on the moralising discourse but were fraught with tensions and contradictions; non-monogamous, heterosexual men were having sexual relations with multiple female partners, including extramarital liaisons. The incongruity between the imposed monogamous Christian marriages and the polygynous sexuality of men was (and still is) so stark as to render sexual penal offences, such as bigamy, prostitution and adultery, impotent.[17] The enactment of such laws, however, clearly facilitated the creation of the slur of 'loose women' on the conception of Ugandan womanhood.

Though English criminal law has undergone considerable amendment, the Ugandan body of criminal law remains largely unchanged from the 1930 model, in particular the offences related to sexuality. This means that many of the blatant, double sexual morality standards between men and women inherent in the sexual crimes starkly violate the constitutional provisions that recognise gender equality and non-discrimination.

The 1964 amendment of the penal code defined prostitutes as females. Although the law on prostitution was again amended in 1990 to define a prostitute in gender-neutral terms, womanhood continues to be firmly engrained on the body of a Ugandan prostitute and it remains an extremely gendered concept. The focus of the legislation against sex work focuses on the 'immorality' of women who engage in promiscuous sex. Indeed, in the penal code, prostitution is listed under the section 'Offences against Morality'. Through the law, the patriarchal state attempts to control promiscuous women and their deviant sexual acts. Further proof of this is the fact that the penal code limits culpability of this offence to the sellers of sex and not to the clients.[18] This reinforces the idea that sex outside marriage makes a woman a *malaya* (whore), but makes a man a 'real man'.

The important element of sex work is the indiscriminate character of women's sexual intercourse. The fact that the law equates female sexual promiscuity with prostitution is evidence that it is attempting to control female sexuality and maintain male control over women's bodies. In implementing the current law against sex work, the Ugandan police use both legal and extra-legal powers to abuse, harass and use violence against sex workers. A comprehensive search of the criminal court records revealed not a single prosecution, let alone conviction, of a prostitution charge. The law against sex work in Uganda is practically impossible to enforce and most law enforcement and judicial officers interviewed for this study described it as redundant. As one magistrate commented: 'It is very difficult to prove prostitution. Sexual intercourse and relations between consenting adults is not criminal so it is difficult to distinguish between "lovers" and a commercial sex transaction ... The law is simply not effective.'[19]

So in practice the law is used as a scarecrow by the patriarchal state to control women's sexuality. Because it is difficult to encounter a prostitute in 'the legal act' of prostitution, most sex workers are arbitrarily prosecuted for the offences of being 'idle and disorderly' or being 'rogues and vagabonds' (Section 167 and 168, penal code).[20] Another common and extraordinary charge levelled against sex workers by local government authorities is that of 'disturbing peace by using violent or scurrilous or abusive term of reproach'.[21] The law has become an instrument of harassment and abuse by the police. Most arrests are not pursued in courts of law.[22] Sex workers are forced to either buy their way out of jails or to succumb to rape by the people who are supposed to enforce the law against them.

There are three main types of sex work in Uganda. The first is street sex work. The second is indoor sex work, which includes a wide array of sites such as brothels, hotels and lodges, bars and clubs, residential homes and massage parlours. The third type is export sex work, whereby Ugandan sex workers ply their services in foreign lands such as Kenya, Dubai, China and Hong Kong. Both the expansion of sex work and state responses to its rapid growth point to the paradoxes and contradictions arising from Uganda's capitalist economy, its embattled patriarchy, globalisation and HIV/AIDS (White 1988, 1990; Davis 2000; Musisi 2001). In the next section, I report on findings through a demonstration of the forms that such paradoxes and contradictions take and the ways that sex workers interrogate Uganda's political economy.

Paradoxes of sex work and sexuality

The study of commercial sex must acknowledge and appreciate the complexities, depths and contradictions inherent in human interactions, needing a clear focus on the social and sexual discourses, both hegemonic and counter-hegemonic, in which sex work takes place in Uganda. By locating some of the paradoxes that crystallise when we analyse the operation of sex work, I hope to lay bare the multiple realities, intersections and disjunctures between and within gendered/classed sexualities.

Of *malayas* and *malaikas*

The ancient whore/madonna paradigm is alive and well in Uganda's patriarchal society. In local parlance the whore is *malaya* and the Madonna is *malaika*. The livelihood of a sex worker goes against the notions of femininity and domesticity for Ugandan women defined and constructed by the patriarchal society, culture, religion and the law. These institutions dictate who with, how and under what circumstances women are supposed to have sex. Patriarchal morality emphasises the need for 'decent women' to be chaste, modest and monogamous, but at the same time secretly desires 'immoral *malayas*'.

Erotic sexuality is constructed as a private and intimate issue and is shrouded in secrecy and taboos, yet when it is peddled in the public realm as work, it throws up challenges to the heteronormative notions of sex, gender and sexuality.[23] As one sex-worker participant stated: 'the most critical persons in this work are our clients. During the day they say one thing and at night they come for our services.'[24]

In an earlier study of a cultural/sexual initiation institution (the *ssenga*)[25] of the Baganda in Uganda, I reported that the basic message passed on to tutees is: 'Be a nice, humble wife, but turn into a *malaya* (prostitute) in your bedroom!' (Tamale 2005: 27) In other words, the performance of a demure and coy woman is only good outside the bedroom; this must be shed when she steps into the bedroom in order to have a healthy sexual relationship with her partner. In this sense ordinary Ugandan women are required to perform a version of femininity that is difficult to reconcile for its sheer perversity. The type of performance that sex workers engage in, on the other hand, is quite different: it is one of defiance and agency; one mostly driven by economic survival but which subverts and parodies patriarchy. The following observations by two Ugandan feminists sum it up very well:

> We are all prostitutes! A married woman is not in control of her sexuality... In order for her to satisfy her man, she must engage in prostitute-like behaviour. Moreover, if she needs a *gomesi* (traditional female outfit) or a car, it's through sexual satisfaction. Isn't that sex in exchange for material gain? Women will remain in a sad marriage for economic gains. So whether you're on the street or in the comfort of your home, we are all prostitutes![26]

> I view sex workers as bold women who do what they want to do. I respect women that have control over their sexuality; they determine when and where they'll exercise their bodies. But clients abuse them because their work is criminalised and perceived as a moral issue. It is the stigmatisation of the profession that makes it a problem. Many sex workers can negotiate safe sex, which is not available to your regular women, including wives.[27]

It is worth noting that regardless of whether a Ugandan woman conforms to the normative *malaika* image that society has constructed for her or defies it and becomes a *malaya*, she is not protected from violence at the hands of either her husband or her client. Ironically, law enforcement agents such as the police ignore violence inflicted by either perpetrator. In this sense, therefore, a sex worker is no more a victim of patriarchy than a wife is.

Notwithstanding, there is a further paradox in the response of organised women's groups to the issue of sex work. The mainstream women's movement in Uganda frowns upon prostitution and alienates women who engage in it or those who support it. Because women's sexuality outside the context of marriage is constructed as sinful and shameful, and because it is entangled with religion, morality and the law, sex work is a sticky issue for the women's movement to engage, and results in a studied avoidance of any critical discussion of the issue. Through Ugandan gender norms, 'good women' (*malaikas*) learn to suppress their sexual desires. Perhaps the relative sexual autonomy and freedom exhibited by sex workers is also a source of some degree of uneasiness and resentment on the part of mainstream women's rights activists.

Gender roles versus women's impoverishment

Women make up only 35 per cent of the waged workforce in Uganda and occupy the lowest-ranking and lowest-paying jobs (UBOS 2006: 34). Almost 68 per cent of female-headed households are also single-parent homes (UBOS 2006: 111). Females spend more than nine hours a day (compared to one for men) doing care labour activities (UBOS 2006: 35).

Women are the primary care providers in Ugandan society and operate in the context of gender discrimination in education, diminished employment opportunities in the structurally adjusted economy, widowhood, single motherhood, increased orphaning due to HIV/AIDS and armed conflicts – all of which drive women into sex work. Most women turn to sex work as the only available means of earning money and many hold very traditional family values, despite the stereotypes depicted in the media:

> Most of us have a side job to mask our involvement in the sex business … Many of us are Owino market vendors officially. Others have a stall in a shop on Luwum street. Some of us are married women. It is important to preserve the dignity of our family members. I don't want my child to be teased that your mother is a *malaya*.[28]

> I am a Muslim and go to the mosque regularly … But I have to do what I have to do in order to survive. I am the mother and father to my children. I have responsibilities.[29]

> I have been able to help my siblings since both my parents passed away and all the property was grabbed by our relatives.[30]

> I have built a house for my mother and invested in a big entertainment establishment in town … I have two expensive cars and I also look after some relatives.[31]

In her study of sex workers in South East Asia, Lisa Law (2000a: 4) observed: 'employment in the sex industry is only one facet of the lives of women who work there'. Similarly, the needs and aspirations of Ugandan sex workers are as ordinary as those of the average Ugandan woman. In my conversations with them, they spoke about their responsibilities as mothers, wives, caregivers, daughters, sisters, students, breadwinners and so on. Most of them enter the sex industry to fulfil these responsibilities. One of the most extraordinary things that I encountered in this study was the way women in this trade metamorphosed from the nocturnal 'sex work act' to looking extremely ordinary when off-duty. As the rather perplexed student research assistant recruited for this study remarked as we departed from our first focus group discussion: 'They are normal people!'

Sex workers put on a strategic performance, much like stage actresses, to achieve a specific goal (Goffman 1956; Butler 1990; Pullen 2005). Inherent in such shifting roles and identities is a nuanced and pragmatic form of agency. Depending on the time of day, opportunities, demands, resources and challenges that a sex worker encounters, her body moves in and out of the various roles that she fulfils. Indeed, the phenomenon of 'shifting identities' that most women are familiar with, such as from mother to wife to career woman, applies to sex workers in similar ways. The boundaries of personal ethics and morality that they draw for themselves constitute their self-actualisation.

There is an apparent disconnect between policy-makers, politicians and their constituents. One member of parliament opined: 'It [prostitution] is a disability of sorts and society should handle it as such.'[32] But Amongi, who paid for her university education through sex work, would vehemently disagree with such a view: 'I lost both my parents to HIV soon after my A-levels. I really had no choice but to sell my body in order to build a sound future for myself ... It was tough but I endured all the hardships until I graduated in 1999.'[33]

Reminiscent of the 1980s discourse on prostitution, there are currently many attempts by NGOs and religious-based organisations with an agenda to 'rescue' or 'rehabilitate' women from sex work.[34] They do this by offering sex workers micro-credit and/or vocational training, such as tailoring, hairdressing, knitting and weaving, and bookkeeping. But because such activities fetch very modest incomes, most trained sex workers invariably return to the industry. An official from one such NGO conceded that the success rate of these programmes was quite low: 'I can think of only three "success" stories; one is a hairdresser and the other one is currently working at our drop-in centre at Nakulabye ... The main problem we face is lack of funding ... women need credit, otherwise they'll stay on the streets.'[35]

Moreover, the fact that most interventions by NGOs are based on the stereotypical social inscriptions of sex workers' bodies (sinned, stigmatised, immoral, dirty, diseased), their prescriptions tend to be too maternalistic and do not tackle the real concerns of sex workers.

'Good' masculinity versus 'real man' masculinity

Analysis of sex work throws into bold relief the incongruence between the dominant Judaeo-Christian norms of heterosexual monogamous masculinity and the Ugandan traditional practices that valorise male promiscuity as a component of virility and competent masculinity. In Uganda, like elsewhere on the continent, active sexual lives and having multiple partners are central in the social repertoire of a powerful man. As people who transact in the business of sex, sex workers are integral in the construction of the idealised heterosexual masculinity in Uganda.

We were curious to find out whether the unequal gender relations in the wider society were replicated in the sex worker/client relationship. Given the fact that transactions take place in an underground economy, under conditions of patriarchy, we would expect the scales of power in the sale of sex to tip heavily in favour of the male buyers. Indeed, the fact that it is the male client who decides on whether or not to have sex with the commercial sex worker gives him some degree of power over her. Furthermore, the extensive evidence of violence against sex workers exposed in this study is a clear indicator of unequal power relations between clients and their customers.

Yet, the relations of power within gender systems in Uganda are not always adhered to for the entire duration of commercial sex encounters. The power dynamics are somewhat destabilised in the face of an active partner (the *malaya*), whose profession involves displaying sexual prowess and expertise. The leverage begins to kick in the reverse direction during price negotiations and the actual sex act, which are largely structured by the female sex worker (Plumridge, Chetwynd and Reed 1997: 228–43). She sets the boundaries of the encounter and even draws the lines in the power game (Izugbara 2005: 141–59):

> No fellatio, no anal sex for us, we do not want to damage our sphincter mus-
> cles! [laughter] [36]

> In our business there is no credit; it is strictly on cash basis. [37]

Hence, even though the work of women in the sex industry renders them vulnerable, through their transgressive activities they also wield some degree of power. Indeed, many times, their skills and experience inevitably subvert the dominant sexual male and subordinate sexual female construct. The paradoxical power dynamics between Ugandan sex workers and their customers are illustrated in the following excerpts from the study interviews:

> Yes, the fact that I seek out the prostitute and buy her services means that I am in control ... I must say though that contrary to common belief about commodifying the prostitute's body, whenever I am with a *malaya* it is me who feels like ... [pause] a commodity, with her telling me what to do and being totally in charge of the whole act ... You literally feel your power over her slipping with every passing minute and you tend to oblige, to kind of resign to fate and ... you know, to pleasure. [38]

> The first time I went to Katanga to buy a prostitute was when I was a university student. Um, I was so naive in these things [laughs] and basically wanted her to teach me the art of making love ... learnt a great deal and even now, whenever I'm with one, I let her take over the whole act ... I am the puppet, she's the puppet mistress and ... she's in total control ... and I love it. [39]

> There are times when I get hooked to a particular *malaya* and I'll keep going back; you know ... those that taste and feel like *akatiko* [mushroom] down under! But it will be strictly for business ... Moreover, they don't want a long relationship because they don't need a man to control them. [40]

> Some customers are very decent and treat you like a human being but many are rude and violent ... But let me tell you this, even the most brutal ones can become all mushy and sentimental on us, especially when you start working on them [laughs]. It's amazing what sex can do to a human being ... They become brutal again when you ask them for your money. [41]

> Most men are emotionally weak and they come to us for TLC [tender loving care]. They can talk, talk and go on about their personal lives, cry like babies ... We offer a listening ear and comfort them then they go back to their bickering wives. So, you can see that we *malayas* do in fact stabilize marriages [laughter]. That is a service that we offer but society overlooks it. [42]

The last quote points to the emotional effort or 'surface acting' (Hochschild 1983) that sex workers usually employ in their work. In fact the erotic performance and emotional manipulation that sex workers summon for their clients' pleasure is often taken for granted (Hochschild 1983; Hochschild and Ehrenreich 2003). Arlie Hochschild (1983) coined the term 'emotional labour' to highlight the commodification of human feelings in service work that requires customer/client communication.

Intimate care work forms a big part of the sex worker's scripted regulation of their emotions and feelings.

The see-saw of power relations during the commercial sex encounter underlies the complexity of gender relations in eroticised situations. As the contours of power are shifted and reconfigured at different points of the encounter, so are the levels of control that participating individuals wield over each other. In other words, the normative femininities of sex workers and the coherent masculinities of their male clients are destabilised at various points during the encounter. The encounter deconstructs the radical notion that views sex work as the quintessential practice of female exploitation and inequality.

Victims versus survivors

As in all patriarchal societies, gender-based violence is endemic in Uganda. We have seen in the preceding sub-section how the gender/power relations that exist in ordinary Ugandan women's day-to-day lives slide in and out of the sex worker/client relationship. At certain points the latter feels that his money can buy the very personhood of the sex worker:

> Some of them are so arrogant … I brought a *malaya* to my flat one night and laid a plastic protective sheet on the bed … don't want these girls' DNA on my bed! I couldn't believe it when the *malaya* questioned what I'd done, like she was above this and I was belittling her … Don't bring an attitude when you're a *malaya*; that's not part of the game. You've sold your body, what else is there for you?[43]

The contempt and disgust expressed by the male client quoted above is reflective of the extreme sexism and misogyny that exists in the sex industry. Paradoxically, he is willing to patronise and share very intimate and personal relations with a person he despises to such a degree. It calls to mind the desire for (and rape of) slaves by their white owners during the era of slavery in Europe and America.

Criminalisation of the trade increases significantly the vulnerability of women who engage in it. Sex workers in this study narrated gruesome experiences of violence at the hands of clients and/or potential clients. Streetwalkers and brothel workers are the most vulnerable to abuse:

> When I was arrested, raped and tortured it hardened me even more. Prison did not take away the problems that got me into prostitution in the first place. The experience just gave me the inspiration to devise new ways of survival in eluding the authorities.[44]

> Sometimes customers pay us to sleep with dogs, particularly *bazungu* (Caucasian) clients. They train their dogs to sleep with women.[45]

> One day a long-time and trusted client asked me to escort him on a visit to his rural-based mother. I accepted the invitation without hesitation. After

driving for over an hour, he stopped atop a lonely hill. When I asked where his mother was, he pointed to a big lizard in a small nearby cave ... He forced me to undress and had this reptile suckle at my breast. It was so disgusting and god knows what diseases we pick up from these animals.[46]

Being on the street is like being on the frontline of a battlefield ... You can get killed any time.[47]

One time a customer took me to his posh Kololo home and once we were inside the fenced compound and inside the house, he took out two bodies of a woman and a young girl and asked me to wash them ... I don't know maybe he wanted me to take away his *kisirani* (curse) or maybe it was some kind of ritual ... I was so scared and helpless.[48]

The ever-present threat of violence in the sex industry has led sex workers to hone their survival skills. One of the most effective ways that sex workers cope with the difficult conditions under which they work is by distinguishing, both conceptually and practically, the material body from the symbolic social spaces that their bodies occupy when they are working. Their bodies invariably have a public dimension but they also struggle to claim rights over their private sexual lives. Their resistance takes various forms, ranging from collaborating with lodge security guards, bartenders and street children to 'look out' for them or substance abuse to numb them from the humiliation and ostracism that they suffer, to using humour to deal with the pain and difficulty associated with their work.

The coping mechanisms and strategies developed by sex workers ensure that they endure and survive the various forms of discrimination and dehumanisation that they suffer. Working in groups bolsters their human capacity and well-being. Infused in these skills is the deployment of 'resistance identities' by sex workers in order to survive in a hostile working environment.

For most sex workers, prostitution is more than an economic activity; it is a lifestyle that offers a social network in a criminal subculture. People who engage in commercial sex often look out for each other and form alliances with other social outcasts, such as homeless street people and lodge operators. Such networks are crucial given the social vulnerability of most sex workers, occasioned by issues such as poverty, to all forms of violence, lack of access to healthcare, denial of their freedom of association and speech and so forth. At the same time, the othering and victimisation of sex workers hardens them: 'Society forgets that we are part of them. We have parents, relatives and friends ... Our clients are from the same society that despises us. My clients are men of status and responsibility.'[49]

Contrary to the popular image of sex workers as 'conveyers of disease' (Ministry of Health 2006: 56), most sex workers encountered in this study were extremely cautious about sexually transmitted diseases, particularly HIV/AIDS. Most insist that their clients use two condoms, one provided by themselves.[50] As one male client recounted: 'One time in the haste to wear a condom, I put it on the wrong way. You know ... inside out. I tried to turn it and wear it the correct way but she insisted that I put on another one. Those girls take no chances.'[51]

In brothels, sex workers do not take kindly to clients who request 'live sex' (unprotected sex). They are appalled at the behaviour of customers who are 'very careless with HIV'.[52] Most of them are enrolled in HIV/AIDS awareness programmes or support groups. This shows that, far from being the problem in the transmission of HIV transmission, sex workers are in fact part of the solution for curbing the pandemic.

Reinforcer of patriarchy versus potentially subversive activity

Sex work reinforces the way in which patriarchal society views and controls women, especially their sexuality, by underpinning the *malaika/malaya* dichotomy that it constructs. Wives are constructed as virginal creatures who are not related to sex for pleasure, except their husband's pleasure. They embody all the ideals of family and sex for procreation. *Malayas*, on the other hand, are constructed as the fallen women who do not get married, but with whom you can play out all sorts of fantasies – ranging from ones about sex simply for pleasure with no responsibility to provide a home, conversation or emotional support, to the truly sordid and debased where power can be played out in ways that would be unimaginable in polite, 'decent' society.

One of the male clients I interviewed confirmed this. When asked why he bought sex, he responded:

> Carnal instinct ... adrenaline rush ... She's not going to ask any questions. No ties ... You can have your way, cross certain boundaries of 'civilized' sexual relations that you have with your wife. Anything goes ... Sex toys, handcuffs, whip, creams, the bondage thing. It's really easier with the 'coalition of the willing'... I create a fantasy in my head and look for someone who will fulfil the fantasy.[53]

By focusing on pleasure (albeit men's), sex work pushes the normative maternalisation of women's bodies to the margins, thus challenging an important pillar of gender inequity.[54] It doubtlessly threatens the traditional notion of female maternalised sexuality. But sex work subverts and destabilises heteropatriarchy[55] in more ways. The politics that the Ugandan sex worker embodies is one that relates her body to struggle. Her subversive expressions of female sexuality strike at the foundations of the established order. Michel Foucault (1984: 83) theorised the human body as both an object of power and the site at which power is resisted (see also Grosz 1989).

By putting the spotlight on the body, sex workers challenge patriarchal gender norms. Law (2000: 9) focuses on the prostitute body as 'an object of power, as a site of resistance, as well as a site from which identity is constructed and performed'.[56] Dominant codes of morality dictate that a respectable Ugandan woman remains chaste and sexually monogamous, and sex workers transgress and breach every rule of the game. And they do so consciously: many sex workers who participated in this study simply rejected the stigmatised, deviant inscriptions that society imposes on their bodies. One said: 'I feel that it is right for me to do this work as it is my body and I cheat nobody in doing this work',[57] and another insisted: 'I don't feel like a sex object because I'm paid for rendering my service.'[58]

By snubbing the patriarchal-religious discourse that views them in negative terms, sex workers create their own positive reality. In fact, during the focus group discussions, we were told several stories of ex-*malayas* who had 'hooked' themselves rich male partners (especially white men) through sex work. This points to the agency (the capacity to make changes) through which sex workers, who might otherwise lead lives of despair, secure empowerment.[59] The survival of their families (both immediate and extended) and their education and shelter pivot on their work.

Other sites of sex workers' subversion include the physical spaces that they occupy – bars, streets, night clubs, brothels, hotels and massage parlours, among others. The way that they negotiate the surveilling authority of law enforcers is a lesson in female ingenuity and perseverance. The (criminalised) bodies of sex workers are thus forced to function in ways that outsmart the law. Furthermore, sex workers subvert spaces of elite businesses, conference venues and even religious crusades – the Sheraton Hotel, Serena Hotel, Grand Imperial Hotel, Nile Avenue and Speke Road in Kampala, and Mayfair Hotel, Amigo Babez, Main Street and Clive Road in Jinja – turning them into nocturnal sites of sexual desire and danger.

The hegemonic way of thinking that pegs women's sexual pleasure to coitus and penetrative sex is flouted by the nature of sex work. Female practitioners in the sex industry naturally explore a wide repertoire of sexual activities in order to meet the demands of their diverse clientele. Pleasure and sexual satisfaction are a performance for most sex workers on duty. These facts come as a shock to some clients, who come with a patriarchal mindset about female sexuality. One male client shared this anecdote:

> One of the most shocking experiences for me with prostitutes is … you know, when you're with somebody and after going with them for hours and you think you've really quenched their sexual thirst, then they freshen up and go right back on the street, peddling again. Man, it makes me feel somehow ineffective.[60]

Moreover, women who engage in sex work have refused to be trapped in the patriarchal, inhibitive language that stigmatises their work. In fact, language helps sex workers re-invent themselves through a more normalising discourse. They have moved away from the historical constructions of *malaya* and describe themselves and the terrain within which they work differently. The poem posted in graffiti on the wall of one of the brothels that is reproduced at the beginning of this essay is a good example of this. Popular stereotypes associate sex workers with sex, not love, but through graffiti these sex workers voice their lives, expressing their artistic feelings and emotions.

But even as they take charge of their lives, most participants in the study expressed a deep sense of hatred for the sex trade that they were involved in:

> I do this work, not because I like it but out of sheer desperation. I do it because I want my child to have a better life.[61]

> If somebody gave me some working capital to start a decent business, I'd leave this work without looking back. Sometimes, I feel so dehumanized that I sit and cry for hours on end.[62]

> There is no pride in this job ... I would not support decriminalising the work we do.[63]

This points, in part, to the limited opportunities and choices that women have in patriarchal, capitalist, underdeveloped economies. I have heard similar sentiments expressed by housemaids, barmaids, factory workers and even nurses. Despite the problems associated with sex work, it offers a relatively lucrative alternative to the low-skilled jobs that these women would otherwise qualify for. The participants' words further stress the stigma and violation of rights that criminalisation renders to commercial sex work.

Class differences in sex work

Despite the popular belief that all sex workers are needy, vulnerable individuals, there are obvious class-related differentials that exist in the Ugandan sex work industry. This study revealed an extremely variegated world of sex work that included 12-year-olds selling sex on the street to a very sophisticated set-up of call girls, charging hundreds of dollars. The stereotype that paints the sex worker as a poor, illiterate, non-skilled woman simply disregards the power and complexities associated with this profession. A study conducted by the NGO the Slum Aid Project, for example, described sex workers as disease-ridden, single mothers emanating from broken families who 'live in groups of three to ten sharing one room and all the basic necessities. It is common for them to share clothes, shoes and beddings. Their "houses" are tinny [sic] made of rusty iron roofs, with mud floors and walls' (Slum Aid Project 2002: 12).

Though many sex workers who operate from Kampala slums such as Kisenyi, Katanga, Kivulu and Bwaise, or Jinja slums such as Loco or Buwenda, would fit the profile depicted above, our own study encountered many sex workers who did not remotely match that stereotype.

High-class prostitutes, who operate from upscale bars and hotels or from their homes, are protected from police harassment, abuse and violence. On the other hand, street prostitutes and those working in slum brothels face the wrath of police brutality and the law. Moreover, the former have more leverage to negotiate safe sex, while the latter are more desperate and have fewer options. Trish provides escort services to rich men who telephone her whenever they need her services: 'I really don't care whether prostitution is legalised or not ... I do my business without any interference.'[64] Most sex workers whom we talked to did not share the class privileges that Trish does. So just as class mediates and brings meaning to the lives of ordinary women, so too does it underpin sex work.

Conclusion

The paradoxes highlighted above reveal that prostitution laws and policies are about the patriarchal state, sexism and classism, propped up by religious moralism. The oppositions set out in the essay surface the complexities surrounding sex work and explode the common and simplistic assumptions that mainstream society holds about sex workers. Transactional sex work is neither clearly liberating nor oppressive; it simultaneously offers both the opportunities of liberation or oppression, with a whole range of experiences and possibilities in between (Law 2000a).

The paradoxes, ambiguities and contradictions discussed in this study also have a significant impact on the relationship between sex workers and government, aid agencies as well as NGOs. Most times these bodies deal with sex workers in total oblivion to the complexities inherent in the lives of the latter. Their lives are often projected against a negative backdrop of immorality, disruption and disease. This partial understanding of the lives of sex workers leads to ineffective policies and rehabilitation programmes.

Most of the findings in this study are in line with the known 'hot spots' of feminist research and scholarship on sex work globally. By exploring the paradoxes and ambiguities of the lived everyday experiences of sex workers in the towns of Kampala and Jinja, this study has provided an alternative way to imagine sex work theory and practice (Law 2000a). In many ways sex workers transgress the bounds of the constructed Ugandan womanhood.

However, in addition to the Western concept of sex work as one form of work and/or an issue of human rights, commercial sex work in Uganda must also be situated within the broader context of underdeveloped economies in Africa. In the context of few education opportunities for women, staggering rates of unemployment, low incomes for farmers and unskilled workers and the extent of gender discrimination and oppression, many women are left with no choice but to engage in sex work. Despite this, it must be noted that the conditions under which Ugandan women enter the trade are highly variable.

The fact is that for most women in Uganda, sex work is neither a criminal nor a morality issue, but rather an economic one. It is economic survival (and therefore emancipating) for the women who engage in the profession. It is a form of work, engaged in primarily for economic and not moral reasons. It is the duty of the state to provide safe working conditions, free of violence and abuse, for all types of work – be it in the home, factory, office, market, bar, street or brothel.

The intersection between the criminalisation of commercial sex work and abortion in the context of extreme impoverishment and the HIV/AIDS scourge reveals the multiple oppressions of gender and class hierarchies. The women in this study revealed the hardships associated with their trade but most refused to author themselves as hapless victims. Through sex work, most are able to meet the basics of life for themselves and their families.

From the analysis of gender and sexuality, particularly commercial sex work, African feminists can draw up a progressive agenda. The movement for the decriminalisation of sex work must be launched within the radical women's movement as a subversive force against patriarchal control and oppression. Organised religion and its hypocritical moral code, which is so influential in the lives of the wider population in Africa, must be engaged with. Feminists should organise against the various fundamentalisms and institutionalised hypocrisy with corresponding meticulousness and thoroughness.

Notes

1. An earlier version of this essay was published in 2009 in the *East African Journal of Peace and Human Rights*, 15(1). Reprinted with permission. I wish to acknowledge with deep gratitude the support extended to me by Baxter Bakibinga and Rita Birungi in collecting data for this study. I also thank J. Oloka-Onyango who read through earlier drafts of this report and provided valuable suggestions and wise counsel.
2. In the most recent example of how the patriarchal state stifles the voices of sex workers, the Ugandan government banned a sub-regional workshop that was scheduled to take place in Entebbe on 26–28 March 2008. The organisers were forced to relocate the meeting, which ironically was to address issues concerning the rights of sex workers, to Mombasa, Kenya (*Saturday Vision* 2008).
3. In this chapter, I use the terms sex work and sex workers strategically to destigmatise the profession and the people engaged in it. Any reference to prostitute or prostitution here is in connection to the structured and stigmatised official uses of the terms.
4. Data collection and analysis of this study was primarily guided by feminist methods of research, which foreground the experiences of sex workers, as well as the meanings and interpretations that they attach to these experiences. Data gathering techniques included five focus group discussions and in-depth interviews with at least 30 female sex workers and six male informants who had interacted with and/or used the services of sex workers. A further 11 interviews were conducted with NGOs that deal with women's rights issues and/or managers of and bureaucrats associated with sex work. Informants were primarily identified using the 'snowball' sampling method.
5. Fenton Bresler (1998: 51) in his book, *Sex and the Law*, puts it bluntly: '[t]he simple truth is that from the beginning of time – and until the end of time – men have been going, and will continue to go, with prostitutes because they are seeking something which, for whatever reason, they cannot get elsewhere. It is such a primaeval need that the law has proved, and will always prove, powerless to control effectively.'
6. For examples of such scholars see Catharine MacKinnnon (1987), Andrea Dworkin (1993), Gayle Rubin (1984) and Carole Pateman (1988).
7. Note that this essay restricts its discussion to adult (hetero) sex work and does not include any arguments about trafficking for prostitution or child prostitution. Following intense lobbying by children's and women's rights activists, the Prevention of Trafficking in Persons Act was passed by the Ugandan parliament in 2009.
8. The African Growth and Opportunity Act (AGOA) is a 2000 US Trade Act with the aim of enhancing US market access to 38 sub-Saharan African countries.
9. Kampala is the cosmopolitan capital city of Uganda with a day-time population of about 2 million people. Jinja is the second largest commercial centre of the country and home to about 70,000 people. Both cities have a thriving night life that beckons sex workers.
10. Prior to that period, non-feminist theorisation of prostitution was based on reductionist arguments regarding male and female sexualities. The male sexual urge (which is supposedly greater than that of females) creates a demand for sexual gratification that might not always be met by women of the same social class, hence the willingness to pay for sexual gratification. For example, see Alfred Kinsey et al (1948) and Abraham Sion (1977).
11. *Aldona Malgorzata Jany v Staatssecretaris van Justitie* (2001) ECR I-8615.
12. Wolfenden Report, Cmnd 247 (HMSO, 1957), para. 226.
13. In Senegal prostitution was legalised through Law No. 66-21 dated 1 February 1966. The enforcement decree of this law, however, is contained in Decree No. 69-616 dated 20 May 1969 (Ndoye 1995).

14. Shaver identifies three types of 'sexual moralism': the overt Victorian moralism; the more covert moralism of contemporary crusaders and legislation hidden behind the nuisanced rhetoric; and the principled moralism of radical feminists.

15. See http://africansexworkeralliance.org/node/1, accessed 27 August 2010.

16. But while the British law focused on the public nuisance aspects – banning solicitation for the purpose of prostitution – in addition the Ugandan law criminalised the sale of sex for money.

17. Recently, the Ugandan women's movement has successfully challenged the double standards inherent in criminal adultery, which allowed it for husbands (excepting only sexual philanderers with other men's wives) but totally prohibited it for wives. See *Law and Advocacy for Women in Uganda v. Attorney General* (2007), Constitutional Petition Nos. 13/05 and 05/06.

18. The persecution of prostitutes is seen further in the Ugandan evidence legislation, which virtually condones the rape of prostitute women by allowing a man accused of rape to put up the defence of 'general immoral character' on the part of the woman in order to impeach her credibility. See section 153(d) of the Evidence Act (Cap 6).

19. His Worship Richard Ndangwa, Grade II Magistrate (2006), interview in City Hall, Kampala, 8 December.

20. Section 167(a) of the penal code provides: 'Any person who being a prostitute, behaves in a disorderly or indecent manner in any public place shall be deemed an idle and disorderly person, and is liable on conviction to imprisonment for seven years.'

21. Contrary to Rules 27(c) and 72 of the Urban Authorities Rules, Statutory Instrument 27–19.

22. This state of affairs is common elsewhere on the continent. In April 2009 the High Court of the Western Cape in South Africa interdicted the police from arresting sex workers unless it was with the intention to prosecute. See judgement in *The Sex Worker Education and Advocacy Taskforce (SWEAT) vs. The Minister of Safety and Security and Ors*. [Case No. 3378/07], http://www.lrc.org.za/lrc-in-the-news/934-sweat-#10, accessed 27 August 2010.

23. The concept of heteronormativity refers to the ideology that views heterosexuality as the normal and only legitimate socio-sexual arrangement of society (see Hennessy and Ingraham 1997).

24. Connie (aged 18–24) (2006), interview in Jinja, 12 December. All the names used in this essay are pseudonyms to protect the identity of participants.

25. *Ssenga* literally means paternal aunt. She performs the role of tutor to her nieces in a wide range of sexual matters, including pre-menarche practices, pre-marriage preparation, erotics and reproduction.

26. Action for Development (ACFODE) (2007), interview in Kampala, 16 May. The analogous proposition that a loveless marriage is no different from prostitution is not new. The German philosopher Kant argued that marriage amounted to a lease of the wife's sex organs (quoted in Bresler 1998: 55). Also see South African case of *S v Jordan* (2001) (10) BCLR 1055, discussed in Bonthuys and Monteiro (2004).

27. Akina Mama wa Afrika (2007), interview in Kampala, 16 May.

28. Focus group discussion (2006), Kiganda Zone, Kisenyi slum, 13 September.

29. Hadija (aged 18–24) (2006), interview in Kampala, 13 September 13.

30. Samali (aged 24–30) (2006), interview in Kampala, 8 December.

31. Trish (aged 24–30) (2006), interview in Kampala, 8 December.

32. Hon Richard Sebuliba-Mutumba (Member of Parliament Kawempe-South) (2006), interview in Kampala, 8 December.

33. Amongi (above 35) (2006), interview in Kampala, 7 October.

34. Such organisations include: Uganda Change Agents Associates (UCAA), Slum Aid Project (SAP), AMREF-Uganda, World Vision and Women at Work International (WAWI).

35. Ms Halima Namakula (WAWI) (2007), interview, 16 October. Also see AMREF (2001).

36. Focus group discussion (2006), with sex workers in Kisenyi, Kampala, 13 September.

37. Ibid.

38. Oola (over 35 years) (2007), interview in Kampala, 20 April.
39. Ibid.
40. Kunya (over 35 years) (2007), interview in Kampala, 16 April.
41. Alaso (above 35 years) (2006), interview in Kampala, 7 October.
42. Samali (aged 24–30) (2006), interview in Jinja, 8 December.
43. Phillip (over 35 years) (2007), interview in Kampala, 16 March.
44. Maria (aged 24–30) (2006), interview in Jinja, 13 December.
45. Focus group discussion (2006), with sex workers in Kisenyi, Kampala, 13 September.
46. Ibid.
47. Ibid.
48. Solome (aged 24–30) (2006), interview in Kampala, 6 December.
49. Aisha (aged 24–30) (2006), interview in Kampala, 11 December.
50. However, depending on how desperate a sex worker is, she may agree to have
    unprotected sex with a client for some additional payment.
51. Phillip (over 35 years) (2007), interview op cit.
52. Focus group discussion (2006). Kiganda zone, Kisenyi slum, 13 September.
53. Gregory (aged 31–35) (2007), interview in Kampala, 5 April.
54. Gender division of labour in Uganda assigns men the public, productive (remunerated)
    roles in the political and market sphere, while the private, reproductive (unremunerated)
    roles within the home and family are assigned to women.
55. That is, heteronormativity with patriarchy.
56. Also see Chapter 1.
57. Maria (aged 24–30) (2006), interview in Jinja, 13 December.
58. Sheeba (aged 18–24) (2006), interview in Jinja, 12 December.
59. Cf. Luise White (1990).
60. Sseti (aged 31–35) (2007), interview in Kampala, 5 April.
61. Hadija (aged 18–24) (2006), interview in Kampala, 13 September.
62. Nabirye (aged 31–35) (2006), interview in Jinja, 15 December.
63. Amongi (above 35) (2006), interview in Kampala, 7 October.
64. Trish (aged 24–30) (2006), interview in Kampala, 8 December.

References

Aderinto, Saheed (2006) 'Prostitution and urban social relations', in Tijani, Hakeem I. (ed)
    Nigeria's Urban History: Past and Present, Lanham, Maryland, University Press of America
AMREF (2001) 'Commercial sex workers' project annual report', Kampala, AMREF
Anarfi, John K. (1998) 'Ghanaian women and prostitution in Côte d'Ivoire', in Kempadoo,
    Kamala and Doezema, Jo (eds) *Global Sex Workers: Rights, Resistance, and Redefinition*, New
    York, Routledge
Arnott, Jayne (2006) 'SWEAT (Sex Worker Education and Advocacy Taskforce)', *Feminist
    Africa* 6: 88–90,
    http://www.sweat.org.za/, accessed 29 April 2007
Aronson, Gregg (2006) 'Seeking a consolidated feminist voice for prostitution in the US',
    Rutgers Journal of Law & Urban Policy 3: 357–85
Bakwesigha, C. (1982) 'Profiles of urban prostitution: A case study from Uganda', Nairobi,
    Kenya Literature Bureau
Barrett, Michele (1980) *Women's Oppression Today: Problems in Marxist Feminist Analysis*,
    London, Verso
Bell S. R. (1994) *Reading, Writing the Prostitute Body*, Indianapolis, Indiana University Press
Bentzon, Agnete, Hellum, Anne, Stewart, Julie, Ncube, Welshman and Agersnap, Torben
    (1998) *Pursuing Grounded Theory in Law: South–North Experiences in Developing Women's
    Law*, Harare, Mond Books
Bernstein, Elizabeth (1999) 'What's wrong with prostitution? What's tight with sex-work?
    Comparing markets in female sexual labour', *Hastings Women's Law Journal* 10(1): 91–119
Bonthuys, Elsje and Monteiro, Carla (2004) 'Sex for sale: the prostitute as businesswoman',
    South African Law Journal 121(3): 659–67

Bresler, Fenton (1988) *Sex and the Law*, London, Frederick Muller

Butler, Judith (1990) *Gender Trouble: Feminism and the Subversion of Identity*, New York, Routledge

Chan, Jason (2007) 'Decriminalization of prostitution in China', *New England Journal of International and Comparative Law* 13: 329–66

Davis, Paula (2000) 'On the sexuality of "town women" in Kampala', *Africa Today* 47(3/4): 29–60

D'Cunha, Jean (1991) *The Legalisation of Prostitution: A Sociological Inquiry into the Laws Relating to Prostitution in India and the West*, Bangalore, Bookmakers

Delacoste, Frederique and Alexander, Priscilla (eds) (1987) *Sex Work: Writings by Women in the Sex Industry*, San Francisco, Cleis Press

Dodillet, Susanne (2004) 'Cultural clash on prostitution: debates on prostitution in Germany and Sweden in the 1990s', paper presented at the 1st Global Conference on Sex and Sexuality, Salzburg, 14 October, http://www.inter-disciplinary.net/ci/sexuality/s1/Dodillet%20paper.pdf, accessed 29 April 2007

Dworkin, Andrea (1981) *Pornography: Men Possessing Women*, London, Women's Press

—— (1993) 'Prostitution and male supremacy', *Michigan Journal of Gender and Law* 1: 1–12

Farley, M. (2004) 'Bad for the body, bad for the heart: prostitution harms women even if legalised or decrimalised', *Violence Against Women* 10(10): 1087–1125

Foucault, Michel (1984) 'Nietzsche, genealogy, history', in Rabinow, Paul (ed) *The Foucault Reader*, New York, Random House

Gangoli, Geetanjali and Westmarland, Nicole (eds) (2006) *International Approaches to Prostitution: Law and Policy in Europe and Asia*, Bristol, Policy Press

—— (2006) 'Prostitution in India: laws, debates and responses', in Gangoli, G. and Westmarland, N. (eds) *International Approaches to Prostitution: Law and Policy in Europe and Asia*, Bristol, Policy Press

Goffman, Erving (1956) *The Presentation of Self in Everyday Life*, New York, Doubleday

Grosz, E. (1989) *Sexual Subversions: Three French Feminists*, Sydney, Allen and Unwin

Gutkind, Peter (1963) *The Royal Capital of Buganda: A Study of Internal Conflict and External Ambiguity*, The Hague, Mouton and Co

Harnández-Truyol, Berta and Larson, J. (2006) 'Sexual Labour and Human Rights', *Columbia Human Rights Law Review* 37: 391–445

Harrison, Rachel (1999) 'The Madonna and the whore: tensions in the characterisation of the prostitute by Thai female authors', in Jackson, P. and Cook, N. (eds) *Gender and Sexualities in Modern Thailand*, Bangkok, Silkworm Books

Hennessy, Rosemary and Ingraham, Chrys (eds) (1997) *Materialist Feminism: A Reader in Class, Difference and Women's Lives*, New York and London, Routledge

Hevener, Natalie (1986) 'An analysis of gender-based treaty law: contemporary developments in historical perspective', *Human Rights Quarterly* 8(1): 70–88

Hochschild, Arlie (1983) *The Managed Heart: Commercialisation of Human Feeling*, Berkeley, University of California Press

Hochschild, Arlie and Ehrenreich, Barbara (eds) (2003) *Global Woman: Nannies, Maids, and Sex Workers in the New Economy*, New York, Metropolitan Books

Homaifar, Nazaneen and Wasik, Suzan (2005) 'Interviews with Senegalese commercial sex trade workers and implications for social programming', *Health Care for Women International* 26: 118–33.

Izugbara, Otutubikey (2005) '"Ashawo suppose shine her eyes": female sex workers and sex work risks in Nigeria', *Health, Risk & Society* 7(2): 141–59

Jeffreys, Sheila (1997) *The Idea of Prostitution*, Victoria, Australia, Spinifex

Jenness, Valerie (1990) 'From sex as sin to sex as work: COYOTE and the reorganisation of prostitution as a social problem', *Social Problems* 37(3): 403–20

Kapiga, Saidi , Noel, S., Shao, J., Renjifo, B., Masenga, E., Kiwelu, I., Manongi, R., Fawzi, W. and Essex, E. (2002) 'HIV-1 epidemic among female bar and hotel workers in northern Tanzania: risk factors and opportunities for prevention', *Journal of Acquired Immune Deficiency Syndromes* 29(4): 409–17

Kempadoo, Kamala and Doezema, Jo (1998) *Global Sex Workers: Rights, Resistance, and Redefinition*, New York and London, Routledge

—— (1998) 'Introduction: globalising sex workers' rights', in Kempadoo, K. and Doezema, J. (eds) *Global Sex Workers: Rights, Resistance, and Redefinition*, New York, Routledge

Kinsey, Alfred, Pomeroy, W.B. and Martin, C.E. (1948) *Sexual Behaviour in the Human Male*, Philadelphia, W.B. Sanders

Kotiswaran, Prabha (2001) 'Preparing for civil disobedience: Indian sex workers and the law', *Boston College Third World Law Journal* 21(2): 161–242

Kuhn, Annette and Wolpe, AnnMarie (1978) 'Feminism and materialism', in Kuhn, A. and Wolpe, A.M. (eds) *Feminism and Materialism: Women and Modes of Production* , London, Routledge and Keagan Paul

Law, Lisa (2000a) *Sex Work in South East Asia: The Place of Desire in a Time of AIDS*, London, Routledge

Law, Sylvia (2000b) 'Commercial sex: beyond decriminalisation', *Southern California Law Review* 73: 523–610

Legal Assistance Centre (2002) 'Whose body is it? Commercial sex work and the law in Namibia, Windhoek', LAC, accessed 8 June 2007

Levick, Margaret (1996) 'A feminist critique of the prostitution/sex work debate: recommendations for legislative change in South Africa', unpublished dissertation, Institute of Criminology, University of Cape Town

Lorde, Audre (1984) 'Uses of the erotic: the erotic as power', in *Sister Outsider: Essays and Speeches*, New York, The Crossing Press

MacKinnnon, Catharine (1987) *Feminism Unmodified: Discourses on Life and Law*, Cambridge, MA, Harvard University Press

—— (1993) *Only Words*, Cambridge, MA, Harvard University Press

Maerov, Arnold (1965) 'Prostitution: a survey and review of 20 cases', *Psychiatric Quarterly* 39: 675–701

Ministry of Health (2006) 'Uganda: HIV/AIDS sero-behavioural survey, 2004–2005', Kampala, Ministry of Health

The Monitor (2006) 'Police arrest 84 over prostitution', 26 April

Morris, H. F. and Read, J. (1966) *Uganda: The Development of its Laws and Constitution*, London, Stevens and Sons

Musisi, Nakanyike (2001) 'Gender and the cultural construction of "bad women" in the development of Kampala-Kibuga 1900–1962', in Hogson, D. and McCurdy, S. (eds) *'Wicked' Women and the Reconfiguration of Gender in Africa*, Oxford, James Currey

Ndoye, Ibra (1995) *La prostitution au Sénégal*, Dakar, Senegal

New Vision (2009) 'Suspected idlers arrested in Fort Portal', 17 November

Obbo, Christine (1980) African Women: Their Struggle for Economic Independence, London, Zed Press

Olowu, 'Dejo (2006) 'Law reform: the promise of the New Zealand Prostitution Reform Act', *Alternative Law Journal* 31(2): 93–4

Omondi, Rose (2006) 'Gender and the political economy of sex tourism in Kenya's coastal resorts', unpublished paper presented at a Conference on Sexual Health and Rights, 19–21 June, Hilton Hotel, Nairobi, Kenya, accessed 29 April 2007

Overall, Christine (1992) 'What's wrong with prostitution? Evaluating sex work', *Signs* 17(4): 705–24

Parker, Richard (2001) 'Sexuality, culture, and power in HIV/AIDS research', *Annual Reviews in Anthropology* 30: 163–79

Pateman, Carole (1988) *The Sexual Contract*, Stanford, Stanford University Press

Pauw I. and Brener, L. (1997) 'Identifying factors which increase risk of HIV infection and mitigate against sustained safer sex practices among street sex workers in Cape Town', unpublished mimeo

Perkins, Roberta, Prestage, G., Sharp, R. and Lovejoy, F. (eds) (1994) *Sex Work and Sex Workers in Australia*, Sydney, University of NSW Press

Pheterson, Gail (ed) (1989*) A Vindication of the Rights of Whores*, Seattle, Seal Press

Plumridge, Elizabeth, Chetwynd, J. and Reed, A. (1997) 'Control and condoms in commercial sex: clients' perspectives', *Sociology of Health and Illness* 19(2): 228–43

Posel, Deborah (1993) 'The sex market in the inner city of Durban', occasional paper 28, Economic Research Unit, Durban, University of Natal

Potter, Kathleen, Martin, J. and Romans, S. (1999) 'Early developmental experiences of female sex workers: a comparative study', *Australian and New Zealand Journal of Psychiatry* 33(6): 935–40

Poulsen A-G., Aaby, P., Jensen, H. and Dias, F. (2000) 'Risk factors for HIV-2 seropositivity among older people in Guinea-Bissau: a search for the early history of HIV-2 infection', *Scandinavian Journal of Infectious Diseases* 32(2): 169–75

Pullen, Kirsten (2005) *Actresses and Whores: On Stage and in Society*, Cambridge, Cambridge University Press

Rubin, Gayle (1975) 'The traffic in women: notes on the "political economy" of sex', in Reiter, R. (ed) *Toward an Anthropology of Women*, New York, Monthly Review Press

—— (1984) 'Thinking sex: notes for a radical theory of the politics of sexuality,' in Carole Vance (ed) *Pleasure and Danger: Exploring Female Sexuality*, Boston, Routledge

Saengtienchai, Chanpen, Knodel, J., Vanlandingham, M. and Pramualratana, A. (1999) '"Prostitutes are better than lovers": wives' views on the extramarital sexual behaviour of Thai men', in Jackson, P. and Cook, N. (eds) *Gender and Sexualities in Modern Thailand*, Bangkok, Silkworm Books

Saturday Vision (2008) 'Government bans prostitutes' meeting', 22 March

Sex Workers Project (2003) *Revolving Door: An Analysis of Street-Based Prostitution in New York City*, New York, Sex Workers Project

—— (2005) *Behind Closed Doors: Bringing Sex Workers' Struggles into the Open*, New York, Sex Workers Project

Shaver, Frances (1985) 'Prostitution: a critical analysis of three policy approaches', *Canadian Public Policy* 11(3): 493–503

—— (1994) 'The regulation of prostitution: avoiding the morality traps', *Canadian Journal of Law and Society* 9(1): 123–45

Sion, Abraham (1977) *Prostitution and the Law*, London, Faber and Faber

Slum Aid Project (2002) 'Manual for working with commercial sex workers', Kampala, Slum Aid Project

Soderlund, Gretchen (2005) 'Running from the rescuers: New US crusades against sex trafficking and the rhetoric of abolition', *NWSA Journal* 17(3): 64–87

Southall, Aidan and Gutkind, P. (1957) *Townsmen in the Making: Kampala and Its Suburbs*, Kampala, East Africa Institute of Social Research

Ssewakiryanga, Richard (2002) 'Sex work and the identity question: a study on sex work in Kampala City', CBR Working Paper 75, Kampala, Centre for Basic Research

Svanström, Yvonne (2006) 'Prostitution in Sweden: debates and policies 1980–2004', in Gangoli, G. and Westmarland, N. (eds) *International Approaches to Prostitution: Law and Policy in Europe and Asia*, Bristol, Policy Press

Tamale, Sylvia (2005) 'Eroticism, sensuality and "women's secrets" among the Baganda: a critical analysis', *Feminist Africa* 5: 9–36

Tannenbaum, Nicola (1999) 'Buddhism, prostitution and sex: limits on the academic discourse on gender in Thailand', in Jackson, P. and Cook, N. (eds) *Gender and Sexualities in Modern Thailand*, Bangkok, Silkworm Books

Thomas, Lynn (2005) *Politics of the Womb: Women, Reproduction, and the State in Kenya*, Kampala, Fountain Publishers

Tinsman, Heidi (1992) 'Behind the sexual division of labour: connecting sex to capitalist production', *Yale Journal of International Law* 17: 241–48

Uganda AIDS Commission (2006) 'The Uganda HIV/AIDS Status Report, July 2004–December 2005', Kampala, Uganda AIDS Commission

Uganda Bureau of Statistics (UBOS) (2006) 'Uganda National Household Survey 2005/06 (UNHS): Report on the socio-economic module', Kampala, Uganda Bureau of Statistics

UNAIDS (2006) 'Senegal 2002 epidemiological fact sheet on HIV/AIDS and other sexually transmitted infections', http://data.unaids.org/pub/Report/2006/2006_country_progress_report_senegal_en.pdf, accessed 5 April 2007

Vanwesenbeeck, Ine (1994) *Prostitutes' Wellbeing and Risk*, Amsterdam, VU University Press

Varga, Christine A. (1997) 'The condom conundrum: barriers to condom use among commercial sex workers in Durban, South Africa', *African Journal of Reproductive Health* 1(1): 74–88

Walakira, Eddy (2004) 'Report on stigmatisation, harassment, exposure to HIV/AIDS/STIs: a situation analysis of sex workers in Uganda', Kampala, Lady Mermaid Bureau

White, Luise (1988) 'Domestic labour in a colonial city: prostitution in Nairobi, 1900–1952', in Stichter, S. and Parpart, J. (eds) *Patriarchy and Class: African Women in the Home and the Workforce*, Boulder, CO, Westview Press

—— (1990) *The Comforts of Home: Prostitution in Colonial Nairobi*, Chicago, University of Chicago Press

Wojcicki, Janet (1999) 'Race, class and sex: the politics of the decriminalisation of sex work', *Agenda* 42: 94–105

Wonders, Nancy and Michalowski, Raymond (2001) 'Bodies, borders, and sex tourism in a globalised world: a tale of two cities – Amsterdam and Havana', *Social Problems* 48(4): 545–71

11

Love, power and resilience[1] – life story

Daughtie Akoth

My name is Daughtie Akoth and I live in Mtwapa, Mombasa. I am 25 years old with a lovely five-year-old son, who I absolutely adore. I have several nicknames: 'Amarula Girl', because of my skin colour and 'Naughty Daughtie' because I am daring, wild and speak my mind. I love watching movies, especially Italian movies because I love Italian men. I like intellectual movies too and I love cartoons because they make me laugh. I am a fun-loving person and I am a very good mother. I dedicate my time to children at an orphanage where I volunteer, and I dream of one day having an orphanage for AIDS orphans. I am also a peer educator and I am HIV positive.

When people ask me who I am, I tell them that I am many things – a mother, sister, daughter, friend, woman, activist and so much more. Yes, I am a sex worker, but that is not who I am, it is just what I do. I'm a bundle of energy and expend that energy during sex (for pleasure) and when I do housework. I'm a neat freak!

Since I was a little girl, I always believed I was special. I am the third born in a family of four children. I lost my parents when I was 14 years old. I was always 'mama's girl' and so I went everywhere with her. My mother discovered she was HIV positive when my father died. She had a stroke when she found out. She died only six months later. But not before she had made sure that each of her children was placed with a relative and would be taken care of.

Most people say I look like my mum. Losing my parents at that young age was very difficult for me because that was an important stage in my life, when I needed to create a relationship with my parents. After they died, I took up the responsibility of being my own mother. Most orphans in Kenya end up abandoned, so I had to learn to love myself. I had also been forced to grow up very fast in the year prior to my parents' deaths. All my siblings were in boarding school so I was the only one at home to take care of them when they were sick. After they died, all of us were split up to live with various relatives. I went to live with an uncle in Nairobi when I was in Class 8.

I grew very close to my uncle because I was seeking love and attention. He was married but his wife was always busy and away, so we ended up spending a lot of time together. They had no child of their own so when I went to live with them, I was like their child. My mum had been raised by my uncle's mother. Since I wanted to know more about my mother, I felt that growing closer to my uncle would bring me closer to her. My uncle took advantage of my need for love and stripped me of my innocence. He raped me when I was 15 years old. I didn't know he was raping me because it was not the first time that he had touched me, so I thought it was normal. On many other occasions before that we would stay up late watching movies and he would play with my body. I was only 14 and mistook this for affection. There wasn't much sex education in school so I really didn't know what was going on. I also never had anyone to talk to about these things. I told a few friends about it and also wrote about it in my diary.

A few days after the rape I started having some abdominal pains so I asked my auntie to take me to the hospital. That is when I found out that I had contracted an infection – I had candidiasis. When we returned home that day, my aunt sat me down and asked where I had got the infection from. I didn't say anything.

I continued to write my stories in the diary that I kept under my mattress. It was my refuge. I remember writing about what had happened. It was like this secret I had and the only release was my diary. I blamed myself, my aunt for not being there, my parents for dying.

One day, I returned from school and found that my diary was missing. That night, my aunt called and said she wanted to talk to me. She wanted us to talk about sex, a topic she had never discussed with me before. I got evasive and she got angry. That was when she pulled out my diary and asked me to explain myself. She thought it was all in my imagination and wanted me to retract it. I told her it was the truth, but she refused to accept it, scolded me and then just acted as if nothing had happened. She continued travelling and my uncle continued to spoil me, buy me presents and have sexual relations with me.

I could see that my aunt had started withdrawing and there was growing tension in the house. She must have discussed the issue with her husband because his attitude towards me also started changing. This situation became unbearable for me and when I was in Form One, I didn't want to continue living in that house. They allowed me to go to Mombasa. I went to live with my sister, who was living with my aunt and her German husband. My aunt mistreated us by calling our parents all sorts of names. It wasn't really home, so after six months I left. I found another school – Koru Girls boarding school. At that age, the only important thing to me was getting my education, so that was what I focused on. My sister had completed high school and was staying at home; my aunt told her that she needed to start taking care of herself.

My aunt was a sex worker and she reasoned that we were women just like her and that we could take care of ourselves. She stopped paying my school fees. The funny thing is that she continued to pay for my older brother's education, and he is now a computer engineer. She is even still paying for my younger brother's education, so it was clearly a gender issue.

Whenever my aunt would go abroad, she would lock up her house without any warning and wouldn't care what happened to us. That was when my sister got into sex work. She had friends in the industry that made a lot of money. One of her friends was paying her own school fees and had a house. She would tell my sister that she could do sex work and pay her way through school and also have things she wanted.

So, when my aunt abandoned us to join her husband in Germany, my sister started working the streets and I eventually joined her. We really didn't have a choice. We were so desperate that we would have just one meal a day and sometimes even went days without eating. At that point, I was not doing sex work as a profession; I was doing it to meet my most basic needs. My sister didn't force me into sex work. She left the choice to me because she knew education was better.

I can't really remember my first client. I remember going on a double date with my sister. It was very awkward to have someone I didn't know putting their hands all over me. It's like taking mud and putting it on a white shirt! Eventually, after having a couple of clients though, I got used to it. I learned that I had to play nice even when I was not in the mood. It was not about sexual pleasure; it was about food and money at the end of the day.

I am a very resilient person – there is something in me that just helps me bounce back from difficult situations. So when I was out there working, thinking that all I needed was a plastic smile to get me a client and some food, I was able to do it. At that point, I hadn't got my son, so it was easier for me. Now that I have a son that depends on me for shelter, education, clothing and everything else, I feel I have the responsibility and the power to offer him the best life that I can. So when I think that the only price I have to pay is a smile to be able to provide him, and avoid constantly worrying about supporting him, I am able to do it. Whatever price I have to pay to have a good life and to offer a good life to my son, I will do it.

My son is five years old now and we have a very close relationship. I met his father randomly almost ten years ago. He was 11 years older than me and at first he was a client, but with time I discovered that he was a very caring person and we started dating. We moved in together and were practically married for five years. As in any relationship, we had our ups and downs, and sometimes we would have very intense fights. We had a serious disagreement one time and I decided to run to my sister in Nairobi for a while. That was when I discovered that I was pregnant.

When I shared the news of the pregnancy with my boyfriend, he was very happy, but at the same time there was a deep sadness in his eyes. He had been in and out of hospital for a while, but I didn't know what he was suffering from. While I was in Nairobi he got tested and found out that he had AIDS. I took the news courageously and got myself tested as well. That was the day I found out that I was HIV positive. He was one of the very first clients that I had, so he knew that he was the one who had infected me.

Initially he thought I would leave him, but I told him it was OK. I had lost my parents to HIV and I didn't want to spread the disease so I wanted us to stay together. I was actually the one who was encouraging him, even though I had just found out and was dealing with my own fears. I realised I couldn't undo the situation though, so I just had to pick myself up and move on. Two months later, my boyfriend died. It was the 12 August 2004. I was with him throughout his last days.

I was just two months pregnant when my boyfriend died. I contemplated an abortion. His family came and took everything we owned from the house and left me with nothing. During the grieving period, we didn't really talk much, but I was always there. He had a huge family and people wanted to know who I was, so some of his family members would introduce me as his widow. His mother, however, refused to acknowledge me and said I was not married.

After the burial, when I returned home, I discovered that they had broken into the house and taken everything. I tried to confront them but that was when they started telling me that I was a prostitute and that I was the one who had infected their son with HIV. They were accusing me of killing him. I think they were grieving and just needed to find someone to blame. Once again, I was on my own, so I turned to my two sisters and a few friends who supported me.

My doctor had advised me against breastfeeding and I was disappointed because I had been told that that was the best way to bond with your child. When I had my son, I resisted the temptation. Fortunately, I was able to build such a close relationship with him, that I think we are even closer than mothers who breastfeed. But life was very difficult for me. I moved into a house where a group of five or six single mothers lived. This is where I got the support and encouragement I needed to maintain a positive attitude. I would watch them and realised that even when they were really frustrated, they would look at peace when they were with their children. I wanted to build a strong relationship with another human being, so I made a commitment to do that with my baby. This is the kind of relationship I have with my son now. Even when things are extremely difficult, he somehow lifts some of the weight off my shoulders.

Sex work has different faces. I've spent ten years in the sex work industry, so I have seen and experienced a lot. Through sex work, I have been able to meet celebrities and diplomats. I have clients who have treated me very well, and taken me to fancy restaurants and hotels. There are certain clients who just want you to listen. Some of these men are frustrated in their marriages, have not slept with their wives and just need someone to let off steam with. That is why sometimes I call myself a sex therapist. These relationships are beyond the sex. People might still see me as a sex worker when I'm hanging out with them, but these are people I now know very well and who play an active role in my life.

And of course, there is the money. I can earn more money in one session than I would in a lifetime if I was doing something else. Sex work is like any other work. A married woman who is a housewife and depends on a man that she doesn't love to provide everything she needs, isn't that also sex work?

My son does not yet know that I am a sex worker. When he gets older, I want to tell him what I'm doing, even though I'm not planning to do sex work much longer. You can never really be out of sex work though, because money is never enough. I want my son to respect women, whether they are sex workers or not. That is why I am going to tell him that I am or was a sex worker. Some of the men who abuse sex workers were actually abused when they were young, so they don't appreciate women and try to degrade them. I am raising my son in an open-mind environment. He is in a public school so other kids might find out about me. Their parents might talk about me and him, and I want him to be able to stand by me. He is my source of strength – everything I do, I do for him.

I am not ashamed of what I do because it has enabled me to provide a good life for my son, which is less than I can say for many other poor, young mothers in Kenya. This morning, for example, I went to pick up a lady to come and do my laundry. This woman has young children who are not in school despite the fact that there is free primary education in Kenya. All she has to do is buy them school uniforms, but she says she can't afford it. When people don't know that their *nyeti* (vagina) is power, they lose out a lot. This woman can even provide these services to her husband and demand that he pays for the family's basic needs.

The lowest that I have earned was 400 Kenya shillings ($5). We had picked up a group of Italian cabin crew members, so we naturally assumed that we would get good money. We didn't negotiate our rates beforehand, so after the sex, when I got 400 bob, I was really shocked and angry. There was an exchange of words, but there was little we could do as we were not in our own territory. We had been snuck into their hotel, so they could easily have called security and had us arrested. I took this as a learning experience. These days I never go with clients to their hotels. I choose the places where we go, and I never go to my house with them, so I make sure I always have the upper hand. I also make sure I know at least one person in the hotels, lodges or clubs where we go.

The highest I have ever been paid was 20,000 Kenya shillings [about US$270] by a client who told me that it was the first time that he'd ever had a blow job and cum. It was quite an achievement for me to get 20,000 for a blow job. I now have an imaginary wall called Daughtie's wall. So many clients have told me that I give the best blow jobs, so I usually ask them to rate me and if they rate me high, I write their name on Daughtie's wall. I have between 20 and 40 names on this wall now.

The sex industry is really what you make it. I have had clients who've made absurd requests like anal sex or group sex. I've never consented to any of these, because I'm not comfortable in such situations. The risk of HIV and STI infection is also higher with these kinds of sexual practices. There's always a concern about the other person's health status. It is very easy to use protection when you are just two people, but when you are a group, interacting under the influence of alcohol as is usually the case, it gets very messy and risky. I also consider the issue of re-infection and because I don't want to get any other strains of the virus, I stay away from such activities.

Sex is an act that is in the Bible, and almost everybody does it but they don't do it openly. So, the fact that sex workers do it in the open is seen as wrong. We are accused of destroying the sanctity of sex as it was meant to be in the Bible – private, within marriage and solely for purposes of procreation. Sex workers are therefore considered immoral. I argue, however, that sex is an act between two consenting adults and there is absolutely nothing wrong with it, whether there is a financial transaction or not. After all, even wives get gifts from their husbands.

These days I don't even need to negotiate prices with my clients because I have been meeting and transacting with clients of a high social class. These men just end up paying me really well, so I don't even have to ask for it. Some of them even give me money without me having to have sex with them. When I am in financial trouble, I can even call some of them and tell them I need money and they don't even have to ask me for a sexual favour because we have an understanding and they are able to offer me that financial support.

So when so-called feminists say that sex workers are victims, that we are being expoited by men and that we are not in control of our lives, I tell them some of the times I have felt most powerful in my life, have been when I was doing sex work. Whenever I get an opportunity to negotiate the price, protection and choose my client, in that moment, the ball is in my court and I have the power. The situation is under my control so I don't feel that I am being taken advantage of by these men. I am the one offering the services, so I take the bull by its horn.

When I meet a guy who tells me, 'I will pay you 500 shillings' for a blow job, you know what I say to him? I say, 'You can give that money to your girlfriend or your wife!' But many know that their girlfriends or wives will not consent to a blow job, so I tell them my price and tell them they can either take it or leave it. This is how I remain in control. The first thing a sex worker has to do is create her own face. Many sex workers have a low self-esteem and they look at themselves as society does – a body with no face. As sex workers, we therefore need to create the face so that our clients can start to look at us as human beings.

I'm very sexual and embrace my sexuality, but I don't want anyone to objectify and degrade me. One of the things that helps me accept my sexuality is that I love myself. Sex is a broad area – there are so many acts of sex – kissing, French kissing, blow jobs, touching, etc. There are times when I just want to let go and lose all the energy that is inside me … move from human to animal. I am the sort of person who has explored my sexuality. I love my sexuality. I would rather explore it now than wait until I am older. I am comfortable with my sexuality because I know what I am comfortable with and what I am not, so I feel free to do whatever I want.

I don't know if I am bisexual but there are certain women that I look at and immediately get turned on, so I have had sex with a woman and I am comfortable with it. That doesn't necessarily mean I'm gay, but these are things about myself that I acknowledge and embrace. I truly believe that there's a little gay in every-one. Unfortunately, many of the gay and lesbian sex workers in Kenya are afraid to accept their sexuality so they hide it, even if they are having sex with people of the same sex. They haven't accepted the fact that this is part of who they are and that it is OK.

I love to love and be loved. Relationships are pretty important to me, whether it is with men I am romantically involved with, or my friends. I don't know if there's something about me that makes my clients want to have more with me than just sex for money. I don't just accept all clients and get into relationships with them, but right now there are three men in my life that I am having serious relationships with. I have spent a lot of time with one of these men. I have shared everything about my life with this person. He understands me and I understand him. He is the kind of person that whatever I am going through, no matter how late in the night, I can feel free to call him, and if he can help me, he will. If he can't help, he'll just be there to listen to me. He is a married man, but he is there for me always. This is what intimacy means to me.

I have never gotten into drugs, but I use alcohol occasionally, especially when I am meeting a client for the first time. The alcohol helps me relax and eases some of the tension, but I have never had alcohol abuse problems. I do not do drugs because I have seen what they can do. I actually lost a friend last year who was also a sex worker who had a serious cocaine addiction problem. I have a lot of information about the consequences of drug abuse, so I stay away.

I also think about what would happen to my son if I ended up getting addicted to drugs. I know my sister would take care of him in the event that I am not here, but she is in a bumpy marriage with an abusive man, and I have seen what this environment is doing to her son. Sometimes her son gets depressed and I would never want this to happen to my kid. As much as I would like my son to have a father figure, when I look at what my nephew is going through it makes me really sad because these are things that children should not be exposed to. So even though I am HIV positive, I want to be here for as long as possible and I want to be able to take care of my son, at least until the point that he can take care of himself.

Sex worker organising is also very critical to me. When you share experiences with others in the same profession, you are assured that you're not alone. We need to be able to stand and speak for ourselves and not have others speak on our behalf. Empowerment to me therefore means letting sex workers speak for themselves. A highlight for me was the first African sex worker conference in February 2008 in South Africa. I was a key facilitator at that conference and even read out the press statement to an audience of more than 150 people. It was a high point because I've been in the industry and I know the good and the bad side of it. Most girls didn't want to do interviews. There was an issue of security and identity and some people didn't want to take that risk. But I did … I'm not a spectator. The press in South Africa the next day had headlines calling me 'Dotty, the naughty girl from Kenya'.

For sex workers to be part of the women's movement, we need to get rid of the distinction between 'us' and 'them'. There are women's organisations that are against abortion, sex work and lesbians, so they tend to exclude anyone that they don't agree with. If we are really committed to movement-building, then we should all be under the umbrella of the women's movement. This is why I keep saying, 'I am not just a sex worker. I am someone's sister, wife, mother and friend.' I am everything that other women can be.

I don't want to be called any name. I just want to be called by my name. I get hurt when I get labelled. Nobody has the right to call me anything because they really don't know who I am. I have been called a witch once by a client's wife who found out that I was seeing her husband. I would rather she called me a prostitute. Instead she claimed I had bewitched her husband because he was always day-dreaming about me. This really hurt me.

I would like to see an East African sex workers movement. There's all this talk of sex worker rights and decriminalisation, but one country can't do it alone. When sex workers in Uganda talk about how their government is tough on them, we, the Kenyan sex workers, feel fortunate that we have a bit more freedom. But we don't want sex workers in one country to be more oppressed than in any other country. We need to speak as one voice in the three countries and fight for the same rights. If we're just sex worker groups in different countries shouting, no one will take us seriously. But if we're a movement, we shall truly be a force to reckon with.

I am now working with the Africa Sex Worker Alliance, where I have just been hired as the country coordinator for Kenya. I will be in charge of coordinating several activities this year. We will be training sex workers as peer educators and not only train them in sexual and reproductive health issues, but also include human rights issues. We are going to train sex worker activists as human rights defenders and paralegals. I am really excited about the job. It is a lot of work, but it is good work. With this job, I actually don't even have to do sex work if I don't want to. I work three days a week and receive a good salary. I get to spend quality time with my son, and I am able to dedicate time to my studies.

When things get really difficult, I just remind myself that bad things may happen along the way, but it is all just a part of life. I can't just sit and whine, so if I don't like a situation, I try as much as possible to change it. Sometimes I surprise myself and even today, I realise that there are parts of me that I am yet to discover.

Note

1. First published in Zawadi Nyong'o (ed) (2010) *When I Dare to be Powerful: On the Road to a Sexual Rights Movement in East Africa*, Kampala, Akina Mama wa Afrika. Reprinted with permission.

12

African LGBTI declaration

As Africans, we all have infinite potential. We stand for an African revolution which encompasses the demand for a re-imagination of our lives outside neo-colonial categories of identity and power. For centuries, we have faced control through structures, systems and individuals who disappear our existence as people with agency, courage, creativity, and economic and political authority.

As Africans, we stand for the celebration of our complexities and we are committed to ways of being which allow for self-determination at all levels of our sexual, social, political and economic lives. The possibilities are endless. We need economic justice; we need to claim and redistribute power; we need to eradicate violence; we need to redistribute land; we need gender justice; we need environmental justice; we need erotic justice; we need racial and ethnic justice; we need rightful access to affirming and responsive institutions, services and spaces; overall we need total liberation.

We are specifically committed to the transformation of the politics of sexuality in our contexts. As long as African LGBTI people are oppressed, the whole of Africa is oppressed.

This vision demands that we commit ourselves to:

- Reclaiming and sharing our stories (past and present), our lived realities, our contributions to society and our hopes for the future.

- Strengthening ourselves and our organisations, deepening our links and understanding of our communities, building principled alliances, and actively contributing towards the revolution.

- Challenging all legal systems and practices, which either currently criminalise or seek to reinforce the criminalisation of LGBTI people, organisations, knowledge creation, sexual self-expression and movement-building.

- Challenging state support for oppressive sexual, gendered, discriminatory norms, legal and political structures and cultural systems.

- Strengthening the bonds of respect, cooperation, passion, and solidarity between LGBTI people, in our complexities, differences and diverse contexts. This includes respecting and celebrating our multiple ways of being, self-expression and languages.

- Contributing to the social and political recognition that sexuality, pleasure, and the erotic are part of our common humanity.

- Placing ourselves proactively within all movement-building supportive of our vision.

18 April 2010, Nairobi, Kenya

13

Two kinds of blue

Connie Mutua

Baby!
Wanna talk?
Bring on the beer
Let's brew candlelight magic.
Here baby!
By the street lamps
I get off on the talk
–Ugh! Man. No!
Only the best sidewalk fever
Want a lover, wife-a high?
Only 50 kalas
I kiss you
Make you my man
Ten minutes before the sunrise.

14

A night in Zanzibar – life story

Jessica Horn

> Oh my body, make of me a [wo]man who always asks questions.
>
> Frantz Fanon – *Black Skin, White Masks*

It was a balmy evening at Mercury's, the beachside restaurant named after the famous lead singer from Queen. I was in Zanzibar for a meeting of African feminists and this was our celebration meal – a buffet of exquisite food and the Indian Ocean stretched all around us, embroidered with memories of dhows and aromatic spices.

A group of local musicians arrived. They set up their instruments on the sand, and the men started to press their toughened brown hands to the warm, stretched hide. Two women had accompanied them, draped in their black *buibuis*.[1] They stood indifferently at the side of the drummers, observing us and ingesting the drums' song. As the rhythm gathered force the women threw off their veils, tied *kangas* around their hips, and began to dance towards us all on the sand, hips moving in agile figure eights along the contours of sound.

The dancers challenged us to join them. But many of us, defiant in our politics yet shy in our bodily expressions, feigned misunderstanding. Finally, one of us submitted to the call, wrapped her scarf around her hips, and entered the dancer's game with the dextrous movements of a woman raised in post-independence Kinshasa. She danced and we stared, entranced.

I was sitting at the edge of the sandy dance floor. As I watched, one of the dancers moved towards me, beckoning me to dance with a mischievous glare in her eyes. Caught off guard, I felt like I had no choice. I stood up and allowed the rhythm to play its game. She was dancing in front of me, and began to move closer and closer until our bodies almost touched. Then she suddenly raised her palm and pushed me backwards, forcing me to kneel with my back flat on the sand as she straddled my body and began to increase the speed and ferocity of her movements, back undulating and hips moving in wizardly circles around my pelvis. I later learned that the on-looking waiters saw this as a sexual provocation. But in that moment I knew that while she expressed herself in the physical movements of sex, it was probably not an invitation to love. It felt like a declaration of war. And I was losing.

As the drums reached a crescendo, the woman laid the final blow with a contraction of her thighs, stood up triumphant, and turned her back to me as she walked nonchalantly across the sand. Although duly humbled, I marvelled at the sheer irreverence of her bodily articulations, at her disinterest in the audience and her absolute confidence in her power to conquer and overthrow with swift movements of her hips.

Walking back to the hotel that night I laughed a riotous laugh in my head. I laughed at the ironies, the stereotypes blown from their fragile cages. I laughed at the strength of our belief in the supposed 'limits' of a veiled woman's sexuality and her capacity for self-expression. I laughed at our careless associations between adornment and desire, our assumptions about subaltern women, the myth of the impotence of our sensuality and the realities of the force of eros, not simply as a sexual force, but as form of power. How naive we are to attempt to straightjacket our bodily expressions as Africans with phrases that begin 'African women do not' or 'African women aren't'. We are so much poorer for not embracing our endless capacity to innovate and create meaning through our bodies.

That night I penned this poem, an homage to the unceasing power of African women to subvert and reinterpret within, and well beyond, the veil of social norms:

Woman, rise!

Glide
the figure eight
across these Mnyarwanda hips
these Mswahili
   Mswazi
Ashanti
   Xhosa
ride
the slow flex
and turn
mould and
build
breeeeaaaaaaaathe
and
transform
the rhythmic rebirth
of Africa's daughters

Mwalimu, Madiba
Lumumba, Nkrumah
asanteni sana!
but it is our turn now....

Incandescent butterfly woman
and river spirit
rise!
impala and ocean mother
rise!
story teller, basket weaver,
yam seller
rise!

mama, dada,
mother, sister
rise!

sister comrade sister fighter
sister lover sister friend
rise!

sister comrade sister fighter
sister lover sister friend
rise!

Woman
rise!

Note

1. The *buibui* is a form of the Muslim veil worn by Swahili women.

15

False memory[1]

Jumoke Verissimo

This my aging delight…
Of birth
    Of worth
        Of earth
            Of a strung
                Lamentation…

Of birth
    I share ache and unnumbered hours
of worth
    I bear fake seconds of ecstasy
Of earth
    I dare a stake to endless calamities

I am war…

War that makes the world go bland.
Housing utopia as dystopia, and
in thin slits creating jealousy,
housing subjugation, and
rearing servitude into advantages?

I am *the* thing.
The memory that clothes
erections into digressions; I break
rigidity into involuntary flaccidity.

I, the receiver,
the container, the abuse-donor

I, language of forced patience,
the torture; the unsolved equation

the joy of grated freedom, the
anger in a platter of condescension

I have earned contraceptive freedom
I stand apart from wholeness.

Maker (are you there?)

There is haggling over
my existence

a pen
is rewriting my ambitions

a vain pro/test
against my resolutions

Maker (are you there?)
Is there a mistake?

Does variance mean disparity?

I am memory

Note

1. This poem first appeared in Jumoke Verissimo (2009) *I Am Memory*, Lagos, Dada Books.
   Reproduced with permission.

16

Dear Diary[1]

Lindiwe Nkutha

Monday 8 May 2006[2]
Today is a sad day in my life. Not in mine alone, in a lot of other people's too, I'm sure, some for different reasons no doubt, but some, I suspect for the same reason as me. Today also marks the last day of our relationship. I am afraid I can't write in you anymore, without risking incriminating myself. Who knows in whose hands these pages might one day end up? And who knows what unreasonable deductions they may seek to make about me, after leafing through you.

I am afraid I can no longer share my innermost thoughts with you. Not my joys either, or my traumas, or my nightmares borne of my past and present. I'm afraid I can no longer come to you at the end of a harrowing day, to tell you, in that honest and sincere way, I seem able to tell only you. I'm afraid that if I should ever get raped, again, and cry wolf (because there really is one), they might make you admissible evidence, and that you might just contribute to my downfall. It's not because I don't love you anymore. Not that you have not provided an outlet for my frustrations and emotional turmoil. If there's anyone who knows all my highs and lows, it is you. It's just that this place that I love with all my heart has made it somewhat unsafe for us to carry on. But I thought it would be unfair if I left without telling you, the best I know how, the reasons why I have to pack away my commas and exclamation marks. I hope you understand.

> Today I woke up in a place that said to me be free
> so long as I kept my mouth shut and made no
> demands that my freedom actually be taken seriously
>
> I woke up in a place that said be what you want to be
> so long as what I wanted to be did not include
> me being a woman who wears a *kanga*,
> has a history of mental illness
> is prone to forgetting
> or has in the past been raped

I woke up to a dream, and I realised that I am stronger than I was
yesterday
but this dream rapidly turned into a nightmare
right in front of my eyes as I began to see
that I had in fact been rendered much weaker than I was,
just yesterday

I woke up in a place where it's the size of your heart that counts not
your fists
and realised that no matter how big my heart was,
these fists would continue to find a landing pad on my face
and that if I am to survive, I needed to pack a punch in mine.

Because yesterday I was digging for gold, and today I am wearing it
on my wrists, around my ankles, across my heart
it shackles my every step,
because now it is expected that I wear my chains with pride,
in line with the dictates of my culture
Yesterday I was burning with frustration; today I am growing big business
and this business of growing ever more sick and tired fuels my anxiety

I woke up and realised that I don't need a gun to make you listen
because the one that hangs from your crotch
isbhamu somdoko as you call it, is more potent
and if that does not make me listen, what else will?

And even if I have nothing, this place can give me everything
on condition that I give it in return every inch of my entire being,
until I am left in the end with much less than what I had when I
started.

All I need do is believe
in nothing, because nothing much is worth believing in anymore
not the comfort in the knowledge that my elders will not hurt me
not the comfort in the fact that if they do the law will protect me
just the ugly reality, that depending on how it's spun
every sexual act I am forced to engage in,
no matter how many times I say no
will be construed as having being consensual

Today I woke up in a place whose cheering can be heard on the other
side of the world
but whose screams land on deaf ears inside my home
A place where my brother is my brother no matter what
and my sister is someone who does not matter, no matter what

Today I woke up in a place that flows with courage
but drowns under showers of cowardice
That laughs,
at me often
that's cried
sometimes with me, (well only a handful)
that says it's okay
go ahead do to her what you please
we will find something in her history
to make her allegations sound like a fairy tale

Today I woke up in a place that sings with hope to the rest of the world
but mutters despair to itself
And I smiled because
well because this morning left me a tad haggard,
and smile to stave off my tears is all I can do sometimes
when I'm feeling like this, besides I hear,
South Africans are creating a new dawn everyday
oh how I wish this dawn would cast its rays my direction too.

Today I woke up in South Africa
and so help me I am never ever going back to sleep
lest those who relish in plotting against me should
devise more schemes while I slumber
lest I miss in my sleep a chance to be part of a legion
that will create for myself, my sisters, my aunts, my mothers, my
daughters
a solid string of incandescent dawns that are truly
Alive with possibility
Unlike the one I woke up to today
that seems to me to be languishing in a state of atrophy.

So you see why this full stop I am about to write has to be my last, from now on I
am holding inside me everything I otherwise would have shared with you, so long.

Notes

1. This chapter was first published in Pambazuka News (2006), no. 254, 11 May. Reprinted
   with permission.
2. This is the day that the Johannesburg high court handed down the judgment in the
   highly publicised Jacob Zuma rape case. Former South African deputy president Zuma
   (and current president) was acquitted of the rape charges.

17

EXPLAIN[1]

Hakima Abbas

To Eudy and Girly and all the sisters whose flame was cowardly extinguished but whose fire lights my soul.

You killed her.

How do I explain this to my child?
People hate that we love women
Their masculinity depends
on our non-existence.
Their whole being is so unsettled
By the mere idea
Of love, pleasure, sex, song and dance between women
Between men, between sheets, behind doors
You don't understand?
Baby, neither do I.

But, they killed her.
And I see the images of her partner,
Her mother, her people, weeping, mourning.
They killed her.
And I can't explain it.
We killed her.
And I just can't explain it.

Sisters scream STOP
The war on our bodies
STOP the violence.
And they are brave
And they are strong.
And they are beautiful.
In their fearlessness, I see vulnerability.
I see pain. I see Black Woman. That I want to keep safe.
And I am scared.
What will you tell my child when they come for me?

Together as men you raped, you killed a woman.
Is that your masculinity?
You proved it? You proved that you hide behind others.
You proved you are not man enough to think.
Not man enough to love.
Not man enough even to fight as equals.
You proved our brutality.
This made you a man, *my brother*?

YOU explain it to my child.
You who is silent.
You who doesn't like them but…
No, of course, you don't condone violence.
You who said it is unnatural.
You who just doesn't have an opinion.
You who thinks God will judge.
You who hides in your closet among our bones.
You who thinks that there are more important issues.
You who doesn't think that my life depends on it.
You who won't join the scream
STOP
And explain this to my child.

Note

1. I wrote this poem after my daughter asked me to explain the picture of Eudy Simelane's partner grieving outside court. Eudy (a South African lesbian) was gang raped, beaten and stabbed 25 times in the face, chest and legs. I didn't know how to explain why she was killed.

18

My love (for Eudy Simelane)

Musa Okwonga

To some people
My love is somewhat alien;
When he comes up, they start subject-changing, and
In some states he's seen as some contagion –
In those zones, he stays subterranean;
Some love my love; they run parades for him:
Liberal citizens lead the way for him:
Concurrent with some countries embracing him,
Whole faiths and nations seem ashamed of him:
Some tried banning him,
God-damning him,
Toe-tagging him,
Prayed that he stayed in the cabinet,
But my love kicked in the panelling, ran for it –
My love! Can't be trapping him in labyrinths –
Maverick, my love is; thwarts challenges;
Cleverest geneticists can't fathom him,
Priests can't defeat him with venomous rhetoric;
They'd better quit; my love's too competitive:
Still here, despite the Taliban, Vatican,
And rap, ragga in their anger and arrogance,
Calling on my love with lit matches and paraffin –
Despite the fistfights and midnight batterings –
Despite the dislike by Anglican Africans
And sly comparisons with those mishandling
Small kids, and his morbid inner chattering
My love's still here and fiercely battling,
Parenting, marrying, somehow managing;
My love comes through anything

Questions for reflection

1.
How are gender, sexuality and power relations linked together in post-colonial, neoliberal contexts?

2.
How do the pluralist legal systems found in Africa affect sexualities? How is the law used as an instrument of controlling and/or regulating people's sexuality? Why the need for control?

3.
What does it mean to be a 'sexual citizen' in the context of pre-colonial and post-colonial exclusions? Are sexual rights part of human rights?

4.
What does the term 'African sexualities' invoke, and why?

5.
What lessons can we learn from existing strategies of resistance and subversion that 'sexual minorities' have employed in Africa?

6.
How does sexuality work to make some people vulnerable?
Who are these people?

7.
How does sexuality work to make some people dominant?
Who are these people?

8.
What voices are heard regarding sexuality and in which spaces? What voices are silenced? What causes silence when it comes to issues of sexuality? Can silence be used as an empowering strategy to subvert dominant sexualities?

Part 3
Mapping sexual representations
and practices of identity

19

Representing African sexualities

Desiree Lewis

Introduction

Although the American cartoon in Figure 19.1 was produced in the 19th century, it features images that still haunt our conceptual landscape, both within and beyond Africa. The cartoon portrays recurring stereotypes of black bodies and sexuality: the image of the lewd black man; the myth of the pure white female body; the portrayal of the black/African body as grotesque, uncivilised and crudely sexual, even when formally dressed. This cartoon conveys stereotypes in particularly explicit ways, yet these are the representations of African bodies and sexuality that continue to surface in present-day popular culture, news media and even in some academic work.

Figure 19.1

The cartoon encourages us to understand what many late 20th-century theorists have argued, namely that the linguistic, visual, scholarly or popular interpretation of human relationships and subjects is inseparable from what some might see as their very essence. A wave of post-colonial theorising from the late 1970s examined dominant assumptions about certain body types and the histories and places associated with them. Among the scholars confronting the racial and colonial significance of represented people, spaces and situations, Edward Said (1978) and V.Y. Mudimbe (1988) have made especially influential interventions.

In *Orientalism* (1978), Said explains ways in which images, preconceptions and myths dominate what is conventionally understood as 'the East' in the form of 'orientalism'. Capturing the cognitive process through which 'the East' is understood, *Orientalism* laid the foundation for many post-colonial writers' explorations of how legacies of colonial-inspired knowledge systems have defined bodies, human subjects and social histories.

Mudimbe's *The Invention of Africa: Gnosis, Philosophy and the Order of Knowledge* (1988) draws on this post-colonial tradition to analyse how African bodies and experiences have been discursively invented. Mudimbe is concerned with 'African societies, cultures and peoples as signs of something else' (Mudimbe 1988: ix). Throughout his book, he argues that: 'until now, Western interpreters as well as African analysts have been using categories and conceptual systems which depend on a Western epistemological order. Even in the most explicitly "Afrocentric" descriptions, models of analysis explicitly or implicitly, knowingly or unknowingly, refer to the same order' (Mudimbe 1988: x).

As this post-colonial scholarship demonstrates, occidental, colonial, Western-centric, imperial and neocolonial paradigms are so entrenched in knowledge production and popular culture that they influence the most seemingly progressive, compelling or disinterested accounts. Consequently, to explore African sexualities carefully means first exploring how they have been thought about; it requires what Kwame Appiah (1992: 240) describes as a 'discursive space-clearing', a way of both acknowledging and analysing how others have historically been imagined.

Scholarly and everyday representations of sexuality usually generate controversy. But the topic of represented sexualities in Africa is particularly charged in both academic and popular accounts. A key reason is that assumptions have been linked to essentialist beliefs – originating with colonialism – about the fundamental bestiality or degeneracy of African bodies. Writers such as Bernard Magubane (2007) and Jan Pieterse (1992) have shown that colonialism linked projections about African sexuality[1] to myth-making about the perceived racial degeneracy of others.

Racism, until the start of the 19th century, assumed that though Africans might be culturally and morally inferior, they remained amenable to cultural assimilation and development. Pieterse captures the shift in Western perceptions from the late 18th century by stating: 'before 1770 blacks were regarded as inferior more on grounds of cultural traits and the traditional association in Christian culture of blackness with evil than on those of any theory of in-bred racial inferiority. In the 1770s several works were published which gave a different turn to the discussion' (Pieterse 1992: 41).

By the end of the 18th century, the onset of colonial conquest had reinforced theories of inbred degeneracy, so that during the mid-1800s a persuasive knowledge system for differentiating African bodies from others had been established. Magubane comments on the evolving stereotypes in relation to eugenics and evolutionary theory:

> The theory of social evolution … relegated African societies to the primeval or decadent stage of human existence. From this perspective, European cultural history was seen as demonstrating an unbridgeable break or convergence from the remote beginning of human history. In the evolutionary continuum, Europeans were at one pole and Africans at the opposite pole. (Magubane 2007: 87)

By the 19th century, therefore, Africans were deemed innately, biologically different and degenerate. And central to this essentialist belief were ideas about their distinctively pathological sexuality.

Today, the legacy of colonialism endures in essentialist attitudes toward African sexuality and corporeal difference. As this essay shows, contemporary forms of othering are not always explicitly and recognisably racist. In fact, they might often be presented as positive and ennobling celebrations of the black body. In explaining this, post-colonial scholarship emphasises that colonial discourses are ingrained as hegemonic truths in mindsets and discursive practices. They are therefore entrenched as normal, neutral or natural in the images and symbols on which societies draw to make sense of their worlds.

Moreover, colonial-inspired scripts have been recrafted by Africans ostensibly concerned with independent self-definition or ennobling views of Africa. For example, many nationalist claims that African men are innately powerful and virile or that homosexuality was non-existent in traditional Africa reinforce colonial projections developed during the 19th century. What follows explores views about sexualities in relation to colonial, racial and gendered scripts. The discussion also focuses on the political and theoretical origins and implications of key assumptions.

Race, gender and African sexuality

Some studies of sexuality, race and gender in Africa have dwelt on the interpretations of colonial writers and artists in the 18th and 19th centuries. In highlighting patterns around representation and subjectivity, much work draws on cultural studies and psychoanalysis. One strand within this work examines how colonial perceptions are constructed through projections of African bodies.

Dealing with texts by travel writers, novelists, artists and poets, critics have analysed ways in which whiteness – and especially white masculinity – is textually imagined. For example, Anne McClintock's *Imperial Leather* (1994) considers links between imperial sexuality and colonial conquest and settlement. McClintock shows that eroticism and sexuality for colonial men were intimately connected to ways in which they 'oriented themselves in space, as agents of power and agents of knowledge' (McClintock: 24). Her study is not simply an attack on triumphant colonial conquest, but an investigation of the way in which eroticism is inscribed in narratives of colonial mastery.

Studies also focus on the obsessive interest in African sexuality expressed by others. Examining the writings of Edward Long, the mental health doctor, Magubane analyses a scientific preoccupation with the projected sexual prowess of Africans. Articulating contemporary thought, Long described Africans in terms of their bestial physicality. In listing features of African physicality, Long wrote:

> Fifthly, their bestial or fetid smell, which they have to a greater or lesser degree; the Congo's, Arada's, Quaqua's and Angolans … The scent in some of them is so exceedingly strong, especially when their bodies are warmed up either by exercise or anger, that it continues in a place where they have been, for nearly a quarter of an hour. (Quoted in Magubane 2007: 78)

As this quotation indicates, the description testifies only to the writer's fears, obsessions and prejudices.[2] By painstakingly describing the invented degeneracy, bestiality and, most importantly, the hypersexuality of Africans, many scientists in the 1700s and 1800s expressed the anxieties of their own social universe.

Much attention has been focused on 19th-century imagining of Sarah Baartman, the southern African (Khoisan) woman, who was exhibited in Britain and France as the 'Hottentot Venus'. Studies show how her display, as well as the wave of popular, scientific, written and visual depictions of her body, reveal tropes that are invoked repeatedly in cultural analyses of African corporeality and sexuality. Work by Sander Gilman (1985) therefore concentrates on how representations of Baartman helped to consolidate 19th-century thought about pathological bodies.

Yvette Abrahams (1997), the South African historian, concentrates on how Western scientists fixated on the genitalia of Sara Baartman. She illustrates the way in which they institutionalised the definition of black female bodies as objects of classification, academic scrutiny and sexual fantasy. Zine Magubane (2001) unpacks the significance of the 19th-century scrutiny of Baartman further, by arguing that the 'discourse of corporeal alterity … was a response to fears about the blurring of class and status differences within the European polity' (Magubane 2001: 820).

Studies of imperial constructions of African (and especially African women's) sexualities have therefore been part of a wave of work on colonial narratives, fantasies and desire during the 19th century and before. This work is directly connected to the colonial discourse studies school originating in the 1980s. Often drawing on the work of post-structuralists in the North, Ifi Amadiume (1987), Mudimbe (1988) and Appiah (1992), among many others, have undertaken psychoanalytic explorations of the links between desire and power in their work on colonial discourses of African bodies.

As part of a broader tradition dealing with the politics of representation, work on projections of African bodies departs from many Marxist-inflected studies, which locate 'desire' squarely in economic and political interests. One such study is Emmanuel Wallerstein's (1976) explanation of Africa's involvement in the world economy. Identifying three stages of Africa's economic incorporation, Wallerstein focuses only on how African bodies and territories served the needs of expanding global capitalism; his account does not therefore address the psychological, existential and sexual motivations of how and why African bodies were imagined (and often policed) in very particular ways. Largely, historical materialist accounts of racist representations of sexuality tend to assume that these straightforwardly rationalise economic and political power. Marxist explanation of the origins of racial ideology in colonial expansion and capital accumulation remains highly relevant. At the same time, materialist determinism can neglect the extent to which representation and projection are linked to subject formation and identity construction.

Increasingly, therefore, scholars are acknowledging how the careful analysis of represented sexualities helps to explain the meanings of race, the persistence of stereotypes, the reproduction of gender and the operation of power. Such work is also important in explaining processes of subjectification from the mid-20th century to the present day. As this essay goes on to show, desire for control and mastery, inscribed on both the land and African bodies, directly connected colonial to nationalist and post-colonial narratives and myth-making in the years after formal decolonisation.

Overall, studies of how sexuality has been represented in narrative, text and image have astutely identified the centrality of imagining, invention and fabrication around sexuality. Echoing the arguments of Michel Foucault (that sexuality is not so much a fact or biological given as it is a social practice and product of discourses), this work broadly identifies the invention of sexuality in relation to power and processes of subjectification.

African masculinities and myths about sexual deviance

Charles Linnaeus, the father of Western-centric scientific classification, established a system for classifying human beings in which Africans featured at the very bottom of the hierarchy. Among Africans, Khoisan people (hunter-gatherers from southern Africa) were considered to be especially inferior. Yvette Abrahams writes: 'From the late 17th century onwards, a widespread belief existed among European scientists that Khoisan men were born with one testicle' (Abrahams 1997: 38). This belief, Abrahams argues, was rooted in genetic theory – the firm conviction that the genitals of Khoisan men were biologically deviant. However absurd such thinking might be from a modern perspective, the theories about African masculinity propounded by Linnaeus reveal indicators of the Western-centric fixation with manufacturing sexual deviance in Africans.

Moreover, the myth complemented prevailing colonial perceptions of the 'unmanliness' and inferiority of African men. Many post-colonial theorists show that the 'emasculation'[3] of colonised men in imperial representations is a recurring pattern. In this trend, colonised men from the East, or from various third-world sites, are represented as weak, degenerate or sickly,[4] with this myth rationalising imperial control and dominance.

Although Linnaeus' theory identified a lack in black South African male sexuality, a far more common pattern, especially with the rise of eugenics from the 1800s, was the perception of sexual potency among black males. Many writers identify this construction in the North American context. Studies such as Carol Henderson's 'Seeking the dry bones of my father: race, ritual and the black male body' (2009) show how control over the African male enslaved body was enforced through myths about the need for such control. Violent methods of policing, punishing or institutionalising black male bodies were therefore rationalised by beliefs about the rapacity of black male sexual desire. Henderson shows that the fantasy image of the black male rapist often justified the extreme violence of the measures taken against black men. For example, lynching and castration were the violent acts that justified claims that particular black men raped or threatened to rape white women.

But Henderson also describes the peculiar fixation with spectacles of violence inflicted on the black male body, often by other black males. These spectacles endure in contemporary globalised culture, often in popular films. Their lasting appeal for many testifies to a public fascination with and bizarre pleasure in (often consciously or unconsciously coded as erotic) watching black men die violently.

Figure 19.2
Robert
Mapplethorpe,
*Thomas and
Dovanna*, 1986

Gelatin silver print
Image: 23 ⅛ x 19 ¼ inches
(58.7 x 48.9 cm),
Sheet: 23 ¹³⁄₁₆ x 19 ⅞ inches
(60.5 x 50.5 cm)
Solomon R. Guggenheim
Museum, New York
Gift, Robert Mapplethorpe
Foundation 1993,
93.4303

And this 'psychosexual imagining' (Henderson 2009: 49) is evidenced in:

> the visual images in modern time that found black males hanging from trees
> along America's eastern and southern thoroughfares or, in recent manifesta-
> tions, shot dead in gangland shootings – real and imagined – on our small
> or large screens (is that not what Denzel Washington won an Oscar for in
> *Training Day*?). (Henderson 2009: 38)

The photographer Robert Mapplethorpe mocks the myth of the hypersexual black
man in *Thomas and Dovanna* (1986). However, even though his image sets out to parody the stereotype of the black male raping the chaste white female body, it perpetuates the standard othering of the sexualised black body – an object of desire that is
here configured as black and homoerotic. Ultimately, then, for Mapplethorpe, as is
the case with the many artists and writers depicting the sexuality of African men in
a previous century, the black male body remains a sexualised spectacle and object
of the colonial imagination.

Yaba Badoe's documentary, *Without Walls: I Want Your Sex* (1991), explores the
projection of the black male body as a signifier of extraordinary sexual potency.
Drawing connections between power, desire and fantasy, she shows how images

of black men's bodies loom large in Western-centric imagining. Thus, science and the popular media promulgate beliefs such as the idea that black men's penises are very large, that black men are more driven by sexual desire than white men and that black men are especially prone to promiscuity. Though studies of African masculinities have proliferated in recent years, it is noteworthy that few of these explore the construction of black male sexuality, or ways in which this construction informs contemporary representations and definitions of subjectivity.

Current scholarship and policy-related research on masculinities can covertly reinforce colonial myth-making about the 'essential' nature of African masculinity in influencing, for example, gender-based violence or the spread of HIV/AIDS on the continent. In their study of how long-held beliefs about sexuality shape recent research on masculinity and HIV/AIDS, Katarina Jungar and Elina Oinas (2003) argue that the implicit project of 'civilising' African men informs much policy research and activism, as well as academic work on masculinities. Frequently, writers and activists sensationalise African male sexuality (as the cause of high-risk behaviour and sexual aggression, for example) and normalise particular Western-centric constructs of heterosexism and patriarchy as desirable. Jungar and Oinas' analysis of othering discourses in ostensibly transformative work is a reminder that even the most seemingly progressive research cannot afford to neglect attention to how the identities and social practices that we explore are coloured by long-established ways of conceiving of them.

African women and sexuality

In some ways, the representation of male sexuality has been reflected in constructions of female sexuality. Both African men and women have been defined in terms of sexual excess, bestiality and bodily deviance. As many feminist scholars have pointed out, however, gender provides a foundation for the further othering of African female bodies. Abrahams therefore observes that the speculation about Khoisan male genitals from the late 17th century revealingly gave way from the mid-1800s to speculation about the 'measurable' and 'analysable' sexual deviance of the African female body. Nowhere was this more clearly conveyed than in the figure of Sarah Baartman. The extravagant myth-making and invention associated with Baartman explicitly indicates how bodies – marked according to racial and gendered inferiority – carry dense cultural meaning and how African female bodies easily became sites for others' inscription.

Systems of power rooted in race and gender have systematically tried to rationalise the regulation and exploitation of socially subordinate human bodies. Thus, myths about sexuality have been linked to definitions of the African female body in terms of domestic work, physical labour, sex work and all activity denying the mind and prescribing service. In recent decades, mythology about the sexualised African female body has been subjected to intense scrutiny by feminist scholars and by radical female African writers and artists. Among others, Amina Mama (1995), Abrahams (1997), Amadiume (1997), Patricia McFadden (2003) and this author (2005) have investigated how black women's bodies and sexuality have been misrepresented and how this connects to power relations. It is noteworthy that these misrepresentations persist in the present, with the policing of African women and efforts to control their bodily presence in the public sphere taking the form of neo-imperial constructions of their sexual excess. Consequently, colonial definitions of women's urban work as peripheral and unlawful, together with the stereotypes surrounding their presence in towns, frequently persist in the post-colonial period.

Public perceptions of women's informal trading in Ghana, for example, have been criticised as 'market women in urban areas as an undifferentiated mass of ... corrupt elements who bear responsibility for Ghana's economic problems' (Dzodzi Tsikata 1997: 399). Tsikata shows how, within new systems of neocolonial patriarchal authoritarianism, Ghanaian market women's bodies have been defined in relation to long-established tropes about the deviant sexuality of the African female body. Similar trends have surfaced in perceptions of women traders in Nigeria: the military government of the 1980s blamed women traders for economic crises, with the state's modernising and disciplining missions instituting an array of mechanisms against working women in cities (Dennis, in Afsar 1987: 21). In Zimbabwe immediately after independence, the government instituted policies of urban population control targeting women in ruthless round-ups (Jacobs and Howard 1987: 39–44).

Pumla Gqola deals with the scripting of the South African female body in literary texts by stating that 'black female characters provide the sale on which the chalk marks of history and black patriarchy are inscribed' (Gqola 2009: 108). In this way, she draws attention to the centrality of tropes of sexual deviance in contemporary popular imagining of black South African women. Throughout Africa, therefore, messages about African women's sexual excess have justified their being scapegoats, their low status and the demonising of their urban economic activity and political empowerment. Such controls are anchored in discursive representations of the sexualised and degenerate female body, a body that threatens to pollute or weaken the 'healthy' national body politic.

Apart from feminist scholars, female artists have played a significant part in unsettling myths about African female sexuality. Examples of these are black South African artists Berni Searle and Tracey Rose. Both challenge myths about the hypersexualisation of the African body. For example, Tracey Rose's self-portrait, 'Venus Baartman' (2001), represents herself as Baartman, with her work functioning to sublimate stereotypes of the black woman as hypersexual, as bestial, as close to nature.

Rose ironically represents herself as a naked stalking beast. In so doing, she analyses both her own identification in discourses of race and gender, and the origin of these discourses in Baartman's othering. Also representing her own body in her installations, Searle focuses on how African women have been defined by colonial myths, by fictions about their hypersexuality, their physical degeneracy and their tantalising exoticism. As these artists indicate, African women's sexuality is inextricably connected to past myths. Like many feminist scholars, therefore, they deconstruct embedded meanings about African female bodies and sexuality.

Although much scholarship dwells on the misrepresentation of African female sexuality, there is a relative paucity of work on African women's sexual pleasure: far fewer writers have constructed women's sexuality in relation to desire and sexual autonomy. Patricia McFadden (2003) conveys this when she writes that African women's 'ideas and political instincts are being muffled … and [their] feminist energies and agencies are being stifled by patriarchal sexual discourses that appropriate and restructure [their] debates about sexuality and lifestyles' (2003: 51).

Boldly imagining female sexuality in new ways, McFadden invokes Audre Lorde to envisage possibilities around female sexuality. In an article published in 2003, McFadden argues that rights-based approaches to their bodily and sexual freedom can continue to confine women to 'routine processes … through which girls and women are persistently reminded that they are the chattels of men in our societies' (McFadden 2003: 13). She overturns deep taboos about what is 'permissible sex talk' among many progressive writers on African female sexuality, by connecting female sexuality to the power of fully 'owning pleasure' (McFadden 2003: 13). The taboos surrounding women's sexuality, which influence research and academic work, are of course not unique to African contexts. But it is interesting that traditions of feminist theory and writing in Western contexts have often been crucially concerned with linking celebratory representations of women's sexuality to broader challenges to patriarchal authority, knowledge and writing.

The absence of similar exploration in traditions of African feminist and gender studies could be attributed to overt or direct rejections of colonial stereotyping of African (and especially African women's) 'hyper-developed' sexuality: in refusing the stereotype, certain writers might have shied away from exploring African women's sexuality altogether. It can also be attributed to an existing emphasis in African studies on what are considered to be pressing collective issues of development and transformation, rather than on more humanistic, psychic and individual dimensions of freedom.

Several issues of African-based feminist journals, such as *Agenda* and *Feminist Africa*, have started to challenge this trend, with contributions (including poetry and artwork) raising the way that bodies and sexuality are not only sites of others' inscribed meanings, but also sources of African women's agency. This trend raises new discussions about pleasure, desire and holistic understandings of sexuality. Increasingly, then, it is complementing the volume of work that concentrates on African female sexuality mainly in relation to its distortion, or to such issues as disease, gender-based violence and patriarchal control.

Heterosexuality, homosexuality and the policing of sexuality

Part of colonial and racist assumptions about African sexuality involved defining Africans as 'natural' beings, whose instincts, it was felt, were wholly different from the sophisticated desires of Westerners. The colonialists believed that Africans were less than human or uncivilised, and so they could not possibly be anything but heterosexual. Busangokwakhe Dlamini (2006) writes that, because the African man 'was perceived to be close to nature, ruled by instincts, and culturally unsophisticated, he had to be heterosexual; his sexual energies and outlets devoted exclusively to their "natural" purpose – biological reproduction' (Dlamini 2006: 132).

African sexuality, therefore, was often defined in relation to reproduction, with the assumption being that Africans could not possibly display homoerotic desires or agencies, which were associated with sophisticated human desires and eroticism. As Dlamini notes, measures for codifying sexual practices extended from colonial administration through to ethnographic scholarship (Dlamini 2006: 132–3). Such work, developed and modified until the mid-20th century, has consistently denied the existence of same-sex practices in Africa. Marc Epprecht, in a chapter provocatively titled 'The ethnography of African straightness', emphasises the centrality of anthropology to evolving knowledge across disciplines. He writes:

> Anthropologists played a central role in documenting the diversity of human sexuality as it is understood and expressed around the world. Scholars in many other disciplines ... are often heavily dependent on their research. However ... at times anthropologists 'conscripted' select evidence and even fabricated 'facts' about the people they studied in order to advance ideals and preferences concerning gender and sexuality in their own societies. (Epprecht 2008: 34)

Colonial and early anthropological representations of sexuality (especially as it has coerced heterosexuality as an institution) have therefore been central to many present-day taboos, laws and attitudes surrounding sexuality in Africa.

Work that seeks to uncover and discover homosexuality in Africa is fairly new, with much of this responding both to entrenched Western-centric myths and to mounting homophobia across the continent: the escalating and often state-sanctioned homophobia evident in countries such as Namibia, Zimbabwe and Uganda, in view of its enormous effect on human freedoms and rights, has begun to receive growing attention. Increasing work has been undertaken on the distinctive forms of same-sex relations in Africa. And much of this work grapples with the trickiness of representation, especially with how non-Western and precolonial subjectivities and practices can be understood within the framework of concepts, languages and conventions that assume or prioritise modernity and Western-centric assumptions. Many draw attention to distinctive ways in which sexual orientation is often codified in parts of Africa. As indicated by researchers such as Sylvia Tamale (2003) working on socially marginalised but extremely resilient lesbian subcultures in Uganda, African trends frequently differ from the celebration of sexuality in Western discussions.

Many other studies address the themes Tamale raises. For example, Rudy Gaudio (1998) highlights attention to the cultural biases of Western feminist and social constructionist theory when he explores homoerotic and homo-relational bonds in Nigeria. In 'Male lesbians and other queer notions in Hausa', Gaudio shows how, among the Hausa *yan dauda*, dress, conduct and work align them with women's domain, while their sexual relations with other men are marginalised so that 'the practice of *dauda* is culturally understood in terms of gender rather than sexuality' (Gaudio 1998: 119).

Gaudio's appraisal of the relativity of the concepts we use to define homoerotic patterns also informs Judith Gay's and Kathryn Kendall's studies of women's lesbian relationships. In 'Mummies and babies and friends and lovers in Lesotho', they describe customary same-sex relationships among young girls. Although involving sexual relations, these are not semantically conceptualised as such, with 'sexual' being a term reserved for heterosexual relations. They go on to observe that women in these contexts are paradoxically often able to enjoy greater sexual freedom and avoid the homophobic backlash faced by many lesbians in the West.

Dlamini's discussion of the homo-relational bonds prescribed by the iconised Zulu leader, Shaka,[5] draws attention to how his strict regulation of male-centred relationships for his warriors might have countenanced and even prescribed homosexuality for young men. Suggesting that homoeroticism among Zulu warriors was central to their definition of aggressive and triumphal masculinity, Dlamini's argument entirely overturns conventional Western-centric ways of defining 'alternative masculinity' in relation to male homosexuality. Some research on homosexualities in Africa has therefore shown that pre-colonial societies were often far more amenable to homoerotic patterns than is suggested by the virulent attacks, ostensibly defending African tradition, associated with figures such as Robert Mugabe.

Studies of homoeroticism in Africa frequently draw attention to individuals' adoption of gendered behaviour that differs from that which is sanctioned 'official'. Indicating that gender is performative, these explorations contribute to insights raised within trans-gender theory, which has recently been expanding discussions of gender in the West. Beth Greene's 'The institution of woman-marriage in Africa: a cross-cultural analysis' (Greene 1998) is particularly noteworthy because it draws connections between different patterns and suggests the theoretical relevance of these to understanding our acquisition or rejection of socially imposed gender.

Transgressive trends in the representation of African sexualities have therefore sought to extricate African sexuality from binaries that define heterosexuality as normatively African and homosexuality as deviant and Western. They have also questioned the usefulness of exploring sexuality, gender and sex in terms of dualisms and binaries. As the research shows, these dualisms and binaries are often embedded in the seemingly innovative theoretical frameworks on which present-day researchers draw. In fact, Greg Thomas' study of sexuality from a Pan-African perspective suggests that much progressive research actively reconstructs imperial, occidental and white supremacist power. Thomas writes:

> An eruption of 'sexual [intellectual] discourse' in the 1980s and 90s changed ... very little ... In certain quarters, the professed social construction of gender and sexuality has acquired the status of a cliché, however controversial it may remain to some. The ideological naturalisation of erotic life is refuted, in principle, by the facts of cultural formation ... The really nasty fact that sexual personas and practices are ritually constructed as well as theorised in the service of colonial imperial structures of 'race', or white supremacy, has not been the subject of academic commerce under Occidentalism. (Thomas 2007: 1–2)

Sexuality and post-colonial discourses of tradition and culture

In the same way that assumptions about African sexuality were central to colonial myth-making, these assumptions have also become central to postcolonial myths. These myths have often supported efforts at nation-building, with dominant political parties, politicians and community leaders claiming to speak in the name of the collective by constructing rigid images of innate sexual identities, relationships and institutions. How sexuality has been represented has therefore been central to the current imagining and crafting of nationalism, as well as to the institutionalising of authoritarian cultures.

Kopano Ratele explores the centrality of sexuality discourses to colonial and postcolonial nation-building in 'Native chief and white headmen'. 'Receptive cultural discourses,' he argues, 'imply open-endedness ... [and] are necessary to re-fertilise the group while engendering a desire for the person to flourish' (Ratele 2007: 75). In contrast, 'reductive cultural discourses refer to those practices associated with culture which are exclusionary and averse to complexity. These tend to be well-served by patriarchal, tribalistic ideologies' (Ratele 2007: 74). Reductive notions of culture therefore assume that cultures are static and fixed, and that certain practices and customs must be endlessly rehearsed for the sake of preserving group identity. It goes without saying that such 'static cultures' do not and cannot exist in reality, and that 'human cultures were ... and still are, always messy' (Ratele 2007: 70). Invocations of static culture are fictions. Even the most seemingly pristine and unchanged cultural practices are affected by history, globalisation and social struggles.

Ratele's explanation of reductive cultures is relevant to understanding two key politicised examples of cultural discourses in relation to sexuality. One is the way that these are linked to colonialism. Dealing with South Africa, Ratele writes:

> There is no need to go far to find one of the clearest expressions of the instru-mentalised political uses and dangers of supposed inflexible boundaries in the configuration of modern culture. In South Africa, this mode of represent-ing and organising culture derives, among other sources, from the muscular truth-regime of segregation. (Ratele 2007: 68)

The other is how discourses of tradition and timeless culture are used for conservative ends, for regulating the sexuality of women as well as men. It is this second role that is of particular importance to considerations about culture and sexuality in contemporary Africa. What follows shows how the policing of women's and men's bodies through fictions of 'normal' sexuality for men and women has been an especially important feature of reductive culture discourses.

Stereotypes about African sexuality, despite their colonial origins and roles in maintaining racial binaries, persist in media representations, popular culture, academic practice and in the everyday imagining of identity. The crude representation of the African man as a virile heterosexual warrior may be starkly captured in colonial writings or the ethnographic studies of the early 1900s. Yet, stereotypes that echo this image persist in much contemporary policy research and academic research.

As indicated earlier in this essay, Jungar and Oinas (2003) describe the ways in which HIV/AIDS prevention strategies and the research driving such strategies define African male sexuality within tropes of excess and barbarism. However oblique, the central argument of this research is that African men need to be taught to cultivate a sense of responsibility about sexual behaviour. Consequently, the developmentalist discourse informing much advocacy, research and policy starkly reconfigures the image of the promiscuous, irrational and highly sexualised African male body.

The persistence of stereotypes about African male sexuality is also evident in ideas – often codified in official national discourses – about homosexuality. Violent public attacks on homosexuality are frequently couched as defences of what is traditionally African from a contaminating Western influence, and homosexuality is a criminal offence in countries including Algeria, Angola, Cameroon, Libya, Malawi, Morocco and Nigeria, to name but a few. The Ugandan Anti-Homosexuality Bill, introduced in 2009 and which has generated a global outcry about the implications of policing sexuality, starkly reveals how African politicians and leaders have invested in efforts to regulate heterosexuality.

Public attacks on homosexuality have been global. But a crucial question is why so many African leaders have publicly condemned and acted to criminalise homoerotic desires and relationships. One reason is that discourses of national belonging have been anchored in familial scripts and the invention of nations as biological families. In constructing sexuality, the family and personality in terms of a familial frame, the 'natural' reproduction of communities and the 'rightful' belonging of individuals within collectivities are assured. On one level, therefore, homosexuality – whether as fact or as possibility – drastically confounds the 'natural' binaries, identities and relationships central to fictions of nation: to belong as citizens, we have legitimate and 'natural' sexual roles to play. When we step out of these roles, we become unnatural, Westernised and traitorous.

One of the most potent instruments used by many contemporary politicians is the performative deployment of power. For many, power has to be demonstrated, enacted and rehearsed in order to galvanise mass support. Exploiting populist appeals to many Africans' desire for 'authenticity', politicians such as Robert Mugabe and Jacob Zuma have worked to demonstrate their allegiance to practices defined as African. The paternal authority of certain leaders has therefore been defined as the index of the pride of an entire group, and ascendant manhood has come to signify the reclaimed pride of the entire community.

Consequently, men and women can become complicit in venerating men's preeminence in the household and the wider community. This explains the unwavering popular support for leaders whose actual contribution to social struggles might be far outweighed by evidence of their abuse of power. The symbolic meaning of their authority can be perceived as being far more important than their unjust or exploitative uses of power. And central to their paternal power is the demonstration of control over others' bodies.

An insightful exploration of the personalised acquisitions of identity associated with this is the novel *Purple Hibiscus* (2003) by the Nigerian novelist Chimamanda Ngozi Adichie. Dealing with a family headed by an extremely violent father, the novel traces the intimate connection between Nigeria's military dictatorship and domestic violence in an individual household. Told from the perspective of a young girl, Kambili, the story captures her sense of entrapment within a system which is at once a protecting home (towards which she feels a powerful sense of obligation and allegiance) and also terrifying for the way it suppresses her independence and sanctions her physical suffering. Importantly, the violence of Kambili's father is seen to be linked to his deep belief in social duty – as a Nigerian citizen committed to building his nation, ensuring the well-being of his employees and promoting democracy and freedom of speech.

Motivated by an obsessive authoritarian paternalism, he often 'fathers' and 'guides' his family in extremely brutal ways, appearing to experience an almost divine sense of the social need for his behaviour:

> Papa was like a Fulani nomad … as he swung his belt at Mama, Jaja, and me, muttering that the devil would not win. We did not move more than two steps away from the leather belt that swished through the air. Then the belt stopped, and Papa stared at the leather in his hand. His face crumpled; his eyelids sagged. 'Why do you walk into sin?' he asked. 'Why do you like sin?' (Adichie 2003: 102)

As Adichie shows, an important feature of individual and collective behaviour in post-colonial Africa – sanctioned both in everyday life and by the state – is discipline and authoritarianism. Although many post-colonial states are committed to good governance, constitutional rights, citizens' bodily integrity and freedom of speech and expression, many repressive and coercive mechanisms are manifested in spectacles, rather than in formal politics, namely institutions, legislation and policymaking. Visual images, acts of display and spectatorship and representations of human bodies have all had tremendous impact within these spectacles.

At one level, we see this in the disciplining of actual women, especially young women. The control of young women's bodies has been central to the construction of masculinist citizenship and nationhood, as well as masculinised ethnicity. At another level, authoritarian cultures draw on and are rationalised by gendered behaviour and language, by somatic symbols and meanings, through which notions such as citizenship, order and the healthy social body are imagined.

Some of the most prominent post-colonial mechanisms for instituting control over women's bodies are associated with customary law and practices.[6] These might include the obvious violations of, for example, virginity testing or female genital mutilation. As revealed by the rape trial of Jacob Zuma in South Africa, rape, recast as 'aggressive male heterosexual behaviour' may sometimes be redefined as the legitimate heterosexual response of 'normal' African men. These responses also include the seemingly benign institution of polygyny, or communally sanctioned forms of verbal abuse and disciplining. Polygyny in particular has functioned performatively in the theatrical display of patriarchal authoritarianism associated with leaders such as Jacob Zuma and Robert Mugabe, among many others.

For many young women involved in 'customary' practices, fantasy meaning revolves around dignity and pride, a sense of respect that seems to defy the negativity associated with subordination on the basis of gender, class, race and youth. Dignity is also conferred through the fictive yet compelling sense of 'tradition', connectedness to some sense of past that appears to be uncontaminated by a present of moral despair, the prevalence of HIV/AIDS, violent crime, unemployment and generally the prospectlessness that neoliberal Africa holds for large numbers of Africans.

For older women, who are often the ones who police young women's bodies, customary practices can confer power, the authority to control the youth and the enactment of older women's dominance even under patriarchy. Such authority offers power and status where the old colonial and apartheid orders of 'tradition' – in the face of rapid urbanisation and the breakdown of communal and traditional networks and belief systems – are fast eroding. For older men, the power is obvious. Many customary practices and laws have worked to reinstate traditional systems of authority, systems based not only on gender, but also on age – through inscribing the bodies of young women. Most importantly, customary practices shroud this authority in ceremonial ritual and offer abundant symbolic resources for all participants (the women who are subjected to them, and those who drive and sanction the process) to create a sense of self through fantasies of belonging and to discover gendered subjectivity through personalised emotional and fantasy meaning.

Reactionary constructions of sexuality are so resilient because individuals often rely on conservative fictions of self to gain acceptance within communities, societies or nations. Both men and women may collude in perpetuating customary laws and practices. This happens not because women and men gain equal measures of power from these, but because many women are able to derive a seemingly enduring and meaningful sense of self and belonging through them. The survival of fictions of sexuality in the myths by which many live and structure their lives is probably the most obvious indicator of our need to interrogate representations of sexuality today.

Conclusion

Our world is dominated by mass media messages, images circulating on the internet and spoken and written messages transmitted through mass communication technologies that have become increasingly ubiquitous and sophisticated. Even the most isolated areas on the African continent are infiltrated by these. These messages might be connected to consumerism, as is the case with advertising or to political organisation, as evidenced in politicians' and political parties' communication. They might also be embedded in news and information, or connected to awareness-raising, development programmes or health campaigns, as indicated in the wealth of posters, leaflets and online material dealing with HIV/AIDS.

Although the digitalised, print and technologically complex forms of these messages have altered dramatically in recent years, their content often remains surprisingly constant. Constructed bodies and sexualities that convey menace, panic

© Zanele Muholi

Figure 19.3. Miss D'vine I

and excess, or that serve the political purposes of various groups startlingly repeat familiar tropes and meanings. Remarking on this, the editors of *Imagining, Writing, (Re)Reading The Black Body* write:

> In two very powerful domains, the mass media and popular literature, images of the black body saturate cultural politics with caricatures and stereotypes about black sexuality ... Sexualisation of the black body continues to impinge negatively on black males and females, manifested in violence, brutality, devaluation of black lives ... These complex messages fuel social concerns and anxieties about the need to contain black bodies, perceiving them to be vessels of disease that threaten and menace stability and order.' (Jackson, Demissie and Goodwin 2009: xiv)

On one hand, therefore, repressive and neo-imperial constructions of sexuality still play an influential role in African popular cultures, everyday life, and academic and policy research. On the other, innovative, critical and subversive representations are flourishing. Ranging from the defiant dress styles of, for example, youth and gay and lesbian subcultures, to the path-breaking research of many radical post-colonial researchers, or contemporary artwork and photography, these reveal the enormous possibilities for rethinking and reconceptualising sexualities in Africa.

It is misleading to attribute these to Africans' exposure to the benefits of modernity or liberal rights discourses. In fact, as this essay has shown, Western modernity and rights discourses often reinforce conservative and damaging representations.

214

Rather, current alternative representations are fascinating echoes of bodily performance and sexual identities that, long before colonialism, were important features of the experiences of men and women in different African contexts. Neither gender oppression nor sexual taboos were invented by colonialism, and pre-colonial African societies exhibited numerous examples of repressive and coercive constructions of bodies and sexuality.

At the same time, as Ifi Amadiume (1987, 1997) reminds us, many cultural meanings attached to gender, sexuality and material bodies – prior to colonialism – transcended the binaries, hierarchies and power relations that characterise the present. The explosion of transgressive representations of sexual identities and meanings today is therefore part of a long tradition, influenced by but neither determined nor initiated by Western modernity, of struggles for and over meanings associated with bodies and sexuality in Africa.

Notes

1. The notion of a single 'African sexuality' indicates erroneous generalisations and essentialising about the wide-ranging behaviours, intimacies, practices and relationships associated with sexuality in different parts of the continent.
2. J.M. Coetzee's novel *Dusklands* (1974) is an important fictional exploration of these travel writings and their political meaning.
3. 'Emasculation' here refers to various ways of defining colonised men as unmanly in relation to the norm of manliness associated with middle-class Western European and Victorian standards of manliness.
4. Joseph Conrad's astonishing accounts of degenerate African labourers in his novel, *Heart of Darkness*, illustrates this. But the tendency to feminise third-world men is probably more pronounced in imperial accounts of men in the East.
5. Shaka instituted strict measures for isolating the young male members of his army from women.
6. It is worth recalling Ratele's observation about the artificiality and constructedness of these. Although 'custom' and 'tradition' may often be invoked to rationalise certain practices, these are often distorted or selected remnants of the past. And colonial methods of policing women and ruling men have played no small part in their late 20th-century reinvention.

References

Abrahams, Y. (1997) 'The great long national insult: science, sexuality and the Khoisan in the 18th and early 19th century', *Agenda* 32

Adichie, C.N. (2003) *Purple Hibiscus*, New York, Random House

Amadiume, I. (1987) *Male Daughters, Female Husbands*, London and New York, Zed

—— (1997) *Reinventing Africa: Matriarchy, Religion and Culture*, New York, Zed

Appiah, K. (1992) *In My Father's House: Africa in the Philosophy of Culture*, New York, Oxford University Press

Coetzee, J.M. (1974) *Dusklands*, Johannesburg, Ravan

Conrad, J. (1902 [1983]) *Heart of Darkness*, London, Penguin

Dennis, C. (1987) 'Women and the state in Nigeria: the case of the federal military government, 1984–5', in Afsar, H. (ed) *Women, State and Ideology: Studies from African and Asia*, London, Macmillan

Dlamini, B. (2006) 'Homosexuality in the African context', *Agenda* 67: 128–36

Epprecht, M. (2008) *Heterosexual Africa? The History of an Idea from the Age of Exploration to the Age of AIDS*, Pietermariztburg, University of KwaZulu-Natal Press

Gaudio, R. (1998) 'Male lesbians and other queer notions in Hausa', in Murray, S. and

Roscoe, W. (eds) *Boy-Wives and Female Husbands: Studies of African Homosexualities*, Bloomsburg, Macmillan Press

Gilman, S. (1985) 'Black bodies, white bodies: towards an iconography of female sexuality in late 19th-century art, medicine and literature', in Gates, H.L. (ed) *Race, Writing and Difference*, Chicago, University of Chicago Press

Gqola, P. (2009) 'Black women's bodies as battlegrounds in black consciousness literature: wayward sex and (interracial) rape as tropes in Staffrider, 1978–1982', in Jackson, S., Demissie, F. and Goodwin, M. (eds) *Imagining, Writing, (Re)Reading the Black Body*, Pretoria, UNISA Press

Greene, B. (1998) 'The institution of woman-marriage in Africa: a cross-cultural analysis', *Ethnology* 37(4): 395–412

Henderson, C. (2009)'Seeking the dry bones of my father: race, ritual and the black male body', in Jackson, S. et al (eds) *Imagining, Writing, (Re)Reading the Black Body*, Pretoria, UNISA Press

Henderson, H. (1999) 'Beyond streetwalking: the woman of the city as urban pioneer', in Anyidoho, K., Busia, A. and Adams, A. (eds*) Beyond Survival: African Literature and the Search for New Life*, Trenton, NJ, Africa World Press

Jackson, S., Demissie, F. and Goodwin, M. (2009) 'Introduction', in Jackson, S., Demissie, F. and Goodwin, M. (eds) *Imagining, Writing, (Re)Reading the Black Body*, Pretoria, UNISA Press

Jacobs, S. and Howard, T. (1987) 'Women in Zimbabwe: stated policy and State action', in Afshar, H. (ed) *Women, State and Ideology: Studies from Africa and Asia*, London, Macmillan

Jungar, K. and Oinas, E. (2003) 'Tragic masculinities, brave girls and prevention strategies – what about treatment ? – a discourse analysis of recent gender-sensitive HIV research', paper presented at Sex and Secrecy Conference, WISER, University of the Witwatersrand, 22–25 June

Lewis, D. (2005) 'Against the grain: black women and sexuality', *Agenda* 63: 11–24

Magubane, B. (2007) *Race and the Construction of the Dispensable Other*, Pretoria, UNISA Press

Magubane, Z. (2001) 'Which bodies matter? Feminism, poststructuralism, race and the curious theoretical odyssey of the "Hottentot Venus"', *Gender and Society* 15, 6 December

Mama, A. (1995) *Beyond the Masks: Race, Gender and Subjectivity*, London and New York, Routledge

McClintock, A. (1994) *Imperial Leather*, New York, Routledge

McFadden, P. (2003) 'Sexual pleasure as feminist choice', *Feminist Africa* 2: 50–60

Mudimbe, V.Y. (1988) *The Invention of Africa: Gnosis, Philosophy and the Order of Knowledge*, London, James Currey

Pieterse, J. (1992) *White on Black: Images of Africa and Blacks in Western Popular Culture*, New Haven and London, Yale University Press

Ratele, K. (2007) 'Native chief and white headmen: a critical African gender analysis of culture', *Agenda* 72: 65–76

Said, E. (1978) *Orientalism*, Harmondsworth, Penguin

Tamale, S. (2003) 'Out of the closet: unveiling sexuality discourses in Uganda', *Feminist Africa* 2: 42–9

Thomas, G. (2007) *The Sexual Demon of Colonial Power: Pan-African Embodiment and Erotic Schemes of Empire*, Bloomington and Indianapolis, Indiana University Press

Tsikata, D. (1997) 'Gender equality and the state in Ghana', in Imam, A. et al (eds) *Engendering African Social Science*, Dakar, CODESRIA

Wallerstein, E. (1976) 'The three stages of African involvement in the world economy', in Gutkind, P. and Wallerstein, E. (eds) *The Political Economy of Contemporary Africa*, London, Sage

Without Walls: I Want your Sex (1991) directed by Yaba Badoe, Fulcrum Productions, Great Britain

20

Pious stardom: cinema and the Islamic revival in Egypt[1]

Karim Mahmoud Tartoussieh

> Stars are a reflection in which the public studies and adjusts its own image of
> itself ... The social history of a nation can be written in terms of its film stars.
> *Raymond Durgnat (1967: 137–8)*

Following the screening of the Egyptian film *Bahibb al-Sinima* (*I Love Cinema*) at the
November 2005 Middle East Film Festival (Cineaste) in New York, attendees met
Usama Fawzi, the Egyptian film-maker and Layla 'Ilwi, the film star, who had flown
in from Cairo for the event. In one of the discussion sessions (the film screened three
times), Fawzi informed the audience – made up mostly of Middle Easterners, save
for roughly 20 people – that he wanted to salute 'Ilwi for accepting her role despite
the controversial nature of the character, an Egyptian Christian wife and mother
whose repressed sexual and artistic energies are unleashed through an extramarital
affair with an artist. Fawzi went on to address the increasing difficulty in finding
an actress who would agree to take roles without first stipulating that she not be
depicted in a state of undress or in a sexual situation. He concluded that, given
Egypt's 'difficult times', Layla 'Ilwi should be applauded for her courage in accepting roles that, due to their sensitive and controversial nature, most contemporary
actors would shy away from.

Fawzi's comments might have seemed strange to the handful of Americans
at the screening. To them, 'Ilwi's role likely appeared far from controversial and
the sex scenes diluted and mild. But the director's salute to 'Ilwi was a commentary on a powerful but under-analysed moment in Egyptian social and cultural
production. Fawzi was vehemently condemning, although not naming, what film
critics and the cinema industry have since the late 1990s termed 'clean cinema' (*al-
sinima al-nathifa*). Fawzi was, in fact, nodding to 'Ilwi's transgression of the clean
cinema's credo – a transgression that risks alienating a substantial sector of her
domestic audience.

Fawzi is not the only voice in the Egyptian film industry to ruminate on the dictates of clean cinema and the threat it poses to a filmmaker's cinematic vision and
artistic projects. The 2003 documentary *Les Passionnées du Cinema* (*Women Who Loved
Cinema*) by Marianne Khoury features the opprobrious voice of Kamila Abu Zikri, a
disgruntled young female director, who, despite a critically acclaimed student film
project, found it difficult to work within the commercial film industry's parameters.
Abu Zikri bemoaned the lack of artistic vision among the new generation of women

actors (mostly those who appeared on the scene after 'Ilwi), who choose their roles based on the moralistic standpoint of clean cinema's ethical/religious register.[2]

A bevy of film critics and journalists have recently lamented clean cinema's stranglehold over cinematic production in Egypt. In so doing, they are frequently also mourning the long-lost glory days when cinema was Egypt's second source of national income after cotton. There have been, however, very few critical academic interventions that sought to understand and analyse the phenomenon discursively or, furthermore, question the term clean cinema and its validity. By mapping the contours of the clean cinema debate and locating it within the broader Egyptian religio-cultural context to which it is inextricably linked, this article fills a gap in scholarly work on this new cultural reality.

Examining the concept of clean cinema entails addressing the phenomenon as a mode of cultural production, consumption, distribution and reception. It also requires charting the Islamic revival movement in Egypt and its relationship to cinema. In looking at what have become known as clean films, I will not be focusing on the content of these films. Their individual narrative content is irrelevant to the task at hand. What I offer here is an analysis of the form and structure of a body of films that share a specific set of conventions that today constitute the new genre of clean cinema. I explore the inter- and extra-textual elements of the clean cinema phenomenon by drawing on the plethora of commentary on these films and the stars who appear in them. My discursive analysis of the clean cinema genre provides a needed exploration of the inter-textual relationship between cinema and the Islamic piety movement as sites of cultural and social production and consumption.

What is clean cinema?

In an article in the *Wall Street Journal*, entitled, 'Egypt TV's veil uproar', Mariam Fam offers a description of the new genre:

> In a country that proudly calls itself the 'Hollywood of the East', a group of actresses has touched off a furor by appearing on television and in movies with a new look: the conservative Islamic veil … At least five actresses are at the heart of the controversy after adopting a devout style of dress not only in their personal lives but also as part of the characters they portray. Their decision has sparked a huge public debate over the role of religion in art and society in one of the most important cultural centers in the Muslim World. (Fam 2006: B1)

Clean cinema is a new mode of cultural production and consumption that is linked to representations of the body in film. Such bodily representations are animated by a reconfiguration of the cinematic bodies of artists (especially female artists) to fit within a normative religio-ethical project that has been gaining momentum and popularity in Egypt since the early 1990s. Central to this religiously inflected ethical project is proper bodily comportment, piety, social awareness and responsibility.

The cinematic adaptation of this religio-ethical project entails devising aesthetic strategies that mirror the ethical and moral vision of such a religious project. On the visual level, clean cinema aims at eschewing any overt or explicit portrayal of sexuality, impropriety or nudity – meaning revealing clothing that shows a woman's cleavage, stomach or thighs.[3] Film critics coined the term to describe, almost always disparagingly, this genre of film that is sanitised of any visual depiction of sex, however oblique, and has given rise to a new generation of actors, who have acquired their stardom through clean films. These stars have become propellers and proponents of the new cinematic genre; they are exemplars of a new screen morality that echoes and constitutes a shifting societal sensibility. Apart from being a mode of cultural production, clean cinema articulates a mode of embodiment, a new way of experiencing and representing the body on the screen and in society. Shifting concepts of gender norms and expectations mark this mode of embodiment. One particularly potent articulation of the gendered implications of clean cinema is the notion of 'repentant actors', which refers to female actors who renounce acting and don the Islamic headscarf. This term, however, is not used to describe male actors who stop acting due to their newly found religiosity. Thus, female stars play a decisive role in upholding a shifting code of cultural production – one that caters to an increasingly conservative consumer base that seeks religiously inflected cultural products.

Despite its seemingly transparent valence, clean cinema is a nebulous term that obscures the complexities of the shifting modes of cultural production and consumption of the past two decades. It immediately conjures its opposite: dirty cinema. If the label clean describes the new mode of cinematic production/consumption in Egypt, it then follows that previous modes of film production/consumption are to be described as dirty – an epithet that the film critics themselves would reject. The hygienic trope assumes a too neat and rigid system of classifying films that simplifies the changing geographies of cinematic production. Certainly, there is a new regime of cleansing films of overt sexuality and that regime can expose a great deal about new modes of cinematic production. Yet, critically engaging the term itself allows for the interrogation of the productive power of Egyptian film criticism and how it entrenches the very object it opposes.

The new regime of bodily discipline in film is inextricably linked to Egypt's upsurge of religiosity that has steadily intensified since the 1990s. One of the starkest aspects of this religiosity is its emphasis on personal piety and bodily modesty. Islamist religiosity in this case destabilises the category of modern; it presents an alternative urban modern lifestyle that is not simply compatible with Islam but, more importantly, faithfully adheres to its purported essence. The upsurge of religiosity has had a discernable impact on clean cinema, whose seminal ethos is *al-fann al-hadif* (purposeful art).

This ethos dictates a vision of an art tinted by religion in order to achieve a constructive social purpose that, in turn, provides the art's *raison d'être* and source of legitimacy. Thus, certain cinematic roles and characters – the prostitute, the seductress and the adulteress, among others – are considered undesirable and are socially and cinematically ostracised. Within these cleansing conventions, the onus is on female artists to uphold the dictates of this form of cultural production.

Female stars, for their part, are increasingly insisting on taking roles purified of overt sexuality. An almost obsessive preoccupation with nudity and sex constitutes a staple feature of interviews with female artists in newspapers, magazines and tabloids. Since the mid-1900s, the same formulaic questions have become standard fare. The interviewer typically asks the actor if she will agree to appear in seduction scenes, if she will agree to be kissed on screen and if she will wear a bathing suit as part of her role.

The highly successful film *Isma'iliyya Rayih Gayy* (*Ismailia, Round Trip*) (1997) was a cultural and social milestone of the clean cinema genre. The film explores the stellar rise to fame of a poor and talented crooner – an exhausted theme in Egyptian cinema – and was a commercial landmark that opened the doors to stardom for a new generation of stars, mostly males but including some females. It is often hailed as the film that enticed audiences back into movie theatres after a long abandonment.[4] The film also initiated a de facto monopoly of slapstick comedy as the hegemonic genre and cash cow of the industry for the coming decade. Signalling the rise of a new generation of Egyptian male comedians and a noticeable marginalisation of female roles, the striking aspect of the film – one that would become a common convention of the whole genre – is its chasteness.

Indeed, *Isma'iliyya Rayih Gayy* is emblematic of the concept of clean cinema in its self-conscious evasion of any representation of explicit sexuality (even the one quintessentially Hollywood-inspired kiss between the male and female protagonists was curtailed). The popularity and prevalence of the slapstick genre, with its reliance on male comedians and its relegation of female actors to the ill-developed supporting characters, was not accidental. As Edgar Morin has argued: 'The comic ... is also a sexual innocent ... He lacks the psychological characteristics of virility ... This desexualised hero is frequently in love. His love is sublime because it is not founded on sexual domination or appropriation' (Morin 2005: 90–92). Thus, the slapstick genre is a vehicle for the sexual chasteness that is so central to the new regime of sexual/visual discipline in Egyptian cinema.

Clean cinema poses a paradox for the people who have named and defined it. On the one hand, as mentioned earlier, many film-makers and critics severely criticise this cinematic phenomenon for holding a religiously inflected moral system as a criterion for evaluating artistic works. They thereby construct a false historical trajectory of a cinema that has hitherto been secular and devoid of religion. Film-makers and critics also criticise clean cinema for its supposed potential to destabilise Egypt's cultural weight as the Hollywood of the East.

On the other hand, it was precisely the clean cinema genre that revived the declining Egyptian film industry, which had reached an unprecedented low in the late 1980s and early 1990s. The massive and unexpected success of the film *Isma'iliyya Rayih Gayy* injected millions of Egyptian pounds into the moribund film industry. The film's revenue propelled producers to invest in production, which resulted in increased film budgets, higher production values and improved post-production services, such as advertising. The success of the formulaic genre also coincided with the rise of the cineplex or multi-screen movie theatres attached to the new shopping malls mushrooming in Cairo and Alexandria. The end result was a general investment in the cinema industry; it was a commercial and industrial boom. Thus, clean cinema came to inhabit a paradoxical space for film critics – it was at once demonised and celebrated.

Between clean cinema and entrepreneur cinema

A cursory look at the trajectory of Egyptian cinema from the 1970s to today reveals some of the major shifts in production and consumption practices. In the past 30 years, two modes of film production and consumption have emerged on the Egyptian cinema screen: *al-sinima al-nathifa* (clean cinema) of the 1990s and *sinima al-muqawalat* (entrepreneur cinema) of the 1980s. These two genres reflect two varying visions of art vis-à-vis religion. The differences between these two modes of film production illustrate the shifting approaches to Islamising public culture in Egypt.

Often referred to as Hollywood on the Nile, Egypt was the first and only Arab country to develop a fully-fledged film industry. With a total output of more than 3,000 films, Egyptian cinema asserted its dominance and hegemonic presence as the only Hollywood-influenced industry in the Middle East. This film industry has historically relied – for the most part – on commercial films fuelled by a star system. Much to the chagrin of those Arab film-makers who characterise Egyptian cinema as lowbrow, commercial entertainment lacking any artistic value, Egyptian films have left an indelible cultural mark on Egypt as well as on the Middle East and beyond during the past 80 years. From the beginning, the Egyptian film industry was not intended solely for local consumption; it was and continues to be eagerly consumed all over the Arab world. Indeed, the very term Egyptian cinema has become interchangeable with Arab cinema in popular Middle Eastern consciousness.[5] The cultural weight of Egyptian films has also transcended national and linguistic borders; Hebrew speakers in Israel as well as people in India and Eastern Europe are also audiences for Egyptian film.

Viola Shafik (2001: 29–33) divides the period from 1971 until today into two parts: the electronic media era (1971–91) and the satellite era (since 1991). The former is characterised by technological developments in the media industry, such as the introduction of the videocassette recorder (VCR), while the latter is marked by the proliferation of transnational satellite broadcasting television channels. Shafik uses this technology-driven classification to map the main political and social changes in Egyptian society that have played an indelible role in shaping cinematic production. These changes include Anwar al-Sadat's economic open-door policy (*infitah*), the spread of a new morality movement characterised by an aggressive religious fervour, the rise of an Egyptian *nouveaux riche* fuelled by petrodollars, and the proliferation of the mostly Saudi Arabian-owned satellite channels that have forcefully entered the field of cinema and television production (Shafik 2001: 37).[6]

It is within this political, social and religious context that entrepreneur cinema and clean cinema emerge. Despite similarities between these two genres, collapsing them into one obscures an important complexity in Egyptian cinema and conflates two different visions of Islamising society. Although both genres were influenced by a highly conservative and moralistic religiosity, there remain salient differences. Entrepreneur cinema boomed in the 1980s and refers to a mode of film production, distribution and consumption that was the product of Sadat's *infitah* policies, the technological innovation of the VCR and the influential role of petrodollars (mainly Saudi Arabian investment capital) in cinema production. These factors gave rise to a new breed of films characterised by mediocre production standards, hasty direction (filming was sometimes completed in a week) and the use of non-star actors. These films were primarily targeted for video distribution and adhered to the strict censorship codes applied in Gulf countries.

Muqawalat cinema was coterminous with the *Wahhabi*-inspired religiosity that triggered a fierce discussion on the sinfulness of art and prescribed the veiling of actresses and belly dancers. This religiosity was widespread during the 1980s and entailed women publicly renouncing acting and their 'sinful' careers. These women artists came to be known as the repentant artists (*al-fannanat al-ta'ibat*). Their choices involved both a renunciation of their previous paths as well as a sort of self-imposed semi-reclusiveness. Writing about this phenomenon, Shafik notes:

> [F]rom 1987 to 1994 up to twenty-five actresses declared their retreat from show business and veiled themselves, complying with the calls of Muslim fundamentalist teaching (that pontificates that art is sinful). The reasons were various: a growing sense of morality, increasing family pressures, age, and maybe even (as some newspapers suspected) bribery. (Shafik 2001: 36)[7]

Whereas *muqawalat* films are primarily produced for export and directed toward a Gulf spectator/consumer, clean films are for the most part directed toward Egyptian audiences. These audiences are comprised mainly of youth, who constitute the bulk of the movie-going stratum and who have come of age at the apogee of a new wave of religiosity, with its changing social codes. In the 1980s, the phenomenon of the repentant artists entailed the termination of the artistic careers of many female artists, based on their belief in the sinfulness of art. However, the 1990s witnessed the return of many of these artists – their heads newly covered – to the screen, mostly in television dramas. The new generation of female actors, unlike the preceding one, does not renounce acting even if they decide to wear the Islamic headscarf. Instead, the continuation of acting careers is sanctioned by the choice of roles. Hence, many young female stars seek chaste roles, sterilised of any representations of sexuality or nudity.

New cinema, new bodies

The striking feature of the new screen and societal morality in Egypt is its unequivocal focus on women and women's bodies. The popular wave of donning the Islamic headscarf is a testament to the success of the piety movement. Women's bodies are the battleground for a societal war on immodesty and immorality. This hygienic trope has worked in many instances in popular culture; cleanliness is a social, semiotic and moral order and the aestheticised body is a body without dirt that does not challenge social control or discipline (Fiske 1991: 99). In the case of clean cinema, the clean body is the chaste female body, purified of the sullying effects of sexuality.

One of the interesting aspects of the new clean cinema is a discernible fear of the visual and a desire to tame and domesticate its potential for impropriety. In clean cinema, with its strong moorings in the larger piety movement, visual representations of desire and sexuality are considered polluting and dangerous. It does not follow, however, that clean films exclude sexual themes or motifs. On the contrary, these films develop a new mode of representing sex and the sexual. To fit within the moral expectation of the genre, clean films develop oral and narrative strategies to convey stories that include strong sexual motifs. For example, Kamila Abu Zikri's most recent film, *An al-'Ishq wa al-Hawa* (*On Love and Passion*) (2006), revolves around extramarital sex, prostitution, abortion and marital infidelity. Yet not a single kiss or amorous embrace is rendered visually; the storylines are instead relayed through narration and symbolism.

Egyptian cinema and the spectre of 'Iranisation'

In October 2006 *The Times* of London published the article 'Hollywood fashion eclipsed by Islam as actresses cover up'. It echoed a sense of panic that secular intellectuals, film-makers, critics and some journalists in Egypt express vis-à-vis the trend of a highly visible cinematic religiosity. The article began by relaying a disoriented alarm shared by the interviewees:

> Something big is happening in Cairo, the Hollywood of the Middle East. Actresses are getting overtly religious and wearing the Islamic headscarf, or even the veil. The move has roused controversy in the country that dominates the Arab film business and where actresses were traditionally a class apart, more akin to belly dancers and entertainers. (*The Times* 2006)

During 2006, prominent journalists, intellectuals and film critics waged a virulent campaign against the genre of clean cinema in general, and female stars who decided to don the Islamic headscarf in particular. They accused both the genre and these stars of plotting to destroy Egyptian art by applying their religious criteria. For example, the famous Egyptian screenwriter Usama Anwar 'Ukasha accused scarf-donning Egyptian actors with intentionally organising the destruction of Egyptian art (*The Times* 2006).

The most rabid attack came against the newly veiled actress Hanan Turk's declarations about how Egyptian cinema should be transformed. In an interview with the Egyptian independent daily *Nahdat Misr* (quoted in *The Times* 2006), Turk proclaimed that Egyptian cinema should take Iranian cinema as its model. She argued that women wearing headscarves did not impede the Iranian cinematic industry from producing internationally acclaimed, award-winning and artistically superior films.[8] Given the current Shi'a–Sunni sectarian divide in many areas of the region, as well as the perceived threat of increasing Iranian regional influence to Egypt's historical hegemony, Turk's comments triggered an aggressive campaign against her. Agence France Presse (AFP) described Turk's comments and the responses they provoked: Turk's 'conversion', the article stated, 'was the latest event to electrify the ongoing debate on the Islamisation of Egyptian society, with artistic circles lamenting her decision but many youths celebrating her as a trendsetter' (AFP 2006).

Turk's case exemplifies the evolution of clean cinema. When I met Turk three years ago, she was not wearing the headscarf, though she had become very religious.

We met on the set of one of her films, at a shoddy nightclub in Cairo. In breaks between scenes, Turk performed prayers and read the Qur'an in an ostentatious display of piety. In interviews with Egyptian newspapers and magazines, Turk, a star of the new generation of Egyptian female actors, underscored that although she considered herself a sinner for not wearing the Islamic headscarf, she did not yet feel ready to take that step, and would not give up acting. Turk went on to describe her new-found religiosity as spiritual (veiling her heart, she explained, is more important than veiling her hair). She was adamant about accepting only those roles that obey the principle of *al-fann al-hadif*.[9]

Turk's comments are similar to those of her contemporaries and bear a great resemblance to the teachings of trendy Islamic preachers, such as 'Amr Khalid, described by a recent *New York Times Magazine* article as 'the world's most famous and influential Muslim televangelist' (Shapiro 2006: 47). Echoing the teachings of Khalid and other preachers, who encourage young women to balance an active life with a pious existence, Turk does not see a contradiction between working as an actor and being religious, a departure from previous opinions that declared acting sinful.

Stars, spectators and embodiment

> When I look back on my acting career before deciding to veil I realize that I wasn't myself. I wasn't happy with myself so I returned to my true self through returning to God.
>
> Shahira, a former actor, interview in *al-Maw'id*, November 2005

Shahira was an actor who donned the headscarf, quit her career and then, after years of semi-reclusiveness, returned as a preacher (*da'iya*) on a television show. She elaborated on her new role by stating that it was her duty as a Muslim woman to practise *da'wa* (preaching). Being an artist, she stated, made her realise that the media provides a powerful venue for reaching a wide constituency. She expressed her joy that through her television programme she could illuminate the lives of many women by showing them the path of true Islam.

Shahira gauged her success by the number of fan letters she received from women who reported donning the Islamic headscarf after watching her television programme, which they averred had been a beacon for their own way back to their true selves. When asked to comment on the fact that her daughter acts in films but does not cover her hair, Shahira retorted that just as no one forced her to wear the headscarf, she would not force her daughter to do so. She pointed out, 'besides, my daughter sets an example of moral correctness, as evidenced by the choice of cinematic and television roles that promote chastity, decency, and righteousness' (interview in *al-Maw'id* 2005: 15–16).

Richard Dyer explains that 'stars have a privileged position in the definition of social roles and types, and this must have real consequences of how people believe they can and should behave' (Dyer 1986: 8). There is a dialectical relationship between female stars and their women spectators. Exploring this dialectical relationship enables us to complicate and move beyond the question: 'are (women) stars a phenomenon of production (arising from what the makers of films provide) or of consumption (arising from what the audience for films demands)?' (Dyer 1986: 9). Female stars of the new clean cinema are, like other stars, both produced and consumed. Production and consumption are not separate processes but part of a larger framework whereby consumers shape and are shaped by production.

Within the cosmology of the piety movement that encourages modesty, spectators produce stars with their expectations that actors embody certain roles and eschew others based on a strict moral code. Concurrently, *al-fann al-hadif* produces spectators as disciplined moral subjects, whose tastes, desires and behaviours are re-educated. Shahira's path to the true self and her guidance of others are tightly wound up in the mutuality of the production and consumption of cultural practice.

The cultivation of this kind of true self is accompanied by the embodiment of a different kind of body. Although clean cinema is not the sole site of production of these new selves and modes of embodiment, the phenomenon plays a salient and highly visible role on the level of both the female stars and their spectators. Women stars occupy a marginal, liminal role in clean cinema; they signify a curious presence/absence. Their presence is shadowed and dwarfed by the male actors and is contingent upon the erasure of their sexuality and the silencing of their bodies. Clean films represent the female characters as simultaneously asexual and potentially threatening to the sexual and social order. The women actors of the new clean cinema inhabit a body that is at once chaste, ascetic and overwhelmingly appealing, even prurient in its modesty and morality.

Proponents of clean films tolerate the presence of unveiled women actors on the screen only if their roles convey modesty by other means. The most important of these performances of modesty is abstaining from enacting any sexual scenes, known in the industry as *mashahid sakhina* (literally, hot scenes). Many Egyptian female stars find themselves obliged to adhere strictly to these dictates in order to maintain their fan base.[10]

There is a strong affiliation between the embodiment of a chaste persona within clean cinematic representations and the cultivation of a new pious body that is one of the main preoccupations of the new Islamic movement in Egypt.[11] The pressure of this project of self-cultivation imposes certain rules on the cinematic representation of women. More importantly, perhaps, it affects the private lives of the female stars, who precariously negotiate a public and private persona loyal to the dictates of the new wave of religiosity. When interviewed on the prohibition against representations of sex, nudity and seduction, many female stars respond in a formulaic manner; these roles are so far removed from their nature as human beings that they are not even capable of embodying them.

A good example that demonstrates the star-spectator dynamic within the religiosity movement is a 2005 interview in *Akhbar al-Nujum* with Mayy 'Izz al-Din, one of the rising stars of clean cinema. This young star's words shed light on female spectatorship's identificatory practices with stars in clean cinema:

> I choose my roles with an eye on the spectator, especially my female spectators, whom I aspire not to disappoint with my role choices. One of the things I do to gauge the reactions of my fans is to make clandestine visits to the movie

screenings to watch how people react to my roles. In one of the screenings, an older veiled woman was watching a scene in which the male character tries to kiss me. The veiled woman hissed in a low voice, 'What are you doing, Mayy? Why do you want to disappoint me by agreeing to be kissed?' And, to the woman's delight, when the scene ended without the male protagonist kissing me, she whispered to herself, 'That's a good girl, Mayy. You have not disappointed me by succumbing to immoral acts'. (*Akhbar al-Nujum* 2005: 47)

'Izz al-Din expressed her happiness that she had not disappointed her fans but, more importantly, she was grateful for the spectator's guidance (the star revealed her identity to the spectator after the screening and thanked her for her comments). 'Izz al-Din reiterated that she would refuse any role that entailed kissing or nudity because her 'essential being' (*takwin*) did not agree with such roles.

This interview focused on the issue of identification as a crucial element in the star–audience relationship. There are different types of identificatory relationships that audiences can enter with film stars. The relationships most relevant to clean cinema are what Jackie Stacey calls cinematic identification (which refers to the viewing experience) versus extra-cinematic identification (which refers to the star identity in different cultural space and time), and identification based on difference versus identification based on similarity (Stacey 1991: 159).

'Izz al-Din's interview revealed the merging of the cinematic and the extra-cinematic identificatory practice. We saw the pious female spectator setting a moral expectation for both the cinematic character that 'Iz el-Din impersonated and the real-life character of the star herself. This expectation inscribed the kiss as a taboo that both the film character and the female star should not transgress in her life if she wanted to remain in favour with her pious female spectators. Thus, this was also a case of identification based on similarity (not difference) between the morality of the spectator, the film character and the female star. Such identification processes between actor and spectator became the source of spectator pleasure.

Another salient point in the 'Izz al-Din interview was the spectator's imaginary conversation with the star as she performed on-screen. This spectator–star conversation (both on-screen and off) revealed the democratisation of censorship as well as a process of internal censorship, both of which are arguable consequences of the piety movement. Historically, censorship as a mode of cultural policing and taste formation in Egypt was the mandate of the state censor. The Egyptian censorship law, issued in 1976, states:

'Heavenly' religions should not be criticised. Heresy and magic should not be positively portrayed. Immoral actions and vices are not to be justified and must be punished. Images of naked human bodies or the inordinate emphasis on individual erotic parts, the representation of sexually arousing scenes, and scenes of alcohol and drug use are not allowed. Also prohibited is the use of obscene and indecent speech. The sanctity of marriage, family values, and one's parents must be respected. Besides the prohibition on the excessive use of horror and violence, or inciting their imitation, it is forbidden to represent social problems as hopeless, to upset the mind, or to divide religions, classes, and national unity. (Quoted in Shafik 2001: 34)

Despite its highly prohibitive claims, the law's enforcement has never been strict. The state's decision to invoke its prohibitions and ban or censor a cultural product is arbitrary (depending on who is in power at the censor's bureau) and politically motivated. For example, in times of crisis, such as the 1967 defeat,[12] when public morale was at a deep low, the censor's bureau loosened the prohibition on depictions of sex. Films of the late 1960s and early 1970s therefore enjoyed a kind of sexual licence not afforded to later works.

The new piety movement, however, is outside the purview of the state and is developing new forms of informal censorship. The work of the state-appointed censor becomes complemented or challenged by the self-appointed censor/spectator. This position provides another disciplinary filter through which cultural products pass. Whereas state censorship is repressive yet arbitrary, self-appointed moralistic censorship is meticulous. In recent years, many films deemed suitable by the state censors were found to be inappropriate by religious spectators. Some movie theatres in Cairo and Alexandria began cutting scenes that spectators objected to. *American Beauty* was one film that was subjected to drastic spectator-driven censorship.[13]

One can thus conceive of the role of censorship in cultural governance through a generative or productive lens. Censorship, whether official (state) or unofficial (Islamist religiosity), is thus 'an ongoing activity of definition and boundary maintenance and reproduced in challenges to, and transgressions of, the very limits it seeks to fix' (Khun 1988: 128). So, on the one hand, despite prohibitive state censorship laws, some Egyptian filmmakers were (and still are) able to circumvent state prohibitions, making use of legal loopholes to stretch their margin of freedom in a productive and creative fashion. On the other hand, the clean cinema genre, through self-imposed regulation, helps produce an ethical, moral subject that has the capacity of 'ethical self-monitoring', thus producing and redefining the prohibition. In this Egyptian cultural industry context, 'prohibition and productivity may be regarded not as opposites, nor as mutually exclusive, but as two sides of the same coin' (Kuhn 1988: 127).

Thus, unofficial censorship can effectively set the contours of permissible representations of the body, desire and sexuality. The religiosity movement's project of refashioning the social body becomes central to how unofficial and mass-based censorship seeks to refashion a certain cinematic body.

Coda

A Cairo daily newspaper announced the return of an actress – now wearing the headscarf – who had renounced acting 13 years before, justifying her return as recognition of the importance of assuming her place in society through socially constructive roles. A popular weekly magazine quoted a young actress who had declined a role in the renowned director Youssef Chahine's latest film because the role involved sexual scenes. A plethora of foreign publications alarmingly signalled their apprehension about the Islamisation of popular culture in Egypt and the Arab world. Such statements have become ubiquitous landmarks of Egyptian cultural geography. They point to the concept of clean cinema and its project of refashioning representations of the body – not just of Egyptian female cinematic roles, but Egyptian visual culture generally. In fact, cinema in Egypt has become a powerful arena in which the Islamist movement successfully triggers the apprehension of an Egyptian state that is increasingly lacking in legitimacy and wanting in popular support.

Female stars of clean cinema represent normative ways of being, feeling and behaving in a society in the midst of a pietistic wave of religiosity. Female stars negotiate a precarious position within this new constellation of power. Cinematic female actors and female societal actors/spectators are not passive products of top-down religious governance. The women discussed here are neither dupes of the cultural industries nor the puppets of an Islamic revival movement. They are active producers of meaning in everyday life and social agents in a new social and political reality.

It is important to note that there are other modes of cultural production that forego the scriptures of this genre. The rise of clean cinema in the 1990s was, in fact, concurrent with the proliferation of transnational satellite television channels. These satellite channels, which are beyond the institutional reach of state censorship, popularise a genre of music videos (known throughout the Arab world as video clips) that rely heavily on highly sexualised representations of women. The salient phenomenon of the video clips transgresses clean cinema's taboos of sexuality and nudity. In fact, these music videos are the source of a major controversy throughout the Arab world and have increasingly become the subject of academic and intellectual gaze.[14] Both clean cinema and the video clip occupy the same cultural space and are primarily directed towards young people. The coterminous existence of these phenomena indicates the coexistence of contradictory models of cultural production in Egyptian popular culture.

In the final analysis, what has emerged is the piety movement's embrace of popular culture's potential to propagate a religio-ethical normative project. The sinfulness of art – a discourse that was prevalent in the 1980s and resulted in many female actors renouncing their artistic careers and veiling – has been replaced by a different discourse that is amicable to popular culture as an arena of social purity and morality. This new approach toward popular culture has enabled the religiosity movement to mobilise, indeed revitalise, cinema as a physical, visual and moral space. Within this new vision of popular culture and its potential in the Islamist project of self- and social ethical cultivation, censorship cannot be simply understood as repressive.

Currently in Egypt, both actors and spectators cooperate and compete with official state censors in formulating the codes of cinematic and social representations. Clean cinema provides many instances in which censorship can be perceived as existing along a repressive–productive axis. In attempting to mirror some of the ideals of the piety movement, particularly vis-à-vis female bodies, clean cinema – a term that started as a journalistic slogan – has been active in an ethical–moral, as well as aesthetic project. In shying away from portraying the illicit, clean cinema has developed new iterations of orality and narrative structure that convey what the visual is restrained from representing.

Notes

1. This essay was first published in 2007 in the *Arab Studies Journal* 15(1). Reprinted with permission.
2. Abu Zikri acquiesced to the hegemonising pressures of the industry with her film *Sana Ula Nasb* (*First Year Crookery*), which is somewhat loyal to the strictures of the clean cinema genre. The film was a commercial success; producers began taking her seriously. Perhaps Abu Zikri's move was only strategic, intended to allow her to gain ground in the industry and ultimately fulfil her artistic vision. Her success in this endeavour is yet to be seen.
3. 'Nudity', in the sense of visual depictions of bare breasts, bottoms or genitals, is unfamiliar to Egyptian cinema. In the Egyptian discourse on clean cinema, however, the term nudity (*'ury*) is used mostly to imply the choice of revealing clothing that shows a woman's cleavage, stomach or thighs. Several actresses wearing bikinis in recent films, for example, have been heavily criticised in the media for their alleged on-screen nudity.
4. By the 1980s, movie theatres in Cairo and Alexandria were in a state of decrepitude, with almost no investment in upgrading existing venues or establishing new ones. This state of disrepair contributed to spectators preferring to watch films on video rather than going to the movies. By the mid-1990s, a revival of sorts took place. New screens were added and old theatres were renovated.
5. In popular usage and consciousness in Arab countries, film *'arabi* (Arabic film) almost always refers to film *misri* (Egyptian film).
6. The bulk of these transnational satellite channels are funded by Saudi Arabian capital. Saudi influence is economically liberal but socially and politically highly conservative. This paradoxical stance can be discerned through the proliferation of profit-making Saudi-owned and financed satellite channels. These channels air what journalists and writers in Egypt have described as quasi-pornographic music videos alongside religious programming, yet in Saudi Arabia a prohibition still holds against the establishment of movie theatres.
7. It is worth noting that in interviews with repentant artists, some recurring tropes are cited as fuelling their decision to wear the Islamic headscarf. These include a supreme calling communicated through dreams and an intense fear of death. The death of a loved one seems to be a major determining factor behind the decision to renounce an acting career and don the headscarf. Similarly, the 1992 earthquake that hit Egypt played a role in the decision of several belly dancers to cover their hair.
8. Turk's comments do not indicate any thorough knowledge of post-revolutionary Iranian cinema or familiarity with the strategies that Iranian film-makers use to avoid a stringent censorship system.
9. An example of these interviews with Hanan Turk can be read online at www.akhbarelyom.org.eg/negoom/april05, accessed 10 November 2006.
10. Historically, female performers were always in a socially precarious position. They were perceived as decadent and loose, in a guilty-until-proven-innocent situation until they earned the respect of the audiences.
11. In her ethnography of the piety movement in Cairo, Saba Mahmood perceptively observes that the piety movement's programme of self-cultivation is an 'an entire conceptualisation of the role of the body in the making of the self in which the outward behaviour of the body constitutes both the potentiality as well as the means, through which interiority is realised' (Mahmood 2005).
12. The 1967 defeat of Arab armies in the war with Israel culminated in an immensely humiliating affair for Egyptian and Arab leaders.
13. I experienced this form of censorship first hand when attending a screening of *American Beauty* (Mendes 1999) in an Alexandria movie theatre. When I asked the theatre manager about missing scenes, I was told that the management cut scenes after receiving complaints from audience members about their inappropriateness, despite their official sanctioning by state censors.
14. The first issue of the *Transnational Broadcasting Studies Journal* (Fall 2005) is solely

dedicated to discussing music videos in the Arab world. The volume is entitled, 'Culture wars: the Arabic music video controversy'. The publication is an example of the growing academic interest in the video clip phenomenon. For a taste of the different debates surrounding this cultural product, see Walter Armbrust (2005) 'What would Sayyid Qutb say? Some reflections on video clips', and Patricia Kubala (2005) 'The other face of the video clip: Sami Yusuf and the call for *al-fann al-hadif* in Armbrust et al (2005). For a more sensationalist take on the phenomenon, see Abdel-Wahab (2005).

References

Abdel-Wahab, M. Elmessiri (2005) 'Ruby and the chequered heart', *al-Ahram Weekly*, 17–23 March

Agence France Presse (AFP) (2006) 'Daring Egyptian actress dons headscarf, calls Iran "role model"', 16 June

Akhbar al-Nujum (2005) interview with Mayy 'Izz al-Din, 4 March

Al-Maw'id (2005) interview with Shahira, 18 November

An al-'Ishq wa al-Hawa (2006) directed by Kamla abu-Zikri, Al-Massa Al-Nasr-Oscar, Cairo, Egypt

Armbrust, W., Amin, H. and Schleifer, S.A. (eds) (Fall 2005) *Transnational Broadcasting Studies: Satellite Broadcasting in the Arab and Islamic Worlds*, Cairo and Oxford, American University and Oxford University

Durgnat, R. (1967) *Films and Feelings*, London, Faber and Faber

Dyer, R. (1986) *Stars*, London, BFI Publishing

Fam, Mariam (2006) 'Egypt TV's veil uproar', *Wall Street Journal*, 31 October, http://www.timesonline.co.uk/tol/news/world/middle_east/article610797.ece, accessed 26 November 2006

Fiske, J. (1991) *Understanding Popular Culture*, London and New York, Routledge

Isma'iliyya Rayih Gayy (1997) directed by Karim Diya' al-Din, Al-Adl Group, Cairo, Egypt

Kuhn, A. (1998) *Cinema, Censorship, and Sexuality*, New York and London, Routledge

Mahmood, S. (2005) *The Politics of Piety: The Islamic Revival and the Feminist Subject*, Princeton, NJ, Princeton University Press

Morin, E. (2005) *The Stars*, Minneapolis, University of Minnesota Press

Shafik, V. (2001) 'Egyptian cinema', in *Companion Encyclopedia of Middle Eastern and North African Film*, London and New York, Routledge

Shapiro, Samantha M. (2006) 'Ministering to the upwardly mobile Muslim', *New York Times Magazine*, 30 April

Stacey, J. (1991) 'Feminine fascination: forms of identification in star–audience relations', in Gledhill, C. (ed) *Stardom: Industry of Desire*, London and New York, Routledge

The Times, (2006) 'Hollywood fashion eclipsed by Islam as actresses cover up', 24 October, accessed 10 November 2006

21

Intersex: the forgotten constituency

Julius Kaggwa

Sexuality has remained a controversial subject in Ugandan society, in which leaders of almost all sectors have chosen to ignore the reality that sexual diversity is naturally present and progressive. Story after story has been told of a young or older person who has confirmed – through much soul searching – that their sexuality differs from what conventional society considers normal.

The issue of what is normal and who determines what is normal has also been contentious among those of us who believe that all human beings remain human beings despite differences in sexual development, belief, race, sex, gender, sexual preferences and inclinations. It is also proven that almost all issues pertaining to humanity typically have to do with popularity as opposed to normality. As a result, the popular has been turned into the normal.

It is the popular thing for a midwife to announce from the delivery room, 'It is a boy!' or 'It's a girl!' Occasionally, the infant will be in between girl and boy, but healthy and normal enough to push their way out of the womb and to give a first cry at their entrance into the world. This, however, is not popular and it is therefore considered strange and abnormal. From the onset, it attracts all sorts of biases and prejudices based in cultural fundamentalism, heteronormativity, patriarchy and homophobia.

When I was born with an atypical body anatomy close to 40 years ago, my peasant mother did not know how to handle the situation because there was simply no space to dialogue on an issue such as that one – it was not popular and therefore not normal for a woman to give birth to a child that could not be clearly classified as female or male. She mitigated my and her own trauma the best way she knew how and that was to find a mystical interpretation for it. There were concerns about whether I would ever have 'normal' sexual relations, whether I would ever marry 'just like a normal person', whether I would be able to have children 'just like a normal person', and whether I would be able to develop mentally and intellectually 'just like a normal person'.

The situation was vexing and, with some nudge from an explanation handed down by family ancestral spirits, a decision was quickly reached to classify me as a girl because it was considered an easier gender to control or manipulate. I was then christened Juliet. Given the absence of appropriate medical and psychosocial support at the time, I believe that my parents took what appeared to them as the best course of action to contain a situation that placed huge questions not only on my sexuality and identity but on their own as well.

The struggle to try to 'be' a girl was harrowing. I did everything a girl 'should not' do socially, and occasional rebuking was not effective. From a very early age, I did not expose my nakedness or engage in communal games or festivities because my mother instilled in me strong inhibitions towards these. This could have contributed to why I became an introvert and never developed a love for sports. Nonetheless, I discovered that I was different from as early as primary six when I had the chance to clearly see 'other' girls naked performing a Kiganda female sexuality ritual. I was blessed because both my parents encouraged me to talk to them about my experiences and my mother gave me a satisfactory explanation for my difference. My father was mostly absent, therefore the weight of my condition lay more on my mother than on him and she paid a great price to maintain the silence while ensuring that I lived as 'normally' as possible.

The climax of my struggle happened during puberty when, in an all-girls' boarding school, I failed to fulfil age-old female sexuality milestones, such as menstruation and sexual attraction to the 'opposite' sex. Although I had negligible breast development, I grew unsightly body hair on my face, legs and arms. The most alarming of all was the progressive development of male genitalia and consequent attraction to some of the girls I associated with.

When I was old enough to fully understand my situation, I also learnt that there was a God who had created me and that He was most powerful, able to do or change anything. I latched on to this new relieving belief and sought a prayer-based solution to my sexuality predicament. While I still believe in the supremacy and omnipotence of God and I still strongly subscribe to prayer, I realise that back then my belief was premised upon a false conviction that I was abnormal, haunted by generational curses, with a questionable future and in need of divine deliverance from the sins of my ancestors. I had no idea that my sexuality was simply a diversion from what was popular and furthermore that it happened more often than acknowledged.

At 20 years old, I realised that I had the power of choice over my sexuality and I decided to tell someone. A series of events followed, which included sexual and spiritual counselling. After two years of counselling, I knew that despite the social stigma that lay ahead of me, I simply could not keep up the female image. In my case, the challenges of being either a woman or a man were equal, but what was most important and delightful was that by letting go of the female image, I would never get romantic advances from a man, I would never be forced to find some man to marry me and I would not have to conceal my sexual feelings for girls. I decided after much, much soul searching that with those thorny issues out of the picture, I was ready to live out the other challenging realities of having been born intersex and those of a gender re-assignment. I stopped the pills, stopped the traditional medicines, stopped the deliverance prayers, took off the skirts, sought medical intervention and 'became' a man.

The interweaving of social and spiritual definitions of sexuality establishes prejudiced categories for human beings in which some are girls and some boys; some single and some married; some divorced and some widowed; some faithful and some promiscuous; some sinful and others saintly; some gay and others straight; some normal and others abnormal; and so on. Such categorisation of people in relation to sexuality leaves no room for fluidity and in my case made me abhor who I was and greatly reduced my ability to rise to my real potential because I was constantly faced with messages that confirmed that something was wrong with my body.

Even after medical interventions years later, there are still aspects of my body, such as surgical scars, that are not quite typical and have had a bearing on my sexuality. It robbed me of the ability to make informed sexual choices in my early adulthood because society – including family relations – indicated that my sexuality was not to be celebrated and anyone who related with me sexually was performing a brave act. This made me a victim of emotional blackmail. I was not supposed to negotiate the terms of my relationships because it was assumed that a partner was actually doing me a favour and placing their own sexuality and reputation on the line by having a sexual relationship with an intersexed individual.

Only after years of exposure and extensive reading have I finally been able to overcome the inhibitions and hindrances concerning my being born intersex and to reclaim my sexuality as a God-given gift of diversity. I have further come to realise that every human being, especially those born with divergent sex development, has a primal desire to express their fundamental nature, and we can all greatly benefit from a paradigm shift in what is 'perceived' and 'real' in our quest for value and meaning in life, love, relationships and sexual intimacy in today's Uganda, which is unbelievably diverse and multicultural. While I chose to pursue an appropriate gender for myself, many intersexed people silently live out their lives in the best guess gender assigned at birth, amid incredible stigma and a low self-image.

That said, heteronormativity and patriarchy still loom large in many ways, including the lack of indigenous expressions for sexual diversity that could be considered 'humane' enough for use in official debates and policy discussions concerning sexual identities, gender identities and sexuality. Cultural and religious fundamentalisms still play a key role in constructing social perceptions on sexuality and related stigma. Despite huge strides I have taken to rise above the deterrent prejudices, I still feel specks of stigma on certain occasions at which my identity is the subject of biased debate in a work, spiritual or family matter.

Of greater interest to me over the years is the irony of society's debates on what is normal and abnormal, right and wrong. For example, there were very strong arguments about the supremacy of white people over non-whites, as well as the supremacy of men over women. The slave trade and the subordination of women were sanctioned and thrived based on these premises. Christianity, too, came to Africa with a strong economic arm, which gave it a powerful social voice, and interpreted African ways and beliefs as primitive and satanic. From as early as the advent of Christianity in Africa, those with the economic means to control have influenced popular perceptions and belief and have made culture and laws based on these.

In conclusion, the issue of sexuality, and particularly the issue of intersexuality, is no different from other issues that have been the focus of rights struggles. The only difference is that in the Ugandan context, as in most parts of Africa, it is an issue that some people would rather was kept silent or at best was addressed only through stigmatising sensational media exposure. It is a forgotten constituency.

The unspoken but predominant message is that positive acknowledgement of sexuality in all its diversity is a destructive and an immoral part of human experience that must be kept in check. This has become a major hindrance in the campaign to challenge heteronormativity and patriarchy in law and policy because there are still deep-rooted beliefs in fixed identities.[1]

Note

1. For further reading about my life, see Kaggwa (1997).

Reference

Kaggwa, Julius (1997) *From Juliet to Julius: In Search of My True Identity,* Kampala, Fountain Publishers

22

The chronicle of an intersexed activist's journey

Sally Gross[1]

I was born to Jewish parents in Cape Town, South Africa in 1953. Although I did not realise this, my genitalia were ambiguous and it is clear, in hindsight, that there were difficulties deciding whether I was to be classified as a little boy or as a little girl. In short, I was intersexed.

In terms of what became standard medical protocol from the mid-1950s, my anatomy at birth would have led to classification as born female. Even as an adult the dimensions of my phallus, which has depth rather than length, is within the range of size which leads to this classification rather than being classified as born male. Back in 1953, though, it was decided to classify me as male. At that time there were certain advantages in law which accrued to those classified as male. Mani Bruce Mitchell, an intersexed activist friend in New Zealand, also born intersexed and classified initially as male (though it was decided two or three years later to reclassify her as female), tells me that a textbook used in New Zealand at that time advised that infants born with ambiguous genitalia should be classified as male if at all possible in order not to deny them 'the prerogatives of maleness'. Perhaps this is what informed decisions taken about the classification of my sex at the time.

In accordance with the Biblical commandment that all Hebrew male infants must be circumcised on the eighth day after birth, there was a circumcision ceremony. Family and friends would have assembled to see it. Usually, the process, which involves removal of the foreskin, is uncomplicated. As scar-tissue testifies, in my case the process was anything but uncomplicated and, as far as I can make out, while it was possible to cut and to draw blood – the 'cision' part of circumcision – it was not possible to cut around, removing the foreskin, and this was due to a dramatic shortfall in what was there which could be cut. The *mohel* – the Hebrew term for a ritual circumciser – evidently struggled with his task in front of my parents' friends and family, explaining the way in which I tended to be treated as different throughout childhood, a sense of whispers and things kept secret from me, and in which there seemed to be things about me that I was not told.

Some months ago, my late father sent me an email in which he expressed anger at the 'stupid' ritual circumciser, who should, on my father's account, have realised that I was a girl and should not have attempted the circumcision. As I have noted, scar-tissue told me as a young adult that circumcision had been problematic. My late father's email revealed something I had not known: that the *mohel* returned a few days later to hack at the still unhealed wounds, presumably also without anaesthetic, in order to try to tidy up the mess. This shocks me.

As for the accusations that the *mohel* was stupid, my sense is that they are unfair. Refusal to attempt a circumcision in that highly public context would probably have had a devastating effect on my parents and on my personal development. The problem, in any case, was not that the *mohel* had stupidly attempted to circumcise a little girl, but rather that I was intersexed: my sexual differentiation, as evidenced by my genitalia, had not taken the typical paths of male and not female, and female and not male. I was not exactly male or female, but somehow had characteristics of both. This sets the context of my life history.

Something which was a bit of a puzzle during my adolescence was that I did not develop sexual attractions – although I found girls and women attractive aesthetically, and indeed sometimes identified more internally with girls and women than with boys and men, albeit without any sense of being a girl trapped in a boy's body, I was not attracted sexually to boys or men either. It bothered me a bit. I eventually realised and came to accept that I am asexual, one of nature's celibates, and it has not bothered me in and of itself since I was an adolescent. Though I do not doubt that this has something to do with the way in which my brain came to be wired in the womb, it is not in and of itself part of the intersex package. There are intersexed people who are attracted sexually to women, there are intersexed people who are attracted sexually to men, there are intersexed people who are attracted sexually to both women and men; and there are also intersexed people like myself who are attracted sexually neither to women nor to men.

Since 2000, I have drafted amendments bearing on intersex for the Alteration of Sex Descriptions Bill and the Promotion of Equality and Prevention of Unfair Discrimination Act (PEPUDA), and these have been lobbied into law. Getting intersex into PEPUDA is the weightier of the two. Lobbying persuaded the South African Human Rights Commission (SAHRC) that intersex is a serious human rights issue. This yielded an SAHRC workshop three years ago, which looked at the imposition of genital surgery on intersexed infants and children and the possible need for legislation.

Through Engender, an NGO on whose board I serve, funds were raised to set up Intersex South Africa (ISSA) formally as an Engender project with a full-time coordinator. My role was advisory. The organisation set up a website and it employed two coordinators who developed literature and ran numerous workshops. As of June 2010, with Engender's encouragement and support, ISSA became independent. I now serve as ISSA's director.

Much needs to be done to educate the public about intersex. They need to learn that it is part of the fabric of human diversity and not a threat, a rights issue and not pathology. Teachers and curriculum need content about it. Medical students need input from a medical ethics and human rights perspective. Religious leaders need to be educated about it to educate others. Research about the prevalence of intersex in South Africa (and indeed the rest of Africa), and about attitudes and practices, is needed. We need legislation to limit and regulate non-consensual genital surgery on the intersexed, and legislation must be screened with implications for the intersexed in mind.

The past three years have convinced me that although NGO involvement is helpful it is not necessarily sufficient. Government needs to be brought on board to act as a catalyst if possible. A modest directorate with a director, a deputy director and one or two administrative assistants-cum-project-officers, with a mandate to engage with other departments regarding the rights and needs of the intersexed, could achieve a great deal at minimal cost, were it to work closely with ISSA. What has been most important, from the perspective of intersex activism, is the amendment of PEPUDA and, through it, the statutory introduction of intersex into the interpretation of the equality clause. Should I die in my bed tonight, be I remembered for it or not, my life and endeavours will have laid the legislative foundations in our law for the significant enhancement of the rights and prospects of people who are intersexed. Knowing this, when I go gently into that good night I can go proudly.

Note

1. Founder and director of Intersex South Africa. See http://www.intersex.org.za, accessed 12 November 2010

23

Gender dynamics: a transsexual overview

Audrey Mbugua

Introduction

I could begin with a definition…

I could try a few paragraphs something like this: transsexualism (also known as gender identity disorder, gender dysphoria) represents a desire to live and be accepted as a member of another sex/gender, usually accompanied by a sense of anguish and torment around one's anatomical sex – because of the way this connotes a gender – and sometimes accompanied by a wish to have hormonal treatment and surgery to make one's body as congruent as possible with the preferred sex. The goal of therapeutic intervention is to help the individual achieve maximum psychological and physical well-being (GIRES 2002).

Some researchers and activists see this as a form of intersex condition and in this case not an atypical genital differentiation of foetuses, but a mismatch of the neurologically wired gender identity in the brain with the sex organs of the person. Not everyone chooses hormonal treatment and/or surgery but the idea is that the hormonal, surgical and psychological procedures of transition reduce the dissonance between the psychological identification as male or female, on the one hand, and the phenotype and associated gender role on the other. Such treatments are regarded as highly successful; one study indicates a degree of satisfaction of 87 per cent in trans women and 97 per cent in trans men (Green and Fleming 1990).

Outcomes depend, however, on the individual's personal strengths as well as the level of social and professional support available during and after the process of transition. It is also significant that although psychotherapeutic treatment remains, for many, a helpful ingredient, the inevitable distress caused by this condition cannot be alleviated by any conventional psychiatric treatment. This is true whether treatment be psychoanalytic, eclectic, aversion treatment or by any standard psychiatric drugs (Green 1999). The aim of psychiatric treatments is, therefore, not to remove the condition, but to mitigate its most stressful aspects (GIRES 2003).

And then I would need a paragraph about how this kind of definition is not integrated into African contexts of understanding about trans people and about what this might mean, in practice, for those of us living in these contexts. I might also need a paragraph about whether or not I think it is even useful to create definitions, and about the difference between medicalised approaches to transsexual and transgendered experiences and political approaches. On and on I could flow.

I am Kenyan; I'm young; I want to engage in questions of definition, and in ideas about the medical and about the political. I need, however, to start somewhere completely different. I need to start at home. It's not going to sound pretty. It's going to be personal. I'll start slowly, though.

The inexplicable fear of transsexual people

I find it intriguing that there is such a pronounced fear of transsexual people among men in Kenya. Among women in my context, I find there is generally an atmosphere of curiosity especially when transsexual women and cisgender women are in spaces such as bathrooms together. I have witnessed comical curiosity on the part of some female friends of mine. They want to know whether I pee while standing or when squatting. Their curiosity spills into a nest of questions. Can I have children? Do I have a boyfriend? or a girlfriend? Can I get an erection? 'Let's feel your "boobs" and if they are real.'

I wish I could say this for some of the encounters I have had with men. In my experience, most Kenyan men are incapable of hiding their deep-seated fear and apprehension of transsexual women. I want to say something about this terror; I want to say something *to* the 'terrorised'.

Two years ago, I was working at an agricultural research station in Nakuru. We had a computer pool, through which members of staff could access internet services. One morning two men and I were doing our stuff and one of the men left the room, closing the door behind him. After some minutes, the other man opened the door and went back to his work. As I was about to finish emailing my friends, he asked me for my name and why I thought he had opened the door. Well, I gave him my name and said that I didn't know why he had opened the door and I didn't think it was necessary for me to know. The gentleman told me that he had opened it because he didn't want people to think he was a homosexual because of working in a room where I was present.

Sir, I'm not a sex object. And the emotional, sexual and psychological stereotyping of transsexual people is effortlessly churned out by cretins who, despite the fact that they call themselves educated, cannot be trusted to act on the benefit of intellect. Let me go on to offer a lecture to Kenyan men.

You are woefully ignorant. And, in your arrogant heterosexuality, you say and think woefully ignorant things. Here are some pointers:

- Not all transsexual women are sexually attracted to men. Some are into other women and some are asexual.
- Being a Kenyan man doesn't remotely mean that you can arouse a morsel of interest in transsexual women. I know some of you men have been made to believe, by Kenyan women who want to get into your wallets, that you are irresistible and you have foolishly bought into this lie hook, line and sinker. But

don't expect me to soothe your turgid egos. Some of you look like the back of my shoe and I would never be caught in bed with you even if my life depended on it.

- You should stop objectifying transsexual women. You should stop objectifying women altogether. Transsexual women, like any woman, are not public sex vending machines. It's not on our agenda to have sex all day long with whatever dummy we meet in the street.

- A transsexual woman is a special type of a woman; she is not a man. She doesn't want to have sex with you unless she chooses to. And she is choosy about her men. Very choosy. The ones who make assumptions about who she is, what she wants, and what she is worth get flushed, faster than a turd.

The lecture continues…

The average Kenyan man, in my experience, in his muddled heteronormative and usually self-aggrandising head, would not want to be seen together with a transsexual woman because he fears that his friends would think he is having 'homosexual-type' sex with the transsexual woman. His terror of her is the terror of 'him'(self).

Discussion of men's fear of transsexual people would be deficient if I failed to elucidate why sexual identities have the kind of gravity they have in Kenyan society. Heteronormativity is deeply embedded in the Kenyan contexts. Whenever we meet someone, we glean certain information from what these people are wearing, their presentation, the way they talk and other outward attributes and then go ahead to label them as female or male. As a national pastime, we become accustomed to the system; the rigidity of this binary system in the life-long assignation of gender. As Kenyans, we are 'comfortable' in our assigned genders and perceived sex; all of our acquaintances are equally satisfied with what they are and we would consider anyone not fitting the system as psychotic. Or worse.

Let me tell you, gentlemen: as you grow up, you will meet some individuals who don't fit in your 'self-sustaining and stable' gender system. Individuals who bend gender, break binaries. Suddenly, what you thought was the natural order of things is now threatened by certain individuals. These individuals are in most cases transsexual people who were assigned one sex and corresponding social rearing, but later are discontent with it all. It's not that they wake up one morning and just decide to shake the foundations of your gender system. Far from it. They feel desperately unhappy in their bodies and the gender roles expected of them by society. It's not a mental illness, but an incongruence of anatomical sex and the psychological sex.

Unfortunately, what most people do when faced with these scenarios is to act without the benefit of intellect. Their thought processes take a break and the beast in them comes out. This is wrong; it's simply wrong. It does not matter that you are ignorant of transsexual concepts or not; it's wrong because the aftermath of your unintelligible actions is borne by transsexual people, who feel the pain of being discriminated against in the labour market while you sip your champagne in your air-conditioned rooms.

You can afford to concoct a number of reasons to justify your irrational behaviour, but know that you are not the only person who has human rights and that your preoccupation with trying to make everyone fit in your system is a threat to any of the democratic gains and freedoms that some nationalists died for. The Mau Mau never sacrificed the warmth of their families for you to use your space as a slaughterhouse for the rights of transsexual people.

We are Kenyans and you have to deal with your psychological fears since we are here to stay. Would you be happy if you were HIV positive and you were discriminated against on that fact? I don't think so. I (and my kind) demand to be respected by everyone and to be treated equally whether I/we fit in your rigid gender system or not. If you cannot learn to live and let others live then I suggest you pack and leave this country. A sane and civil Kenya cannot accommodate such malignancies.

That's my lecture to you, my brothers.

Post-lecture notes (answers to possible questions from 'the brothers'?)

Religious doubt

Scott Bidstrup defines a fundamentalist religion as 'any religion, that when confronted with a conflict between love, compassion and caring, and conformity to doctrine, will almost invariably choose the latter regardless of the effect it has on its followers or on the society of which it is a part (Bidstrup 2001). Religious fundamentalism in Kenya presents a formidable threat not only to democracy in Kenya but also access to medical care for transsexual people.

To explore these claims, I draw primarily upon some of my experiences during my transition to support my claim that the delusion of the existence of a god who does not want people to interfere with his wonderful creation is the primary reason some healthcare providers are hesitant to treat transsexual people. It's also the cauldron of the intolerance, hatred and discrimination that transsexual people face in Kenya.

It is not god's will

During my early years of gender dysphoria, I sought a bilateral orchidectomy from a clinical officer in our district hospital. Who else was I to get help from? The moment the know-it-all clinical officer opened her mouth, I realised she was in the wrong career: she told me that her god did not wish me to change my sex.

If I had wanted some religious babble, I am sure I would have found my way to our local church. I was seeking medical services and this caring healthcare provider denied me medical care just because Jehovah had sent her a transmission signal articulating his agenda on transsexuals? What's the point of training a healthcare provider who, instead of following standards of care, feels compelled to confer with her deity to make sure he approves the treatment of some humans? I hope she went to a bible school to serve god better and give other people a chance to live decent lives, otherwise she is part of the problem and not the solution.

There was a clinical officer in the college I graduated from. I told her how my head was spinning because of the feeling I had and the dissonance between who I felt I was and my anatomy, and she opened her drawer, took out some King James version religious heap and started 'treating' me with the word of god!!! No diss to Kenya's clinical officers; I don't know if that's what they are taught in college. But we have to concentrate on what is important in the treatment of transsexual people and not escape into flights of fancy whenever their concerns are presented. I admit that there are competent clinical officers out there who are passionate about what they do, and then there are the horrible incompetent clinical officers who, despite the fact that they graduated from whatever college they had enrolled in, come last in their course work. The latter are malignancies in the lives and well-being of transsexual people. Transsexual people, watch out. They don't come with labels.

Let me make it crystal clear to those silly enough to expect me to obey the 'message' of their god: I don't care what god told you about transsexual people. We cannot have a system whereby god has to approve provision of medical care to a particular minority in Kenya.

Making more people

'You will never get children.'

For the love of god, will somebody tell me something that I don't know? Here it is: I don't want to have kid(s). I have had the honour of listening to some preposterous reasons as to why people have kids and why, therefore, I – and all women – should have kids as a core relationship to our social value.

Here are a few comments I get, enough to give me an anger stroke:

- What if my parents had decided not to have kids? Would I be alive?
- If all of us decided not to have offspring, then how would the world look in 150 years to come? There would be no people.
- Our mighty and loving god told us to multiply and fill the earth. If you don't do that, you are a sinner. (Mind you, more than 10 million Kenyans are currently faced with starvation. Will people ever learn?)
- Nobody will be named after you.

Okay! I know our teachers and parents told us it's wrong to laugh at silly arguments but these are super silly. Overpopulation is a major political and economic concern; the argument that 'if you don't have children, you wouldn't have been born' is bizarre, and the idea that if one woman decides not to have children, all people will follow her lead is preposterous. Some of the geniuses who have made these arguments to me are in our civil service. That is so reassuring.

What to do, what to do?

How then do we, as intelligent and emancipated *homo sapiens* capable of making informed decisions about our own lives, deal with the ignorance – religiously inspired or not?

The first technique, and one which requires measurable amounts of self-control, is to ignore their self-righteousness. Ignore them. Walk away from them if you can and if that's not possible, use the pull-the-rug-under-their-feet technique.

This is the second technique and, owing to the fact that we are knowledgeable in science, this should be a pushover. Mention research work that has been done in the field of transsexualism and point out that you believe in facts, not fables. This method often works. If you are armed with facts and figures in the moment, no one will fault you.

I should point out that religion is a threat not just to the well-being of transsexual people but to any democratic gains this country has achieved so far. This is how it goes: stand in the pulpit in front of some ignorant and (under)educated mass and say something hateful about a particular group, then followed by 'praise god'. People will start talking in tongues and in the next minute you see this mass demonstrating over trifles, such as propositions to ordain gay priests or women.

The sheer power of the opposition? Can we 'walk away'?

An irony that comes out with all the screeching, arm-twisting, obfuscation of details and social injustices against transsexual people done by Christian fundamentalists in Kenya is the denial of the power of god. Look at it from this angle: you claim that sex reassignment surgery is not the will of god. On the other hand, we 'know' that god is powerful and is everywhere (omniscient and omnipotent, respectively). If thousands of sex reassignment surgeries are taking place, how is it so?

At any rate, that's settled.

And where does the 'T' stand in LGBT?

I need to mention that some lesbian, gay and bisexual (LGB) individuals have made significant contributions in the transgender movement. I highly laud their input. But we cannot ignore the marginalisation and abuse some LGB individuals and organisations have imposed on transgender people. This ranges from the constant lumping of trans people with gays/lesbians to the insensitive reference of trans women as men and trans men as women, to sidelining their issues. Such practices are an embarrassment to the LGB community and breed suspicion and hostility between these communities.

The transgender community exists within the LGBT movement not because of their sexual practices or sexual orientation, but because of their gender identity. If people cannot respect that fact and cease calling transgender people gays, MSMs and lesbians, then these groups should separate. The pecking order of LGBT should simply be dismantled.

Final comments

Surveying the myriad problems transsexual people face in Kenya, I argue that though transsexual people are divided by the diversity of their backgrounds, almost invariably they have similar concerns derived from the commonality of the oppressive mentality they face. It is detrimental to assume that African communities historically had no transsexual people in their midst and that one's assigned sex was immutable. But even if transsexualism was a foreign culture ('unAfrican') it would still not justify the injustices transsexual people face. Human beings have the right to practise the culture of their choice without having to look over their shoulder in case some 'true African' is watching and listening.

Transsexual people are not the same. They are individuals, with distinctive educational, class, religious and ethnic backgrounds. Though it is impossible to speak of 'Kenyan transsexual persons' as if they are a ready-made collective, one story that consistently emerges about Kenya's transsexual people and makes their voice a collective is that they have and continue to endure discrimination in the labour market, violence, ridicule and exclusion.

Despite a plethora of gender-based programmes initiated by the Kenyan government and NGOs, transsexual people have been left out and probably because of the incompetence in these agencies nothing tangible has been achieved. It is not surprising that some women continue to demonstrate double standards in their policies and deliberations in respect of transsexual people in Kenya. In August 2008, a newscaster working with a leading TV station laughed after airing a video of a transgender woman being beaten up and stripped by men and women.[1] No sane and civil woman would encourage peace and freedom to express one's gender and simultaneously be part of the brutal system that transgender people face in Kenyan society.

Kenya, in recent years, has witnessed an increase in human insecurity, injustices, rights abuses and lack of adequate medical care to transsexual people. Transsexual women are survivors amid insurmountable odds and regressive traditions, poor governance and bad political and economic choices which compound and complicate their situations. Transsexual women are doubly disadvantaged on account of their stigmatisation, yet their positions are barely accounted for in mainstream development programmes. To add salt to the injury, those in formal structures suffer from institutional patriarchy together with cisgender women. Discrimination in the labour market not only denies them a source of livelihood but also any sense of human dignity. This is encouraged by both our government's and Kenyan civil society's complicity in these injustices.

I believe that the links between protection of the rights of transsexual people, academics and economic empowerment are intrinsically entwined. Legal integration of the rights and freedoms of trans communities is a prerequisite for the empowerment of transsexual people in the overall development of any nation. However, the key lies primarily with transsexual people, who must articulate their cause and contest the numerous social injustices they face. Too often, when the subject of transsexualism crops up, we get to see some 'experts in gender' spouting garbage and a skewed perspective of transsexual and transgender concepts. Take for example the bishop who claims that god created a man and a woman and nothing else, or the nurse trying to 'cure' (with a bible) a transsexual who is recovering in hospital after genital mutilation.

If anyone wants to help us, please talk to us; we are the ones who face discrimination in the labour market, get arrested by the police on some flimsy pretext while they hope they make headlines and perhaps secure a promotion. At least we have intimate knowledge of the experiences and problems we have faced. 'Gender experts', on the other hand, speak from different realities remote from the everyday experiences of transsexual people. Let's not be naive on this one. It's either you are with us or against us.

For the economic prosperity of Kenya to trickle down to all citizens, human rights violations against transsexual people have to be addressed with the seriousness and urgency they deserve, concentrating on ways to eradicate the vectors of discrimination that they face. What's the importance of singing the hit song 'gender mainstreaming' if the very vocal protagonists are the antagonists of the transsexual cause. If cisgender women cannot accommodate and tolerate transsexual women in the war against patriarchy, then I kindly request the sexists of this country to oppress cisgender women further. If transsexual women can't have it, cisgender women will not have it. That's my mantra when dealing with transphobic women.

It is important for public policymakers to listen and act on the needs of transsexual people. Our justice and education system should be a key to the fight to end social injustices against transsexual people in Kenya. Let public policymakers listen to the experiences of transsexual people and determine if any human being deserves such bile.

In the end, I believe there are human beings out there who have the courage to take their responsibilities seriously. Maybe their reality tunnels are not so narrow and they are not prone to trivialise the needs of transsexual people simply because their children are not transsexuals or because the wiretap in their head (made by god) tells them to do so.

Maybe.

Notes

1. See http://www.youtube.com/watch?v=SR8k9HnIAy4, accessed 12 March 2009

References

Bidstrup, Scott (2001) 'Why the fundamentalist approach to religion must be wrong', http://www.bidstrup.com/religion.htm, accessed 24 October 2010

Gender Identity Research and Education Society (GIRES) (2002) 'Unacceptable standards of care proposed. A reasoned critique of the proposals issued for national consultation regarding "Gender identity disorder in adults – Guidance for the management of transsexualism"', Ashstead

Gender Identity Research and Education Society (GIRES) et al (2006), 'Atypical gender development: a review', *International Journal of Transgenderism* 9(1): 29–44

Green, R. (1999) Report cited in *Bellinger v. Bellinger* British court of appeal judgment, 17 July 2001, TLR 22-11-2000

Green, R. and Fleming, D. (1990) 'Transsexual surgery follow-up: status in the 1990s', *Annual Review of Sex Research* 1: 163–74

24

Barrenness and sexuality in the Ndau community

Rebecca Magorokosho

The Ndau are part of the Shona people who live in the eastern part of Zimbabwe, near the border with Mozambique. They follow a patrilineal kinship system and practise Christianity and African traditional religion. Today, among the Ndaus, the age-old custom of *lobola* (bridewealth) has been transformed and has mutated into one that transfers the woman's total self (productive and reproductive rights) to her husband's family. Part of the bridewealth, known as *rusambo* or *danga*, is the main part of *lobola* and is 'paid' in monetary form in addition to some animals. Currently, *lobola* signifies total transfer of the woman's rights to the husband's clan.

Once acquired, the woman's sexuality remains a resource for the whole clan and neither barrenness nor death terminates this chain of obligations between the two clans. In the event that the woman is not able to bear children, her family organises a girl from among her brothers' daughters to go and stay with her and bear children for her, with no additional *lobola* changing hands. The young girl (*chigadzamapfihwa* – the one who lights fire where there is no fire) can remain in the family, act as the man's second wife and continue to bear children for him.

Where the woman has reached menopause or is too old to sexually satisfy her husband, her family again organises for a daughter of her brother to live with her, to bear children and meet the sexual needs of her brother-in-law. The young girl, commonly known as *chimutsamapfihwa* (the one who blows to life the dying out fire), can also be the second wife to that man, with no additional *lobola* changing hands. Where the man feels the woman is too old and he needs somebody just to entertain him in bed, without necessarily bearing children (commonly known as 'sprucing up'), again her family organises a girl from the woman's family to go and entertain her brother-in-law, with no additional *lobola* being required. The girl, commonly known as *chitsaraimvi* (the one who singles out the grey hair), is usually given to the brother-in-law who has proved to be resourceful and good.

With respect to the man, it is slightly different. Where the man has proved infertile, his family secretly makes an arrangement for his brother to sleep with his wife and have children. It is strategically arranged in such a way that the infertile man won't even detect it. Usually, it is done when the man is away from home. This practice poses health risks in light of HIV/AIDS but the man's brother (*babamunini*) and the woman (*maiguru*) involved undergo testing first before the *babamunini* 'plants his seeds' into the *maiguru's* uterus.

However, with urbanisation and the women's rights movement in Zimbabwe, some of these practices are increasingly dying out. The 2007 Domestic Violence Act strictly prohibits child pledging and identifies these practices as acts of domestic violence. In this way we see feminism slowly chipping away at the oppressive patriarchal Ndau traditions.

Questions for reflection

1.

What is the difference between presentation and representation? What about misrepresentation? How can we relate these terms to African sexualities?

2.

How has this Reader facilitated the deconstruction and reconstruction of mainstream African sexualities?

3.

What is the difference between gender identity, sexual identity, sexual orientation and sexual practice? Are these concepts fixed for each of us? Do they have a linear relationship?

4.

How are lesbians, gays, bisexuals, transgendered and intersexed (LGBTI) individuals 'gender-benders'? What effect do Western-specific labels such as LGBTI have on African sexual (re)presentations and practices of identity?

5.

How has the AIDS epidemic influenced African representations and identities?

Part 4
Integrated and positive sexuality

25

'Osunality' (or African eroticism)

Nkiru Nzegwu

Introduction

In a trend toward cosmopolitanism, African elites and urbanites are rapidly adopting erotic practices circulated by North American and European media houses and conglomerates. Some theorists[1] argue that in light of this development and of modernity it makes no sense to talk about African eroticism as something fundamentally different from what occurs in other parts of the world. Whatever erotic might have been in Africa's cultural past, it has now been radically reshaped by the world's two major patriarchal religions – Christianity and Islam – as well as by colonial modernity and capitalist ideology. On this viewpoint, the emphasis on globalisation – brought on by the acceleration of Westernisation from the second half of the 20th century, and the avid consumption by urban dwellers of romance, erotic and pornographic materials – has promoted the adoption of a universal and uniform meaning of eroticism. This universal view of the erotic belies the racialisation of bodies and the stigmatisation of black women inherent in the sexual scheme.

Even as this argument on universality is being made, other theorists are contesting the erosion of African notions of sexuality and eroticism, and showing the robustness and resilience of the deeply rooted cultural practices that are thriving in diverse locations of Africa and the world (Abdoulaye 1999; Biaya and Rendall 2000; Biaya 2004; Diallo 2004; Ikpe 2004, 2006; Nyamnjoh 2005; Nzegwu 2005; Tamale 2005; Arnfred 2007; Undie et al 2007). Tshikala Kayembe Biaya and Ly Abdoulaye reveal that even after 10 centuries of Islamic influence of the Lawbé/Laobé and Wolof, pre-Islamic social structures of sexuality and eroticism continue to define standards of sexuality and eroticism in modern-day Senegal, a predominantly Muslim country (Abdoulaye 1999; Biaya and Rendall 2000: 712; Nyamnjoh 2005). Signe Arnfred reveals a similar trend in northern Mozambique, where Makhuwa sexual structures respond subversively to the puritanical prescriptions of the Baptist Union Church (Arnfred 2007: 154–5). In all these encounters, slippages and shifts occur as elements of oppositional colliding value schemes adjust and fuse.

The issue at stake here is not whether the fusion takes away the authenticity of the Lawbé/Laobé or Makhuwa sexual practices. Rather, it is whether or not we are sufficiently grounded to recognise the enduring character of Lawbé/Laobé and Makhuwa sexual norms and criteria. Usually, there is a deep-seated belief in Africa's deficiency that undermines the value of African sexual practices. This provides the fuel for disparaging comments to end these practices, while also failing to critically engage with how Western societies' conceptual universes lead to a confusion of forces of erasure.[2] A careful study of this universe reveals a profusion of ideas and practices that show that African sexual ontology is not Western sexual ontology in a black face; that it has its own defined history; that it is in fact quite progressive and a resilient stronghold of female power. On this reading, ideas and practices that are heavily informed by Western erotic activities do not count as African eroticism in this work.

So what was African eroticism before the impact of Western hegemonic influences? An explication is important not just to provide a baseline for analysing Africa's contemporary ideas and attitudes toward sex, for understanding the different ways of thinking about sexuality within the African spatial universe and for revealing the logic of those practices. Ultimately, the goal is to uncover how African cultures set up their sexual schemes such that sexual pleasure and fulfilment were equally expected for both women and men, and sensuality was neither pornographic nor the basis of women's subjugation and domination as was the case in Europe (MacKinnon 1989; Vuorela 2003). The point to take away is that, though the Western notion of sexuality has made tremendous gains in various parts of the world, this does not mean its view of the erotic is correct (MacKinnon 1989), or that it is the only appropriate way of thinking about the erotic (Lorde 1984). I should state that, in this chapter, my uses of the word 'sex' refer largely to sexuality.

Moving the framework

A widely held view within the Western intellectual tradition is that philosophising about sex began in ancient Greece (Soble 2005a: xxiii). Eroticism derives from the Greek word *eros*, meaning sexual desire or libidinal passion. Eros, the Greek male god of love and sexual desire, overthrew his mother, Aphrodite – the goddess of love, beauty and sexual rapture – to become the personification of love, creative power and harmony.[3] That the son became the purveyor of sensuality, sexual desire and fertility and the force that propels individuals to actualise their wholeness is hardly surprising (Gould 2005: 800–11). Such a view is consistent with the patriarchal ideology of Greek, Roman, pre-modern and modern European worlds that establishes a moral framework for exerting control over women's bodies, and in which the creative life force is characterised as male.

The resultant European/Western conception of eroticism underwrites theoretical, literary and fictional narratives of sexuality from a phallocentric position that emphasises and legitimises the privileging of men's needs, desires and fantasies (MacKinnon 1989). To expose the exploitative nature of this notion of sexuality, Western feminist research on battery, rape, incest and child sexual abuse, prostitution and pornography has demonstrated that women within this European and European-derived sexual scheme are objects of pleasure rather than subjects who ought to have pleasure. The sole exception are women deemed to be of low or easy virtue and forced to live the exploitative life of prostitution. Virtuous women, by contrast, are required to be pure, chaste and monogamous.

This sexualised gender hierarchy of the West eroticises male dominance and female subjugation as sexual (MacKinnon 1989: 127–9). Far less obvious is that sexual right is a political right, and that women lack any of this right, which is the purview of men. Religion and the state historically reinforced this ideology through a series of laws and precepts that politically and socially regulated women's sexual activities, making eroticism and sexuality a basis for women's moral anguish, conflict and downfall (Pateman 1988, 1991, 2001). With sex outside marriage and reproduction as taboo, the idea of female sexuality and eroticism acquired transgressive overtones and attracted moral strictures from the church and state. For African women in particular, Christianity and the chattel plantation slavery of the Americas projected hypersexuality and lasciviousness on black bodies, rationalised black women's subjection to rapes and sexual exploitation and the lynching of black males for the imagined ravishing of white women (hooks 1981; Collins 1990; Brown 1995; Harris 1995; Giddings 2009). Capitalism further entrenched all women's subjugation and sexual exploitation by regulating and controlling their sexuality and reproductive capacities (Mackinnon 1989). Imperialism racialised sexuality worldwide, and colonialism, apartheid and corporate globalisation reconstituted only white women into paragons of purity and beauty and deserving of love and affection, and fetishised non-white bodies as expendable and worthless.

Additional conceptual complications occurred in the Western universal understanding of eroticism. These were added to by excursions into the perverse by theoreticians, such as Marquis de Sade (1740–1814), Sigmund Freud (1856–1939) and Georges Bataille (1897–1962). The injection of a counter-natural quality linked eroticism to sexual practices, such as bestiality, paedophilia, homosexuality and sadomasochism, considered perverse, taboo and transgressive. The dissolution of the boundaries of normality also eroticised demeaning practices on women (particularly prostitutes and black women) and induced disruptive and disorderly activities for the delayed gratification of men. In time, eroticism within the Western intellectual frame became distinguished as male-defined, perverse sexual excitement and was fused with pornography (MacKinnon 1989 ch. 7; Lorde 1984: 53–9).

It should be of concern that this is the universal, putatively uniform, cosmopolitan notion of eroticism that is moving into the African landscape. The question that this notion raises for cosmopolitan Africans is: what is the justification for embracing a notion of eroticism that is steeped in an ideology of gender inequality, that promotes men's sexual hierarchy and the domination of women and that construes the bodies of black African women as undesirable?

Cheikh Anta Diop's (1923–1986) groundbreaking work on the material culture of Africa provided a theoretical means for dissolving or resolving the dilemma, for pushing back this notion and for articulating a different model of the erotic (Diop 1978, 1991). His work on the cultural unity of Africa effectively shifted Friedrich Engels' (1820–1895) European patriarchal framework used to theorise African cultures and highlighted the matriarchal (mother-centred) ideology of African societies. Diop countered the prevailing singular evolutionary theory of human society used to anchor European hegemony, racism and the theory of women's universal subordination. Instead, he advanced a more convincing thesis of two cradles of civilisation in which two broad types of societies developed in relation to their geographic and climatic conditions.

Diop argued that the Indo-European civilisation was patriarchal, a reflection of the existential uncertainties of the nomadic way of life and the social organisational principle that emerged as a result. This patriarchal social ideology differed fundamentally from the matriarchal one that emerged in the southern cradle of civilisation, where the mode of life was sedentary. Diop argued that this sedentary living positioned mothers as the anchors of families and communities and fostered a complementary social ideology that reflected how mothers value equally their offspring.[4] Advancing the matriarchal viewpoint, Ifi Amadiume (1987a) argues that this ideology and its valuation of both female and male children is reflected in the cosmogonies of societies. The thrust of this line of research is that although women and mothers exist in both cradles of civilisation, the socio-political statuses and ideological meanings of women and motherhood differ.

The value of Diop and Amadiume's analyses is threefold: they highlight the unifying mother-centred logic of African societies regardless of their cultural differences;[5] they alert us to the danger of naively assuming conceptual equivalence between European and African ontologies and conceptual frameworks; and they highlight the error in believing that terms such as erotic and sexual pleasure have the same meaning in the mother-centred African cultural universe as they do in the patriarchal European cultural universe. In short, we do epistemological violence to Africa and the conceptual schemes of similarly situated cultures when we fold their underlying matri-focal ideology and principles of complementarity into Europe's patriarchal structure.

Given the deep difference between the ontologies of the two modes of civilisation, the conventional Western definition of eroticism with its male-privileged view of the erotic (in which the emotion is located within a framework of male dominance) does not represent an understanding of sexual pleasure in the African universe. The two frameworks are fundamentally different. So what then was the conception of eroticism in the African sexual universes before the imposition of European hegemony? What do we mean by sexual pleasure? I address these questions in the following section, first, by relocating to Africa's intellectual framework and, second, by analysing the sexual institutions of some African communities.

Philosophical roots

Africa's recorded philosophical ideas on eroticism go back to the ancient civilisations of the Nile valley, specifically to ancient Egyptian philosophy (2780–2260 BCE),[6] to *The Pyramid Texts*, the *Inscription of Shabaka*, the *Instructions of Kagemni*, the *Maxims of Ptahhotep* (Obenga 2004: 6), the more than 50 surviving secular love songs from the New Kingdom (1567–1085 BCE) and the erotic paintings from the New Kingdom burial chambers (Meskell 2002; Graves-Brown and Cooney 2008). Although *The Pyramid Texts* (sometimes referred to as the *Book of Going Forth by Day* or *Book of the Dead*) can be read as philosophical treatises on divine love, divine adoration and eternal love, the images of sexual intercourse in the burial chambers speak eloquently and audibly through the secular love songs of the Chester Beatty Papyri I.

Specifically, these are Songs of the Heart's Sublime Delight, Songs of Joy, or Beautiful Sons of Joy for Your Loved One, Beloved of Your Heart, When She Comes from the Fields, Under the Protection of Hathor, My Heart Flutters Hastily, It Is Her Love that Gives Me Strength, among others (Fox 1996; Obenga 2004: 599). The songs are passionately charged declarations of love and intense sexual desire. They speak in smouldering erotic tones about the male lover whose 'heart is afire with desire for [his beloved's] embrace' (Obenga 2004: 598); or the female lover whose 'heart flutters hastily / When I think of my love of you / . . . / It lets me not put on a dress' (Chester Beatty Papyri 1).

Clearly libidinal, these songs also address the totality of the human subject, speaking frankly, openly and publicly about romantic love, passionate needs and intimate desires. The tone and graphic nature of the songs are extraordinarily contemporary, in fact, strongly suggestive of the poetic songs of present-day Lawbé/ Laobé performers of Senegal (Abdoulaye 1999; also see Marame Gueye's Laabaan song in Chapter 66 of this volume) and Makhuwa dance songs of eroticism (Arnfred 2007: 153). No sense of abashment seems present in the society that had conceptualised sexual desire and sexual intercourse as a legitimate part of life for both men and women (Meskell 2002; Graves-Brown and Cooney 2008).

Both the female and the male lover stand as equals, with no psychological anxieties about purity and decency. A man sings of his beloved beauty and declares his wish to approach her; a woman passionately sings of her longing for her chosen one, whom her mother might not approve of; another man despairs of even reaching the woman of his affection; a woman struggles with her desires for her beloved; a man exalts in seeing his beloved but chafes at being separated from her; and after seven days of separation a man publicly declares that he is sickened and insists that only she can cure him (Obenga 2004: 598).

The sheer openness of the songs, the unabashed willingness to expose the depths of desire, and the frankness between lovers yield a conception of passionate desire that aims for sexual pleasure and satisfaction. The 'brother' and 'sister' terms of endearment reference not an incestuous relationship, but a relationship of equality and belongingness that approximates that of siblings (Lichteim 2006). It appears that in the matri-centric ideology of ancient Egypt, in which sons and daughters were equally valued, the society held up the sibling equality relationship as a model for intimate loving relations.

Visual art, literatures (oral and textual), social institutions and ontologies are the living repositories and archives of communities' views on quintessential questions of reality, nature and humanity. Using the *longue durée* and other 'methods of historical linguistics based on comparative and inductive techniques', Egyptologists Théophile Obenga and Diop established genetic kinship affinities between ancient Egyptian cosmogony, language, concepts and thought and other continental African languages and cosmogonies (Obenga 2004:16, 20; Diop 1991).[7] Their work mapped out an older African conceptual universe that not only provided a better interpretation of cultural phenomena in diverse regions of Africa, but also, when supplemented with archival records in Greek, Ge'ez and Arabic, a robust, intellectual universe of discourse many millennia old. Further reinforcing the articulation of this conceptual universe are the new archaeological discoveries, architectural artefacts, art history scholarship and tales of migrations along the Nile Valley highway that links southern and northern Africa and the trans-Saharan routes that link East and West Africa and the western and northern parts of the continent.

Although ancient Egyptian literatures and ontology are millennia old, they share important elements with Yoruba religion, which developed in remote antiquity. A point of contiguity is the cosmogony that suggests some form of connectedness or overlap. In Egyptian cosmogony, for instance, Hathor – the divinity of joy, love, fertility and childbirth and the protector of women – is the divine daughter referred to as The Eye of God (Obenga 2004: 176). In turbulent moments when she manifests as the destroyer of conspirators of the Supreme God, Ra, she wields a dreaded incarnate power that transforms her into Sekhmet.[8]

This dual creator/destroyer identity of Hathor can be found in the Yoruba divinity Òsun,[9] whose distinguishing traits are preserved in the sacred texts of the ancient Odù Ifá divination system that go back to remote antiquity. Òrìsà Òsun is the divinity of fertility, wealth, joy, sensuality and childbirth, protector of women and giver of children to barren women. Like Hathor, she possesses a special relationship to Olódùmarè, the Supreme Creator Force (Badejo 1996; Ogungbile 2001: 190) and an equally dreaded power known as Àjé, which she uses to destroy violators (Badejo 1996; Washington 2005).[10]

Although Òsun is the sole female divinity among 16 male divinities, she is the one that 'the Creator-God placed all the good things on earth in [her] charge making her "the vital source"' of life (Abimbola 2001; Abiodun 2001:18). Known as 'the source', this archetypal female 'conduit through which all life flows' and epitome of sensuality and sexual pleasure (Badejo 1996: 12) speaks to female sexual knowledge and agency. In the Yoruba diaspora of the Americas and the global world of Yoruba religion, Isabel Castellanos proclaims that Òsun 'rules over the erotic component of human nature', including Latin female sensuality (Castellanos 2001: 39).[11]

Functioning as a philosophical treatise on society and human nature, the chapters of Odù Ifá present a conception of human sexuality and of female sexuality that can best be described as Òsun-sexuality. In symbolising a sexual and maternal conduit, Òsun represents a pronatalist, female-centred, life-transforming energy that courses through and animates life. The Òsetúrá chapter of Odù Ifá presents this force as highly sensual and sexual. Women who typify this Òsun force brandish their sexuality openly and quite unselfconsciously.[12] Because Odù Ifá does not rest on a simple correspondence theory of truth between Òrìsà and humans, a philosophical reading of this Òsun force construes it as a dynamic creative energy connector between the intervening phases of the sexuality–fertility paradigm. In explicit terms, Òsun force outlines a sequential energy flow from desire, arousal, copulation, pleasure, fulfilment, conception, birth and growth.

The flow need not result in conception and birth, but it does entail the principle of pleasure at the heart of copulation. This pleasure principle at the heart of the creative energy is metaphorically referred to as Òsun's 'honey',[13] which I call 'osunality'. Osunality affirms the normality of sexual pleasure and the erotic. When absent in life, the result is suspended animation or stasis, and as the Òsetúrá chapter chronicles, life effectively halts.

The activation of Òsun's 'concealed power', or osunality, revitalises and renews life. This energy, which is shared with other women (Abimbola 2001; Abiodun 2001; Ogungbile 2001; Washington 2005), is located in the female creative organs – reproductive and genitalia – not solely in the clitoris as Rowland Abiodun (2001: 24) posited. The act of copulation spiritually and psychologically activates this force of change, transformation and growth, and the feeling of sexual fulfilment it produces ensures social harmony and stability.

Osunality is a dynamic, dialectical force that sets up dualistic relationships of actuality and potentiality in the cycle of life and death, as well as rich and complex dualities in women's sexual identity, deepening their persona to include: maternal figure and paramour; home builder and courtesan; confidant and gossip; drawer of children; and igniter of the sexual or osunic fire. Òsun's 'honey' and the 'good things' it portends are offered to partners in order to build communities through the birth of children, and to build harmony through intimacy and bonding.

Yoruba ontology, similar to other ancient African ontologies, seems to emphasise fertility over sexual pleasure and satisfaction. That sexuality appears hidden, concealed or glossed over is because the philosophical grammar of the ontologies is becoming lost to modern Africans, who are disengaging from indigenous worldviews. No such loss of meaning occurs in the diasporas in the Americas, where Òrìsà worship is prevalent.

Epistemologically, Òsun is constituted by two principles – sexuality and fertility – and an elaborate sequence of processes. The former principle yields sexual pleasure and the latter, children. Constructed as a female divinity to function as a mnemonic device, Òsun, like other female deities of fertility all over Africa,[14] authorise and reinforce female sexuality without negating male sexuality. These forces are not simply guardians of fertility, but also theoretical articulations of sexuality and fertility processes. Thus, relocation to an African ontological scheme and an examination of its foundational beliefs highlight the sexuality component, as well as a different picture of sexual desire and passion. Deemed a personal and social good, sexual fulfilment is highly valued by families and communities because it produces well-adjusted individuals.

This becomes obvious when we turn to the vast numbers of sexuality training schools in Africa created to facilitate the transmission of this valued ideology. Though the emphasis in the following section is on the Sande *kpanguima* (school) of the Mende, Susu, Vai, Temne, Sherbro, Gola, Bassa and Kpelle of Guinea, Sierra Leone and Liberia, I also draw insights from other similar schools, such as the Lawbé/Laobé (Senegal); *Dipo* of the Adangme (Ghana); *Isong* of the Ibibio and Ekoi, *Iria* of the Kalabari and Ijaw, *Mbobi* of the Efik and *Iru-mgbede/Ima Ogodo/Nkpu* of the Igbos (Nigeria); *Ssenga* of the Baganda (Uganda); *Nkang'a* of the Ndembu, *Chisungu* of the Bemba and Tonga (Zambia); *Unyago* of the Kizaramo (Tanzania); *Olaka* of the Makhuwa, Yao and Makonde (Mozambique); *Efundula* of the Ovambo (Namibia); and *Musevhetho* of the Tsonga (South Africa).

Notwithstanding the variation in detail and duration, the schools create spaces for women to transmit indigenous ideas on sexuality and pleasure, to fashion a group identity and then to emerge with a female-identified consciousness to work in a complementary relation to men with male-identified consciousness.

Teaching 'osunality'

The prevalence of female fertility forces all over Africa speaks to the historical social ideology that, before the overlay of patriarchal structures and beliefs, accorded autonomy to women. The complementarity principle, built on ancient matri-centric foundations, ensured that men and women in differing cultures controlled their respective sexual socialisation. Within the female sphere, women of various communities learned the meaning of being an adult female, of marriage, sexual intercourse, conception, childbirth, and personal maintenance and aesthetics. They learned that the centripetal force of these activities resided in coitus, in which a powerful force of pleasure is coiled. The pan-ethnic Sande and Bundu *kpanguima*, and all other similar sexuality schools, taught young women about the force of this pleasure, as well as its value in taming and controlling spouses.

The discourse on sexuality typically begins from the standpoint of understanding, mastering and directing this powerful energy (Boone 1986; Tamale 2005). It treats osunality as a critical dimension of not just life, but a seat of women's power. The osu-nic force is vital because it modulates men's propensity for aggression, acting like an opiate to produce calmness and equanimity. It produces emotional interdependency, which causes people to avoid conflict because it is perceived as not worth the risk.

Because the theorisation of sexuality takes place in the context of producing a good society and healthy social living, Sande instructors work on firmly moulding girls into self-assured women. They induct them into community-wide fellowships of women and transform them into Sande *nyaha* or mature adult women, complete with an adult personal aesthetics and a female-identified consciousness. Next, they develop their charges' artistic and aesthetic capacities in dance, songs, mime, adornment, personal comportment, hygiene and contraception. They consolidate these young women's self-esteem through a series of personal development exercises that transforms them into artistically proficient and socially aware beings (Boone 1986: 55).

Sexuality discourse in the *kpanguima* curriculum lays out the culturally approved boundaries of behaviour, the culturation of the natural body for sexual expression, and the conditions under which sexual encounters can be pursued and with whom. Coitus is presented as a normal part of adulthood and as something that should be rightly explored under proper conditions, not furtively. Because sexual pleasure is a social good, sexual desire is not subject to punitive laws unless one engages in prac-tices that are deemed culturally unacceptable. For communities that permit some form of youth sexual activity before the completion of the last of the protracted mar-riage rites, students are informed of the limits. Teachings about male physiognomy, sexual desire and its relationship to sexual pleasure are important parts of the cur-riculum because communities emphasise the right of women to enjoy sex. Students learn about the critical stages – pre-coital, coital and post-coital – as well as a range of techniques[15] for the different phases.

As for any skilled task, performers must acquire relevant knowledge and gain proficiency in the art of pleasuring. Students learn sexual cues, ways of issuing invi-tations for sex, and the use and value of sexual enhancers. Foremost on the list of enhancers are waist beads made of glass, pearls or clay, which function as sex toys. The soft muted sound of these beads act as a powerful sexual stimulant (Biaya and

Rendall 2000; Biaya 2004; Diallo 2005; Tamale 2005; Arnfred 2007). They also learn the art of igniting passion by means of gestures, the look, the walk, dance moves, spatial configurations,[16] modes of dressing,[17] food initiators (Ikpe 2006; Arnfred 2007: 152), knowledge of erogenous zones and rhythmic pelvic movements. Knowledge of sexual pharmacopoeia is also important to satisfying sexual relations. Students learn about herbal stimulants and mood-enhancing effects, tree barks that sustain erection, and leaves that when added to drinks or consumed can tighten the vaginal walls, and either enhance vaginal lubrication and maintain its warmth or dry it. Lastly, they also learn coital sound stimulants or 'lovemaking noises' (Tamale 2005).

The discourse and underlying notion of osunality encourages the treatment of sexual pleasuring and enjoyment as of optimal importance. The institution of nuptial advisers, for example, emerged to facilitate pleasurable experiences, and to instruct young women and couples in the art of lovemaking. These advisors are found in different regions of Africa, and include the Sande *sowei* (Boone 1986) and the *laobé* in Senegal;[18] the *nwang abe* of the Ubang of Nigeria (Uchendu 2003); the *magnonmaka* of Mali (Diallo 2005); the *ssenga* of Buganda (Tamale 2005); the *shwen-kazi* among the Banyankore in Uganda; the *tete* among the Shona of Zimbabwe; the *alangizi* of the Yao of Malawi and the *chewa* of Zambia; the *nacimbusa* of the Bemba of Zambia (Richards 1956); the *mayosenge* in parts of Zambia and the *olaka* of the Makhuwa of Mozambique (Arnfred 2007), among others.

In Mali, for example, the *magnonmaka* joins the couple in the room on their wedding night to instruct them on the procedure required for a pleasurable experience (Diallo 2004). She ensures that intercourse proceeds smoothly with both parties correctly executing the necessary moves. Similar practices exist among the Itsekiri of Nigeria, who ensure that a mature female relative supervises a girl's first sexual encounter; she literally walks her and her carefully chosen experienced male partner through the act. The adviser not only ensures that the girl's first sexual experience is pleasurable, but reassures her and allays her anxiety. From the prevalence of these practices, it is safe to infer that communities place a high premium on women's positive sexual experience and psychological health. In fact, the existence of the institution strongly suggests the centrality of sexuality in the promotion of well-being of both the individual and the society.

Because in some cultures body aesthetics stipulate the production of a particular female body, I will briefly address in the following section the issue of genital surgery and genital modification at the heart of sculpting the sexual body.

Sculpting the erotic body

Most theories of African sexualities seldom treated the natural body – both female and male – as ready for sexual experience until after the completion of certain modifications. Body or genitalia sculpting was essential to create a sensual body. On the aesthetic grid of African cultures, natural bodies required some modification to bring them within the communities' sexual scheme. Varying degrees of genital surgeries, ranging from nicks to the clitoris to excision, were performed in the past, though these practices are rapidly dying out.

Among the Efik, for instance, *mbobi* (circumcision)[19] was important for *nkugho* (a girl's rite of passage) rites, and as Ikpe (2006) explains, its objective was 'to enhance the erotic by "beautifying" the genitalia' and marking it as cultured. That Diallo (2004) and Boone (1986) offer the same explanation for the surgeries in Mali and Sierra Leone, respectively, tells us that the procedure was probably used to distinguish between two types of women: those with cultural legitimacy who belonged, and those who lacked legitimacy and, for whatever reason, did not belong. Like the scarifications that many African communities performed, the sculpting of the genitalia as well marked ethnic identity, social hierarchy and perhaps the boundaries of legitimacy in intimacy matters.

It is quite conceivable that the children of mothers with non-culturated bodies might occupy a lower social category, forcing mothers in this category to adopt the practice for their daughters in order to eliminate for them any structural barriers. Though the origin of and rationale for genital surgeries remains obscure, they do not seem to have been for curbing women's sexuality – the much-hyped explanation that many feminists propound. Such an explanation is unpersuasive given the efforts made in African cultures to reinforce female sexuality and sexual agency and to make a woman's lack of sexual fulfilment legitimate grounds for divorce.

In addition to genital surgery, another prevalent practice of genital sculpting has been stigmatised by the World Health Organisation (WHO), although it does not involve cutting. This is the practice of manually elongating the inner folds of the labia minora to create the culturally approved organ modification, which is deemed sensuous and critical for enhanced sexual pleasure (see Brigitte Bagnol and Esmerelda Mariano's discussion of this practice in Mozambique in Chapter 26). The practice is widely common in east and southern Africa, including in Uganda, Rwanda, Malawi, Lesotho, Zimbabwe, Tanzania, Namibia, Botswana, Mozambique and South Africa.[20]

Labia stretching, in addition to acculturating genitalia, introduces young girls to their genitalia. It encourages them to explore, massage and become familiar with them; in effect introducing them to the act of self-stimulation or masturbation and thereby leading to the discovery of other erogenous zones. As Tamale makes clear, labia elongation 'enhances the erotic experience of both the male and the female (when touched during foreplay or mutual masturbation, they intensify the pleasure of the couple); [it] serve[s] as a cultural identifier or "stamp of legitimacy"' (Tamale 2005: 40). It is the ultimate sexual toy.

Again, the reasons for labia elongation are obscure though it seems to be an identity marker as well. The practice provides a model of female sexuality that invites pre-pubescent girls to begin exploring their bodies. Within Africa's broad sexual universe and its many cultural schemes, there is an awareness of the complex nature of sexuality and an understanding that female pleasure is not exclusively located in the clitoris, so the former is not compromised by the removal of some parts of the latter.

There seems to be an awareness of other erogenous zones and a knowledge of how to reach them during intercourse. There is also an appreciation of the value of sexual pleasure and fulfilment for an individual's mental health and social stability because the same societies that practised female circumcision also took steps to mitigate the negative effects of genital surgeries for women's sexual health. The effectiveness of this mitigation is evident in the famed sexual reputation of women from societies that practice female genital surgery and who apply the lessons of their sexuality schools. There seems to be an awareness in the locales in which genital modification is performed that sexual pleasure and orgasm depend on a totality of sensuous stimulation, the engagement of the imagination and the stimulation of fantasies.

This is not to say that genital surgeries are good for women and must be restored. It is more to state that dispensing with sexuality schools and their grounded approach to sexuality simply because of female genital surgeries is totally misguided. The sexuality schools have a lot to offer to young women. Genital surgeries can be eliminated without dispensing with the schools' important curriculum. Although the practice of genital surgeries might seem at odds with the idea of women's rights to sexual pleasure, which is at the heart of this essay (McFadden 2003), the oddity lies in the following: the lack of knowledge about what the sexuality schools do, and a hostility toward practices that are perceived to be harmful to women or dictated by men to control women and deny them sexual pleasure. Interestingly, such beliefs are based on an illegitimate substitution of European/Christian/Muslim sexual values for African values, resulting in the demonisation of Africa through erroneous and negative projections.

That the matri-centric substructure of African societies still generates a notion of sensuality that differs qualitatively from the notion circulating in the patriarchal universe (Arnfred 2007: 150–152) cannot be overemphasised. After decades of the overlay of patriarchal ideologies, the undertow of matri-centric ideologies and osunality are still strong enough to exert the sexual rights of women and to protect their right to sexual enjoyment. In diverse societies in Africa, osunality circulates definitions of sexuality which engage both women and men, and which privilege both the vulva and penis. Sexual desires, fantasies and pleasures focus on the totality of the being and tend to avoid the domination/subjugation complex of patriarchal ideology, which infuses current understandings of the erotic and eroticism (MacKinnon 1989: 130). The sexual creative energy underpinning the African notion of sexuality authorises mutual pleasure.

The devouring vagina

Although Òsun sexuality disseminates an ideology that views human sexuality in a positive light, it is necessary to establish what happens when women are positively affirmed; how our understanding of sexuality differs when the vagina is perceived as an important organ. At the very least, cultural songs and dances are rich with sexual allusions to the power and strength of this organ. Cultural dances and contemporary dance moves, such as *makossa, mapouka, ndombolo, soukous* and *ventilator* speak of this power in fluid, circular gyrations of the hips and quick forward and backward thrusts of the pelvis. These dances can be energetically or slowly enacted, delivering the osunic or sexually charged moves that suggest the penis will be devoured.

The imagery of a devouring vagina joins food, sexuality and dance together in one aesthetic experience (Nzegwu 2005). Dancers – both male and female – appreciate that the penis is eaten because it is filling and flavourful. The apparent incongruous assimilation of copulation to consumption is not value-neutral: it assigns agency to the vagina that is absent in Western notions of the erotic and it assigns a measure of passivity to the penis, which is seen as the organ of dominance in the Western frame.

The idea of the vagina as a devouring agent comes from the penis's invisibility during copulation. The engulfing of the penis by the vagina reverses normative Western sexual wisdom by positioning the male in a subordinate position, though he may be atop the woman. Being on top does not imply a superior psychological or physical position, because severe damage can be done from the underside, as evidenced in the penis being enveloped, swallowed and made to disappear. This concept of intercourse as an enveloping act grants the vagina great power. After all, to devour or to eat something is to assert one's power and will over it, yet that act does not deny power to that which is eaten, because what is eaten provides nourishment to the eater. Indeed, the penis's frantic activity of withdrawal, being pulled in (re-swallowed) and withdrawing again might appear as resistance, but its effort is really futile because its seed is pulled from it by the demanding vagina.[21]

Copulation as unidirectional consumption derives from the fact that only men give up something of themselves. After the semen's extraction, the depleted male is physically and emotionally drained, while females are powered to continue. Ordinarily, eating involves something's demise, but there is no death in the devouring act of the vagina, except for the seeds that are absorbed and die. In the heat of the moment the owner of the penis relishes the consumption, oblivious to the cycle of life and death and to the energy expended in each act, the end of which leaves him emotionally drained and compliant. Copulation forces the man to replenish speedily his vital force so he can function as a man, even when procreation is not the goal of intercourse. The script of extraction and expulsion, the disappearance (symbolic death) and re-emergence (symbolic re-birth) of the penis chronicles the drama of life and death.

It is to their credit that African cultures created a positive role for the vagina without castrating male libido. Men still play an important role in sexual matters, but the emphasis is different. The positive conception of the vagina derives from its vital role as a conduit through which all people come, regardless of sex, class and social status. Because of its importance in the continuation of birth and the expansion of families, the vagina becomes the seat of women's power. It is a cavernous chamber that works with the uterus to incubate life and later delivers it into the world.

The capacity and functionality of the vagina makes it both a desirable and dreaded organ. Its moist (or dry), warm chamber allures and arouses men and drives them to seek copulation. Its muscular walls rhythmically grip and pull the penis into its recesses and impel the male to an emotional peak. It is feared also, because its concealed inner depths are the receptacle for the origin of life. As owners of this passage, women dictate the terms of entrance. They can make entrance a pleasurable experience through muscular rhythmic contractions or they can frustrate that experience by lack of cooperation.

Copulation entails notions of reciprocity and acknowledgment of pleasure with gifts. The positive conception of vagina and the recognition of women's sexual autonomy yields a richer description of the vagina as 'mature and experienced', 'taunting' (referring to dexterous pelvic movements during intercourse), 'assertive', 'firm', 'tight', 'moist', 'warm', 'rhythmic', 'textured' and 'pulsating'. A corollary of these linguistic developments is that the penis equally comes up for review. Is it long and big enough? Is it experienced and adequate? How long can it retain turgidity? Women decide the criteria for judging penises and their evaluations are required so men can improve performance and ensure their own fulfilment and satisfaction. These evaluations arguably accommodate the interests of both sexes in achieving fulfilling intercourse.

Contrarily, under the normative Western framework, the dominant sexual being is (or largely has been) the man, and sexual discourse privileges male anatomy. The penis is represented as the central and dominating copulatory organ; the vagina is merely a sheath for the penetrating penis, a passive receptacle that receives the invading penis that drives deep into the woman. Questions are not raised about why a little organ is likened to a sword; why it seeks a sheath; or why it expends energy. Rather, the erect little organ is pictured both as a weapon that can harm and an object that can give pleasure.

Whatever the preferred description, glossing Protagoras (c. 480–410 BCE), it is always the man as the measure. In this framework, no analogous imagery of the vagina existed. Even in a loving relationship, the penis was primarily an instrument of pleasuring for men. Women were not pictured as desiring subjects that copulation might stimulate; good women were not expected to enjoy sex; and 'fallen women' (nymphomaniacs, prostitutes) were thought to crave sex and were labelled 'pathological'. It was only after a liberalisation of this perspective in the 1960s that some sexologists began to explore female sexuality and clitoral orgasm.

Conclusion: post-colonial sex and implication

A true story: A hip African university professor sallied to one of the neighbouring villages to find a 'real' village girl for post-colonial sex (a mish-mash of techniques picked up in male secondary schools and college campus bathrooms, spiced with moves gleaned from sex magazines and pornographic videos). He aimed to dazzle. The girl looked to ensnare a 'big man'. But the plan went awry. The don focused on his moves, his skill and his pleasure, believing he was delivering the best sex ever. The girl was astounded, wondering how anyone with so much book knowledge and a 'doctor' title could be so inept. He was groping, and flailing and thrashing about with no sense of engagement, like a novice. Seconds passed. Peering with barely concealed annoyance, she took charge and issued a string of commands: 'Put your foot on the wall, eh. Place your foot on the wall and push. Ee he. Push, good. Push, the drum the Creator fabricated will not break.'

It is tempting to read the village girl as a symbolic representation of Africa's indigenous sexual practices and the don as a signifier of cosmopolitan sexual knowledge. Others might infer from this that educated women too must be inept;

that this is a commentary on urban and rural living. Other than suggesting that knowledge is not necessarily the monopoly of those formally educated, such a reading is far too simplistic and limited. The narrative is intended neither to symbolise urban/rural or old/new dichotomies, nor to state that only those in rural areas are sexually knowledgeable. It is rather an invitation to begin a re-evaluation of positive sexual values and to consider the mode of preservation of these elements.

Although sexually proficient, the village girl's minimal education is a drawback in our present reality. Knowledge of osunality must be consistent with our level of progress, and must involve an astute analysis of traditional practices to ensure the elimination of the myths of male privilege that are based in patriarchal religious and military ideologies, in the values of capitalism and corporate globalisation, in male dormitory living in gold and copper mines and in other similar contexts. In re-articulating the values of osunality for contemporary life, uncritical representations of tradition and traditional practices are unacceptable. Teachings of osunality must occur on a template that protects women's sexual rights, as well as the right of those whose sexual preferences are non-heterosexual. Sexuality is far too important an area of human life to be left in the realm of ignorance, patriarchal forces and market-driven economics.

Notes

1. I have in mind theorists –African feminists, non-feminists, as well as non-Africans operating under an imperialist ideology of gender and development, who view anything African, traditional or indigenous as backward, outmoded and in cases reprobate. Constructions of African values and practices as necessarily violating women's rights, bodies, health and well-being deploy false and problematic imageries to prop up whatever derives from the Western value scheme of development experts, foundation donors and funders. In this vilification of whatever is African, no attempt is made to highlight the shortcomings of the values and practices of the European or European American schemes that are under severe criticism in their own cultural contexts.
2. Some might construe this reference to an African sexual universe and later to African sexual ontology as a gross homogenisation of Africans, at best, and of essentialism at worst. I should state that I am well aware of the diversity of cultures and heterogeneity of the peoples of Africa. However, recognition of differences does not automatically preclude identification of similarities. One of the benefits of writing this chapter was discovering the underlying structural commonalities in the patterns of beliefs, family systems, social ethos, and ideology and practices that need to be articulated. Linguistic differences and cultural accents, notwithstanding, these areas of deep cultural overlap or unities call for detailed investigation. It is these areas that this essay explores.
3. Other suggestions of Eros' parentage abound (Leadbetter 1997): Aristophanes states 'he was born from Erebus and Nyx (Night)'; another mythology makes him the offspring of Aphrodite and Ares; Hesiod disagrees and makes him Aphrodite's attendant, not her son; and another makes him the son of Iris and Zephyrus.
4. Although some work is being done in this area by Ifi Amadiume and other independent scholars, more African scholars need to undertake ground-up research to better grasp their theoretical analysis. Until they do, their work is a mish-mash of disconnected ideas that on the one hand fail to explain African phenomena, and on the other totally distort the logic of African reality.
5. The quick, but unsound, assumption that many people make on hearing about a unified African cultural universe is to advance the flawed post-modernist argument that this amounts to over-simplification and essentialisation.

6. This is the starting point only because the records from Kush and Qustul Nubia that predate Egypt have yet to be deciphered.

7. They did this because of the European scholarly agenda to represent Egypt as either a European civilisation or an Asiatic Semitic civilisation. Martin Bernal has discussed the role of racism/aryanism in scholarly research in his two-volume work, *Black Athena* (1987). The fact that Africans developed anything seems inconceivable within the post-17th century European frame of reference.

8. This divinity is also known as Nyabinghi in the upper sections of the Nile, toward the borders of southern Sudan and Uganda, in ancient Kush and Nubia.

9. I chose to make this linkage with Òsun rather than with any other African female divinity because of the global spread of the Yoruba religion. Unlike other African religions, adherents of the Yoruba religion can be found in Africa, South and Central America, the Caribbean, the USA, Canada and Europe. Also, the philosophical analysis of the Yoruba religion arguably exceeds that of any other African religion, hence providing a solid basis for arguments.

10. Obenga, Diop and a number of African researchers have identified a corpus of Egyptian concepts and words with the same meaning in numerous languages all over Africa including Wolof, Yoruba, Igbo, Fang and Luganda, among many others. Other cultural parallels exist but are not the focus of this essay. Their investigation is worthwhile, though still underdeveloped.

11. It is important to stress that this notion of Òsun is held by practitioners of Òrìsà religion in Latin America and the USA, as well as in Brazil among practitioners of Candomblé.

12. Òsun deployed her sensuality to seduce and marry multiple spouses – Orumila, Ogun, Erinle and Sango. This portrait of Òsun is a composite picture gleaned from multiple sources including Diedre Badejo (1996), Rowland Abiodun (2001), Wande Abimbola (2001) and Theresa N. Washington (2005).

13. Wande Abimbola (2001: 149) and Castellanos (2001: 40) talk about Òsun's 'honey', but not in the sense in which I discuss it. In the Odù Ifá text, the term 'honey' is a coded symbol, which I have chosen to interpret as a sexual allusion.

14. Notable ones include Ani/Ala, Idemmili and Ogwugwu for the Igbos of Nigeria; Nagaddya, the goddess of marriage and fertility in Buganda; Nyabingi in Rwanda; Isong, the divinity of the face of love of the Ibibio and Ekoi; and Eka Obasi, the divinity of sensuality, sexuality and fertility of the Efik of southeastern Nigeria.

15. Tamale (2005) provides a comprehensive discussion of the three stages. Biaya and Rendall (2000) and Nyamnjoh (2005) present some of the pre-coital stages in their descriptions of the activities of the Senegalese *drinaké/diriyanke* (experienced, self-assured matrons) and *diskette/disquettes* (relatively inexperienced slender young women). Ikpe (2006) alludes to this in her description of the *mbobi*.

16. In the Islamic regions of West Africa, incense, or *thiuraye*, is utilised to mark the body and to transfigure space.

17. Embroidered or lacy *bethio* – handmade wrappers with strategically placed holes that reveal more than they cover, are erotic enhancers in intimate settings. They heighten a partner's imagination, setting up a dialectics of availability and non-availability, and create *mokkeu pojje* or 'soft thigh' (Biaya and Rendall 2000).

18. Although the Lawbé/Laobé are a sub-group of the Toucouleur, in this instance the word functions as a marker of 'nuptial advisors'. I am grateful to Babacar M'Bow, who provided this information in a personal communication on 25 July 2010.

19. The surgery results in the cutting of the tip of the clitoris to sculpt the labia into a culturally approved erotic shape.

20. Anecdotal accounts suggest that some white South African women are getting in on the act in order to keep their men from crossing racial lines.

21. In the West, these ideas often hint at the 'castration' of the male. Freud wrote in his book *Fetishism* (1927: 154), 'probably no male human being is spared the terrifying shock of threatened castration at the sight of the female genitals'.

References

Abdoulaye, Ly (1999) 'Brief notes on eroticism among the Lawbé, Senegal', Dakar, *CODESRIA Bulletin* 3 & 4

Abimbola, Wande (2001) 'The bag of wisdom: Òsun and the origins of Ifá divination', in Murphy, J.M. and Sanford, M. (eds) *Òsun Across the Waters: A Yoruba Goddess in Africa and the Americas*, Bloomington, Indiana University Press

Abiodun, Rowland (2001) 'Hidden power: Òsun, the 17th Odù', in Murphy, J.M. and Sanford, M. (eds) *Òsun Across the Waters: A Yoruba Goddess in Africa and the Americas*, Bloomington, Indiana University Press

Amadiume, Ifi (n.d.) 'Sexuality, African religio-cultural traditions and modernity: expanding the lens', Africa Regional Sexuality Resource Centre (ARSRC), http://www.arsrc.org/downloads/features/amadiume.pdf, accessed 21 June 2010

—— (1987a) *Afrikan Matriarchal Foundations: The Igbo Case*, London, Karnak House

—— (1987b) *Male Daughters, Female Husbands: Gender and Sex in an African Society*, London, Zed Books

Antelme, Ruth and Rossini, S. (2001) *Sacred Sexuality in Ancient Egypt: The Erotic Secrets of the Forbidden Papyri*, Rochester, VT, Inner Traditions

Arnfred, Signe (2004 [2005]) 'Introduction', in Arnfred, S. (ed) *Rethinking Sexualities in Africa*, Uppsala, The Nordic Africa Institute

—— (2007) 'Sex, food and female power: discussion of data material from northern Mozambique', *Sexualities* 10(2): 141–158

Badejo, Diedre (1996) *Òsun Seegesi: The Elegant Deity of Wealth, Power, and Femininity*, Trenton, NJ, Africa World Press

Bataille, Georges (1957 [1986]) *Eroticism: Death and Sexuality*, San Francisco, CA, City Lights

Baumeister, R.F., Maner, Jon K. and DeWall, C. Nathan (2006) 'Theories of human sexuality', in McAnulty, Richard D. and Burnette, Michele M. (eds) *Sex and Sexuality, Volume 1*, Westport, CT, Praeger Publishers

Becker, Heike (2004 [2005]) 'Efundula: women's initiation, gender and sexual identities in colonial and post-colonial northern Namibia', in Arnfred, S. (ed) *Rethinking Sexualities in Africa*, Uppsala, The Nordic Africa Institute

Bernal, Martin (1987) *Black Athena: The Afroasiatic Roots of Classical Civilization*, New Brunswick, NJ, Rutgers University Press

Biaya, Tshikala Kayembe (2004) 'The arts of being beautiful in Addis Ababa and Dakar', *West Africa Review* 5

Biaya, T.K. and Rendall, Steven (2000) '"Crushing the pistachio": eroticism in Senegal and the art of Ousmane Ndiaye Dago', *Public Culture* 12(3): 707–720

Boone, Sylvia Ardyn (1986) *Radiance From the Waters*, New Haven, Yale University Press

Brown, Elsa Barkley (1995) '"What has happened here?": The politics of difference in women's history and feminist politics', in Hine, D.C., King, W. and Reed, L. (eds) '"We Specialise in the Wholly Impossible"': A Reader in Black Women's History*, Brooklyn, NY, Carlson Publishing Inc

Castellanos, Isabel (2001) 'A river of many turns: the polysemy of Ochún in Afro-Cuban tradition', in Murphy, J.M. and Sanford, M. (eds) *Òsun Across the Waters: A Yoruba Goddess in Africa and the Americas*, Bloomington, Indiana University Press

Collins, Patricia Hill (1990) *Black Feminist Thought: Knowledge, Consciousness, and the Politics of Empowerment*, Boston, Unwin Hyman

Diallo, Assitan (2004 [2005]) 'Paradoxes of female sexuality in Mali. On the practices of Magnonmaka and Bolokoli-kela', in Arnfred, S. (ed) *Rethinking Sexualities in Africa*, Uppsala, The Nordic Africa Institute

Diop, Cheikh Anta (1978) *The Cultural Unity of Black Africa: The Domains of Patriarchy and Matriarchy in Classical Antiquity*, Chicago, Third World Press

—— (1991) *Civilisation or Barbarism: An Authentic Anthropology*, Brooklyn, NY, Lawrence Hill Books

Diorio, Joseph A. (2005) 'Sex education', in Soble, A. (ed) *Sex from Plato to Paglia: A Philosophical Encyclopedia*, Westport, CT, Greenwood Press

Fox, Michael V. (1985) *The Song of Songs and the Ancient Egyptian Love Songs*, Madison, WI, University of Wisconsin Press

Freud, Sigmund (1927 [1961]) *Future of Illusion*, trans. James Strachey. New York, Norton and Company

Giddings, Paula J (2009 [2008]) *Ida: A Sword Among Lions: Ida B. Wells and the Campaign Against Lynching*, New York, Amistad

Goldman, A. (1991) 'Plain sex', in Soble, A. (ed) *Philosophy of Sex*, Lanham, MD, Rowan and Littlefield

Gould, Carol Steinberg (2005) 'Plato' in Soble, A. (ed) *Sex from Plato to Paglia: A Philosophical Encyclopedia*, Westport, CT, Greenwood Press

Graves-Brown, Carolyn and Cooney, Kathlyn M. (2008) *Sex and Gender in Ancient Egypt*, Cardiff, Classical Press of Wales

Harris, Cheryl I. (1995) 'Whiteness as property', in Crenshaw, K., Gotanda, N., Peller G. and Thomas, K. (eds) *Critical Race Theory: The Key Writings that Formed the Movement*, New York, The New Press

hooks, bell (1981) *Ain't I a Woman: Black Women and Feminism*, Boston, South End

Ikpe, Eno Blankson (2004) 'Human sexuality in Nigeria: a historical perspective', Understanding Human Sexuality Seminar Series, ARSRC, 29 July

—— (2006) 'Culture and pleasurable sexuality in southeastern Nigeria', *Sexuality in Africa Magazine* 3(3): 4–5, 8, http://www.arsrc.org/publications/sia/sep06/feature.htm, accessed 21 June 2010

Leadbetter, Ron (1997) 'Eros', in *Encyclopedia Mythica*, http://www.pantheon.org/articles/e/eros.html, modified 2 March 2006, accessed 5 July 2010

LeMoncheck, Linda (1997) 'Introduction', *Loose Women, Lecherous Men: A Feminist Philosophy of Sex*, New York, Oxford University Press

Lichtheim, Miriam (2006[1976]) *Ancient Egyptian Literature—A Book of Readings, Volume II: The New Kingdom*, Berkeley, CA, University of California Press

Lorde, Audre (1984) *Sister Outsider: Essays and Speeches*, Freedom, CA, The Crossing Press

MacKinnon, Catharine (1989) *Toward a Feminist Theory of the State*, Boston, Harvard University Press

McFadden, Patricia (2003) 'Sexual pleasure as feminist choice', *Feminist Africa* 2: 50–60, http://www.feministafrica.org/index.php/sexual-pleasure-as-feminist-choice, accessed 11 July 2010

Merriam-Webster Online Dictionary (2010) 'Eroticism', Merriam-Webster Online, http://www.merriam-webster.com/dictionary/eroticism, accessed 5 July 2010

—— (2010) 'Pornography', Merriam-Webster Online, http://www.merriam-webster.com/dictionary/pornography, accessed 5 July 2010

Meskell, Lynn (2002) *Private Life in New Kingdom Egypt*, New Haven, Princeton University Press

Mysliwiec, Karol (2004) *Eros on the Nile*, trans. Geoffrey L. Packer, Ithica, Cornell University Press

Nyamnjoh, Francis (2005) 'Fishing in troubled waters: disquettes and thiofs in Dakar', *Africa* 75(3): 295–324

Nzegwu, Nkiru (2005) 'African philosophy', in Soble, A. (ed) *Sex from Plato to Paglia: A Philosophical Encyclopedia*, Westport, CT, Greenwood Press

—— (2006) *Family Matters: Feminist Concepts in African Philosophy of Culture*, Albany, SUNY Press

Obenga, T. (2004) *African Philosophy: The Pharaonic Period: 2780–330 BC*, Dakar, Per Ankh

Ogungbile, David O. (2001) 'Eérìndínlógun: the seeing eyes of sacred shells and stories', in Murphy, J.M. and Sanford, M. (eds) *Òsun Across the Waters: A Yoruba Goddess in Africa and the Americas*, Bloomington, Indiana University Press

Pateman, Carole (1988) *Sexual Contract*, Stanford, Stanford University Press

—— (1991) '"God hath ordained to man a helper": Hobbes, patriarchy and conjugal right', in Shanley, Mary Lyndon and Pateman, C. (eds) *Feminist Interpretations and Political Theory*, Cambridge, Polity Press

—— (2001) 'Genesis, fathers and the political theory of sons' in Evans, M. (ed) *Feminism: Critical Concepts in Literary and Cultural Studies Volume 1: Feminism and the Enlightenment*, London, Routledge

Pereira, Charmaine (2003) '"Where angels fear to tread?" Some thoughts on Patricia McFadden's "Sexual pleasure as feminist choice"', *Feminist Africa* 2: 61–65, http://www.feministafrica.org/index.php/where-angels-fear-to-tread, accessed 16 July 2010

Pluth, Ed (2005) 'Sigmund Freud', in Soble, A. (ed) *Sex from Plato to Paglia: A Philosophical Encyclopedia*, Westport, CT, Greenwood Press

Pritchett, James Anthony (2001) *The Lunda-Ndembu: Style, Change, and Social Transformation in South Central Africa*, Madison, Wisconsin University Press

Quinn, Carol V. (2005) 'Objectification, sexual', in Soble, A. (ed) *Sex from Plato to Paglia: A Philosophical Encyclopedia*, Westport, CT, Greenwood Press

Richards, Audrey I. (1956) *Chisungu: A Girl's Initiation Ceremony Among the Bemba of Northern Rhodesia*, London, Faber and Faber

Samuels, Herbert (1994) 'Race, sex and myths: images of African-American men and women', in Bullough, Vern L. and Bullough, Bonnie (eds) *Human Sexuality: An Encyclopedia*, New York, Garland Publishing

Soble, Alan (2005a) 'Introduction', in Soble, A. (ed) *Sex from Plato to Paglia: A Philosophical Encyclopedia*, Westport, CT, Greenwood Press

—— (2005b) 'Overview of philosophy of sex', in Soble, A. (ed) *Sex from Plato to Paglia: A Philosophical Encyclopedia*, Westport, CT, Greenwood Press

—— (2005c) 'Personification, sexual', in Soble, A. (ed) *Sex from Plato to Paglia: A Philosophical Encyclopedia*, Westport, CT, Greenwood Press

—— (2008) 'The analytic categories of the philosophy of sex', in Soble, A. and Power, N. *The Philosophy of Sex: Contemporary Readings,* Lanham, MD, Rowan and Littlefield

Spronk, Rachel (2005) 'Female sexuality in Nairobi: flawed or favoured?', *Culture, Health and Sexuality* 7(3): 267–77

Tamale, Sylvia (2003) 'Out of the closet: unveiling sexuality discourses in Uganda', *Feminist Africa* 2: 42–9, http://www.feministafrica.org/index.php/out-of-the-closet, accessed 11 July 2010

—— (2005) 'Eroticism, sensuality and "women's secrets" among the Baganda: a critical analysis', *Feminist Africa* 5: 9–36, http://www.feministafrica.org/uploads/File/Issue%205/FA5_feature_article_1.pdf, last accessed 16 July 2010

Uchendu, Chinturu (2003) 'Equal encounters: gender, language and power in an African society – the case of Ubang-Obudu, Nigeria', PhD dissertation, Bethesda, University of Maryland

Undie, Chi-Chi and Benaya, Kenaya (2006) 'The state of knowledge on sexuality in sub-Saharan Africa: a synthesis of literature', *Jenda: A Journal of Culture and African Women Studies* 8: 1–33

Undie, C., Crichton, J. and Zulu, E. (2007) 'Metaphors we love by: conceptualisations of sex among young people in Malawi', *African Journal of Reproductive Health* 11(3): 221–35

Vuorela, Ulla (2003) 'Motherhood in the naming: mothers and wives in the Finnish/Karelian cultural region', *Jenda: A Journal of Culture and African Women Studies* 4: 1–16

Washington, Teresa N. (2005) *Our Mothers, Our Powers, Our Texts: Manifestation of Àjé in Africana Literature*, Bloomington, Indiana University Press

Weeks, Jeffrey (2000) *Making Sexual History,* Cambridge, UK, Polity Press

World Health Organisation (WHO) 'Female genital mutilation', http://www.who.int/mediacentre/factsheets/fs241/en/, accessed 8 August 2010

26

Politics of naming sexual practices[1]

Brigitte Bagnol and Esmeralda Mariano

Introduction

Women, in different periods of their lives and with various motivations and purposes, carry out interventions on their genital organs. These might include incisions, elongation, ablation of the labia minora and majora or clitoris; the stitching up of the labia majora or minora, the ritual breaking of the hymen; and incisions in the vaginal and perineal area. Some women modify the diameter of the vagina, its temperature, lubrication, humidity and consistency through steam baths, smokes and application or ingestion of various preparations.

References to vaginal practices can be found in studies of various countries of Asia, Africa and the Americas. Daily or regular hygiene methods to wash the vagina, eliminate secretions and semen or odours, using various products through topical or internal application, are the most widespread of these and can be observed in various countries and on different continents (Ombolo 1990: 149–50; Joesoef et al 1996; Preston-Whyte 2003; Utomo 2003; Martin Hilber et al 2010a, 2010b).

Reasons for the various practices include, but are not limited to, the control of women's sexuality and the sexual satisfaction of one or both partners. They are also connected to personal hygiene, health and well-being, and socialisation of the woman's body and fertility (Brown and Brown 2000; Van de Wijgert et al 2000; Bagnol and Mariano 2008). These practices are the result of a learning process. They are representations of gender behaviour generally associated with femininity and masculinity and incorporated as a result of social norms, among which heterosexuality and reproduction play a fundamental role (Butler 1990). The incorporation and imposition of these gendered behaviours are based on the sexed body of the 'woman', but modified to adapt to prevailing values. These practices express an ethics of sex and sexuality, and an *ars sexualis* in many respects similar to that described by Michel Foucault (1984).

According to the WHO/UNICEF/UNFPA Joint Statement (WHO et al 1997), 'all procedures that involve partial or total removal of female external genitalia and/or injury to the female genital organs for cultural or any other non-therapeutic reason' are considered female genital mutilation (FGM) and should be banned. With the exception of excision and infibulations[2] found on the African continent (Hosken 1979; Boddy 1989; WHO 2000) and defined as female genital mutilation (WHO et al 1997) of Type I, II and III, vaginal practices have been scarcely documented or studied, especially as far as their links to sexual pleasure are concerned. Little has been written about the role of non-surgical interventions defined as FGM Type IV, which include the insertion, application or ingestion of various substances to attempt to tighten the vagina and/or change the level of its lubrication and the elongation of the labia.

According to the definition, Type IV FGM includes: 'pricking, piercing or incising of the clitoris/or labia; stretching of the clitoris and/or labia; cauterisation by burning of the clitoris and surrounding tissues; scraping of tissues surrounding the vaginal orifice (*angurya* cuts) or cutting of the vagina (*gishiri* cuts); introduction of corrosive substances or herbs into the vagina to cause bleeding or for the purpose of tightening or narrowing it; and any other procedure that falls under the definition given above' (WHO et al 1997). Curiously there is no description of its prevalence in the world or in particular countries, neither a description of the health implications of the practices. The new statement on FGM (OHCHR et al 2008: 4) is more careful and aware of the debate and includes in Type IV 'all other harmful procedures to the female genitalia for non-medical purposes, for example: pricking, piercing, incising, scraping and cauterisation'. However, 'stretching' and 'introduction of harmful substances' are still included and described in the document (OHCHR et al 2008: 27).

This article, based on ethnographic data collected in 2005 in the Tete province of Mozambique as part of the WHO multi-country research project on gender, sexuality and vaginal practices (Bagnol and Mariano 2008; Martin Hilber et al 2010a, 2010b), provides detailed information on non-surgical vaginal practices and advocates for their removal from the classification of FGM of Type IV (WHO et al 1997). It shows that considering the elongation of the labia minora[3] and the use of vaginal products as FGM is inappropriate because it ignores both the motivations and the consequences of the practice. In addition, the article stresses that, in Mozambique, this line of labelling runs the risk of antagonising women and being counterproductive.

The stretching of the labia minora: an overview

On the internet, several websites publicise the elongation of labia minora as an erotic asset based on an 'ancient art' to enhance sexual performance and also used by Western women.[4] This adoption of the practice shows its wide attraction for the enhancement of sexuality. In the southern African region the elongation of the vaginal labia minora is quite widespread and is practised by many ethnolinguistic groups (Parikh 2005). It is found among the Venda (Blacking 1967) and Lovedu (Krige and Krige 1980) of South Africa and among several groups in central and northern Mozambique (Arnfred 1989, 2003; Ironga 1994; Enoque 1994; Bagnol 1996, 2003; Geisler 2000). It is a common cultural practice in the south of Tanzania among the Makonde-speaking people (Dias 1998; Johansen 2006), in Uganda among the Baganda linguistic group of the central region (Tamale 2005) and in some groups in the western region (Parhik 2005) and in Zimbabwe among the Shona (Gelfand 1979: 19; Aschwanden 1982: 77; Lafon 1995: 179). The Khoisan are also reported to have elongated labia minora. However, none of these authors gives a full account of the motivations of this practice and the voices of women who perform it are rarely expressed.

The idea that elongation of the labia minora is part of sexual education and aims at improving the sexuality of both partners is shared by several authors who have described the practice. Shanti Parikh explains that in Uganda, despite the fact that girls' sexuality is manipulated essentially in order to respond to male desires, the pulling of the 'little lips' increases the women's sexual desire and the pleasure arising from masturbation (Parikh 2005: 132–139). The author also stresses that the 'girl received a stern warning that if she did not pull she would either be unable to give birth or would experience complications during delivery' (Parikh 2005: 133). Michael Gelfand (1979: 19), referring to the Shona linguistic group, says that the process begins one or two years prior to menarche. Herbert Aschwanden, in relation to the same group, notes that a woman who has not elongated her lips is called a 'cold woman' or even 'a man' and stresses its importance in the construction of female identity (Aschwanden 1982: 77).

These practices are part of the context of preparation for sexuality, which also includes scarifications on women's bodies in order to increase eroticism (Aschwanden 1982: 77–78). John Blacking observed that among the Venda 'this operation is begun often long before puberty, its importance is emphasised at *vhusha* [puberty school]' (Blacking 1967: 83–4). Recent data from both Mozambique and Tanzania indicates that the practice aims at transforming young girls into real women and that it is very much connected to sexuality and reproduction (Johansen 2006; Bagnol and Mariano 2008).

In the WHO (2000) report, 'Systematic review of the health complications of female genital mutilation including sequelae in childbirth', there is no mention of the stretching of the labia, except in the definition of FGM. No negative consequences of the stretching of the labia minora were found in the literature except in a report by Makerere University and the Uganda AIDS Commission, which states that the practice influences young girls to start their sexual life earlier and makes them vulnerable to HIV (Etyang and Natukunda 2005).

In a different line, authors such as Arnfred (2003) have encouraged research on this practice to better understand the motivations behind it and to accumulate evidence of the fact that it does not constitute a form of genital mutilation. Tamale (2005), a Ugandan scholar describing the *ssenga* institution among the Baganda, which is set up to educate women specifically in relation to their sexuality, stresses its role in women's empowerment and the part it plays in women's silent struggle against colonialism and post-colonial forces including religion, which aimed at imposing a 'modern' view on sexual behaviour. In her article, one of the first African voices on the practice of elongation, she contextualises 'the strict regulation and control of African women's sexuality' and reproduction (Tamale 2005) and its importance for capitalism. She also synthesises Marxist[5] and feminist theories to show how capitalism, colonialism and religious proselytism attempted to modify African beliefs and practices.

In Mozambique, elongation of the vaginal labia was first reported by Henri Alexandre Junod, a Swiss missionary, in an annex written in Latin in the French version of his book on the Ba-Ronga of southern Mozambique (Junod 1898: 482–85).

Today, in Mozambique the practice is quite common in the central and northern regions of the country (Organização da Mulher Mozambicana (OMM) 1983; Ironga 1994; Enoque 1994; Arnfred 1989, 2003; Bagnol 1996, 2003). In an effort to trace discourses around these practices it is necessary to mention that after independence, in 1975, following the efforts of the colonial state and the missionaries, the Frente de Liberação de Moçambique[6] (Frelimo), the OMM[7] and other mass organisations fought against traditional practices such as African medicine, initiation rites, *lovolo* (bridewealth), polygyny, extramarital relations and early marriages. Frelimo's position on tradition is well expressed in the following:

> Traditional ... society is a conservative, immobile society with rigid hierarchy ... [It] excludes youth, excludes innovations, excludes women. (Vieira 1977, quoted in Honwana 1996)

> [In traditional society] women are regarded as second class human beings, subjected to the humiliating practice of polygamy, acquired through a gift made to their families (*lovolo*) ... and educated to serve men passively. (Machel 1970, quoted in Honwana 1996)

Obscurantism, superstition, religious belief, ignorance and rituals such as initiation and *lovolo* were considered by Frelimo to be mechanisms by which women were alienated. It was felt that these mechanisms were used both in the context of colonialism and capitalism to oppress men and women, but also by men to maintain women in a position of subordination and passivity. This view of women and of initiation rituals reflected how the revolutionary leadership had adopted Christian and colonial views of their own culture, rejecting it violently.

During our research, some interviewees stressed that after independence foreign doctors, mainly from the former USSR, would cut the elongated labia during childbirth because they found them cumbersome. These mutilations of women's labia appear to have been based on the discretion of individual doctors rather than any political decision. These actions showed a lack of awareness of female identity construction and total disrespect of women's bodies and rights. These occurrences, in a political context of rejection of traditional values, fuelled women's fear for both their physical integrity and their right to make decisions about their bodies, and it discouraged them from attending hospitals to give birth.

In contrast to Frelimo's official discourse, however, elongation of the labia 'was highly praised by women as well as by men, as a contributing factor to a pleasurable life' (Arnfred 2003), during preparations for the OMM conference 1983/84. A conference report from Tete province indicates that 'during coitus they (elongated labia) increase the sexual pleasure of the man, and later when the woman is older, the lips are used to strengthen the diameter of the vagina'[8] (OMM 1983). The same report, in analysing initiation rituals and practices aimed at the elongation of the labia or to increase the size of the penis, states that 'neither boys nor girls should use products which may damage their health and sexual organs' (OMM 1983). The focus on health issues is important and shows that these practices were not considered as those that should be eradicated, although health-related consequences were to be avoided and monitored.

Signe Arnfred (2003), who participated in the preparation of the OMM conference 1983/84, has contrasted the discourses on initiation rituals by colonialists and religious and independence movements with the voice of women who support what they consider an important part of their femininity construction and an instrument for their empowerment. She juxtaposes the meanings that women give to these practices with interpretations of the rituals by outsiders and shows the need for a participatory approach to the subject (Arnfred 2003: 16). Brigitte Bagnol (1996, 2003) has also analysed the implication of the elongation of the labia minora on homo-attraction and gender roles. She argues that the elongation of the labia aims at achieving womanhood, 'as a woman without long labia is not a woman' (Bagnol 2003: 11).

Some authors refer to this practice as responding to a male request, inasmuch as it enhances sexual pleasure (Raimundo et al 2003), or they suggest that its absence might constitute a ground for divorce (Ironga 1994). More recent research relates to the importance of elongation and application of vaginal products for women's health and well-being and for eroticism (Bagnol and Mariano 2008, 2009).

Stretching of the labia in Tete province

In Tete province, one of the most widespread vaginal practices is the elongation of the vaginal labia minora (*kukhuna, kupfuwa* or *puxa-puxa*). It is part of the process of initiation to female sexuality, which includes the use of a belt of beads and scarifications on the body, as well as the modification or alteration of the genital organs. This initiation is led by godmothers, who are chosen by the girls' mothers or aunts. They are remunerated for providing teachings and following the tradition of the elongation. Normally this process starts from the age of 8–12 and lasts for four to six months.

The first time that a godmother demonstrates elongation, she pulls the young girl's labia (*matingi*) herself and makes sure that the girl is proceeding correctly. The labia are massaged and stretched from top to bottom, with the tips of the thumb and index finger of each hand. Oily substances extracted from the kernel of the *nsatsi* (castor-oil plant) are used. The interviewees insist that one does not pull the clitoris and that the latter remains withdrawn between the two lips. However, others say that the clitoris is also stretched. Although most women indicate that they are stretching only the labia minora, other information suggests that in some cases the labia majora might also be elongated.

The elongation is done daily, generally early in the morning and at sundown, and in discreet places. The labia are elongated by the individual or sometimes in a group of girls who pull each others' labia. According to a nurse, 'They pull each other in order not to feel pain, among friends, one in front of the other, and they pull each other at the same time for thirty minutes every day. Only the unmarried girls pull each other, when they are young' (mother-and-child health nurse (2005), interview at Tete provincial hospital).

Although the above interviewee speaks of pain, another explains that the process can be pleasurable:

> When the girls or women do *puxa-puxa*, they feel sexual pleasure … when
> she's grown up. Also as an element to amuse oneself and masturbate when
> she doesn't have a man beside her … When she reaches around fifteen years
> of age she starts to do it, to feel pleasure. (Potter, about 45, (2005) interview in
> Chipembere, August)

The above quotation shows that even if the official goal is heterosexuality and
'holding onto one's partner', young women explore many aspects of their sexuality,
pain but also pleasure, individually or with girlfriends. The elongation of the labia
is ritualised learning in autoeroticism and homoeroticism, as various interviewees
explained and as suggested in previous works (Bagnol 1996, 2003).

The elongation process may take several months, until the ideal length of three
to four centimetres is achieved. Feminine beauty is thus partially evaluated by the
presence or absence of the *matingi* and by their length. If they are too short, the
woman is considered 'lazy', but when they are too long, they 'can create water'
in the vagina. According to the interviewees, the right size of the lips allows the
vagina's dampness to be drained and ideal vaginal dryness to be obtained. A female
traditional healer in the city of Tete summarises this idea well:

> When the *matingi* are very long water comes out, because they perspire. When
> they are average, they absorb water at the time of sex, the man doesn't feel
> that there's water, because of those *matingi* … if she doesn't have them, the
> water fills up because it's only a hole. (Healer, 38, a widow with four children,
> (2005) interview in Filipe Samuel Magaia)

Elongating the labia minora is related to a basic notion of femininity. The primary
motivation is to use the *matingi* to close the vaginal orifice naturally open at birth,
but also by regular coitus or after the birth of a baby. The elongated vaginal labia
are often described by the metaphor of a 'door' (Bagnol and Mariano 2008, 2009).
Prior to the sexual act the partners should 'open the door', 'the man can't come in
just like that'. These notions illustrate the importance of the woman being closed –
perhaps as a form of protection – and possible foreplay prior to penetration. People
use the word 'hole' when the labia are not elongated as a form of ridicule or insult
to a woman who does not have *matingi*. The interviewees also explained that if the
girl does not elongate the labia, she will not manage to keep her partner, because he
will prefer to have sex with a woman who has the *matingi*. If girls are not 'prepared'
(sexually initiated and familiar with the manipulation of genitals), later on they
may be disrespected as women and even considered to be men.

It is a widespread belief that the labia tend to shrink after childbirth and with the
menstrual cycle. Therefore, to attain the ideal size of the labia, every woman continues to pull them and 'maintain them', ensuring their length and smoothness are
constant and that their elasticity remains as long as they are sexually active, until
menopause. The male partners also help their female partners to stretch the lips,
'making use' of them as an erotic stimulus through massages and oral sex.

Some interviewees considered the clitoris irrelevant, all the emphasis being
given to the labia, whereas others considered it fundamental because it is the point

of departure for the sensation that propagates along the labia. At times, the labia are placed inside the vagina in order to reduce its diameter and make the entry of the penis difficult on first attempt, creating greater friction and increasing the 'heat' in the sexual act. Using metaphorical language, they may be referred to as 'the firewood to light the bonfire'.

Use of vaginal substances: an overview

In parts of Asia (Hull and Budhiharsana 2001) and Africa, women use various substances to reduce the size of the vagina and its lubrication to increase friction, thus creating favourable conditions for men's and sometimes women's pleasure (Martin Hilber et al 2010a, 2010b). E. Judith Brown et al (1993: 991) explain that in Zaire women use little balls of ground leaves, which they insert in the vagina prior to coitus, to increase sexual pleasure. The authors mention the need to avoid noise during the sexual act (Brown et al 1993: 990). Practices aimed at tightening the vagina are also found in central and southern Africa and have been documented by several authors (Runganga et al 1992; Civic and Wilson 1996; Morar and Karim 1998; Reed et al 2000; Braunstein and Van de Wigjert 2002). Jean-Pierre Ombolo, analysing sexuality in central and southern Cameroon, explains that a wide vagina is considered a serious problem, because the vagina is ideally 'narrow and hot' (Ombolo 1990: 51–52). Ombolo underlines that this attitude is also common in sub-Saharan Africa (Ombolo 1990: 52). A study on STIs carried out in Mozambique explains that the use of products 'in order to reduce lubrication and increase friction' aims at increasing men's sexual pleasure to the detriment of that of women (Mahomed et al n.d.: 27).

Literature on these practices focuses mainly on their health impacts and only a few in-depth ethnographic studies have been carried out to better understand the motivations (Awusabo-Asare et al 1993; Green et al 2001). The increased susceptibility to infections and disease transmission due to the modification of the vaginal flora is mentioned by some authors, as well as the risks of inflammation and irritation of the genital organs of both partners (Brown et al 1993; Dallabetta et al 1995; Orubuloye et al 1995; Sandala et al 1995; Baleta 1998; Kun 1998; Brown and Brown 2000; Braunstein and Van de Wigjert 2002).

Many studies have shown that some sexually transmitted infections facilitate HIV transmission. However, vaginal infections, such as bacterial vaginosis (BV), as well as yeast infections which are likely to result from vaginal practices, have not yet been clearly established as co-factors for HIV infection (Myer et al 2005). Some studies also suggest that different products might have completely distinct effects, with some limiting and others increasing the risks of disease transmission (Myer et al 2005), and that outcomes might differ according to the product and the quantity used. A recent systematic review of prospective longitudinal studies concluded that it is plausible that intravaginal cleaning practices and vaginal infections increase susceptibility to HIV infection, but conclusive evidence is lacking. However, a meta-analysis of data from 11 prospective cohort studies involving 14,874 women suggests an increase in the risk of acquiring HIV infection amongst women who use cloth or paper to wipe out the vagina or apply products, insert products intended to dry or tighten the vagina, or clean with soap intravaginally (Low et al 2010).

Thus, further research is needed to discern which practices and products are potentially harmful and which have a high potential association with STIs and HIV. In addition, studies should also investigate variations in practices within the same culture, or among women of different social classes and cultural backgrounds (Bagnol 1996, 2003; Awusabo-Asare et al 1993; Green et al 2001).

Insertion of substances into the vagina in Tete province

As in the case of the elongation of the labia minora, the majority of women use a variety of substances in order to contract or narrow the vaginal canal. These products are called *mankwala ya kubvalira*, which literally means 'medicine to put' because they are to be used specifically in the vagina. Most women who are sexually active and of childbearing age use products to 'prepare' their vagina. Moreover, many women use products after childbirth to close up the vagina as rapidly as possible, so as to resume having sex with their partner.

Among the various reasons for the use of vaginal products is the association of the idea of virginity with narrowness of the vaginal orifice. Many interviewees used the expression 'to seem to be a virgin' as the ideal condition for a more satisfactory sexual encounter. The vagina ought to be tight, dry and hot in order to allow friction, sexual pleasure for both partners and women's well-being. The following quotation highlights the sexual pleasure of the two partners:

> When the woman gets together with a man [has sex], the body doesn't usually end up well ... the body gets separated [because the vagina is too open], so with *kubvalira* the body returns [the vagina is tightened], that's the way the men like it ... The women also like it. (Widow, 64 (2005) interview in M'padwe)

Friction is thought to be fundamental for sexual pleasure and, to that effect, the penis should not enter the vagina easily. This condition is also associated with good health, according to another interviewee:

> One has to put the *kubvalira* product in order for the man not to end up entering right away, just like that ... If she doesn't put the *kubvalira* product, she ends up as if she had just been with another man, she's open, very open, without feeling right herself. (Female traditional healer (2005) interview in M'padwe)

When 'excess water' is mentioned, women are said not to be 'sweet' or to be 'tasteless'. Seeking heat, sweetness and friction implies a certain way of having sex '*nyama na nyama* (flesh on flesh), which appears to be the most satisfactory. When a woman has a very lubricated vagina, her partner complains and might accuse her of having had another partner beforehand, or of not having 'prepared' herself properly. If he is angry with the woman and if this partner is casual, he may even comment on this as a way of insulting her or in the form of ridicule with his friends. However, many women think that men do not know that women place products in their vaginas in order to modify its lubrication. This is quite a highly guarded 'secret', inasmuch as women want this to appear to be a natural, individual characteristic.

Speaking of a sexual encounter with a 'watery' woman, the man may say: 'it's like having sex in a glass of water', in reference to the absence of friction and to the resulting noise. Sometimes 'water' is related to some disease or to 'a rending'. 'When the woman gets a tear, water comes out constantly,' explains a (female) traditional doctor who is also a potter and midwife in the village of Chipembere in Changara District. Thus products ought to be inserted into the vagina so as to treat it. A traditional doctor explains as follows:

> Amongst some women there has been that white dirt that doesn't smell, that is normal, but in others there has been one that smells, which comes out a lot, it usually being linked to a dirty uterus, but with that drug all of the water comes out and it's dry. (Healer, 38, a widow with four children (2005) interview in Filipe Samuel Magaia)

Following childbirth, the vagina may also end up 'torn' and it is necessary to close it up once again by inserting products into it. Usually, products are provided by women's relatives (godmothers, aunts, grandmothers) or by traditional doctors. These different *mankwala* can be bought in the market in the city of Tete from itinerant vendors (Zimbabwean or Mozambican women) who circulate in the rural areas or from traditional doctors, or they may be prepared by family members, neighbours or the user herself. The *mankwala* produced locally are leaves, roots, and dried and pounded tree bark (reduced to a powder), applied in three ways: placed in the panties, in the vaginal orifice with the fingertip or inside the vagina.

There are also kinds of 'vaginal eggs' made with natural substances, similar to those mentioned above and mixed with an egg in order to form little balls. Eggs are used in the preparation because they are impenetrable and are consequently considered to have the characteristics of the desired vagina.[9] Within the *mankwala ya kubvalira*, we might find household products, such as Colgate and Vicks. The massive immigration of women from Zimbabwe has intensified and diversified the use and type of substances. Among the *mankwala* coming from Zimbabwe are stones and alum or copper sulphate.

As explained by health workers interviewed in a focus group in the city of Tete, the majority of women use *mankwala ya kubvalira*: 'Eighty per cent use them here. We Africans ought to use such products … In the city it's 80 per cent and in the countryside it's almost everyone' (focus group, health personnel (2005) interview in Tete). All sexually active women tend to use *mankwala ya kubvalira*, but pregnant women stop using them after the third month of gestation. In some churches, women are advised against using traditional products. The opinion is widespread that women in menopause cease having sex[10] and also very frequently abandon the use of these products. However, some continue to use them in order to 'be well' and to have 'weight' as opposed to the lightness they feel when their labia are open. In a situation of sexual competition with others, whether in rural or urban areas, women tend to make greater use of vaginal products.

According to the majority of women, *mankwala* inserted or applied in the vagina, or ingested, tend to improve their sexuality when they are concerned about keeping an unfaithful or polygynous partner. Sex workers also tend to use vaginal products in order to be able to provide satisfactory sexual performances and ensure that the sexual partner 'doesn't suspect that they have just had sex with another man'. Thus, the frequency with which vaginal products are used varies according to the needs of differently positioned women and the efficacy of the substance.

Perceived consequences of the practices

Most women and men in the province of Tete see the elongation of the labia minora as having a very positive effect on men's and women's sexual lives and relationships. It is extremely rare to register negative effects. However, excessive length of the labia 'creating water', or the fact that the elongating process is painful, especially at the beginning, were mentioned. Sometimes, some products used for elongation can also cause lesions. In relation to the vaginal products, a large majority of the women interviewed who use them stated that they did not have negative effects. However, excessive use of these products as well as new products can in fact have unexpected effects. Some women reported experiences of exfoliation of the vaginal mucosa, vaginal lacerations, burns, swellings and increased secretions:

> I know the *kubvalira* which I bought and inserted. I started to moan, then straightaway I fell ill, on that day I had to take a fan and direct it on [my vagina] … The next day, that exfoliated, something white scaling right off and that ruins the uterus … that thing is salt from Zimbabwe, small stones. (Focus group, OMM (2005) interview in Tete)

Despite their awareness of the high prevalence of vaginal products, discussions of the issue among health personnel are still extremely limited. Not much research has been conducted on them in relation to public health, to understand their cultural dimension or their impact on the transmission and prevention of STIs/HIV.

Pain reported by men and women during intercourse is generally a consequence of vaginal products. Lacerations on the penis and in the vagina are said to result from the effort needed to penetrate and the friction occurring during coitus. The vaginal products appear for some as being in direct opposition to the use of a condom, the argument being that with the insertion of vaginal products the sex act ought to be unprotected (with no condom) in order to allow direct contact between the vagina and the penis and to obtain greater sexual pleasure. It was found that the majority of the interviewees did not use a condom. However, some people, including sex workers, explained that *mankwala ya kubvalira* may be used simultaneously with condoms. Yet, they leave no doubt that the lubricant on the condom leads many people to question the reason for its existence. Because most men and women seek to reduce lubrication in the vagina in order to create greater difficulty for penetration, using a lubricated condom is an absurdity that is difficult to justify.

During the meetings held with health workers, it was noted that frequently, during clinical observations, women show residues of vaginal substances or vaginal complications (discharges) assumed to be caused by the use of vaginal products, as explained by a (male) nurse:

> After inserting the stones (women) had a reaction involving discharge which never passes, a vaginal discharge ... When they arrive here [in the Health Post] they [women] seem to have an STI which is not STI ... The roots may provoke lesions outside or inside the vagina and represent a danger ... with this problem of STIs and HIV/AIDS, she goes along there with those lesions and it's easier to catch them. (Male health-care provider (2005) interview in Mpadwe)

Daily or regular washing with soap and other products used with water is not seen as having any negative consequences and is even recommended by most nurses. The possibility of infection and laceration as a consequence of a daily or regular internal washing process has, however, been mentioned.

According to some health workers, cancer of the uterus may have its origin in the insertion of some products into the vagina because these practices might provoke infections, inflammations or lacerations. Daily washing of the inside of the vagina with various substances destroys the vaginal flora, thus modifying its pH (acidity). Some health workers say that this leads to a greater vulnerability to STIs, including HIV.

Can these practices be considered FGM?

To understand our effort to remove the elongation of the labia and the introduction of products in the vagina from the definition of FGM, some background information is necessary. In the 1960s and 1970s the debate around sexuality and the role of women in society exploded. Several feminists from the South, such as Awa Thiam (1978) and Nawal El Saadawi (1980) engaged in the debate, presenting their personal experiences of FGM. In the same period Fran Hosken (1978) published the first comprehensive article on the epidemiology of FGM worldwide.[11] The debate was extremely fierce, with French feminists such as Benoite Groult (1979) condemning the practices and anthropologists from the French Association of Anthropologists (AFA) publishing a collective text aimed at showing 'how a certain feminism resuscitates (today) the moralistic arrogance of yesterday's colonialism' (AFA 1981: 37–9). They urged people to look at the context and to understand the motivation of the practices. The article concluded:

> Let's stop making the Africans look like savages, let's stop imposing on them our models for living and now our models of pleasure, let's stop to perceive horror in others to better deny them in our society. For now to whom is the scandal benefiting? Isn't the barbarian the one who believes in barbarism? (AFA 1981: 39)

In the same period the WHO was pressured to condemn the practices. The first joint statement appeared in 1997 (WHO et al 1997). The second statement reviewing the knowledge gained over a decade was issued in 2008 (OHCHR et al 2008: 27). The debate about the issue is still very intense. In recent research and publications, a need to 're-think sexualities in Africa' has emerged in order to reconceptualise old colonial and post-colonial paradigms and to give voice to an African understanding of health, sexuality and eroticism. Far from a vision of African sexuality that focuses on otherness and difference, new points of view on the issue stress the diversity and the contextualised ways in which individuals shape their sexuality in light of myriad factors, including the linguistic group to which they belong, their religion, social class, gender and race/colour.

The book *Female Circumcision and the Politics of Knowledge, African Women and Imperialist Discourses*, edited by Obioma Nnaemeka, opens with the sentence by Claude Levi-Strauss that ended the French anthropologist's article 24 years earlier: 'The barbarian is first and foremost he who believes in barbarism'. The questions and debates seem to be the same. There is no disagreement about the need to put an end to harmful practices; the argument is rather about the lack of respect for the practices within the discourses. Labelling some practices 'barbaric' or a 'torture' without contextualising them promotes negative effects instead of helping to eradicate them. It disempowers and antagonises women. As Rogaia Abusharaf writes: 'In large part because of the European animosity toward circumcision, the practice became a focus of African resistance to foreign encroachment and interference' (Abusharaf 2001).

The question remains: why are elongation and the use of vaginal products considered to be female genital mutilation, while aesthetic vaginal surgery[12] such as labiaplasty, vaginoplasty, vaginal reconstruction, vaginal rejuvenation or tightening are promoted, and well-known surgeons and clinics are allowed to perform definitive modification of the vagina? Why is the use of play lubricants[13] bought in shops in the West not defined as female genital mutilation, if the use of products with the same objective and results are considered as such when they are home-produced in Africa or bought in a shop in Asia? Who decides who is barbarian? Who decides what is FGM and what is not? The answer lies in the understanding of the ethnocentrism underlying the production of discourses and the objectification of the African and Asian female body, in the othering and the stigmatisation of others' practices.

People are both objects and subjects – within a dynamic process of submission and resistance – of a process of transformation, which places them within the local culture and overall concept of society, including notions of sexuality, health, social well-being and relationships between persons and spiritual forces. It is in the process of transformation and care given to bodies and their functions (essentially sexual and reproductive) that the biologically male and female individuals become men and women, learning the appropriate gender behaviours at each phase of their lives. Thus, the biological body acquired at birth is one of the elements that determines the way individuals behave as men or as women, but in itself it is not sufficient. Interacting in particular institutions and with particular people, individuals invent and define their belonging to the categories man and woman. And it is in this context that individuals continually negotiate and exercise their agency.

The data collected strongly demonstrates that the practices under study (elongation of the labia minora, use of vaginal products or ingestion of potions to modify the condition of the vagina) do not constitute mutilation. The findings from Tete province bring evidence of the need to remove from the definition of FGM the mention of vaginal practices that do not involve surgical interventions, such as the insertion, application or ingestion of various substances. The consequences of the elongation of the labia minora and the use of vaginal products do not require a ban as in the case of FGM Types I, II and III, and these practices cannot be targeted through human rights legislation on violence against children and/or women, bodily harm and child abuse.

Nevertheless, some practices can result in injuries, such as lacerations and tears, and might need to be discouraged when evidence of an increase in STIs and HIV/AIDS transmission is confirmed. As is the case in Uganda (Tamale 2005), vaginal practices constitute an institution in which women develop their knowledge of interaction with others and transmit it to younger women in Tete province. It is a female institution and a locus of expression of women's power over their own bodies and their sexual relationships. These aspects have to be taken into consideration in the development of an approach that empowers women to control their sexuality, but also recognises vaginal practices as their secret to influence their partners' sexuality.

Acknowledgement

We would like to thank Dr Adriane Martin Hilber of the Department of Health and Reproductive Research of the World Health Organisation (WHO) in Geneva for the coordination of the research project at the international level. Our particular thanks are directed to Dr Ana Dai (MISAU), Dr Filipa Gouveia and Dr Frederico Brito, the Tete Provincial Health Director. A big 'thank you' is addressed to Dr Touré Boukar, WHO representative in Mozambique and to Dr Alicia Carbonel for the immense support they provided. This research was implemented by the International Centre for Reproductive Health (ICRH) and is being supported by the UNDP/UNFPA/WHO/World Bank special programme on research, development and research training in human reproduction, the International Partnership for Microbicides research, the Flemish government and Australia Aid (AusAID).

Notes

1. The text of this paper was originally published in 2008 in the *Finnish Journal of Ethnicity and Migration* 3(2): 42–53. Also published in 2009 in *Outliers, A Collection of Essays and Creative Writing on Sexuality in Africa*, Volume 2, New York, IRN Africa. Reproduced with permission.
2. Infibulation is the excision of parts or all of the external genitalia and stitching or narrowing of the vaginal opening.
3. In this paper we refer to the labia minora, as women interviewed explained that they elongate the 'little lips'.
4. See, for example, http://www.labiastretching.com, accessed 28 November 2010.
5. Engels viewed the establishment of private property and the development of agriculture

as the 'historical defeat of thefemale sex'. He believed that women's oppression would cease with the dissolution of private property. This analysis has been criticised by feminists who refute the association between the origin of man's control over woman and the establishment of private property or patriarchy.

6. The Mozambican Liberation Front, which, after fighting an armed struggle against colonial rule, proclaimed Mozambique's independence in June 1975. Frelimo took a socialist and Marxist approach, which rejected some values of the so-called 'traditional' society. This agenda was in many ways similar to that of the missionaries of the pre-independence era.

7. The Mozambican women's organisation (OMM) was conceived as a wing of Frelimo, and implemented Frelimo's strategy. The process by which the 'new' woman would be 'constructed' included women's participation in productive activities, the development of scientific and cultural education, and the modification of relationships between couples.

8. Here the document refers to the possibility of introducing the labia inside the vagina in order to reduce the diameter of the orifice.

9. Janice Boddy (1989), in her book *Wombs and Alien Spirits. Women, Men and Zār Cult in Northern Sudan*, also refers to the egg as a sexual symbol in the context of Sudanese society, which practices infibulation.

10. Because the sexual act is linked to procreation, in this phase of the woman's life the sperm would not result in conception and would be disposed of. The respondents explain that because the sperm is not evacuated with menstruation, it gets rotten inside the woman's body and she gets a swollen belly, which can result in health problems and death.

11. In 1979 a book entitled *The Hosken Report: Genital and Sexual Mutilation of Females* was published.

12. See the following websites (all accessed 28 November 2010): http://www.urogyn.org/aestheticvaginal.html; http://www.labiaplastysurgeon.com/; http://www.boloji.com/wfs5/wfs648.htm; http://www.onlinesurgery.com/plasticsurgery/vaginal-rejuvenation-default.asp.

13. See http://www.durex.com/en-US/Products/Lubes/Pages/LubesHomepage.aspx, accessed 28 November 2010.

References

Abusharaf, Rogaia Mustafa (2001) 'Virtuous cuts: female genital circumcision in an African ontology', *Differences: A Journal of Feminist Cultural Studies* 12 (1): 112–40

Association Française des Anthropologues (AFA) (1981) 'Tribune libre. A propos de l'excision en Afrique', *Bulletin de L'AFA* 4: 37–39

Arnfred, Signe (1989) 'Notes on gender and modernisation', paper presented at ROAPE conference, Warwick, UK

—— (2003) 'Contested construction of female sexualities: meanings and interpretations of initiation rituals', paper presented at the Conference on Sex and Secrecy, Johannesburg, 22–25 June

Aschwanden, Herbert (1982) *Symbols of Life*, Gweru, Mambo Press

Awusabo-Asare, Kofi, Anarfi, K. John and Agyeman, K. Dominic (1993) 'Women's control over their sexuality and the spread of STDs and HIV/AIDS in Ghana', *Health Transition Review* 3: 69–84

Bagnol, Brigitte (1982) 'Photographic chapter', in McLean, S., Longo, G., Visca, D. and Marziale G. (eds) *Circoncisione Feminile, Escissione e Infibulazione: Realtá e Proposte di Cambiamento*, Rome, Ed. Bulzoni

—— (1996) 'Assessment of sexual orientation in Maputo and Nampula', consultancy report, Maputo, Royal Netherlands Embassy

—— (2003) 'Identities and sexual attraction: female adolescent rituals in northern Mozambique and healers in southern Mozambique', paper presented at the 4th International IASSCS Conference, University of the Witwatersrand, Johannesburg, 22–25 June.

Bagnol, B. and Mariano, E. (2008) 'Vaginal practices: eroticism and implications for women's health and condom use in Mozambique', *Culture, Health and Sexuality* 10(6): 573–85
—— (2009) 'Cuidados consigo mesmo, sexualidade e erotismo,' *Physis* 19(2): 387–404
Baleta, Adele (1998) 'Concern voiced over "dry sex" practices in South Africa', *The Lancet* 17, 352: 1292
Beksinska, E. Mags, Rees, Helen V., Kleinschmidt, Immo and McIntyre, J. (1999) 'The practice and prevalence of dry sex among men and women in South Africa: a risk factor for sexually transmitted infections?', *Sexually Transmitted Infections* 75: 178–80
Biesele, Megan (1993) *Women Like Meat. The Folklore and Foraging Ideology of the Kalahari Ju/'hoan*, Bloomington, Indiana University Press
Blacking, John (1967) *Venda Children's Songs*, Johannesburg, University of Witwatersrand Press
Boddy, Janice (1989) *Wombs and Alien Spirits. Women, Men, and Zār Cult in Northern Sudan*, Madison, University of Wisconsin Press
Braunstein, Sarah and Van de Wijgert, Janneke (2002) 'Cultural norms and behaviour regarding vaginal lubrication during sex: implications for the acceptability of vaginal microbicides for the prevention of HIV/STIs', New York, Population Council
Brown, E. Judith, Okako, Bibi Ayowa and Brown, R.C. (1993) 'Dry and tight: sexual practices and potential AIDS risk in Zaire', *Social Science and Medicine* 37: 989–94
Brown, E. and Brown, R.C. (2000) 'Traditional intravaginal practices and the heterosexual transmission of disease: a review', *Sexually Transmitted Diseases* 27(4): 183–87
Butler, Judith (1990) *Gender Trouble, Feminism and the Subversion of Identity*, New York and London, Routledge
Civic, Diane and Wilson, David (1996) 'Dry sex in Zimbabwe and implication for condom use', *Social Science and Medicine* 42: 91–8
Cole, M. Catherine, Takyiwaa, Manuh and Miescher, Stephan F. (2007) *Africa After Gender?*, Bloomington, Indiana University Press
Dallabetta, Gina, Miotti, Paolo G., Chiphangwi, John D., Liomba George, Canner, Joseph, K. and Saah, Alfred, J. (1995) 'Traditional vaginal agents: use and association with HIV infection in Malawian women', *AIDS* 9: 293–97
Dias, Jorge (1998) *Os Maconde de Moçambique*, Lisboa, Instituto de Investigação Cientifica Tropical
El Saadawi, Nawal (1980) *The Hidden Face of Eve, Women in the Arab World*, London, Zed Press
Enoque, M.A. (1994) 'Mulheres maniyka contam ... sexualidade e família (micro estudo exploratório)', Maputo, INDE/FNUAP/UNESCO
Etyang, Jude and Natukunda, Carol (2005) 'Visiting the bush linked to HIV', Kampala, New Vision, http://www.aegis.com/news/nv/2005/NV050820.html, accessed 28 November 2010
Feliciano, José Fialho (1998) 'Antropologia económica dos Thonga do sul de Moçambique', *Estudos* 12, Maputo, Arquivo Histórico de Moçambique
Foucault, Michel (1984) *Histoire de la Sexualité 3, Le Souci de Soi*, Paris, Editions Gallimard
Geisler, Gisela (2000) 'Women are women or how to please your husband: initiation ceremonies and the politics of "tradition" in southern Africa', in Goddard, Victoria Ana (ed) *Gender, Agency and Change: Anthropological Perspectives*, London, Routledge
Gelfand, Michael (1979) *Growing up in Shona Society from Birth to Marriage*, Harare, Mambo Press
Green, Gill, Pool, Robert, Harrison, Susan, Hart, Graham J., Wilkinson, Joanie, Nyanzi, Stella and Whitworth, J.A.G. (2001) 'Female control of sexuality: illusion or reality? Use of vaginal products in southwest Uganda', *Social Science and Medicine* 52: 585–98
Green, Maia (1999) 'Women's work is weeping: construction of gender in a Catholic community', in Moore, L. Henrietta, Sanders, Todd and Kaare, Bwire (eds) *Those who Play with Fire. Gender, Fertility and Transformation in East and Southern Africa*, London, The Athlone Press
Groult, Benoite (1979) 'Les mutilations sexuelles', *F Magazine* 14: 50–6
Honwana, Alcinda (1996) 'Spiritual agency and self-renewal in southern Mozambique', PhD thesis, London, University of London

285

Hosken, Fran (1978) 'The epidemiology of female genital mutilation', *Trop Doctor* 8: 150–56
—— (1979) *The Hosken Report: Genital and Sexual Mutilation of Females*, 2nd ed., New York, Women International Network News (WIN)
—— (1982) *The Hosken Report: Genital and Sexual Mutilation of Females*, 3rd ed., Lexington, Mass, WIN
Hull, Terry H. and Budhiharsana, M. (2001) 'Male circumcision and penis enhancement in southeast Asia: matters of pain and pleasure', *Reproductive Health Matters* 9(18): 60–7
Ironga, Ignês (1994) 'Mulheres Chuabos contam … sexualidade e família' (micro estudo exploratório)', Maputo, INDE/FNUAP/UNESCO
Joesoef, M., Sumampouw, H., Linnan, M., Schmid, S., Idajadi, A. and St Louis, M. (1996) 'Douching and sexually transmitted diseases in pregnant women in Surabaya, Indonesia', *American Journal of Obstetrics and Gynecology* 174: 115–19
Johansen, Elise (2006) 'Sculpted female bodies. Discourses and practices on genital manipulation in the context of globalisation', paper presented at Nordic Africa Days, Uppsala, The Nordic Africa Institute, 30 September–2 October 2005
Junod, A. Henri (1898) *Les Ba-Ronga. Étude Ethnographique sur les Indigènes de la Baie de Delagoa, Moeurs, Droit Coutumier, Vie Nationale, Industrie, Traditions, Superstitions et Religion*, Neuchatel, Imprimerie Attinger Frères
Krige, Eileen Jensen and Krige, John D. (1980) *The Realm of a Rain Queen*, Johannesburg, Juta and Company
Kun, Karen E. (1998) 'Viewpoint: vaginal drying agents and HIV transmission', *International Family Planning Perspectives* 24(2)
Lafon, Michel (1995) *Le Shona et les Shonas du Zimbabwe. Recueil d'Information sur la Langue et la Culture*, Paris, L'Harmattan
Low N., Chersich, M.F., Schmidlin, K., Egger, M., Francis, S.C., van de Wijgert, J.H et al (2010) 'Intravaginal practices, bacterial vaginosis and HIV infection in women: individual woman data meta-analysis', *PLoS Medicine*
Mahomed, Aida, Paulito, Coutinho and Balbina, Santos (n.d.) 'Envolvimento do parceiro no desiste e tratamento das ITS em mulheres grávidas', relatório draft, Maputo, MISAU
Mariano, E., Samucidine, M., Boaventura, I.B. and Sousa, C.P. (2010) 'Healers, nurses, obstetrics-gynaecologists dealing with women in the quest to become pregnant in Southern Mozambique', in Social Aspects of Accessible Infertility Care in Developing Countries: Facts, Views and Visions, *Scientific Journal of the Flemish Society of Obstetrics and Gynaecology Monograph* 43–50
Martin Hilber, Adriane, Hull, Terry, Preston-Whyte, Eleonor, Bagnol, Brigitte, Wacharasin, Chinta, Smit, Jenny and Widyantoro, Ninuk (2010a) 'A cross cultural study of vaginal practices and sexuality: implications for sexual health', *Social Science and Medicine* 70: 392–400.
Martin Hilber, Adriane, Hull, Terry, Chersich, Matthew, Bagnol, Brigitte, Prohmmo, A., Smith, Jenny, Widyantoro, Ninuk, Utomo, Iwu, François, Isabel, Tumwesigye, Nazarius M. and Temmerman, Marleen, on behalf of the GSVP study group (2010b forthcoming) 'Prevalence of vaginal practices in Africa and Asia: findings of a multi-country household survey', *Journal of Women's Health*
Martin Hilber, A., Francis, S.C., Chersich, M., Scott, P., Redmond, S., Bender, N., Miotti, P., Temmerman, M. and Low, N. (2010c) 'Intravaginal practices, vaginal infections and HIV acquisition: systematic review and meta-analysis', *PLoS ONE* 5(2), e9119: 1–11
Moore, L. Henrietta, Sanders, Todd and Kaare, Bwire (eds) (1999) *Those Who Play with Fire: Gender, Fertility and Transformation in East and Southern Africa*, London, The Athlone Press
Morar, Neetha S. and Abdool Karim, Salim (1998) 'Vaginal insertion and douching practices among sex workers at truck stops in KwaZulu-Natal', *South African Medical Journal* 88(4): 470
Myer, Landon, Kuhn, Louise, Stein, Zana A., Wright, Thomas C. Jr. and Denny, Lynette (2005) 'Intravaginal practices, bacterial vaginosis and women's susceptibility to HIV infection: epidemiological evidences and biological mechanisms', *Lancet* 5: 786–94
Office of the High Commissioner for Human Rights (OHCHR), UNAIDS, UNDP, UNECA,

UNESCO, UNFPA, UNHCR, UNICEF, UNIFEM, WHO (2008) 'Eliminating female genital mutilation: an inter-agency statement', Geneva, WHO

Ombolo, Jean-Pierre (1990) *Sexe et Société en Afrique Noire*, Paris, L'Harmattan

Organisação da Mulher Moçambicana (OMM) (1983) 'Preparação da conferência extraordinária da mulher: relatório da provincia de Tete', Tete, OMM

Orubuloye, I.O, Caldwell, P. and Caldwell, J. (1995) 'A note on suspect practices during the AIDS epidemic: vaginal drying and scarification in southwest Nigeria', *Health Transition Review* 5: 161–5

Parikh, A. Shanti (2005) 'From auntie to disco: The bifurcation of risk and pleasure in sex education in Uganda', in Adams, Vincanne and Pigg, Stacy Leigh (eds) *Sex in Development*, London, Duke University Press

Preston-Whyte, M. Eleonor (2003) 'Contexts of vulnerability: sex, secrecy and HIV/AIDS', *African Journal of AIDS Research* 2(2): 85–90

Price, Janet and Shildrick, Margrit (1999) *Feminist Theory and the Body, A Reader*, New York, Routledge

Raimundo, Inês, Saùte, Aida, Saide, Antonio, Mucamisa, Carlos, Bonifácio, Maximo, Maruassa, Leão, Ndango, Augusto and Mariano, Esmeralda (2003) 'Pesquisa rápida socio-cultural: provincia da Zambezia', Maputo, Centro de Estudos de População (CEP), Universidade Eduardo Mondlane (UEM) and United Nations Population Fund (UNFPA)

Reed, D. Barbara, Ford, Kathleen and Wirawan, Kathleen (2000) 'The Bali STD/AIDS study: association between vaginal hygiene practices and STDS among sex workers', *Sexually Transmitted Infections* 77: 46–52

Runganga, Agnes, Pitts, Marian and McMaster, John (1992) 'The use of herbal and other agents to enhance sexual experience', *Social Science and Medicine* 35(8): 1037–42

Sandala, Luciano, Lurie, Peter, Sunkutu, M. Rosemary, Chani, Edgar M., Hudes, Esther S. and Hearst, Norman (1995) '"Dry sex" and HIV infection among women attending a sexually transmitted disease clinic in Lukasa, Zambia', *AIDS* 9: S61–68

Simonsen, Jan K. (2000) 'Webs of life: An ethnographic account of Cisungu female initiation rituals among Mambwe-speaking women in Zambia', unpublished PhD thesis, Oslo, University of Oslo: Institute of Social Anthropology

Tamale, Sylvia (2005) 'Eroticism, sensuality and "women secrets" among the Baganda: a critical analysis', *Feminist Africa* 5: 9–36, http://www.feministafrica.org/2level.html, accessed 30 July 2007

Thiam, Awa (1978) *La Parole aux Négresses*, Paris, Denoël-Gonthier

Utomo, Iwu (2003) 'Vaginal drying and cleansing in southeast Asia: notes for future research', paper presented to the Asia Pacific Conference on Sexual and Reproductive Health and Rights, Bangkok, 6–11 October

Van de Wijgert, Janneke H.H., Mason, Peter R., Gwanzura, Lovemore, Mbivzo, M.T., Chirenje, Z.M., Iliff, V., Shiboski, S. and Padian, N.S. (2000) 'Intravaginal practices, vaginal flora disturbances and acquisition of sexually transmitted diseases in Zimbabwean women', *Journal of Infectious Diseases* 181: 587–94

World Health Organisation (WHO), UNICEF, UNFPA (1997) 'Female genital mutilation: a joint WHO/ UNICEF/UNFPA statement', Geneva, WHO

World Health Organisation (WHO) (2000) 'Systematic review of the health complications of female genital mutilation including sequelae in childbirth', Geneva, WHO: Department of Women's Health Family and Community Health

27

My American Jon[1] – fiction

Chimamanda Ngozi Adichie

There is something forlorn about Baltimore; I thought of this every Thursday when my taxi sped down Charles Street on my way to the train station to visit Jon in New York City. The buildings were connected to one another in faded slumping rows, but what really held my attention was the people: hunched in puffy jackets, waiting for buses, slouching in corners, making me wonder again and again why the dankest, drabbest parts of all the American cities I knew were full of black people. My taxi drivers were mostly Punjabi or Ethiopian. It was an Ethiopian who asked where my accent was from and then said, 'You don't look African at all,' when I told him Nigeria.

'Why don't I look African?' I asked.

'Because your blouse is too tight.'

'It is not too tight,' I said.

'I thought you were from Jamaica or one of those places,' he said, looking in the rear-view with both disapproval and concern. 'You have to be very careful or America will corrupt you.'

Later, I told Jon about this conversation and how the driver's sincerity had infuriated me and how I had gone to the station bathroom to see if my pink blouse was too tight. Jon laughed. But I was sure he understood; this was during the early months, the good months of our relationship.

We met at a poetry reading. I had come up to New York to hear the new Nigerian poet Chioma Ekemma read from her *Love Economies*. During the Q&A, the questions were not about why she chose to write poems without active verbs, or which poets she admired, but what could be done about poverty in Nigeria and would women ever achieve equality there and wasn't she lucky that she could come to America and find her voice? She was gracious – too gracious, I thought. Then Jon raised his hand from two rows ahead of me and said tourism was the easiest way to fix the Nigerian economy and it was a shame Nigeria was not tourist friendly. No hostels. No good roads. No backpackers. He spoke with absolute authority. Chioma Ekemma nodded enthusiastically. I raised my hand and said one could fix an economy in other ways that did not involve richer people going to gawk at the lives of poorer people who could never gawk back. There was some scattered clapping; I noticed the most vigorous came from the black people. Chioma Ekemma said something conciliatory and moved on to the next question. She was clearly thinking of keeping the peace so that as many people as possible would buy her book.

Jon was staring at me; a white man wearing a metal wristband who thought he could pontificate about my country irritated me. I stared back. I imagined him taking in my Afro-shaped twists, my severe black frames with distaste. But there was something else between us, between the chairs and people separating us: a sparkle, a star, a spark. His face was solemn when he came over after the reading and said I had really felt strongly back there and did I want to get coffee and have a little bit more of a debate? It amused me, the way he said 'debate'. But we did debate, about devaluation and deregulation and debt, and later, when we kissed at Penn station in a sudden press of our bodies before I got on the train, it was as if the debate was continuing, the way our tongues darted around inside our mouths without meeting.

He had never been with a black woman; he told me this the following weekend with a self-mocking toss of his head, as if this were something he should have done long ago but had somehow neglected. I laughed and he laughed and in the morning sunlight that streamed in through the windows of his apartment, his skin took on a bright and foreign translucence. After we broke up two years later, I would tell people that race was the reason, that he was too white and I was too black and the midway too skewed in his favour. In truth, we broke up after I cheated. The cheating was very good, me on top gliding and moaning and grasping the hair on the chest of the other man. But I told Jon that it had meant nothing. I told him that I had hated myself although I was filled with well-being, with a sublime sense not just of satisfaction but of accomplishment.

At first, Jon was disbelieving. 'No, you didn't have a one-night stand. You're such a liar.' I did lie to him sometimes, playful little lies like calling to say I could not come that weekend when I was just outside his door. But I did not lie about the big things.

'It's true,' I said.

He got up and turned down the volume of the stereo and paced and looked through the tall windows at the cars and people below. 'Unknown Soldier' was playing. Jon loved Fela Kuti; it was the reason he'd visited Nigeria and attended Nigerian events, perhaps the reason he thought he knew how to save Nigeria.

'Why?' he asked finally.

I should not have been pleased by the prospect of telling Jon why I had cheated. I sat down on the sofa and said, 'It was desire.'

It was desire. It felt as though gentle peppers had been squirted at the bottom of my stomach, a surge of pure aching desire that I was grateful for feeling and was determined not to waste.

'Desire?' Jon was watching me. Maybe he was thinking that it had always been good between us. So I got up and held him close and said that even though it had been a physical desire, the act itself had meant nothing because my self-loathing made pleasure impossible. Jon did not push me away. He said, 'The sin is not the sex, Amaka, the sin is the betrayal. So it doesn't matter whether or not you enjoyed it.'

That all-knowing tone of Jon's had always made me stiffen. If the circumstances were different, I would have asked him, 'Did the people at Yale teach you how to talk with such authority about things you know nothing about?' I had often asked him this in the past. Such as when, two or so months into our relationship, I arrived at his apartment and he kissed me and gestured to the table and said, 'Surprise. Tickets to Paris for three days. We leave tonight. You'll be back in time to teach Tuesday.'

'Jon, I cannot just jet off to Paris. I have a Nigerian passport and I have to apply for a visa.'

'Come on, you're an American resident. You don't need a visa to go to Paris.'

'I do.'

'No you don't.'

After I showed him on the internet that Nigerian citizens who were resident in America did in fact need a visa to get into Europe – a process that required bank statements, health insurance, all sorts of proof that you would not stay back and become a burden to Europe – Jon muttered 'Ridiculous,' as though it was the French embassy and not he who had been wrong. We did go to Paris, though. Jon changed the ticket dates. We went together to the French embassy but I went alone to the window where a woman wearing silver eyeshadow glanced at me, at my passport, back at me, and said she would not approve the visa because Nigerian passport-holders were high risk and it seemed suspicious to her that I was going to Paris for just three days.

'But…' I started to say and she made an impatient gesture and pushed my documents across under the glass. Jon got up then, tall and sinewy and angry, and told her I was going to Paris as his guest and my documents included his bank statements and my employment letter and insurance and everything else, if only she'd look at them. 'We're together,' he added, as if it was necessary to make it clear. The woman smirked. She said I should have explained myself better. She made a show of looking through the documents and said the visa would be ready for pick-up in two days.

It filled me with a dizzying pride, how Jon would often stand up for me, speak for me, protect me, make me omelettes, give me pedicures in the bubbling foot bath, slip his hand into mine as we walked, speak in the first-person plural. 'O na-eji gi ka akwa: he holds you like an egg,' Aunty Adanna said admiringly when she finally accepted that I was serious with a white man and asked me to bring him to lunch. Aunty Adanna was one of those Nigerian immigrants who, when they spoke to white people, adopted a risible American accent. I took Jon to her seven-room home in Columbia, outside Baltimore, and suddenly she was calling her son 'Mek', my bewildered teenage cousin whom we had always called Nnaemeka, and talking about how good he was at golf. She spoke of *fufu* and soup, which Jon had eaten many times before in New York, as if Nigerian food could not be worthy unless it was like something American. This is like your mashed potatoes, she told him, this is just like your clam chowder. She spoke of her swimming pool needing to be drained. She told anecdotes about the patients at her medical practice.

Jon asked when last she had been back in Nigeria and she said it had been six years; she could not bear the dirt and chaos and she did not know what the matter was with all of those corrupt people in government. 'Matter' came out sounding like 'marah.' Even though Jon had not asked, she proudly told him she had lived in America for 18 years, that she had sponsored my trip here eight years ago after my Nigerian university kept going on strike after strike. I stabbed the chicken in my soup and said nothing. I was ashamed. I was ashamed that she did not have books in her house and that when Jon brought up Zimbabwe, she had no idea what was going on there and so to cover my shame I muttered 'Philistine' as we drove away.

'Nigerian doctors and engineers and lawyers don't read anything unless it has the possibility of leading them to bigger paycheques,' I said. Jon laughed and said it had nothing to do with Nigeria, it was the same for the American bourgeoisie and, leaning over to kiss me, said that Aunty Adanna had been sweet, the way she was so keen to make him comfortable. It wasn't sweet, it was pathetic, but I liked that Jon said that and I liked that he wanted to be liked by my family.

I had never felt that love I read about in books, that inexorable thing that made characters take all sorts of unlikely decisions. By the time I met Jon, I had convinced myself that the feeling was like an orgasm; a certain percentage of women would never have one after all. At first, each long weekend with Jon in New York was a pleasant break to look forward to after teaching three days a week at the Shipley school. Soon, each weekend became something I longed for, and then something I needed. I realised that what I felt for Jon was becoming an inexorable thing when I saw the flyer advertising a teaching position in a New York City private academy on a board outside the general office and immediately went in to ask the secretary, Nakeya, if she knew more. She shook her head and said it wasn't a good idea.

'They like you here and you'll rise quickly if you stay, Amaka,' she said. I persisted. She said the academy was a good place although the pay at Shipley was better; the student body there was richer, though, and the class size smaller. She added in a lower voice that they were a little conservative and it was best if I took my twists out for the interview. 'You know how our hair can make them feel threatened?' Nakeya asked with a smile.

I knew. Why adults would feel threatened by hair has never ceased to amaze me but, after I called the academy and was asked to come in for an interview, I removed my twists and straightened my hair with a hot comb that burned my scalp. I was even willing to buy blonde dye. I wanted the job. I wanted to be in New York City with Jon. I had been rashly honest at my Shipley school interview, telling them that I had just graduated from Johns Hopkins graduate creative writing programme, had published only a few poems in journals, was struggling to complete a collection and was unsure how to make a living. For the academy interview, I decided I would be more circumspect. I told the two white men and one Hispanic woman that teaching was my first love and poetry my second.

They were attentive, they nodded often as if to show approval. I didn't tell Jon about it because I wanted to surprise him but after I got the email only three days later, thanking me and telling me they had selected a better-qualified applicant, I told Jon. He smiled, his big generous smile. He asked me to resign from the Shipley school, to move in with him and take some time off and focus on my poetry and, if I was worried about not paying rent, I could do so in kind. We laughed. We laughed so often during the early months. I put up an advertisement for subletting my Baltimore apartment, put my furniture in storage and moved in with Jon.

Later, almost two years later, on the day I told Jon that I had cheated, I wondered whether my moving in had contributed in some way; perhaps things would have been different if I had stayed in Baltimore, visiting for long weekends. That day, it took hours of sidestepping each other, of drinking tea, of Jon lying face up on the couch, before he asked, 'Who is he?'

I told him the man's name: Ifeanyi. We had met years ago at the wedding of a friend of Aunty Adanna's. He had called me a few times and then, recently, he moved from Atlanta to Harlem and we met for coffee and the desire happened and we took the train to his place.

Jon said, 'You gave him what he wanted.'

It was an odd thing for Jon to say, the sort of thing Aunty Adanna, who persisted in speaking about sex as if it were something a woman gave a man at a loss to herself, would say. I corrected Jon gently. 'I took what I wanted. If I gave him anything, then it was incidental.'

'Listen to yourself, just fucking listen to yourself!' Jon's voice thickened and he got up and shook me and then stopped, but did not apologise. 'Amaka, I would never have cheated on you. I didn't even think about it in the past two years, I didn't think about it,' he said and I realised that he was already looking at us through the lens of the past tense. It puzzled me, the ability of romantic love to mutate so completely. Where did it go? Was the real thing somehow connected to blood since love for children and parents did not change or die in the way love for romantic partners did?

'You won't forgive me,' I said.

'I don't think we should be talking about forgiveness right now.'

Jon was the kind of man for whom fidelity came easily, the kind who did not turn to glance at pretty women on the street simply because it did not occur to him. He sat down on the couch and I felt a terrible loss because I had become used to knowing that he was undisputedly there, to the cultured ease in the life he gave me, to his upper-class tickets and his boat and house in Connecticut and the smiling uniformed doorman in his apartment building. Even though I had shrugged, non-committal, the two times he brought up marriage, I often thought of it. The first time I told him I was not sure I wanted to get married. The second time I said I was uncomfortable about bringing mixed-race children into the world. He laughed. How could I buy into the tragic mulatto cliché? It was so much bullshit. He recited the names of our – his, really – biracial friends who seemed perfectly fine with being as they were. His tone was arch, superior, and perhaps he was right and it was bullshit but this was truly how I felt and it did not help that Jon approached my misgivings about race with an intellectual wave of his hand.

And who says that race did not play a role in our break-up? Who says we were not lying all those times we clung to the comforting idea of complexity? It wasn't about race, we would say, it was complex – Jon speaking first and me promptly agreeing. What if the reasons for most things didn't require blurred lines? What about the day we walked into a Maine restaurant with white-linen-covered tables, and the waiter looked at us and asked Jon, 'Table for one?' Or when the new Indian girlfriend of Jon's golf partner Ashish said she had enjoyed her graduate experience at Yale but had disliked how close the ghetto was and then her hand flew to her mouth after 'ghetto' and she turned to me and said, 'Oh, I'm so sorry,' and Jon nodded as if to accept the apology on my behalf.

What about when he, Jon, said he hated the predatory way a black man had looked at me in Central Park and I realised I had never heard him use the word predatory before? Or the long weekend in Montreal when the strawberry-haired owner of the bed and breakfast refused to acknowledge me and spoke and smiled at Jon and I was not sure whether she disliked black people or simply liked Jon and later in the room, for the first time, I did not agree that it was complex, at least not in the way I had agreed all the other times. I shouted at Jon, 'The worst thing is never being sure when it is race and not race and you'll never have this baggage!' And he held me and said I was overreacting and tired.

What about the evening we attended a reading at the Mercantile Library and afterwards Jon's friend Evan, who wrote travel books, told me he was sure it had to feel like shit when ignorant people suggested I had been published in the *Best American Poetry* because I was black and Jon merely shook his head when I told him that the ignorant people had to be Evan himself because nobody else had suggested this. And what about the first time I met Jon's mother? She talked about her Kenyan safari in the 1970s, about Mandela's majestic grace, about her adoration for Harry Belafonte and I worried that she would lapse into Ebonics or Swahili. As we left her rambling house in Vermont, where she had an organic garden in her backyard, Jon said it was not really about race, it was more complex than that, it was that she was too hyperaware of difference and consequently too eager to bridge it.

'And she does that with me, too. She likes to talk about only the things she thinks I'm interested in,' he said. This he did often: a constant equalising of our experiences, a refusal to see that what I experienced was different from his.

And what about Jon's wife? Jon was divorced from a woman who he described as brilliant and needy. She lived in Cambridge but was on sabbatical in Europe and so did not feature in our lives during the first months, the good months. Then she came back and began to call often. She was unhappy, she wasn't sure what she wanted to do, she wasn't tenure-track, she had given up on her book. Jon often put her on speaker and said soothing things to her about hanging in there and ended the conversation by mentioning me, 'I have to go, Amaka and I are late already.' 'I have to go, I'm cooking Amaka dinner.'

On the evening we were to go and see Thom Pain off-Broadway, she called and hung up after only a minute or so and he said she was awfully drunk and had called to confess that she still loved him and felt bad that he was with someone else and worse that the someone else was black. He was laughing. I wanted to cry. I am tough, believe me, but that day, as I stared at the high-heeled sandals I was about to slip on, I wanted to cry. All I said was, 'I can't go to the theatre.' This woman whom I did not know had brought out in Jon something I loathed with a visceral lurch in my chest: an inability to show necessary outrage. For this new power of hers, I resented her. When, finally, we met, her unremarkably small breasts delighted me, the lines around her eyes and the saggy skin of her neck delighted me. It was at Ashish's garden party. She wore a pretty jersey dress and a limp string of green beads around her neck and smiled too brightly as we were introduced.

'Jon has told me so much about you,' she said.

'You sound different,' I said.

'What?'

'When you call Jon puts you on speaker so I can follow the conversation and you sound nothing like you do on the phone,' I said, smiling.

She looked away and then back at me before she excused herself to go find a drink. When I went to the bathroom, I was not surprised that she had followed me.

She was standing by the door when I came out.

'It's not real,' she said.

'What's not real?' I asked. I was bored with her. I was a little disappointed that Jon had not been with a less predictable woman.

'What you're doing isn't real. If it was, he wouldn't be trying so hard.'

I turned and walked back outside to the party, hoping she thought I was taking the high road when the truth was that I had no idea what to say in response. On the day that I told Jon I had cheated, about eight months after that garden party, I repeated her words to Jon and said I had never told him about it because a part of me had always suspected that it was true.

'That what was true?' Jon asked.

'You were trying too hard to prove that my being black didn't matter and it was as if it wasn't a good thing and so we had to pretend it wasn't there and sometimes I wanted it to matter because it does matter but we never really talked, truly talked, about any of this.'

Jon started to laugh. 'This is rich,' he said. 'Now you blame it on race? What are you talking about? We've always talked about everything. And you told me you didn't even remember I was white!'

I had indeed said that and it was true, but only when we were alone, when we were silent, when we sat side by side and watched a film, or lay side by side and passed *New York Times* sections to each other. And yes, we did talk about race, either in the slippery way that admitted nothing and engaged nothing and ended with that word 'complexity'; or as jokes that left me with a small and numb discomfort; or as intellectual nuggets to be examined and then put aside because it was not about us (such as when he read somewhere that mainstream women's magazine sales fall with a light-skinned black on the cover and plummet with a dark-skinned black).

Jon was still laughing, his bitter laughter.

'I should leave,' I said. 'I'll go and stay with Aunty Adanna for a while.'

'No, wait.' Jon got up. 'Will you see him again?'

I shook my head.

'Does he mean anything to you?'

Again, I shook my head.

'We can talk. Maybe we can work through this.'

I nodded. He placed his hand on my chin and gently tilted my head up and looked into my eyes. 'You don't want to, do you? You want to make this look like my decision but it's really yours. You don't want to be forgiven. You don't want to work through this,' he said, with that all-knowing authority of his and I stood there and said nothing.

A week later, I was back in Baltimore, a little drunk and a little happy and a little lonely, speeding down Charles Street in a taxi with a Punjabi driver who was proudly telling me that his children did better than American children at school.

Note

1. The text of this story was originally published in 2007 in the literary journal *Conjunctions* 28: 231–40. It was also published in 2009 in *Mechanics Institute Review* 6: 27–37. Reproduced with permission.

28

Questions, questions – life story

Lucy Nambajjwe

A few months ago, just as I was preparing to turn off the light and go to sleep, there was a quiet knock at the door. I was tempted to ignore it. The day had been a long and arduous one, and I was looking forward to seeing the back of it. Again a knock – a little more determined this time. On my asking who it was, my 12-year-old daughter appeared slowly and meekly behind the opening door.

'Mummy, can I ask you a question?' On her face was a very sheepish but earnest look. My heart sank. The last thing I needed on that of all nights was another question. I made ready to tell her that it was late and that she should get to bed and that we should discuss it in the morning since 'mummy' had had a long day at work and that she was so tired, blah, blah, blah. Then I hesitated. It occurred to me that what she had to ask must be important, given the tactics she employed in approaching me (quiet and respectful as opposed to the bold and brassy stance normally applied).

'Yes,' I looked at her searchingly, 'What is it?'

Silence, her head bowed.

'Has something happened at school?' No response. I pull the covers back on the bed and invite her to join me, which she does readily. I try to reassure her. 'If you don't ask I can't help you.' Silence.

Then suddenly, 'Mummy, is it wrong to touch yourself down there?' Her hand is covering her face with embarrassment. I am filled with tenderness for her. A thousand thoughts fill my mind as I try to prepare my response. I know it was difficult for my daughter to ask and I don't want to disappoint her with my answer. But just to ensure that I understand her meaning, I ask her some questions of my own. I ask her what she means by touching. She responds, 'Touching and stroking.' I ask what she means by down there. She rolls her eyes at me, 'Mummy, I mean my vagina!' I ask if she touches herself often. She says, 'Not so much.' I ask how she feels when she touches it. She says, 'Mmm, it's okay,' all the while gauging my mood and expression. On and on we go.

I feel so honoured that she has felt it safe to ask me (I would not have even dreamt of asking my mother this kind of question! It was difficult enough to tell her that I had begun to menstruate). But I also feel a weight of responsibility that is a little overwhelming. How do I help her negotiate the discovery of her body, her sexuality, against the terrible judgement meted out by societal values and social dictums, mired as they are in disgust, loathing, guilt and anger at anything sexual, especially if it is a woman's body? How do I help my daughter to be in this world but not of it? That was what was before me at that particular moment.

Some years ago, when my daughter was about five or six, we were in a grocery store doing some weekly shopping. My daughter was wearing a pair of shorts and tee shirt. In the queue for the check-out counter, I remembered an item I had forgotten and asked my daughter to get it for me. I turned after a few seconds to monitor her progress. And there before me was a man, a full grown-ass man staring at my daughter's bottom as she made her way down the aisle with what can only be described as a lecherous, dirty, dirty, lecherous look. I was stunned; filled with horror and fear and anxiety (as well as anger). I asked him what he was staring at. He turned, licked his lips, smiled menacingly at me and sighed, 'Hmmm,' and walked off. Just like that. Just like that. No embarrassment, no acknowledgement of any transgression whatsoever. The young woman at the counter, who had also witnessed this scene, quietly mouthed the word 'Sorry' to me.

My reaction after this incident was to monitor and censure everything my daughter wore in order to deflect any such unwanted attention from ever coming her way again. This was one time I felt totally helpless. How could I protect my daughter from this violation? The violation that allows and even enables men not to take responsibility for their sexual conduct; that enables them to feel totally at ease with lusting after a child and expressing that desire with all the freedom in the world in a public place?

You read it in the papers, you hear it on the radio, in conversations, all the time, everywhere, the way that society sanctions this kind of conduct – 'What's the harm, he was only looking?' 'You are overreacting!' 'Eh, these days these girls are growing fast, they have buttocks of a big woman!' 'But why do they wear such clothes?' You, who challenge it, become the crazy one. In some contexts as a feminist activist, I am used to being the crazy outsider. But in this one, I was caught between a rock and a hard place as I saw it. I wanted to challenge that bastard and others like him. And I do. But I know that the change I desire is a long way down the line. In the meantime I want my daughter safe and free of this or any other kind of abuse. My helplessness resulted in my policing her dress. I felt completely disempowered to control any other variable in this equation but my daughter's dress. But what had she done wrong?

As a mother I often find myself rather clumsily navigating the world that I would like to see against the world that we are in. And nowhere is this more trying than on the issue of my daughter's discovery of her sexuality. I want her to have a healthy, happy, enjoyable and respectful relationship with her body. I want her to be free of those awful notions of false pride, piety and modesty that are so debilitating and eating away at our societies like a cancer. And yet this is the world in which she lives. How do I help her celebrate but at the same time withstand the condemnation that will come with these 'outsider' notions?

On her question, we talk intimately for an hour or so. We laugh. I tell her my thoughts. She asks more questions and challenges some of my responses. We go to sleep. It is in my role as a mother that I second-guess myself the most. But on this night, I take something away. She came to me to ask. That must count for something?

29

Penitence: hurry hurry, no speed[1] – fiction

Derrick Zgambo

A warm cloud of dust blew into the air as he brought the bike to a halt outside the house. Beatrice was not on the *khonde* to greet him as she usually did. He looked round. The villagers greeted him with little clapping gestures, but he felt from their eyes that they knew he was a prodigal.

He knocked on the glass part of the door.

'Odini.'

He entered, unable to see at first in the gloom. She was standing very straight with her hands on her hips, her face unsmiling.

'You found us then?'

'Yes, I've come.'

'Sit, I must give you *nsima*.'

He sat on a rickety chair, terrified and fascinated by the anger that shook from her every gesture. She laid the table with precise, hard, studied movements. Samson brought in the steaming *nsima* and the *ndiwo* of greens in groundnut sauce. The three of them ate together with noisy lip-smackings. Andrew tried to break the tension by asking about Samson's uniform. He received short, factual answers. She was not to be trapped into gratitude. When he mentioned Felix's impending return it was the same. Every clatter of the plate, as Samson cleared away the meal, made Andrew jump with fear. Beatrice sat in a deck-chair and scowled. When Samson had finished and left them alone, she smiled with a remarkably chilling, wide-teethed grin.

'So you found another sweet pussy. You tired of this one?'

'No, Beatrice, it was a mistake. I was drunk.'

'You want spare wheel, what can I do?'

She shrugged her shoulders as if dismissing the subject, still almost smiling.

'I want to apologise, Beatrice. I was wrong. I'm sorry.'

She suddenly jumped up from the chair, her lips pursed and eyes twisted into a furious ugliness.

'Sorry. Sorry didn't mend a broken leg. You think you're clever. I'm stupid because I keep this pussy for you. You're *mzungu*, you're clever. You think I can't find good boyfriend?'

'Of course, Beatrice…'

'SHUT UP! You make me stupid, bloody fool bastard. You think because I'm savage…'

'Beatrice, stop it, you've gone crazy, honey…'

There was another sudden change – she dropped on to her knees at his feet and placed her head in his lap. The head, with the hair pulled into little square braids, seemed very small as it bounced on his thighs, and he could feel her tears soaking into his jeans. Andrew felt partly embarrassed, partly flattered, and partly exhilarated by the erotic tension. At last she lifted her face, the tears glistening on the tribal scars. The voice now was warm and maternal. Each change of mood drew him closer to her with a cunning he could recognise but not resist.

'You stupid, Andrew. If you want leave me, you don't want marry me, okay, you're free. Do what you wish. But slow slow. Hurry hurry, no speed. You fuck that bitch and get disease. It's no good.'

'It's not that, Beatrice. I was drunk. I want you really. I think maybe I want to marry you.'

'True? Lying bastard!'

She cupped her hand carefully over her left breast as if it hurt her.

'You kill my heart, true. I'm jealousy because I love you too much.'

'I'm sorry, it's too late now, Beatrice. It's done. How can I make you feel better?'

'You can help.'

'How?'

She stood up in a more authoritative mood.

'Take off your shirt.'

Andrew obeyed automatically, trembling as he undid the buttons.

'Kneel.'

He knelt before her. She attacked him like a swoop of birds, nipping, scratching, slapping. She took the flesh on his chest or back and twisted it slowly till he almost cried out in pain, and he closed his eyes, feeling in his loins like some raped Belgian nun, that he was expiating all the crippled, crushed Samsons of Africa. She stopped the punishment with equal abruptness and led him to the bedroom. The sun on the iron roof made the room greenhouse hot. She felt his enlarged cock.

'You been to the doctor, sure?'

'Sure.'

'All disease finished?'

'Finished.'

She tore her clothes off and they made love like a pitched battle and with animal speed. It was a circuit reconnected, in an urgent unexpected flash. The second time was more tender. She made him play with her long soft labia, and explained how she was taught to pull them by an auntie when she was a young girl as a way of satisfying her future husband. It seemed another stage in his passage rite.

Note

1. First published 1978, Lusaka, NECZAM. Also published 2008 in *Passages* (Chapter 22), Southern Illinois University Carbondale (SIUC), Brown Turtle Press, pp. 84–6. Reprinted with permission.

30

Love beads[1] – fiction

Yaba Badoe

We looked at each other and laughed. We had been awake for over 32 hours and both of us knew that we wouldn't sleep, until our courtship, begun on midsummer's eve, was satisfied. An excess of daylight and the deftness of your touch made me gleam in expectation. The zimmer dim invariably has that effect on me; but so soon after having slipped through a crack, the play of light combined with the grace of your presence, conspired in a surreal dance of the senses. I was adrift in a haze between spirit and flesh. Every sound was magnified and colours, luminous in crystalline purity, bathed me in perpetual day.

My mother would have said that I was flying higher than a kite, and that women of my sort, those incapable of commitment, are prone to losing ourselves before claiming a man; because for us, sex, if not quite a religion, is definitely a drug of choice. If that was indeed the case, and you were my intended prey, then, by an odd quirk of fate, you were the falconer as well.

You wiped a trickle of sweat from my brow; you caressed my hair, my ears, and couldn't help but look at me, as we strolled hand in hand to Vierra Lodge. I quickly prepared a picnic of fruit and cheese, while you rummaged for blankets upstairs. Then, armed with champagne, we made our way to the beach where you first kissed me. There you kissed me again.

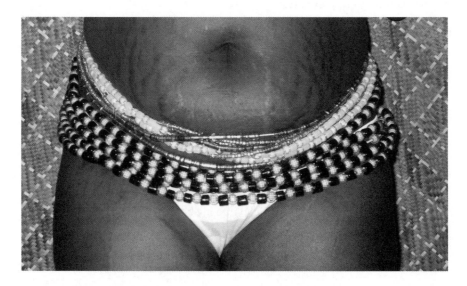

There was no urgency in your kiss this time, simply an assurance that the future was ours, and that even if our passion should subside into friendship, all would be well. That was what I told myself, unbuttoning your shirt as you pulled off my jacket. I was convinced by you; persuaded that what others deemed exotic in me, you seemed quite at home with. We shared a continent, and something deeper, a lightness that put me at ease.

I slipped out of my silk blouse, you slid your finger along the line of my neck, and, inclining my head in your hand, I sensed an ache in your sigh, so that taking you in my arms, I wanted to satisfy you immediately. Any inclination I might have had to subject you to habits honed over the years, subtle games designed to keep love in its place, had dissipated in the short time that I'd known you.

Between our kisses, we stripped naked, and as we savoured our bodies with our tongues, we tentatively explored them with our hands. Tall and lean, you were strong. Your arms were shapely, while mine, slender and lithe as a leaping cat, gently clawed your back.

There was clumsy symmetry in our movement, the tremulous call and response of a couple finding a voice. Impatient at first, yet measured in intent, you gradually deciphered the drift of my mood, and then, gleeful, our senses alight, our tempo quickened.

Your hands fluttered to my face. You gazed at me, and in the landscape of your eyes I heard the call of gulls from the caves of Scabra Head. Your lips nibbled my breasts, then as you licked the curve of flesh leading to my waist, your mouth descended, and you found it; the string of beads I took from my mother at puberty. They belonged to a distant ancestor on my great-grandmother's side, a Fulani beauty whose history, my mother assured me, when she realised that I'd filched the beads, I am repeating.

Bright in colour, made of stone, they fascinated you. I was surprised you hadn't encountered them before; adornments on the waist of a girlfriend, some woman you'd spent time with in West Africa. I had been wrong about you. It appeared that my beads and I were a revelation.

I thought at the time that you would fondle them for hours; so, once I retrieved your lips, I slid my body over yours, and my waist rippled along the length of your thigh, as I displayed the artistry of the *ahweniee*. Excited by the motion of soft stone on your skin, a tremor passed through you and you began kissing me again; long, languorous kisses that tasted of the sea and lured me to the whirlpool at your centre. Then, sinking, almost drowning, my senses sparkled with joy. I tasted the hard bite of copper in my mouth and was blinded by a cascade of pink light as she emerged splashing, like a goddess of the sea: the siren who sang for you alone. We were yours and in that instant you wanted me with the same fierce urgency as the night before.

Rolling me over, you folded me in your arms and pinned me down. Yet gauging my distance in the dream saturated brightness of my eyes, you pursued me, and descending to where I was adrift, glided into my body. You came to me gently, and while you did so, I felt the ebb and flow of water, soft at first, behind the crescendo of the Fulani's song. We heard waves lapping on Vierra cove, the splash of an echo in Enyhallow Sound.

When I surfaced and glimpsed the dream passing from my eyes, you were with me. With a hand resting against your cheek, you stroked my eyebrow in a gesture of tenderness that made me shiver. 'Are you cold?' you asked.

I wasn't cold. But were I to have the same skin as you, I would have flushed crimson, terrified by what you'd awoken in me. I shook my head. All the same, grabbing a spare blanket, you wrapped it around me, saying: 'I'm lucky to have found you, Cuba.'

Note

1. Extract from *Possessed*, the forthcoming (2011) novel by Yaba Badoe. Reproduced with permission.

31

Cinnamon[1]

Gabeba Baderoon

I fall outside
the warm stole
of history.

Eyes run down my skin
like a single finger.

I find you

Open as a tent.
You are
cinnamon curved around me.

Note

1. First published in 2005 in Gabeba Baderoon's *The Dream in the Next Body*, Cape Town, Kwela Books. Reproduced with permission.

32

Covert sexuality

Coumba Toure

Low down
The beads I wear under my clothes are beautiful
So beautiful
I change them according to my mood
They slide in different shapes and colours
Some glow in the dark
They are my hidden beauty

For me to feel sensual
I keep them on even when I am lying naked
Next to you
When I touch, when you touch
I burn with desire

When I walk down the streets of Dakar, Bamako and Ougadougou
You can't see them but I can feel them
They remind me that I am beautiful
So beautiful inside
The promise of pleasures and tenderness

You cannot hear their noise from afar
But they provide the rhythm of my gait
When I pass by
If you pay attention
Or if I decide to get your attention
You will hear the subtle sound of my waist beads

I keep so much underground
So much creativity
Woman to woman
Secrets exchanged between the initiated
The crochet underwear, knit like a net
That no fish can slip through

The *bethio* – small pieces of underwear cloth
With thousands of holes
The incense, to intoxicate you, leaves you gasping
Laughter, rolling eyes, intricate henna
A bare shoulder to caress
The hanging head wrap catches your eye

Sexy, sensual, invisible
Yet there, terribly present
You between my legs, if I so wish

But even I didn't know about the bed sheets
with different provocative positions of intercourse…
Low down

33

The dream in the next body[1]

Gabeba Baderoon

From the end of the bed, I pull
the sheets back into place.

An old man paints a large sun striped
by clouds of seven blues.
Across the yellow centre each
blue is precisely itself and yet,
at the point it meets another,
the eye cannot detect a change.
The air shifts, he says,
and the colours.

When you touched me in a dream,
your skin an hour ago did not end
where it joined mine. My body continued
the movement of yours. Something flowed
between us like birds in a flock.

In a solitude larger than our two bodies
the hardening light parted us again

But under the covering the impress
of our bodies is a single, warm hollow.

Note

1. Previously published in 2005 in Gabeba Baderoon's *The Dream in the Next Body*, Cape
   Town, Kwela Books. Reproduced with permission.

34

Nature's dance

Olivia Coetzee

Two bodies rising to chance
A moon and sun setting
in the far distant horizon,

Clouds lost in the skies of passion
The twelfth night of the ninth month, twenty O' nine
She declares 'You are, without equal in my life'

I look to find the source of
Perfection that flows from her crimson petals
As I oblige, further and deeper into her wholeness

Drums, beating beneath our hills of
Gaia
As we are swallowed by essence,
Burning up and down the soft of our thighs

Flesh on flesh
As I touch, tracing the
brown in and around her eyes

I grab kisses from her lips
Planting them gently
on the back of her behind

my fingers disappearing into
her heat, painting, gently, fiercely
on the moist of her pleasure walls

she guides her sword of
wisdom, down under, tasting,
dipping in the fullness of my heavens

as soft groans breathe on
the long hair carpet, sprawled,
beneath our womanly caves

above the moist grass, we
emanate, sculpting the wind
with aching, screaming bodies

Under a blanket of lust
Holding you and me tight under
a blanket of purity and deep trust

The fourteenth night of the ninth month
Twenty O' nine, beads of all sorts
She strung, through and around my spine

In lust and love fulfilled
Two of the same kind
Became one.

35

Untitled

Juliane Okot Bitek

My fingertips burn
With the memory of a tweaked nipple
One hot afternoon

You clasp my wrist
To your chest
I wrestle with the drummer
Whisper

It's time to eat

Your eyes flash open
Hot with desire
You steal a quick hard kiss
As I escape captivity and walk away
Watching you
Glow.

Questions for reflection

1.
Why is pleasure rarely part of the public discourse on sexuality today? Has this always been true in African sexuality cultures? When was the paradigm shift to sexual reticence? What does African history teach us about sexual pleasure and what factors have influenced this discourse?

2.
Is sexual pleasure important to quality of life? What is the association between pleasure and power? Can we speak of the right to sexual pleasure? What is the link between sexuality and African women's subordinate status?

3.
How have women's erotic desires been suppressed in patriarchal African societies? To what end?

4.
How does the resurgence of various fundementalisms (cultural, religious, economic) threaten Africans' (particularly women's) bodily integrity and right to sexual pleasure?

5.
How have African cultures adapted to the scourge of HIV/AIDS?

Part 5
Reproduction and rights

36

Sexual and reproductive health and rights

Beth Maina Ahlberg and Asli Kulane

Introduction

This chapter focuses on sexual and reproductive health and rights (SRHR) as they have been articulated in recent years in debates, policies and development strategies on the African continent. During the past few decades, a rights-based approach to sexual and reproductive health has evolved. The fundamental principles of this approach to the sexual and reproductive health of women and men highlight not just the rights, but more importantly, how and who should implement and safeguard these rights. The rights approach stipulates that as individuals we have the right to the highest attainable standard of health, including the right to life and survival, the right to control our sexual and reproductive life, and the right to make reproductive decisions, including the number and spacing of our children, without interference or coercion.

Because the rights approach is rooted in the Universal Declaration of Human Rights – based on the idea that everybody is born with, and possesses, the same rights regardless of where they live, their gender, sexual orientation, race or religious, cultural or ethnic background – it ensures and upholds non-discrimination and therefore respect for difference. The principle of indivisibility recognises that individual women and men cannot, however, realise their sexual and reproductive health and rights without also realising their broader human rights. The right to choose the number and spacing of their children can, for example, cannot be realised unless they can also afford transport and user fees for services, such as family planning. Moreover, they must be free from poverty, and must have access to information and education and also be free from violence, whether from their partners (especially in the case of women) or from the state.

The rights approach therefore obliges governments and other authorities to ensure equal access to healthcare for everyone and at the same time to address the unique needs of women and men. As a framework, the rights-based approach not only provides value and ethical frames for healthcare providers, but can also empower care users and communities by instilling a sense of entitlement, therefore creating room for advocacy.

The discourse and view promoted by the 'pro-family' group that called itself the NGO Caucus for Stable Families during the preparatory committee meeting in March 1999 for the United Nations General Assembly Special Session's five-year review of the International Conference on Population and Development – commonly referred to as the Cairo +5 preparatory meeting – was that the basic needs approach is ethically and socially superior to the human rights approach. In opposition to this, Rosalind Petchesky argues that:

> Rights are merely the codification of needs reformulated as ethical and legal norms and thus implying a duty on the part of those in power to provide all the means necessary to make sure those needs are met … The terminology of 'human' and 'universal' simply says that there should be no distinctions of class, gender, race, ethnicity, age, religion, and so on; the rights belong to all persons and the duties to fulfil them to all authorities. Rights are meaningless, in other words, without needs. But needs cannot stand on their own as ethical principles, because they lack any intrinsic methods for a) determining whose and which needs should take precedence b) assigning obligations to specific parties for fulfilling those needs and c) empowering those whose needs are at stake to speak for themselves. (Petchesky 2000: 21)

It is implied, in other words, that there is need for the principle of moral agency to prevent states, medical experts or religious authorities from deciding, for example in the area of sexuality and reproduction, what is good for women, men, young people or people with different sexual orientations.

This chapter explores the way the discourse on reproductive rights has evolved globally, but more specifically within Africa and the initiatives undertaken at various levels. It also questions why, despite the enhanced articulation of the rights principles and some very progressive initiatives at international, regional, national and local levels, the state of sexual and reproductive health remains poor or has even deteriorated in the African region. In an attempt to understand what enhances or limits achieving the progressive goals articulated in SRHR, the chapter examines a number of issues. In particular, it addresses the broader issues and challenges posed by the cultural and religious contexts, the shortcomings within the biomedical model, and the interplay with international development discourse and practice – especially the way development has been conceptualised within a globalised neoliberal economic and political order that promotes and structures global inequalities. The chapter also reflects on how African feminists, women's movements and human rights advocates are innovating, using the spaces provided by the rights-based approach. Before delving into this, we focus briefly on the legal conventions adopted during the past decades.

Toward universal sexual and reproductive health and rights

The rights approach to sexual and reproductive health is rooted in the post-Second World War human rights debate, when the United Nations created international standards for a range of human rights including the right to health. Since then, a number of international conferences and declarations have reinforced the rights debate with formulated programmes of action. In 1979, the Convention on the Elimination of All Forms of Discrimination against Women (CEDAW) was adopted by the UN General Assembly. This convention provides the basis for realising gender equality by ensuring women's equal access to opportunities in political and public life, including the right to vote and to stand for election, and the right to education, health and employment (UN Women 2010).

In 1993 the World Conference on Human Rights took place in Vienna and affirmed women's rights as human rights. This meant the rights of women should not be subordinated to cultural or religious traditions. The conference also marked a breakthrough in acknowledging that human rights should be extended to incorporate issues of sexuality and reproduction. The 1994 International Conference on Population and Development (ICPD) in Cairo made another breakthrough by creating a more comprehensive framework to realise reproductive health and rights (Sadik 2000). This marked a move from policies focused only on reducing fertility, by incorporating gender equality, equity and empowerment of women, reproductive rights and reproductive health (UN 1995). The 1995 Fourth World Conference on Women in Beijing confirmed and built on the links established in Cairo between women's reproductive health and human rights. Not only did the Beijing Platform of Action focus on governments' obligations to fulfil and create the conditions to enable women and men to realise their rights to health, but it also took a holistic view of health and the social, political and economic factors affecting health.

In 2000, reproductive health received a boost through the UN Millennium Development Goals (MDGs). Four of the eight goals, namely promoting gender equality and empowering women, reducing child mortality, improving maternal health and combating HIV/AIDS, malaria and other diseases, focus directly on SRHR. Furthermore, poverty, which is a major determinant of poor health and a threat to SRHR, was put high on the development agenda in the MDGs, which all the 191 UN member states pledged to achieve by 2015 (UN 2008). Yet another initiative taken by the world body in the area of HIV/AIDS was to institute a global fund with which WHO, UNAIDS and other partners vowed in 2003 to provide antiretroviral therapy in poor countries. This came to be known as the '3 by 5' initiative, the goal being to provide antiretroviral therapy to three million people by 2005.

The African Union (AU) took a similarly progressive initiative in July 2003, when the protocol to the African Charter on Human and Peoples' Rights on women's rights was adopted. This came into force in November 2005 (Manji et al 2006) and by 2009 had been ratified by 26 countries (SOAWR 2008; Winyi 2009). This protocol, which added the rights missing in the existing African charter on human and people's rights, provides broad protection for the rights of women, including sexual and reproductive rights, thus affirming reproductive choice and autonomy as a key human right. Accordingly, the protocol became the first international document to explicitly articulate the right of women to medical abortion when pregnancy results from sexual assault, rape or incest, or when continuation of pregnancy endangers the life or the health of the pregnant woman or in the case of grave foetal defects (SOAWR 2008). Furthermore, the protocol made history as the first international document to explicitly call for the legal prohibition of female genital mutilation.

It is against this progressive legal backdrop in the area of sexual and reproductive health and rights that this chapter addresses the advocacy and work of civil society organisations in Africa. It appears, however, that there are many challenges and that critical questioning and reflexivity are required in part to locate the gaps and some explanations for the challenges in realising SRHR. One question that needs to be addressed is why the state of sexual and reproductive health remains poor in most of Africa. But before that we briefly describe the current status of SRHR.

The state of sexual and reproductive health and rights in Africa

Despite the impressive legal progress described above, the state of SRHR within Africa is still poor. The African Partnership for Sexual and Reproductive Health and Rights of Women and Girls (AMANITARE) sums up the status quo thus:

> The majority of women in Africa lack access to basic sexual and reproductive health services and information, safe labour and delivery services, emergency obstetric care, essential drugs and contraceptive supplies. They are also in danger of labour complications, unsafe abortion and HIV and other sexually transmitted infections which remain the leading causes of illness and death among women aged 15–49. Women now represent two-thirds of those infected with HIV in sub-Saharan Africa. (Karanja 2007)

An estimated 22.5 million or 68 per cent of the global total of 33.2 million people living with HIV and AIDS are in Africa south of the Sahara (UNAIDS 2007). Though HIV infects both women and men, women are disproportionately affected and constitute 61 per cent of those living with HIV. Furthermore, of the 20 million women worldwide who experience unsafe abortions every year, 18.5 million are in the global South; of the 67,000 – 70,000 women who die, almost all (97 per cent) are in the global South; and countries in sub-Saharan Africa report 680 deaths per 100,000 abortion procedures (Okonofua 2004; Grimes et al 2006; WHO 2007).

In Kenya, a study carried out in 2004 found that 300,000 abortions occur each year, 48 per cent of them among young women aged 14–24. More than 20,000 women are hospitalised with abortion-related complications each year (Mushtaq 2008). Apart from the severe consequences to the health of individual women, families and communities, abortion-related hospitalisation ranges between six and 16 per 1,000 in different countries in Africa (Singh 2006). Finally, harmful practices such as female genital mutilation and early marriage expose young women to the risk of infection with sexually transmitted diseases, including HIV/AIDS, while early child-bearing and related reproductive health risks continue.

The scenario above is the result of the interplay of many factors, including gender power imbalances, cultural and religious forces, poverty, stagnation and deteriorating socio-economic conditions – most acute in many countries in the African region. The issue of poverty was articulated by the African Union ministers of health meeting in Maputo in September 2006. Poverty in Africa has, according to the ministers, increased rapidly, with most member states having poverty rates above 50 per cent since the 1990s. Wangari Maathai (2009) stresses that by 2001 the number of Africans living in extreme poverty had nearly doubled to 316 million from 164 million 20 years earlier.

Because poverty is a major determinant of poor health, including sexual and reproductive health, it is important to explore how poverty is created and how it is conceptualised in theory and in practice within the international development discourse. The following section focuses on the various phases in the development process during the past century. The aim is to illuminate the parallel processes: one articulating rights and the other political and economic development interests and ideologies, with a language that often conceals political interests and ideologies. We believe that reflecting on this development process, which has promoted poverty and maintained global inequalities, will increase our understanding not only of what limits the realisation of sexual and reproductive health and rights, but also what might indicate the way forward.

Development discourse and practice

The imposition of Western influences, starting with direct colonisation at the end of the 19th century was followed, after the Second World War, by the 'age of development' (Sachs 1992: 2). The term development was coined in 1949 by Harry Truman, then US president, when he described, in his inauguration speech, the southern hemisphere as 'underdeveloped areas'. The following period saw development aid in the form of material and Western experts as the main tools for development and as the major elements to facilitate what Jeffrey Sachs (2005) has called 'catching-up' with development or modernisation. The development ideology of 'catching-up' was nonetheless strongly embraced by the African nationalist leaders taking over after independence. According to Adebayo Olukoshi and Francis Nyamnjoh, the promise of development or, more specifically, 'modernisation' was so rich that 'it served as a credible platform for the mobilisation of the entire populace, who in turn bought into it in varying degrees and with an equally varied menu of expectation' (Olukoshi and Nyamnjoh 2005: 1).

But although the African leaders had such strong faith in 'modernisation', in reality development aid has led to what Yash Tandon (2008: 129) calls the 'aid trap' or what Wangari Maathai (2009: 63–82) describes as the 'aid dependence syndrome'. These sentiments are elaborated by Hakima Abbas and Yves Niyiragira, editors of the recent book, *Aid to Africa: Redeemer or Coloniser?*:

> While Africa is the biggest recipient of aid globally, the terms, conditions and principles upon which aid is conceived and delivered are not defined by the people of Africa for whom, at least rhetorically, this aid is supposed to create positive change. In the global politics, aid is often flaunted as a golden carrot to African states by established and emerging powers alike. Lofty pledges are pronounced during crises or when political clout is being wielded. Aid in itself has created an unparalleled debt crisis in Africa compounded by an acute dependency syndrome. (Abbas and Niyiragira 2009: vii)

Moreover, Africa has been relegated to the position of producing raw commodities for export with prices dictated, often unfairly, by the international market. On the heels of independence, a cold war period stretching from the 1960s to the 1980s saw Africa divided once again into spheres of influence for either the Western capitalist or Eastern communist economic and political systems, and thus dragged into their ideological confrontations. The period then was characterised by competition for Africa's resources and support from the competing powers, mostly of the military kind to dictatorial regimes such as that of Mobutu Sese Seko in Zaire, was the order. In this context, though the word 'help/aid' might sound or appear to be an innocent notion within the development discourse and practice, it has, as Marianne Gronemeyer argues, been 'an instrument of the perfect, that is elegant, exercise of power' (Gronemeyer 1992: 53), that is, perfected to conceal who actually depends on whom.

That the poor countries in the global South continue to pay to the rich countries in the North more than they receive in aid was the point articulated in the UN General Assembly in 2005 (UNDPI 2005). Moussa Dembele puts it more strongly that aid is 'a drop in the ocean' (Dembele 2009: 114) compared to the huge outflows in the form of debt repayments, capital flight, tax evasion and profit repatriation, not to mention the extensive brain drain in which large numbers of Africa's skilled professionals have migrated to the West. In reality it is Africa and the rest of the global South whose immense wealth is transferred to the North. More recently, yet another mechanism for transferring resources from the South is the vulture funds, otherwise known as distress debt funds, whereby an investment company buys (at bargain prices) distressed investments for a future high return. In the case of debt relief for the poor countries:

> These companies buy the debt of poor countries at a big discount from the original owners (either government or a commercial creditor) with the purpose of suing the indebted country once the poor country has some money (often after debt cancellation) to recover the original face value of the debt or close to it. (Africa Action Campaign Resource 2008: 2)

When a poor country receives newly freed money from debt cancellation, the vulture fund investors take legal action and sue the poor country in courts in Europe and the USA for much more money than they bought the debt for. An example of this was in Liberia, where in 2008 a British court ordered its government to pay $20 million to two vulture fund investors, Hamsah Investment of the British Virgin Islands and Wall Capital of the Cayman Islands. The claim was based on a $6.5

million loan to Liberia by former US bank Chemical Bank in 1978 (Puopolo 2010). Other countries sued in the same manner include the Democratic Republic of the Congo (DRC) and Zambia. The International Monetary Fund (IMF) reports that at least 54 vulture fund companies have taken legal action against 12 of the poorest countries in the world (Elliott 2007).

Thus, even when debts are cancelled, instead of the money being channelled to poverty alleviation or improving education or health, including sexual and reproductive health, in the poor country, it can end up in the bank accounts of vulture fund investors. Moreover, to reach the point of receiving debt relief, there are many other conditions a poor country must fulfil. The country must be eligible to borrow from the World Bank's International Development Association (IDA), which provides interest-free loans and grants to the world's poorest countries, and from the IMF's Poverty Reduction and Growth Facility (PRGF), which offers subsidised loans when poor countries face an unsustainable debt burden that cannot be addressed through traditional debt relief initiatives. The country must also have established a record of sound reform policies through IMF- and World Bank-supported programmes and to have developed a poverty reduction strategy (Mabheju 2010).[1] These are some of the reforms and conditions within the structural adjustment programmes (SAPs) that have in the first place harmed the health sector, as discussed below.

The SAPs as promoters of social inequality

The end of the Cold War and the fall of the Berlin Wall toward the end of 1980s ushered in a period of neoliberal economic development in which African countries were forced by the international financial institutions, namely the World Bank and the IMF, to institute structural adjustment programmes. Through SAPs, poor countries were forced to privatise essential services (including healthcare) as a condition of receiving development aid in grants or in loans. The assumption then was that leaving market mechanisms to their own devices would ensure competition, leading to economic growth or at least 'poverty reduction' – the concept or term which had by then replaced development.

Contrary to expectations, however, the SAPs' economic policies led to stagnation and deeper poverty. Walden Bello and Soren Ambrose (2006) argue that the conditions imposed by the IMF and the World Bank – that governments of poor countries cut spending on public institutions, cut subsidies to farmers and privatise public services such as healthcare, education, water and electricity – as prerequisites for receiving help (including loans) have deepened poverty.

In another twist, although the poor countries are forced to cut subsidies to their farmers, the rich countries in the North not only subsidise their farmers, but also in essence close their markets to products from the poor countries. Moreover, the flooding of products from the North to the South pushes local farmers out of business (Maren 1997). In addition to poverty, a major challenge for African countries resulting from these different phases of 'modernisation' is the shaping of a leadership that has, in turn, destroyed the continent through lack of foresight, mismanagement and corruption (Maathai 2009) and what Olukoshi calls the 'erosion of the state' (Olukoshi 2004: 2).

So, in our view, to achieve the goals articulated in the rights to sexual and reproductive health or to reverse vulnerability, we need to reflect critically on what we have come to know as development. In this context, we agree with Angela Ndunga-Muvumba's (2010) conclusion about the MDGs: that to believe they would stem HIV is a mere wish if social inequalities, including the structural inequalities discussed above, are not tackled. Priya Nanda (2002) too shows how user fees, introduced as part of cost recovery within SAPs, have led to a decrease in health service utilisation in Ghana, Swaziland, the DRC and Uganda. This shift has led to health being regarded as a market commodity rather than a human right (Mayhew 2002).

The structural inequalities created and maintained in the development discourse and practice outlined above have led to the poor state of SRHR. The impact of the user fee, the main element in health sector reform, is well articulated by the Women's Global Network for Reproductive Rights (WGNRR):

> The introduction of user fees has led to a decrease in access to health services for women around the world. In the early 1990s a clear correlation was established between the introduction of user fees for health services and a marked fall in women's attendance at antenatal clinics in Zimbabwe, one of the first African countries to experience reforms. In Harare General Hospital, mortality rate among children born to mothers who did not attend antenatal clinics was almost five times that of their registered counterparts. In other African (Nigeria, Tanzania) and Latin American countries (Argentina and Guatemala) pregnant women are unable to access pre-natal and emergency care because they cannot afford it.
>
> In several countries, the introduction of user fees has actually led to an increase in maternal mortality rates. Between 1983 and 1998, when user fees were introduced for most health services in Nigeria, maternal deaths in the Zaria region increased by 56% and there was a threefold increase in obstetric complications. User fees increase the risk of sexually transmitted diseases (STDs) while at the same time making it more difficult for women to access treatment. Reductions in the utilisation of STD services were noted in Kenya and Zambia due to user fees being introduced. (WGNRR 2009: 4)

The language used to describe development or the way language has shifted is yet another area of concern, especially given the way it manages to conceal what is going on or the development ideology that maintains inequalities and poverty.

Language that conceals the development ideology

During the past two decades, the language and concepts used in the development discourse and practice described above have been changing. Robert Chambers argues that the words are both 'formative and adaptive' (Chambers 2004: 3) and that they influence and express conditions, ideologies, perceptions, practices and priorities. In other words, they reflect the shortcomings and challenges arising from the way development has been conceptualised. But above all, the impression created is that a new concept would somehow accelerate development.

Andrea Cornwall and Karen Brock (2005) describe how the use of what they call buzzwords – empowerment, participation and poverty reduction – shapes a global development industry that is removed from the world in which poor people go about their everyday lives. Such lofty-sounding concepts also appeal to the moral authority of different stakeholders, but in essence imply 'business as usual' and conceal the development ideology. Indeed, this is reflected in the narrative of the MDGs and poverty reduction strategies.

The MDGs focus on measuring change rather than making a deep analysis of the forces that produce poverty. As time-bound numerical targets, for example, reaching the MDG goals by 2015, they represent a way of world-making that lacks the sense of place. Similarly, Dembele (2009) argues that the MDGs will not solve structural problems of poverty and underdevelopment because they are framed within the neoliberal paradigm that maintains inequalities. Moreover, as if to acknowledge the toll of SAPs on the healthcare sector, the case is being made for adjustment 'with a human face' (Olukoshi 2004).

Because buzzwords are fuzzy, they have a propensity to shelter multiple meanings, making them politically expedient and lending the possibility of common meaning to extremely disparate actors (Cornwall and Brock 2005), thus shielding from attack those who use them. Reflecting on the statement, 'at the Summit there was a global commitment to eradicate poverty', Else Øyen (1999) notes how the UN has developed a language of poverty reduction inaccessible to outsiders and very difficult even for insiders to learn. The statement that appeared in the report of the Special Session of the UN General Assembly on the implementation of the outcomes of the World Summit for Social Development and further initiatives in 1998 was political rather than empirical, but its repetition in the many documents following the summit could be viewed as a conscious deception, which further demonstrates ignorance of the processes leading to poverty reduction. Such language is wrapped in diffuse statements to give it moral legitimacy, but stresses simultaneously the non-committal character of an institutional organisation run by actors with many conflicting interests. Poverty reduction is thus devoid of political landscape within which policies are supposed to operate and neither is there any discussion or analysis of conflicts built into poverty reduction.

It is in the context of such language that the politics of poverty reduction or ending poverty – as orchestrated by Jeffrey Sachs (2005), who played a pivotal role in the international policy design as the director of the UN MDGs from 2002 to 2006 – is important. What is at stake is not a lack of concern or enthusiasm to end poverty. Rather, it is the way Jeffrey Sachs and others conceptualise poverty in poor countries as an initial, rather than a final, stage of an economic paradigm which, according to Vandana Shiva (2005), the Indian property rights advocate, has been responsible for the plunder and destruction of the ecological and social systems that maintain the life, health and sustenance of the planet.

By defining the poor as those who were left behind in the pursuit of progress or modernity even as the crisis of modernity is calling for a rethink of the way in which disaster capitalism has created poverty in poor countries (Klein 2009), Sachs misses or avoids the point that the poor are those who were and continue to be pushed out and excluded from access to their own wealth and resources by the forces of modernisation. Any serious attempt to end poverty would therefore require acknowledging that poverty was and continues to be created in the context of the global capitalist economic paradigm and that the interconnectedness between the wealthy North and the poor South is much more complex and requires going beyond simple technical fixes, such as distributing mosquito nets (Mkandawire 2006) or establishing the so-called Millennium Villages. Since 2004 a total of 12 Millennium Villages have been established in Ethiopia, Ghana, Kenya, Malawi, Mali, Nigeria, Rwanda, Senegal, Tanzania and Uganda as the way to end poverty.[2] It remains to be seen how such experiments in single villages will be translated to the rest of the populations living in poverty.

Nonetheless, the use of concepts with diffuse meanings is critical. Chambers (2004) examines three more concepts, two of which are in popular use currently, and the other of which is hardly ever used. He argues that new concepts or those that are recycled, for example 'social capital' and 'sustainable livelihoods', have been selectively used to refer to the poor and their contexts, but are never used to reflexively address or question the powerful themselves or the relations of power. Compared to social capital or sustainable livelihoods, the concept 'responsible well-being' has not been embodied in research or policy programmes, although it is more commonly used by poor people to describe their conditions and how they can move forward. According to Chambers, this is because of the moral overtones of the term 'responsible well-being'. This means that it is not politically neutral and, moreover, it draws attention to inequalities in power relations and property rights (Chambers 2004: 19). Responsible well-being derives from words and concepts such as health, family life, respect and social values, which poor people use instead of income and wealth (Chambers 2004: 9). Use of such terms would naturally embrace reflexivity and critical analysis of how poverty is created, thereby questioning or addressing the responsibilities of the powerful.

In the context of SRHR, the silence about the responsibility of the powerful and the use of confusing language aimed at concealing the interests and ideologies of the powerful have created ambivalences, especially when it comes to sexuality. Researchers see 'African sexuality' as being responsible for HIV and AIDS in the African context (Caldwell et al 1989) and for the high fertility rates as argued further below.

Broken pledges and selective funding in sexual and reproductive health

Despite the growing concern about poverty reduction, whatever its shortcomings, it is imperative to mention two other paradoxes. The first is the failure by donors to honour their pledges. That the poor global South pays more to the rich countries of the North than they receive in aid has been noted (UNDPI 2005). More recently, during the UN summit on the global financial crisis in June 2009, the UN Secretary-General noted the hypocrisy of Western donors for lagging behind with their aid promises. For the past 50 years, according to the secretary general, donor countries have given some $2trillion in aid, but during 2009, the year of the financial meltdown, $18 trillion was raised to bail out banks and other financial institutions, which were in fact responsible for the crisis in the first place (Deen 2003, 2009).

The second paradox is the selective funding that is most dominant in the area of SRHR. During the Countdown Africa 2015 conference on sexual and reproductive health rights in London, the United Nations Population Fund (UNFPA) painted a scenario in which, ten years after the Cairo pledges, maternal mortality continued to rise and pregnancy and childbirth remained the leading causes of maternal deaths among young women in Africa between the ages of 15 and 19 years (Godia 2004). Moreover, annually, 40 per cent of abortions in Africa ended in death. The UNFPA also noted that donor funding to African countries for contraceptives had dropped from 30 per cent in 1992 to 20 per cent in 2004. Many health facilities offering contraceptive services had been forced to close and the shortage of condoms was, according to the UNFPA, so severe that if all available condoms in Africa were evenly distributed there would be only three condoms per man per year (Godia 2004). The South African HIV/AIDS advocacy group, the Treatment Action Campaign (TAC), cited the figure of 35 condoms per man per year in South Africa (TAC 2005).

Underlying this scenario is the growing religious fundamentalism advocating a moralist approach to sexual and reproductive health and rights, whether the focus is contraceptives, condoms or abortion. More than any other aspect of donor funding, SRHR is the one in which selective funding is most exercised. The policies and related restrictions of some donor countries have become most explicit through the US government's 'gag rule', instituted first in 1984 by then President Ronald Reagan and also known as the Mexico City Policy. The policy prohibited aid being given to international family planning organisations that provided abortion services or abortion counselling, or advocated for abortion access. The ban was suspended during the Clinton administration in 1995, reinstated by the Bush administration in 2001 and again suspended by US President Obama (US Mexico City Policy 2007; IPPF 2009).

The policy has been strongly supported by religious organisations, notably the Catholic church and the Holy See, which has observer status at the UN. At international conferences, the Catholic church frequently uses its power to block any reference to contraception and family planning (Maguire 2003), an action that intimidates and enforces consensus or silence among delegates from largely poor Catholic countries. During the ICPD in Cairo in 1994, the Catholic church in Kenya accused the government of Kenya of promoting abortion. Two years later there was a public display of burning condoms and sexual education books (Wanyeki 1996). In 2010, religious groups were opposed to the inclusion of abortion in Kenya's new constitution (Anyangu-Amu 2010; Maina and Ciyendi 2010). In 2002, the government of Uganda complied with the request of the Cardinal of Uganda to cease in its efforts to promote emergency contraception and to deem such contraception an abortifacient.

Another consequence of the gag rule, as observed in both Kenya and Ethiopia, was that NGOs stopped publicising the success of post-abortion care programmes for fear of reprisal from the religious community (Shuster 2004). The opposition by the church is not, however, uncontested. At the private level, women take action, as was evident in central Kenya, where women were observed to use contraceptives and secure abortions for teenage daughters, but deny such actions in public

(Ahlberg 1991). Reproductive health and rights, and specifically women's bodies, have become the site of the battle between the powerful moralist agents and people who advocate a human rights approach to public health.

In the area of HIV/AIDS, the swords are similarly drawn along moral grounds. Notable here is the funding from the US President's Emergency Plan for AIDS Relief (PEPFAR), which is channelled, as shown in a study by Nandani Oomman et al (2007), mostly through international organisations (mainly US) including faith-based organisations. These organisations predominantly orchestrate the moral message of sexual abstinence until marriage (Lancet 2007), disregarding the growing evidence suggesting just how risky marriage is for women.[3] Those donors who promote abstinence-only education can and have refused to support the use of condoms (Booker and Colgan 2004). Moreover, they aggressively discredit the condom for being ineffective, arguing further that premarital sex leads to unhappy marriages in the future and causes depression and suicidal feelings among teens (Bader 2005). Abortion is never presented as an option.

The Reverend Donald Messer, a New American Methodist priest, has described the church as 'the second virus' (Messer 2004). Local organisations receiving PEPFAR funds for HIV/AIDS are required to sign a pledge not to support prostitution in their programmes (Saunders 2004; Bristal 2006). Organisations funded for HIV/AIDS are thus reluctant to include the forbidden aspects of sexual and reproductive health for fear of losing funding (Okello 2004; Sindig 2005) – a kind of carrot and stick strategy and response. Uganda, known for its openness from the start of the epidemic, is an example of a country forced to retreat from such a position in dealing with the epidemic, as a condition for receiving the PEPFAR funds during the Bush administration years (Booker and Colgan 2004).

The healthcare infrastructure was also affected. As indicated above, the gag rule forced many clinics offering contraceptives and abortion services to close. In the context of HIV/AIDS, apart from emphasis on abstinence-only education and faithfulness within marriage, there has been in the recent past a tendency for some donors to focus on treatment only. Treatment is of course an urgent need currently, but when donors engage up to 30 per cent of the staff of an already weakened healthcare service to set up a service parallel to the official one, it has led to what McCarthy (2007) calls 'internal brain drain'. This refers to a situation in which healthcare workers in the public sector are lured from existing facilities and services to more lucrative donor-funded programmes. This trend has become a real burden for some countries, not to mention the rather vertical biomedical focus that results and excludes the preventive aspects of sexual and reproductive health.

This point is well articulated by the TAC when it argues that treatment and prevention go hand in hand and that people need to be educated about treatment and diet among other important things related to living with HIV/AIDS (TAC 2005). Moreover, argues the TAC, instead of preaching ABC ('abstain, be faithful, use condoms'), the emphasis should be on the right of every person to a full, healthy, sexual, reproductive and family life (TAC 2005).

In Kenya, faced with a choice between losing all its funding and technical aid from USAID, and therefore having to cease work on safe abortion, Family Health Options Kenya (FHOK) chose to forfeit the aid to be free to advocate for the health and well-being of Kenyan women. This resulted in the closure of three FHOK clinics, the reduction of services in its remaining clinics and the slashing of funding for outreach programmes and created a situation in which poor Kenyan women found it much harder to access family planning information and services, with the consequences of more unwanted pregnancies, unsafe abortions (IPPF 2009) and maternal deaths.

Largely because of the moralist approach described above, discriminatory laws and policies that curtail the freedoms of citizens, civil society and the media have been legislated across Africa, resulting in the (re)criminalising of abortion, HIV transmission and homosexuality. These laws not only violate basic human rights to privacy and confidentiality, sexual integrity and autonomy, bodily integrity, freedom from discrimination, and health, including sexual and reproductive health, but they also serve to perpetrate violent attacks on sexual minorities, mostly homosexual men, lesbian women, transgender and bisexual people, sex workers and people living with HIV/AIDS. The anti-homosexuality bill introduced in the Ugandan parliament in October 2009 is a good example (Kaoma 2009a); also see Chapter 47 of this volume). The prominent involvement of religious conservatives in the US in the resurgence of homophobia and the (re)criminalising of homosexuality in many parts of Africa deserves further discussion.

In his research, Reverend Kapya Kaoma (2009b), an Anglican priest from Zambia, has observed how US Christian conservatives in particular have used a number of tactics to infiltrate and manipulate African churches both to promote homophobia and persuade African clergy to adopt American-style methods to wage anti-gay battles. Political conservatives in the USA, along with religious renewal groups and the more conservative elements within the mainstream churches, have joined with conservative African religious and political leaders to promote homophobia in both Africa and the USA. Their efforts have resulted in the mainstream churches appearing neocolonialist, working to destabilise and corrupt African moral values. Another key tactic that this conservative bloc has employed is to accuse mainstream churches of supporting homosexuality and terrorism, thereby alienating them from the African churches they are in partnership with and thus promoting alignment of the African churches with the conservative right.

By claiming that homosexuality is un-African, for example, the US religious conservatives exploit the politics of post-colonial identity that reject Western influences. They then use the tactic of highly personalised and unrestricted funding for only those African bishops who have US connections. During the United Methodist general conference in 2008, for instance, the Institute on Religion and Democracy (IRD) and the United Methodist Church gave African delegates to the conference free cellphones before urging them to vote strongly against homosexuality. With such funding, some African religious leaders view the American conservatives as more generous than the progressive groups, whose conditions might demand stricter accounting and oversight.

Yet another tactic has been to alter texts written by African religious leaders in an attempt to make them conform to the position of the US religious conservatives. A case of this kind of manipulation occurred when the IRD altered a statement written by Reverend Jerry Kulah of Monrovia, Liberia that was taken as the position of African church leaders during the 2008 United Methodist general conference.

Reverend Kaoma, however, concludes that contrary to claims that homosexuality is un-African, homosexuality has been in Africa since time immemorial and it is homophobia that is un-African. In his foreword to Kaoma's report, Tarso Luis Ramos writes:

> Just as the United States and Northern societies routinely dump our outlawed or expired chemicals, pharmaceuticals, machinery and cultural detritus on African and other Third World countries, we now export a political discourse and public policies our own society has discarded as outdated and dangerous. (Kaoma 2009a: iv)

Additionally, the dominant Western biomedical research model has tended to medicalise sexuality and reproduction. It has, in essence, not only moved sexuality and reproduction from its sociocultural contexts, but also promoted a view of sexuality as simply a problem for technical interventions. This phenomenon is the focus of the next section.

A Western biomedical focus

In this section, we take up the issues of fertility control and HIV/AIDS as examples in which biomedical technical interventions have been particularly dominant. In the case of HIV/AIDS, prior to the discovery of the link between HIV and sexual behaviour in the early 1980s, there was little serious research on issues of human sexuality in African contexts (Ahlberg 1994). The advent of AIDS changed this situation, but research and other interventions continued to follow in the footsteps of population studies, in which the major interest was fertility control.

The history of fertility control goes back to the 1950s when the population explosion alarm was raised (Ehrlich and Ehrlich 2009). The history provides insights into the ideological background and political interests shaping fertility control and its organisation. Population, especially that of the global South, became the object of control interventions because population increases in countries emerging from colonial domination were seen as not only key causes of poverty, but also as threats to global social and economic progress (Frank and McNicoll 1987). The goal then was to stem the population growth and thereby ensure economic growth. Demographers and economists argued that, should a decline in birth rates not follow the declining mortality rates, as they did in industrialised Western countries, the impact on progress would be catastrophic (Caldwell et al 1988, 1989). Fertility control, through family planning and more specifically contraceptives, became a very prominent part of the international aid package, largely targeting married women.

Universalised research methods, including knowledge, attitude and practice (KAP) surveys, became the primary approaches used to generate knowledge and to evaluate and assess the impact of interventions on fertility behaviour-change among women (see Part 1 of this volume). The assumption was that giving women information about contraceptives would lead to an increase in their use. Subsequent evaluation studies observed the paradox that women acquired a good deal of knowledge about contraceptives, but this did not necessarily translate, as expected, to greater use of contraceptives.

Interesting here are some of the ways the women resisted the interventions. We use the concept 'positive resistance' to describe the phenomenon observed in Central Kenya. Women responded in the affirmative when asked if they used contraceptives. At the same time they discouraged each other, by spreading rumours about terrible contraceptive side effects (Ahlberg 1991). This did not mean that women were not concerned about fertility issues. In the same study, they expressed great concern about having several children in short periods of time. Elderly women in particular wondered whether younger women who gave birth every year could not control their sexuality as the custom had been in this area during the pre-colonial period. What was not clear to them was how the society had been affected by colonisation and subsequent development practice.

Some of the reasons for the paradoxes in the fertility control paradigm can be traced to the development process, which did not take account of people's knowledge systems or realities, but also specifically to the use of KAP as a research method. The KAP studies have limitations in their assumptions, conceptualisation and design. For example, they assume that knowledge is associated with attitude and behaviour change in a linear form (Warwick 1993; Hauser 1993). Moreover, in their design and implementation, KAP surveys assume that informants understand or have thought about the issues or questions they are asked about in an interview that is often the first, and perhaps the only, interaction between the researcher and the researched. Through case studies, Akosua Adomako Ampofo (2006) illustrated the discrepancies in preferences among women and men overlooked by KAP survey data used to define and measure the unmet needs in fertility control programmes. She stressed the need for method mix in part to generate data that better reflected underlying processes, such as gender/power dynamics, which often explain the real preferences.

Bagele Chilisa (2005) similarly argued, using her experiences in AIDS research in Botswana, that questionnaire surveying is a top-down method that mirrors the worldview of the researchers or their perception of the research question. The generated knowledge is then treated as the truth, the argument being that it is objective. In our view, the major problem here is that informants, researchers and users of the knowledge generated are detached from each other. The world view of the researched is ignored or even erased.

The detached way of generating and using knowledge is, however, nothing new. It is the philosophy underlying Western modernity and the concomitant idea of development or progress that shaped European thinking and colonial practice toward the end of the 18th century (Foucault 1970; Smith 1988; Escobar 1992; Airhihenbuwa 2007).

Notwithstanding, the focus on individual behaviour change assumes that individuals execute their preferences or choices regardless of societal pressures around them, the complex contexts within which reproduction takes place and the colonial histories that disrupted the many cultural systems of regulating reproduction (Ahlberg 1989, 1991, 1994; Chikovore et al 2002). By targeting married women only, the fertility control programmes ignored other social groups including men, adolescents and elderly women or the generational and gender power structures and relationships relevant to fertility and its outcome. They also overlooked the contexts within which fertility decisions are made in different social and cultural settings (the complexities of choice are ably analysed by Chi-Chi Undie in Chapter 54 of this volume).[4] Furthermore, the targeting of medical technology in the form of contraceptives medicalised reproduction and narrowed a complex cultural and social phenomenon to coitus. In our view, it is as a result of this narrowing that contraceptive use too became stigmatised, forcing women who choose to use contraceptives to fetch them from clinics far away from where they live in an attempt to avoid being identified (Ahlberg 1991).

Despite such experiences from the fertility control paradigm and indeed some of the concerns taken up in the Cairo population and development conference and the Beijing women's conference, HIV/AIDS research and interventions followed the same model, reinforcing the idea of seeing sexuality not as a positive part of human life, but rather as a health problem. This biomedical focus, as argued by Chilisa (2005), results in interventions to prevent the spread of HIV/AIDS marginalising other knowledge systems and in this way alienating people from their own knowledge systems, or making them ambivalent about these systems, and thereby reducing their capacities to deal with issues of sexuality (Ahlberg et al 2009).

Nonetheless, early in the AIDS epidemic, biomedical research established the causes of AIDS and identified what were then categorised as risk groups (Ankrah 1989; Packard and Epstein 1991; Schiller et al 1994). Although it was considered important to have multidisciplinary teams, the social science contribution remained modest and rather narrow, because social scientists were mostly invited as team members within the biomedical framework, often in already designed research projects (Ahlberg 2008). They too mostly used the KAP surveys and similarly focused on the risk groups (Packard and Epstein 1991). Because risk groups referred to already marginalised social groups, such as sex workers and homosexual men, the concept tended to distance the problem from what would be considered as the 'normal' population (Schiller et al 1994) while at the same time reinforcing stigma associated with those already stigmatised social groups. As in fertility control, the assumption in HIV/AIDS control was that providing information on sexual risks for transmission of the virus would enable the individual to make rational decisions to avoid the risk.

In summary, we have discussed some of the challenges, dilemmas and paradoxes in interventions in sexual and reproductive health and rights. We have argued that in order to understand why reproductive health remains poor or has deteriorated, there is a need to understand the parallel processes – on the one hand the articulation of SRHR and on the other a development paradigm based on international aid that has paradoxically created and sustained inequalities in poor countries in the global South, making them more vulnerable and incapable of realising their obligations for SRHR.

In our view, attention should also be focused on the use of language, particularly the tendency to conceal the ideological and political interests of international financial institutions and donors. Critical reflection is needed about the intervention methods of research and education, so as to ground them in social contexts and meanings that promote sexual wellness and well-being, rather than notions of sexuality as a medical problem. Now we want to focus on some developments that appear to address many of these challenges, paradoxes and dilemmas. Although these are not strictly new, they provide some hope that SRHR can be realised in Africa. One such development is the questioning, at a global level, of approaches and models based on individual sexual behaviour change described above (Scalway and Deane 2002; Scalway 2003) and a growing shift toward approaches that empower communities to tackle AIDS stigma and discrimination (UNAIDS 2005). Also necessary are effective communication, theories and models relevant to local situations and needs and a shift away from the assumption that sex is subject to rational thinking.

According to UNAIDS (1999a), community interventions must be within the domains of government policy, socio-economic status, culture, gender relations and spirituality. There is an evolving consensus that previous behaviour-change strategies have been at best insufficient (UNAIDS 1999b), and at worst have undermined indigenous responses to the epidemic. Such critical questioning or reflexivity is important for any positive change to take place. We would like to believe that this is serious reflexivity that will lead to real and fundamental changes to overcome the problems of development this chapter has illuminated in limiting the realisation of SRHR. However, considering that the rights-based approach itself and various global conventions on rights are about such reflections at different times, there is still room for concern about what happens in reality. Is this another tactic or language that conceals ideology, leaving business as usual? As if to answer the question, Zo Randriamaro (2003) cautions about the way in which women's voices have been turned into instruments or are co-opted to legitimise economic processes imposed by the World Bank and other donors.

Without disputing such a consequence given the history described in this chapter, we devote the rest of it to an examination of how these developments have also shaped some of the most determined struggles in the global South for realising sexual and reproductive rights. The first is the emerging scholarly work from the global South that has criticised the way Western development practice has been presumed to be universal. Most of this scholarship has stressed the need to tap into local knowledge systems for the development of Africa. The second is the ways in which women's and human rights movements have used the spaces offered by the rights-based approach to make advocacy alliances locally, regionally and globally, to demand their rights and, more significantly, to initiate institutional building in very innovative ways.

Tapping local knowledge for development in Africa

Scholars from the global South have stressed the need to interrogate and challenge the representations which essentialise or create a natural state of being for both the colonised and colonising cultures. In the context of what we discussed earlier in this chapter, interrogating international aid could, for example, reveal how poverty is created and maintained in the global South. This is of course nothing new when we take into account the works of scholars such as Andre Gunder Frank (1966), Walter Rodney (1972) and Samir Amin (1976), to name only a few, who articulated the structural mechanisms of development and underdevelopment as part of the same process. More recently, many other scholars have called for methodologies to interrogate the essentialist perspectives about African conditions perpetuated by Western thinking. Ifi Amadiume (1997), the Nigerian sociologist, has criticised the universalistic tendencies in Western feminism, for example, and has explained, using a comparative and historical analysis, how African gender systems strikingly differ from European ones. She points to some decisive differences between the material and ideological worlds of African and Western women.

Although the fundament of power of African women is the household organisation, the power base of oppression of Western women is the patriarchal family. In the latter, there is no distinction between the household and the family, so crucial to the power division between men and women, the woman being the head of the household and the man the head of the family. Amadiume argues further that in rural economies, where women are the backbone, the economic sphere is a social and cultural realm in which people interact in multiple relations, and in which African women participate in their varied identities. There is therefore no separation of the housewife/home/unproductive/non-political from the public/production/politics, as was the case in the patriarchal fabrications of European capitalism, which colonial education and the socialisation of women and men attempted to create.

Understanding these differences has been a large focus in the black African feminist scholarship, in part to identify resources as well as to work out how to tap into them. Uma Narayan (2000), like Amadiume, advocates using the history of change as methodology for analysing and understanding cultural change. To her, this helps to avoid essentialist views that have been marked by an unwarranted universalism – Western conceptions being assumed to be globally valid. Others have emphasised the need to re-examine 'the insider'[5] much more closely and critically to identify and tap its resources. Mary Kolawole (2003), for example, reasons that in order to unpack the celebrated image of African women as passive victims, marginalised and without voice, which she argues is part of the politics of appropriation that indeed silences the voices of African women, the idea of self-naming is appropriate and she proposes the use of the concept womanism, rather than feminism. The term womanism arose in relation to the predominantly white Western feminist movement, in which the focus was on gender oppression at the expense of issues of race, class and sexuality.[6]

Moreover, Kolawole highlights the importance of referring not only to academic research, but also to African women literary writers to articulate African women's struggles, with an emphasis on cultural relevance, conciliation and inclusiveness of family and motherhood among others. Pragmatic research that draws from local resources including ceremonies, songs, folklore and proverbs could, according to Kolawole, help identify spaces and avenues to elicit gender concepts that mobilise insider perspectives which, as we have argued throughout this chapter, is one major missing link when Africa is defined from outside.

Similarly, Patricia McFadden (1997) puts the African women's movement at the centre but calls for an education that helps women to understand what has sustained African systems in the face of all odds and also how rituals facilitate power relations. In our view, it is only through this kind of interrogation, not to mention making knowledge accessible to people at all levels of society, that we can hope to reverse the order by making the represented represent the self. This does not mean cutting ties with international partners, because in the increasingly globalised world, this might not be feasible. Rather, we make the case that only when there is self-representation can there be true partnership and dialogue among people within their own communities, regionally and with the rest of the world.

This point was well summed up by Simi Afonja, the Nigerian sociologist, who argued using the concepts of decolonisation and deconstruction in search of a new model of development in the context of globalisation and economic reforms:

> [W]e must recognize existing collaborative work among feminists internationally, advance this process and strengthen collaboration with other feminists internationally to insert cultural realities into contemporary knowledge, policies and policy making. An international research agenda on understanding equity may be a good means of reinvigorating international collaboration, respecting diversity and advancing the achievements of feminism internationally. (Afonja 2005: 18)

Institutional innovations by movements in Africa

In conclusion, we turn to a brief discussion of the way women's movements and human rights advocates have used the emerging spaces to forge alliances nationally, regionally and globally. It is important to point out that African women's movements have for the most part been in the forefront of pushing for the rights-based approach to sexual and reproductive health and rights. In this section, we focus on three of the many women's rights groups: Gender and Economic Reform in Africa (GERA), African Partnership for Sexual and Reproductive Health and Rights of Women and Girls (AMANITARE) and Solidarity for African Women's Rights (SOAWR) to demonstrate the ways in which the women's movement in Africa is using spaces for institutional building within the rights-based approach. Furthermore, we discuss the TAC and its innovative work around HIV/AIDS. We highlight these organisations to show how, through networking, they address the complex issues that arise when implementing SRHR. The organisations also represent what the African women's movements bring to the global scene by representing the self. The three women's organisations are pan-African, with global links.

Gender and Economic Reform in Africa, according to Zo Randriamaro:

> is a Pan-African research and advocacy programme, which aims to increase understanding of the different impact of economic reforms on men and women in the African setting, and ensure greater participation of African research organisations and women's groups in research, analysis and advocacy. (Randriamaro 2003: 44)

The critical and strategic concerns addressed by GERA include the depoliticisation of economic policy. This refers to the practice by which global institutions depoliticise economic policies through liberalisation and privatisation or reduce them to a set of technical prescriptions that become the monopoly of experts, as exemplified in the SAPs discussed earlier and the World Bank's current Poverty Reduction Strategy Papers or the Poverty Reduction Growth Facility, now advocated by the IMF. Moreover, GERA calls for the governance of multilateral trade and a reconceptualisation of human security, the main argument being that the structural causes of women's subordination are not addressed in these policies. According to the organisation, this requires transforming policies and institutions not just at the micro level, but more importantly at the level of global economic governance.

Since its initiation in 1996, GERA has provided support for 16 research and advocacy projects on gender dimensions of economic reforms in 12 African countries. In its use of action research, GERA has taken a step away from the type of top-down research discussed earlier, which privileges the views of the researchers, and adopted an approach in which the perspectives of all participants in the research are valued in the production of knowledge. The organisation uses the growing wealth of knowledge on participatory methodologies, including participatory action research (PAR), which was developed by researchers from the global South, among them Paulo Freire (1972), Borda Fals (2001) and Ansur Rahman (2004), as suitable for enabling poor people to become participants in exploring their own conditions.

As a social science research approach, PAR has two goals: to generate knowledge and to simultaneously use the knowledge to change the situation of those collaborating in the research. The research involves mobilising a broad base of actors who participate collaboratively, learn through reflection, innovate and develop. In our view, GERA is involved in the type of conscietisation articulated by Freire, whereby the micro, meso and macro levels are connected both vertically and horizontally with women's organisations in different countries, and through this vertical and horizontal involvement institutional innovations take place.

GERA focuses on gender aspects of economic policies, be they economic reforms, trade or human security, while AMANITARE is a partnership more directly concerned with sexual and reproductive health and rights. The partnership was launched in 2000 and adopts the name of a queen of ancient Nubia, to invoke a legacy of African women's leadership and agency. The major motivation, as described by Jessica Horn (2003), is the observation that in spite of reproductive health and sexual health being part of African policy statements for decades, the issues have been dominated by campaigns for safe motherhood and family planning. Furthermore, public debate and policymaking has tended to focus on women's prescribed roles, ignoring their right to choice and individual freedoms. The AMANITARE partnership notes that the single-issue campaigns, such as safe motherhood, fail to tackle the complex nexus of gender inequality, cultural norms and poverty within which sexual and reproductive health and rights concerns are rooted and that their effectiveness has, in fact, been undermined by the introduction of reforms led by the World Bank, including those that promote privatisation and user fees in the public health sector.

It is clear that AMANITARE too takes a holistic perspective, noting for example the omission of women from initiatives such as the New Partnership for Africa's Development (NEPAD), the continued presence of discriminatory laws and the lack of representation in national governments and legislatures. Like GERA,

AMANITARE works at the micro level, providing skills to women and girls in respect of their rights, at regional level by advocating for progressive implementation of SRHR policies and at the international level by facilitating African women's contribution to the UN and other global negotiations. Through research and capacity building, the partnership also works to challenge conservative support for the notion of culture, religion and community as the basis for denying women their rights.

Solidarity for African Women's Rights (SOAWR) is the third organisation we briefly describe. It was launched in 2005 as a coalition of 33 civil society organisations across Africa and the diaspora, working largely to ensure that the Protocol to the AU Charter on the Rights of Women in Africa remains on the agenda of policymakers and to urge African leaders to safeguard women's rights through the implementation of the protocol. An update on this campaign in October–December 2008 is an example of the organisation's quarterly campaign activities and reporting on the progress regarding ratification, domestication and popularisation of the rights of women in Africa. This particular update shows the intensity of activities and the broad range of actors involved at all levels and in different African countries. The activities range from workshops with different audiences, such as the youth, parliamentarians and Muslim communities, to lobbying governments and relevant ministries in different countries and translating the protocol into local languages to make it accessible to more people.

The last organisation is the TAC, a movement started by and for people living with HIV and AIDS in South Africa. The TAC managed to mobilise national and international support for universal access to antiretroviral drugs. According to Sisonke Msimang (2003), the group started the campaign using pregnant women's right to nevirapine as the rallying point, and then broadened the campaign to include all people living with HIV. Through the work of the TAC, the South African government was encouraged to take the pharmaceutical industry to court, and won. This paved the way for a win at the World Trade Organisation (WTO), which ensured that patents could not supersede the rights of human beings to access lifesaving technology (ICTSD 2001).

In conclusion, we have described in this chapter two parallel processes – one articulating the human rights-based approach and the other a development approach that has created and maintained structural inequalities, resulting in poor countries finding it increasingly difficult to meet their healthcare obligations and to address the state of sexual and reproductive health in Africa. The essay highlights the challenges, but also the paradoxes, whereby countries receiving development aid end up paying out more to donor countries than they have received. Apart from this reversed order in the movement of aid, pledges made are often not honoured and language is used to cover up actual ideology and practice.

Despite these challenges, the women's and human rights movements on the continent have used the spaces provided in the rights-based approach for institutional innovations through networking at the local, regional and global levels. This is perhaps what we could call 'people's power', which gives hope to the African continent.

Notes

1. For the long list and types of documents required by the World Bank and the IMF before a poor country is granted debt forgiveness and new loans, see Easterly (2002).
2. It is reported that the villages were selected to represent each of the agro-ecological zones in sub-Saharan Africa, representing 93 per cent of the agricultural land area and 90 per cent of the agricultural population. Each Millennium Village is located in a reasonably well-governed and stable country and in a hunger hotspot, an area with the highest rates of rural poverty and hunger, as identified by the UN Millennium Project. This intervention has reportedly turned the villages from places of chronic hunger to high crop production, with the surplus being sold in nearby markets (Millennium Project 2002–2006, n.d.).
3. For a discussion of the vulnerability of women to partner violence and to HIV and AIDS see Mathole et al (2006), Crichton et al (2008), Trenholm at al (2009), Magoni (2009).
4. For a more elaborate discussion of fertility control interventions in sub-Saharan Africa see Ahlberg (1989, 1991, 1994).
5. The concept of the 'insider' is used to refer to a situation where knowledge, realities and perspectives of the people are told by the people themselves, rather than being represented by others.
6. See also Alice Walker (1983), the African-American scholar who first used the term womanism.

References

Abbas, H. and Niyiragira, Y. (eds) (2009) *Aid to Africa: Redeemer or Coloniser?*, Oxford, Pambazuka Press

Adomako Ampofo, A. (2006) '"Whose unmet needs?" Dis/agreements about childbearing among Ghanaian couples', in Arnfred, S. (ed) *Re-thinking Sexualities in Africa*, Uppsala, The Nordic Africa Institute

Airhihenbuwa, C.O. (2005) 'Theorising cultural identity and behaviour in social science research', Dakar, *CODESRIA Bulletin* 3 and 4: 17–18

—— (2007) *Hearing Our Differences: Crisis of Global Health and the Politics of Identity*, Boulder, CO, Rowman and Littlefield Publishers

Afonja, S. (2005) 'Gender and feminism in African development discourse', lecture for visiting fellows at Indiana University, Bloomington, October/November

Africa Action Campaign Resource (2008) 'Understanding vulture funds: key terms to know', June, http://www.africaaction.org, accessed 12 June 2009

Ahlberg, B.M. (1989) 'A critical review of family planning programmes with special reference to sub-Saharan Africa', *International Journal of Prenatal and Perinatal Studies* : 397–416

—— (1991) *Women, Sexuality and the Changing Social Order: The Impact of Government Policies on Reproductive Behavior in Kenya*, New York, Gordon and Breach

—— (1994) 'Is there a distinct African sexuality? A critical response to Caldwell', *Africa* 64(2): 220–42

—— (2008) 'Dare we dream of a future without AIDS? Challenges and opportunities for responsive social science research', in Flam, H. and Carson, M. (eds) *Rule Systems Theory: Explorations and Applications*, Berlin/New York, Peter Lang

Ahlberg, B.M., Kamau, F., Maina, F. and Kulane, A. (2009) 'Multiple discourses on sexuality: implications for translating sexual wellness concept into action strategies in a Kenyan context', *African Sociological Review* 13(1): 105–123

Amadiume, I. (1997) *Reinventing Africa: Matriarchy, Religion and Culture*, London, Zed Books

Amin, S. (1976) *Unequal Development: An Essay on the Social Formations of Peripheral Capitalism*, New York, Monthly Review Press

Ankrah, E.M. (1989) 'AIDS: methodological problems in studying its prevention and spread', *Society, Scence and Medicine* 29: 265–276

Anyangu-Amu, S. (2010) 'Kenya clash over abortion rights in new constitution', 14 January, http://ipsnews.net/print.asp?idnews=49984, accessed 29 January 2010

Bader, E. (2005) 'Reproductive rights: abstinence only education', January, http://zmagsite. zmag.org/jan2005/baderrpr0105.html, accessed 14 September 2006

Bello, W. and Ambrose S. (2006) 'Take the IMF off life support', 24 May, http://www. commondreams.org/views06/0524-22.htm, accessed 12 April 2008

Birdsall, K. (2005) 'Faith-based responses to HIV/AIDS in South Africa', http://www.cadre. org.za/pdf/FBO-report.pdf, accessed 12 December 2007

Booker, S. and Colgan, A. (2004) 'Compassionate conservatism comes to Africa', 24 May, www.africaaction.org, accessed 20 May 2005

Bristal, N. (2006) 'US anti-prostitution pledge decreed unconstitutional', *The Lancet* 368(9529): 17–18

Caldwell, J.C., Caldwell, P. and Quiggin, P. (1988) 'Is the Asian family planning programme model suited to Africa?', *Studies in Family Planning* 19(1): 19–28

—— (1989) 'The social context of AIDS', *Population and Development Review* 15(2): 185–233

Centre for Reproductive Rights (2006 [2009]) 'The protocol on the rights of women in Africa', briefing paper, February, www.reproductiverights.org accessed 18 February 2011

Chambers R. (2004) 'Ideas for development: reflecting forwards', Institute for Development Studies (IDS) Working Paper 238, Brighton, Institute for Development Studies, University of Sussex

Chikovore J., Lindmark, G., Nyström, L., Mbizvo, M.T. and Ahlberg B.M. (2002) 'The hide and seek game: men's perceptions of abortion and contraceptive use within marriage in a rural area in Zimbabawe', *Journal of Biosocial Science* 34(3): 317–32

Chilisa B. (2005) 'Educational research within postcolonial Africa: a critique of HIV/AIDS research in Botswana', *International Journal of Qualitative Studies in Education* 18(6): 659–84

Cornwall, A. and Brock, K. (2005) 'What do buzzwords do for development policy? A critical look at "participation", "empowerment" and "poverty reduction"', *Third World Quarterly* 26(7): 1043–60

Crichton J., Musembi, C.N. and Ngugi, A. (2008) 'Painful tradeoffs: intimate-partner violence and sexual and reproductive rights in Kenya', working paper 312, Brighton, Institute of Development Studies, University of Sussex

Deen, T. (2003) 'Rich nations fail aid pledge to the poor', http://www.foodfirst.org/en/media/ display.phpid375, accessed 3 March 2010

—— (2009), 'Western aid declines, financial bailouts mount', http://www. ipsnews.net/print. asp?idnews=47374, accessed 27 June 2009

Dembele, Moussa (2009) 'Africa: official development assistance and the Millenium Development Goals', in Abbas, H. and Niyiragira, Y. (eds) *Aid to Africa: Redeemer or Coloniser?*, Oxford, Pambazuka Press

Easterly, W. (2002) 'The cartel of good intentions: bureaucracy versus markets in foreign aid', working paper 4, Center for Global Development, http://www.cgdev.org/content/ publications/detail/2786/, accessed 22 January 2011

—— (2009) 'The cartel of good intentions', *Foreign Policy*, January, 5: 77-81

Ehrlich, P.R. and Ehrlich, A.H. (2009) 'The population bomb revisited', *The Electronic Journal of Sustainable Development* 1(3): 63–7

Elliott, L. (2007) 'Vultures in pursuit of £1bn threaten debt-relief deal', *The Guardian*, 22 October

Epstein, H. (2005) 'God and the fight against AIDS', *The New York Review of Books*, 52(7): 2005

Escobar, A. (1992) 'Imagining a post-development era? Critical thoughts, development and social movement', *Social Text* 31(32): 20–56

Fals, Borda O. (2001) 'Participatory (Action) research in social theory: origins and challenges', in Reason, P. and Bradbury, H. (eds) *Handbook of Action Research: Participative Inquiry and Practice*, London, Sage Publications

Foucault, M. (1970) *The Order of Things*, New York, Vintage Books

Frank, A.G. (1966) 'The development of underdevelopment', *Monthly Review* 18 September: 17–30

Frank, O. and McNicoll, G. (1987) 'An interpretation of fertility and population policy in Kenya', *Population and Development Review* 13(2): 209–243

Freire, P. (1972) *Pedagogy of the Oppressed*, London, Penguin Books

Godia, J. (2004) 'Tragedy of three condoms a year', *The Sunday Standard*, 2 September

Grimes, D.A., Benson, J., Singh, S., Romero, M., Ganatra, B., Okonofua, F.E. and Shah, I.H. (2006) 'Unsafe abortion: the preventable pandemic', *The Lancet* 368(9550): 1908–1919

Gronemeyer, M. (1992) 'Helping', in Wolfgang S. (ed) *The Development Dictionary: A Guide to Knowledge as Power*, London and New Jersey, Zed Books

Hauser, P.M. (1993) 'The limitations of KAP surveys', in Bulmer M. and Warwick, D.P. (eds) *Social Research in Developing Countries: Surveys and Censuses*, London, Third World UCL Press

Hoodbhoy, M., Flaherty, M.S. and Higgins, T.E. (2005) 'Exporting despair: the human rights implications of US restrictions on foreign health care funding in Kenya', *Fordham International Law Journal* 29(1): 1–26

Horgan, J. (1991) 'Exporting misery: a US abortion ruling affects women's health worldwide', *Scientific American* 265(2): 16–17

Horn, J. (2003) 'AMANITARE and African women's sexual and reproductive health and rights', *Feminist Africa* 2: 73–9

International Center for Trade and Sustainable Development (ICTSD) (2001) 'Drug companies drop case against South African government', *Bridges Weekly Trade News Digest* 5(15)

International Planned Parenthood Federation (IPPF) (2009) 'President Barack Obama rescinds the global gag rule', 23 January, www.ippf.org/en/News/Press releases/President +Barack+Obama+rescinds+the+Global+Gag+Rule.htm, accessed 29 January 2010

Kaoma, K. (2009a) 'The US Christian right and the attack on gays in Africa', The Huffington Post, http://www.huffingtonpost.com/rev-kapya-kaoma/the-us-christian-right-an_b_387642.html, accessed 5 February 2010

Kaoma, K. (2009b) 'Globalizing the cultural wars: US conservatives, African Churches, & homophobia', Political Research Associates, http://www.publiceye.org/publications/globalizing-the-culture-wars, accessed 10 August 2010

Karanja, G. (2007) 'Defending sexual and reproductive health rights', 2 July, http://www.brettonwoodsproject.org/print.shtml?cmd[884]=x-884-554267, accessed 11 June 2009

Kolawole, M. (2003) 'Re-conceptualising African gender theory: feminism, womanism and the Arere metaphor', in Arnfred, S. (ed) *Re-thinking Sexualities in Africa*, Uppsala, The Nordic Africa Institute

Klein, N. (2007) *The Shock Doctrine*, London, Penguin Books

Lancet (2007) 'Editorial PEPFAR and the fight against HIV/AIDS', *The Lancet* 369(9568): 1141

Lines, T. (2008) *Making Poverty: A History*, London, Zed Books

Maathai, W. (2009) *The Challenge for Africa*, New York, Pantheon Books

Mabheju, S. (2010) 'Debt relief: vulture funds', *The Herald*, 8 February

MADRE (2005) 'The UN millennium development goals: obstacles and opportunities', 1 March, http://www.madre.org/index.php?s=4&news=53, accessed 19 May 2006

Magoni, P. (2009) 'Untangling HIV, GBV and cultural practice', http://ipsnews.net/africa/focus/countdown/opinion23.asp, accessed 3 March 2010

Maguire, C. (2003) 'A papacy's 25 years of unfulfilled potential', *Los Angeles Times*, 17 October

Maina, B. and Ciyendi, C. (2010) 'Women's rights and Kenya's constitution: challenging "men of faith"', 29 April, http://pambazuka.org/en/category/features/64050, accessed 30 May 2010

Manji, F., Mohammed, F. and Musa, R. (eds) (2006) *Breathing Life into the African Union Protocol on Women's Rights in Africa*, Oxford, Fahamu Books and Pambazuka Press

Maren, M. (1997) *The Road to Hell: Effects of Foreign Aid and International Charity*, New York, The Free Press

Mathole, T., Lindmark, G. and Ahlberg, B.M. (2006) 'Knowing but not knowing: providing maternity care in the context of HIV/AIDS in rural Zimbabwe', *African Journal of AIDS Research* 5(2): 133–139

Mayhew, S. (2002) 'Donor dealings: the impact of international donor aid on sexual and reproductive health services', *International Family Planning Perspectives* 28(4): 220–224

McCarthy, M. (2007) 'Report calls for changes in US global AIDS efforts', *The Lancet* 369(9568): 1155–6

McFadden, P. (1997) 'The challenges and prospects for the African women's movement in the 21st century', 18 October, http://www.hartford-hwp.com/archives/30/152.html, accessed 26 March 2001

Messer, Rev Dr D.E., (2004) *Breaking the Conspiracy of Silence: Christian Churches and the Global AIDS Crisis*, Minneapolis, Augsburg Fortress

Millennium Project 2002–2006 (n.d.) 'Millennium Villages: A new approach to fighting poverty', http://www.unmillenniumproject.org/mv/mv_closer.htm, accessed 23 August 2010

Miller, A.M. (2001) 'Uneasy promises: sexuality, health and human rights', *American Journal of Public Health* 91(6): 861–4

Mkandawire, T. (2006) 'The intellectual itinerary of Jeffrey Sachs', *Africa Review of Books* 2(1): 4–5

Msimang, S. (2003) 'HIV/AIDS, Globalisation and the international women's movement', *Gender and Development* 11(1): 109–113

Mushtaq, N. (2008) 'Kenya: ready for new abortion law?', 16 September, http://allafrica.com/stories/printable/200809170075.html, accessed 24 February 2010

Nanda, P. (2002) 'Gender dimensions of user fees: implications for women's utilisation of health care', *Reproductive Health Matters* 10(209): 127–34

Narayan, U. (2000) 'Essence of culture and a sense of history: a feminist critique of cultural essentialism', in Narayan U. and Harding, S., *Decentering the Center: Philosophy for a Multicultural, Postcolonial and Feminist World*, Bloomington, Indiana University Press

Ndunga-Muvumba, A. (2010) 'Stemming HIV is a mere wish if social inequality is not tackled', *Africa Countdown to 2015*, 7 November, www.ipsnews.net/africa/focus/countdown/opinion3.asp, accessed 15 July 2010

Okello, R. (2004) 'Health: the divergence of AIDS, and sexual and reproductive rights', 8 September, http://www.ipsnews.net/interna.asp?idnews=25397, accessed 16 June 2009

Okonofua, F.E. (2004) 'Breaking the silence on prevention of unsafe abortion in Africa', *African Journal of Reproductive Health* 8(1): 7–8

Olukoshi, A. (2004) 'Neo-liberal globalisation and its social consequences', 15 July, http://pambazuka.org/en/category/features/23194

Olukoshi, A. and Nyamnjoh, Francis B. (2005) 'Rethinking African development: editorial', *CODESRIA Bulletin* 3 & 4: 1–4

Oomman, N., Bernstein, M. and Rosenzweig, S. (2007) *Following the Funding for HIV/AIDS: A Comparative Analysis of the Funding Practices of PEPFAR, the Global Fund and World Bank MAP in Mozambique, Uganda and Zambia*, Washington DC, Centre for Global Development

Øyen E. (1999) 'The politics of poverty reduction', *International Social Science Journal* 51(162): 459–65

Packard, R.M. and Epstein P. (1991) 'Epidemiologists, social scientists and the structure of medical research on AIDS in Africa', *Social Science and Medicine* 33: 771–94

Petchesky, R.P. (2000) 'Rights and needs: rethinking the connections in debates over reproductive and sexual rights', *Health and Human Rights* 4(2): 17–29

Puopolo, R. (2010) 'Vulture funds: ugly name for an ugly reality', 9 February, http://www.afjn.org/focus-campaigns/other/other-continental-issues/82-general/791-v, accessed 25 February 2010

Rahman, Ansur (2004) 'Globalisation: the emerging ideology in the popular protests and grassroots action research', *Action Research* 2(1): 9–23

Randriamaro, Z. (2003) 'African women challenging neo-liberal economic orthodoxy: the conception and mission of the GERA Programme', *Gender and Development* 11(1): 44–51

Rodney, W. (1973) *How Europe Underdeveloped Africa*, London, Bogle-L'Ouverture

Romer, D. and Hornik, R. (1992) 'HIV education for youth: the importance of social consensus in behaviour change', *AIDS Care* 4(3): 285–303

Sachs, J.D. (2005) *The End of Poverty: Economic Possibilities for Our Time*, New York, Penguin Group

Sachs, Wolfgang (ed) (1992) *The Development Dictionary: A Guide to Knowledge as Power*, London and New Jersey, Zed Books

Sadik, N. (2000) 'Progress in protecting reproductive rights and promoting reproductive health: five years after Cairo', *Health and Human Rights* 4(2): 7–15

Saunders, P. (2004) 'Prohibiting sex work projects, restricting women's rights: the international impact of the 2003 US Global AIDS Act', *Health and Human Rights* 7(2): 179–92

Scalway, T. (2003) 'Missing the message? 20 years of learning from HIV/AIDS', London, Panos Institute

Scalway, T. and Deane, J. (2002) 'Critical challenges in HIV communication: a perspective paper', London, Panos Institute

Schiller, N.G., Crystal S. and Lewellen D. (1994) 'Risky business: the cultural construction of AIDS risk groups', *Social Science and Medicine* 38: 1337–46

Shiva, V. (2005) 'How to end poverty: making poverty history and the history of poverty', 5 November, http://www.zmag.org/Sustainers/Content/2005-05/11Shiver.cfm, accessed 14 November 2005

Shuster, P. (2004) 'Advocacy in whispers: the impact of the USAID global gag rule upon free speech and free association in the context of abortion law reform in three East African countries', *Michigan Journal of Gender and Law* 11: 97–126

Sindig, S.W. (2005) 'Does "CNN" (condoms, needles and negotiation) work better than "ABC" (abstinence, being faithful and condom use) in attacking the AIDS epidemic?' *International Family Planning Perspectives* 31(1): 38–40

Singh, S. (2006) 'Hospital admissions resulting from unsafe abortion: estimates from 13 developing countries', *The Lancet* 368: 1887–92

Smith, Linda Tuhiwai (1988) *Decolonising Methodologies: Research and Indigenous Peoples*, London, Zed Books

Solidarity for African Women's Rights (SOAWR) (2008) 'Update on the campaign on ratification, domestication and popularisation of the protocol on the rights of women in Africa', *Equality Now*, October–December, http://www.soawr.org/resources/oct_dec_2008_en.pdf. accessed 14 August 2010

Tandon, Y. (2008) *Ending Aid Dependence*, Oxford, Fahamu Books

Treatment Action Campaign (TAC) (2003–2005) 'We are [still] dying: every AIDS death is a loss for every member of the body politic from the Union Buildings all the way down', chairperson's political report, unpublished

Trenholm J., Olsson P. and Ahlberg B.M. (2009) 'Battles on women's bodies. War, rape and traumatisation in eastern Democratic Republic of Congo, *Global Public Health Journal*, September 28: 1–14

UNAIDS (1999a) 'Communications framework for HIV/AIDS: a new direction', January, http://www.unaids.org/publications/IRC-pub01/jc335-commramew_en.pdf, accessed 18 August 2004

—— (1999b) 'Sex and youth: contextual factors affecting risk for HIV/AIDS. A comparative analysis of multi-site studies in developing countries', May, http://data.unaids.org/publications/IRC-pub01/jc096-sex%26youth-3_en.pdf, accessed 27 January 2010

—— (2005) 'HIV-related stigma, discrimination and human rights violations: case studies of successful programmes', April, http://data.unaids.org/publications/irc-pub06/jc999-humrightsviol_en.pdf, accessed 10 November 2010

—— (2007) 'AIDS epidemic update'

United Nations (1995) 'Cairo Programme of Action, DPI/1618/POP', March, http://www.un.org/ecosocdev/geninfo/populatin/icpd.htm, accessed 27 January 2010

—— (2006) 'Short history of CEDAW convention', http://www.un.org/womenwatch/daw/cedaw/history.htm, accessed 25 January 2010

—— (2008) The Millennium Development Goals Report, http://www.un.org/millenniumgoals/pdf/The%20Millennium%20Development%20Goals%20Report%202008.pdf, accessed 17 September 2009

UN Department of Public Information (DPI) (2005) 'Our challenges: voices for peace, partnerships and renewal', conference overview, 58th Annual DPI/NGO Conference, New York, 7–9 September

UN Women (2010) United Nations Entity for Gender Equality and the Empowerment of Women, http://www.unwomen.org/facts-figures/, accessed 5 October 2010

US Mexico City Policy (2007) 'Abortion funding in foreign countries', 27 April, http://www. religioustolerance.org/abo_wrld.htm, accessed 17 September 2009

Walker, A. (1983) *In Search of Our Mothers' Gardens: Womanist Prose*, New York, NY, Harcourt

Wanyeki, L.M. (1996) 'Kenya-population: church burns condoms and AIDS materials', 5 September, http://www.aegis.com/news/ips/1996/IP960901.html, accessed 12 December 1999

Warwick D.P. (1993) 'The KAP survey: dictates of mission versus demands of science', in Bulmer, M. and Warwick, D.P. (eds) *Social Research in Developing Countries: Surveys and Censuses*, London, Third World UCL Press

Winyi, Norah Matovu (2009) 'A call to action: implement the Africa women's rights protocol', 25 June, http://pambazuka.org/en/category/features/57219, accessed 22 January 2010

Women's Global Network for Reproductive Rights (WGNRR) (2009) 'Health sector reform: hazardous to women's health', http://www.choike.org/nuevo_eng/informes/1942.html, accessed 5 April 2010

World Health Organisation (WHO) and UNAIDS (2003) 'Treat 3 million by 2005 (3 by 5) initiative', http://www.who.int/3by5/publications/doc?uments/isbn9241591129/en/, accessed 27 September 2005; and http://www.unaids.org/en/treat3millionby2005initiative. asp, accessed 21 November 2005

World Health Organisation (WHO) (2005) 'World Health Organisation: Millennium Development Goals', http://www.who.int/mdg/en/, accessed 20 November 2005

—— (2007) 'Unsafe abortion: global and regional estimates of the incidence of unsafe abortion and associated mortality in 2003', 5th ed, WHO, Geneva

37

Morality, justice and gender: reading Muslim tradition on reproductive choices[1]

Sa'diyya Shaikh

In the build-up to the 1994 United Nations International Conference on Population and Development (ICPD) held in Cairo, many Muslim communities and leaders expressed suspicion toward the UN initiatives for family planning and population control (Noakes 1995: 100–1). The Saudi Arabian Council of Ulama, that nation's highest body of religious authorities, condemned the Cairo conference as a 'ferocious assault on Islamic society' and forbade Muslims to attend (Gorman 1994). Sudan, Lebanon and Iraq then joined Saudi Arabia in announcing that they would not send delegates to Cairo.

Among other things, the conference agenda, specifically those items relating to issues of family planning and birth control, was seen as an imposition of Western values on the Muslim people and an attempt to revive 'colonial and imperial ambition' (Noakes 1995: 100–1). Although this by no means represented the whole spectrum of Muslim voices in the debate, since there were many Muslim participants who were involved and committed to the goals of the conference, the voices of resistance were loud and well documented by the media.

This type of vociferous antipathy to family planning in some Muslim communities presents a fairly sharp contrast to the way in which Muslims have historically addressed the issue. Even a cursory investigation into the Islamic intellectual legacy will demonstrate that eight out of nine classical legal schools permitted the practice of contraception and that the Islamic legal positions on abortion range from allowing various levels of permissibility of abortion under 120 days to prohibition (Omran 1992: 145–83). Furthermore, medieval Muslim physicians had documented detailed and extended lists of birth control practices, including abortifacients, commenting on their relative effectiveness and prevalence, and Arabic Islamic erotic literature provided detailed descriptions of popular understandings of contraceptive techniques (Musallam 1983: 60–104). These facts illustrate the level of incongruity between the Islamic legacy, in which family planning was widely permitted and even encouraged in certain contexts, and some prevailing Muslim perspectives that reject family planning as contrary to Islam.

To understand some of the contemporary Muslim resistance to this topic, one needs to contextualise the debate within the present matrix of post-colonial power relations. Over the past several centuries the shift in the balance of power between Islam and Western powers has contributed to the prevalence of a polarised 'Islam vs the West' schema (Daniel 1960). The historical colonial presence in many Muslim countries has shaped some of the forms of political and cultural resistance to Western presence. In the current era this is exacerbated by the fact that Euro-American cultural forms, through the processes of globalisation, are perceived as encroaching and increasingly threatening to Muslim societies (Akbar and Donnan 1994). Within this context family planning, contraceptive usage and access to abortion are regularly framed as either a conspiracy by Western powers to limit the growth and power of the Muslim world or as a reflection of the permissive sexual mores of Western society (Zahra 1962; Maududi 1974; Noakes 1995: 100–1). Thus, the issues relating to birth control are submerged within a larger minefield of political and cultural polemics.

As a result, many Muslims have assumed a defensive posture in these debates, contributing to a particular myopia in significant pockets of the Muslim world. The need to resist what is perceived as a colonising Western discourse has ironically resulted in the reality that Muslims are being defined, albeit oppositionally, by that very discourse. Such denunciation of family planning as a Western concept becomes defining in some Muslims' discourses to the extent that their own positions become largely determined by resisting a perceived adversary. Contemporary Muslim rejection of family planning endeavours becomes particularly salient in light of an investigation into the Islamic legacy, which is characterised by rich diversity and a remarkable openness to issues of family planning. In fact scholar Norman Daniel shows how medieval churchmen found the Islamic permissiveness regarding contraception as another of the sexual 'horrors' of Islam (Daniel 1960: 142).

In this chapter I draw on a number of traditional Islamic resources in delineating a more 'self-referential' and less defensive Islamic approach to the questions of family planning, contraception and abortion. I discuss a diverse Islamic legacy with varying approaches to the questions of family planning.

In exploring Islamic perspectives on family planning, contraception and abortion, it is necessary to understand some of the fundamentals of Islam that inform such ideas. I begin by discussing some of the essential Islamic teachings about God and humanity, which form the basis for an Islamic approach to addressing ethical concerns and contemporary challenges of population growth, family planning and human well-being. I argue that the central Islamic concept of human moral agency (*khilafah*) demands that we address these challenges holistically. This includes a response to structural injustices relating to economic and gender hierarchies, as well as an informed approach to particulars of family planning.

God and humanity: *tauhid, fitrah* and *khilafah*

The belief in the oneness or unity of God, known to Muslims as the principle of *tauhid*, is the centre from which the rest of Islam radiates. It is a foundational ontological principle anchored within the deepest spiritual roots of the religion, suffusing different areas of Islamic learning that include theology, mysticism, and law and ethics in varying ways. While transience, finitude and dependence define everything else, God is the only independent source of being (Q. 55: 26–7). As such, God is primary to our understanding of the very meaning of reality and is constitutive of the ultimate integrity of human beings (Q. 59: 19).

According to the Qu'ran, human beings are uniquely imbued with the spirit of God and in their created nature have been granted privileged knowledge and understanding of reality (Q. 15: 29). Human weakness, on the other hand, is presented primarily as the tendency to be heedless and forgetful of these realities. God's revelations through the various prophets in history are an additional mercy intended to remind us about what is already ingrained at the deepest level of our humanity. Mediating between faith and heedlessness is the human capacity for volition and freedom of choice. This uniquely endowed human constitution with an inborn capacity for discernment is called the *fitrah*.

Within Islam therefore, although humanity is primed for goodness, our moral agency is bound to the freedom of choice and the active assumption of responsibilities that ensue from such agency. This understanding of human purpose and potential is reflected in the pervasive Qu'ranic concept of *khilafah*, which can be translated as trusteeship, moral agency or vice-gerency (deputyship), and where the subject of this activity, the human being, is referred to as the *khalifah*, that is the trustee, the moral agent or the vice-gerent. This core Qu'ranic concept provides the spiritual basis for understanding ethical action in Islam. Within this framework, each individual as well as every community is responsible for the realisation of a just and moral social order in harmony with God's will (Rahman 1980: 18). In Islam, enacting one's moral agency is intrinsic to a right relationship with God.

Social and ethical implications

One of the crucial secondary principles that flow from the *tauhidic* view that God is one and that all human beings are God's *khalifah* is the notion of the 'metaphysical sameness of all humans as creatures of God' (Al-Hibri 2000: 52). Each person, irrespective of gender, race and nationality, possesses the birthright to be God's *khalifah* in this world. According to the Qu'ran, the only real criterion for distinction among human beings is that of *taqwa*, which can be translated as God-consciousness and righteousness (Q. 49: 13).[2]

Moreover, the Qu'ran repeatedly describes the true believer as one who enacts the moral imperative for justice in the world (Q. 4: 135). Within the Qu'ranic worldview the belief in the unity of God explicitly relates to the striving for the unity of humanity for which justice is a prerequisite.[3] Thus the theological concepts of *tauhid* and *khilafah* explicitly intersect – bearing witness to God's absolute oneness in Islam is intrinsically related to enacting that awareness in the world for the purposes of justice and human well-being. As foundational Islamic constructs, they have an overarching relevance to the Islamic approach to family planning because the concept of *khilafah* is replete with the importance of human moral agency, the distillation of our inner conscience, freedom of choice and the striving for an ethically alive social order.

I would argue that in working toward an ethical order, particularly in addressing the challenges of population growth, it is imperative to look at the question holistically, situating it within the relevant social, economic and political forces of the day. To this end I focus, first, on poverty and economic justice and second, on sexism and gender justice as concerns that are structurally implicated in the concern for family planning.

Poverty and economic justice

In addressing the state of human well-being globally, the issues of poverty, resources and wealth distribution are paramount. The previous chapter, by Beth Maina-Ahlberg and Asli Kulane, clearly pointed out that contemporary concerns with population growth and sustainable resources are intimately connected with the inequitable distribution of wealth. Frequently the multiple levels of socio-political inequity in the world are connected to questions of how wealth and resources are controlled.[4]

An Islamic response to these economic realities begins with the Qu'ranic view that wealth is part of beneficence and the bounty of God and in reality belongs to God; it is entrusted to human beings to be used wisely and with a responsibility to the well-being of all (Q. 59: 7). The poor, the orphaned and the needy have a right to a portion of one's wealth and Muslims are obligated to pay a welfare tax called *zakat*. The root meaning of the term *zakat* is 'to purify' or 'to grow', which is particularly relevant since wealth is also a means through which God tests humanity (Q. 64: 15–17). Wealth sharing purifies the individual from greed and material attachment while simultaneously increasing the giver's good deeds and spiritual wealth.

The circulation of wealth among all segments of a society is seen as a duty placed on the individual *khalifah* and the larger Muslim community (Q. 59: 7).[5] Not only does the Qu'ran encourage us to share wealth, it also categorically condemns greed and selfish hoarding (Q. 47: 38; Q. 89: 16–26). There is an explicit link between those who decline to pay the poor their due and the idolaters (Q. 41: 6–7). Given that the belief in God's oneness (*tauhid*) is so central in Islam, this association between idolatry and miserliness is among the harshest criticisms of the concentration of wealth among the few at the expense of the rest. It speaks to the incongruity between genuine belief in God and a disregard for the needs of others and to the inextricability between an individual's well-being and the well-being of others. In terms of this ideal it is unacceptable to have a society characterised by the co-existence of extreme wealth and poverty, and Muslims are urged to work toward generating systems of socio-economic justice that foster the common good.

These ethics of wealth sharing and socio-economic concern for the economically marginalised have a pressing urgency in a world characterised by huge economic disparities between nation states.[6] The reality that economic marginalisation occurs most brutally at the nexus of race, nationality and gender hierarchies is illustrated by the fact that women, primarily in the poorer nations, constitute 70 per cent of the world's 1.3 billion poorest people and own less than 1 per cent of the world's property, but work two-thirds of the world's working hours (Maguire and Rasmussen 1997: 3). Even within the heart of capitalist wealth, the USA, we find significant pockets of poverty and neglect in the inner cities that are generally divided along racial lines.

These realities reflect a paradigm that is contrary to *tauhidic* teaching, in which human lives are not equally valued but rather are prioritised on the basis of race, nationality, gender and class stratification. The lives of those who do not belong to privileged groups or nations are removed from the radar of social concern and moral responsibility. Here the Qu'ranic critique points us to the reality that economic injustice, a lack of appreciation of lives outside the centres of power and privilege, and the maldistribution of wealth reflect a failure of human beings to carry out their trusteeship (*khilafah*) from God. In addressing human well-being in the world, transforming systems of economic injustice and exploitation and establishing a more equitable distribution of wealth are as crucial spiritual and ethical concerns as are issues of family planning and population control.

Sexism and gender justice

Another pivotal area of concern relates to Islamic perspectives on gender relations, marriage and their implications for family planning. The notion that God's unity is reflected in the equality and unity of humankind provides a basis for a strong critique of sexism and gender hierarchy. The Qu'ran explicitly asserts the fundamental equal worth of male and female believers as well as the fact that gender relations are intended to be cooperative and mutually enriching (Q. 9: 71; Q. 16: 97; Q. 33: 35). This ethos of reciprocity between women and men is further reinforced in the Islamic understanding of marital relationships.

The Qur'an presents marriage and children as a gift from God to be cherished and enjoyed (Q. 16: 72; Q. 25: 74). As such, marriage is valued and encouraged in most Muslim cultures. Despite this incentive to have a family, neither marriage nor children are considered obligatory in the life of a Muslim man or woman. In fact the Qu'ran also warns that if marriage and parenting are not approached with the right attitude and awareness, these too can have a negative impact in people's lives (Q. 64: 14–15). For those who fear such a possibility and do not have the wherewithal for marriage, the Qu'ran even permits them to remain unmarried (Q. 24: 33).

Al-Ghazzali (d.1111), one of the most renowned Islamic intellectuals, discussed some of the potential disadvantages of marriage. Among these he included the possibility of excessive financial burden on a family or that people might become ensconced within the enjoyment and needs on family, and thereby become distracted from the true purpose of life, which is the individual's journey to Allah (Farah 1984: 71–4). Marriage, like many lawful things in Islam, if approached correctly, is an opportunity for growing closer to God. However, if it is approached as an end in itself, it can become destructive.

I would argue that one of the ways in which marriage becomes an obstacle instead of an aid to God-consciousness is when the notion of male superiority or privilege emerges as a defining aspect of the relationship. Systems of patriarchy and sexism, which place male human beings above female human beings solely on the basis of their gender, are a denial of the essential equality of humanity, thereby constituting a negation of the reality of *tauhid*. Although this position is not uncontested, there is certainly a strong Qu'ranic basis for developing a hermeneutic of gender justice in marriage and in society more broadly.[7]

A number of contemporary Muslim scholars have argued that the Qu'ranic view of the inviolable sanctity of every human being, both male and female, implies a duty to protect each person's physical, emotional, psychological, social and intellectual integrity (Wadud 1999: 94–104; Hassan 2000: 241–248). This implies that the whole range of explicit violations of women's personhood, including physical violence against women, honour killings and cliterodectomy, constitutes a transgression of spiritual sanctity of the individual and therefore a disregard for the principle of *tauhid*.

At the more insidious level, socialisation processes and cultural ideals of womanhood in many Muslim communities are premised on male-centred norms. Social ideals that promote women's silence and subordination to men, that deny or limit women's access to education, that restrict their mobility and agency in the world, that define women primarily in terms of their sexuality, or that fix women's roles or value solely as mother and wife constitute structural violence to women's full humanity.

These types of sociocultural constructs also often reinforce structural economic inequities, where resources, skills and education are dominated by men, thereby perpetuating patriarchal power relations. It is no coincidence that the world's poorest people are women – patriarchy and classism are structural injustices that intersect and reinforce one another to create the most brutally impoverishing conditions for many women in the world, including some Muslim women. Within this context, the burden of numerous pregnancies and children can be fundamentally debilitating, threatening women's very survival and well-being. Moreover, in conditions of poverty, undernourished and weak offspring are more a source of anxiety and stress than the 'comfort' or 'allurement' of the parent's eyes, as the Qu'ran intends (Q. 25: 74).

These varying levels of systematic injustice operating against women violate the essential *tauhidic* notion of the equality of human beings. This includes the reality that poor women often do not have access to information and education around issues of family planning, including religious rights and medical information. Moreover, the fact that many women are deprived of educational, intellectual, social and economic opportunities often traps them into accepting notions that they are obliged to reproduce and serve their husbands. The fact that in many Muslim societies the important roles of wife and mother are presented to the exclusion of other avenues for women's intellectual and spiritual development violates Muslim women's access to the fullness of moral agency or *khilafah*. Although Islam encourages marriage and family life for both men and women, no Muslim is obligated to marry or reproduce. However, every Muslim woman, like her male counterpart, is obligated to undertake her *khilafah*, which includes realising her full potential for intellectual, economic and social agency in the world.

In articulating a relevant Islamic response to contemporary challenges, including the realities of population growth, it is imperative to focus on addressing the problems of economic and gender injustice. In our context, it is inadequate, if not irresponsible, for any religious or ethical framework to address questions of human well-being, family planning and birth control without looking at the related systems of socio-economic injustice that directly restrict human agency and freedom and exacerbate human misery in the world. An Islamic ethical vision needs to address the issues of social justice as an organic component of family planning and population control. This nonetheless has to be coupled with a responsible and informed approach to the specifics of family planning.

Family planning

In addressing the question of family planning from an Islamic perspective, it is necessary to consult the various sources of guidance within the religious tradition. These include the Qu'ranic revelation and the prophetic traditions, as well as the inner moral capacities of discernment in human beings. In addition, it is valuable for Muslims to inform themselves of the relevant aspects of the Islamic legal legacy as well as all the contemporary advances in knowledge on the subject.

The Qu'ran and prophetic traditions, which are both considered primary sources of authority in Islam, do not have unambiguous and explicit teachings relating to family planning. Within Islamic legal philosophy, issues that require independent intellectual exertion and moral circumspection in light of a changing context and varying individual circumstances are called *ijtihadi* issues. *Ijtihad* is based on the assumption that in dealing with issues that are not explicitly addressed in the primary sources, jurists, informed by the spirit of the Qu'ran, use their moral capacities for creative reasoning and judgement to arrive at relevant legal solutions (Moosa 1997: 140). This opens up the possibilities for more dynamic Islamic approaches to understanding the issues of family planning in the current context.

Proponents and opponents of family planning both derive their positions from their understandings of what constitutes 'the good' and interpret broader Qu'ranic injunctions to inform and support their respective positions. The possibility to sustain contrary readings of the divine text speaks to the reality that exegesis is a hermeneutical enterprise informed by the varied human capacities for understanding and moral reasoning. All readings are not equally convincing or legitimate and in reviewing the arguments provided for both, it is my contention that family planning is, in fact, a legitimate and important Islamic priority.

Opponents of family planning often base their rejection of both contraception and abortion on their reading of the following verse: 'Kill not your children, on a plea of want, we provide sustenance for you and for them' (Q. 6: 151; Zahra 1962; Maududi 1974).

It is important to look at the context of revelation of this verse. This verse was a response to the pre-Islamic Arab custom of burying female children alive (Rahman 1982: 286–7). It was therefore a condemnation of infanticide and of the deep misogyny of that culture. Proponents of family planning have argued that using these Qu'ranic verses to counter all family planning initiatives is therefore a misreading of the text.

Furthermore, opponents of family planning base their resistance to it on the basis that it constitutes a lack of trust in God and in God's sustenance, and that it is an assertion of human will vis-à-vis God's will (Omran 1992: 89–90). The verses that they use to support this position are the following:

> There is no creature on earth, but its sustenance depends on God. He knows its habitation and its preservation. (Q. 11: 6)

> And whosoever is conscious of God, He will find a way out (of difficulty) for him, and He will provide for him in a manner beyond all expectations, and for every one that places their trust in God, He alone is sufficient. (Q. 65: 2–3)

Indeed trust in God and in God's sustenance is an integral dimension of Islam. These verses speak to the reality that in Islam ultimately the outcome of all things resides with God, for God is without doubt the Sustainer, the All-Powerful. I do however disagree with the conclusion that this absolves human beings from any responsibility for agency in the world. On the contrary, I would argue that this type of reasoning is contrary to the very fundamental Islamic notion of human *khilafah*.

We have established that *khilafah* implies that humanity is entrusted with moral agency which demands a God-conscious, active and responsible attitude to ourselves, to fellow human beings and to the world. It includes using the faculties of reason, judgement and God-consciousness that are part of our *fitrah*, to plan our lives, to seek out sustenance and to strive actively for the well-being of self and society in relation to the challenges of our age. In the current context of living in world characterised by increasing populations with limited access to resources, being a *khalifah* includes responding constructively to these difficulties instead of further exacerbating the over-burdened resources of the world. Though Muslims trust that ultimately all lies within the power of Allah, human agency is intrinsic to the Qu'ranic worldview and the prophetic teachings.

The Qu'ranic narrative of Joseph's planning and preservation of food in anticipation of the famine is an act of agency that does not demonstrate a lack of trust in God's sustenance. Similarly, there are prophetic traditions that address the combination of human agency with trust in God, as is reflected in the Prophet's advice to a man to tie up his camel and then trust in God, or the caliph Umar's statement that reliance on God means to plant the seeds in the earth, then trust in God for a good crop (Omran 1992: 91). Family planning, including contraceptive usage, can be seen as an extension of the human capacity to plan, to respond to and to actively make choices in terms of contextual needs and emerging realities.

Contraception

Contraception has a long history in Islam that needs to be situated in relation to the broader Islamic ethos of marriage and sexuality. In Islam, if one chooses to marry, this is not automatically linked to procreation. Within the Islamic view of marriage an individual has the right to sexual pleasure within marriage, which is independent of one's choice to have children.[8] This approach to sexuality is compatible with a more tolerant approach to contraception and family planning.

Historically, the overwhelming majority of the various Islamic legal schools have permitted *coitus interruptus*, called *azl*, as a method of contraception (Omran 1992: 145–182; Ministry of Information Egypt 1994: 27–34). This was a contraceptive technique practised by pre-Islamic Arabs and continued to be used during the time of the Prophet with his knowledge and without his prohibition (Omran 1992: 115–142). The only condition the Prophet attached to the acceptability of this practice, which was reiterated by Muslim jurists, was that the husband was to secure the permission of the wife before practising withdrawal. Since the male sexual partner initiates this technique, there needs to be consensual agreement about its use by both partners for two primary reasons. First, the wife is entitled to full sexual pleasure and *coitus interruptus* might diminish her pleasure. Second, she has the right to offspring if she so desires (Musallam 1983: 31–6). These requirements speak to the priority given in Islam to mutual sexual fulfilment, as well as consultative decision making between a married couple in terms of family planning.

As early as the ninth century female contraceptive techniques, such as intravaginal suppositories and tampons, were also a part of both medical and judicial discussions in Islam (Musallam 1983: 37–8, 77–88). Although medical manuals listed the different female contraceptive options and their relative effectiveness, legal positions differed about whether the consent of the husband was necessary or not with the use of female contraceptives. In classical Islamic law, which informs contemporary Islamic jurisprudence, the majority position in eight out of the nine legal schools permits contraception (Omran 1992: 145–67).

Because of this broad-based legal permissibility of contraception in Islamic law, Muslim physicians in the medieval period conducted in-depth investigations into the medical dimension of birth control, which were unparalleled in European medicine until the 19th century (Musallam 1983: 60–89). Ibn Sina in his *Qanun* lists 20 birth control substances, and physician Abu Bakr al-Razi in his *Hawi* lists 176 birth control substances (Musallam 1983: 60–89). The permissibility of contraceptive practice in Islamic history at the level of both theory and practice is abundantly evident in both its medical and legal legacies.

Although different legal scholars discussed the acceptability or reprehensibility of particular individual motives for using contraceptives, this discussion did not contest the overarching permissibility of contraceptive practice. The scholar Al-Ghazzali supported the use of contraceptive practice for different reasons, including economic factors or situations in which a large number of dependents would impose financial and psychological hardship on the family (Farah 1984: 111). He reasoned that a large family might cause us to resort to unlawful means to support these excessive responsibilities. Fewer material burdens, he added, are an aid to religion.

He also supported the decision to use contraception in order to protect the life of the wife, given the possible physical dangers that childbirth posed to the mother. In addition, he considered the need for the wife to preserve her beauty and attractiveness for the enjoyment of the marriage as a reasonable justification for contraception (Farah 1984: 111).

Although the last-mentioned rationale might characterise a patriarchal emphasis on the primacy of the wife's appearance to the enjoyment of the marriage, it nonetheless simultaneously illustrates the high levels of tolerance for contraceptive practices in the Islamic legacy. This is reflected in the fact that there are many other influential jurists and theologians in different historical periods who discussed the permissibility of *azl* or contraception for similar and additional reasons.[9]

In the present context there are a number of considerations that speak to the urgent need for family planning in Muslim societies. At the national level, Professor Abdel Rahim Omran, the physician and demographer, demonstrates through population statistics that the population in the Muslim world is growing at a rate that is not matched by economic and service development. Because of these realities he states that:

> Muslim countries have been forced to acquire debt, import food and rely on foreign aid to cope with the needs of growing populations. The result is a vicious cycle of poverty, ill health, illiteracy, overpopulation and unemployment being compounded with social frustration, extremism and social unrest. (Omran 1992: 212)

There are significant internal social and economic reasons to focus on family planning in the Muslim world. Arguments by religious scholars, who see family planning as an external Western conspiracy aimed at curtailing the growth and strength of the Islamic world, appear to be uninformed of both the socio-political and demographic realities in many Muslim countries as well as the historical permissibility of contraception within the Islamic legacy (Zahra 1962; Maududi 1974). In fact, I would argue that, given the profound socio-economic and political difficulties in various parts of the Muslim world, a lack of family planning and increasing populations would weaken and curtail the strength of Islam.

At the more personal level, the demands of a large family impact on the quality of life of all its members, including parents and children. Numerous offspring make it less possible for parents to provide for the full range of their children's needs, including spiritual, emotional, psychological and financial dimensions, resulting in children experiencing a reduced quality of life. Similarly, multiple demands on parents generally create the need to work harder to provide for these numerous needs. This in turn often reduces their quality of life, including the fact that they have less time and energy for the necessary spiritual and religious introspection also required in Islam.

It is noteworthy that the majority of contemporary Islamic leaders who are well educated in the Islamic legacy and are aware of social needs, with few exceptions, state the religious permissibility of contraception (Ministry of Information, Egypt 1994; Bowen 1998: 150). The fairly widespread encouragement of family planning and the permission to use contraceptive practices are reflected in a number of different conferences and religious publications participated in by leading Islamic scholars in various parts of the Muslim world (Omran 1992: 201–24). Some of the key arguments in these books and conference publications involve an application of Qu'ranic ethical principles to the perceived needs of the age. The following represent some of the recurring elements in many of these conferences and publications (Omran 1992: 201–24):[10]

- Islam is a religion of ease and not of hardship. Moderation is the recommended approach to life (Q. 2: 185; Q. 22: 78). Thus large families in the context of a limited access to resources often impose difficulties on the provider.
- In Islam there is a prioritisation on the quality of life rather than a large quantity of lives.
- Planned spacing of pregnancies will allow the mother the time and opportunity to suckle and care for each child. The Qu'ran recommends that a mother should suckle her child for two years.
- Undernourished and weak offspring are more a source of anxiety and struggle than the 'comfort' or 'allurement' of the parent's eyes as the Qu'ran intends.
- In Muslim countries that are underdeveloped, have limited resources and are overpopulated, an absence of family planning will result in a weak multitude enduring more hardships, instead of a smaller but stronger and healthier population.
- Contemporary contraceptive methods that temporarily avert pregnancy are analogous to the Islamically sanctioned practice of *coitus interruptus* (*azl*) and are thus permissible.
- Sterilisation or any type of contraceptive that would cause permanent infertility are impermissible unless there are exceptional reasons.
- People should not be coerced to stop childbearing.

In some Muslim countries, the authorities have emerged with guidelines for contraception. For example, an official Egyptian manual on family planning which was compiled by religious scholars included a discussion on the acceptability of various forms of modern contraceptives including condoms, the cervical cap, the loop device, the contraceptive pill, the contraceptive injection and the IUD (Ministry of Information, Egypt 1994: 34–66).

A forum that made some particularly noteworthy and progressive declarations was the International Congress, which took place in Aceh, Indonesia in 1990. The Aceh Declarations included an emphasis on responsibility that the present generation owes to the future generations because the lifestyle and decisions of the former affect the quality of life of future generations. As part of a family planning programme, they also recognised the importance of the empowerment of Muslim women, their informed participation in decision-making processes and the need to improve maternal care and childcare facilities (Omran 1992: 220).

It is noteworthy that gender relations and women's rights are also key aspects of the argument, although used in a different way, among the religious scholars who oppose contraception. For example, Maulana Maududi of Pakistan condemns the entry of women into the public labour force and gender desegregation in society. He argues that in this type of permissive society:

> [T]he last obstacle that may keep a woman from surrendering to a man's advances is fear of illegitimate conception. Remove this obstacle too and provide women with weak character assurance that they can safely surrender to their male friends and you will see that the society will be plagued by the tide of moral licentiousness. (Maududi 1974: 176)

This type of argumentation is underpinned with a gender ideology that sees women's roles as restricted to the domestic realm under male control. Moreover, women are seen as moral minors, whose abstinence from illicit sex is only due to fear of external sanctions, and who are easily influenced by the sensual wiles of men. Paradoxically, responsibility for sexual morality of the community is seen to reside with activities of women, for it is their entry into public space that will cause sexual anarchy.[11]

These notions are expressly masculinist and patriarchal, and counter the very basic Islamic notions of the *khilafah* or full moral agency of every human being. Not only is it a violation of the personhood of women but also it considers men as sexual predators who are driven by the needs of their uncontrollable libidos and will at any given opportunity seek out illicit sexual relationships. Accordingly, men too are depicted as lacking in moral agency because their proper conduct is premised on the absence of females in their company. Pervading this argument is the view that sexual morality is dictated by external constraints.

This type of sexual ethos contradicts the very basis of Islamic morality – that every human being is endowed with the capacity to be an active moral agent and that no soul bears the burden of another. Moreover, Qu'ranically, human morality and ethics are intended to emerge fundamentally from that all-pervasive internal locus of control called *taqwa* or God-consciousness. Accordingly, I would reject Maududi's argument against contraception and family planning as being contrary to some of the very basic premises of an Islamic worldview.

Despite the kind of perspective that Maududi represents, it appears that the right to family planning is certainly part of the contemporary scholarly Islamic discourse. Based on sociological fieldwork in Morocco, researcher Donna Lee Bowen demonstrates that many of the local religious leaders who oppose contraception have relatively limited education in Islamic scholarship and their views are in sharp contrast with those who come from the more educated *ulama* class (Bowen 1998: 150–151). Given the Islamic scholarly legacy, as well as the demands of the current period, I would argue that opponents of family planning are not only inadequately informed but are lacking in judgement and the ability to articulate a dynamic and socially relevant Islamic response to challenges of the time.

In summary, it would appear that the contemporary need for family planning in the Muslim world is premised on the view that smaller families first reduce hardships on the family and on national resources and, second, support the conditions for the flourishing of human life. Both of these, I believe, are authentic and essential Islamic imperatives found in the fundamentals of the Qu'ranic worldview.

I would like to reiterate that, although the views of the learned scholars might be illuminating and helpful (or not), in Islam the individual believer retains the right to make his or her own decisions on the basis of being a moral agent (*khalifah*). For Muslims, these decisions need to be informed by the primary sources and the Islamic principles of justice, human well-being, mercy and compassion in which freedom is always accompanied by moral and spiritual responsibilities.

Abortion

In Islamic scholarship the positions on abortion are more varied and less consensual than the approaches to contraception. Historically, the Muslim legal positions range from unqualified permissibility of an abortion before 120 days into the pregnancy, on the one hand, to categorical prohibition of abortion altogether, on the other. Historically, even within a single legal school, the majority position was often accompanied by dissenting minority positions (Musallam 1983: 57–9).

Some of the key ethical and legal considerations in addressing the abortion question relate to understanding the nature of the foetus, the process of foetal development and the point at which the foetus is considered a human being. Though scientific inquiry has illuminated the process of foetal development with progressively more clarity, the question of when a foetus is considered a human being is open to varying interpretations. The following Qu'ranic verses are central to understanding some of the ways in which Muslim thinkers approach these issues:

> He creates you in the wombs of your mothers
> In stages, one after another
> In three veils of darkness
> Such is Allah, your Lord and Cherisher. (Q. 39: 6)

> We created the human being from a quintessence of clay
> Then we placed him as semen in a firm receptacle
> Then we formed the semen into a blood-like clot
> Then we formed the clot into a lump of flesh
> Then we made out of that lump, bones
> And clothed the bones with flesh
> Then we developed out of it another creation
> So Blessed is Allah the Best Creator. (Q. 23: 12–13)

Given these scriptural teachings, Muslim scholars have understood that the foetus undergoes a series of transformations beginning as an organism and becoming a human being. An authenticated prophetic tradition (*hadith*) of the Prophet provides a more detailed timeframe for understanding the pace of foetal development: 'Each of you is constituted in your mother's womb for 40 days as a *nutfa* (semen), then it becomes an *alaqa* (clot) for an equal period, then a *mudgha* (lump of flesh) for another equal period, then the angel is sent and he breathes the *ruh* (spirit) into it.'

Together the Qu'ranic verses and the prophetic tradition have been understood to describe a sequential process in which the foetus undergoes a series of changes and finally culminates in becoming a full human being when it is 'ensouled' (Qayyim al-Jawziyya 1933: 374–5). According to the Qu'ran, this culmination point denotes a significant shift because the foetal organism is transformed into something substantively different from its previous state, as is reflected in the verse 'then we developed out of it another creation' (a human being). In the prophetic tradition this same point of transition into a human being is described as the point at which the angel breathes the spirit into the foetus at 120 days.

Medieval Islamic scholars also found support for the Qur'anic position and the prophetic teachings from Greek medicine, which had a corresponding understanding of the stages of foetal development (Musallam 1983: 54). Contemporary medical technology has developed such that we are now able to detect vital signs of a foetus, such as brainwaves and heartbeat. Though these advances in medical knowledge are informative and help to illuminate decisions, they still do not provide us with definitive criteria for determining when a foetus becomes fully 'another creature' (a human being). Science can contribute to a description of the foetal development, but it is outside of scientific method to determine the point of spiritual transition into the full human essence. For human beings any designation of when a foetus constitutes a full human life can be contested because we are unable to know this unambiguously. Thus, revelation and prophetic inspiration remain crucial to understanding this issue from an Islamic perspective.

The narratives from the primary Islamic sources provide Muslim thinkers with a way to generate an estimated criterion for establishing personhood during the process of foetal development. This in turn has direct implications for the ethical and legal approaches to the question of abortion in Islam. The view that the foetus is ensouled at 120 days, thereby becoming a human being and thus a legal personality, was integrated into Islamic jurisprudence.[12] For example, if someone injures a pregnant woman causing her to miscarry the foetus, the amount of compensation due to her is based on the stage of foetal development. Causing the miscarriage of an ensouled or what is called a 'formed' foetus, is considered a criminal and religious offence and the mother must be compensated for the full blood money (diya) as though it were a case of a child already born (Musallam 1983: 57). A lesser remuneration is due if the foetus is considered 'unformed'. According to Islamic law, only a formed foetus which is miscarried or accidentally aborted has the right to inheritance (to pass on to relatives), to be named and to have a ritual burial. From this perspective, the abortion of a formed foetus (after 120 days) is considered a criminal offence and prohibited by all Islamic legal schools. Exceptions to this prohibition, however, include situations in which the mother's life is in danger, where the pregnancy is harming an already suckling child or where the foetus is expected to be deformed (Omran 1992: 192).

Relating to an abortion prior to the 120-day period, there are four different positions in classical Islam, which have been summarised by Shaykh Jad al-Haq (1983: 3093–109) in the following way:

> 1) Unconditional permission to terminate a pregnancy without a justification or foetal defect. This view is adopted by the Zaydi school, and some Hanafi and Shafi'i scholars. The Hanbali school allows abortion through the use of oral abortifacients within 40 days of conception.
>
> 2) Conditional permission to abort because of an acceptable justification. If there is an abortion without a valid reason in this period it is considered to be disapproved (makruh) but not forbidden (haram). This is the opinion of the majority of Hanafi and Shafi'i scholars.
>
> 3) Abortion is strongly disapproved (makruh). This is the view held by some Maliki jurists.

> 4) Abortion is unconditionally prohibited (*haram*). This reflects the other Maliki
> view, as well as the Zahiri, Ibadiyya and Imamiyya legal schools.[13]

Such diversity in perspectives characterises the Islamic legal canon, which contains contrary positions in which both permissibility and prohibition of abortion are considered legitimate. This range of positions suggests flexibility in the way that Muslim societies have historically approached the issue of abortion. Moreover, the extensive discussions of specific types of abortifacients in medical manuals of the classical Islamic world reflect that historically it was a part of the social reality.

However, the range of approaches in the legal canon is not to be confused with a casual approach to human life – this is evidently not the case, as any perusal of the Qu'ran and Islamic legal texts will demonstrate. In fact, the minority of classical legal scholars who forbid abortion do not differ with other scholars on the process of foetal development, but prohibit abortion because of their religious reverence for the potentiality of human life. Islam teaches the sanctity of human life and shows a profound respect for its potential. Nonetheless, the rightful concern for a foetus needs to be situated in a larger context, juxtaposed and weighted in relation to the broader well-being of the mother, the family and the society. Islam is a religion of balance and moderation that seeks to maximise the well-being of all elements in a society.

This type of circumspection and balanced judgement characterise the statement of the former Grand Shaykh of Al-Azhar, Sayed Tantawi (d. 2010), who supported the *fatwa* (juristic response) that abortion was permissible in the case of rape and that the rape survivor had the right to privacy about her experience (Tadros 1998). In 2000, the Ayatollah Ali Khameni in Iran issued a *fatwa* in favour of abortion for foetuses under 10 weeks that were tested with a genetic blood disorder of *thalassemia* (*Iranian Times* 2000) Also in Iran, the Grand Ayatollah Yusuf Saanei issued a *fatwa* that permits abortion in the first trimester and not only for reasons of the mother's health or foetal abnormalities. In an interview reported in the *Los Angeles Times* he stated that Islam is a religion of compassion and that in the event of serious problems, abortion is permitted (Wright 2000).

In a submission to the South African parliament, the Judicial Committee of the Islamic Council of South Africa recognised the right to terminate a pregnancy for a reasonable cause before 120 days. This included, among others, the impairment of the mental capacity or the integrity of the woman as well as the ability and willingness of the woman to accept the responsibility of parenthood (Islamic Council of South Africa 1995). Finally, contemporary legal scholar Ebrahim Moosa, drawing on the legal opinions of Abd al-Hayy al-Laknawi, the 19th century Indian Hanafi scholar, illustrates how some traditional legal thinkers also permitted abortion in the case of pregnancy outside of wedlock (Moosa forthcoming) He speculates that Al-Laknawi's legal reasoning was possibly informed by the fact that the future prospects of an unwed mother would be radically reduced in his society, and thus the Indian jurist recommended the radical act to terminate advanced pregnancies arising from sex out of wedlock. For him it was a case of the lesser of two evils.

It is not surprising that, despite the diversity characterising Islamic legal perspectives on abortion, which even include views of its permissibility, the realities of many contemporary Muslim societies reflect a tendency to adopt a more rigid approach.

Part of this motivation, rightfully, is to ensure that people do not adopt an uncritical acceptance of abortions, because the decision to terminate a potential realisation of a human life is a grave decision not to be taken lightly or without circumspection. Indeed, the gravity of this whole enterprise bolsters the case for a responsible approach to family planning, including reliable use of contraception, which would for the most part pre-empt the need for abortion.

In fact, some of the contemporary practices of abortion based on the gender of the foetus are ethically very problematic. From the 1980s there has been a growing practice in India, China and South Korea of aborting female foetuses based on ultrasound tests (Dugger 2001). This reflects misogyny and constitutes a direct contrast to Qu'ranic ethics, which strongly condemn the hatred of 'femalehood'. Thus I would propose that from an Islamic ethical perspective aborting a foetus on the basis of gender is unjustifiable.

For more people, however, abortion is neither based on the gender of the foetus, nor is it an easy or thoughtless decision. It involves much anguish and internal struggle. In the event that such a decision is deemed necessary, it is important to remember that the God of the Qu'ran is consistently described through the divine qualities of mercy and compassion. In fact these two portals of God's self-revelation are constantly invoked by Muslims throughout their daily activity. It is vital to move from invocation to enactment. The ways in which the realities of compassion and mercy manifest themselves in difficult situations require an awareness of and a response to the suffering and complexity of human lives.

For those who oppose abortion, a compassionate and merciful attitude would include focusing on transforming social structures so that having children does not create hardships for the mother, the family or for the society. This would be a more socially constructive use of energy than the crusade against abortion. A concern for the welfare of the foetus without a concern for its continuing welfare as a human being reflects a limited, if not hypocritical, approach.

In Islam, if an individual or a couple is considering the possibility of an abortion, it is imperative that they do so with a full awareness of the gravity of such a decision. In this situation, I would present that being a *khalifah* or moral agent requires careful consideration of all the factors, weighing up the different demands and needs of the specific situation and, as in all things, intentionally keeping a sense of *taqwa* or God-consciousness at the forefront. Islamically, the freedom to act as the *khalifah* is intrinsically accompanied by accountability and responsibilities at the personal, social and religious levels. Often the specifics of a given context determine what the most responsible alternative is. Given these considerations, from within the Islamic perspective there is room for a pro-choice perspective wherein individuals' *khalifah* engages all sources of Islamic guidance – the Qu'ran, the prophetic traditions, the legal positions, as well as a human being's own intellectual, moral and ethical capacities to inform a decision about abortion.

In conclusion, it is my view that a contemporary Islamic ethical perspective on family planning, contraception and abortion requires a holistic vision of the problems of our era. We are confronted with the realities of socio-economic injustice, sexism, overpopulation and diminishing resources, to name but a few. There is a need for Muslims to assess the needs of the time in terms of an understanding of the political, social and economic realities of their respective contexts. It is crucial that Muslims move beyond purely defensive posturing and undertake *khilafah* by adopting a genuinely engaged and informed approach to the world.

The Islamic legacy provides a rich heritage of human agency and creative, socially relevant thinking. As a religion, Islam provides its adherents with multiple resources to implement progressive social visions premised on the values of human freedom accompanied by responsibility, of human well-being with optimal spiritual development, and of justice tempered with mercy and compassion. It is in the interests of humanity that Muslims bring all these spiritual treasures to the discussion about family planning, contraception and abortion.

Notes

1. This article was first published in 2003 under the title 'Family planning, contraception and abortion in Islam: undertaking *khilafah*: moral agency, justice and compassion' in Daniel C. Maguire (ed) *Sacred Rights: The Case for Contraception and Abortion in World Religions*, Oxford, Oxford University Press. Republished with permission.
2. Moreover, in situating Qur'anic revelation in seventh century Meccan society, this notion of *taqwa* as being the sole criterion for human worth provided a sweeping critique of the very basis of the social formation that was characterised by socio-economic, gender and tribal hierarchies.
3. This synergy is encapsulated by the Sufi teacher Shaykh Bawa Muhaiyaddeen, who states, 'If we are true believers, we will not see any difference between others and ourselves. We will see only One. We will see Allah, one human race, and one justice for all. That justice and truth is the strength of Islam' (Muhaiyaddeen 1987: 26).
4. The realities of structural economic imbalances internationally were borne out by a 1996 UN development report, which stated that the world's 358 billionaires were wealthier than the combined annual income of countries with 45 per cent of the world's population (Loy 1997). By 1995 the average CEO of a large US corporation received a compensation package of more than $3.7 million annually (Korten 1995: 218). This coexists with the reality of an estimated 900 million malnourished people worldwide, 40 million of whom die from hunger and poverty-related causes (Ponting 1991: 245). From these statistics alone, it is clear that the question of equitable wealth distribution and economic justice are urgent human ethical concerns.
5. Moreover, it is noteworthy that in defining the believer, the Qu'ran repeatedly includes wealth sharing as a criteria of genuine belief in God (Q. 9: 71; Q. 13: 22; Q. 23: 1–5). Accordingly, the category of worship (*ibadat*) in Islam is not restricted only to ritual prayers but includes various types of socio-economic responsibilities, such as giving charity to the needy, feeding the hungry and taking care of the orphans. Even the ritual worship (*salat*), which is a duty prescribed to every Muslim to perform five times a day, is itself imbued with various levels of social responsibility. For example, one Qu'ranic rationale for *salat* is that it creates a pervasive God-consciousness, thereby enabling people to refrain from injustice – in other words, 'establish regular prayer for prayer restrains from shameful and unjust deeds and remembrance of God is the greatest thing in life without doubt. And Allah knows the deeds that you do' (Q. 29: 45). Furthermore, one's worship is only considered spiritually meaningful when accompanied by ethical behaviour in relation to social need: 'Do you see the one who gives a lie to the faith? Such a one is he who repulses the orphan and does not encourage the feeding of the indigent, so woe unto the worshippers who are neglectful of worship who only want to be seen but deny the needs of those around them' (Q. 107: 1–7). Hence prayer that does not coexist with the worshippers' awareness of the plight of other human beings and related ethical actions is contrary to spiritual truth and thus does not constitute real prayer.
6. With the advances of global capitalism, increasing numbers of multinational corporations

from richer nations in the world move their factories to poorer countries with the cheapest labour and where governments are most tolerant of exploitative labour practices in order to retain foreign investment. For a detailed account of the impact of corporate capitalism on global markets, see Greider 1997.

7. Muslims committed to ideals of human equality advocate a holistic reading of the Qu'ranic text, which places the different verses on gender in relationship to one another and historically contextualises the revelation to derive a full picture of the relevant Qu'ranic teachings (Wadud 1999). For a recent analysis on the deep spiritual roots of gender equality and its practical implications in the legal sphere, see Shaikh (2009). This type of exegetical work provides a stark contrast to the approach of Muslim patriarchs who interpret and prioritise specific Qu'ranic verses in ways that buttress their ideologies of male hegemony.

8. Islam also recognises the spiritual dimensions of sexuality, as explored by medieval mystical philosopher Ibn Arabi, who stated that in accordance with the spiritual state of the partners, the act of sexual union has the possibilities for unparalleled mystical unveilings and experiences of the divine (Al-Arabi 1980: 274).

9. These include Abu Jafar Tahawi (d. 933) in his *Sharh Maani al Athar*; Ibn al Qayyim (d.1350) in his *Zad al Ma'ad'*; Ibn Hajjar Al-Askalani (d.1449) in his *Fath al Bari*; and Al-Shawkani (d.1830) in his *Nayl al-Awtar*.

10. Here I have summarised some of the key arguments found in the discussions and declarations of these various contemporary conferences and publications.

11. For a discussion on the construction of gender ideology and sexuality, see Shaikh's (1997) article on exegetical violence.

12. For detailed legal implications of the religious view of foetal development, see Muhammad Salaam Madkur (1969).

13 The Zahiri, Ibadiyya and Imammiyya schools all have limited followings.

References

Abu, Zahra (1962) 'Tanzim al Nasl', *Liwa al Islam* 16(II), cited in Omran, Abdel Rahim (1994) *Family Planning in the Legacy of Islam*, London, Routledge

Akbar, Ahmad and Donnan, Hastings (1994) *Islam, Globlisation and Postmodernity*, London, Routledge

Al-Arabi, I. (1980) *Bezels of Wisdom*, trans Austin, R.W.J, New Jersey, Paulist Press

Al-Haq, Jad Ali Jad al-Haq (1983) 'al-Fatawa al Islamiyya min Dar al-Ifta al-Misriyya', *Wazara al-Awqaf/ al Majlis al-A'la li al Shu'un al-Islamiyya* 9: 3093–109

Al-Hibri, Azizah (2000) 'An introduction to Muslim women's rights', in Webb, G. (ed) *Windows of Faith: Muslim Women Scholar-Activists in North America*, Syracuse, Syracuse University Press

Bowen, Donna Lee (1998) 'Interpretations of family planning: reconciling Islam and development' in Waugh, E. and Denny, F. (eds) *The Shaping of an American Islamic Discourse*, Atlanta, Scholars Press

Daniel, N. (1960) *Islam and the West: The Making of an Image*, Edinburgh University Press

Dugger, Celia (2001) 'Abortion in India is strongly tipping scales against girls', *New York Times*, 22 April

Farah, M. (1984) *Marriage and Sexuality in Islam: A Translation of Al-Ghazali's Book on the Etiquette of Marriage from the Ihya*, Salt Lake City, University of Utah Press

Gorman, C. (1994) 'Clash of wills in Cairo', *Time Magazine*, 12 September, http://www.time. com/time/magazine/article/0,9171,981409-1,00.html, accessed 14 December 2010

Greider, William (1997) *One World, Ready or Not: The Manic Logic of Global Capitalism*, New York, Simon and Schuster

Hassan, Riffat (2000) 'Human Rights in the Qu'ranic Perspective', in Webb, G. (ed) *Windows of Faith: Muslim Women Scholar-Activists in North America*, Syracuse, Syracuse University Press

Islamic Council of South Africa, Judicial Committee (1995) 'Memorandum on abortion: submission to the parliamentary committee on abortion and sterilisation', Cape Town, May

Korten, David (1995) *When Corporations Rule the World*, Connecticut, Kumarian Press

Loy, David (1997) 'Religion and the market', http://www.religiousconsultation.org /loy.htm, accessed 20 January 2011

Madkur, Muhammad Salaam (1969) *Al-Janin wa Ahkam al-muta'alliqa bihi fi al-fiqh*, Cairo

Maguire, D. and Rasmussen, L. (1997) *Ethics for a Small Planet: New Horizons on Population, Consumption and Ecology*, Albany, State University of New York Press

Maududi, Maulana (1974) *Birth Control*, trans Ahmad, K. and Faruqi, M.I., Lahore, Islamic Publications Ltd

Ministries of Waqfs and Information (1994) 'Islam's attitude toward family planning', Cairo, Egypt Ministries of Waqfs and Information

Moosa, Ebrahim (1997) 'Prospects for Muslim law in South Africa: a history and recent developments' in Cotrane, E. and Mallat, C. (eds) *Yearbook of Islamic and Middle Eastern Law*, The Hague, Kluwer Law International

—— (forthcoming) *Essays in Islamic Law*, The Hague, Kluwer Law International

Muhaiyaddeen, M.R. Bawa (1987) *Islam and World Peace: Explanations of a Sufi*, Philadelphia, The Fellowship Press

Musallam, B. (1983) *Sex and Society in Islam*, Cambridge, Cambridge University Press

Noakes, G. (1995) 'Cairo population conference still controversial', *Washington Report on Middle East Affairs*, April/May

Omran, Abdel Rahim (1992) *Family Planning in the Legacy of Islam*, London, Routledge

Ponting, Clive (1991) *A Green History of the World*, New York, Penguin Books

Qayyim al-Jawziyya, Ibn (1933) *Al-Tibyan fi aqsam al-Qur'an*, Cairo, Fadak Books

Rahman, Fazlur (1980) *Major Themes of the Qu'ran*, Minneapolis, Bibliotheca Islamica

—— (1982) 'The status of women in Islam: a modernist interpretation', in Papanek, Hannah and Minault, Gail (1982) (eds) *Separate Worlds: Studies of Purdah in South Asia*, New Delhi, South Asia Book

Shaikh, Sa'diyya (1997) 'Exegetical violence: Nushuz in Qu'ranic gender ideology', *Journal for Islamic Studies* 17: 49–73

—— (2009) 'In search of *Al-Insan*: Sufism, Islamic Law and Gender', *Journal of the American Academy of Religion* 77(4): 781–822

Tadros, Mariz (1998) 'The shame of it', *Al-Ahram* (weekly online), 3–9 December

The Iranian Times (2000) 'Doctors refuse abortion for blood disorder', 18 September, http://www.iranian.com/Times/2000/Septemberc/Haraz/rights.html#187, accessed 14 December 2010

Wadud, Amina (1999) *Qu'ran and Woman: Rereading the Sacred Text from a Woman's Perspective*, New York, Oxford University Press

Wright, Robin (2000) 'Iran now a hotbed of Islamic reforms', *Los Angeles Times*, 29 December

38

Guilty until proven innocent: politics versus the press in defence of reproductive rights in Zambia

Wilma Nchito

> I wanted them to see the suffering of a mother, instead they called it pornography.
> *Chansa Kabwela, News editor*, The Post, *Lusaka, Zambia*

Background

The case of Chansa Kabwela made headlines between July and November 2009. It generated interest both in Zambia and internationally not because of the 'crime' allegedly committed but because a news editor of *The Post* – a newspaper critical of the ruling government – was involved and the government had instigated the arrest. The events unfolded as follows:

9 June – A distraught husband presented to *The Post* digital photographs of a woman in the process of giving birth to a lifeless baby in breech position. He wanted the paper to publish the pictures. Nurses and other health workers were on strike and the woman had been to two clinics before trying the University Teaching Hospital, where the controversial photographs were taken.

10 June – Chansa Kabwela, *The Post's* news editor, sent a letter with photographs attached to the Zambian Vice-President George Kunda, the Minister of Health, the Non-Governmental Organisations Coordinating Council (NGOCC), the Council of Churches and women's groups, to try to get them to do something about the strike, which had been going on for more than a month with no end in sight.

24 June – President Bwezani Banda addressed a press conference at which he brought up the issue of the photographs, referring to them as 'pornographic', and expressed his wish that the photographer be arrested.

29 June – The strike by medical workers ended.

13 July – Chansa Kabwela was arrested and charged with one count of 'circulating obscene materials ... with intent to corrupt morals'. She faced a minimum of five years in prison.

5 August – Chansa Kabwela's trial commenced.

16 November – Chansa Kabwela was acquitted.

Labour is labour

The president's reference to the photographs as 'pornographic' was based on two assumptions, both later proving to be embarrassing. First, he assumed that the photographer worked for *The Post* and, second, he assumed that the person behind the whole saga was male. As it turned out, the person responsible for the grotesque photographs was the father of the dead child and husband to the poor woman. He had nothing to do with the newspaper. It also turned out that the person who would eventually appear in court was Kabwela, an extremely feminine and petite woman and the news editor of *The Post*. Because Chansa is a unisex name among the Bemba people, the president could not confirm her gender from the name. He said:

> Just because you are morbid and peculiar you sent photographers to go and
> take pictures of your mother naked. Shame on you! And I hope that there
> are laws in this country to stop young men from taking pornography. I hope
> those responsible for the law of this country will pursue this matter. (*The Post*
> 2009a: 4)

The president claimed that he had been unable to look at the picture but later contradicted himself when he said that he had looked at the pictures and had thrown them away (*The Post* 2009a: 4). At this point very few people in the country were aware of the existence of the said photographs and, instead of stirring collective outrage against the photographer or the newspaper, many could not understand the context of the president's reaction. The question of whether the photographs were pornographic became a laughing matter, as people found it extremely odd that the president referred to them as such. The other embarrassing point was that the editor was female. It was clear to all that the target of the president's wrath had been the editor of *The Post* and he had missed his target badly.

From whatever angle we might scrutinise the said photographs, they would never pass as pornographic and it seems this became clear to the police, who could not come up with an appropriate charge and instead charged Chansa with distributing obscene material contrary to section 177(1)(a) of the Penal Code Act. Muna Ndulo (2009), a professor of law, highlighted the failure of three institutions: the police service, the judiciary and the office of the director of public prosecutions (DPP).

The first time that the nation heard about the photographs was from the president's press conference. He had been complaining about how deceptive *The Post* had become and had given an illustration of the picture, featured in an earlier edition, of himself and a female minister (who had earlier resigned) appearing to be sitting next to each other. He had not been sitting next to her but the angle at which the picture had been taken made it appear so and he was not happy about the inference. He remarked, 'This is manipulation, this is lies, everybody knows that *The Post* lied … what are you trying to imply?' (*The Post* 2009a: 4). This incident led the president to bring up the issue of the photographs, which had been sent to the vice president, of a poor woman who had given birth to a baby in breech position. The nurses had been on strike for close to six weeks and the situation was dire. Patients were being sent home and some hospital wards were closed and occupied by police officers.

It is against this backdrop that the poor woman had gone into labour and, after two futile attempts to get help from private clinics, the desperate husband had brought her to the main University Teaching Hospital where the fateful pictures had been taken in the car park. By the time the woman reached the hospital the baby had been partially born and its head was still stuck inside the mother, presenting a disturbing sight. It is probably the fact that no nursing staff ran to assist the woman, despite her condition, which prompted her husband to take pictures of her, throwing all morality and African taboos to the winds. It is even possible that for some time the man had considered the possibility of losing his wife and had wanted final pictures of her and their son who had not been given a chance to live.

Could this man have possibly had pornography on his mind when he took the pictures? His actions in the days that followed made his intentions explicitly clear. He had two photographs printed and delivered them to *The Post* editorial room, demanding that they publish the pictures to show the devastation of the strike. He did not anticipate that the photographs would lead to the incarceration of the news editor; if he had known, he would have probably acted otherwise.

The news editor happened to be the 30-year-old Kabwela who, after some in-house consultations, decided not to publish the photographs because they were too distressing and graphic. Instead, she decided that in order to bring the drastic effects of the strike to the attention of the highest authority in the land, the pictures should be sent to a few prominent and influential people and groups. This is how the pictures found their way to the desks of the vice-president, the secretary to cabinet, the Archbishop of Lusaka, the minister of health, Women for Change (an NGO) and the NGOCC. The president was at the time in South Africa, which is why the pictures were sent to the vice-president. The letter accompanying the pictures stated that the newspaper wanted the recipients to intervene in the strike by health workers and bring it to an end as quickly as possible. Part of the letter read:

> I write to bring your attention to images that we have difficulty to publish in our newspaper of the very desperate situation at our hospitals arising from the ongoing strike. I am doing this in the hope that these pictures will move you and your colleagues to take quick action and bring this strike to an end. Enclosed are the very disturbing pictures from the University Teaching Hospital (UTH) in Lusaka that have been brought to our newsroom. (MISA 2009)

Axe or applaud?

Whereas the action taken by *The Post* would have been commendable under normal circumstances, in this case the newspaper was castigated by a sector of society – a typical case of 'shooting the messenger'. It was inconceivable that the head of state would focus on the photographs and not the rationale behind sending them. Why had the strike been allowed to continue for such a long time? What was government doing about it apart from threatening to fire the nurses and recruit replacements from neighbouring Zimbabwe? The fact that there was silence on the part of government concerning responsibility for the situation, or to express empathy with the woman in the picture and her family, spoke volumes.

Ordinarily one would have expected the recipients to have engaged the health workers in dialogue and used the story in the pictures as a tragic example, but instead the paper faced condemnation. The first to openly condemn the paper was the president. After the president's tirade, the women's movement and the NGOCC wrote a letter of complaint to *The Post* stating that the paper had not taken into account the woman's right to privacy. The women's movement had also concluded that the paper was the originator of the photographs and thus sought to remind them to consider women's rights. The news editor dutifully wrote an apology to the women's movement, which was published in all the dailies. In this case it would appear that the women's movement chose to look at the issue from one angle and ignore other facets of the case. Many questioned why the women's movement, for example, was not advocating for the woman's right to access safe reproductive health facilities, which had been crippled by the strike and the government's uncompromising stance.

The president's displeasure with the newspaper probably influenced his decision to focus on the photographs and the originator, rather than the reasons why a woman was delivering a baby outside a hospital. The strike had not been called off at this point and the president could have used the photographs to appeal to the conscience of health workers to pick up their tools and return to work. Instead of ensuring that he had the correct facts, the president and his handlers acted on incorrect assumptions. It should be noted that during the strike there was at least one other case of a woman giving birth in the open, this time at a hospital bus stop on the Copperbelt. This case did not receive any coverage or mention by the president.

Describing the photographs as pornographic generated a lot of interest and the news spread like wild fire across the internet. Everyone wanted to see if they were really pornographic and if the president's accusation had merit. Many who saw the pictures totally disagreed with the president and questioned the exact meaning of the term 'pornography'. The following week the media was awash with comments from the public, most rejecting the president's 'pornographic' label. 'Labour is labour not pornography' read the inscription on a tee-shirt worn by a prominent Zambian musician who had escorted Kabwela to court. Many could not understand how the president could find the process of childbirth pornographic. This led to many discussions on what legally constituted pornography. It was pointed out that pornography constituted images that were sensual and arousing and it followed that people questioned how the president could have found the pictures of the distraught woman giving birth arousing. This led many to conclude that *The Post* was being targeted and the issue was not about the content of the photographs. The general public repeatedly called upon the police to withdraw the case.

The lack of independence of the police immediately became clear when the charge was considered. The charge also exposed the president's assumptions that the person behind the lens was employed by *The Post*. At this point the government could have saved face if the DPP had withdrawn the case. It was very clear even to a lay person that the police had no case. First, the material was not of the nature that could corrupt morals and, second, giving the photographs to five prominent leaders did not amount to circulation. Should the person who showed the photographs to the president also have been charged with circulating obscene materials? Why, for instance, did the police not pursue the husband for having taken the pictures? It was very clear that government had its daggers drawn and was not going to retreat whether or not it was on the right path, and so the case against Kabwela went to court.

Within the context of the strike we might well have excused the actions of the news editor. The situation was extraordinary and very serious so it was understandable that the news editor took drastic measures to try to highlight the gravity of the situation. The intended purpose was to bring the strike to a swift end and thus save lives. Put in its proper context, we would have expected the president to exercise restraint. He himself confessed to having opted to seek medical attention in South Africa because the nurses were on strike. At the time he addressed the press conference, nurses were picketing outside hospitals and clinics, refusing to work.

The president, though displaying anger toward *The Post*, showed no compassion for the woman; he did not sympathise with her or her family about the loss of a child, as would be expected in Zambian society. He also did not take responsibility as head of state. His actions showed that clearly he did not care about what had transpired but cared more about the woman's privacy or lack of it. He did not take the opportunity to appeal to health workers to go back to work after the strike had endangered a life and caused the death of the infant.

The women's movement also missed the opportunity to raise its voice for reproductive rights. Zambia has one of the highest maternal mortality rates in the world and the photographs could have been used to raise awareness of this fact. Instead of fighting for improved conditions of service for medical staff to improve healthcare service delivery, the women's movement joined the president in castigating the newspaper for distributing 'offensive' material and not considering the woman's privacy. The chairperson of the NGOCC wrote: 'We have been extremely shocked and disgusted at the pictures you have circulated of a woman in child birth ... Not only is it a gross violation of the woman's privacy and dignity but more so of the sanctity of human life' (*The New York Times* 2009). In her rather sarcastic response, Kabwela wrote:

> We know very little about women's issues. Our intention was not to violate the rights of that woman or to offend yourselves as your letter indicates. And for that we are extremely sorry. We have learnt our lesson, and we will know how to conduct ourselves in the future over issues of this nature. Please excuse and forgive our ignorance, we are not polymaths. (*New York Times* 2009)

The fact that *The Post*, which is known to publish images of topless initiates and skimpily dressed revellers, opted not to publish these particular pictures because they were too graphic should have said something about its motives, but the women's movement chose to overlook this. Many felt that the response of the women's movement was a letdown. Instead of holding the government accountable for developing policies that uphold reproductive rights, the movement was more concerned with privacy.

Improved health services are part of reproductive rights (Corrêa 1994), but in this case the woman in the pictures was denied her rights and the women's movement did not stand up for her. We can only speculate as to why this route was chosen by the women's movement. It appears the latter somehow found it prudent to castigate the newspaper and not hold government to account for its failure to provide and ensure adequate health services. The women's movement should have advised the president that the photographs were not pornographic.

Apart from a few entries on the internet, no one said anything about the husband. He had taken the photographs and initially the president had said the photographer should be locked up. Why is it then that the police did not call him for questioning? Didn't *The Post* need to prove that it was not the originator of the said photographs? This exposed the failure of the police to 'act as an independent professional force' (Ndulo 2009). The police deliberately overlooked the photographer and targeted *The Post*. During the same period a woman gave birth in a police cell because the officer on duty had ignored her cries of distress. Strangely enough the officer on duty was charged with negligence and locked up. The president and his sympathisers focused on the messenger and did nothing about the message. As Kabwela herself said, 'I wanted to bring and end to suffering; instead, they saw pornography' (*The New York Times* 2009).

Acquittal

After hearing the testimonies of 10 state witnesses over a period of three months, the magistrate was ready to deliver his ruling. The reports of the witnesses, who were mostly women, focused on how they had been shocked, embarrassed or upset at the sight of the photographs. It was not surprising that none reported experiencing the 'corruption of their morals', which would have spoken directly to the charge against Kabwela. Some witnesses had testified that by presenting the images of childbirth, which is taboo, Kabwela had violated local customs. One testified that she 'felt the woman's integrity was exposed and a Zambian woman's pride was at stake' (*Zambia Daily Mail* 2009). Some witnesses queried whether the photographs had really been taken in the hospital carpark.

However, the witnesses failed to prove that the photographs were obscene or had in any way corrupted their morals. They also failed to prove that they were independent and not biased. It was difficult to explain, for instance, why one of the witnesses, an obstetrician, testified that they had cried upon seeing the photographs. In a country in which only half of the births are assisted by medical staff (Bryne 1994: 34) and maternal mortality is at 729 per 100,000 women (CSO et al 2009: 259), we would expect that such a professional had seen similarly horrific sights before. It was also surprising that none of the witnesses expressed concern that the woman had been forced to give birth in the car park. Instead, issues of culture, morality, pride and even whether the photographs had actually been taken in the car park were raised.

Kabwela was eventually acquitted on 16 November by Magistrate Kafunda. The magistrate ruled that by sending the photographs to the five people, the defendant had indeed circulated them and this had not been contested. He, however, ruled that 'conduct that may depart from such morals is not obscene' (*The Post* 2009a: 4). The magistrate expressed his sympathy with the witnesses about the emotional turmoil the photographs might have caused them but said that did not amount to 'corruption of morals' (*The Post* 2009a: 4). The prosecution had failed to prove two things: obscenity and corruption of morals. So what had the president seen? Many felt that the magistrate had ruled correctly and had acted independently.

The editor's view

After the acquittal, Kabwela had the opportunity to air her views on the saga. She gave a number of interviews to various media. She was very clear about one thing – her innocence. She stated that from the time she was arrested she waited for her day in court. Kabwela knew that it was not she who was the target, but her employer, *The Post*, and its proprietor Fred M'membe. According to Kabwela, the saga should not have happened and many Zambians agreed with her. She received immense support – people from all walks of life thronged to the court each time the case was being heard. Human rights activists, feminists, musicians, the press and ordinary citizens expressed their solidarity with Kabwela and *The Post*.

In Kabwela's view, if people were prepared to be strict moralists, then they should have been concerned that the woman had had no privacy while being carted around town in search of medical attention. As she said, 'If as a country we value culture very much and we want to promote morality, then, let's provide the necessary services for the people. Let's provide medical care so that people are not exposed' (*The Post* 2009a).

Medical staff have over the years demanded a living wage but have been ignored. Staffing levels in government health institutions have been drastically reduced and the remaining staff are overworked and frustrated. The Kabwela case should have exposed the government's shortcomings in the provision of healthcare for Zambian citizens, but instead it served to discredit a newspaper with which it has had serious and frequent confrontations in the past. Unfortunately, the case was extremely weak and the president was exposed.

Conclusion: what next?

In conclusion, it is not wrong to suggest that things could have been done differently. If the president had not raised the issue at the press conference, the existence of the photographs would not have been exposed to the nation. Perhaps it was a good thing that the president brought the issue into the limelight, although he was driven by a different motive. It might be a beneficial reference point when health workers contemplate withdrawing their labour in future.

It is not possible at this stage to predict the impact of the Kabwela case on the collective conscience of health workers. It is also not possible to predict whether the president will stop exerting undue influence on the police force. Further, it is impossible to predict the reaction of the public to future cases that might be frivolous and vexatious.

That the case saw the light of day reaffirmed the suspicion of many that the police worked under orders from the president. When President Banda said, 'I hope that there are laws in this country to stop young men from taking pornography. I hope those responsible for the law of this country will pursue this matter' (*The Post*, 2009b), it was just as good as saying 'go and arrest them whether or not you have a prima facie case'. How else could the prompt reaction of the police be explained? They had not seen the photographs and therefore had to first search the offices of *The Post* and the news editor's house. An attempt was made to link a payment of an amount of money to the distribution of the photographs so Kabwela's bank accounts were probed as well. The allegation was that she had been paid by someone to do what she did. This angle of the investigation was a dead end. We were left wondering whether the president would have reacted in the same manner had he known that his accusation was directed at a young woman and not a man, as he had expected. Would he have come out so strongly?

The Kabwela case showed that the police service was not as independent as it should have been. The cry for help by the woman's husband went unheard and instead he had to deal with being responsible for the possible incarceration of a newspaper editor. The whole affair could have and should have been handled differently in a more discreet manner because it was clear that no crime was committed. The case also showed that the general public did not agree with the sentiments of the head of state. Although many were relieved at the acquittal, the feeling was that the case had been a waste of time and should have been stopped by the DPP. The women's movement also failed to take a stand for the improvement of reproductive rights, choosing instead to stand for the right to privacy.

It is hoped that all those who reacted on impulse in this case will refrain from doing so in future. At the end of the day the case gave the Zambian media a new heroine in the diminutive form of Chansa Kabwela.

References

Bryne, B. (1994) 'Gender profile of Zambia', *BRIDGE*, Institute of Development Studies, Brighton, University of Sussex, http://www.bridge.ids.ac.uk/reports/re29c.pdf, accessed 6 November 2010

Corrêa, S. (1994) *Population and Reproductive Rights: Feminist Perspectives From the South*, London, Zed Books in association with DAWN

Central Statistical Office (CSO), Ministry of Health (MOH), Tropical Disease Research Centre (TDRC), University of Zambia and Macro International Inc (2009) *Zambia Demographic and Health Survey, 2007*, Calverton, CSO and Macro International Inc

Media Institute of Southern Africa (MISA) (2009), 'Trial against Post news editor Chansa Kabwela commences', 28 August, http://www.misazambia.org.zm/media/news/viewnews.cgi?category=2&id=1251455273, accessed 12 September 2009

Ndulo, Muna (2009) 'The Chansa Kabwela trial: a comedy of errors', *The Post*, 17 July

The New York Times (2009) 'In Zambia, pictures of birth, mailed as protest, bring arrest', 14 July, http://www.nytimes.com/2009/07/14/world/africa/14zambia.html?_r=1&pagewanted=print, accessed 12 September 2009

The Post (2009a) 'Kafunda acquits Kabwela', 17 November
The Post (2009b) 'The Chansa Kabwela trial', 29 November
Zambia Daily Mail (2009) 'Labour picture circulation wrong say witnesses', 7 August.

39

Abortion: a conversation with a taxi driver

Hope Chigudu

It is 8.30 in the morning, close to Christmas, a busy time in Nairobi's heavy traffic. The organisation I am visiting is close to a Catholic church in Kariobangi, a high-density area outside 'the green city in the sun'. It will take me about 45 minutes to get there. It is therefore important that I get a good comfortable taxi and use the time to prepare for the meeting. I approach a fairly new taxi cab.

HC: Could you kindly take me to organisation X? It's close to the Catholic church in Kariobangi north.

TD: I know where it is, I am a Catholic.

(*HC settles down in the back seat of the taxi in a reflective mood but TD starts a conversation. He does not seem to realise that HC has closed her eyes. He is probably being friendly and wants to introduce himself.*)

TD: I started working as a taxi driver two years ago, after retirement. Before that, I was working for the Canadian embassy. I am still strong and want to continue working. Are you Kenyan?

HC. No, I'm from many places including Uganda and Zimbabwe.

TD: I know Uganda very well. When I was working for the Canadian embassy, I went to every part of Uganda with my bosses. For example, I have been to Gulu and other parts of northern Uganda. In Kampala I used to stay at Grand Imperial Hotel while my boss stayed at Serena. He wanted me to stay close to him. I used to walk across the hotel and eat *matooke* with the ordinary people. Aha! Those were great days.

HC: (*without interest*) You know Uganda.

TD: (*warming to the conversation*) There are many prostitutes in Kampala. Just walk around the Grand Imperial and the Sheraton at night. It's really bad. How can a person decide to earn money by selling her body? Some of these women have the potential to be great wives. But they live in sin. Do you know that one time I saw a pregnant prostitute near Grand Imperial but a few days later, her stomach was as flat as the stone we use for grinding millet? I asked her what happened and she simply said, 'Aborted'. Then she swung her body and walked away. (*Is TD salivating? Can't see his face properly.*) She uprooted what some man had planted in her garden. She killed a man's baby.

HC: (*The body wants to ignore him but the spirit is restless.*) Have you ever engaged with the women you call prostitutes so as to know and probably even appreciate their story?

TD: (*disdainfully*) Engaged with prostitutes? Madam sister, I told you I was a good Christian. Do you really think it is all right for a woman to uproot a seed a man put in her garden? How would you feel if someone uprooted your crops without your permission?

HC: (*Seeds/garden ... why is he using these words?*) If it's my garden, then it is mine; I own it and I know what is good for it and what is poisonous. Whoever sows in it does so at his own risk. I have the right to determine what kinds of seeds are suitable for my garden and when they should be sown. It's also my right to assess if the resources (money, energy, ability and state of mind) I have can nurture and tend to the crops. However, you are using the wrong imagery. You call children crops but crops come and go; children don't. They are more demanding.

TD: Huh?

HC: Anyway, to continue with your seed story, some seeds are poisonous and some are even forcibly sown. Others are planted without consideration of the situation and circumstances. You don't have to go far, look at the streets of Nairobi and you will appreciate the dangers of random, malicious, poisonous and careless seeding. All those street children; where are their fathers?

TD: The children are on the streets because of women who don't want to be wives. A man sows; a woman takes care of the garden and its products.

HC: (*Must not lose temper, this is an interesting conversation.*) If it's a woman's own garden, should she not choose when...

TD: (*He turns to look at me as if I have insulted him.*) Do women have their own gardens? Madam, it was Mrs Eva Adam whom we read about in the bible who sinned and not Adam. Come to think of it, the Original Sin mentioned in Genesis was a blessing in disguise; it's on account of that sin that God gave a woman's garden to a man, to till and control: 'Woman, you will always submit to a man', thus sayeth Jehovah God. The garden you are talking about belongs to a man; he uses it to sow his seeds. The resulting crop is his. It does not matter if a woman is as educated as you are or as illiterate as my wife. You are both women and your fate is the same, you belong to men. Are you married, madam?

HC: (*He is right, the fate is sometimes the same for womanhood, but I won't tell him class matters. Ignore the question about marriage.*) Sowing and leaving a woman to nurture the crops might be a good thing for a man, but is it productive for a woman?

TD: Madam, is there a woman who does not like children here in Africa? What kind of a woman uproots that which God has given her? Did you not eat breakfast this morning? What if someone had uprooted the banana tree from which the bananas you ate came from? Does not every plant have a right to live and bear its own fruit? At least if you uproot, have the grace to be sorry for your crime. This woman was swinging her sinful body...

HC: The woman you keep talking about seems to have disturbed you. She is empowered, and you are getting agitated with her decision to refuse to play victim. Mr

369

TD, many women have good instincts for self-preservation and will do that which is right for their bodies or gardens as you call them. She is not an isolated case. Women have abortions all the time! You taxi drivers, I'm sure, talk about women when you have no customers, making exaggerated claims to each other about the power you have over your women.

TD: Ah! What else is there to talk about but the daughters of Eva? Actually, madam, when I shared the pregnancy and killing baby story with my brother taxi drivers, we all agreed that the church should organise a day of prayer for the prostitutes and all the women who kill babies.

HC: It is not killing but simply abortion. Anyway, who in the church will pray for the sinners since we know that even some of the priests are guilty of sodomising young men and raping the women they invite to their houses to pray for? Don't some of them plant their seeds and run away without any sense of responsibility? And do you also know that some of your fellow Christians are the bread and butter of the sex workers? Do you think that the people who buy sex are from Mars? And Mr TD, who are the fathers of the children you see on the streets of Nairobi? Go and look at them closely, you will be amazed that some of them closely resemble your fellow churchgoers.

TD: The way you are talking... Do you believe in God?

HC: My faith and beliefs are immaterial in this conversation. We should engage with all people, without judging; the founder of your religion never judged. Why don't you allow yourself to understand the experiences, fears, hopes and dreams of the women you are talking about? As a Christian you are supposed to be compassionate; remember that sometimes hunger, violence, death and beatings are so much part of the women you are condemning. And Mr TD, differences on matters of faith and politics should not stand in the way of human relationships. Talking to another human being has nothing to do with faith.

TD: You have a point there.

HC: (*capitalising on this moment of weakness*) When you go to Gikomba market, don't you see men carrying huge sacks, some even coughing blood as a result of the dusty sacks they carry, stuff that should not be carried by human beings. Do you think that they chose to do that kind of work?

TD: No, I think it's because of poverty and lack of job alternatives. Such men have no choice; they have to support families. It's hard being a man, you are supposed to give what you don't have. Wives don't respect men who go home without bread. Look at me; I dropped out of school because of lack of money. Had I continued, I would have been a big man in a huge office with several people serving me.

HC: (*now fully awake, reflection abandoned*) The issue of choice is important! I am surprised, though, that you are quick to understand the fate of men and their lack of choice and not the women who want choices in life. You know the women you are condemning have probably paid school fees for some of the people who keep your country going. Apart from supporting us all one way or the other, earning a well-needed income provides them with purpose and meaning; and some are actually self-sufficient, they manage and protect their families. I am sure we make a mistake when we talk about them as if they are powerless or as if they are murderers.

TD: You could be right, but then selling one's body is one thing but surely to uproot…? Ay!!! We men don't want to see our seeds wasted. Do you know that some women's groups even wanted to include uprooting in our recent Constitution? To make abortions legal?

HC: You are funny. You seem to think that a man's sperm is the most precious thing in this world. Does every seed result in what you are calling crops? If that was the case, how many people would be in this world? Would the world accommodate them?

TD: But madam…

HC: Mr TD, I think there is little listening going on in your world and the world of some of your fellow Christians and taxi drivers. The reality is, when you do listen to people who are different from you, you might find that you and your fellow friends don't have all the answers or values, even about abortion.

TD: …but am listening, it's only…

HC: (*my turn to be a bad listener*) Just out of curiosity, let me ask, I'm sure you don't support the use of condoms, so how can a woman who does not want to get pregnant protect herself?

TD: Why would a single woman want to have sex? That is a sin; it's promiscuity.

HC: Hey, I am not familiar with the world of sins. I am more familiar with the world of human beings. And I am not talking about marriage, I'm talking about sex and pregnancy. Are you saying that in marriage, sex always results or should result in pregnancy?

TD: Ideally it should unless the field is no longer fertile. Madam, there is pride and a sense of accomplishment that comes from sowing and seeing the crops flourishing. I have nine children. My wife just stopped having children. If God had not fenced off the garden, we would have gone on and on. I have raised my children as Catholics. They say grace, recite the rosary and go to mass fairly regularly. I love seeing all my children gathered together for baptisms, weddings and funerals. They are my wealth, my pride, my power and my joy; the fruits of my labour. I want them to go out there and produce, as the bible says.

HC: Which labour? Do you call disseminating seeds labour?

TD: Madam, you are now making fun of me.

HC: No, I wouldn't, but back to your children. I am sure that all the nine are different; they all have their own identity. This means that you with your big family should appreciate the respect for diversity and not just think that all people are Catholics or that they believe in what you believe in. It's my turn to say that you should ask your church to pray for you. With dwindling resources, poor health and education facilities in this country, how do you expect all those children to have as many children as you did and cope? What will they eat?

TD: But madam, the birds of the air…

HC: Let us talk about human beings, we don't know much about the birds of the air. After all they steal our seeds (I mean real seeds)… If your children and grandchildren follow the example of the birds of the air, they will be imprisoned for theft. Women's bodies are not fields to be ploughed whenever men feel like it. What women want is choice; choice to accept to be ploughed, to say no when they don't want to, to enjoy themselves without thinking about seeds and crops, and to remove the seeds if they don't want them. Above all to smile and swing their bodies once they have courageously removed the seeds.

TD: The way you are talking, like you are not an African?

HC: (*first not Christian and now not African. Ignore.*) Back to the sex workers, why do men buy sex?

TD: Madam, (*am happy to be called madam, keeps conversation focused*) when a man is not happy, he goes out to find happiness. It's women's fault. Once married, they feel confident and comfortable and they change! They are angels during courtship, but they turn into chameleons after marriage. It's always difficult to know which colour you will find at home after work. You can't claim to know a woman, that is why they wear headscarves! Take my wife, for example. When we were courting I thought I knew her but in actual fact, I only knew her for real six years after our marriage.

HC: What do you mean by that?

TD: At the beginning what mattered was love. It was pure, alive and something rousing. The ease with which we talked to each other was amazing. I was confident about her and about our future. After six years, I discovered she was not the woman I thought she was. Her true colours became visible and bright for all to see, just like the Kenyan flag colours.

We have had many differences but we have stayed together and produced children. I have had a few girl friends, but only on those occasions when my wife was not treating me like a man. You are an African and I am sure you know that in Africa if a woman does not take care of her husband, he will wander in other directions. It's important, though, that the wife never gets to know. We are not like whites, who will go out with another woman and report the experience to the wife. I worked with them; I swear to God it's true. A man sleeps out and the wife asks him if he had a great time.

HC: I guess we are all different and handle our sexual lives differently. Back to your wife, do you think that you have not changed? Are you still the person that you were when you were courting her?

TD: I have not changed! If she allowed me, I would show her the roaring lion in me. You know this thing of yours, when the period stops, what do you call it? Now my wife is that way. She does not want to have sex with me anymore. She does not want my seed. I even went to see a doctor about it. He said that with age, women lose interest in sex. But you see, for us men we remain as sharp as a razor till we die. So what should I do with this energy that is threatening to burst my body? I feel I am being wasted… Ah madam, I am wasted. (*He is almost in tears.*)

HC: With menopause many changes happen to a woman's body. I am sure that men's bodies also change. (*Maliciously*) I have no doubt that you are still a razor but a blunt one.

TD: (*He turns to look at me with a sly grin.*) I tell you I was very strong. We used to have sex every day. Our children have only nine months' difference. We could not stop. We were wild and vibrant. There were many times when I went to work late, just because I was making my wife happy…

HC: Has it occurred to you that you might be the cause of problems because you don't want to change? You are still living in the past but life is about change. People change, organisations change and almost everything in this world changes. I suggest that you make an appointment with yourself and think about your life. It sometimes takes a lot of courage – it's not easy – just sitting with yourself and trying to work with your own heart.

TD: Yes, things change, but madam, ah! You have insulted me; I'm still as sharp as I was many years ago. Am approaching 70 but if you give me an 18-year-old-girl, she would live to tell the story to the next generation.

HC: (*full-blown malice*) Old man, forget-18-year olds; they want young men, smooth skins, vitality and black, thick hair. Go and be nice to your wife. Take her out to a movie or go to a restaurant and eat good food. Court her again. Fall in love. Create a romantic mood and she might respond positively, who knows? Forget 18-year-olds. You talk about uprooting seeds. Why, for example, would an 18-year-old want to keep a grandfather's child?

TD: Eh, go out? Cinema? (*He has chosen not to talk about 18-year-olds.*)

HC: Yes, you have educated your children. If you bring a new wife, they will abandon you. And you know what? You will lose everything you have worked for. They will take their mother and take care of her; (*enjoying myself*) she might even find an old loving man! You will start producing other children, some will be aborted, and you will die a lonely, bitter, dissatisfied and angry man.

TD: So I must take my wife to a restaurant?

HC: Yes, you have allowed your mind to be waterlogged. Open your eyes and see. I am sure she is still beautiful, in a different way.

TD: Really?

HC: Really. Take your wife out; it will help both of you. Tomorrow we shall return to the topic of abortion. Before I leave, let me remind you that the founder of your religion grounded his work and commitment in the experience and narratives of those who suffered and had needs. And in his work he included women and sex workers (remember the story of the woman who was caught committing adultery). I am sure if the issue of the right to choose abortion had arisen during his time, he would have been pro-choice because he respected women. And, on every other issue related to reproductive health and rights, he voted for women! That is why he was killed.

TD: But madam…

HC: Yes, Jesus knew that transformative change always starts with people who live on the margins. Have a good day, and eh, I need a receipt.

TD: How much should I write on the receipt; who is paying?

HC: (*Smile – the Catholic wants to help me cheat!*) Never mind who is paying. We agreed on 1,500 shillings.

40

The shedding of blood[1]

Unoma Azuah

I can't sleep tonight...
My ovaries are set on a war of fire and stones
It's been a night of wishes and dry pain
a night of silent phones and shortened cords
Painkillers are sucked up in the storm that is my womb
I am a woman with succulent but un-suckled breasts–
The lips that taste the pain and pleasures these mounds house, I pick.
And this night is a night of absent tongues and fingers, forgotten
A night buried in a cackle of thunder and rain
——as a lightening flashes
the shadow of death hunches in a corner like a wet rock.
And I refuse to WooMAN
Dear uterus, if it takes only the sprouting of seeds
to quieten you down, then rage on–
You are a garden I possess–
I pick and choose the crops I grow...
If any.

Note

1. First published in Sentinel Poetry (online), in March 2005, E. Amatoritsero (ed).
   Reproduced with permission.

41

Ode to my uterus

Everjoice J. Win

So here you are. Lying all dead and shrivelled in a jar of formaldehyde. I am not sure why the doctor thought I needed to actually see you in person, so to speak. It's not like you are a familiar relative, killed in an accident and I need to ID you. I had never actually seen you. So you could very well be anybody else's uterus for all I know. I just knew you existed. Oh boy, did you make me know that you were in there! You have given me so much more grief than joy over the years. That is why I decided to get rid of you.

We have had a long 41 years together, you and I. I no longer want to be defined by your presence. Neither do I want to feel like I have to schedule my travels and social life around your 'time of the month'.

In my teenage years I became aware of just how much having you in there defined a woman's life. Every so often, one or other of my female relatives would declare, 'I don't feel so good in my uterus.' It was never very clear to me what this meant. Over time I got to know this meant anything from; I have a period pain, to I have a sexually transmitted infection, to my sex life is generally miserable! I grew up fearing these various illnesses emanating from you. Just after my 13th birthday, I finally got to know. As you contracted and expanded painfully for a whole week, I writhed in such agony I wished you could be ripped out of me immediately.

When I shared this with an older aunt she laughed at my silliness at first, and then got really angry. What kind of woman was I wishing to take out her uterus? Did I not know that without you I was not a real woman? Did I not know if I failed to have children (plural!), I was not a real woman and would be divorced instantly by my husband? She even told me nasty words used in my two languages for women whose uteruses were 'not functional' – *ngomwa* in Shona, or *nyumbwa* in Ndebele. Mean little words that have sent many women into spirals of depression or led them to commit suicide.

Later on I got to appreciate just how much you define women's worth and value. In my two cultures, bride price is paid for a woman's reproductive capacity. The higher the amount, the higher the number of children you are expected to have – preferably boys, of course. The desirable quota is never clearly spelt out. You stop reproducing when the one who pays says so. If you don't produce boys you get divorced, or he can take another wife and that should be okay by you. In days gone by this could be your younger sister or niece. And they had no choice in the matter. The uterus had to deliver.

The unmarried woman was not spared either: 'Ah how can you die without a child?' 'Just have one, it doesn't matter who with.' 'You are a woman. You must have at least one,' chided aunties and complete strangers. The uterus had to be productive, couldn't just be wasted. But no sooner had a woman chosen to exercise this option than she would learn this was not her decision to make unilaterally. Fathers, uncles and/or brothers would demand 'damages' from anybody who had illegitimate sex with a woman/girl, that is without paying bride price first. Everyone demanded their cut.

I think that South African politicians got it all wrong. It is not the vagina that is 'isibhaya sika baba'akhe' (her father's cattle kraal). It is the uterus. You, dear uterus, are the cash cow.

There is nothing like a hysterectomy to remind us that the earth is still flat. So after I got rid of you, I never expected the avalanche of responses that I got. In group one was what I called the back-to-biology-class lot. One woman burst into tears when she heard why I was going into hospital. She asked me how I was going to have sex without the uterus! There were several other responses of this kind. I now move around with a pen and piece of paper so I can draw the female reproductive system. And this is not in the village, mind you. No wonder we are not getting very far with our HIV awareness work.

Group two were worried about my future prospects. What will I do if the man I am involved with decides to have a baby – with me? No matter how stridently I argue that I am done with babies and that I don't want to have another one, they still agonise over what this man will say. Whatever happened to the concept of *choice*, I keep asking? But I forget, to these people, women are not entitled to choice. Again these are not uninformed people I am talking about. These are smart young activists, NGO workers and others who really should know better.

Group three have been the most surprising. One of the key reasons I decided not to have any more kids is because I stopped having unprotected sex twelve years ago, thanks to the impact AIDS has had on my family and on the quality of my personal life. Everybody who has been around me knows this very well. Surprisingly, I keep getting told that is a small matter. One of my friends even dared to say, 'Oh EJ, you make it sound so bad.' This is Southern Africa. I am Zimbabwean. Life expectancy for women in my country is now 34 years. And this is not *bad*? Maybe I am on the wrong planet.

So, dear uterus, rest in peace. I can't say I am going to miss you, because I definitely will not. I look forward to living out the rest of my days without being reminded of your presence every month. More than anything, I am now a free agent. The rest of my body belongs only to me. Nobody is going to get a cut from you, my little reproductive machine.

42

Ob/gyn experiences – life stories

Sylvia Tamale

Many women have visited a 'modern' obstetrician/gynaecologist several times in their lives and know how it feels to bare their most 'private' body parts to the glare of the doctor's lights and the probe of his (or her) gaze.

It is possible to list a wide range of reasons for our visits: routine check-ups, prenatal and postnatal care, delivery, pap smears, IUD insertion and birth control advice, abortion, STD diagnosis and treatment, abnormal bleeding, fibroid treatment, artificial reproductive techniques, menopause management, hysterectomy, cosmetic surgery, hymen reconstruction and sexual advice, among others. Each term in the list, however, goes beyond the identification of a reason for a particular woman to seek the training and expertise of a gynaecologist. The terms hint at a complex set of realities, interlocking questions of health, bodies, power and potential together in ways which have demanded the attention of feminist activists and thinkers worldwide. In African continental contexts (and, indeed, in others) 'modern' gynaecological/obstetric systems operate simultaneously within the legacies of development-oriented approaches to the 'needs' of women and, sometimes, at the cutting edge of feminist political interventions aimed at empowering women and claiming their rights to sexual and reproductive health.

Institutional and medical control of reproduction, through the medicalisation of women's bodies, was one of the issues that first outraged Nawal El Saadawi (see Chapter 6 in this volume), revolutionised her thinking about 'doctoring' and women in Egypt and began her activist and theoretical journey into fighting for women's rights, especially their rights to their own bodies. At the other end of the spectrum, we can read in the journal *Feminist Africa* of the radical work of gynaecologists Drs Lynette Denny and Nomonde Mbatani at Groote Schuur Hospital in Cape Town, who have been jointly responsible for critical new approaches to the early diagnosis and treatment of cervical cancer among poor women in South Africa (Dosekun 2007). Thinking about women's relationships to the work of gynaecologists and obstetricians is to move into a key set of debates about the meaning of 'womanhood' and the gendered politics of embodied agency.

In more ways than one, the relation between gynaecologists and their women patients is quintessentially one of power. Apart from the ever-present feelings of vulnerability and a sense of 'being invaded' that women may have on the examination table, power is also wielded through gender (the majority of doctors who specialise in ob/gyn in Africa are men), language, age, class, ethnicity and so forth. A woman patient's (or client's) feelings of anxiety are exacerbated by the ways in which heteronormative notions of women's overt sexuality associate them with reproductive 'successes' and 'failures'.

When preparing this Reader, I put out a call for African women to share their stories of the ways, in practice and in diverse contexts, they have experienced the deployment of gynaecological/obstetric power. The women who responded to my call were diverse but all middle-class, and in this chapter you will find a sampling of a dozen varied experiences that middle-class African women have had regarding their reproductive healthcare. The absence of stories from rural-based African women signifies both their lack of access to the technologies that would enable them to respond to my call, and the fact that the majority do not have access to professional obstetricians and gynaecologists.

The stories reveal that there is a price to be paid for the 'luxury' afforded by class, that women might pay in succumbing to the technologically advanced methods of managing our reproductive and sexual health (completely abandoning the traditional options, in different contexts, for support in childbirth, sexual education and protection from illnesses). To note this is not, in any romanticised way, to suggest that traditional approaches to women's sexual and reproductive bodies do not demand feminist exploration. It is clear, however, that the value of women sharing their ob/gyn stories lies in the importance of truth-telling about modern, middle-class, African lives.

The stories that follow certainly document the 'nonsense' that goes on in our often substandard and highly gendered healthcare systems, but more importantly, through the act of autobiographical narration, offer one path toward a certain liberation. In writing about what we have encountered as the objects of the medical gaze, we move ourselves into angles beyond the pain, psychological damage and humiliations that might have marred our capacities for sensual and erotic enjoyment. By naming (and even laughing at) the ways in which professional/medical discourses have found us 'pinned' (like butterflies in entomological museums) as we seek health, advice and support, we find the courage to discover our bodies anew.

It is my hope, of course, that the accounts will also raise the awareness of many health providers to treat their patients in a more humane and dignified manner. If a Lynette Denny and a Nomonde Mbatani are possible, this is undoubtedly because they, as African feminist gynaecologists/obstetricians, have listened to stories such as those that follow.[1]

Story 1: Mumbi

Walking into an obstetrician/gynaecologist's office is never an easy thing to do. One goes there because they have issues that need to be addressed. Visiting a male ob/gyn is even more unnerving because of the invasion of one's private space by a person they would not ordinarily let into that space. I have had male ob/gyns for many years. This has not been out of choice but is rather necessitated by the institutional pool that my employer and medical insurer have. To be fair, I believe my current ob/gyn is in the top league internationally. He is a good academic as well. That said, I

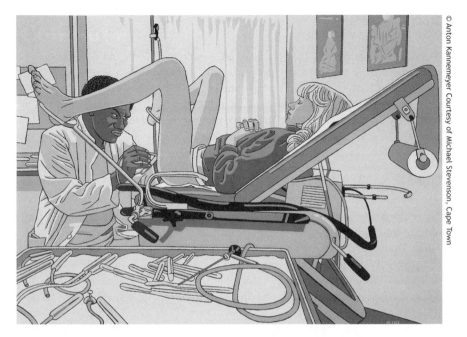

think he talks a little bit too much. Because his clientele is largely women, he has an ease with which he talks that can cross the boundaries of professional interaction.

This is the context within which you must understand my beef with my ob/gyn. I pulled myself out of my home voluntarily to see him for my annual pap smear. A pap smear is not a pleasant experience, but women have to do it. When I had positioned myself in the requisite posture, my only thought was getting over and done with the excision of all the relevant matter. It is not usual for obs/gyns to talk as they are getting their specimens so I was rather surprised to hear my ob/gyn asking me in a rather amused tone as he peered down under, 'Did you know that you have grey hair?' I was utterly shocked but my posture did not give me much space to react.

After he was done, I dressed, left his office and went into a reflective mode for an hour at the hospital café and buried this in a space of 'gravely offended'. I went back for my results after a week but thereafter chose to do my pap smear tests elsewhere. Now, I insist on a woman taking the specimen.

Story 2: Hilda

The one I have never forgotten is an experience I went through in Zimbabwe. I went to do a pap smear, which I hate like nothing. The white male doctor probed and pinched and when he was through he told me I could go. Just as I had dressed and was ready to leave, he looked at the sample and said, 'Oh no, I made a mistake, let's do that again!' I felt I could murder him.

Story 3: Ndanatsei

A colleague of mine says she was asked by a male gyn, 'How old did you say you were again?' This was when she had spread out her legs as much as she could. Could the question have been raised because she looked older or younger down there? I have since given up wanting to think what the gyn (male or female) thinks of me when they do what they do! It's all a waste of time; they all think I am younger than I actually look, only after I have spread my legs!

Story 4: Nana

My personal story is moving to the UK and registering with a clinic. I was 19 years old and told I would need to do a smear test. So I booked an appointment to see the nurse. I had heard from my best friend that smears were uncomfortable and painful so I psyched myself up for the ordeal. The nurse asked me how many sexual partners I had had and I responded, 'None'. She said there was no need to do the test because otherwise she would be 'taking my virginity with a spatula'. That phrase has always stuck with me.

I have always felt that preparing for a smear test should be a bit like foreplay before sex. The doctor/nurse should give you time to get relaxed and perhaps encourage you to think sexy thoughts so that we get naturally lubricated. What are your thoughts?

Story 5: Wangari

Around this time last year I went through the most godawful procedure called a hysterosalpingogram (HSG). It involved the shooting of a coloured dye through my vagina, into my uterus and through my fallopian tubes. The purpose of this HSG was two-fold: (1) to detect my uterine and fallopian health; and (2) to annoy me.

I went to one of those diagnostic centres in Nairobi and waited my turn. Before the procedure, a male attendant took me into a room for what he called 'routine preparation', which went something like this:

Him: How are you?
Me: Fine.
Him: Are you sure?
Me: Yes.
(pause)
Him: You are Wangari?
Me: Yes.
Him: Are you married? Where is your 'hubby'?
Me: Huh? Why?
Him: Just asking.
Me: Irrelevant.

Him: Okay, are you trying to conceive?

Me: Not particularly.

(pause)

Him: Ai! Why did the doctor send you for an HSG then?

Me: I have an acute pain in my lower abdomen. It's all in the notes.

Him: Are you a doctor?

Me: No.

Him: Anyway it's a painful procedure, especially afterwards. Many women cry. Some shout and wail. You know women.

Me: Great news.

Him: We will inject a liquid into your uterus and then take a picture using our latest state-of-the-art equipment.

Me: Great news.

Him: You have to remain relaxed throughout because if you clench we will have a problem called 'back flow'. The liquid will not go where it needs to go. We will take the picture and then send the results to your doctor. Is that okay?

Me: Yes. When do we start?

Him: When you are ready.

Me: Let's do it. Can I get a female technician please?

Him: No problem. We have one – she is new.

Minutes later I'm lying naked on cold stainless steel, legs apart, with the same man peering into my vagina. The female technician is there, but it becomes apparent that her role is in fact to soothe me and ask me to relax. I cannot – because he annoys me. I have 'back flow' three times. The woman says *'Wacha nijaribu'* ('Let me try'). He leaves and goes to operate the x-ray machine. She and I are finished in 15 seconds – without backflow. He takes the picture, out of earshot. She says *'Wachana na yeye, nilimwambia kutoka mwanzo afadhali nifanye. Anapenda tu kuona wanawake wakilia'* ('Leave him alone, I told him from the beginning that I should do it. He just likes seeing women cry').

Story 6: Lesley

What a great idea to collect our stories. I have had many such terrible encounters. The most recent is that I developed a little pimple on my vagina and worried that it was something ominous. When I told the gyn about it he asked, 'Have you been to the harbour lately?'[2] I was horrified! He thought it was funny. Turned out I had an allergic reaction to soap.

Story 7: Cecilia

Just yesterday I went to a GP to do a general medical test. When it came to the gyn/ob issues the doctor said, and I quote, 'I am not doing the finger thing, it's disgusting.'

Story 8: Takyiwaa

The things we have had to endure! The ob/gyn story I want to share occurred when I was about 19 years old, just after I had entered university. I used to experience very painful periods, and went to see this gynaecologist. After or during the examination, he asked me what course I was pursuing and I responded, 'Law.'

'Well,' he said, 'that course is too difficult for a woman; that is why you are experiencing painful periods!'

I responded that my mother, who had never stepped inside a classroom, also experienced painful periods and that clearly that could not be related to any difficult course she had pursued.

I left the hospital deeply disdainful of the knowledge and expertise of the gynaecologist.

Story 9: Zeedah

I was new in Switzerland and a friend recommended a gynaecologist. No one seemed to know a female one so I went along as the recommended one was ranked as 'very female-sensitive and friendly'. There had even been a newspaper article on him as he was a supporter of women's rights to safe, state-paid abortions.

So I called and booked an appointment and went as planned, on a typically cold and rainy November day. After the initial greetings and handshakes, I explained that I wanted my IUD (coil) removed. I was invited to remove my lower clothing and lie on the notorious gyn table. Standard practice, no problems.

As he put his gloves on, he asked me where I was from and I said, 'Kenya'.

'*Mamangu weeeee*!!' His narration took off! He was so pleased, because, he said, Kenya is nice and has this and that. The usual tourist palava!!

He then started telling me about his trip to Kenya, some ten years ago, and he was trying to remember the names of the parks, the names of the waiters who served him, and the number of zebras and giraffes he saw.

All this while, I am lying with my legs open, with him placing a hand on one of my knees, totally oblivious to the ticking clock or to my look of annoyance.

I tried to prompt him by offering names of known game reserves, and he would say, 'No, it was something else!' After what seemed like hours, but was actually an agonising 35 minutes, he had his 'eureka moment' and proudly announced '*Hakuna Matata*!' That was the name of the park and he wanted to know whether I knew it. I quietly said, 'Yes, I know that park,' and added that I was a bit late for my next appointment.

As he did his gyn check, he continued sharing his Kenya experience, all the while pausing with his hand on my knee and my vulva exposed to the elements!

I left after a good hour, for which he later billed me, never to return and with a life-long irritation for the words *hakuna matata*.

Story 10: Linda

I lived in Kinshasa, the Democratic Republic of Congo from 2004 to 2006. In 2004, I tried to get an appointment with a doctor because I was not feeling well. The trick turned out to be that because of the breakdown in services in the DRC as a whole due to the civil war, the available doctors and/or consultants were 'mobile'. That is, they moved from hospital to hospital offering their services and they were in huge demand.

The GP I saw asked me to first have an ultra scan done. When the technician started doing the scan, he let out an involuntary exclamation. I asked what was wrong and he said, 'Nothing'. I then asked him to turn the screen so I could also follow what he was doing. He refused and said I should wait for my doctor. I insisted. Very reluctantly, and he made no effort to hide his displeasure at this woman, he turned the screen toward me. When I asked him to explain what the matter was, he insisted that I speak with my doctor.

The GP said I was pregnant and also asked that I see my ob/gyn to further discuss what the results of the scan were. The ob/gyn, by the way, could only be seen from 6pm each day. He would switch off his cellphone during the day. When I eventually saw him, he just said I had fibroids and did not understand why I had wanted the technician to explain what the issue was, nor why I had wanted to also see the screen as the scan was being done. He also wondered where I had heard that pregnant women needed to take iron tablets in the early trimester.

The next time I had to go for another scan, I went to the 'best' hospital in Kinshasa at the time. I went with my husband. The consultant tried not to acknowledge my presence. Each time I asked him a question; he would try to ignore me. He asked me to take off my jeans for the scan and I said I could pull it down and he performs the scan. He refused and in fact said my maternity jeans were not suitable for pregnancy.

Then to my utmost amazement, he pulled out what looked like a funnel and proceeded to dig painfully into my sides, trying to get a heartbeat! I was speechless for a few seconds. I asked him to ease the pressure a bit and he turned to James and said the baby's heartbeat was strong.

That was it, no more discussions!

Story 11: Hope

I told my friend Sara that I was going to Dr X for a pap smear. She remained silent for a moment – allowing, I now understand, for me to fully take measure of what I was saying and the doctor I was going to see.

It was early morning in August, the light was clear, quiet and translucent. I was happy, an odd sort of happiness. I was about to do something I had been postponing for months.

Before going to the clinic I spent the day basking in the fold of nature. Then in the afternoon I drove to the clinic. The image of the famous Harare jacarandas accompanied me all the way – either side of the road, tall black trees tightly knit together, standing guard. Mesmerised by the beauty of the landscape, thoughts came softly to me. It's time for women to build alliances as never before, to support each other. Time for feminists and women's rights defenders to exercise regularly, have medical check ups and eat well.

In I went to see the doctor. In readiness, I had washed my vagina well, my underwear was clean and I was even clean shaven. The good doctor requested that I remove my underwear, as if he needed to ask. I was not sure whether to put the underwear in my handbag, his chair or just hold it. I placed it in the bag. I lay on the bed, spread my legs and waited. He put on his gloves, spread my legs wider and what I had been dreading most happened – invasion of the body, my body.

I closed my eyes so that I would not see, feel or hear. I numbed my feelings. Then I heard his voice as if coming from far. He was asking me if I was enjoying myself and if I was having fun!

I did not respond. I simply pushed his hand out of my vagina, got off the bed, and without putting on my underwear, I marched out of his office. I have never been back.

When I narrated my story to Sara, she said she had been through the same experience with Dr X but had hesitated to warn me because she was not sure if the experience was unique to her.

Story 12: Mansah

Nulliparous. Primiparous. I first came across these terms when I was expecting my first child. I was 35 years old and considered weird to have lived all that time without trying to have a child. The truth is that I had been studying until age 30 and never thought I could simultaneously handle motherhood and my studies. So I made sure I never became pregnant when I was a student. Then, after my studies, I relocated from Europe to my native West Africa. I was single, and hadn't met anyone I thought would have been a suitable father for my children. But why am I trying to explain myself? That is the problem. Why should a woman have to explain why she does not choose to have a child 'early' in life? Oh, I got a lot of pressure from everyone. Friends, cousins, siblings, workers at the university where I work: 'So you do not have a child?' 'But you have such a nice house with so much space.' 'Don't you want to have a child?' 'When will you be ready?' 'God will provide for you and the child.' 'Go on and have one. A husband is not necessary.'

This was the kind of advice I kept getting.

Then I met someone, but it took me about four years to take a decision to 'settle' with him. So finally after four years of dating, I became pregnant. I was cool with my decision and the results thereof, but the medical people were not, it seems. That is when those words were used to describe my condition: nulliparous; primiparous.

I grew to hate those words. And then there was the pressure I had to undergo. I was supposed to have a caesarean delivery. My doctor thought I was too old to have a normal delivery. My bones and muscles were no longer flexible, he said, and anything could happen to me during childbirth at my age. I went to see the next doctor. He mumbled something about an 'elective caesarean', so I moved to the next one.

Of course they were all men. I do not know if it would have made any difference with a female gynaecologist. They all seemed to say the same thing.

Primiparous or nulliparous at 35 meant that my baby was at risk and I should not be allowed to go through a normal, natural delivery. The most important thing was for me to have a baby. Now completely frustrated, I tried another doctor. He was not really my choice, he had a swanky clinic and charged exorbitant fees I could not really afford. And rumour had it that he was the first lady's doctor. But I went to see him anyway. He was more accommodating than the other doctors I had seen and agreed to let me try to have the baby naturally. 'But remember that we will have to cut as soon as any problems crop up,' he warned. I settled with this doctor and even began to find the routine visits pleasant. He appeared to think I would be alright and this gave me a little confidence.

When the time came I was naturally very afraid. Who wouldn't be? At age 35 and primiparous? I was admitted to the clinic a few days before the birth because I had false contractions. In our culture women are not supposed to make any noise during the birth process but I threw caution to the winds and screamed at every contraction. Looking back, I know it was the fear that made me shout like that. After about two hours of labour, I gave birth to a baby boy any woman would have been proud of. It all happened at night, and the doctor was not on the premises when I had the baby.

All done naturally, without a caesarean. I did have some awful vaginal tears from the delivery, though. The midwife who delivered the baby later told me she could not bear to cut me up. When the doctor arrived the next morning and examined me, he cautioned her about that and sewed me up quickly, without sedation.

As long as the baby is fine, anything goes, I think.

I gave birth to another child, two years later, without the need for a caesarean section. But there were other complications. And that is my second story. Actually I think it is quite an amazing one, too.

After my success at giving birth without the need for an operation at age 35, I decided to have the next child at a maternity home. This time I wanted no fuss from doctors who thought they knew what was best for me. The midwife (I shall call her Aunty Agnes) had about 40 or more years of experience. She could have been my mother or grandmother. I warmed up to her from the beginning and was completely fearless when my time came. My partner accompanied me and sat quietly outside, waiting for the child to be born. I did not scream. When I was well into labour, Aunty Agnes told him to go home and wait.

'No men needed here,' she said.

Aunty Agnes took charge of the birth process with authority. She told me how to breathe and when to push. She must have noticed that something had gone wrong at some point because suddenly she told me to stop pushing. She told me firmly that she and her staff would take care of everything from that point. Then she called for four cloth wrappers and quickly tied them together. She tied the long cloth under my breasts, and with two nurses on each side of the bed, pulling the cloth as if in a game of tug of war, the baby was eased out of my body. It was a boy. She lifted him high up, turned him upside down and gave him two gentle whacks on the bottom. 'You bad boy,' she said. And then she explained to me that the reason why she asked me to stop pushing during the birth process was that the child had not presented as expected. He had not turned face down as is normally the case, and he had his arm firmly placed round his head.

Her quick reactions and experience had saved me. In a hospital I most probably would have had surgery.

Notes

1. There is no claim to generalisation of the personal stories in this chapter.
2. Going to the harbour refers to prostitution, servicing sailors.

Reference

Dosekun, Simidele (2007) 'Medicine and activism: institutionalising medical care and compassion for rape survivors', *Feminist Africa* 8: 111–16

43

Reflections on my journey with my womb – journal excerpts

Akabotho Kaluwa

Part 1 November 2006

One of the real wonders of living in our age is that we exist in an era in which women are able to read about health concerns that affect them and that have been written by other women, and, more importantly, that allows us to at least make decisions on the basis of being informed. I am amazed at how much more I now know about fibroids compared to when I had my first operation in December 1995. Almost 11 years to the date I find myself preparing for yet another operation of the same kind, to have my fibroids removed, or a myomectomy, in medical parlance.

I realise now as I have grown older that from the onset my relationship with my womb has never been an easy one. I guess the first time I ever really thought consciously about having a womb as a distinct part of my anatomy was when my paternal aunt, who is known more for her direct speech than her marriage to the first black Anglican Bishop of Zimbabwe, in an attempt to dislodge a thorn that had taken root in my foot, made the remark that if I could not even bear such little pain, what on earth was I going to do when faced with the pain of childbirth.

'So having a baby is painful,' I remember thinking to myself and burying this deep in my subconscious for future reference. For the immediate term, my concern was with the thorn that had taken advantage of a six-year-old running barefoot, as thorns are wont to do. In less than eight years my womb and I were to consciously engage with each other in ways that were to leave an indelible mark compared to the conversation that I had had with my aunt. My periods started at the age of 12 going on 13. At first they politely came and went away without drama. But that period of peaceful monthly co-existence was short lived. Within two years or so from the time I started menstruating, my monthly cycle became a time of dreaded encounter. The pain was unbearable. I would writhe in extreme agony and throw up. Painkillers such as aspirins, panadols were weaklings hardly worthy of their name. They had absolutely no effect other than making me even more nauseous. Relief generally came after hours of lying completely still in bed and consciously willing my mind to separate itself from the pain of my body. I guess what I found disturbing as I grew older and reflected on this time in my life when my menstrual cycle was such hell, was how I was expected to bear with it. Periods were a natural part of a woman's life cycle, so the reasoning went, and discomfort during this time was in keeping with what could be expected.

My mom, in particular, was at the forefront of these 'naturalist theories'. She vocalised that the pain would go away with time and, in any event, with childbirth, if nothing else. *Jeko* is what she told me the condition was called in our language. For her a painful period was not deemed sufficient cause to visit a doctor, even though I often had to miss school because of the pain. A visit to the doctor had to be founded on something more dramatic of which there were no shortages on my part in my earlier years.

The one time we did visit a doctor on account of my dysmenorrhea and he suggested that I could try to regulate the periods with a contraceptive, my mother cut him off even before he could finish articulating his thought. I must have been about 17. To her, that would have been tantamount to giving me a licence to indulge in sex. I could tell she thought the white doctor most irresponsible for even fathoming that kind of remedy in the initial instance. We did leave his offices though armed with a prescription for a stronger painkiller.

It did bring some relief even though not considerable. In retrospect, I know that the perception that I should have borne the pain as a woman was misplaced. I cringe when I read feminist articles that devalue the fact that women have such different experiences with their menstrual cycles and that for some of us the experience was hell. By age 27, I was told that I had fibroids. 'Hormonal related,' the doctor surmised. In a sense it did not come as a surprise that there was something wrong with my womb, as we seemed to have had not so happy encounters right from the outset. The fibroids were small and no cause for concern, although my periods were somewhat heavy. The drop which made the bucket overflow regarding my decision to have them removed was months of pain in my right upper leg, as if my nerve was being pinched. I was told that a fibroid was probably pressing on a nerve. It was an irritating pain to have to bear day in and day out, so I decided enough was enough and bit the bullet.

I was only 34 then but I remember the gynaecologist putting forward the suggestion that I have a hysterectomy. I told him I still wanted to try to have a baby. He respected my wishes and I had the myomectomy. I was an ardent gym goer and so my recovery was amazingly swift. However, I still vividly remember the pain in the initial two weeks. As I prepare for this second operation, I find myself somewhat burdened by these memories of having been cut in half. I remember thinking at one time that it would be a miracle to have this pain as a 'thing of the past'. But yes, the miracle did happen. One of the memorable discomforts was not being able to pass a stool for a few days after I was discharged. When it finally happened, thanks to a neighbour who had worked as a nurse and recommended castor oil, it was like releasing the hardest golf ball ever! I thought I would need a stitch or two at the end of it all. I did not. After that, recovery was smooth sailing.

It later turned out (about a year or so down the line) that the real cause of the pain in my leg was not the fibroids, because the pain returned, but a muscle, which needed to be stretched thoroughly after gym. Not that the fibroids were not there. They were and in fairly sizeable proportions. I got this diagnosis about the cause of the pain from a female doctor at the Well Woman Clinic. What struck me then was that she knew what I was talking about because she was a woman and that a male doctor would not have known the kind of pain I was talking about. I put her suggestions to stretch thoroughly into practice, with discernibly positive results. To this day, one of my virtues is stretching wholeheartedly after an exercise regime.

To get to the present. I have made a decision yet again to have my fibroids removed rather than my actual womb. In the period since my operation, they have grown with a vengeance. My bleeding is out of control. More like opening a tap and letting it run. The inconvenience to my life would fill its own pages. Another operation has not been an easy decision to come to. Over the years, doctors have tried to persuade me to have a hysterectomy as the best option despite the wealth of information especially from women, and in particular those in the medical profession, that it should be the last option. I have become an internet patient, reading as much as I can on fibroids and alternative remedies. I even came across an organisation in the United States called HERS Foundation[1] that deals with women who have had hysterectomies. I wrote to them and they sent me some literature. It has made me wonder whether doctors here in Zimbabwe really keep up with the information out there. The eagerness, even by women medics, to throw parts of women's bodies into the incinerator seems somewhat baffling.

The option of a hysterectomy seems to be given here as an operation of first choice and is often wrapped in a shocking cloak of ageism and the perception that once over a certain age you do not need a uterus. As I write this, I will be 44 in a few days. I would like to remember this timeframe in my life in years to come. I am assuming that I will survive the operation. But what exactly would I like to remember? I think the process that has led me to the decision is a fascinating one. I feel I have played the artful dodger with doctors on this issue over the last couple of years.

I distinctly remember my visit to Dr X. She had been recommended as a female gynaecologist and generally the word was that she was good even if somewhat abrupt and acid tongued. I saw her in 2003, I think it was. I will cut out on unnecessary details for fear of defamation, save to say that my experience led to my awarding her my trophy for the rudest person I have ever met in the medical profession. When I went to see her, I tried to discuss some of the options I had read about at that time concerning the treatment of fibroids, such as embolisation, and taking a certain abortion-related pill which was said to shrink fibroids. These she contemptuously dismissed and within five minutes she had recommended a hysterectomy and given me a date in the following week when she was available to do the operation. Her advice also centred on the fact that I was carrying unnecessary weight because of the fibroids and that I would lose an instant 3–4kg if I had the operation. I never returned. I thought that her approach was too rushed, too hurried, too much premised on maximising the number of clients that she had to see that day. My emotional and spiritual concerns about the connections and connectedness with my womb were not an issue for her. In five to ten minutes flat, I was supposed to have made a decision. What rubbish!

I guess my greater disappointment compared to what she had to say really emanated from the fact that I had expected her approach to be different because she was a woman. I associated the dismissiveness concerning women's bodies mainly with male doctors. But as I have had to learn on this important journey, things are not always black or white. Not day or night. Not always male or female. Although these distinctions do matter and cannot be dismissed in their entirety, the truth is you will find female doctors who are 'full of it' as much as you will find male doctors who are willing to lend you an ear. I did see my GP, also female, over the years, who always expressed dismay that I still had not had the hysterectomy. She too insisted that I would feel good and that one of the benefits – now wait for this – would be that instant flat tummy. OK, I do admit that with fibroids that were the size of a 24-week pregnancy, I must have made a humorous spectacle for those who like to laugh at others, since year in and year out despite looking pregnant I never seemed to give birth. I know there were many who revelled at being better than me by dint of a smaller girth.

But compared to the consequences of hysterectomy that I had read about, a distended stomach seemed a small price to pay compared to the long-term effects of a hysterectomy ranging from bladder problems, back pain, heart conditions and lack of sex drive. Also having been brought up not to put too much store on outward appearances, I never really saw the size of my tummy as worthy of priority number one on my list of concerns. To make this a priority among the plethora of world problems seemed narcissistic in the extreme. I think the turning point in making a decision came when I visited the Well Woman Clinic and met a really sympathetic doctor who was willing to listen and not look at my case from an ageist perspective. She had just had her first child in her mid-forties. OK, fine, having never had children, the thought was still an attractive one and had been part of the reason why I had decided against a hysterectomy.

Part 2 January 2007

Isn't it amazing how quickly time flies? It is more than seven weeks since I had the operation and yes, I have lived to see another day. I never got a chance to go back to my reflections pending the operation because life became so hectic. I had to move house, having finally taken the decision that it would be a good idea to recuperate in my new place. Also I would not have to worry about thieves breaking into an empty house if I moved into it. Anyway, suffice to say that by the time the date of my operation arrived, I was pretty sure that I wanted a myomectomy. Having been given time to think about it at my last visit and to let him know my decision, I had emailed my new gynaecologist a sentence to the effect that this was the operation of my choice. I had done the necessary medicals.

I had received a call from his nurse about a week before the operation that the doctor wanted to see me the morning before I checked into St Anne's Hospital. I wondered whether he wanted to dissuade me from having a myomectomy. His email response had been brief and to the point that he had noted my wishes. I had discussed the issue with some of my friends and family members. Both a good and a bad thing! Both therapeutic and exhausting. Everyone had her own opinion as to how best to proceed. It was like a debate. There were those for the myomectomy (thankfully the majority) and those who were against and who thought that, this being the second attempt at it, perhaps I should call it a day with my womb. Let me not sound ungrateful for the myriad views. I appreciated them. In the end, however, I let my spirit be my guide and felt that 'those in the winds', my grandmothers and great-grandmothers, would intuit the direction I was supposed to take.

On the morning of the operation I went to see the doctor. I was still strong in my resolve to retain my womb. The doctor did a quick scan to assess once again 'whether the operation was possible'. He reiterated that his view was that a hysterectomy would be the best way to proceed.

Was I signing my own death warrant then by insisting on a myomectomy? I had told him during an earlier visit of an article that I had read from the Hysterectomy Foundation in the USA about the dire consequences of disposing of that part of your anatomy (your womb) willy nilly. I had promised to copy the article for him but hadn't got round to doing so. I still stood my ground and he conceded that he could detect my reluctance to have a hysterectomy. We reached a happy compromise in that we agreed that if he formed an opinion once he had opened me up, that it would be dangerous and foolhardy to proceed with my wishes as per request, then in order to save my life he could proceed with a hysterectomy.

What I did not tell him was that I had read a book by Christiane Northrup (1998), a renowned female gynaecologist, who says that very rarely does a myomectomy turn into a hysterectomy if you are in the hands of a good surgeon. I also liked her approach to fibroids as manifesting blocked energy. I could relate to that. She saw a hysterectomy as an operation of last choice. I had received this book a few years earlier from my friend, Judy, as a birthday present. A good example of the useful kind of gifts women can give each other. I still rank this gift as one of the most useful I have ever received as it played a critical informational role in the decisions I made about my body. Knowledge is indeed power!

The surgeon I had been referred to was said to be one of the best and came highly recommended in terms of his skill, if not his mental attitude toward hysterectomies. He certainly needed some persuading about keeping my womb. So when I left his surgery to head home to get my stuff for the hospital, I can honestly say that I did not know if when I woke up after the operation I would have a womb or not. I promised to drop off the article for him, which I did. My sister-in-law was at hand to pick me up from home and take me to the hospital. I needed to check in on the Tuesday afternoon for preparation. Friends and family were great. Magazines, books, flowers were dropped off that afternoon, sending the comforting message that I would be around to read them. I got into a private ward, having decided to relax about spooks. Also I did not quite fancy sharing a ward with four others in this era of strange illnesses. My vitals were checked. The anaesthetist came in to see me – a chatty woman who assured me Jesus would be with me. I did not volunteer the information about my laxity toward church. Although I had signed the hospital card as Anglican, I had omitted to state 'by baptism' as opposed to 'in practice'. This meant that, that afternoon I already had a visitor from the church – an embarrassing moment as I was asked which parish I go to and had to mumble something about not having been to any for a long time. It turned out that the woman who represented the church was a cousin of a cousin, if you know what I mean, African style. She therefore felt in her heart to visit more than once over the next few days.

Anyway, to cut this part of the journey short, I ate well, slept well and was woken at about 4.45am to take a sip of water with my blood pressure medicine. I had been informed the previous day that I was the first on the operation list for the doctor that day and that he could not come before 1pm. He must have finished early with his patients because just after 12 noon when I was still musing in my head, a horde of nurses came to wheel me out. As they were doing so, I remembered that I still had my contact lenses in and asked to remove them. I would not see my assassins and would be unable to identify clearly who to spook should I not come back. But there was no time to worry about my possible activities in the afterlife.

Before I knew it the anaesthetist was inserting needles into my veins ignoring my protest about the pain she was inflicting. What kind of people are these who happily and smilingly jab others with needles? I hate needles. Well, I don't think anyone loves needles either. I am sure drug users merely tolerate them. At what point I became unconscious to the world, I do not recall. It seemed instant. The last thing I remember was the anaesthetist telling the doctor to change into his robes. I have no recollection of any dream or of even sleeping so I won't lie that I glimpsed heaven or hell. Both eluded me so I have absolutely nothing to report in that regard. I was totally and completely lost to the world.

When I next woke up, I was in the ward and the doctor was telling me that he had read the article the previous night and had been amused by it. What a sense of humour at the expense of women's real concerns! OK, the article wasn't exactly gentle about male gynaecologists or their motives for cutting up women with such frequency and lack of hesitation, if not hidden glee. But at least he had read it, and he seemed to have absorbed its contents, even if somewhat reluctantly.

He mentioned that he had removed 30 fibroids, which meant that my womb had survived to see another day. I was so heavily sedated that barely had the doctor finished delivering his news, than I had fallen asleep again. I had not realised then that I was in the high dependency unit and breathing with the aid of an oxygen mask. He left instructions to be contacted should anything untoward be observed. I was bleeding and the nurse was not sure whether it was from the wound or the vagina. They were also measuring my stomach to ensure that it did not balloon. At one time, I heard the nurse call the doctor to inform him that I was bleeding. A sign of impending death! I had been warned of the danger of over-bleeding if the fibroids were removed and that I might need a transfusion. So when she made that call I thought, 'This is it.' When the doctor did not come rushing to my bedside after the call, I was comforted that I lived in hope. The nurses changed my linen, I think twice. Quite painful, as I had to be moved sideways for the process to be effected.

Morning came soon and it was such a comfort to see my little sister. She had come the previous day but I had lost all sense of time and space. She was smiling as usual, bless her heart! She had also come to sit with me the day I checked in and had protested at my chosen night wear and the fact that I did not own a morning gown. What did she expect would happen to me in the hospital corridors I wondered? That I would be raped for wearing a full slip with spaghetti shoulders? Please! She was joined in chorus on this issue by another friend and in a matter of hours before the operation, some maternity looking morning gowns had been purchased and dispatched without delay to the hospital. Public indecency had been averted!

Anyway, to return again to my first morning without the 30 fibroids in my womb … when the doctor came, he seemed happy with my progress and ordered that my blood count be taken to determine whether I needed to be transfused. The anaesthetist also came to check how I was doing. The doctor said he wanted to show me what he had removed. I told him I did not have my contact lenses in. When he came back later in the day, I still did not have my lenses in so they were brought to me. Being squeamish in the extreme, I did wonder at the wisdom of a full frontal viewing of the fibroids. But curiosity got the better of me. I had heard of people being shown their body parts whether for shock value, a practical lesson in human anatomy, or for whatever unexplained reason. In my case I must say I was *not* prepared for what I saw.

When the fairly large silver hospital dish was brought to me, its contents shocked me. I had not expected that the fibroids would be that large or that many. Four of them seemed to be the size of fully-grown pears, a large orange or a grapefruit. Take your pick. Apart from size, they hardly resembled the benign nature of these fruits! They were ugly and distorted and looked like white, tightly twisted intestines. Even the so-called smaller ones were in reality, fairly large in size. It was hard to believe that my womb had carried such a huge mass. I must have looked pregnant. I was to later learn that my uterus was the size of a 28-week pregnancy. I asked the doctor how much they weighed. 'Approximately 800 grams,' he volunteered. I was forlorn. I had expected that I would instantly wake up 10kg lighter – alright, a bit exaggerated – but an entire dish load of stuff plucked out of me and only accounting for a mere 800 grams of my body weight! Well, would you not be disappointed? I got over my disappointment by reminding myself that it was politically incorrect for a feminist, let alone an African woman, to want to look like Barbie.

I stayed in the high dependency unit for two nights and was wheeled to the ordinary ward on the third day. I liked the care I received in the unit. In the general ward the nurses were not exactly at your beck and call. They were not negligent or monstrous either. Just not as available. I suffered from nausea and did not have an appetite for much. In fact the mental vision of the fibroids aided and abetted the puking process. My dreams, once I got back to my private ward, were vivid. I dreamt of bright colours and posh places. It must have been the pethidine injections they were giving me.

Let me wind my walk on this path by briefly reminiscing on my journey toward recovery. One thing this second round of being cut up has taught me is the depth of female friendships and liaisons. The toil and unconditional support I got from my female 'sisters' was amazing and always with good cheer. Elly, thanks for being such a wonderful understanding colleague. Tricia, you were an angel. Thanks for the walks and for putting me in shape before the op and for your support thereafter. Judes, words fail me. Your calls and text messages kept me alive and smiling. Mabs, you were grieving the loss of your mom and yet still found time to comfort others. Never one to miss an opportunity to engage in a philosophical discussion, you mercilessly came to tax my brain both in and out of hospital, as a result of which my cells certainly did not atrophy. Eve, you were with me on this one. Sarah G, your energy and zest for life are truly amazing. Your forward-looking strategies in coming to work the garden will bear fruit long after the op is forgotten. And hey, thanks for bringing your family over on Xmas day. Celina, your warmth and culinary skills brought great joy. Sheila, without your humour, days would have been dull. Tanaka, thanks for being there in the past and now. Sara M, good to see you and your support was appreciated. Barbara, thanks for the plant. A positive celebration of life.

There were also a few good men who lent their support. But as I was to learn from this experience, making sacrifices for ill friends does not come as easily to men as it does to women. As one of my male friends who is out of the country stated: 'I can't come to that place [Zimbabwe]. What! With no water and electricity? It would drive me nuts. Worse than visiting Baghdad.' Food for thought. Fibroids and dead-end relationships!

To my family, thanks for being the solid rock. You shopped, you ferried, you comforted and you provided your teenage children as rare orchids with palliative effects. They were indeed palliative because rather than risk eating cremated food, I learnt to get up and cook faster than lightning. Love you all!

Note

1. Hysterectomy Educational Resources and Services. See www.hersfoundation.com.

Reference

Northrup, Christiane (1998) *Women's Bodies, Women's Wisdom: The Complete Guide to Women's Health and Well-being*, London, Judy Piatkus Publishers

Questions for reflection

1.

One of the questions that kept popping up during the course of developing this Reader was: what has reproduction got to do with sexuality? Has reproduction always been conceptually separated from sexuality in African cultures? What factors have operated to detach reproduction from sexuality and with what consequences?

2.

An examination of reproductive health and rights in Africa must inevitably engage with issues of development. How have the reproductive lives of poor African men and women been lived out under economies that have undergone structural adjustment programmes (SAPs — prescribed by the IMF and World Bank), with the attendant user fees for healthcare, privatisation of public hospitals, retrenchment of government health workers, the internal brain-drain, inequalities created and magnified by neoliberal policies?

3.

What benefits lie in conceptualising reproductive health as a human right? What significance does this right hold for African women's autonomy and self-determination, and ultimately for loosening the patriarchal stranglehold that is exercised over their reproductive capacities?

4.

What is the conceptual relationship between African cultures and the medicalisation of reproduction? What, for example, does it mean for the average African woman to be removed from 'social care' during childbirth and shifted into the 'modern' hospital facilities that are very individualistic, impersonal, unfamiliar and 'professional'? What has it done to the age-old technologies of traditional birth attendants?

5.

Because women (and girls) are the people most directly affected by reproduction, there is a tendency for them to monopolise the reproductive health agenda and to ignore men's involvement (as perpetrators, partners, clients). What is the importance of examining the link between healthy human reproduction and gender equality, as well as the gendered character of reproductive health?

6.

What is the significance of emerging trends in the area of reproductive health and rights on the continent, for example the forced sterility and lack of freedom to procreate for women living with HIV/AIDS, the criminalisation of HIV and the abandonment of babies by HIV-positive mothers?

Part 6
Sex and masculinities

44

Male sexualities and masculinities

Kopano Ratele

Introduction

In many parts, if not all, of post-colonial Africa, a significant theme of being a man revolves around sex. Indeed, from the massive popularity of and profits from sexual aids for erectile dysfunction, such as Viagra, sex as an important, constitutive theme of manhood appears to be true for other countries of the world as well.

Sex is only one of several thematic factors that resource the dominant masculinity narrative, but it is without doubt a significant one. Nearly everywhere in the world manliness is closely associated with our sexual partner(s), the sexual appeal of our partner(s), the size of our penises, the claims we make about our sexual stamina, whether we can maintain a healthy erection and how virile we are. These are just a few examples, yet they go to the heart of how sex is used to construct a particular form of masculinity and manliness.

To a significant extent, 'real sex' is nearly always associated with the penis (but see Plummer 2005). That said, the significance of the penis in any man's life is never just with the organ as a physical object. Rather, the consequence of a penis is more about the powerful meanings that the organ accretes in different cultures. And so boys who grow up to support the grand narrative of what being a man is about must also learn the meaning of womanhood. They must learn to talk about the penis in a particular way and the vagina in another way. The penis is, for instance, a *koto* (in seSotho) or *induku* (in isiZulu) (both meaning a stick); the vagina is a *mokoti* (seSotho for hole). As such, a man who is perceived not to be using his stick or not filling holes is in isiZulu referred to as *isishumane* – an object of ridicule.

This essay is intended to show that the meanings a man gives his penis and those of other men, their sexual behaviours, feelings, fantasies and problems are decisive elements in the construction of masculinity. It must be noted that such meanings are always realised within interpersonal and institution-mediated relationships. Thus, in more collectivist cultures such as those found in African societies, the relational accomplishment of the meaning of manhood and of sexuality is even more pronounced.

In the equation of dominant masculinity with heterosexual sex – which says a true man is that male who has awe-inspiring sex with a beautiful woman – women who are attracted to women give the first lie to the dominant sexual story of

BOX 44.1

Women with vibrators and dildos

Do women penetrating each other not suggest that they want a real man's penis? This is one of the most common questions heterosexuals are often troubled by. One must not deny that possibility outright: some women who like being penetrated with a vibrator or dildo might find it a substitute for a man's penis. However, it has to be acknowledged that possibly many women prefer vibrators, tongues, dildos, fingers or fists for other reasons. Here are four of them:

- The woman who desires to be penetrated might not want the whole man but rather might only want a finger inserted into her. Or she might lust after a tongue at the door of her vagina. That finger or tongue could be her own or that of another woman. Tongues or fingers, perhaps we should state, do not have a gender.

- Very few women who want coitus will have it with just anybody else. For most individuals, women and men, the desire for sexual congress has a specific object in mind, which may take the form of a real person, a part of a person, a figure of one's fantasies such as a film or television, or a character from a book. Actually, many people have a freer and better fantasy sexual life, including in dream life, than real life. And so the sexual object of woman's fantasy life might be fulfilled by another woman or her own self, with the help of fingers or dildos.

- The impact of scientific, medical, psychological and technological developments over the centuries on people's sexual lives. One of these developments has been the invention and access to the contraceptive pill for women. Closely related to the contraceptive pill has been the availability of the morning-after pill, legalised safe abortion and other pregnancy-related prophylactics. And still other developments – some of which prefaced the pill by centuries – have been the manufacture of sexual aids such as books on sexuality, dildos and vibrators, erotica films and others. The point to be appreciated here is that ever since

masculinity. For this reason, of equal importance to men's actual or proclaimed sexual relationships, and at times with greater consequence than their own and other men's sexual practices, prevalent forms of manhood in many parts of contemporary Africa are defined by women's sexual relations. Even more specifically, the big story that is told of manhood in many countries in Africa starts with the question: how, and with whom do women have sex?

This is where we shall start to try to understand the connection of sexuality to the dominant construct of manhood in much of contemporary Africa, through an examination of what it means to men for women to love other women. I look at African female same-sex desires and the struggle to legitimate their existence. I consider what such desires mean to dominant conceptions of African heterosexual masculinity. What will hopefully become clear is that, without understanding the reproduction was decoupled from sex by the advent of the pill and other reproductive and sexual technologies, women have been enabled to have more and more control over their sexual lives. Men's violence against women and coercive sexual practices are, in this regard, one other set of factors or mechanisms that aim to reassert men's control over women and to impede women from having fun with their bodies. Other issues that dis-able women sexually include patriarchal sanctions against sexually free women, personal inhibitions, dislike of one's body, lack of privacy, lack of knowledge about sexuality, the lack of a skilled partner or the unwillingness of one's partner to try new things that one might like to do.

- Finally, the most important thing that a vibrator or dildo or her own fingers do for a woman is to give her control. She is able to direct the apparatus so that she is able to caress the clitoris as lightly or as hard as she wants it. She manipulates the depth of penetration. She regulates the speed. She has the power when to stop and when to start. She can do it at her own time. She can practise with it until she knows what gives her the most pleasure and what will make her orgasm more intense. All of these she cannot do with a man because, for one reason, he is likely to have his own needs. Any woman who is looking for a man who performs like her favourite dildo – the perfect sexual partner – will die before she finds a man who will be pliable and willing to learn about her pleasure and to satisfy her every time. But here is the most troubling aspect for men about women with vibrators or dildos: women penetrating themselves or sexually enjoying each other make penis-centred masculinity or phallocentric sexuality superfluous.

Ultimately, when coupled with lowered inhibitions, lack of fear of pregnancy, lessened societal reprimands and no men's violence, the use of sexual toys by women on their own or between themselves implies that any woman can choose to be penetrated by or to penetrate other women if she so desires. This is the greatest fear at the heart of a particular form of patriarchal heterosexual masculinity: that women can live happily without men's erection.

psychological 'disorder' and social distress that female same-sex sexuality generates in the ruling African masculinity, we would almost certainly misperceive what it means to be a man in today's Africa.

I further look at another category of subjects that belies the dominant view of what makes individual subjects manly. As with women who love other women, this category also introduces or otherwise widens the rupture that inheres in the dominant shape of African masculinity. This category of subjects is thought to especially betray the dominant ideologies of manhood in Africa because these subjects are expected to naturally support the ideology. These are African men who are gay, so we must examine males who prefer to have sex with men rather than women and see what this suggests about the ruling form of heterosexual masculinity.

In the third section of the essay I consider individuals who find both sexes sexually desirable. What are the implications of their practices on dominant masculinity and its sexual inventory? Although space does not allow us to go into much depth, the objective in discussing bisexualities is to highlight more of the complexities of sexual practices that are to be found among African men. The goal is to show that the perspective that views African masculinity simplistically and purely as heterosexual is absurd.

In the fourth section I discuss how the notion of manhood has come to be understood in global critical studies of men and masculinity. I especially consider the question of why non-heterosexual sexualities and genders generate so much anxiety and disorder in the masculinity order. Students of masculinity in Africa will want to know whether the dominant forms of masculinity in their countries mean the same thing as ruling masculinity in other parts of the world. The final section will address this question.

Female same-sex desire and its implications for dominant masculinities

There are many African women who do not like being fucked by men and instead prefer fucking other women. I will explain. My earlier statement that sexuality is a major preoccupation of the dominant form of masculinity in Africa (and the rest of the world) was too general. More specifically, research reveals that for men who ardently subscribe to the aggressive configuration of masculine heterosexuality, the point of relating to women is to fuck them (Plummer 2005). It is not about making love. It is about possessing. The more women a man possesses and the more sought-after he appears in the eyes of other men, the more a 'man' he is.

It is this very fact that informs the struggle of African feminists against gender-based violence. That said, I should also note that some African feminists have appropriated the language of fucking, in contradistinction to the language of making love, when talking about sex. There are many women around the world, as Plummer (2005: 190) notes, who 'not only want to have fun, they also want to fuck'. But by noting that many African women do not like being fucked by men, it has to be agreed that some women instead like fucking *with* men, as opposed to being fucked *by* them.

A variety of forms of love exist in Africa, including the lustful, the companionable, the mad and the romantic woman-to-woman forms – for the simple reason that modern Africa is not distinctive in any essential way from the rest of the contemporary world. Just as lust, companionship and romance exist for heterosexuals on the continent, so too they exist between women. There are many African women who love other women – women might or might not identify as lesbians (Chan Sam 1994). This is part of the dynamic, elusive character of sexual desire: that a woman who has little feeling for being penetrated by a man's penis might otherwise feel excited by being penetrated by another woman with an artificial penis (see Box 44.1).

Activism around the rights of lesbians, gays, bisexuals, transgendered, queer and intersexed (LGBTQI) persons is steadily growing on the continent. Examples of such organisations working in this area include Lesbians, Gays, Bisexuals of

Two women cuddling
each other

Botswana (LeGaBiBo), Gays and Lesbians of Zimbabwe (GALZ), the Gay and Lesbian Coalition of Kenya (GALCK), Behind the Mask, Sister Namibia, Sexual Minorities Uganda (SMUG) and the Coalition of African Lesbians (CAL). Fanny Ann Eddy, the lesbian founder of the Sierra Leone Lesbian and Gay Association, put it very well: 'We do exist' (Human Rights Watch 2004a). Zanele Muholi, the South African photographer, has documented the existence of some of these women in her work. About her 2007 show, staged at the Michael Stevenson gallery in Cape Town, Zanele Muholi wrote:

> *Being* is an exploration of both our existence and our resistance as lesbians/ women loving women, as black women living our intersecting identities in a country that claims equality for all within the LGBTI community, and beyond. The work is aimed at erasing the very stigmatisation of our sexualities as 'unAfrican', even as our very existence disrupts dominant (hetero) sexualities, patriarchies and oppressions that were not of our own making. (Muholi 2007)

Hard as it might be for many countries to accept the right of women to sexual choice and equality, the question that must be asked is: what significance does the phenomenon of women sexually desiring other women have for heterosexual masculinity? The acceptability and legitimacy of same-sex female desires are often attacked, maligned and not fully represented in social life as in the popular imagination. The main aim of such denunciation, assaults and vilification is not simply to exorcise society of same-sex desires. It is part of societal forces aimed at controlling all female sexuality and at subordinating female bodies and desires to men's commands.

Unomah Azuah (2009), a Nigerian poet and teacher of writing, has remarked that 'allusions to same-sex desire have, historically, been rare in African literature and film'. She draws attention to some works by African writers and film-makers from the late 1990s, which challenge the prevalent views about same-sex desire. She further notes how women who have sex with women are represented in popular media:

> If the issue is acknowledged at all, such desire is typically characterised as either a pathological condition that deserves to be punished or eliminated, or an exotic influence ... Homophobic characterisation continue in much popular culture, including in the Nigerian film industry known as Nollywood. In movies like *Last Wedding*, *Emotional Crack*, *Beautiful Faces*, and *End Times*, women who have sex with women are first objectified, presumably for the enjoyment of the male audience, then come to violent ends. Popular media, such as the daily press, throughout Africa commonly treat the topic with mocking humour or anger and contempt against 'the West'. (Azuah 2009: 184)

The concerted erasure, stigmatisation, criminalisation and assaults on women's sexual relations with women are seen in the form of 'corrective rape' and other violent assaults. FannyAnn Eddy poignantly testified in April 2004 at the United Nations Commission on Human Rights:

> I would like to use this opportunity to bring to your attention the dangers vulnerable groups and individuals face not only in my beloved country, Sierra Leone, but throughout Africa. My focus of interest is the lesbian, gay, bisexual and transgender community, which most African leaders do not like to address. In fact, many African leaders do not want to even acknowledge that we exist. Their denial has many disastrous results for our community. We do exist. But because of the denial of our existence, we live in constant fear: fear of the police and officials with the power to arrest and detain us simply because of our sexual orientation ... We live in fear that our families will disown us, as it is not unusual for lesbian, gay bisexual and transgender people to be forced out of their family homes when their identity becomes known ... We live in fear within our communities, where we face constant harassment and violence from neighbors and others. Their homophobic attacks go unpunished by authorities, further encouraging their discriminatory and violent treatment of lesbian, gay, bisexual and transgender people. (Human Rights Watch 2004a)

In September of that year, FannyAnn Eddy was gang raped, stabbed and had her neck broken. She left behind her 10-year-old son.

Zanele Muholi, *Dada* 2003

A woman putting on a
strap-on penis

Human Rights Watch has noted: 'sexuality has become a cultural and religious battleground. The danger comes from the weight, political importance, and emotion increasingly attached to issues of gender and sexuality' (Human Rights Watch 2009: 3). Even in a country like South Africa, where the post-apartheid constitution was the first in the world to explicitly prohibit discrimination on the basis of sexual orientation and to recognise sexual equality, women who love women are still victimised.

ActionAid researchers have reported that South Africa 'is now witnessing a backlash of crimes targeted specifically at lesbian women who are perceived as representing a direct and specific threat to the status quo. This violence often takes the form of "corrective" rape – a way of punishing and "curing" women of their sexual orientation' (Martin et al 2009: 5). Since 1998, at least 31 women who had sexual relations with women were killed in anti-lesbian violence, with activist groups indicating that the real numbers are probably higher given the difficulty of finding out about hate crimes on the basis of sexual orientation (Harrison 2009). The most telling aspect about these murders is that they happen in spite of the legislation that protects queer people from discrimination and offers them legal equality.

Homophobic violence, threats of assaults, psychological abuse, discrediting of women and men who support same-sex sexuality and proscription of homosexual love are not confined to Africa. There are as many African as non-African states – including those states usually referred to as developed – and non-African social groups around the world that do not like women having sexual relations with women. In all the cases, the main aim is to discipline female sexuality, to drive females into 'servicing' heterosexuality and thus to perpetuate masculine domination. The fact that as many non-African as African states and groups are homophobic should put to rest the argument that homosexuality is 'unAfrican'. But it has not. Human Rights Watch (HRW 2002; 2004b; 2005) has documented cases from countries such as the USA, China, Latvia, Poland and India, in which politicians and other national figures have actively sought to prohibit sexual relations other than those between a man and a woman.

Explaining the prohibition and often violent refusal to recognise the fact of women who prefer women to men, Patricia McFadden said:

> A fundamental premise of patriarchal power and impunity is the denial and suppression of women's naming and controlling their bodies for their own joy and nurturing. In all patriarchal societies, women and girls are taught, consistently and often violently, that their bodies are dirty, nasty, smelly, disgusting, corrupting, imperfect, ugly and volatile harbingers of disease and immorality. The redemption of the pathologised female body is seen to come through males of various statuses: fathers, who protect and defend the family honour through them; priests, who experience holiness and godliness through them; brothers, who learn through women and girls how to become authoritative and vigilant; husbands, who realise their masculinity through sexual occupancy and breeding; and strangers, who wreak misogynistic vengeance upon them for an entire range of grievances, imagined and otherwise. A denied right, misinformation, a frown, a disapproving scowl, a raised voice, an angry reprimand, a verbal insult, a shaken fist, a shove, a slap, a punch, rape, a slit throat – these are part of the routine processes of socialisation and gendered identity construction through which girls and women are persistently reminded that they are the chattels of men in our societies. (McFadden 2003: 56)

One very important point to underline from McFadden is how gender power functions. Women who are sexually attracted to women (as men who are sexually attracted to men) are subjected to harassment, violence and medical, psychological or pastoral treatment to reorient them sexually (Cock 2003) because the gender of their sexuality bothers patriarchy.

The link between sexualities and gender has long been explained by feminists and critical scholars of masculinity. Tim Edwards puts it thus: '(G)ender and sexualities … are intricately linked, and it is often far more accurate to talk in terms of gendered sexualities and sexualised genders than of gender and sexuality as if they were two distinct categories' (Edwards 2005: 54). And so it is helpful to understand that women who love women are oppressed for having 'masculinity in the wrong body', 'for being the wrong sort of woman' (Edwards 2005: 54). The case of Caster Semenya, the South African athlete who won the women's 800 metre race at the 2009 International Association of Athletics Federations World Championships in

Berlin, Germany is possibly the best recent example of the discourses from around the world about 'masculinity in the wrong body' or 'being the wrong sort of woman' (Moyo and SAPA 2009).

Violent practices and stigmatising language against women who dare to love women rather than men arise from the fact that patriarchy – especially expressed as patriarchal heterosexual masculinity – instanced by sexual and marital relations between an older man and younger woman, cannot abide such freedom for women. The most important reason for this oft-violent intolerance to women's sexual and gender freedom is because such women's sexual preference of other women over men is indicative of lack of control of men over women's bodies and lives. Such intolerance is often supported by structures such as the law, media, custom, employment policies, family organisation, religious codes and practices and education systems. Women who cannot be subjected to men's social power are dangerous to patriarchal power and masculinity. '[T]he organisation of desire is the domain of relations of power … What is at issue here is power over women' (Carrigan et al 1985: 596).

The same kind of violent and stigmatising sexual and gender discourse applies when women are seen to be too unlike women should be. Patriarchy can only stomach 'ugly women', for example, if they keep their heads down and are content to be seen as ugly. Again, the reason women, unlike men, cannot be allowed to 'own' their bodies and faces, that is, cannot have full rights to look however they do or want to look, is because if women are allowed to be 'ugly' and still think of themselves as wonderful, what is the use of patriarchy?

In sum, the main objective for introducing African masculinities by talking about same-sex female desire is to point to other forms of love, beyond the heterosexual norm, that exist in Africa. The argument is that if all kinds of love to be found in the world are also found in Africa, 'lesbian' love must perforce exist in African societies – unless there is something unimaginably aberrant about Africans. Similarly, if other, non-sexual affectionate feelings can be conceived to exist between African women, why would romantic affections between two African women be inconceivable? Indeed, many African countries proscribe such love, and this is one of the main reasons for its invisibility.

We have highlighted the effects of same-sex female desire on masculinities. Now we turn to men who desire other men.

Male same-sex desire and ideas of manliness

For its sustenance, the power of patriarchy and certain forms of masculinity needs the majority of men and women to believe in it and support its ideology and systems. At a minimum the system of gender domination needs men and women not to mobilise against its structures, to remain acquiescent and not rock the patriarchal boat. Another fundamental premise for the rule of men over women is the denial of male sexualities other than heterosexuality. Even then, research and personal testimonies of men attest to the fact that many African men are sexually attracted to other men (Moodie et al 1988; Harries 1994; Kleinbooi 1994; Mclean and Ngcobo 1994; Nkoli 1994; Epprecht 2005).

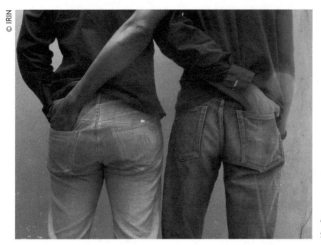

© IRIN

Anonymous gay couple
showing affection

The mere existence of male-to-male African sexuality makes those who swing that way objects of fear and hate within the dominant sexual system. Males who like penises rather than vaginas are made into outlaws. Where it does not attract overt loathing and phobia, the sexual love of a man for other men almost always makes the man a marginal figure, an outsider within those societies in which patriarchal heterosexual masculinity is normative. Men who love other men end up as objects of homophobic rage because such love disturbs a cornerstone of patriarchal heterosexual power in that it shows that men are not of one mind and feeling when it comes to sexuality. Men who eroticise men instead of women engender a potential crisis in ruling ideas of true masculinity (Edwards 2005).

The potential crisis engendered within the ruling ideology of masculinity is not only because of the contradiction of the idea of gay masculinity. Also, the behaviour and desires of men who love other men indicate that there is neither one, homogenous, untroubled masculinity, nor one form of masculine subjectivity and identity. According to Stephen Whitehead, 'some of the most important lessons we have learned from the critical study of men concerns their diversity, their multiplicity and their differences. We know that men are not all the same. We know that there is more than one expression of masculinity'(Whitehead 2006: 2). And we know that gay masculinity is one form of African masculinity.

The criminalisation, widespread phobia and violence against men who prefer sexual relations with other men are a result of and perpetuate the fact that there are many shapes of manhood. Many societies are organised to support one predominant form of manhood – the heterosexual form. The underside of this organisation of male sexual desire is that it is forbidden, often with the help of violence, for men to find other men desirable. In these societies such men must learn, surely against themselves, that, for instance, the way another man smells can never be arousing; the way the buttocks of another man look in their pants should not be allowed to stimulate sexual feelings; or the way another man smiles must not stir up thoughts of love. In many societies, if a man goes against heteronormative masculinity and finds other men desirable he might well be ostracised, routinely harassed, often jailed, violently assaulted and even murdered.

Any male who desires men sexually, whether or not he identifies as gay, is unacceptable in most African societies because he belies patriarchy. A man who finds pleasure in kissing another man's lips or other body parts indicates that there is no natural link between being male and heterosexual desire. To love sucking penises as opposed to clitorises and women's breasts turns out to be more than simply an act between two individuals. Contrary to prevailing depictions, a man who chooses to suck a penis, just like the woman who chooses to eat a vagina, is not simply engaging in a deeply subjective act or a way of relating between two persons in their private lives. Their actions boldly reveal that sex acts are highly social and political. Men penetrating each other, just like women having sex with each other and the sexual congress between men and women, can be and are always useful in ordering society and politics. Therefore:

> The history of homosexuality obliges us to think of masculinity not as a single object with its own history, but as being constantly constructed within the history of an evolving social structure, a structure of sexual power relations. It obliges us to see this construction as a social struggle going on in a complex ideological and political field, in which there is a continuing process of mobilisation, marginalisation, contestation, resistance and subordination. (Carrigan et al 1985: 589)

The disgust that some men and women experience when imagining a man being penetrated by another man cannot be regarded as merely instinctive and biological. The stigma exhibited by many men and women on seeing men showing sexual tenderness to each other is not just an emotional and cognitive reaction. Sexual disgust, hatred and stigma are the end products generated by patriarchal heterosexual structures, integral to the very constitution of patriarchy and heterosexuality. Conversely, the sexual guilt or shame we experience when men feel sexually stirred up by other men is thus also an effect of the prevailing structures. How we sense, feel and think about others and our own desires and pleasure is not only hormonal or genetic. Sexual sensations, feelings, thoughts and behaviours are as much social and political practices as they are physiological and psychological. Roger Lancaster addresses not 'the role of heterosexual norms in establishing homosexual stigma and minority status, but the role of homosexual stigma in structuring male sexual and gender norm' (Lancaster 1999: 99).

The prevalent heterosexual form of masculinity is thus not a fact of nature, but practice that emerges from the life of power within a society – from the indigenous political and economic forces operative in that society as well as forces imposed from outside. But it is important to underline the fact that masculinity is not a mere artefact of political forces (such as military rule) or economic forces (such as the market), even though it intersects with these forces. Many countries in Africa and around the world discourage same-sex male relationships, sometimes with state-sanctioned violence, including whippings, homophobic laws and prison terms (Reddy 2001; Reuters 2005).

In short, any discussion of manhood in Africa is obviously inadequate if it does not include same-sex male desires. Discussing men who have sex with men is important because the simple (but violently resisted) point that all forms of sexual

---

BOX 44.2

A brief word on terms: what to call women who prefer women and men who prefer men?

Women who refuse to be sexual objects of men and opt to seek sexual happiness with other women — who in African countries often do so under threat of death (Huisman 2006; Orford 2006) — have come to be referred to as 'women who have sex with women' or WSW (Epprecht 2008). The equivalent term for men who prefer men's sexual company is 'men who have sex with men' or MSM (Epprecht 2008). The terms are supposed to obviate the cultural and political baggage freighted by the terms homosexual, lesbian and gay. But they are, I am afraid, lifeless. They fail to fully represent the array and dynamism of sexual relating.

Yet the uncritical use of terms gay and lesbian in many places in Africa is no less problematic. 'This notion of gayness and lesbianism as "identities" involving choices is politically dangerous and can be expected to provoke strong reactions,' argues Jacklyn Cock (2003: 42). She goes on to say:

> The assertion of a public gay identity is particularly problematic in an African context. To illustrate, Kendall found that the notion of 'lesbian' was not helpful in understanding female — female relationships in Basotho. She found widespread, apparently normative erotic relationships among Basuto [sic] women, but this (including instances of cunnilingus) was not defined as sexual, and not a single Mosotho — to Kendall's knowledge — defined herself as a lesbian. Kendall concludes that 'love between women is as natural to southern Africa as the soil

---

desires exist in Africa needs to be reiterated until such time that great numbers of African people acknowledge this fact without getting all knotted up. Talking of African males who desire other males is important because the desires of African males are part of the larger world where such desires exist. Many African countries prohibit men having sex with other men. Given this backhanded acknowledgement of the existence of male-to-male sexual love, it is not that African countries do not know that there is such love, but rather that the powers that be believe that it undermines the naturalised socio-sexual order.

Are you straight or what?

Besides same-sex desires, there are many individuals who enjoy sexual relations with both women and men. Such people might desire both sexes because they find that they are not fully true to themselves sexually if they restrict themselves to one sex. They are available for sexual mating with either men or women because they find both sexually attractive, what the *Daily Nation* newspaper in Kenya referred to as 'bi-curiosity' and Gloria Wekker named 'multiplicitous sexualities' (Machera 2004).

itself, but that homophobia is a Western import' (Kendall 1998: 224). She emphasizes that Basotho society has not constructed a social category 'lesbian'. Basotho women define sexual activity in such a way that makes lesbianism linguistically inconceivable. (Cock 2003: 42)

One of the terms I have used here is 'sexual relations', which I employ more or less interchangeably with sexual relating. I feel it better embraces both the breadth, drive yet also elusive character of behaviours, attitudes, emotions and ideas through which human beings sexually interact with each other or one person relates to herself or himself. The behaviours, attitudes, emotions and ideas range from a woman touching another woman or her own body in a sexual manner; the attitudes she has towards another's genitalia and secondary sex organs, and other body parts not usually considered sexual (such as hair or calves); the way others dress; feelings of joy, tenderness, shame, disgust or guilt about particular body parts or certain acts; and imagining oneself or someone else engaged in certain acts, which might include writing about or video recording the acts.

The point of all this is that what we call what we do, how we identify ourselves and others is very important. The act of naming — calling ourselves or being called homosexual or bisexual men or women, *stabane* or *moffie*, *supi*, women who love women, women who have sex with women, for instance — is soaked with politics. One has to be careful about one's words then, for at times, the terms of engagement can be more rather than less confusing of what we wish to relate. Words can be an act of submission or resistance, supportive of the status quo or defy prevailing structures. Naming, as part of discourse, is then a central element of the process of making ourselves as sexual beings and the world in which we express that sexuality.

Individuals with this preference might call themselves bisexual if they are aware of the lifestyle and identify with it. But, as is often the case with terms that arise out of a specific society and its politics, the label 'bisexual' conveys specific culturally mediated meanings, and might not have ready equivalents in African communities and cultures. In other words, many African individuals who like both women and men might not necessarily express a bisexual identity and lifestyle. They might just prefer to be loved in a sexual way by a woman or man or both at any point in time of their lives (Reid 2005).

There are three lessons that we learn from practices shown by the work of scholars such as Dunbar Moodie (1988), Patricia McFadden (2003), Graeme Reid (2005), Sylvia Tamale (2005) and Marc Epprecht (2008). First, it is clear that for sexualities to be fully appreciated, they must be seen in the context within which they are expressed (see Box 44.2). Whereas it might be relatively easy to flourish as a gay man or lesbian woman in some of the big cities of the world and some locales in Africa, a different form of sexual expression of same-sex attraction might be common in other cities, towns, townships and villages. In these other places, men and women might publicly be heterosexual while privately engaging in other forms of sexual relating.

The second lesson is that some people do not explore the full potential of their sexuality, for a variety of reasons. Some men, for instance, have not had rings inserted into their anuses, been covered in chocolate, had their nipples in a clamp or worn latex for sexual purposes, not because they abhor such practices but simply because they are not aware of these possibilities. Often people do what they do sexually because parts of themselves remain obscured and cowed by the dominant discourses about sexual personhood or because they have not had exposure to other possible sexual worlds. Hence, many of the things we sexually desire often remain unknown to us through our lifetime.

The third lesson is that sexual relating, which incorporates not just physical acts but also sexual knowledge, desire and identification, is always 'a work in progress'. Sexual relating (which expresses this idea better than the term sexual relationship) is also more unsettled than is usually represented in renditions of sexual life. Individuals are not born knowing what they desire sexually. They have to work at finding what turns them on and what they do not like.

Clearly, the fact that there are individuals who have sexual preference for both sexes further complicates the picture of sexual relations of African men and women. In their attraction to both men and women these individuals constitute another set that actively (or by the mere fact of their existence) questions the universality and naturalness of heterosexuality, especially its core act of penile-vaginal penetration. Individuals who love both men and women as sexual partners challenge the controlling power of ruling men to set the rules of sexual relating.

There are many other sexual acts, ideas, preferences, lifestyles and identities indicative of the heterogeneity of sexual life in Africa, but these three make the point well enough: there is no singular, stereotypical African sexuality. Heterosexuality might be the dominant form of sexual practice, in the sense of having many more subscriptions and structural support, but it exists alongside many other practices.

In short, it is ludicrous to think that any manner of sexual love that exists today cannot be present in post-colonial Africa. Modern Africa is of course part of the world and all its loves and hatreds, laws and restrictions. And so to argue that Africans who engage in same-sex copy foreign, un-African activities is to claim a different, marginal and otherworldly identity for Africa in the world – an identity of Africans who do not experience the same kinds of feelings and thoughts as people on other continents. There is nothing particularly different about Africans, nothing that essentially distinguishes them from Americans, Asians, Europeans and any other group of human beings except their historical and contemporary social conditions. If Africans are not singular in the feelings they have for others, the antipathy for the existence and the talk about foreignness of bisexualities can only mean that non-heterosexual sexualities are a serious disturbance to the dominant shape of African masculinity and thus the need to suppress and outlaw them.

But why do sexualities other than heterosexuality generate a disturbance for the dominant form of masculinity?

Why non-heterosexual masculinities convulse dominant masculinity

Fucking women might be an important theme in the narrative of how a male is identified as appropriately manly in many cultures. However, it is crucial to note that not every man who has sex with a woman is part of the forces that actively suppress women or is against same-sex relations. Many men who have sex with women might just do so because that is the done thing, oblivious as to how their sexual acts – as long as they are not being overtly violent or abusive – fit snugly into the larger social organisation of men's gender relations with other men. Others might, of course, be afraid to express what they would really like to do, and keep doing what they have always done. And there are men who simply do not know anything else, who are ignorant of their own sexual desires.

It is when a man has multiple sexual partners with women but does not allow the same freedoms to a woman that he moves into the zone in which he actively participates in the heterosexual masculine domination of women. Even then, however great the number of women a man has sex with, this on its own does not exhaust the meaning of dominant masculinity or the resources from which a particular form of manhood draws its hegemony. Although it might be enlightening to examine the practices of a man who possesses many women when trying to comprehend the maintenance of ruling masculinity – because such form of masculinity usually denounces women who have many sexual partners – ruling masculinity cannot be reduced to sex. And so the only analysis that is likely to be convincing in examining the practices of a male who has multiple, concurrent sexual female partners at this point in many societies in Africa at least is one that shows such practices as indexing the larger relations of gender. That is, the relation of dominant masculinity to those of femininity and non-dominant masculinity.

Masculine dominance in all societies in which it is encountered is propped up by several premises. In addition to encouraging men to sow their wild oats, a society that supports men's domination of women also needs to teach boys and girls that female bodies are dirtier and weaker than those of males; that females are not as intelligent or as strong as males; it needs to deny the rights of girls and women to equality before the law, to education, to equal pay, to bodily integrity, to safety, to the right to own property and to many other rights; and it needs to pathologise the bodies of males who have sex with other males or females who have sex with other females. Above all, it needs vertical and horizontal violence against girls and women, as well as against men who undermine the sexual gender order. Ultimately, men who have sex with multiple women concurrently are expressing the might of the dominant form of manhood while, in contrast, women who are caught in such situations live out the powerlessness of womanhood.

Men who come out as loving to have sex with other men stand at the margins of a society that supports men's domination of women. Indeed, gay men often find that they are expelled or marginalised from the social category called 'men'. Testimonies such as that of Kipkemboi (see Chapter 51 of this volume) abound.

Masculinity cannot therefore be reduced to sexuality. It also cannot be equated with the roles men play (such as the breadwinner or father), or the male body (such as men who pump iron so that they look big), or male identity (Carrigan et al 1985). However, Robert Morrell has correctly pointed out that the term masculinity is often employed to talk about 'a specific identity, belonging to a specific male person'. He adds:

> While this gender identity is acquired in social contexts and circumstances, it is 'owned' by an individual. It bears the marks and characteristics of the history which formed it – frequently with salient childhood experiences imparting a particular set of prejudices and preferences, joys and terrors. Masculinity viewed in this particular way can be understood as something that can be deployed or used. Individuals can choose to respond to a particular situation in one or another way. While there are criticisms of this conceptualization as voluntaristic, such a construction allows for the examination of individual masculinities at work. It also promotes the examination of micro aspects of masculinity, particularly of the body – that major bearer of masculine value and symbolism. (Morrell 2001: 7–8)

Even then, the idea of being a man does not refer to any one man's idea but rather many ideas, of men and women, about what turns a male person into a man; to things done not by any one man but by many men and women (such as what is done in raising a boy-child, or what in acquiescing to, affirming or challenging what a boyfriend, or husband, brother or father does). The bits and pieces that make up manhood are produced in interaction between males, and between males and females. The common thing among the stuff of masculinity is 'a claim to authority that puts [some men] at the top of some hierarchy ... whether it be the structure of an institution, the structure of society, the nature of someone's knowledge, or the nature of someone's experience' (Kiesling 2001: 252). Masculinity therefore has to be seen as a set of actions, relations and discourses that groups men from other men, rendering some men more powerful and others not so powerful. The stuff of men is not necessarily the same from one group to the next, or stable from one historical moment to the next.

Things that one society refers to as 'masculinity' are not the same things that another refers to and, indeed, if they are, might be valued differently by various social groupings. Even within a single society, though, there often exist clashing ideas from one group of men to another about what it means to be a man. The clash of ideas might be generated by the fault lines of ethnicity, culture, religion, political affiliation, age, race, marital status, income, geographical location, school ties and sexual orientation (Ratele 2008). Therefore, it has been common among critical students of men to talk of masculinities rather than masculinity.

The hegemonic form of masculinity tends to occupy a ruling position in a society or group, while other masculinities occupy complicit or subordinate positions (Connell 1995). Non-hegemonic forms are categorised as marginalised, subordinate or complicit. Morrell asserts that 'generally speaking, these other forms of less powerful masculinities develop outside the corridors of power. Minorities, defined in terms of race, class, ethnicity or sexual orientation, all characteristically understand what being a man means differently from members of the ruling class or elite and from each other too' (Morrell 2001b: 7). As far as sexuality is concerned, aggressive heterosexual masculine practices tend to occupy the dominant position in many societies, while other practices such as homosexual, peaceful sexual practices occupy less powerful positions.

A highly influential concept that has been employed in critical studies of men and masculinities is that of 'hegemonic masculinity' (Connell et al 1982; Kessler et al 1982; Connell 1983; Carrigan et al 1985; Connell and Messerschmidt 2005). It is important to note that the concept of hegemonic masculinity is not indigenous to Africa and therefore employing it and theorising the conditions of men in Africa requires careful consideration. But the concept has influenced many researchers and theorists of male lives and relations on the continent and has utility in the thinking about the things that men and boys do (Luyt and Foster 2001; Morrell 2001a; Fouten 2006; Shefer et al 2007).

Hegemonic masculinity refers to the things males (for the most part, but also some females) do that support the subjugation of girls and women as a group (Connell and Messerschmidt 2005). The origins of the concept are in Australia, where in the early 1980s a group of Australian researchers began to think seriously and critically about the gender of men (Connell et al 1982; Kessler et al 1982; Connell 1983; Carrigan et al 1985). Hegemonic masculinity is also evident in how economic, political, scientific, religious, educational, sporting and cultural institutions, among others, are structured to support the male domination of females. Things that men do could and do include such acts as having multiple concurrent sexual partners and not reflecting about it; demonstrating self-composure and not disclosing too much feeling; exhibiting arrogance and not being too concerned with others' feelings; toughness; and driving at high speeds.

The practices and institutions that define this sort of manhood have become hegemonic because they are usually deliberately or unconsciously encouraged by society and its constituent parts. This encouragement comes in the form of the cultivation of boys' experiences in families, schools, sports clubs, religious institutions and from peers, as well as the approving portrayals in movies, television, newspapers and magazines. The most revealing part about all of this is that the same behaviour that receives active or tacit support when expressed by boys and men is almost always vehemently discouraged or at least frowned upon when engaged in by girls and women. It is in this differentiation between boys and girls that the production of male gender power and a thus a certain kind of ruling masculinity is found. This gender-differentiated development of males and females forms a certain type of dominant masculinity. It is evident each time a male gets knowing, encouraging looks if he is seen with a new girl, but a female is met with disapproving looks and considered trash if she is seen with more than one boy.

'Hegemonic masculinity is ... a mesh of social practices productive of gender-based hierarchies, including violence that supports these hierarchies; that is, the unequal relations between females and males as groups' (Ratele 2008b: 516). What this conceptualisation of men's gender practices allows is a search for differences between men, for versions of masculinity (Ratele 2008a: 33). If there are heterogeneous and differently positioned masculinities around the world, within different societies and in different institutions of any society, we need to find out how different individuals and groups of men are positioned in relation to the dominant men and form of masculinity in any given place. At the same time though, there is still the important project of understanding how in different places there are varying but also similar elements that define the powerful version of masculinity.

According to Russel Luyt, around the Cape Flats in the province of the Western Cape, South Africa, the three factors that define the dominant version of masculinity are toughness, control and sexuality (Luyt and Foster 2001, 2005). Others have suggested that the prized expression of manhood in that country is defined by money power, leadership in public life, hardiness, intellectual superiority and sexual prowess (Ratele 2008a). To be regarded as a successful masculine subject, a man's man, then, it has been argued a person needs to be well-employed, smart, a leader of other men and women, physically tough but also sexually strong (Ratele 2008a).

It seems there is agreement that one of the central ideas defining the hegemonic, ruling or dominant configuration of masculinity in some parts of Africa (and thus, contrastingly, what has been referred to as emphasised femininity) is sexual activity and passivity, sexual domination and submission, sexual prowess and availability. In her work on the construction of masculinity among young Namibian males, Heike Becker (2005) has said that, along with violence and alcohol abuse, sexual prowess is 'central to the discursive construction of masculinities among young, urban Owambo', but she also cautions that it is important to be mindful of the 'gaps between discursive constructions of masculinity and the lived experience of men' (Becker 2005: 36), to bear in mind that what men say is not always what they do in daily life.

Nevertheless, the powerful form of heterosexual manhood in many societies of the world is defined by men's sexual prowess, as shown by the number of women with whom they have sex, the sexual attractiveness of their female partners, the claims about the number of 'sexual rounds' they can go with women, among other sexual games and concerns. Viagra is perhaps the best-known example that attests to the fact that sexual prowess is central to heterosexual manhood. There are many other sexual aids on the market that support men to 'keep it up' or 'satisfy women', some preceding the arrival of Viagra, others that have followed it.

Furthermore, African cultural traditions are replete with examples of herbal products used by men to treat erectile dysfunction – a tradition that plumbs the essence of heterosexual masculinity (a popular one found in South Africa, which originates from Zulu tradition, is *umvuza induku* – wake up the stick). In contrast, the prevalent style of heterosexual womanhood is defined by expressing passivity, submission and availability to men as shown by how a woman dresses, sits, satisfies her man and the power of her male partner. The key sexual lesson then, as far as masculinity is concerned in most societies, is that a 'real' man needs to have sex with beautiful women, primarily because the prevailing configuration of masculinity in Africa is heterosexual masculinity. Ultimately, the struggle around sexuality is a political struggle, to be aimed at power structures and social practices, in addition to widespread psychological theories that support ordering of men's and women's sexual relations in a hierarchical structure, and that sexuality has to do with men's power over other men and women.

Men and women who have sexual preferences that are other than heterosexual generate anxiety and disorder in the dominant order of masculinity because they identify around acts other than those that uphold the order of gendered sexualities, hence complicating the picture of sexual relations of men to women. As Rob Pattman and Fatuma Chege (2003: 100) observe, 'it is in those societies in which sexual desire is presumed to be synonymous with heterosexual desire that gender identities tend to be most polarised'. The current global gendered sexualities order requires that women submit to men sexually and in other ways. The relations of women to men are those in which the latter do sexual things to the former, and those that dramatise a colonising penis and colonised vulva. Men who are attracted to men (or both) and women who are attracted to women (or both) by the mere fact of their existence question and potentially mess up the power (besides the apparent universality and naturalness) of ruling heterosexual masculinity.

Conclusion

The main argument in this essay has been that there are naturally multiple forms of female sexual desires in modern Africa, some of which are permitted by power and others forbidden and thus largely invisible. Suggestions that certain types of sexualities are unAfrican are absurd and baseless. There cannot be anything essentially different about Africans that distinguishes them from non-Africans. In other words, there is nothing essentially uncommon about the sexual desires and practices of Africans, no apparent sexual distinctiveness that can be traced to the historical and contemporary social developments that have shaped Africa.

Given that African men and women are not naturally different in the sexual feelings they have for others, the hostility towards homosexualities and bisexualities can only mean that such sexualities disturb the dominant shape of African masculinity and hence the need to suppress them. What we hope is clear from this discussion is that without understanding the psychological disorder and social distress that same-sex sexuality and bisexualities generate in the ruling African masculinity we miss an important piece in the story of what being a man in Africa is supposed to mean.

References

Azuah, U. (2009) 'Same-sex sexuality issues in some African popular media', *Canadian Journal of African Studies* 43(1): 184–187

Becker, H. (2005) '"I am the man"': rethinking masculinities in northern Namibia', in Gibson, D. and Hardan, A. (eds) *Rethinking Masculinities, Violence and AIDS*, Amsterdam, Het Spinhuis

Carrigan, T., Connell, R.W. and Lee, J. (1985) 'Toward a new sociology of masculinity', *Theory and Society* 14(5): 551–604

Chan Sam, T. (1994) 'Five women: profiles of black lesbian life on the reef', in Gevisser, M. and Cameron, E. (eds) *Defiant Desire: Gay and Lesbian Lives in South Africa*, Johannesburg, Ravan Press

Cock, Jacklyn (2003) 'Engendering gay and lesbian rights: the equality clause in the South African constitution', *Women's Studies International Forum* 26(1): 35–45

Connell, R.W. (1987) *Gender and Power: Society, the Person and Sexual Politics*, Palo Alto, University of California Press

—— (1995) *Masculinities*, Cambridge, Polity Press

Connell, R.W., Ashenden, D.J., Kessler, S. and Dowsett, G.W. (1982) *Making the Difference: Schools, Families and Social Division*, Sydney, Allen and Unwin

Connell, R.W. and Messerschmidt, M. (2005) 'Hegemonic masculinity: rethinking the concept, *Gender Society* 19: 829–895

Edwards, T. (2005) 'Queering the pitch? Gay masculinities', in Kimmel, M.S., Hearn J. and Connell R.W. (eds) *Handbook of Studies on Men and Masculinities,* Thousand Oaks, Sage

Epprecht, M. (2005) 'Male-male sexuality in Lesotho: two conversations', in Reid, G. and Walker, L. (eds) (2005) *Men Behaving Differently: South African Men since 1994*, Cape Town, Double Storey

—— (2008) *Heterosexual Africa? The History of an Idea from the Age of Exploration to the Age of AIDS*, Athens, Ohio University Press; Scottsville, University of Kwazulu-Natal Press

Fouten, E.S. (2006) 'Exploring how adolescent boys negotiate regulatory conceptions of masculinity', unpublished masters psychology (research) thesis, Bellville, University of Western Cape

Harries, P. (1994) *Work, Culture and Identity: Migrant Labourers in Mozambique and South Africa, c.1860–1910*, Portsmouth, Heinemann

Harrison, R. (2009) 'Gangs use rape to "cure" lesbians', *Mail and Guardian online*, 13 March, http://www.mg.co.za/article/2009-03-13-gangs-use-rape-to-cure-lesbians, accessed 15 December 2009

Huisman, B. (2006) 'Teen beaten to death for being a lesbian', *Sunday Times*, 19 February

Human Rights Watch (HRW) (2002) 'India: epidemic of abuse: police harassment of HIV/ Aids outreach workers in India', 1 July, http://www.hrw.org/en/report/2002/07/01/ epidemic-abuse, accessed 14 November 2010

—— (2004a) 'Sierra Leone: Lesbian rights activist brutally murdered', 5 October, http://www.hrw.org/en/news/2004/10/05/sierra-leone-lesbian-rights-activist-brutally-murdered#_Eddy_Testimony, accessed 11 December 2009

—— (2004b) *In a Time of Torture: The Assault on Justice in Egypt's Crackdown on Homosexual Conduct*, New York, Human Rights Watch

—— (2005) 'China: Police shut down gay, lesbian event: government persecutes civil society groups that address HIV/AIDS', 20 December, http://hrw.org/en/news/2005/12/19/china-police-shut-down-gay-lesbian-event, accessed 13 November 2010

—— (2009) *Together, Apart: Organising around Sexual Orientation and Gender Identity Worldwide*, New York, Human Rights Watch

Human Rights Watch (HRW) and The International Gay and Lesbian Human Rights Commission (2003) *More Than a Name: State-Sponsored Homophobia and Its Consequences in Southern Africa*, New York, Human Rights Watch

Kendall, Kathyrn (1998) 'When a woman loves a woman in Lesotho', in Murray, S. and Roscoe, W. (eds) *Boy-wives and Female Husbands: Studies in African Homosexualities*, New York, Palgrave

Kessler, S.J., Ashenden, D.J., Connell, R.W. and Dowsett, G.W. (1982) *Ockers and Disco-Maniacs*, Sydney, Inner City Education Centre

Kiesling, Scott Fabius (2001) '"Now I gotta watch what I say": shifting constructions of masculinity in discourse', *Journal of Linguistic Anthropology* 11(2): 250–327

Kleinbooi, Hein (1994) 'Identity crossfire: on being a black gay student activist', in Gevisser, M. and Cameron, E. (eds) *Defiant Desire: Gay and Lesbian Lives in South Africa*, Braamfontein, Ravan

Lancaster, R.N. (1999) '"That we should all turn queer?" Homosexual stigma in the making of manhood and the breaking of a revolution in Nicaragua', in Parker, R. and Aggleton, P. (eds) *Culture, Society and Sexuality: A Reader*, London, UCL Press

Langa, M. and Eagle, G. (2008) The intractability of militarised masculinity: a case study of former self-defence unit members in the Kathorus area, South Africa', *South African Journal of Psychology* 38(1):152–175

Lesbians, Gays, Bisexuals of Botswana (LeGaBiBo) (2006) 'About us', http://www.legabibo. org.bw/, accessed 21 December 2009

Luyt, R. and Foster D. (2001) 'Hegemonic masculine conceptualisation in gang culture', *South African Journal of Psychology* 31(3): 1–11

—— (2005) 'The male attitude norms inventory-II: a measure of masculinity ideology in South Africa', *Men and Masculinities* 8(2): 208–229

Machera, M. (2004) 'Opening a can of worms: A debate on female sexuality in the lecture theatre', in Arnfred, S. (ed) *Rethinking Sexualities in Africa*, Uppsala, The Nordic Africa Institute.

Martin, A., Kelly, A., Turquet, L. and Ross, S. (2009) *Hate Crimes: The Rise of Corrective Rape in South Africa*, London, ActionAid

McFadden, Patricia (2003) 'Sexual pleasure as feminist choice', *Feminist Africa* 2: 50–60, also available at: http://www.feministafrica.org/index.php/sexual-pleasure-as-feminist-choice, accessed 15 December 2009

Mclean, H. and Ngcobo, L. (1994) '"Abangibhamayo bathi ngimnandi" (those who fuck me say I'm tasty): gay sexuality in a reef township', in Gevisser, M. and Cameron, E. (eds) *Defiant Desire: Gay and Lesbian Lives in South Africa*, Johannesburg, Ravan Press

Moodie, T.D. with Ndatshe, V. and Sibuyi, B. (1988) 'Migrancy and male sexuality on the South African gold mines', *Journal of Southern African Studies* 14(2): 229–245

Morrell, R. (ed) (2001a) *Changing Men in Southern Africa*, Pietermaritzburg, University of Natal Press

—— (2001b) 'The times of change: men and masculinity in South Africa', in Morrell, R. (ed) *Changing Men in Southern Africa*, Pietermaritzburg, University of Natal Press

Moyo, P. and South African Press Association (SAPA) (2009) 'Under-fire Semenya set to run, says athletics body', 19 August, http://www.mg.co.za/article/2009-08-19-underfire-semenya-set-to-run-says-athletics-body, accessed 17 May 2010

Muholi, Zanele (2007) *Being*, Cape Town, Michael Stevenson, http://www.michaelstevenson.com/contemporary/exhibitions/muholi/being.htm, accessed 15 December 2009

Nkoli, S. (1994) 'Wardrobes: coming out as a black gay activist in South Africa', in Gevisser, M. and Cameron, E. (eds) *Defiant Desire: Gay and Lesbian Lives in South Africa*, Johannesburg, Ravan Press

Orford, M. (2006) 'The deadly cost of breaking the silence: A tribute to Lorna Mlosana', *Feminist Africa* 6: 77–82

Pattman, R. and Chege, F. (2003) *Finding Our Voices: Gendered and Sexual Identities and HIV/AIDS in Education*, Nairobi, UNICEF Eastern and Southern Africa

Plummer, K. (2005) 'Male sexualities', in Kimmel, M.S., Hearn J. and Connell, R.W. (eds) *Handbook of Studies on Men and Masculinities*, Thousand Oaks, Sage

Ratele, K. (2008a) 'Masculinity and male mortality in South Africa. African safety promotion', *A Journal of Injury and Violence Prevention* 7(2): 19–41

—— (2008b) 'Analysing males in Africa: certain useful elements in considering ruling masculinities', *African and Asian Studies* 7: 515-536

Ratele, K., Swart, L. and Seedat, M. (2009) 'South Africa', in Hadfield, P. (ed) *Nightlife and Crime: Social and Governance in International Perspective*, Oxford, Oxford University Press

Reddy, V. (2001) 'Homophobia, human rights, and gay and lesbian equality in Africa', *Agenda (African Feminism 1 Special Issue)* 50: 3–86

Reid, G. (2005) 'A man is a man completely and a wife is a wife completely: gender classification and performance amongst "ladies" and "gents" in Ermelo, Mpumalanga', in Reid, G. and Walker, L. (eds) *Men Behaving Differently: South African Men Since 1994*, Cape Town, Double Storey

Reuters (2005) 'Polish PM candidate says homosexuality unnatural', 3 October, http://www.redorbit.com/news/international/258443/polish_pm_candidate_says_homosexuality_unnatural/index.html, accessed 15 December 2009

Shefer, T., Ratele, K., Strebel, A., Shabalala, N.J. and Buikema, R. (eds) (2007) *From Boys to Men: Social Constructions of Masculinity in Contemporary Society*, Landsdowne, University of Cape Town Press

Tamale, S. (2005) 'Eroticism, sensuality and "women's secrets" among the Baganda: a critical analysis', *Feminist Africa* 5: 9–36

Tau, P. (2007) 'Night of fun ends in death', *The Star*, 9 July

Whitehead, S.M. (ed) (2006) *Men and Masculinities: Critical Studies in Sociology* (Vol. 5: *Global Masculinities*), London, Routledge

45

Multiple meanings of manhood among boys in Ghana[1]

Akosua Adomako Ampofo and John Boateng

Introduction

Since 1995, one of the authors of this chapter, Akosua Adomako Ampofo, has taught two graduate courses in African studies: 'Gender and culture in African societies' and 'Gender and development in Africa'. These have been among the most satisfying in her career as a university teacher. Although male students normally outnumber females in these classes – a function of male/female ratios at the University of Ghana as a whole – in 2004, for the first time, the 'Gender and culture' class included only male students. Also, for the first time it focused on men and masculinities and was co-taught by Aloysius Denkabe, a male faculty member from the English department. The material they used came from the social sciences and humanities and included novels as well as a significant number of works by male authors.

Three variables had changed from earlier years: the class composition, the course focus and the sex of the co-instructor, and it seemed that simultaneously so did the level of engagement of the male students with the idea of transformative gender relations. However, what was most enlightening for the instructors was how the shift in focus from (1) gender relations and women's oppression (even though the students looked at these issues in very concrete ways) to (2) how masculinity is constructed and sometimes operates to marginalise women as well as oppress some men was associated with a much greater level of commitment among the (male) students to the equal treatment of females. In other words, there was a shift from a typical oppressor/oppressed conceptualisation of gender relations. Both Adomako Ampofo and Denkabe felt that such a binary construction was overly simplistic and not particularly helpful because it reduced masculinities to 'good' and 'bad' masculinities (Robinson 2001).[2]

We, the authors, are both unabashedly biased in our approach. We feel that men and women, but especially boys and men, must undergo transformations if we are to see more equal gender relations, and that men, especially, must understand how masculinity operates and what it does to women and men. When men are led to intimate perspectives on men, often through the eyes of other men, they are better equipped to recognise so-called hegemonic masculinities and their deleterious effects, not only on women, but also on children and on other men.[3] In this chapter, we seek to open a window on some of the meanings of manhood among boys aged between 11 and 15 in the hope that this will expand our understanding of masculinities and contribute to the development of 'new' men (Morrell, 2002).[4]

Masculinity

Robert Morrell (1998) points out that over the last three decades increasing numbers of researchers, especially from Europe and North America, have devoted some attention to the study of masculinities. Indeed, by the 1990s, men's studies had become an accepted discipline and the study of masculinities seemed almost to have become the flavour of the moment.[5] Feminist researchers, however, have always analysed and categorised practices, attitudes, beliefs, relations and concepts of masculinity and femininity in the context of gender. Indeed, a core focus of feminist theorising and practice has been to examine and address the ways in which being a social male impacts on the lives of people who are female.

Within population and family planning discourse, a small corps of researchers who have focused on the male role in Africa (for example, the work of Alex Chicka Ezeh and Francis Nii-Amoo Dodoo, among others, on reproductive decision making in Ghana) have also pointed out how influential women's partners were in determining whether, and when, pregnancies would occur, and whether, and which kind of, family planning methods would be used. A 2003 volume titled *Men and Masculinities in Modern Africa*, edited by Lisa Lindsay and Stefan Miescher is, as far as we know, the first contemporary volume on Africa that theorises and problematises masculinity as gender rather than merely describing or valorising the experiences of men (Lindsay and Miescher 2003).[6] Nonetheless, the idea of studying men and masculinities is still viewed with scepticism, if not dismissed outright in many academic programmes in Africa. Further, by and large, unlike in Europe and North America, it is largely female scholars who have examined these issues.[7]

The term masculinity signifies a collective gender identity and not a natural attribute. It is socially constructed, fluid, resulting in diverse forms across different times and contexts and mediated by socio-economic position, race, ethnicity, religion, age, geographic location and other local factors,[8] making it more appropriate to refer to masculinities (Connell 1998; Morrell 1998; Ratele, 2002; Adomako Ampofo and Prah 2009). Masculinity also defines how boys and men should behave, be treated, dress, appear, what they should succeed at and what attitudes and qualities they should have (Bhasin 2004) and this is why there are variations across societal and social groups.

The study of masculinities is an effort to make sense of the relationships between individual males and groups of males as well as between males and females. In many contexts there is an attempt to disrupt so-called dominant or hegemonic masculinities. Our own aim as researchers and teachers is to understand and explain normative as well as marginal or unconventional masculinities, and the tensions within and between them. Morrell (1998) notes that it is through the investigation of these masculine points of view that a platform for the deconstruction of stereotypical masculinities and the reconstruction of new norms can be formed.

Though much work has been done on adolescent sexual behaviours, most of this work has come from a public or reproductive health perspective rather than gender studies, and has focused on young people's so-called risky behaviours. Less attention has been paid to understanding how young people construct their gender identities, and how these constructions might be related to sexual and other lifestyle choices. The age structure of Ghana's population is youthful, with 51.4 per cent being under the age of 20 – 52.2 per cent of males and 50.4 per cent of females (Republic of Ghana 2002). There are several reasons why we should be interested, indeed concerned, about the current and future gender orientations of children and youth. Children under the age of 14 represent the so-called window of hope for managing HIV/AIDS because generally they have not begun their sexual lives.[9] The Ghana AIDS Commission notes that increased attention to this age group is crucial for the future response to the epidemic.

Much has already been written about the relative 'powerlessness' of girls and women in heterosexual relationships in Africa, and hence the limitations of the ABC (Abstinence-Be faithful-use a Condom) approach (Adomako Ampofo 1998; Dodoo and Adomako Ampofo 2001). Nonetheless, since the spread of the virus predominantly through heterosexual contact persists, the transformation of gender relations remains critical in stemming the tide of the epidemic.[10] Styles of gender and sexual interaction between males and females are 'rehearsed' during adolescence, and research carried out with and among adolescent boys around the world suggests that viewing women as sexual objects, use of coercion to obtain sex and viewing sex from a performance-oriented perspective often begins in adolescence or even in childhood and can continue into adulthood (Jejeebhoy 1996; Adomako Ampofo 2001). At the same time, a handful of studies suggest that this is also the time when boys and young men learn to challenge normative, hegemonic forms of masculinity and to construct less hegemonic notions and expectations (Morrell 1998; Yon et al 1998; Wight 1999). Understanding these alternative masculinities can help suggest possibilities for transformation of particular kinds of masculinities.

Understanding masculinities

Although there are diversities of masculinities – making it difficult to place individual men in separate, seemingly discrete categories – theories of masculinity are important in that they provide opportunities for understanding the social legitimisation, among both males and females, of the unequal treatment of women. Such conceptual arrangements allow us to understand the different kinds of masculinities, make sense of the power aspects of masculinity and suggest how particular constructions might be used as models to transform more hegemonic forms of masculinities.

Hegemonic masculinity is described as the dominant form of masculinity in a society and pertains to the relations of cultural domination by men. In addition to being oppressive of women, hegemonic masculinity silences other masculinities, placing these in opposition to itself in such a way that the values expressed do not have currency or legitimacy, and present a version of how men should behave and how putative real men behave as the cultural ideal (Morrell 1998). Boys and men who fail to live up to this form of masculinity are ridiculed and named; among the Akan of Ghana they are referred to as *bemaa-basia*, 'female-man' or *Kojo basia*.[11] The concept of hegemonic masculinity therefore provides a way of explaining the fact that, though a number of masculinities coexist, a particular version of masculinity has supremacy and greater legitimacy in society.

Feminist research on decision making between spouses, domestic gender role arrangements and sexual and reproductive behaviours carried out in Africa during the past two decades – the period in which many countries assumed democratic governance and established women's machineries – indicates that male dominance remains pervasive and accepted in Ghana and much of sub-Saharan Africa. Studies on gender-based violence, for example, show not only that male-on-female violence is common, but also that many women appear to accept violence from intimate partners as inherent to the relationship (Coker-Appiah and Cusack 1999; Adomako Ampofo and Prah 2009).

Yet, there are several traditions in Ghana that seek to ensure that women are protected in marriage, albeit often for instrumental reasons, such as protecting their reproductive and care-giving roles. Modernisation, liberal feminist and now liberal economic theories have not necessarily brought with them enhanced rights for women, the promised effects of development and democratisation. Indeed, in some instances development has only led to the further marginalisation of (African) women and it would seem that, currently, new hegemonic masculinities are emerging, making it important to understand not only how such identities are transmitted intergenerationally, but also how they are (re)invented or contested.[12]

The stratification of gender roles is often reinforced by traditions passed down from one generation to the next. Among the Akan, a son does not inherit from his father, but fathers are expected to set up their male children in life through training and the giving of gifts, such as land and guns, and to help their sons to 'acquire' their first wife. In the traditional system, this practice involved apprenticing the son to either the father himself or to a master craftsman, an orator or a statesman. In times of war, sons fought alongside their fathers (Awusabo-Asare 1990). During this apprenticeship process, definitions of appropriate masculinity were transmitted. Male characteristics that were approved or encouraged included virility, strength, authority, power and leadership qualities, the ability to offer protection and sustenance, intelligence and wisdom, and the ability to bear physical and emotional pain.

Hence girls are taught to defer to men and boys as stronger, wiser and more responsible and boys are accordingly taught to lead and control women.[13] A boy whose lifestyle does not measure up to the prescribed expectations is branded *banyan-basia*, meaning man-woman. Conversely, a girl who veers from the prescribed feminine roles into the domains prescribed for boys is branded *bemaa-kokonin*, meaning 'a woman-cock' or 'male-woman' (Adomako Ampofo 2001).

Oral literature and proverbs are frequently used to explain and describe, and tend to hold in place stereotypes about women and men. How men behave in their families is strongly influenced by expectations of their fellow men, the community in which they live and the society at large, about what it means to be a man. When a man does not conform to the norms or behaviours prescribed for men, he is often ridiculed. Carrie Paechter (2003) suggests that masculinities and femininities can be considered as local communities of practice. Indeed, children participate in adult communities in which constructions are legitimated or punished. Paechter argues that, in order to sustain gender power differentials, society requires children to behave in particular ways and rewards or punishes them for conformity to or deviance from the norm.

Although hegemonic forms of masculinity persist, other forms have always existed and continue to exist. Writing on gender attitudes among youth in urban Jamaica, Ian Boxill (1997) finds little polarisation between the attitudes about gender roles of urban young men and young women. Several other studies point to individual men who contest these hegemonic forms, despite ridicule or physical threats (see Ramphele 1997; Adomako Ampofo 2001; Narismulu 2003).

What's sex got to do with it?

Akosua Adomako Ampofo (2001) discusses the paradox whereby gender norms tend to expect girls to display little knowledge about sexual matters ('Good girls don't know such things'), while boys, who are permitted some sexual licence and knowledge about sex, are rarely provided with the information, counsel or guidance on issues of sexuality that they need. Several studies suggest that boys are actively encouraged by peers and family members to engage in sexual experimentation during their adolescent years (Mensah Kumah et al 1992; Zelaya et al 1997; Nzioka 2001; Adomako Ampofo et al 2007), yet girls are expected or encouraged to remain virgins until marriage. At the same time, girls are expected to defer to men and their elders, thus reinforcing the notion that boys pursue and seek out girls, girls acquiesce, and that boys and men may enjoy a measure of sexual latitude over girls and women. Young men who do not conform to the norms of sexual supremacy are often ridiculed and their masculinity is brought into question. The results are what we see today, wherein a majority of HIV-infected women are from monogamous relationships, often with their first sexual partner (Awusabo-Asare et al 1993), and sub-Saharan Africa has the unhappy distinction of being the only region in the world in which more women than men are infected with HIV (UNAIDS 2006).

When it comes to AIDS, there is a growing consensus that the behaviour of some men and boys is largely driving the epidemic in sub-Saharan Africa, because in many settings males have a dominant role in deciding the nature and context of sex and whether condoms are used (Dodoo 1998; Rivers and Aggleton 1999; Adomako Ampofo 2001; Adomako Ampofo et al 2007). About half of all people infected with HIV are younger than 25 years; teenage girls in sub-Saharan Africa are five times more likely to be infected than boys; and 62 per cent of young people aged 15 to 24 who are HIV positive live in sub-Saharan Africa (UNAIDS 2006). Given the nature of the transition from HIV infection to AIDS, the high incidence of the syndrome among young people in their 20s indicates that many contracted HIV before the age of 20. The younger people are when they become sexually active, the more likely they are to have several sexual partners and thus the greater their likely exposure to STDs, including HIV (McCauley and Saltes 1995).

McCauley and Saltes (1995) further show that sexually active young men know less about STDs or how to prevent them than young women. Even if they do know about STDs, inexperience or denial, as well as cultural pressures, can make them take unnecessary risks. For instance, Adomako Ampofo et al (2007), writing on youth in Ghana, note that almost all the young men surveyed reported that they had heard of HIV/AIDS, yet despite this knowledge most did not think that they faced much risk of HIV infection, even when they were sexually active. Charles Nzioka (2001), writing on the perspectives of adolescent boys aged 15 to 19 attending schools in rural, eastern Kenya, noted that the young men exhibited high-risk behaviour despite a high knowledge of sexual risks, fear of HIV and awareness of the protective value of condoms. They felt the need to conform to social prescriptions of male prowess, early sexual experience and having more than one partner, yet their feelings about this behaviour were ambiguous and contradictory. They considered getting girls pregnant and having had a treatable STD as marks of masculinity, would blame girls (and girls' parents) for girls' failure to protect themselves, and wanted to boast about their sexual conquests to their peers. Yet they felt embarrassed and reticent about discussing sexual issues with adults, and were unwilling to get condoms from places where anonymity was not assured because they knew their sexual activity was not sanctioned.

Weiss et al (2000) argue that the power imbalance characteristic of sexual relations among adults – with women generally having less access to critical resources than men – has many of its roots in adolescence. Thus, if we are to ensure that the next generation is not condemned to life with AIDs, we have to enhance our understanding of youth sexuality and the manner in which dominant norms contribute to the spread of sexually transmitted diseases. Social norms of masculinity are particularly important in this regard, because the manner in which 'normal' men are defined – such as through the acquisition of multiple partners, power over women and negative attitudes toward condoms – is often in conflict with the true emotional vulnerabilities of young men.

Making decisions and granting permission

Since the late 1990s, a number of significant developments have helped push the issues of masculinity, culture and power to the fore in the public discourse on women's empowerment in Ghana. Since 1998, Ghana has recorded increasing reports of violence against women and children (mostly female) by men in a variety of situations, including brutal serial and spousal killings of women that generated headlines and attention in the public domain from 2000 to 2002. The spousal killings were justified under various framings of male rights and privilege. Media reports, for example, suggested that the wife killings were frequently related to husbands' constructions of their roles as family heads and providers, or to women's failures to accord men their due respect by seeking permission before embarking on certain ventures, or were related to perceptions about women's sexuality.[14]

There are several studies that attest to the financial autonomy and even economic might of Ghanaian women (Robertson 1976; Aidoo 1985; Manuh 1998; Clark 1994) and to the fact that women were expected to be diligent and enterprising. When an Asante girl attained puberty, she was given resources or later cash to serve as seed capital for her own economic enterprise. Further, women traditionally had their own spheres of power and authority in societies guided by a fair amount of complementarity in sex roles. Nonetheless, the myth induced by colonialism and the Victorian moral principle of the male as breadwinner and overall head of household has created a situation currently in which men feel compelled to 'provide' for their families and experience their masculinity as threatened if they are unable to fulfil this role (Adomako Ampofo 1998).

According to a UNFPA report (2000), attempts to live up to the ideals of masculinity are frequently compromised by harsh and changing realities, especially for men who are poor, uneducated, un(der)employed or marginalised in other ways. Using an example from Kisii in Kenya, the report shows how men's self-esteem can be undermined as they lose control of land and livestock and are reduced to the mercy of women's homestead farming as a result of the increasing cost of living. Victor Agadjanian (2002) describes how male street vendors in Maputo become more overtly 'masculine' in their domestic relationships, presumably to compensate for doing 'women's work'. As most men have not been appropriately socialised to handle such situations, the stress and frustrations often become unbearable and result in violent consequences. According to the studies cited in the UNFPA report (2000), violence was least prevalent in households in which spouses communicated and shared responsibility for decisions. In households in which no decisions were made jointly, 25 per cent of couples reported that the husband had hit the wife. Where all decisions were made jointly, the incidence of domestic violence was six per cent.

Male-on-female violence also erupts when women fail to seek permission from their partners before taking 'major' decisions, such as going on a journey, engaging in a new economic activity or even visiting a friend (Coker-Appiah and Cusack 1999). A 'real' man also does not tolerate his wife questioning him about his sexual adventures or, worse, refusing to have sex with him as a result. Sometimes the violence that ensues leads to death. Clearly, although women frequently end up as 'victims' of violence, men are themselves under a great deal of pressure to fit the hegemonic norm of what it means to be a 'man' and frustrations around this are linked to both stress and gender-based violence.

Masculinities and men's well-being

Although in this chapter we are primarily concerned with the potential impact of meanings of manhood on women, a note on masculinity and men's well-being is in order. Boys and men also suffer from hegemonic masculinities. As noted, they are discouraged from showing perceived feminine emotions, such as admitting to fear or pain, and are ridiculed for being effeminate if they are not aggressive. Chinua

Achebe, best known perhaps for his strong positions when it comes to the state and politics in Nigeria, provides several very important descriptions of manhood, or masculinity, in Igbo society as well as in Nigeria more generally. In *Things Fall Apart* (1958) Achebe's character Okonkwo is the patriot who rules his household with an iron hand. Wives and children, even adult children, are expected to obey his commands. Okonkwo acts this way in part to compensate for his own father's perceived weakness (his father, Unoka, died in debt and humiliation when Okonkwo was very young). Shame for Unoka, and a fear of being a failure, drives Okonkwo to work tirelessly.

Nwoye is Okonkwo's son with his first wife and Okonkwo has high expectations for him. However, Nwoye does not quite fit Okonkwo's expectations of a real man; he is sensitive and thoughtful, preferring the friendlier, more female-oriented stories about the tortoise or the bird Eneke, rather than the masculine stories of violence and bloodshed. Fearing that Nwoye will turn out like Unoka, and because he wants him to grow into a tough young man 'capable of ruling his father's household when he is dead and gone to join the ancestors', Okonkwo is harsh with his son.

In Nwoye, Achebe shows us an alternative masculinity, one crushed by Okonkwo's dominance. Achebe shows us that Okonkwo's brand of masculinity and obsession, it seems, with being a 'real' Igbo man, becomes his undoing. His harshness and insensitivity eventually drive his own son away. When Ikemefuna – a young boy given to Okonkwo's village, Umuofia, by a neighbouring village as tribute – is sacrificed to prevent a war, and Okonkwo participates in the boy's death, Nwoye is shaken because Ikemefuma had become his best friend and brother. Okonkwo's rashness also leads to his exile from his beloved village and home. In Uchendu, Okonkwo's elderly and wise uncle, we see yet another counterpoint to hegemonic masculinity, and we also see in Okonkwo's submission to his uncle's authority the possibility of an alternate, gentler masculinity.

Camara Laye (1954) provides a poignant description of the anxieties an African boy might go through in his initiation into 'manhood' in his autobiography *The African Child*. In the account, Laye participates in several rituals and ceremonies and describes the fear that he and his peers felt when they had to go into the forest to encounter they knew not what, on the path to manhood – a fear they were not supposed to name. He also describes the pain of the circumcision itself, and the longing he felt to be with his mother – a longing he dared not verbalise and that he was not allowed to satisfy. After his transition to 'manhood' Laye moves into a separate hut with other age-mate boys, and describes his longing for the nights spent alone with his mother in her hut. When Laye becomes an adult he accepts the rite of passage as a necessary step in his development as a member of his society; however, we also see him questioning whether the pain and anxiety are a necessary part of the journey to adulthood (manhood).

Men and boys are forced into leadership and breadwinner roles that many cannot live up to. Often the desire or pressure to 'perform' as a man leads boys into high-risk activities such as joining gangs and using drugs. Beyond the physical threats that come with attempts to live up to such constructions, boys and men who cannot live up to the expectations of being strong, aggressive providers and leaders can be excessively stressed, especially in their relationships.[15] Moreover, men who cannot live up to these expectations that men should be powerful and competent in all things might respond by retreating into passivity and escape through drugs, alcohol, by resorting to violence towards weaker individuals or by engaging in sheer bravado and risk taking (UNFPA 2000).

What are men (and boys) really like? What do they have in common? In what ways do they differ in their conceptions of manhood? Why are men the way they are? How and when are particular masculinities constructed and used? And perhaps most importantly, how can answers gleaned be used to promote more gender-equitable attitudes between men and women? This chapter presents a small window into the deconstruction of masculinities.

Decision making

Respondents asserted the man's position as the head of the household and therefore as the one responsible for major decision making. Reproductive decision making remains a contentious area for many couples, with disagreements between couples leading to 'unwanted' or 'mis-timed' births for many women (Dodoo 1998; Adomako Ampofo 2002, 2004). We asked boys questions about marital decisions around having children, having more children, ceasing childbirth, contraceptive use and having sex. They displayed a high level of pragmatism, generally according women the final say when it came to having no more children, and according men the final say when it came to having (more) children. This is consistent with the preferences of older men, suggesting that ideas about masculinity remain linked to concepts of biological fatherhood: 'The man should be responsible for family planning in the marriage' (Adomako Ampofo 2004).

Some boys rationalise that women who are not willing to 'give' men the children they need can be divorced, or the man can take a second wife; their perspectives are exemplified in the following comments:

> If the man insists on having a child and the woman also says no, and if the man gets angry, the man can divorce the woman for another woman.
>
> Me what I will say to the woman is that if she says she is tired and she does not want to have any more children then she should allow the man to go and marry another woman he can have a son with. If she does not want then she should understand what he is saying.

Additionally, if a woman is being ridiculed for being childless when in fact it is her husband who wants to delay childbearing, the husband should be considerate. Boys recognise the important ways in which biological parenthood is tied to a normal identity. However, when the interviewer linked cessation of childbearing to the male provider role, a man's ability (or not) to take care of more children, then the boys would usually revert the decision-making power to the husband.

> The woman does not have the power ... because that is part of the benefit (children) that you get from the money you provided for performing the customary rites. It is the man who will take care of the children.

And when a caveat was introduced by the interviewer, that the wife had assured her husband that she could 'look after the child', then some boys said it is alright to have another child even though the husband feels financially challenged and that this in no way diminishes the husband's power:

> I: When you say that, it means that it is the woman who has gotten power over the issue?
> R: What I mean is that you have given her the power. You mean that you don't have money to take care of the child if she gives birth again. And she also means that even if you don't have money to take care of the child, she has money that she will use to help you take care of the two children.

There were many boys, even those who had earlier reflected clear gender divisions in terms of household work allocation, who recommended discussion and compromise on matters of reproduction, such as when the woman wants a child and the man is not ready, or who recognise that unwanted pregnancies and children might be experienced by women more profoundly than by men. Here boys recognised that, although the husband has a titular headship position, his wife may have a more valuable or sensible position on certain issues that he should acknowledge:

> The woman should be responsible for family planning because if she does not make sure that they have family planning, she can get pregnant.
>
> Maybe, I can tell the woman to be patient a bit and if with time I get some money we can have children.
>
> You are saying that the woman wants a child and the man says no, the man should go and see a doctor or a nurse to discuss the issue (about family planning).

Or, in the reverse case, when the man wants a child but his wife is not ready:

> Maybe it will help both of you (to postpone childbirth) so you will have to be patient with her.
> I: So the man, you want to say that he does not have much power in the marriage?
> R: He does but sometimes he has to listen to what the woman says. Sometimes what the woman says is also valuable and so he has to listen because it will help both of them.

Very few children indicated in the survey that they had ever had sex, and even among these, some of the experiences had been non-consensual and/or one-time. Therefore, we pursued questions about sexual activity with a great deal of caution. It might be because the boys were not yet sexually active, and had not begun to engage in peer discourse around actual sexual experiences and on how manhood and sex are linked, that they claimed a high level of respect for a woman's decisions when it comes to sex. Clearly, this presented a unique opportunity to reinforce the notion that men and women have equal rights and desires when it comes to sex.

We asked boys how they would deal with a situation in which a wife did not want to have sex, or turned away from her husband's advances because she was tired. As authors it was heartening to us to find reflected the following thought: 'You have the chance and she also has the chance. So if she says that she is tired you have to respect that.'

We also presented the reverse scenario when the wife wanted sex and the husband didn't and the boys gave similar responses, none indicating that it was an unlikely scenario.[16]

Conclusion: does masculinity matter?

The boys in our study evidenced different meanings that they attached to manhood, and they also differed in the extent to which they reflected so-called hegemonic masculinities. What seemed clearest to them was that there were distinct differences in gender identity according to household tasks as they moved from boyhood to manhood, especially the status of being married. Typical female chores such as cooking, cleaning and laundry must be forsaken, or only performed to 'help' out or if one was (still) single. The boys also seemed to recognise that masculinity is something to be achieved (or a place to be arrived at) in stages, and over time, and that it must be won and defended.

Indeed, as we note, that transition from being single to being married is a status enhancer for men, a sign that one has taken on more responsibility, while for women it means that one is simply transferring one authority figure, or set of authority figures (parents), for another (husband). This would mean that marriage would be very important for males because it not only frees them from the mundane responsibilities of household management, but also confirms manhood in the sense that one moves up from 'female', androgynous or even 'boyish' tasks to manly ones and hence from a more female or genderless state to a masculine one.

These responsibilities of manhood (in marriage) include being a provider for wife and children, as well as the authority over the nuclear family. The authority derives, it seems, not simply from the fact of being a man, but also from the bride-wealth payments that are made. This is an area that has received contradictory comment. For example, in India the opposite concept of a dowry paid by the bride's family to that of the groom has been explained as the reason why women as wives are valued less than men. In sub-Saharan Africa, where men pay bridewealth, some women have argued that the failure to pay bridewealth is evidence that they are disrespected, devalued and can thus be mistreated by their 'husbands' (Adomako Ampofo 2000).

In any case, being the husband accords the man the rights to take major decisions affecting the family and to dispense with permission for his wife to do or not to do certain things. In rare cases, a wife's 'disobedience' even justifies a beating. Further, the assumed importance of marriage to femininity is implied by the boys when they talk about divorcing a recalcitrant wife, or returning her to her parents, presumably a scenario no woman wants. If boys are conditioned to see marriage as a major step in the trajectory towards manhood, with its attendant privileges relative to women, boys can be expected to seek marriage and to enforce these gender divisions once they get married.

And yet the fact that some boys do not see marriage as necessarily conferring these rights and privileges on them suggests that alternative models can be introduced and reinforced. This, it seems to us, is particularly hopeful because none of the boys in our study seemed to see this alternative, less dominant form of masculinity as a deviant or less normative or legitimate form. Whether the Ghanaian boys in our study accepted or rejected some of the more common notions of masculinity, it was certainly clear that they recognised that such notions were imbued with power, and they were in no doubt that men have more power and authority than women.

Feminist theorising and activism has tried to understand and dismantle patriarchy as a social system, and often there has been a backlash from both women and men in society. Working with men to understand and change their behaviours and attitudes has a strong potential for minimising problems brought about by the excesses of masculinity. It is time for men themselves to challenge harmful concepts of masculinity. Commonly held attitudes of men and boys that harm the welfare of girls and women, as well as other males, should be targeted for change. The way men and boys view risk, as well as the way boys are socialised to become men in society, need particular attention. Boys need to be 'captured' and socialised appropriately at an early age. Rob Foels and Christopher Pappas (2004) indicate that it is possible, through socialisation, to 'learn and unlearn' gender myths. They found that the sex difference in social dominance orientation is mediated by gender socialisation (and decreased as a function of feminist identity acquisition).

Herbert Barry III et al, surveying certain aspects of socialisation in 110 cultures, found that, while differentiation of the sexes is unimportant from infancy through the first few years of life, by the time children can walk and talk greater pressure is put on girls and boys to fit expected gender roles. They observe that the best time to capture and socialise boys would be their childhood years when the most pressure is put on boys to fit the expected gender roles. And yet the importance of the home setting in defining gender politics has received insufficient attention compared to the influence of schools and peers. Ongoing analysis of the data from the current study suggests to us that the role of significant adults, either through direct instruction, observation or through a system of rewards and punishments, can be powerful in setting the stage for the acquisition of particular male identities.

Indeed, from a study among African American adolescents, Alison Bryant and Marc Zimmermann (2003) found that, although having paternal role models had the most positive impact on school outcomes, the presence of female role models, in contrast, was associated with psychological well-being, such that adolescents with maternal role models reported the least distress. Adolescents, both male and female, without female role models had the lowest grades and most negative school attitudes. These findings remained when parental support, family conflict and father presence in the household were controlled, suggesting that role model effects are separate from parenting effects.

Thus, it would seem that having someone to look up to is critical for African American youths' development, and thus having significant adults in a young person's life (who do not need to be parents) can be a powerful influence. The importance of having gender-sensitive adults in the community as 'role models', not in the active, formal and public sense normally applied today, but simply as people to live with and observe, is thus important. This means that one cannot bring about transformation without working in the community, letting people see the harmful effects of hegemonic masculinities and the positive effects of alternative forms.

There are many other spaces in which boys could be socialised in ways that diffuse the harmful notions of masculinity and help them transform their understanding of the multiple meanings of manhood to a responsible adulthood. These 'safe' spaces, in which boys can be boys while learning to unlearn certain attitudes and behaviours, could include youth camps, religious groups, boys' clubs and even apprenticeship and other societies.[17]

However, much remains to be known as we theorise around the reproduction and contestation of hegemonic masculinities. How, for example, is the socialisation of these boys different and how are gender-equitable women formed? Also, as we pay more attention to men and masculinity, especially within heterosexual contexts, it remains important to understand how feminist girls and women are born, because to change the power dynamics between the sexes so that young women also experience a sense of entitlement to autonomy, both females and males need to experience transformations in their gender politics, and the gender politics of both girls and boys need to be understood.

Notes

1. Reproduced with permission from Shefer, T., Ratele, K., Strebel, A., Shabalala, N., Buikema, R. (eds) (2007) *From Boys to Men: Social Constructions of Masculinity in Contemporary Society,* Cape Town, UCT Press.
2. Although the elective on culture and gender in African societies was but one of several offered at the Institute of African Studies in the 2003/04 academic year, all but one of the students taking the course decided to write their theses in an area of gender focusing on masculinity.
3. For example, Camara Laye's (1954) descriptions of his initiation and circumcision experience in his book *The African Child,* which we describe later, had a profound impact on the students in the men and masculinities class. They recognised that a practice intended to serve as a transition from boyhood to manhood could be fraught with anxieties and fear for the initiate.
4. Organisations such as GETNET in South Africa have been working with men and women in organisations to catalyse 'new' masculinities that are caring, supportive, non-violent and responsible.
5. Men and masculinities is still a fledgling discipline in many African and third world countries, a notable exception being the Caribbean (see Reddock (2003), who describes its beginning in the 1980s in the anglophone Caribbean).
6. This volume includes chapters that take a historical perspective as well as some that speak to contemporary data. However, what ties them together is an analysis of how 'a cluster of norms, values, and behavioural patterns expressing explicit and implicit expectations of how men should act and represent themselves to others' was and is gendered.
7. A notable exception on the continent is South Africa, where male scholars such as Morrell (1998, 2002) and Ratele (2002) have written on aspects of the constructions of masculinity.
8. For example, in the 19th century USA, though some boys were described as 'sissies' by their peers, and sometimes castigated by them, they were still celebrated by their families

for being caring and home loving (Grant 2004). Little boys were considered to be the province of their mothers and not expected to adhere to strict gender boundaries. With transformations in child rearing, peer culture and adult masculinity, the behaviours of little boys began to be more closely monitored for signs of deviance from these new normative masculinities.

9. Although the peak ages of infection in Ghana from the 2003 and 2004 sentinel surveys are 25 to 29 for females and 30 to 34 for males, and the incidence of the virus among those aged under 20 remains low, the infection rate is growing fastest among the population aged 15 to 19 (Ghana National AIDS Control Programme 2004, 2005).

10. Addressing the poor economic situations of many girls and women that enhance this 'powerlessness' is also critical, of course. However, economic 'powerlessness' should not be seen as a discrete variable separate from gender relations and cultures that have specific gender contours.

11. *Kojo* is a male name and *basia* means female, hence a 'female Kojo'.

12. Colonialism is frequently held particularly culpable for undermining the position of women in African societies, by introducing Victorian values with rigid gender ideologies and for removing certain traditional structures that allowed women considerable autonomy, thereby excluding them from the decision-making and power structures. However, there is evidence that the stratification of gender roles in so-called traditional societies held to hierarchical power structures in which women, as a group, had less authority and power than men. Colonial rule came to reinforce these hierarchies and to create new ones.

13. Of course there are always notable exceptions and women are generally expected to acquire wisdom and even supernatural insights (as in priestesses) as they age (as in the wise old woman). However, men do not necessarily require the characteristics of age or the position of priesthood to attain such influence.

14. In November 2000, the first author joined with other members of women's organisations in Ghana on a demonstration in Accra to protest against the serial killings and the failure of the then government to identify and arrest the perpetrator(s). During the march, some men we met on the way assured us that so long as they were men and we were women they would 'discipline' us if they felt we were out of line.

15. Data from the USA shows that social stress diseases are much more common among men than women and are on the increase (Pietila 1997; Oakley 2005).

16. There was only one boy who, having said that a man who didn't want to have sex (presumably because he linked sex with pregnancy) should go and buy a condom or let his wife use the pill, recommended force be used if the wife was the unwilling partner: 'Then you may really have to force her so that she might think that when she doesn't yield you might go out and take another woman and leave her.'

17. Some calls have been made for the significance of having so-called role models, such as popular artists, sports and TV stars, talk to children about 'responsible' behaviour. However, this direction must be pursued with caution because children are quick to discern when an individual's message is contrived and at odds with their own life.

References

Abu, K. (1991) 'Family welfare and work dynamics in urban northern Ghana', UNFPA/WEP Document No. 13

Achebe, C. (1958) *Things Fall Apart*, Oxford, Heinemann

Adomako Ampofo, A. (1998) 'Framing knowledge, forming behaviour; African women's AIDS-protection strategies', *African Journal of Reproductive Health* 2(2): 151–174

—— (2000) 'Resource contributions, gender orientation and reproductive decision making in Ghana, the case of urban couples', *Research Review NS* 15(2): 93–125

—— (2001) 'When men speak women listen: Gender socialisation and young adolescents' attitudes to sexual and reproductive issues', *African Journal of Reproductive Health* 5(3): 196–212

—— (2002) 'Does women's education matter? A case study of reproductive decision making from urban Ghana', *Ghana Studies* 5: 123–157

—— (2004) '"By God's grace I had a boy": Whose "unmet need" and "dis/agreement" about childbearing among Ghanaian couples', in Arnfred, S. (ed) *Rethinking Sexualities in Contexts of Gender*, Uppsala, Nordic Africa Institute

Adomako Ampofo, A., Alhassan, O., Ankrah, F., Atobrah, D. and Dortey, M. (2007) *Children and Sexual Exploitation*, Accra, UNICEF

Adomako Ampofo, A. and Prah, M. (2009) 'You may beat your wife, but not too much: the cultural context of violence in Ghana', in Cusack, K. and Manuh, T. (eds) *The Architecture for Violence Against Women in Ghana*, Accra, The Gender Centre

Adu-Poku, S. (2001) 'Envisioning (Black) male feminism: a cross-cultural perspective', *Journal of Gender Studies* 10(2): 157–167

Agadjanian, V. (2002) 'Men doing "women's work": masculinity and gender relations among street vendors in Maputo', *Journal of Men's Studies* 10(3): 329–342

Aidoo A.A. (1985) 'Women in the history and culture of Ghana', *Research Review NS* 1(1): 44

Amoah, E. (1991) 'Femaleness: Akan concepts and practices', in Becher, J. (ed), *Women, Religion and Sexuality: Studies on the Impact of Religious Teaching on Women*, Philadelphia, Trinity Press International

Arnfred, Signe (2001) 'Questions of power: women's movements, feminist theory and development aid', in Sisak, A. (ed) *Discussing Women's Empowerment: Theory and Practice*, Stockholm, SIDA

Awusabo-Asare, K. (1990) 'Matriliny and the new intestate succession law of Ghana', *Canadian Journal of African Studies* 24(1): 1–16

Awusabo-Asare, K., Anarfi, J.K. and Agyeman, P.K. (1993) 'Women's control over their sexuality and the spread of STDs and HIV/AIDS in Ghana', *Health Transition Review* 3 (Supplementary issue): 69–83

Barry III, H., Bacon, M.K. and Child, I.L. (1973) 'A cross-cultural survey of some sex differences in socialization', in Scarr-Salapatek, S. and Salapatek, P. (eds) *Socialisation*, Columbus, Merrill

Barry III, H., Josephson, L., Lauer, E. and Marshall, C. (1979) 'Traits included in childhood: cross-cultural codes', *Ethnology* 15: 466–508

Bhasin, K. (2004) *Exploring Masculinity*, New Delhi, Women Unlimited

Boxill, I. (1997) 'Perceptions of gender roles in urban Jamaica', *Humanity and Society* 21(2): 182–89

Bryant, A.L. and Zimmerman, M.A. (2003) 'Role models and psychosocial outcomes among African American adolescents', *Journal of Adolescent Research* 18(1): 36–67

Clark, G. (1994) *Onions are My Husband: Survival and Accumulation by West African Market Women*, Chicago, University of Chicago Press

Coker-Appiah, D. and Cusack, K. (1999) *Violence against Women and Children in Ghana*, Accra, Gender Studies and Human Rights Documentation Centre

Coker-Appiah, D. and Foster, J. (2002) 'Advocacy for better implementation of women's rights in Ghana', Convention on the Elimination of all Forms of Discrimination against Women (CEDAW) advocacy paper, Accra, Ghana

Connell, R.W. (1998) 'Masculinities and globalisation', *Men and Masculinities*, 1: 3–23

Dodoo, F.N. (1998) 'Men matter: additive and interactive gender preferences, and reproductive behaviour in Kenya', *Demography* 359(2): 229–242

Dodoo, F.N. and Adomako Ampofo, A. (2001) 'AIDS-related knowledge and behavior among married Kenyan men: A behavioural paradox?', *Journal of Health and Human Services Administration* 24(2): 197–231

Foels, R. and Pappas, C.J. (2004) 'Learning and unlearning the myths we are taught: Gender and social dominance orientation', *Sex Roles: A Journal of Research* 50(11–12): 743–757

Ghana AIDS Commission (2005) 'Extract from the 2004 HIV sentinel survey', report presented by Dr N.A. Addo, Programme Manager, Accra, National AIDS Control Programme, http://www.ghanaids.gov.gh/main/results_detail.asp?story_id=116, accessed 6 June 2007

Grant, J. (2004) '"A real boy" and not a sissy: gender, childhood and masculinity, 1890–1940', *Journal of Social History* 37(4): 829–851

Jejeebhoy, Shireen J. (1996) 'Adolescent sexual and reproductive behaviour: a review of the evidence from India', ICRW Working Paper No. 3, December

Kabeer, N. (1994) *Reversed Reality: Gender Hierarchies in Development Thought*, New York, Verso

Kemp, D. (1898) *Nine Years at the Gold Coast*, London, Macmillan

Kumah, O. Mensah, Odallo, D. and Shefner, C. (1992) *Kenya Youth IEC Needs Assessment*, Baltimore, Johns Hopkins University Press

Laye, C. (1955) *The African Child*, London and Glasgow, Collins

Lindsay, L.A. and Miescher, S.F. (2003) *Men and Masculinities in Modern Africa*, Portsmouth, Heinemann

MacPhail, C. (2003) 'Challenging dominant norms of masculinity for HIV prevention', *African Journal of AIDS Research* 2(2): 141–149

Manuh, Takyiwaa (1998) 'Women in Africa's development: overcoming obstacles, pushing for progress', Africa Recovery Briefing Paper, No. 11, April

McCauley, A.P. and Salter, C. (1995) 'Meeting the needs of young adults', Population Reports Series J(41), October, http://www.jhuccp.org/pr/j41edsum.stm, accessed 6 June 2007

Morrell, R. (1998) 'Of boys and men: masculinity and gender in southern African studies', *Journal of Southern African Studies* 24(4): 605–630

—— (2002) 'Men's movements and gender transformation in South Africa', *The Journal of Men's Studies* 10(3): 309–327

Nabila, P. (2001) 'Traditional socialisation practices and women's empowerment: a study of adolescent gender socialisation in Dagbon', M. Phil thesis presented to the Institute of African Studies, Legon, University of Ghana

Narismulu, P. (2003) '"Now I am suffering, I've got no place to stay": experiences of insecurity in a Durban shack settlement', presentation at conference Uncertainty in Contemporary African Lives, Arusha, 9–11 April

Nukunya, G.K. (1992) *Tradition and Change: The Case of the Family*, Accra, Ghana University Press

Nzioka, C. (2001) 'Perspectives of adolescent boys on the risks of unwanted pregnancy and sexually transmitted infections: Kenya', *Reproductive Health Matters*, 9(17): 108–17

Oakley, A. (2005) 'Design and analysis of social intervention studies in health research', in Bowling A. (ed) *Handbook of Health Research Methods*, Maidenhead, Open University Press

Odendaal, W. (2001) 'The men against violence against women movement in Namibia', *Development*, 44(3): 90–93

Paechter, C. (2003) 'Learning masculinities and femininities: Power/knowledge and legitimate peripheral participation', *Women's Studies International Forum*, 26(6): 541–552

Pietila, H. (1997) 'Violence against women: An obstacle to peace. Four Conferences – A new vision. Report on four conferences in 1997', [CD-Rom], Brussels, European Profeminist Men's Network

Prah, Mansah (2002) 'Gender issues in Ghanaian tertiary institutions: women academics and administrators at Cape Coast University', *Ghana Studies* 5(1): 83–123

Ramphele, M. (1997) 'Teach me how to be a man: An exploration of the definition of masculinity', in Das, V., Kleinman, A., Ramphele, M. and Reynolds, P. (eds) *Violence and Subjectivity*, Berkeley, University of California Press

Ratele, Kopano (2002) 'Contradictions in constructions of masculinity', in *News from the Nordic Africa Institute*, 2(S): 2–5

Rattray, R.S. (1927) *Religious Art in Ashanti*, Oxford, Clarendon Press

Reddock, R. (2003) 'Men as gendered beings: the emergence of masculinity studies in the anglophone Caribbean', *Social and Economic Studies* 52(3): 89–117

Republic of Ghana (2001) *Population and Housing Census of Ghana*, Accra, Ghana Statistical Service

—— (2002) '2000 population and housing census: summary report of final results', Accra, Ghana Statistical Service

Rivers, K. and Aggleton, P. (1999) *Adolescent Sexuality, Gender and the HIV Epidemic*, London, UNDP HIV and Development Programme

Robertson, C. (1976) 'Ga women and socioeconomic change in Accra, Ghana', in Hafkina N.J. and Bay E.G. (eds) *Women in Africa: Studies in Social and Economic Change*, Stanford, Stanford University Press

Robinson, Sally (2001) 'Pedagogy of the opaque: teaching masculinity studies', in Gardiner, J.R. (ed) *Masculinity Studies and Feminist Theory: New Reflections*, Columbia University Press

The Hunger Project (2001) 'AIDS in Africa: a crisis of leadership', briefing on the strategy to stop the spread of HIV/AIDS in Africa

Tsikata, Dzodzi (2000) 'Introduction', in Tsikata, D. (ed) *Gender Training in Ghana: Politics, Issues and Tools*, Accra, Woeli

UNAIDS (2006) 'Report on the global AIDS epidemic: executive summary', in *UNAIDS 10th Anniversary Special Edition*, Geneva, UNAIDS

UNFPA (2000) 'Men, reproductive rights and gender equity', in UNFPA, *State of World Population 2000: Lives Together, Worlds Apart, Men and Women in Time of Change*, http://www.unfpa.org/swp/2000/english/ch01.html, accessed 6 June 2007

UNICEF (2004) 'At a glance: Ghana. The big picture statistics', 18 January, http://www.unicef.org/infobycountry/ghana_statistics.html, accessed 24 September 2006

Weiss, E., Whelan, D. and Gupta, G. Rao (2000) 'Gender, sexuality and HIV: making a difference in the lives of young women in developing countries', *Sexual and Relationship Therapy* 15(3): 233–245

Wight, D. (1999) 'Cultural factors in young heterosexual men's perception of HIV risk', *Sociology of Health and Illness* 21(6): 735–758

Yon C., Jimenez, O. and Valverde, R. (1998) 'Representations of sexual and preventive practices in relation to STDs and HIV/AIDS among adolescents in two poor neighbourhoods in Lima: relationships between sexual partners and representations', paper presented at the seminar on Men/Family/Formation and Reproduction, Buenos Aires, 11–15 May

Zelaya, E., Marin, F.M., Garcia, J., Berglund, S., Liljestrand, J. and Persson, L.A. (1997) 'Gender and social differences in adolescent sexuality and reproduction in Nicaragua', *Journal of Adolescent Health* 211: 39–46

46

'Mombasa morans': embodiment, sexual morality and Samburu men in Kenya[1]

George Paul Meiu

Introduction

'See that guy with the dreadlocks,' David pointed out, 'him too, he has a *muzungu mama* [white woman] in Mombasa.' David and I were having tea at the Jadana motel when this young man passed by. He was a tall, skinny-20-year old, dressed in red shorts and a gray Puma shirt, wearing a large gold chain around his neck, and carrying a cellphone in his hand. David continued:

> He fucks the old lady, and she sends him money and gold. She bought him a bicycle and some goats. She is taking care of him and then she is proud she has a Maasai. Yeah, Maasai she says. Even those dreadlocks, those aren't Samburu. Us, Samburu, we don't have that.

David went to talk to an elderly Samburu man sitting at the next table. They laughed. He explained to me afterwards:

> You know even the *apayaa* [old man] was laughing at this guy. Some years ago, he used to work at this hotel. He was cleaning the toilets here. And now, every time he is in Maralal, he comes and takes a room here. His parents live close by in a *manyatta* [huts compound]. But him, he can no longer sleep there … there're too many flies [laughing].

David's criticism of his age-mate speaks to the reconfiguration of Samburu masculinities in the late 20th century. More specifically, it is an instance of moral discourse that resituates Samburu masculinities in relation to white women's sexual travel.

This chapter examines some of the ways in which young Samburu men who migrate seasonally to coastal tourist resorts, mostly to Mombasa, and engage in relationships with white female tourists come to embody both the effects of a neo-imperial commodification of their bodies for tourist consumption and the effects of a moral criticism phrased in terms of sexuality. Their seemingly miraculous accumulation of wealth attracts a vociferous criticism, repositioning them within the moral economies of their home community: they became the Mombasa morans (warriors). Herein, contrasts in sexual behaviour constitute a moral issue supplementing a rationalisation of economic inequalities.

This reconfiguration of gendered identities in relation to global processes is ultimately about the inculcation of different bodily dispositions. The re-situation of Samburu masculinities with regard to female sexual tourism constitutes an embodied political matter. It is about the ways in which colonial and post-colonial histories of bodily stereotyping are generative of bodily dispositions. The body is thus the very site of cultural hegemony and its 'tangible processes are eminently susceptible to the kind of ethnographic scrutiny that may divulge the hidden hand of history' (Comaroff and Comaroff 1992: 41).

Strangely enough, the theorisation of 'sex tourism', and more recently of 'female sex tourism', does not include embodiment as one of its analytical concerns. Even when the body is present in these discussions, it is disembodied; that is, it is treated merely as an object of consumption, a consuming object or a form of representation. It is conceptualised through what Judith Farquhar called 'a naive faith in the existence of material natures that are, in theory and essence, untouched by human history' (Farquhar 2002: 8). In studies of 'female sex tourism', as I will show, this tendency results from the fact that the tourist site – the place where hosts and guests meet – is taken as an apparently isolated unit of interaction upon which all analytical energies are focused, and which is therefore defined merely in terms of situated power statuses and 'sexual-economic exchanges' (Kempadoo 1999, 2001).

Accordingly, the recurring question of these studies is whether or not women can be in a dominating position as consumers of sex tourism. Whereas some scholars argue that travelling women engaging in sexual relations with local men are occupying the same exploitative position as their male counterparts (Albuquerque 1998; Phillips 1999; Kempadoo 2001; Sanchez Taylor 2000), others argue that, in fact, women are doing something else, less exploitative, often referred to as 'romance tourism' (Dahles and Bras 1999; Jeffreys 2003). I argue that this very question, however helpful for comparative studies of tourism, leads inevitably to the de-historicisation of the tourist site, and the analytical objectification of bodies and sexualities. Consequently, local men, for example, tend to be dealt with in an essentialist manner, either as 'embodied commodities' (Sanchez Taylor 2001) or as mere consumers of female tourists' sexuality (Jeffreys 2003).

Meanwhile, in the recent studies of men and masculinity in Africa, the analytical implications of embodiment have not yet come to be fully recognised. Responding to Luise White's (1990) early call to theorise men in Africa, an emerging literature on African masculinities (Lindsay and Miescher 2003; Silberschmidt 2004; Miescher 2005; Ouzgane and Morrell 2005) underlines the role of the dynamic social and historical processes in the continuous reconfiguration of masculinities on the continent. Herein, education, religion, wealth and sexuality are only a few of the social forces that shape masculinities and that are – in their turn – (re)shaped in the gendering process. Nevertheless, the embodied effects of such dynamic gendering processes have yet to be explored.

This chapter offers an alternative analysis of the effects of these relationships, and of thinking 'how to conceptualise these delicate and dramatic figurations and refigurations of local embodiments, identities and imaginaries' (Povinelli and Chauncey 1999: 442). Based on my fieldwork in Kenya in 2005, this study is about the re-shaping of Samburu masculinities through the embodiment of the effects of multi-contextual social processes.[2]

Context: 'moran mania'

At the end of the 20th century, on a global scale, transnational travel reached the unprecedented level of 625 million international arrivals (WTO 1999). In 1999, the number of tourists visiting Kenya was estimated at 969,000. By 2004, it had increased as much as 40 per cent, reaching 1,361,000 (ECPAT n.d.). Since Kenya's independence in 1963, the profitability of agricultural production has fluctuated but the tourist market has grown, and more and more people, mostly from western European countries, have turned to Kenya as a holiday destination.[3] As such, since 1987, tourism has represented Kenya's leading foreign exchange earner, and now employs eight per cent of the country's wage-earning labour force (Omondi 2003).

Early on, the Kenyan post-colonial state foresaw some of the great financial opportunities opening up in the international market. In addition to wildlife safaris, it began commodifying a certain 'cultural heritage' that drew intensively on colonial paradigms. Within discourses of Kenyan cultural diversity, fashioned at the interface of the state's nationalist politics and the demands of the global market, the Maasai 'emerged as the epitome of Kenya's national heritage', as local journalists put it, while '[t]he western tourist's love of them has only boosted their image' (Obonyo and Nyassy 2004: 2). The same journalists observed:

> Considered the main selling point of Kenya's tourism, the Maasai are, indeed, one of the most photographed, filmed and written-about indigenous communities on earth; and their culture probably the most commercialised and exploited world over. (Obonyo and Nyassy 2004: 3)

In the 1980s, most safaris already included visits to Maasai settlements in their schedules, and hotel administrators were periodically hiring groups of 10 to 20 Maasai or Samburu men to perform dances for their customers. Meanwhile, women from European countries (but also, to a lesser extent, from Australia, North America and Japan) began visiting Kenya armed with a clear image of the tall, slim bodies of the 'vanishing' Maasai morans (warriors), walking half naked, covered only by their red *shukas* (body blankets) and proudly carrying their spears and clubs. In the early 1990s, Kenya emerged as yet another international sexual destination, and among other forms of sexualised entertainment (Schoss 1995; Omondi 2003),[4] its draw relied intensively on eroticised representations of the Maasai and Samburu.

In Kenya, the Maasai became, as Edward Bruner put it, 'the quintessential pastoralists and the moran (junior warrior) [became] the quintessential Maasai'

(Bruner 2005: 35). In December 2004, the *Lifestyle* magazine of Nairobi's *Daily Nation* announced a global tourist 'mania' for the Maasai morans.[5] There was, as such, a great awareness evidenced in the Kenyan public discourse with regard to the almost mesmerising qualities of the Maasai image in opening tourist wallets. In this sense, the same article observed how this 'moran mania' quickly gave rise to a 'lucrative business', and how consequently 'scores of morans – genuine and fake alike – are flooding the coastal beaches to make a living from the trade' (Obonyo and Nyassy 2004: 2).

Among the Samburu of northern-central Kenya, this context was generating new opportunities for earning cash while performing a long-standing (post-)colonial paradigm that accentuated the relative 'cultural relatedness' of the Samburu to the Maasai. The fact that Samburu people are identified in various circumstances with the better-known Maasai plays out in 'both historical reality and current cultural politics' (Kasfir 2002: 371).[6] Like the Maasai, the Samburu are a Maa-speaking ethnic group of semi-nomadic pastoralists. And whereas the Maasai live mostly in southern Kenya and northern Tanzania, the Samburu inhabit predominantly the semi-arid lands of the north-central savannah of Kenya. Most of the Samburu people raise cattle and, to a lesser extent, goats, sheep and, in some areas, camels (Spencer 1965, 1973). By the mid-20th century, many had also taken up agriculture, livestock trade or migratory wage labour (Fumagalli 1977; Konaka 2001; Holtzman 2003).

Here, the relative freedom associated with the status of the *lmurrani* (moran) is important for understanding why migration is prominent mainly among this age-grade. The period during which a man is *lmurrani* (plural: *ilmurran*) is an interval of up to 15 years, when a boy is initiated with circumcision and which ends with the initiation of a new age-set. During this period, the young men are forbidden to marry and have to spend most of their time outside the domestic unit of their parents.[7] Some *ilmurran* herd the cattle of their fathers away from home. Others, especially those who went to school, orient this period of their lives towards earning cash. Some become soldiers, watchmen or police officers all over Kenya, but others seek to profit from tourism and orient themselves toward the tourist niche that has developed on the coast (Holtzman 2003). Whether it is done through cattle raids, wage labour or tourism, an *lmurrani* is expected by his father to have at least some cattle ready for bridewealth when he becomes a junior elder.

When I began my fieldwork in 2005, David was a Lmooli *lmurrani* (member of the age-set initiated in 1990; now in his late 20s). His family was living on some hills close to the town of Maralal in the Samburu district (northern Kenya). Because his father had died four years prior, David was living with his siblings and his mother in the compound of his father's brother and his two wives. He had finished secondary school a couple of years before and ever since had been coming daily to Maralal, where he waited for tourists and travellers to hire him as a tour guide. The money he earned in these circumstances was spent mostly on food, cattle vaccines and clothing for himself and his family. In August 2005, a new age-set (the Lkishami) was to be initiated, and David was preparing to become a junior elder. However, he had neither enough cattle for bridewealth nor any stable source of income. His years of being an *lmurrani* had not allowed for any accumulation of wealth. Becoming a junior elder would subject him to the social pressures surrounding marriage and David's inability to respond financially to these demands would put him in a difficult position.

David's was not an atypical case. Numerous young men found themselves in similarly contradictory situations. The year 2005 had been one of particular economic hardship for many Samburu. First, the initiation of the Lkishami age-set was making high economic demands on families who had sons to be circumcised. The *emuratare* (circumcision) ceremonies called for livestock to be sacrificed, for large amounts of sugar and rice to be bought, for new clothing and ritual fees. Many families had to move long distances to the *lorora* (ceremonial compound) of their clan. There, the elders in charge of the ceremonies would demand money and alcohol.

Second, with the initiation of the Lkishami age-set, their predecessors, the Lmooli, would become junior elders and would have to marry. Preparing bride prices of eight to 16 cattle for each Lmooli son, sometimes as many as three to six to a polygynous family, placed an additional demand on local domestic economies. Third, the summer of 2005 marked a time of general crisis in the national labour market. Numerous workers' strikes that took place across the country proved ineffectual. In a public speech broadcast in early June 2005 on a national radio station, President Mwai Kibaki threatened workers who would not return to work with immediate replacement. As such, for many young Samburu men the lack of capital coming with the crises on the national labour market and the demands for investment in the age-grade ceremonies, framed a particular situation of economic hardship and social tension.

David's critique of his *murata* (age-mate), quoted at the beginning of the chapter, should be understood within this context. It was meant to question the morality of wealth accumulated 'overnight'. Not unlike accusations of witchcraft, so well documented in the different post-colonies of Africa south of the Sahara (Comaroff and Comaroff 1999), the criticism of the sexual morality of local men engaging in sexual relationships with white female tourists has to be seen as responding to the production of new inequalities. Attacking the sexual morality of men enriched through their relationships with white women became a discursive genre of gossip and scandal widespread among the inhabitants of Maralal.

At the time that David was levelling his critique, others had already come to form a new local elite displaying the material advantages of such relationships. For the past 10 years, men had built themselves large villa-type houses on the edge of Maralal, in an area known as belonging to the Mombasa morans (and probably some officials). Many of these men opened hotels and pubs in the heart of Maralal. They also opened stores or built commercial spaces for rent. Furthermore, most of them owned TVs and VCRs, cell phones, cars, large cattle herds, and had at some point travelled to Europe. All these were symbolic markers of wealth and socio-economic prestige. This accumulation of wealth and economic prestige, in its turn, placed these men in an ambiguous position, sometimes attracting relatives and friends who could benefit from their wealth, at other times becoming the target of moral criticism directed primarily at their sexuality.

Representing bodies, embodying representations

Up until now, I have drawn out some of the general characteristics of the context of moran mania. Now, I turn to a more concrete discussion of the role of the body in certain neo-imperial representations, that is, specific visual idioms inherited from a colonial era and recoded in the post-colonial tourist industry. I will also address some embodied effects of such representations.

The moral criticism targeting men who enriched themselves through relationships with female tourists is a discourse generated by and generative of bodily dispositions. When David spoke of his age-mate, the tone of his voice trembled with disgust, the features of his face strained with resentment. He had guided many female tourists around the district in the past, but never had sexual relationships with any of them. Ultimately, as he came to find out, he was 'too short' and 'too chunky', and thus could barely pass as a 'Samburu warrior'. The possibility or impossibility of participating in the enactment of neo-imperial fantasies within the moran mania phenomenon presupposed, as such, not only a mere performance of specific bodily representations, but also the embodiment of the effects of such a performance.

And it is these particular embodied effects that are omitted in discussions of (female) sexual tourism, when the body is treated merely in terms of its objectification (commodification). With the sexual travel of women to the Caribbean, it is argued, local men become exoticised objects of desire. Carefully performing the Rasta body style, they play out onto a 'cultural' attraction (Pruitt and LaFont 1995: 425; Albuquerque 1998: 91) that turns them into 'embodied commodities' (Phillips 1999: 199–200; Sanchez Taylor 2000). 'Sellers of "cultural experiences"', Sanchez Taylor observes, 'have to be the bearers of very specific racialised and gendered identities' (Sanchez Taylor 2000: 48). Nonetheless, we need to ask: what are the effects of assuming these identities, of trying to embody these cultural images?

In these studies, the effects of the commodification of bodies remain undertheorised, whereas the representations of bodies are also dehistoricised. In Kenya, it was a specific political and historical context that required the representations of Maasai or Samburu bodies to be performed in certain ways, at the same time that this performance materialised its effects in embodied dispositions and moral criticisms.

First, it shall be noted that representations of bodies are not free-floating signifiers, but culturally and historically situated discursive productions. The aesthetics of the current representations of the Maasai or Samburu bodies has to be understood as being based on politically informed discourses and certain hegemonic paradigms inherited from colonial representations. If, on one hand, these new aesthetics emerged in response to the dialogue between national politics and the demands of the global market, on the other hand there was a certain historical continuity in the ways in which the Maasai/Samburu bodies were envisioned. The commodification of colonial and post-colonial representations for tourist consumption was a reinvention of old colonial paradigms, some of which go back to the second half of the 19th century.

Early travel accounts and colonial ethnographies set the path for what was to become a metropolitan fascination with the 'change-reluctant' Maasai/Samburu (Kasfir 1999, 2002; Hughes 2006). Furthermore, coffee-table books, postcards, films and movies concretised this image, inscribing it into a colourful visual archetype, with 'nostalgia being voiced for physical perfection itself' (Kasfir 1999: 73). The imperative of physical perfection was continuously carved out in the social relations of this aesthetic phenomenon, and ultimately determined what bodies were eligible to partake in its benefits (Meiu 2008).

Second, these representations were actively challenged in different contexts, especially when the question of who was legitimised to perform the persona of the Maasai/Samburu moran was posed in terms of ethnicity and bodily aesthetics. With a general awareness in Kenyan public discourse of the ongoing moran mania came a certain sense of chaos associated with the unfolding of the phenomenon, along with a certain anxiety among Kenyan authorities.[8] This anxiety was evidenced in relation to the diffuse image of those who stood to benefit from 'the trade'. Nairobi's *Daily Nation* observed:

> As the moran mania grows, the fake ones have become a source of both envy and loth [sic] ... Luckily for the fake operator, virtually all tourists polled by *Lifestyle* could not tell the bogus moran from the genuine ones although some admit having had intense interactions with the locals ... Mrs Brigit Wurth, a tourist from Germany, confesses her ignorance over the true identity of the moran. 'I have interacted with a number of them, most of whom asked me to assist them to go to Europe. But I couldn't tell a fake from a genuine moran,' says the 67-year-old woman. (Obonyo and Nyassy 2004: 3)

Genuine morans, fake morans and ignorant tourists. The concern with the 'authenticity' of the men benefiting from this moran mania phenomenon emerged at a time when individuals crossed ethnic identity boundaries in order to take up this highly ethnicised persona. Those benefiting from this phenomenon would soon, the concern went, no longer be identifiable in terms of ethnicity. Therefore, the article also provided advice on 'how to tell a fake from a genuine Maasai moran':

> A true moran has a distinct look, facial appearance and dress that the fake moran must ape. The change to 'moranism' involves braiding the hair and dying it red with ochre. The candidate adorns himself in a red-white *shuka*, multi-coloured chokers, earrings and bracelets, with a club to match. For a rare perfectionist, knocking out the two front teeth on the lower jaw is a must. (Obonyo and Nyassy 2004: 2)

Fake morans could appropriate bodily decorations, earrings and bracelets and they could even go as far as 'knocking out the two front teeth' in order to 'ape' moran identity for ignorant tourists. But, it seemed to be implied that there was something deeper, something that they could not appropriate and that made them fake to begin with. And if, for these Kenyan journalists, the signs through which the 'true moran' could be both recognised and 'aped' were more about bodily adornments, for many tourists these signs were also about the forms of the body itself. Thus, the Samburu whose bodies did not match the image of the tall, slim and light-coloured moran persona were often thought not to be Maasai or Samburu. Participating in tourism and developing relationships with white women was not a choice equally available to everyone. The aesthetic paradigms that framed the image of the Maasai/Samburu male body within the moran mania discussed above determined decisively what bodies were eligible to compete for its material advantages.

The colonial and post-colonial visual archetype of the tall, slim Maasai/Samburu warrior as it materialised in the social relations surrounding this phenomenon had created its abject others: namely, short bodies, fat bodies or any bodies that did not fit the stereotypical vision. The issue of who benefited from the tourist niche became an embodied matter: for only certain bodies would have been eligible to employ the aesthetics of this post-colonial persona. During my research, numerous Samburu men whose bodies did not match these paradigms complained to me that they could not 'pick up' tourists on the coast. Others told me of how, when a German film company came to Maralal to shoot *The White Masai* in 2003, many were rejected at a pre-selection gathering because they were 'not tall enough', 'not slim enough' or 'not light-coloured' enough to pass as 'Samburu' (Meiu 2008: 18).

Finally, this essentialised body/ethnicity equation, playing out onto neo-imperial fantasies, became itself a motif of the moral criticism directed at the Mombasa morans in their home communities. As the post-colonial imaginaries of the Samburu moran phrased their limits in terms of bodily aesthetics and excluded abject bodies from contexts of wealth accumulation, those men whose bodies were left out transposed this issue into their criticism of a morally weak form of neo-imperialism. They ridiculed thus their age-mates' participation at the enactment of a primitivist spectacle for sexual purposes. As David sarcastically put it:

> The *muzungu mamas* want the morans that are dressed with *kangas* [body cloth] and have spears. They don't want the ones who have pants and shirts. They say that the ones with *kangas* walk freely and have big dicks ... They want the ones that have long hair dyed with ochre. The boy probably went here to school and used to wear pants, but there [in Mombasa] they put on the *kanga* and take the spear to find *wazungu* [white people]. (Maralal, August 2005)

The criticism of the immorality of a certain objectification of tradition revealed a particular cultural logic. According to Samburu men who did not participate in the sexual tourism of the coast, the objectification of tradition within nationalist propaganda (schools and district festivals) constituted a way of dignifying Samburu cultural identity, at the same time that in Mombasa it represented a vulgar way of performing primitivist fantasies for sexual purposes. Nevertheless, as was often the case, many young men would participate alternatively in both forms of objectification.

In short, the strategic performance of post-colonial imaginaries of Maasai/Samburu bodies by Samburu men has not been a mere theatrical play enacted on the stages of tourist resorts but, foremost, a moralised process resulting in embodied dispositions. Moreover, the objects of representation – the representations of bodies – have been historically and politically phrased paradigms that transpose their limits unto the actors' embodied dispositions, and have reshaped these as they announce which bodies are eligible to compete for the material advantages of tourist performances.

Masculinities, moralities and 'Mombasa morans'

The reconfiguration of Samburu masculinities in relation to white women's sexual travel was phrased, as such, within this particular moral geography, and was animated by the new embodied dispositions that it inculcated. The Mombasa morans came to form a different masculinity, one discursively set apart from other masculinities by moralised notions of wealth and sexuality. An emphasis on the moral criticism phrased in terms of their sexuality can help capture the complex circumstances under which masculinities are reshaped in relation to each other.

In Maralal, for example, we encounter a variety of 'sexual scripts' (Gagnon and Simon 1973) or sets of socially prescribed sexual behaviours. Distinct sexual scripts correspond more or less to different masculinities. Thus, school-educated Samburu men aim for the embodiment of 'modern' masculinities different from those of the men who spend their lives herding cattle in the bush. More specifically, the masculinities of the wage labourers, the teachers, the missionaries, the merchants and so on involve not only slightly different patterns of dress and behaviour, but also, and quite importantly, different sexual scripts phrased in moral contrasts to each other. Among the Samburu, masculinities have been reconfigured within a certain moral geography and with particular reference to wealth and new sexual scripts.

At some general level, Samburu men distinguished themselves as either 'traditional' or 'modern' (idiomatic terms), and derogatorily called each other respectively 'bush' *ilmurran* and 'plastic' *ilmurran*. Unlike the former, the latter went to school, spoke more than one language and had a quite different dress code. Dorothy Hodgson (2003) identified a similar primary distinction of masculinities among the Maasai of Tanzania. Hodgson (2003: 119–21) showed, for example, how the Maa term *ormeek* (modern), initially designating non-Maasai men, was derogatorily attached by Maasai elders to those Maasai men who attended school and worked for cash. Later on, the term *ormeek* acquired rather positive meanings, with elders blaming themselves for their ignorance when it came to bureaucracy and the state. 'In contrast to earlier meanings of *ormeek*,' Hodgson observed, 'such differences are more external and not mutually exclusive: one can both speak Swahili and speak Maa, or one can wear red cloth in the morning, put on pants to go to town, then return in the evening to home and the red cloth again' (Hodgson 2003: 223). Similar usages can now be found among the Samburu.

In my interviews with Samburu men, these categories were often invoked when individuals constructed themselves in opposition to each other. Simon explained:

> These people in the bush don't know how to have sex. Boom, boom, boom, and everything is finished. They don't even kiss. Now, I went to school and I kiss my wife. But them, if they come to Maralal and see on TV someone kissing, they turn around and spit: 'The *wazungu* [white people] are not normal' they say. (Maralal, August 2005)

During my research, Simon was a Lmooli *lmurrani*, awaiting the status of a junior elder. He had had several relationships, in Mombasa, with women from Europe, had travelled several times to Germany, invited by these women, and had recently settled

445

down in Maralal with a Samburu wife.[9] He owned a hotel and a large house there. Throughout our interview, Simon, not unlike the other school-educated men I interviewed, reinforced the distinction between 'bush' *ilmurran* and 'modern' *ilmurran* (like himself) in order to position his sexuality in a relationship of superiority to that of the 'ignorant people in the bush'.

'Bush' *ilmurran*, Simon explained, get most of the stimulation through their palms and from having their loins touched. It is in this sense that one can often see an *lmurrani* rubbing his palms against his loins as he talks to a girl. Also, during the sexual act (*neciaman* or *nárà*), the man rubs his palms against a special set of beads that a girl hangs around her loins to provide stimulation. 'But us,' he pointed out, 'we went to school. We don't do that.'

'The morans in the bush, when they come, they make some loud growls,' Mohammad (another school educated man) told me, laughing, 'and you can hear them from the other hill.' (Maralal, August 2005)

Meanwhile, however, these 'modern' men would occasionally and nostalgically identify their sexuality with the 'heroism' of being an *lmurrani* in the bush.

'They can reach up to seven or even 10 orgasms in one night,' Simon explained. 'If you stay at the *lale* (cattle compounds in the forest) for a long time, and you take *seketet* or *surukoi* (wild plants), you can do that.'

In this way, the morality of different sexual scripts, of various bodily ways of pleasure, was an active discursive differentiator as these 'modern' men both distinguished themselves from or occasionally identified with their relatives in the bush. The sexual body acted in these discourses not only as a figure of discursive distinction, but also – and most importantly – as a figure generative of bodily dispositions, for example, alternating contemptuous dissociation or nostalgic identification.

School education, herein, was invoked to mark the decisive break between these two general categories of masculinity. Simon added that 'before you go to school, you look at people kissing, and you say: how stupid, how disgusting. When you come back, you can't believe how stupid your people are (because they don't kiss)' (Maralal, June 2005). The boarding school played an important role in framing particular sexualities and notions of gender, yet the articulation of different forms of 'modern' masculinity was determined by the various occupations men adopted after graduation, especially in the years of *ilmurran*-hood.

As such, the various types of masculinity emerging from boarding schools, all known as 'modern', were further differentiated in the process of making a living. The missionary Samburu men, for example, would distinguish themselves from wage labourers or 'Mombasa morans', among others, through a moral discourse on sexuality. Moses, who had graduated from the Good Shepherd Seminary of Maralal (a Catholic school) spoke to me about the 'ignorance' of the people in the bush, and about the 'sinful degradation' of the 'adulterous' wage labourers, and 'Mombasa morans'. Paradoxically or not, he would often look up at his cousin who had married a Norwegian woman and settled down with her, and would ask him for financial support.

Similarly, other Samburu men also distinguished themselves from the Mombasa morans through moral discourses on sexuality. Many would criticise the sexual immorality of men sleeping with white women in Mombasa, both in terms of age and in terms of race transgressions. 'In our culture,' David argued, 'you can't marry older women. It's like marrying your own mother. The Mombasa morans sometimes marry women that could be their grandmothers' (Maralal, June 2005). Mohammad also explained:

> Here if a woman is my mother's age, I call her *yieyo* [mother]. If she is my grandmother's age, I call her *nkoko* [grandmother]. One time when this one old, ugly British woman came to see her moran, I went over to her to say hi. I said politely, 'How are you grandma?' She got so furious. 'Don't call me grandma … I'm not your grandma' [laughing]. (Maralal, July 2005)

The generic use of the 'old', 'ugly', white woman in these moral critiques was not arbitrary. Both age and race were used to signify immoral transgressions. On the coast, Samburu men engaged most often, but not exclusively, in relationships with women older than themselves. And if some women were their seniors by only a few years, some indeed would be in their 50s or 60s. Moreover, their whiteness indexed perverted sexuality.

Neville Hoad suggests that discursive attacks on Western sexualities, in Africa, 'can be seen as responses to … prior attributions of primitiveness [to Africans], and as a reversal of the racist charge of retardation and/or degeneration' (Hoad 2007: 56). He adds:

> These attacks consistently locate the origin of perversion (and, with greater political urgency, AIDS) in the West. While Christian dogma, with its rhetoric of universal brotherhood of man, can and has mitigated against some of the racism in these imperialist formations, and the sign of 'marriage', Christian or not, can render the other grave threat to Christian sexual norms (polygamy) somewhat recuperable, imperial 'civilised' sexual norms can remain in place and can paradoxically be defended as authentically African. (Hoad 2007: 56–57)

These attacks on Western sexuality constitute a response to the 'register of sexual "perversion"' attributed to Africa in the context of the HIV/AIDS pandemic, (Comaroff 2007). White women then tended to be perceived through a similar prism of immorality, rendering their sexuality un-Christian and un-African. When I once described my research to a man in Nairobi, he furiously pointed out, 'You know, people say AIDS comes from Africa. It's not true. It is women like these that have money, and come and sleep with these poor men who brought AIDS to Africa.'

And whereas the origin of perversion (here, HIV/AIDS) was explicitly placed in the West, those men who engaged in sexual relationships with these women were nevertheless seen as participating in the same un-Christian and un-African perversion.

This moral criticism of the sexuality of men sleeping with older white women was constitutive of a stigma that was contagiously transferred to the wealth they accumulated. 'I better stay poor my whole life,' David assured me, 'rather than sleep with ugly women for money.' At the same time, the same stigma became essential, along with the stigmatised wealth, in the differentiation of other masculinities from the Mombasa morans.

Conclusion

For David, as for many of his age-mates, ridiculing those men who slept with 'ugly', 'old' white women 'for money' was both a way of discrediting the morality of Mombasa morans and a way to express an embodied disposition produced in response to a particular moral geography and the late reconfiguration of Samburu masculinities.

For those Samburu men whose bodily forms had placed them at an advantage over their fellow age-mates, in the sense of allowing them to play out certain neo-imperial fantasies, relationships with white female tourists constituted an opportunity of upward economic mobility. Migrating to the coast of the Indian Ocean, embodying the performance of post-colonial representations of their bodies and committing to a pattern of circular migration, these Samburu men came to be repositioned within the moral imagination of their home communities. As their accumulated wealth became the object of envy, their 'foul' sexuality became the object of public criticism. These types of moral discourses on sexuality, prevalent in the everyday life of Maralal, were orchestrated by specific bodily dispositions that shaped and distinguished different types of masculinity among the Samburu.

Notes

1. Reprinted with permission from the 2009 *Canadian Journal of African Studies*, vol. 43, no. 1.
2. This article is based on ethnographic research undertaken in 2005, both in the town of Maralal (Samburu district) and in the coastal city of Mombasa. The data was gathered through participation in and observation of everyday life, and formal and informal interviews with Samburu men of different backgrounds.
3. Immediately after independence, the government of Kenya encouraged the development of the tourist industry, establishing for this purpose, in 1965, the Kenyan Tourist Development Corporation. And if, from 1972 to 1982, the number of visitors stagnated at 350,000 per annum, throughout the 1980s the number increased twofold, reaching in 1989 a total of 700,000 visitors per annum (see Schoss 1995: 36–8).
4. Kenyan coastal towns constitute relatively heterogeneous sexual destinations. First, they appeal to female tourists not only through the primitivist spectacle of Maasai and Samburu men, but through a highly nuanced co-presence of various 'beachboys', and 'gigolos' (Schoss 1995). Second, coastal towns are also known for male sexual tourists. Although it is very rare that Maasai or Samburu women engage in relations with male tourists, female sex work is generally widespread on the coast. Third, child-sex tourism is part of the dynamics of the destination, and in spite of state struggles towards its abolition, it persists in underground networks (Omondi 2003).
5. The word moran was adopted in English and Swahili during the colonial era from the Maa *lmurrani* (plural: *ilmurran*), meaning young man, or warrior. The term is widely used in Kenya to refer to both Maasai and Samburu young men who have undergone circumcision and become part of the 'warrior' age-grade of their communities.
6. The occasional merging of Maasai and Samburu identities is a generalised phenomenon in post-colonial Kenya. Both the Samburu and the Maasai are Maa-speaking pastoralists. They share numerous similarities in terms of material culture, rituals, kinship and age-grade system. Although initially part of the same group, since the relocation of the Maasai to parts of southern Kenya and northern Tanzania, the Samburu Maa-speakers of northern Kenya have shaped their own distinct identity. Despite the current almost mythical antipathy of the Samburu toward the Maasai, the Samburu often continue to contextually identify as Maasai or as a clan thereof, in circumstances where such a link could prove beneficial (see Kasfir 2002).

7. Holtzman suggests that *lminong*, or the prohibition of *ilmurran* eating food seen by women, prescribes the removal of the young men from the domestic economy in order to reduce competition over the otherwise limited resources of food (see Holtzman 2003: 234).
8. This concern has most probably to do with controlling tourist cash by maintaining the travellers in well-defined tourist networks (hotels, lodges, restaurants and safari trails). In these discourses, beaches emerge as dangerous spaces of interference, where tourists can interact with local 'beach boys', and where tourist money can uncontrollably be extracted by individuals who are not officially members of the tourist industry. Being no longer able to pinpoint exactly where the morans frequenting these beaches come from generates a certain sense of anxiety. Moreover, the uncontrolled presence of locals on tourist beaches is seen as diminishing the tourists' sense of security. Further research needs to be undertaken in this direction.
9. Simon's case was one of the few instances in which an *lmurrani* was permitted to marry before actually becoming a junior elder. Although the elders of some clans began allowing such early marriages, other elders, predominantly from the Lmasula clan, radically forbid marriages before the end of *ilmurran*-hood.

References

Albuquerque, Klaus de (1998) 'Sex, beach boys, and female tourists in the Caribbean: sex work and sex workers', *Sexuality and Culture* (special issue) 2: 87–111, New Jersey, New Brunswick

Bruner, Edward M. (2005) *Culture on Tour: Ethnographies of Travel*, Chicago, University of Chicago Press

Butler, Judith (1993) *Bodies That Matter: On the Discursive Limits of 'Sex'*, New York, Routledge

Comaroff, Jean (2007) 'Beyond bare life: AIDS, (bio)politics and the neoliberal order', *Public Culture* 19(1): 197–219

Comaroff, John L. and Comaroff, Jean (1992) *Ethnography and Historical Imagination*, Summertown, Westview Press

—— (1999) 'Occult economies and the violence of abstraction: notes from the South African postcolony', *American Ethnologist* 26(2): 279–303

Dahles, Heidi and Bras, Karin (1999) 'Entrepreneurs in romance: tourism in Indonesia', *Annals of Tourism Research* 26(2): 267–93

End Child Prostitution, Child Pornography and Trafficking of Children for Sexual Purposes (ECPAT) (n.d.) 'Child sex tourism in Kenya', www.ecpat.org.uk/downloads/kenya05.pdf, accessed 26 July 2006

Farquhar, Judith (2002) *Appetites: Food and Sex in Postsocialist China*, Durham, Duke University Press

Ferguson, James (1999) *Expectations of Modernity: Myths and Meanings of Urban Life on the Zambian Copperbelt*, Berkeley, University of California Press

Fumagalli, C.T. (1977) 'A diachronic study of change and socio-cultural process among the pastoral nomadic Samburu of Kenya, 1900–1975', PhD dissertation, Buffalo, State University of New York

Gagnon, J.H. and Simon, W. (1973) *Sexual Conduct: The Social Source of Human Sexuality*, Chicago, Aldine

Geschiere, Peter (1997) *The Modernity of Witchcraft: Politics and the Occult in Postcolonial Africa*, Charlotteville, University of Virginia Press

Gupta, Akhil and Ferguson, James (eds) (1997) *Anthropological Locations: Boundaries and Grounds of a Field Science*, Berkeley, University of California Press

Hoad, Neville (2007) *African Intimacies: Race, Homosexuality, and Globalisation*, Minneapolis, University of Minnesota Press

Hodgson, Dorothy L. (2003) 'Being Maasai men: modernity and the production of Maasai masculinities', in Lindsay, L.A. and Miescher, S.F. (eds) *Men and Masculinities in Modern Africa*, Portsmouth, NH, Heinemann

Hofmann, C. (2005) *The White Maasai*, tr Peter Millar, London, Arcadia Books

Holtzman, Jon D. (2003) 'Age, masculinity, and migration: Gender and age among Samburu pastoralists in northern Kenya', in Clark, G. (ed) *Gender at Work in Economic Life*, Walnut Creek, Altamira Press

Hughes, Lotte (2006) '"Beautiful beasts" and brave warriors: the longevity of Maasai stereotype', in Romanucci-Ross, L., De Vos, G., and Tsuda, T. (eds) *Ethnic Identity: Problems and Prospects for the Twenty-First Century*, Lonham, Altamira Press

Jeffreys, Sheila (2003) 'Sex tourism: do women do it too?', *Leisure Studies* 22: 223–38

Kasfir, Sidney (1999) 'Samburu souvenirs: representations of a land in amber', in Phillips, R.B. and Steiner, C.B. (eds) *Unpacking Culture: Art and Commodity in Colonial and Postcolonial Worlds*, Berkeley, University of California Press

—— (2002) 'Slam-dunking and the last noble savage', *Visual Anthropology* 15: 369–85

—— (2004) 'Tourist aesthetics in the global flow: orientalism and "warrior theatre" on the Swahili Coast', *Visual Anthropology* 17: 319–43

Kempadoo, Kamala (1999) 'Continuities and change: five centuries of prostitution in the Caribbean', in Kempadoo, K. (ed) *Sun, Sex, and Gold: Tourism and Sex Work in the Caribbean*, Lanham, MD: Rowman and Littlefield Publishers

—— (2001) 'Freelancers, temporary wives, and beach boys: researching sex work in the Caribbean', *Feminist Review* 67: 39–62

Konaka, Shinya (2001) 'The Samburu livestock trader in North-Central Kenya', *Nilo-Ethiopian Studies* 7: 63–79

Lindsay, Lisa A. and Miescher, Stephan F. (eds) (2003) *Men and Masculinities in Modern Africa*, Portsmouth, NH, Heinemann

Livingstone, Julie (2005) *Debility and the Moral Imagination in Botswana*, Bloomington, Indiana University Press

Meiu, George Paul (2008) 'Riefenstahl on safari: embodied contemplation in East Africa', *Anthropology Today* 24(2): 18–22

Miescher, Stephan F. (2005) *Making Men in Ghana*, Indianapolis, Indiana University Press

Obonyo, Oscar and Nyassy, Daniel (2004) 'Moran mania: the good, the bad and the ugly in the commercial use of Maasai culture', *Sunday Nation*, 12 December

Omondi, Rose Kisia (2003) 'Gender and the political economy of sex tourism in Kenya's coastal resorts', paper presented at the International Symposium on Feminist Perspectives on Global Economic and Political Systems, Tromso, Norway, 24–26 September

Ouzgane, Lahoucine and Morrell, Robert (eds) (2005) *African Masculinities: Men in Africa from Late 19th Century to the Present*, New York, Palgrave MacMillan

Phillips, Joan L. (1999) 'Tourist-oriented prostitution in Barbados: the case of the beach boy and the white female tourist', in Kempadoo, K. (ed). In *Sun, Sex and Gold: Tourism and Sex Work in the Caribbean*, Lanham, MD, Rowman and Littlefield Publishers

Pigg, Stacy Leigh and Adams, Vincanne (2005) 'Introduction: the moral object of sex', in Adams, V. and Pigg, S.L. (eds) *Sex in Development: Science, Sexuality, and Morality in Global Perspective*, Durham, Duke University Press

Pohl, Otto (2002) 'Kenya cracking down on "beach boys", gigolos serving tourists', *The New York Times*, 14 February, www.nytimes.com/2002/02/14/world/kenya-cracking-down-on-beach-boys-gigolos-serving-tourists.html, accessed 1 February 2006

Povinelli, A. Elizabeth and Chauncey, George (1999) 'Thinking sexuality transnationally: an introduction', *Gay and Lesbian Queries* 5(4): 439–50

Pruitt, Deborah and LaFont, Suzanne (1995) 'For love and money: romance tourism in Jamaica', *Annals of Tourism Research* 22(2): 422–40

Ryan, Chris and Michel Hall, C. (2001) *Sex Tourism: Marginal People and Liminalities*, London and New York, Routledge

Sanchez Taylor, Jacheline (2000) 'Tourism and "embodied commodities": sex tourism in the Caribbean', in Clift, S. and Carter, S. (eds) *Tourism and Sex: Culture, Commerce and Coercion*, London, Pinter

—— (2001) 'Dollars are a girl's best friend? Female tourists' sexual behaviour in the Caribbean', *Sociology*, 35(3): 749–64

Schneider, Leander (2006) 'The Maasai's new clothes: a developementalist modernity and its exclusions', *Africa Today* 53(1): 101–31

Schoss, Johanna (1995) 'Beach tours and safari visions: relations of production and the production of "culture" in Malindi, Kenya', PhD dissertation, Chicago, University of Chicago

Silberschmidt, Margrethe (2004) 'Masculinities, sexuality and socio-economic change in rural and urban Africa', in Arnfred, S. (ed) *Rethinking Sexualities in Africa*, Uppsala, The Nordic Africa Institute

Spencer, Paul (1965) *The Samburu: A Study of Gerontocracy in a Nomadic Tribe*, London, Routledge and Kegan Paul

—— (1973) *Nomads in Alliance: Symbiosis and Growth Among the Rendille and Samburu of Kenya*, London, Oxford University Press

Sperling, L. (1987) 'Wage employment among the Samburu pastoralists of northcentral Kenya', *Research in Economic Anthropology* 9: 167–90

Waller, Ulla and Bawa, Yamba (1986) 'Going north and getting attached: the case of the Gambians', *Ethnos* 15 (3–4): 199–222

White, Luise (1990) 'Separating men from boys: constructions of gender, sexuality and terrorism in Central Kenya', *International Journal of African Historical Studies* 23(1): 1–25

World Tourism Organisation (WTO) (1999) *Yearbook of Tourism Statistics*, Madrid, WTO

47

Sexual orientation and human rights: putting homophobia on trial

Makau Mutua

Introduction

The subject of sexual orientation, as understood in all its complexity, is extremely charged in Africa because of the deeply socially conservative landscape and the domination of the political space by Christianity and Islam, the two prevalent messianic faiths in the region. Homophobia has long been a hallmark of the two Abrahamic faiths. As I have argued elsewhere, 'homophobia is not necessarily home-grown' in Africa because 'much of the revulsion of homosexuality can be traced to Christianity and Islam, the two religious traditions that express homophobia in their doctrinal teachings' (Mutua 2009a).

That is why it is paradoxical when African Christians and Muslims attack homosexuality as alien to Africa while embracing the two foreign faiths. However, it is a fact, no matter its origin, that homophobia is deeply embedded in the social fabric of Africa. The question is how to understand the resilience of homophobia in the region, stoke public debate on the subject, and agitate for the recognition and protection of sexual orientation as a basic human right. This is a challenge that will require thoughtful analyses, courageous advocacy and fundamental reforms. It is the normative obligation of civil society, and human rights groups in particular, to lead such a struggle. In this chapter I argue that homophobia is an irrational fear that is used to deny basic rights and which society has an obligation to overcome.

At the core of the human rights project, in spite of misgivings that I have expressed elsewhere (Mutua 2002), is the humanist impulse to re-affirm faith in our common humanity both as individuals, but also as members of the many groups to which we belong (UN Charter 1945; Khan 2009). Although a lot of progress has been made over years, some rights claims have achieved more success than others. The rights language now pervades the struggle against human powerlessness in areas where it was unthinkable only several decades ago.

For example, economic, social and cultural rights seem to have entered the mainstream of rights discourse in the last decade. Claims which were at the margins only recently are now moving, albeit slowly, to the centre. This process of demarginalisation of certain rights claims speaks to the growing acceptance of the complexity of the human condition. Even so, rights claims based on certain identities still meet with stubborn resistance. In some cases, they face outright rejection. In no other identity issue is this truer than with respect to sexual orientation. In a sense, sexual orientation claims might be among the last impenetrable frontiers.

As a result, any discussion of sexual orientation – not just in Africa but the world over – must acknowledge the resilience of homophobia and the taboo of the subject, but that opposition on the basis of tradition cannot be a reason for passivity or the acceptance of bigotry. If anything, it must be the impetus for action. While it is true that a conversation about sexual orientation is not an easy one in any social context, it must take place nevertheless, no matter our personal positions. It is a discussion that every society must have because it touches on the most fundamental of all human values (Terry 1999).

How the issue is debated, and the manner in which the disputants treat each other, says a lot about what a society is, and what it thinks it ought to become. Would the conversation, for example, be held in an atmosphere of civility, or would the contending sides exhibit only contempt, disdain and intolerance toward each other? The ways in which societies debate incendiary and highly emotive questions reveal much about their inherent makeup.

In Africa, the debate on gay rights has been at times acrimonious and rancorous. This reflects the fear that some people have of the unknown, but also the fear of naked bigotry. The young democratic experiments on the continent owe it to themselves to learn how to contest important questions – and to agree to disagree amenably – without diminishing the humanity of those who are dissimilar. Contesting the meaning of sexual orientation – and understanding homosexuals as fellow human beings entitled to full rights – cannot be avoided any longer. The time is now.

This chapter probes the cultural, social and legal bases for homophobia in Africa and argues for inclusivity of homosexuality in the understanding of sexual orientation. It acknowledges the deep-seated nature of homophobia in Africa, but contends that there is nothing inherently African about it. The chapter begins with a broad introduction, which places sexual orientation and homophobia in context. I then discuss the nature and purposes of political society with a particular focus on the tenets of liberalism and the foundational norms of human rights. I build a case for a holistic understanding of sexual orientation as a part of the project of liberalism. Next, I discuss the law and sexual orientation and the reasons for homophobia, and exploding the myth that it is un-African to be gay, I conclude with a call for the equal protection for gays and lesbians.

The purposes of political society

Political society, organised as a state, exists for a variety of reasons but none is more compelling than the welfare of its inhabitants. Citizens are the raison d'être of the state. Thus the norms and structures of the state must respond to the needs of the populace. In the rights language, the state is no more than an instrument for the fulfilment of the will of citizens (Cover 1987). This is the foundation for the notion of popular sovereignty, the democratic will of the electors and the right of the citizens to resist an oppressive state. In exchange for agreeing to be governed by the state, citizens expect accountability, not oppression by the state. This is the reason for the existence of individual rights – entitlements that individuals hold within the state. One of the most important categories of rights pivots on identity. Protected traditional identities or suspect classifications that raise the need for higher legal scrutiny have included race, gender, religion, political opinion, nationality and social status. Over the years, constitutional and human rights law have added other protected identities. These now include marital status, disability and sexual orientation in an increasing number of jurisdictions. This fuller understanding of identity recognises the complexity of the human condition.

The state should therefore be understood not as a master, but a servant. It is not an instrument for oppression, but a servant of the people, an enabler that should allow each individual to try to realise their potential. The state would not exist but for its inhabitants – people are its foundation and with whose consent and on whose behalf it governs. In this regard, the state must not be tyrannical, otherwise the citizens have a right to forcibly overthrow it and institute a more democratic order. The best state exists to enhance liberty and freedom, not to restrict those it represents. The default position of the best state – the one that submits itself to the popular will – is that things are permitted, not prohibited. Prohibition, a limitation on freedom or liberty, requires a compelling logic and a high bar for the state to meet. This is a dynamic process of constant negotiation between the state and the populace to find the balance of acceptable limits on state power and the outer reaches and constraints on individual freedoms and liberties.

Liberalism: principles and tenets

Today, there are core universal values that bind all people no matter where, who and what they are, what they believe, who they worship, how they look, what they eat, the language they speak and how and whom they love. In short, human beings are now protected by universal norms and values in their basic identities and human conditions (Steiner et al 1996 [2008]). But these protections – for the weak or the strong, the poor or the rich, the big or the small, the male or the female, no matter the colour, creed, race and ethnicity – are not possible without two fundamental tenets of liberal theory and philosophy. These two tenets are formal equality and abstract autonomy.

As Henry Steiner has put it, the traditional liberal understanding of the state requires that it protect citizens by guaranteeing their abstract autonomy and formal equality (Steiner 1988). The individual is accorded this exalted status because he is regarded in liberalism as the foundation of human civilisation. S/he is the centre of the moral universe. There is a large consensus today that no modern society, as the term is understood, can prosper without a measure of fidelity to the two key tenets of formal equality and abstract autonomy.

These tenets are the foundations of a modern political democracy. Similarly, it is not possible to think of the idea of human rights without them. Although it is true that other notions of human dignity can be constructed without reference to individualism – long cherished as central to political society in the West – it is inconceivable that elected governments with three co-equal and independent arms of the state in which the judiciary is the guardian of liberties could be possible. Foundational concepts, such as the right to life and freedom from slavery – not to mention freedom of individual conscience – would be hard to fathom.

Formal equality seeks to guarantee a simple notion – that every individual is endowed with inherent and intrinsic worth as a human being and that no one human being is more important than another in terms of their inherent worth. This notion is categorically captured in the Universal Declaration of Human Rights, which provides in its opening stanza that 'All human beings are born free and equal in dignity and rights' (Universal Declaration of Human Rights 1948). That statement is unequivocal and does not condition equality on identity such as sexual orientation.

Equality might be a legal fiction that liberal philosophy encodes, but nevertheless it is impossible to defend living in a society that is explicitly based on the inequality of human beings. Even a casual survey of states and conditions of explicit inequality, such as the former apartheid South Africa, the caste system in India, the Hutu/Tutsi dichotomy in Rwanda and Burundi, female subordination and the enslavement of people of African descent in the United States, evokes a barbarism that cannot be defended in the modern age. Although it is true that these and other privations still exist, it is their defence that is unimaginable.

The second important tenet of liberalism is abstract autonomy, which means that as individuals we are autonomous entities and free from the caprice and control of others. This means that no one can legally or morally own another. As a sovereign being, every human being is their own master/mistress. This is the foundation of democratic citizenship, that humans are rational beings who have the right to make individual choices about their own fate. Of course these two tenets are formal entitlements. They do not, in and of themselves, guarantee the substance of what they promise. It is up to the project of democracy to give them substance in politics and policy, otherwise they will remain empty and vacuous.

Arising from these tenets of formal equality and abstract autonomy are two basic principles on which human freedom and liberty pivot: equal protection and anti-discrimination. In reality, these principles are the flip side of one another. Equal protection guarantees against discrimination and vice versa. Discrimination is prohibited because equal protection is required. It is these two principles that are the cornerstones of the human rights ideal. If these two principles are removed, the whole human rights ideal would collapse. Every human rights treaty or ideal is based on equal protection norms and anti-discrimination notions. Think of conventions on race, women and children and thematic treaties on any subject and their internal logic is based on equal protection and anti-discrimination. In fact, the whole question of rights and the rights regime would be meaningless without them.

The logic of human rights

What are human rights and where do they come from? These are critical questions to interrogate in order to put gay rights protections in a holistic context. There is no serious argument that human rights are a genre of rights, or entitlements, that are socially constructed. In other words, like all rights, human rights are claims on society, but they are higher species of claims than ordinary 'negative' rights that individuals hold against the state. But human rights are socially constructed and do not emanate from above in a mysterious universe. Human rights arise directly from human struggles for freedom and identity and over resources (Klare 1991).

In other words, rights are the bulwark that sits between people and tyranny – whether that tyranny is vertical, from the state, or horizontal, from individual citizens and private entities. But fundamentally, human rights are a set of entitlements that come out of struggles for material resources and human identities. That is, human rights sit at the intersection of power and powerlessness in a location that allows them to check the arbitrary and capricious use of power and the domination of the weak by the strong, the oppression of the minority by the majority, the subordination of the unpopular by the popular.

This narrative suggests that without rights human beings would have little protection from the state (Panikar 1982). Indeed, life would be short and brutish. But rights are fought for, negotiated and socially constructed. They do not come from above like 'manna' from heaven. Rights start as claims by a group and only become rights when those claims have achieved a measure of success and a social ceasefire has been declared by the contending forces or interests. It is because of the nature of the specific struggle over each individual right that different rights are inherently unequal. Thus any conversation about rights must acknowledge the hierarchy of rights. This is an admission that some rights are more important than others. In this respect, some perceptions of rights view human rights as more important than other rights. For instance, human rights would be ranked higher than the rights granted under a commercial contract. In the official human rights universe itself, economic, social and cultural rights have always occupied a less exalted status than civil and political rights (Alston 1988).

Human rights are supposed to represent a higher form of human intelligence. Basic human rights are even more precious and inviolable because they are universally accepted and no state can be permitted to deviate from them. Such rights protect identities and persons from discrimination or capricious treatment. To date there are a number of protected classes of rights and peoples from which no deviation is permitted. These classes and identities are race, religion, sex, gender, language, national origin, marital status, age, racial and ethnic minorities, social standing, ethnicity, disability and political opinion. The question is whether sexual orientation, which includes homosexuality, is or should be, among these protected identities and classes.

What is sexual orientation?

Sexual orientation refers to the state and practice of emotional, sexual and romantic attraction to men, women, both genders or no gender. Sexual orientation is a human condition and is a matter of personal and social identity (Reeves 2009). The three main categories of sexual orientation are heterosexual, homosexual and bisexual – all of which exist in a continuum that ranges from exclusive heterosexual to exclusive homosexual with many variations of bisexuality in between. But this is a simplification of the term because it leaves out complex aspects of sexual identity that are closely related to sexual orientation, for instance those who are asexual, transsexual, queer, which are also forms of sexual orientation. It is important to note that none of these sexual orientations is normal or abnormal; it is, in fact, a misnomer to refer to any of the orientations as normal or abnormal because each is an existential condition.

Every society on earth has had a substantial minority that is gay. By that I mean that there is no one natural sexual orientation because whatever orientation one has is natural. Nor should there be a socially preferred sexual orientation because the preference is individual. That is why it makes little sense to ask Catholic priests, for example, what their sexual orientation is because the question has virtually no practical relevance since they are not supposed to be sexually active. Nor is the question relevant to those who are chaste, impotent or unable to engage in sexual relations for other reasons. The point is that when we think of sexual orientation, we should not automatically imagine one sexual orientation. We have to imagine a plethora of possibilities without privileging one orientation over the others. This is an important point because the dominant social view is to privilege heterosexuality as the natural sexual orientation.

The law

Domestic municipal laws have traditionally protected and privileged heterosexuality and heterosexism as it is entrenched in the traditional Western or European conception of the family. In many societies, this is the idyllic image of one man, one woman, two children and a dog. This is the ideal that has been constitutionalised in many societies. The question is whether the law should protect other forms of sexual orientation apart from heterosexuality. The debate on sexual orientation is critical in Africa. In recent times the issue has preoccupied news and discussion in countries such as Nigeria, Senegal, Malawi, Kenya and Uganda, where the highly controversial Anti-Homosexuality Bill has been under consideration.[1] This unique bill, also known as the Bahati Bill, after David Bahati, the Member of Parliament for Ndorwa West who presented it in October 2009, has caused an international firestorm (Tamale 2009). The bill provided for the death penalty against gays.[2] The US President Barack Obama, among others, condemned the bill as 'odious' and called for its withdrawal (*New York Times* 2010a).

Although the reaction to the bill in Uganda has been mixed, its condemnation at the international level has been unmistakable. This is partly because international sensibilities are moving in the direction of more, not less, recognition of sexual orientation as a human right. International human rights bodies and treaties now tend to protect gay rights, and certainly prohibit discrimination based on sexual orientation. The United Nations Human Rights Committee, the treaty body that interprets the International Covenant on Civil and Political Rights, a premier human rights instrument, ruled against an anti-gay law in the Australian state of Tasmania, which criminalised homosexuality.[3] The European Court of Human Rights in several cases struck down Irish laws that criminalised homosexuality.[4] There is little doubt that international law is moving towards the recognition and protection of gay rights, even if some of the case law suggests that the basis for such recognition is privacy. It is fair to argue that the protection of other forms of sexual orientation besides heterosexuality, which enjoys protection by virtue of the sanctity of marriage and the traditional family, is an emerging international norm.

At the municipal level, states are increasingly moving to protect gay rights, with some extending the right of gay people to marry and found a family. South Africa has taken the lead here on the African continent. The 1996 post-apartheid South African constitution includes the right to privacy and the right to dignity. It explicitly states that 'the state may not unfairly discriminate directly or indirectly against anyone on one or more grounds, including ... sexual orientation.'[5] This equal protection clause is one of the first in the world to guarantee gay rights. The constitutional court of South Africa subsequently declared the common law offences of sodomy between males and similar statutory crimes to be in violation of the constitution.[6]

This enlightened approach by South Africa has not been replicated elsewhere in Africa although the gay rights movement is emerging on the continent against great odds. In May 2010, a court in Malawi convicted two gay men for 'unnatural acts and gross indecency' for holding an engagement ceremony (*New York Times* 2010b). They were sentenced to 14 years in prison. But the universal denunciation of Uganda's Anti-Homosexuality Bill and its rejection by a cabinet committee suggests that the most draconian anti-gay laws cannot expect smooth sailing in the future (*New York Times* 2010c).

The trend for the recognition of gay rights appears unstoppable. Even sections of the clergy in Africa support gay rights. In South Africa, progressive sections of the Anglican Church, of which Archbishop Tutu is the most prominent member, have come out strongly in favour of gay rights. Gay ministers and priests have been ordained in a number of countries around the world. Several states in the USA have either legalised gay marriage or permitted civil unions for same-sex couples. This is a trend that is likely to grow as more states acknowledge gay rights. It behoves other groups in society to protect gay people – even if we find homosexuality morally objectionable – because human rights are not about protecting only those people we like. It is, moreover, about safeguarding the rights of people who are socially or politically unpopular and shunned.

The story of Pastor Martin Niemoller, who supported Hitler and stood by as Nazis persecuted those who were unpopular and then was disillusioned when Hitler went after the church, should serve warning to the silent majority who fail to speak up against the persecution of gays and lesbians. That is why bills of rights exist in any constitution: to protect certain core rights from the herd and the mob mentality of majorities against minorities, or those who are unpopular. The core of the human rights project is not about buttressing prejudices, but creating a firewall so that power, wealth, superior numbers and state control do not entrench those prejudices.

Homophobia

Homophobia is best defined as a range of feelings and prejudices against homosexuality. These negative feelings can take the form of apathy, contempt, prejudice, irrational fear and aversion and can sometimes manifest themselves in discrimination, violence or even murderous rage. What are some of the reasons for homophobia, or the hatred of gays? The first and most enduring reason for the hatred of gays is based on religious interpretations of the Abrahamic faiths – Christianity, Islam and Judaism. There are dangers in arguing with holy texts, but the interpretation of religious doctrine has been used to advance bigotry and prejudice based on the description of same-sex relationships as sinful.

There are instances in history in which religion has been used as a basis for irrational hatred. The Dutch Reformed Church tried to justify apartheid by using the Bible to depict Ham as the forefather of blacks. The Old Testament, the Torah and the Qu'ran contain passages that advocate homophobia. The question is how to interpret these passages in view of history and how to separate religious doctrine from the cultures in which those doctrines are incubated. The other question is whether these texts should be interpreted literally in light of the current advances in human knowledge and science. Even if the texts are taken literally, should they be the basis for legislating against a significant minority? Why should secular states take their dictates from religious law?

At the same time, it is important to realise that there is no unanimity among religions about homosexuality. Not all religions believe that God hates gays or adopt the view that homosexuality is a sin. Some American First Nation traditions venerated homosexuality (Williams 1986; Roscoe 1998; Gilley 2006) and, in the United Kingdom, the Hindu council has taken the view that it does not condemn homosexuality.

Is it un-African to be gay?

The statement that it is un-African to be gay is said effortlessly by many an African. But empirical evidence suggests the exact opposite. This claim is not only historically false, it can be argued as un-African to claim such because gays have always been part of the social fabric (Tamale 2009). Evidence suggests that in pre-colonial Africa, the matter of sexual orientation was not generally contentious. In fact the hatred of gay people and homophobia that are exhibited today have virtually no basis in African culture. In Uganda, as in many other African states, homosexuality and related sexual practices were criminalised for the first time by the colonial state. There are few epithets in African languages for gays. Where such epithets exist, as in Kiswahili, they are mostly likely derived from the Arabic. It seems that in pre-colonial, pre-Christian, pre-Islamic Africa something akin to a policy of 'don't ask don't tell' might have prevailed. This author remembers growing up in Kitui and wondering why two male neighbours who lived together did not have children. My mother told me that they 'have no kids because they have no kids'. Only later when I was grown up did I realize that was her way of telling me that the two men were gay (Mutua 2009a).

There is duplicity and inconsistency among homophobes in Africa (Gatiti 2009). They paradoxically attack homosexuality as alien and embrace Christianity as authentic. When President Robert Mugabe of Zimbabwe attacks gays as sinners, he does not say gays have sinned against the African God. He means that they have sinned against the Christian God, who was imposed on Africa as a part of the colonial project (Shropshire 1938). That particular God came to Africa to pave the way for colonialists and to pacify Africans for domination by European colonial powers. We have to wonder how consistent Mugabe is when he uses a foreign religion (Christianity) while speaking a foreign language (English) to claim that it is un-African to be gay.

Homophobes and the family

Homophobes attack homosexuality by claiming that it is a threat to the institution of the family (Mutua 2009b). There is neither empirical evidence nor sound reasoning for this hateful statement. Even so, homophobes have blamed everything from natural catastrophes to man-made disasters on homosexuality. The reality is that the institution of the family is imperilled not by gays, but by government policies and corrupt practices that fail to invest in education, job creation, public works and crime control (Khan 2009). Families are imperilled by the institution of patriarchy, or rule by men who are cruel and who routinely engage in domestic violence against their spouses and children. Poverty, not gay people, is a key problem for families. But scapegoating is easier than addressing deeply embedded social legacies and distortions that stand at the root of human powerlessness.

Homophobes seek to restrict marriage to that between a man and a woman. What they forget is that in many African societies, same-sex marriages took place in countries as diverse as Kenya, Tanzania, Nigeria and Sudan (Tamale 2009: 510). There is historical evidence to suggest that in Uganda, the site of one of the most intense anti-gay drives on the continent, some members of the Kabaka royalty, the rulers of Buganda, were gay. In any case, marriage is acknowledged in many forms – monogamous, polygynous, polyandrous and heterosexual – so there seems to be no justification for excluding homosexuals who wish to join together in a consensual relationship. Besides, what does a homophobe whose brother, sister, son, father, daughter, uncle or aunt is gay do? Does he shun them, and advocate that they should be discriminated against, or put to death, as the Ugandan bill provides? That is why those who advocate discrimination or punishment of gays need to think a little harder.

Gays/paedophilia/HIV/AIDS

There is no doubt that HIV/AIDS has taken a heavy toll on gays in the West, but in Africa the disease has primarily been among heterosexuals. Nor is there any scientific evidence that HIV/AIDS is a gay disease. What gays and heterosexuals need to do is to practice safe sex – or abstain – the two precautions that will cut down the spread of the virus. There is the benighted view that gays are paedophiles, a charge that has zero credibility. Paedophiles are sick people who prey on children and evidence suggests that most of them are heterosexuals. Who knows why so many Catholic priests have been paedophiles? There is no evidence that paedophile priests are gay.

Conclusions

There are several incontestable truths. Being gay is not a choice – it is, like other identities, a human condition or a state of being. Most gay people are born gay. Sexuality is nuanced – most people are neither wholly gay, nor wholly straight because sexuality is on a pendulum, a sliding scale. Most homophobes are afraid of their own sexuality and are more afraid to think about what it would be like to be gay. Homophobia is a subset of the system known as hetero-patriarchy, or rule by straight men. Homophobia is fear that the hetero-patriarchs will lose control and power over women and children. Tribalists, racists, sexists, homophobes, exploiters, misogynists and religious zealots and extremists of all kinds have one thing in common – they are hateful and live by controlling others.

Any successful fight and struggle against the powerlessness that victimises gays and other vulnerable groups must be carried out through the prism of three concepts – intersectionality, multidimensionality, and anti-subordination. Intersectionality means that discrimination is both vertical and horizontal and takes place at multiple levels among various identities. Thus racists are likely to be homophobes and sexists. Multidimensionality suggests that oppression takes place in multiple dimensions. We can be oppressed as women but also women who are lesbians.

Anti-subordination is the notion that it is futile and hypocritical to fight one form of oppression or discrimination while supporting another form of oppression. Thus, it is hypocritical to fight sexism if we support homophobia. Genuine liberation requires that all oppressions be fought on all fronts at the same time. This is the normative obligation of those who believe in human rights and human dignity. Finally, societies are judged by how they treat their most vulnerable populations and their minorities, not how they treat the strong, the wealthy and the powerful. That is why it is odious to exclude gay people from legal protection, or to propose the barbaric idea of putting them to death on the basis of their sexual preference or otherwise. The death penalty has no place in any civilised society.

Notes

1. The Anti-Homosexuality Bill was presented in the Ugandan parliament in 2009.
2. Section 3.2 of the Anti-Homosexuality Bill provides for the offence of 'aggravated

homosexuality'. Following the tabling of this bill, in October 2010, a local tabloid, *The Rolling Stone,* published an article outing alleged gays and lesbians with a caption that read 'Hang them' and promising to out more in future publications. One of the people whose photograph appeared on the cover page was gay activist David Kato. Together with two others, Kato successfully petitioned the Uganda high court to have the newspaper stop publishing these photographs. After the 3 January 2011 judgment, Kato started receiving death threats and three weeks later, on 26 January, he was brutally murdered.

3. *Toonen v. Australia,* Communication No. 488/1992, Views adopted 31 March 1994, UN Doc. CCPR/C/50/D/488/1992.
4. *Norris v. Ireland,* European Court of Human Rights, 1989 (Ser. A, No. 142).
5. South African Constitution (1996), Section 9(3).
6. *National Coalition for Gay and Lesbian Equality v. Minister of Justice,* CCT 11/98, 1999(1) SA6 (CC), 1998 (1) BCLR 1517 (CC).

References

Alston, Philip (1988) 'Making space for new human rights: the case of the right to development', *Harvard Human Rights Yearbook* 1: 3–40

Cover, Robert M. (1987) 'Obligation: a Jewish jurisprudence of the social order', *Journal of Law and Religion* 65(5): 65–74

Gatiti, Reverand Father James (2009) 'I differ with Don on gay rights', *Sunday Nation,* 31 October

Gilley, Brian Joseph (2006) *Becoming Two-Spirit: Gay Identity and Social Acceptance in Indian Country,* Omaha, University of Nebraska Press

Khan, Irene (2009) *The Unheard Truth: Poverty And Human Rights,* New York, London, W.W. Norton

Klare, Karl E. (1991) 'Legal theory and democratic reconstruction: reflections of 1989', *University of British Columbia Law Review* 69: 69–103

Mutua, Makau (2002) *Human Rights: A Political and Cultural Critique,* Philadelphia, University of Pennsylvania Press

—— (2009a) 'It is nonsense to assert that being gay is unAfrican', *Sunday Nation,* 31 October

—— (2009b) 'Why homosexuality is not a threat to the family', *Sunday Nation,* 6 November

New York Times (2010a) 'Obama calls for "civility" at prayer breakfast', 4 February

—— (2010b) 'Gay couple, arrested after engagement ceremony, are convicted of indecency in Malawi', 19 May

—— (2010c) 'Uganda panel gives setback to antigay bill', 8 May

Panikar, Raimundo (1982) 'Is the notion of human rights a Western concept?', *Diogenes* 120: 75

Reeves, Anthony R. (2009) 'Sexual identity as a fundamental human right', *Buffalo Human Rights Law Review* 215: 15

Roscoe, W. (1998) *Changing Ones: Third and Fourth Genders in Native North America,* New York, St Martin's Press

Shropshire, Denys W.T. (1938) *The Church and the Primitive Peoples,* London, SPCK

Steiner, Henry J. (1988) 'Political participation as a human right', *Harvard Human Rights Yearbook* 1: 109

Steiner, Henry J., Alston, Philip and Goodman, Ryan (1996 [2008]) *International Human Rights in Context: Law, Politics, Morals,* Oxford, Oxford University Press

Tamale, Sylvia (2009) 'A human rights impact assessment of the anti-homosexuality bill', *East African Journal of Peace and Human Rights* 15(2): 509–19

Terry, Jennifer (1999) *An American Obsession: Science, Medicine, and Homosexuality in Modern Society,* Chicago, University of Chicago Press

United Nations (1945) United Nations Charter, Article 55(c)

United Nations (1948) Universal Declaration of Human Rights, 10 December, http://www.un.org/en/documents/udhr, accessed 13 November 2010

Williams, W. (1986) *The Spirit and the Flesh: Sexual Diversity in American Indian Cultures,* Boston, Beacon Press

48

'I am not *tassa*, he is not a man like other men':[1] feminising infertility and masculinising fertility in South Nyanza, 1945–1960

Agnes Odinga

Introduction

Reproduction is an aspect of human function through which various forms of power and identity have been constructed. As a gendered practice, the Luo of South Nyanza province in Kenya constructed masculinity, manhood and fertility through the ability of the man to have children. Because the Luo historically perceived the male as inherently fertile, infertility and childlessness were considered feminine. Therefore, women who were unable to help men achieve their manhood were ascribed an identity of *tassa*.[2]

Being *tassa* relegated women in childless marriages to the periphery of the society. As *tassa*, they had no status or voice and were beaten by their husbands. However, in this chapter, records from Rongo tribunal court reveal that women struggled against the Luo construction of fertility as male. Using evidence such as citing their husbands' previous marriages where they had failed to have children, these defiant women were able to demonstrate that they themselves were not *tassa*. And while they were expected to keep quiet about male infertility, they publicly spoke about male impotence in court and in some instances became pregnant with other men and publicly spoke about their secret lovers. There were childless women who chose to remain in their marriages but wanted to be treated fairly and have access to property, identity and status. Similarly, these women used the court to demand wealth and respect.

Courts have normally been viewed as instruments of patriarchy to serve the interests of men, chiefs and the state hegemony. Although this might have been the case in the 1920s in other parts of Africa, evidence from South Nyanza shows that childless women used the courts to voice their interests and to construct an identity that was far from what the Luo society had ascribed to them. Indeed, in the cases cited herein, fathers testified on behalf of their daughters and were willing to reimburse the bridewealth in order to free their daughters from abusive marriages. In that sense the father-state-chiefs collaboration paradigm that sought to control women and young men's sexuality did not hold true for South Nyanza in the 1950s fertility cases examined in this chapter.

Although the reasons for this difference in activity might be more complicated than explained in this paper, it is a subject that merits exploration for other parts of Africa. Fertility might have been a much more sensitive issue than others in which fathers and the state collaborated. The fact that some women were granted divorce clearly illustrates the extent to which they were able to influence judges to rethink the masculinisation of fertility and the feminisation of childlessness and infertility.

Marriage, childlessness and the social construction of manhood and masculinity, 1950-1960[3]

The Luo word for an infertile woman is *lur* (literally, barren woman)[4] and a woman whose children constantly died was referred as *jakisoni*. Though the word *lur* refers to an infertile woman, there is no equivalent word for an infertile man in the Luo language. What is often confused with being an equivalent is the word *buoch*, which many of my oral informants explained to mean a man with erectile dysfunction. These men could not perform sexually and the Luo often believed that this was due to infertility and sometimes witchcraft. While there was an awareness of the phenomenon of male erectile dysfunction, or *buoch* and infertility, it was a woman's responsibility to ensure that her household had children. No one was allowed to discuss male infertility. This was a guarded secret and women were required to help guard it and were forced by the social conventions to prove fertility.

The inability to have children for whatever reason brought a great deal of attention to a woman and her husband. Not only because of her inability to participate in the social reproduction of the family, but also because of the symbolic, material and spiritual meaning the Luo attached to childlessness.[5] A woman without children had no voice or social status and could not participate in communal events. She was nobody and was perceived as a liability. A household without children was considered incomplete and, invariably, the woman was considered the guilty party. Writing about the attitude of the Luo towards children in the 1970s, Simeon Ominde noted:

> The idea of the perpetuation of their kind is so deeply rooted in the minds of the Luo people that a childless marriage generally culminates in the breaking up of the home concerned, the husband usually being advised by his relatives to marry a second wife. Although results may prove that it is the husband who is defective, priority is always given to men to prove their fecundity. If through the second marriage the husband is proved to be sterile, he may wish to carry on his name through the secret office of the woman's brothers-in-law. (Ominde 1987: 65)

It is against this background that women went to court.

In 1958, Peresia Kisibwa refused to be called *tassa*.[6] She appeared in the Rongo court seeking divorce from her husband, Ezekiel Kisibwa. In her testimony she said:

> My husband Ezekiel Kisibwa calls me *Tassa* but he can't have sexual inter-course. He beats me and has asked me to leave his home since I'm a liability wasting food for nothing. He has threatened to kill me if I continue living with him. When I could no longer bear his cruelty I decided to return to my home. He followed me, called an elders meeting (*jodong gweng*) and demanded his bridewealth. But my father declined to give him his wealth because he pre-ferred to do so before this court. My bridewealth was seven cows and three hundred shillings. We have lived together for five years.[7]

Ezekiel Kisibwa was present in court and in response denied Peresia's claims:

> I refuse to divorce my wife because I love her very much. I don't beat her. I've never called her *Tassa* and neither have I chased her from my home. Her testimony is a fabricated lie. I agree I paid seven cows and three hundred shil-lings as bridewealth, a bull, three calves, and three female cows. I don't want to divorce my wife on baseless grounds.[8]

Peresia not only refutes being called *tassa* but violates the conventions of the time which required Luo women to keep quiet about male infertility and erectile dys-function. By speaking publicly about the unspeakable, she challenged traditional authority, which institutionalised the constructions of female identity based on their reproductive function and sexuality, especially a woman's ability to procreate. Though in the past Peresia's father might not have supported his daughter's claims, he supported her desire for divorce. In his testimony before the court he noted:

> I am the father of the Peresia Kisibwa, the Plaintiff. I received seven cows and three hundred shillings from the Ezekiel Kisibwa, the defendant. But as a father I cannot continue to watch the defendant beat my daughter. On one occasion he beat and chased her demanding his bridewealth back because of her inability to have children. It has been difficult for my daughter and I want to bring closure to her misery. For the past five years Ezekiel has mistreated her. I agree to pay back his wealth.[9]

Peresia's brother was also present in court and agreed to return Ezekiel's bridewealth.

> I'm Peresia's brother. I know Ezekiel Kisibwa, the defendant. His bridewealth for my sister was seven cows and three hundred shillings. He beat my sis-ter, called her *Tassa* and chased her from his village and demanded back his wealth. Without a doubt I'm ready to return his wealth.[10]

Although control and subordination of women might have occurred in many parts of Africa in the 1920s, the court records and testimony of the case of Peresia Kisibwa suggest that by the 1950s fathers did not collaborate with the state and other men to control women's reproduction and sexuality. Peresia's father was present as a witness and agreed to return the bridewealth received from his son-in-law, Ezekiel Kisibwa. The court tribunal's decision to grant Peresia her divorce was based on the testimonies of her father and brother and particularly their willingness to return the bridewealth.

> We listened to the testimony of the Plaintiff, her father, brother, her husband and her brother-in-law Josheck Endemba. The Plaintiff and her witnesses testified that Mr. Ezekiel Kisibwa beat, chased and called her *Tassa*. Mr. Ezekiel Kisibwa, the defendant has denied all the charges against him and has declined to divorce his wife. However, since the Plaintiff's father and brother agree with divorce and are willing to return Mr. Kisibwa's wealth, the court has no objection but to grant Peresia divorce. The court orders the defendant to pay forty two shillings for expenses the Plaintiff incurred filing this case and proceedings.[11]

Four months after the Rongo court granted Perisia Kisibwa her wish, Olum Asiyo, the daughter of Odongo, filed a petition to divorce her husband, Gudu Asiyo. This was a case in which the plaintiff used Gudu Asiyo's previous marriages as evidence to make her case about Asiyo's inability to perform sexual intercourse and his infertility. It reveals the extent to which the Luo silenced women about discussing male infertility. Olum was a replacement bride when her older sister, previously married to Gudu Asiyo, could not give birth. While her sister and two other women deserted Gudu Asiyo, Olum stayed and endured the agonies of childlessness, but when she could no longer tolerate it, she broke her silence in court:

> I am petitioning to divorce my husband Gudu Asiyo. His bridewealth was four cows. We've lived together as husband and wife for seven years but have no child. I am asking for divorce because Gudu Asiyo cannot impregnate a woman. I had sexual intercourse with someone other than Gudu on the first day of my marriage. Gudu did not consummate our marriage and for the last seven years we have not had sexual intercourse. Gudu was previously married to three other women. One of these women was my sister for whom I was a replacement bride because she couldn't give birth. All his women were unable to conceive. They left him and now they all have children. I am not *Tassa*; Gudu Asiyo is not a man like other men.[12]

Scholars have recently begun writing about the social construction of masculinity in African societies (White 1990; Shear 1996; Mutongi 2007). Fundamental to the court testimony was the meaning and the essence of being a man. What did it mean to be a man among the Luo? Scholarly research on the subject among the Luo is very minimal but there is a corpus of scholarship on other societies in Africa. Among the Kikuyu of Central Kenya, for example, masculinity was constructed through the act of circumcision (White 1990). A man who was not circumcised was considered a boy and was treated as such.

It is clear from Olum's testimony that the Luo conceived of manhood and the masculine through male sexuality and fertility. A man unable to have children remained a boy. By testifying that her husband was not a man like other men, Olum was denouncing and raising questions about the feminisation of childlessness as well as the social construction of manhood and masculinity based on a man's ability to perform sexual intercourse and impregnate a woman.

Gudu Asiyo did not appear before the court to answer the witchcraft, infertility and childlessness charges against him. But Gideon Majiwa, his nephew, who represented him in court, had the following to say:

> My uncle, Gudu Asiyo, sent me to answer divorce charges against him. He is very ill and therefore unable to appear before the court. We agree with the plaintiff's desire to divorce. The plaintiff and my uncle had a very difficult marriage for so many years. The plaintiff's bridewealth was six cows. She was a replacement bride on her sister's behalf. Her sister's bridewealth was thirty cows. However, when she deserted, my uncle wanted thirty cows back, which they were unable to produce and instead opted to replace her with sister Olum. We would like all our cows returned before this court.[13]

It is possible that Gudu Asiyo was impotent and infertile. He accepted Olum's request and demanded his bridewealth back. Although Olum's father was not in court, her brother, who testified on behalf of her family, noted, 'This marriage can't work. Gudu paid four cows as bridewealth for the Plaintiff and thirteen cows for my sister who deserted him. In total they are seventeen cows and I agree to pay back his wealth.'[14] Olum's brother was far from being a collaborator with other men to oppress his sister. On his family's behalf, he agreed to return Gudu Asiyo's wealth in order to allow his sister to leave her husband. The court ordered Gudu Asiyo to pay 40 Kenya shillings and Olum was granted permission to leave.

More insight about the complexity of issues of identity, motherhood, constructions of manhood and masculinity is provided by the cases of pregnant *tassas*. Odero Odumbe, the daughter of Otung, asked the court to grant her divorce from Ayoo Odumbe because he constantly abused her and referred to her as *tassa*. In her testimony, she told the court that she lived with him for two years and he paid 15 cows for bridewealth. She explained that her husband had warned her that she would die 'if she did not wake up', a threat that she did not 'know how to interpret'.[15]

In his defence, Ayoo Odumbe told the court that this was the second time his wife had sued him for divorce and that her earlier claim for divorce before the same court was dismissed. He asked the court to deny her request because she was six months pregnant and that he would not like his wife to go away with their unborn child.[16] Otung, the father of Odero Odumbe, testified that a previous claim for divorce by his daughter was denied. He added that after the rejection of that claim his daughter, the plaintiff, only stayed with her husband for five days and fled. He told the court that he did not see a future for the marriage.[17]

In its ruling the court found that there was an acrimonious relationship between husband and wife and that they had been living separately for a long time, because the plaintiff ran away only five days after a previous claim for divorce had been denied. They also considered the fact that the matter had come before the village elders and no solution had been found. Because the parents of the woman had agreed to return all the animals given as bridewealth, the court granted the divorce and asked the defendant to pay 42 shillings.

Another pregnant *tassa* was Nyadie, the daughter of Ocharo. She also used the court to challenge the masculinisation of fertility. Nyadie 's reasons for filing for divorce were:

> I do not like his habits. Wagome forced me to lie down upon which he shaved all the hair on my body and took away my clothes and inner-wear. I know he wants to bewitch me. I don't want him anymore. Moreover he called me *tassa* but now I am pregnant. My father has agreed to return his bridewealth of fourteen cows and eight goats. We have had this case before our parents and Wagome had nothing to say.[18]

Wagome acknowledged that he shaved his wife's body but denied calling her *tassa*. He pleaded with the court to decline her divorce request because she was pregnant. He admitted that, though she was pregnant, the child was not his because Nyadie deserted him and lived with her parents for more than six months. However, since he had paid fourteen cows and eight goats and still loved Nyadie, he didn't want her to divorce him. Nyadie's father agreed to return Wagome's wealth because 'Wagome chased my daughter Nyadie for being *tassa* and now that Nyadie is pregnant I don't see why he should want her. Wagome and his people also took my daughter's body away. His wealth was fourteen cows and I agree to return them when Nyadie gets married.'[19]

Clearly, this was a case in which the man admitted he did not impregnate his wife but was willing to take her back with someone else's child. Nyadie was granted a divorce on the grounds that Wagome admitted practising witchcraft on her and the fact that her father was willing to return the bridewealth. Although the case raises issues of paternity and fatherhood in South Nyanza,[20] it illustrates the cultural biases that were inherent in the way Luo conceived fertility, fatherhood and masculinity. Far more important in a man's life were children, because his image and status within the Luo society was dependent on that, and many men were willing to keep quiet about their wives' extramarital relationships so long as they became fathers. Fatherhood, sexuality and masculinity were central to a man's identity, role and place among the Luos in the 1940s–1960s.

Notes

1. *Olum d/o Odongo vs. Gudu Asiyo, Bura Rongo*, Case No: 170/58, KNA: AKF/2/201.
2. *Tassa* is a Swahili word for an infertile chicken. The Luo word for an infertile woman is *lur*. But the Luo adopted the word *tassa* and used it frequently to refer to childless women.
3. In this section I analyse court cases I found at the Kisumu National Archives. During the periods 1995, 2002, 2006 and 2007, I collected 100 court cases. Although not properly catalogued, there is an extensive collection of divorce, land cases and paternity suits deposited at this archive. I deliberately chose to focus on divorces filed by women between 1950 and 1960. At the centre of the court battles was female infertility, a

contentious issue that tore families apart and set men against women in protracted legal fights through brief and sometimes extremely elaborate deliberations involving presentation of arguments, strategies and counter-strategies in English, customary and traditional laws. As a result, norms, customs and traditional institutions were re-assessed, reworked, negotiated and reconfigured. Most important, these cases reveal how gender, patriarchy and cultural perception of reproduction shaped the identity and the lives of childless Luo women and the ways in which they circumvented these obstacles.

4. However, the use of the word *tassa* to refer to a barren woman was very widespread among the Luo.
5. A barren woman was described as dry bones, an empty river, poor and sad. Wealth was measured by the number of cattle and children. As such, a barren or childless woman was considered a failure.
6. Court proceedings provide limited information about the identity of Perisia Kisibwa. Most cases are sketches, but provide valuable information and insight into gender struggles, the social construction of maleness and the basis of motherhood.
7. Peresia Kisibwa, in *Peresia Kisibwa vs Ezekiel Kisibwa*, Case No: 46/58, KNA: AKF/2/80.
8. Ezekiel Kisibwa, in *Peresia Kisibwa vs Ezekiel Kisibwa*, Case No: 46/58, KNA: AKF/2/80.
9. Angogo s/o Kiduyo, in *Peresia Kisibwa vs Ezekiel Kisibwa*, Case No: 46/58, KNA: AKF/2/80.
10. Thomas Kiduyo, in *Peresia Kisibwa vs Ezekiel Kisibwa*, Case No: 46/58, KNA: AKF/2/80.
11. *Peresia Kisibwa vs Ezekiel Kisibwa*, Case No: 46/58, KNA: AKF/2/80.
12. *Olum d/o Odongo vs. Gudu Asiyo, Bura Rongo*, Case No: 170/58, KNA: AKF/2/201.
13. Gideon Majiwa, in *Olum d/o Odongo vs. Gudu Asiyo, Bura Rongo*, Case No: 170/58, KNA: AKF/2/201.
14. Olum's brother, in *Olum d/o Odongo vs. Gudu Asiyo, Bura Rongo*, Case No: 170/58, KNA: AKF/2/201.
15. *Odero d/o Otung vs Ayoo Odumbe*, Case No: 161/58, KNA: AKF/2/200.
16. Ayoo Odumbe, in *Odero d/o Otung vs Ayoo Odumbe*, Case No: 161/58, KNA: AKF/2/200.
17. Otung, father of Odero Odumbe, in *Odero d/o Otung vs Ayoo Odumbe*, Case No: 161/58, KNA: AKF/2/200.
18. *Nyadie d/o Ocharo vs Wagome Guya*, Bura Rongo, Case No: 236/54, KNA: AKF/2/61.
19. Ocharo, father of Nyadie, in *Nyadie d/o Ocharo vs Wagome Guya*, Bura Rongo, Case No: 236/54, KNA: AKF/2/61.
20. Fatherhood as a social construct is a subject beyond the scope of this paper but would be insightful to explore using the court cases discussed in this chapter.

References

Mutongi, Kenda (2007) *Worries of the Heart: Widows, Family and Community in Kenya*, Chicago, University of Chigaco Press

Ominde, S.H. (1987) *The Luo Girl: from Infancy to Marriage*, Nairobi, Literature Bureau

Shear, Keith (1996) '"Not welfare or uplift work": white women, policing and masculinity and policing in South Africa', *Gender and History* 8: 393–415

White, Luise (1990) 'Separating the men from the boys: construction of gender, sexuality, and terrorism in Central Kenya, 1939–1959', *International Journal of African Historical Studies* 23: 1–25

49

The phantoms of my opera

Lombe Mwambwa

One demands I keep the first seat in my life empty always
    Yet he does and can not sit in it
One shows me only the best part of his face
    He keeps the dark side hidden
One sneaked into my life slowly but boldly
    He is like a room of mirrors, all sorts of images
One always watches me
    His shadow is what I see only
One has claimed me as his forever, without my consent
    He believes he loves me
One seized me by the hand and dragged me through the lake of deceit
    It was the only reality I knew
One holds me captive in the dark
    It's a maze of empty passion
One has not come to my opera yet, he is my true love, he will rescue me
    … If he comes

50

The kiss[1]

Frank M. Chipasula

This marble kiss will never erode, never fade,
From the stone lips sealed with sweetness.
The rock's fine fingers are wings on her marble skin;
The birds of his palms are flying over her,
Softly sifting love onto her bared thigh.
His body, kissing hers, suddenly surges awake:
Music burns through his veins, every cell sings.
In his arms flow a million gallons of blood
That flowed through the arms of generations.

Her lips, having carefully read his body,
Rest on his own, read the Braille of his lips,
Her palm fronds fan the fire.
As they dance up the ancient fig tree,
His fingers fanning the flame he kindled in her loins,
Oils welling from her secret river anoint him,
Coating him as he stirs her soul in the flesh bowl
Where their lives blend and thicken forever—

At both ends where they are neatly joined
He is pouring his turbulent life into her—
Their tongues stirring storms in their mouths.

As she laves him with her own,
His needle dances in the grooves of her song,
Their tongues licking songs inside their mouths:
The double kiss doubles their joy.

Note

1. Reproduced with permission from F.M. Chipasula (ed) (2009) *Bending the Bow: An Anthology of African Love Poetry*, Carbondale, IL, Southern Illinois University Press.

51

The diamond in the G... – life story[1]

Kipkemboi [jeffrey moses]

It must surprise many people, who know me and who don't, that I chose to create a blog that touches on such a controversial issue, and reveal my true identity. What a great risk I took! 'How foolish a risk', you must be thinking.

Let me clarify here and now, that I am not ashamed of who I am. All my life I have carried the burden of shame and self-disrespect. I have hidden behind walls of fear. I was always afraid what my family and friends would think of me. Just their mere perception and opinion of me mattered more to me than my very being.

I have spent many long days and sleepless nights praying that I would be healed from that horrible disease that I had. As society condemned homosexuality, I condemned myself ten times more. I carried the shame of the world on my bare back, I was extremely disappointed in myself for thinking, acting and being a homosexual. I became utterly furious with myself. I planted a seed of self-hate, deep in my heart. The constant judgement, condemnation and shame from around me nurtured this seed.

Eventually I tried to become someone I was not. My life became a script that I had to memorise and act out the moment I stepped into the public eye. My audience was my family, friends and society at large. What they didn't like I struggled to change, when I couldn't I punished myself with more self-loathing. I knew I deserved nothing, I was, after all, unable to heal from homosexuality. How could I expect anything good? I was happy to be reprimanded, I looked forward to my fair share of suffering, I begged to be validated, I needed desperately to be accepted. I lost all sense of self.

Subsequently, I could not find a reason why I was here, on earth. What was my niche? I defined myself through the eyes of society. Inside I was an empty, worn out tool. So why live? What was the point? I could find none, I was utterly useless. I had done my part, I had acted my role and finally I was so exhausted. I lost all sense of responsibility, I became unfeeling and detached. I did not give a damn whatsoever, whatever happened, happened. I wandered the earth aimlessly, expecting the worst, anticipating disaster and misunderstanding any goodwill extended to me. Until the day a part of me died and a new one was born.

I was ostracised and shunned. I became the ridicule of many, the example by which children would be taught. I was the biggest sinner, everybody was relieved for their miniature, trivial, understandable sins. They did not need me anymore, they had run out of 'popcorn for the show', channels were swiftly flipped. They had been the water that my tree of hate needed to keep growing. The stream dried up and eventually that tree died. But those soils remained fertile.

I love myself no matter how much the world hates me. This is me and there will be no other. If I have to be imprisoned for being open, honest and truthful then I shall serve my time. I will die if I must, I shall peacefully face the gallows.

I will not change the identity of this blog. For all those reading, incensed and planning an attack, my gates lay[sic] wide open.

To those members of my family and friends who are ashamed of me and want to break away, good riddance. I am convicted to say that my clear conscience will illuminate the path that lies ahead of me. I refuse to play the chameleon when really I was meant to be the prince of my own destiny.

To the haters, please hate on. I will not be intimidated. I am stronger than you think. I am in my element in the midst of the storm. In the very centre of the furious flames I derive my comfort. I can be changed by what happens to me, I refuse to be broken by it. And why? Because I am a diamond and nothing can break me. Every other fire refines me, every other sharp cut adds to my glisten and worth. I have been through the seven fires, I can certainly survive seven more.

Note

1. Reproduced with permission from Kipkemboi's blog (2008), 6 August, http://rainbowapples.wordpress.com/, accessed 24 December 2010.

Questions for reflection

1.

How are masculinities constructed in African cultures?
Is there a perceived hierarchy among these masculinities?
What role do such hierarchies serve?

2.

What is the link between heterosexuality and
masculinity in Africa? Did black Africans practise
homosexuality before Arabs and Europeans arrived in
their lands? How do African states maintain a culture
of 'heteronormativity'and 'heterosexism'?

3.

What 'foreign' influences have coloured the constructions
of masculinities, and what are the consequences?

4.

How have subordinate masculinities organised to assert
their rights and empower themselves? What strategies have
they adopted and what challenges do they face?

5.

Does Africa need to transform its ideology of masculinity?
How would changing the ways that communities in Africa
think about being a 'man' (and a 'woman') move the
continent closer to gender equity and inclusiveness?

Part 7
Who's having sex and who's not?

52

Unpacking the [govern]mentality of African sexualities[1]

Stella Nyanzi

> The myth of black sexuality was simply a myth of excessive sexuality: it held
> that 'with the Negro, everything takes place at the genital level'.
>
> *Franz Fanon (quoted in Vaughan 1991: 131)*

Introduction

Although sexuality is largely a private and personal affair, the sexual terrain is also
very political. Part 2 of this volume explored sexual politics and power in Africa,
including issues of contestation and activism when individuals and communities
are discontented with how their sexualities are restricted through laws, social controls and prohibitive prescriptive norms. This chapter focuses on unpacking the
governance layers of sexualities in Africa. Acknowledging that the sexual domain is
vested with power and powerlessness – hence the political – and that the subversive
or alternative forms of sexuality often yield resistance through activist initiatives,
the chapter explores the notion of controlling in order to govern the sexual lives of
Africans.

Central to the historical, social and political interactions of Africans with people
from other continents, the 'otherness' of African peoples was important to establish and accentuate to justify ethnocentric superiority – be it in the form of slavery,
colonialism or neo-imperialisms. As various essays in this volume have argued, the
subjugation and dominance of diverse African peoples was justified on the grounds
that their barbaric, savage, primitive, backward, uncultured, uncouth and uncivilised character needed taming, improving, civilising, modernising and rescuing.
Among the principal excesses of the homogenised African that needed taming was
a highly promiscuous, irresponsible, contagious and libidinous sexuality. In order
to curb such excesses, it was important to curtail, hem in, regulate and intervene
in this minutely conceptualised African sexuality. Attaining control and dominion
over African sexuality thus symbolised total subordination of the continent. Hence
the cliché, 'control African genitals and you control Africa'.

From this perspective, it is evident that assumptions were made about who was
having sex and who was not; or indeed more precisely – who was having 'good,

civilised', that is normative, normal, moderate and acceptable sex, and who was having bad, backward, dangerous, disastrous, wild, excessive, subversive and high-risk sex. Assumptions were made about sex that was good and what sex was bad. The bad sex was deemed as needing control, regulation and sometimes even negation through castration or sterilisation so as not to reproduce more of the danger.

Notions of good sex and bad sex continue in society today. In addition to legal instruments and social policies that outlaw certain sexual practices, sexual identities, sexual behaviours and sexual orientations, these subtle notions of good sex and bad sex police how we allow ourselves and others to have meaningful sexual encounters. Preconceived notions of good sex and bad sex determine our acceptance of who, what, when, where, why and how others and ourselves can experience sexualities in forms we deem acceptable. The meanings we bring to and take from diverse sexualities inform the standards with which we judge good sex versus bad sex. They also impact on how we interpret the sexualities of other individuals and groups of people who are different or similar to ourselves. They colour even the most basic indices we use to label some acts as sex or not sex, and some people as sexual or not sexual beings.

Several questions lie at the heart of this essay: who is having sex? And who isn't? Who do we think is having sex? And who do we think isn't? Who can have sex? And who can't? Who should have sex? And who shouldn't? Who must have sex? And who must not? And what is sex, anyway? And what is not sex? And who cares what the answers to these questions are?

The discussion examines academic and lay bodies of knowledge about the regulation and control of sexualities in Africa. It starts by contextualising the issue, using a set of exploratory questions about some common assumptions that abound about certain sexual cultures. The next section outlines five theoretical approaches to understanding how sexual bodies and cultures are governed, controlled and regulated: 1) governmentality, 2) sexual and reproductive health, 3) the charmed circle, 4) sexual stereotypes and 5) sexual citizenship and rights. Thereafter, we provide a brief historical description of the governance of sexualities in colonial Africa. Then a range of systemic, institutionalised and structural mechanisms through which sexualities in Africa are governed are presented. This is followed by an in-depth exploration of the construction of the sexualities of the elderly and children, who offer a case study of social groups whose sexualities are often stereotyped.

Here, we mainly focus on areas of overlap and disjuncture between the underlying assumptions made by outsiders who regulate these groups, versus the reported realities of the individuals and groups within these circles. The discussion problematises whether or not the governance of sexualities is in order. Beyond the question about whether or not outsiders can successfully regulate the sexual lives of others, this section helps readers to consider the appropriateness of protecting some social groups from being sexual.

Exploration of common sexual cultures

There is an abundance of scholarship, popular culture and information that homogenises sexualities in Africa. The Caldwellian hypothesis of a distinct African sexuality is a case in point. However, contemporary scholars have variously critiqued this body of knowledge and exposed its numerous inherent fallacies. In addition to being essentialist – that is, falsely concluding that because one is African one therefore has a specific innate African sexuality – this body of knowledge denies the rich diversities inherent among the different African peoples. It also negates the variations, transformations and dynamic flux over time and space in how Africans appreciate and enact their sexualities. Just as there is not one fixed way of being African, so, for Africans, there are multiple ways of being sexual. Even one individual African undergoes changes in how they conceive, construct and enact sexuality over time, space and with different sexual partners.

Thus, understanding African sexual culture is a delicately complex, multilayered and dynamic enterprise. Regulating or indeed governing African sexualities is an even more fragile venture that unconditionally requires deep insider understanding of the finer workings of each unique sexual culture. Failure to comprehend local meanings, nuances and enactments of local sexualities results in irrelevant, inappropriate, meaningless and time-wasting interventions that are bound to be oppressive to the target communities or individuals. Failure to examine the inherent diversities yields foolhardy generalisations that are an injustice to the rich terrain of sexuality that is always vibrant in specific African settings.

Consider the assumptions you have about each of the following case studies. Grey-haired, wrinkled, toothless and bent over with age – do senior citizens have sexual needs? Do the elderly have sexual desires? Does anyone find them sexually attractive? Do they consider themselves sexually appealing? Do the elderly have sex? Is the aged body still a sexual body?

What about paraplegics, amputees, adult polio survivors, the lame, maimed and anyone representing the range of physical disabilities, including blindness and deafness, among others? Do they have sexual rights? Do they perceive of themselves as erotic, sensual beings? Should they be granted sexual citizenship similar to able-bodied people? Does one qualify as a sexual pervert for sexually desiring a severely physically challenged individual, such as an adult with Downs Syndrome or epilepsy? Does an adolescent who suffered cerebral palsy in childhood have legitimate sexual desires? Do the physically challenged have sexual needs?

There is also the issue of the sexuality of people with mental illnesses, ranging from social stress to diverse forms of psychosis. Should the sexual lives of mentally ill people be regulated or allowed free expression? Does this also equate to the treatment of mentally retarded adults, such as a 21-year-old man with a physically mature body but a mental ability fixed at two years, when he suffered cerebral malaria? What about the 'village madwoman' – shoddily dressed in heaps of rags – who talks seeming nonsense to herself, and roams about on end to no particular destination? Does she have sex? Can she ever have consensual sex? Or is sex only exploitative to her? Does she have sexual desires? Doesn't she have the ability to choose to be sexual? Can she be allowed a sexual life? Should she be allowed to be sexual? Or does sex with her always only equate to rape? Shouldn't she be protected against herself? Shouldn't society be protected against the sexuality of the insane? What if the subject were male – the 'village madman'? Is he always a rapist? Or is he always only raped? How do the rules, fears and opportunities shift when the focus is moved from the sexuality of a woman with mental illness to a man suffering from the same?

Are children sexual beings? Should they always be protected against being sexual and sexualised? Social protectionism of children, youths and minors against sexual activity highlights ethical, moral, legal, biological, psychological and social cultural concerns. However, who does the 'age of consent' maxim serve? Is it the child, the adults or society in general? Are age of consent observances and premarital sex prohibitions really about protecting children? Are they still relevant in today's society?

What about adults who cannot access regular sexual partners? For example, what issues does the sexuality of widows, widowers, divorcees, prisoners, first wives and outside wives in polygynous unions, 'small houses' women[2] and people in long-distance relationships uncover? What is known about how individuals in these social groups negotiate their sexuality? How do their lived experiences compare with stereotypes and assumptions about their sexuality?

What about rape and forceful sex? Is marital rape an antithesis in Africa? Are husbands always entitled to have sex with their wives regardless of anything else? Does having a sexual partnership mean having sex? Do married people have sex and if so, how often? Do they have sex with each other or with others outside the marriage? Do the people in a marital union have equal sexual rights? Should they? If two people are married, does it mean sex with each other is always acceptable? Or indeed is it possible for a husband to rape his wife? And anyway, is sexual intercourse a preserve for only 'the married', however one defines this?

What does sexual dysfunction mean to an individual's sexuality? Do impotent men and frigid women have sexual lives? Are post-menopausal women entitled to sex? Can circumcised women have pleasureable sex? Do they have sex? Does a vasectomy or testectomy negate sexuality? Does a man have a right to sexual fulfilment after surgical removal of his prostate gland?

There is also the conflicted matter of people living with HIV and AIDS. Do HIV-positive people have sexual rights? Can sex with an HIV-positive person ever be considered safe? Why should governments continue spending limited resources on the sexual and reproductive health of HIV-positive people? Should society blame HIV-positive people for bringing the virus onto themselves as a result of reckless sexual lifestyles? Does HIV kill libido? Are HIV-positive people entitled to a sexual life? Can they afford to have reproductive health rights? Is it not in the public health interest of society to negate the sexual entitlements of HIV-positive individuals, particularly considering the high possibilities of transmitting HIV, or indeed of reinfection? Should HIV-positive women be allowed to conceive and deliver babies who might also acquire vertically transmitted HIV? Should an HIV-positive couple be allowed to produce children, when there are possibilities that their lifespans could be cut short, resulting in their children being orphaned and adding more burden to the already limited social support services in sub-Saharan Africa?

Lastly, consider those outwardly attractive, seemingly have-it-all types of people. Often it is the voluptuous beautiful woman with perfect makeup, nice clothes, the flashy car, posh home in an upper-end neighbourhood who also happens to be unmarried. Sometimes it is the lithe-bodied, smooth gentleman with a prosperous business that yields a fat bank account and dual residencies. Are these people necessarily hot-bodied and promiscuous? When a woman makes it up the ranks, is she always only sleeping her way to the top? When a single woman owns her own residence, is it solely for purposes of importing an assortment of lovers? Are these stereotypes or facts based on reality?

Indeed, who is having sex? And who is not? The answers we immediately give to these questions reveal diverse levels of governmentality and how we relate to the notion of governmentality. The questions and answers generated are relevant to subsequent sections of the essay. It is important to reflect on the sexual cultural scenarios delineated above as we engage in the following discussion.

Theoretical approaches to governing sexualities

This section presents five theoretical frameworks that are instrumental to understanding the politics of sexualities, sexual labelling and sexual hierarchies, and important in unpacking and examining how individuals and societies consciously and unconsciously govern sexualities – their own and those of others.

Governmentality

Governmentality is a concept credited to Michel Foucault, the French philosopher. The concept is 'understood in the broad sense of technologies and procedures for directing human behaviour' (Rose et al 2009: 1). The meaning of governmentality is three-pronged:

1. The processes through which governments produce governable citizens, who respond accordingly to policies to create a happy society.

2. How citizens think about and respond through organised practices – for example, mentalities, rationalities and techniques – to the modes through which their conduct is governed.

3. The inter-relationship between these two levels of meaning.

Beyond hierarchical state politics of government control, governmentality also considers how conduct is governed through, for example, individual self-control, parental and family guidance for children, management of the household, the biopolitical control of populations and the relationship between *savoir* – knowledge, power and self-governance – and social control in disciplinary institutions such as the school, the hospital or the psychiatric institution (Foucault 1991; Lemke 2000). This concept facilitates the examination of governance within settings of de-centred power, such as liberal or neoliberal societies in which individuals in the free-market political economy self-govern from within, mainly using internalised knowledge. Our knowledge impacts on our power.

Although the concept of governmentality originates from the West, it is an important analytical tool for scholars of African sexualities because it facilitates the analysis of the locus and dynamics of power in sexual relationships and sexual cultures. Governmentality allows the examination of the interactions between external regulation and self-control of sexual conduct. Discussing the centrality of governmentality to Foucault's work, Thomas Lemke asserts:

> It plays a decisive role in his analytics of power in several regards: it offers a view on power beyond the perspective that centres either on consensus or on violence; it links technologies of the self with technologies of domination, the constitution of the subject to the formation of the state; finally, it helps to differentiate between power and dominion. (Lemke 2000: 3)

Explaining how individuals within cultural groups learn acceptable behaviour, socialisation relies on imparting normative behaviour to individuals who are usually new initiates to a particular social cultural context, so that they govern their own conduct as well as that of others. These individuals are expected to align their behaviour, attitudes and actions to socially accepted standards. The main aim of socialisation is similar to that of governmentality of the self, in other words, 'the shaping of citizens with a certain mode of self-reflection and certain civilised techniques of self-government' (Rose et al 2009: 20). Thus the relevance of governmentality in studying culture becomes imperative because 'culture in itself, then, could be analysed as a set of technologies for governing habits, morals and ethics – for governing subjects' (Rose et al 2009: 20).

Sexual and reproductive health

Based on justifications aimed at improving performance indicators for sexual and reproductive health, the sexual behaviour of most sub-Saharan Africans has been subjected to multiple and rigorous mechanisms of monitoring, control and forced compliance. Examples of these indicators include birth rate, death rate, fertility rate, maternal morbidity rate, maternal mortality rate, infant mortality rate, sexual debut, coital frequency, occurrence of premarital/extramarital sex, number of sexual partners, condom use ever, condom use in the last year, gravida, prima gravida (first pregnancy) between 15 and 19 years, presence of sexually transmitted infections, knowledge of modern contraceptives and prevalence of modern contraceptive use, among others.

Initially the focus of these biomedical interventions was mainly on population control through maternal and child health (MCH) programmes, safe motherhood initiatives and family planning models. However, the focus later moved to integrated approaches for reproductive health and more recently expanded to sexual and reproductive health and rights (see Part 5 for a detailed discussion). The driving principle of this effort is the underlying objective of improving sexual and reproductive health. The main public health mantra advocated is practising safe sex in order to prevent unwanted pregnancies and transmission of sexually transmitted infections, including HIV/AIDS.

This approach relies heavily on demography, epidemiology, public health and biomedicine to inform its interventions. Positivistic theories, large demographic surveys, randomised control trials and statistical analyses are important sources of evidence upon which policy and programmes are based. A major criticism of this approach is, however, that it is often about reproduction and disease. Rarely (if ever) is it about sexual pleasure, well-being or indeed about non-reproductive sexualities – unless the individuals concerned are unwell or have health complications (Dixon-Mueller 1993; Oomman 1998; Miller 2000). So, the focus on sexualities is too narrow to capture their inherent complexities and diversities (Nyanzi 2006). Attention is primarily on risk factors, disease, danger and death – all negative factors that necessitate interventions of rescue, deliverance, elimination and change.

In this paradigm, social groups are divided up and labelled in terms of high-risk or low-risk population groups based on their group sexual dynamics. So, commercial sex workers, men who have sex with men, truck drivers, fishermen and barmaids are labelled high-risk groups, while housewives, peasants and minors are labelled low-risk groups. Human sexuality is conceptualised as a problem to be curtailed, controlled, subdued and governed. Although sexuality is a private affair, the state intervenes using the instrument of the biomedical and public health specialist.

The charmed circle

The charmed circle is an analytical model situated within anthropologist and feminist scholar Gayle Rubin's concept of sexual hierarchy, which appears in her influential paper entitled 'Thinking sex: notes for a radical theory of the politics of sexuality' (Rubin 1984). Based on her analysis of modern Western societies, Rubin proposes a metaphorical tool of the erotic pyramid through which sex acts are appraised according to a hierarchical system of sexual value, with marital, reproductive heterosexuals at the top of the erotic pyramid, and unmarried monogamous heterosexuals in couples, and most other heterosexuals, clamouring below (Rubin 1984). Solitary sex floats ambiguously. The powerful 19th-century stigma about masturbation lingers in less potent, modified forms, such as the idea that masturbation is an inferior substitute for partnered encounters.

The notion of an erotic pyramid presupposes that society undertakes a process of mapping to identify and then categorise all available sex practices within the diverse sexual cultures. Thereafter these sex practices are plotted in ascending order of merit from the least to the best. Position on the pyramid is accorded value judgement relative to other sexual practices, and thereby either rewarded with social approval or else denigrated as vice. The erotic pyramid is a useful model that scholars of African sexualities can adapt to their research about the values that societies attach to the range of sexual possibilities in a particular context. Results of such studies can be compared to and contrasted with Rubin's (1984) discussion, to either confirm it or to offer alternative local interpretations of sexual practices.

Following from this, Rubin propounds the concept of a sex hierarchy, whose value is informed and influenced by various constituencies, including religions, psychiatry, popular culture and politics. Sex is awarded a value. Delineation is made between socially approved and highly rewarded sex on the one hand, and socially condemned and therefore punished sex on the other hand.

A clear distinction is made between 'the charmed circle', which comprises good, normal, natural, blessed sexuality and 'the outer limits', which include bad, abnormal, unnatural, damned sexuality. The different influencing constituencies, such as religions, psychiatry, popular culture and politics continually redraw the lines between these two frames of the charmed circle and the outer limits. Furthermore, Rubin (1984) questions the criteria for plotting particular sex practices in either frame, and finds it wanting, because it 'has more in common with the ideologies of racism than with true ethics' (Rubin 1984: 283).

Transcending the singular framework for judging or valuing sexuality, Rubin advocates for plural sexual regimes, and sexual variation because of the diversity in propensity to appreciate, participate in and enjoy the range of sexual practices. Although Rubin's work has been variously critiqued by diverse scholars (Bristow 1997; Schueller 2005; Ho 2006), it is important because it facilitates analyses of how dominant ideologies construct, control and constrain sexualities. Comparative application of this model to diverse settings and across a range of places, people and periods highlights the multiple systems of valuing sexual conduct, activities, desires, orientations, feelings and behaviours. The concept of sex hierarchy is a useful model for scholars of African sexualities engaged in the analysis of the hegemonic control of sexualities by diverse social powers, be they religious, biomedical, heteronormative or patriarchal. It is important to test this concept of sexual hierarchy with data collected about the experienced and lived realities of Africans in diverse communities. This 'Africanises' the concept.

Of relevance to Part 7 of this volume, Rubin's (1984) work introduces the concepts of good sex and bad sex. Often people are deemed not to be having sex (or ought not to be having it) because there are aspects of their sexuality that are socially labelled 'bad'. Rather than appreciate these aspects as sex in and of itself, their sexual practices are instead reinterpreted in a variety of disparaging ways, including as crime, illness, insanity, delinquency, sin and a form of perversion, to name a few. When dominant discourses interact with local subjectivities in different African societies, then judgements are made about good sex, which gets reaffirmed. Similar judgements are made about bad sex and attempts are made to minimise if not altogether eradicate these 'vices'.

Sexual stereotypes

In order to unpack the concept of sexual stereotypes, I start with an examination of stereotypes in general. Adopted from the printing industry, the word stereotype originally referred to a one-piece printing plate cast in type metal from a mould (or matrix) taken of a printing surface, as a page of set type. Following from this imagery, stereotypes of people refer to an unvarying form or pattern; specifically a fixed or conventional notion or conception of a person, group or idea that is held by a number of people. Stereotype is also Greek for solid, so the term often refers to fixed, unchangeable perceptions of people. Stereotypical representations do not allow for individuality, critical judgement, diversity within groups or even non-conformity. Stereotypes are generalisations made about a collection of people based on gender, age, race, religion, ethnicity, nationality, sexual orientation or any other classification. Stereotypes can be positive or negative, but are often erroneous, hackneyed, simplistic and mostly negative because they are commonly based on presumed difference, prejudice, ignorance and bigotry.

Sexual stereotypes are sweeping statements and general beliefs about the sexual conduct of particular groups of people. Often not based on evidence, these generalisations are misrepresentations which assign uniformity to all within particular social groups. They tend to reduce individuals to a rigid and fixed image, which negates the complexity, transformation and multidimensionality of human beings. They also deny the uniqueness of group members and dehumanise people by claiming sameness for all members of one overly simplistic category. Sexual stereotypes are instrumental to othering people and thereby accentuating assumed differences between 'us' and 'them'. Several sexual stereotypes negate the potential and diversity within groups, for example:

- Black men have high libido.
- Veiled women are passive, submissive lovers.
- Sex repels post-menopausal women.
- Men are dogs!
- Teenagers are sexually innocent.
- Married women are true.
- Men with guns are rapists.
- Homosexual men are paedophiles.

Sexual stereotypes can be dangerous when erroneously attributed to group members who do not conform to the mould description. They can be harmful to members of a group with different traits or choices. Often they are blind generalisations that contain false assumptions about social groups different from those to which we belong. Sexual stereotypes can be tools of falsification, scapegoating, discrimination, injustice, persecution, violence, genocide, hate speech, hate crimes, homophobia, heterophobia, transphobia and xenophobia. It is critical for scholars of African sexualities to identify the politics of sexual naming and acknowledge sexual stereotypes for what they are.

Sexual stereotypes about Africans have masqueraded for too long as pseudoscience and have promoted ethnocentric theorisations in some academic scholarship. Specific reference is made here to the Caldwellian thesis of an African sexuality as intrinsically different to a Eurasian sexuality (see Part 1 for a discussion and critique). Another example is Nakanyike Musisi's (2002) historical discussion, which critically analyses colonial doctors' representation of Baganda women's pelvises. Musisi shows how the missionary doctor Albert Cook linked Baganda women's 'harmful native customs' (such as carrying heavy loads on their heads and preferring local therapies to Western medicine) to poor reproductive outcomes. According to Cook, these women were likely 'to suffer from "degenerate," "flattened," "deformed," and "contracted" pelvises and reproductive organs' (Musisi 2002: 100). This analysis of archival materials on the debate about Cook's theory 'exposes the danger of accepting scientific knowledge at face value' (Musisi 2002: 96) because the knowledge generation process in this case was found to be 'not only partial but also ideologically committed and culturally biased' (Musisi 2002: 96).

Sexual stereotypes are therefore dangerous, particularly when they are not recognised for what they are. Alternative sexualities, sexual minority groups and non-conforming sexual conduct can be ruthlessly targeted for elimination and punishment simply based on sexual stereotypes and prejudices that the majority groups hold regarding these manifestations of difference. Many times there is nothing errant about the alternative sexual conduct, but ethnocentric thinking by the majority, or a powerful group therein, judges and finds wanting any divergence from the assumed norms. Sexual stereotypes based on ignorance about, and fear of and prejudice towards difference yield discrimination, alienation, marginalisation, criminalisation and being ignored, rendered invisible or denied existence in national policies, programmes and service delivery.

Sexual citizenship and rights

Sexual citizenship is a concept that is attributed to David Evans (1993) who, based on a neo-Marxist perspective, challenged social construction theories of sexuality to consider and include the material foundation of sexualities. The concept focuses on the multipronged interactions between politics and erotics. At its heart is a critique of classical theories of citizenship – those that tend to focus on a narrow definition of the citizen principally as a male adult operating in a free market. In this approach, the citizen has neither sexuality nor embodiment. Sexual citizenship on the other hand broadens the scope to include cultural, ethnic, gendered and sexual aspects, all of which interact with politics.

Central to this paradigm shift in examining citizenship are key principles of 1) freedom of expression, 2) bodily autonomy, 3) institutional inclusion and 4) access to space. Working within the framework of sexual citizenship allows for the articulation, advocacy and contestation of the rights of marginalised and minority groups, such as women and LGBTQI. Therefore, very close to the heart of sexual citizenship is the growing discourse of sexual rights (Richardson 2000).

The notion of sexual rights derives from the historic 'paragraph 96', which was highly negotiated in diction, syntax and imputed meaning and then adopted by national delegates to the Fourth World Conference on Women (FWCW) in Beijing in 1995:

> The human rights of women include their right to have control over and decide freely and responsibly on matters related to their sexuality, including sexual and reproductive health, free of coercion, discrimination and violence. Equal relationships between women and men in matters of sexual relations

and reproduction, including full respect for the integrity for the person, require mutual respect, consent and shared responsibility for sexual behaviour and its consequences. (UN FWCW 1995)

Sexual rights extend international human rights protection to the terrain of sexuality. However, the concept of sexual rights is ambivalent (Richardson 2000). Various stakeholders on the sexual and reproductive health and rights scene have different interpretations of sexual rights. Although claims for sexual rights in Europe are mainly motivated in relation to sexual orientation (Klugman 2000), in the African context the lack of sexual rights often results from poverty and gender inequalities, particularly in sexual relationships. Cultural, religious, political and social diversities within Africa also introduce layers of differentiated meaning attributed to sexual rights. Sometimes sexual rights claims necessitate challenges to existent legal regimes that criminalise some sexual preferences (Amado 2003).

There were Africans at the FWCW who opposed sexual rights. Their main justifications were based on religious fundamentalisms, patriarchal subjugation of women, societal claims of communal rights taking predominance over individual rights claims, that this was a Western-driven agenda, and that African priorities should be centred around development (see also Freedman 1995: 331–334). However, there were many other African country delegations and NGOs that took a strong position in Beijing, advocating in favour of sexual rights. The debates highlighted the complexity of sexual rights and how much they are contested: they are complex, layered and not always straightforward. For example, in articulating the sexual rights of people living with HIV and AIDS (PLWHA), we have to counter questions about transmission and re-transmission of HIV, the right to have children who might or might not be infected with the virus through vertical transmission, the possibilities of increased demand on health services, and the repercussions for the health systems and support networks.

Marc Epprecht captures this complexity well:

> Sexuality rights – how to define them and how to achieve them – is another prickly question in much of Africa (as indeed, let us not forget, it still is elsewhere in the world including Canada). Not only is there a problem of perception, whereby leading advocates of broad definitions of sexual rights in Africa or female empowerment are coming from the West, often with a missionary or colonising tone in their voice that alienates potential African allies. There is also the problem that even narrow definitions of sexual rights pose profound challenges to hegemonic, heteropatriarchal culture. Should girls and boys be taught the health benefits of masturbation, for example, and at what age? How far should the state go to coach wives on their right to refuse husbands' sexual demands? Should prostitution be legalised (and prostitutes unionised), and so on? A large social, cultural, and political edifice stands to crumble when such specific rights are recognised, as conservative African leaders intuit all too well. (Epprecht 2009: 7)

So although sexual rights can be an empowering platform from which to operationalise social justice, advocacy and activism for sexual diversities and citizenship, they are also shrouded in complexity, ambivalence and ambiguity. Three examples drawn from the principles of sexual citizenship highlighted earlier will be discussed below to illustrate this complexity. These examples include freedom of expression, the right to sex work and the sexual rights of minors.

On the one hand, sexual minorities demand they are given their right to freedom of (sexual) expression. The lesbian, gay, bisexual, transgender and intersex (LGBTI) activists, advocates and scholars campaigning for the sexual rights and sexual citizenship of the LGBTI fraternity and individuals make claims for the freedom of sexual expression of alternative sexualities, such as those that do not conform to heteronormative standards of society. Some inroads have been made on this front in countries such as South Africa, Seychelles and Comoros. However, (re)criminalisation is simultaneously on the increase in several other countries, such as Uganda, Burundi, Malawi, the Gambia, Zimbabwe and Chad. On the other hand, freedom of expression as a right of rightist, fundamentalist, culturalist, traditionalist and other conservative groups can by the same token become the basis for articulating homophobic, misogynist and other forms of oppressive hate-speech against sexual minorities. Religious zealots can insult, abuse and even incite violence against LGBTI and other sexual minorities, whose preferred sexual expression is seen to be contrary to religious dogma, doctrine and teachings.

Likewise so-called African traditionalists can articulate homophobic hate-speech in the name of protecting some reified African norms. Both groups of extremists would be exercising their right to freedom of expression. Although it is important to advance the cause of freedom of (sexual) expression of LGBTI, we must be cautious and aware that homophobes and other intolerant extremists can use the very same claim to freedom of expression to oppress sexual minorities. If freedom of expression can be empowering to LGBTI, it can also be the basis for hate-speech in which homophobia is dispensed by the powerful majority (sometimes using state machinery, religious pulpits or, indeed, public health institutions).

Radical feminists have argued for the right to sex as work because some sex workers perceive of their services as labour that accrues a paid wage. In Senegal, for example, commercial sex work is legal and protected by state institutions, such as the Ministry of Health, which offers mandatory routine testing services, and the police, who offer protection in the red-light districts. Other public services might include registration, licensing and regular issuing of permits. Although this right to work as a sex worker is empowering to women and men who choose this line of employment, it can also be the premise for exploitation of the weak by the powerful. For example, child sex trafficking, child prostitution, sex tourism, production of pornography especially while under the influence of drugs or alcohol, can all be exploitative modes of oppressing the poor.

A final example of the ambivalence of the sexual rights paradigm pertains to the sexual rights of minors vis-à-vis legal provisions for the 'age of consent'. To what extent should minors be availed their sexual rights and freedoms? Is a degree of protectionism in order for infants and children? Shouldn't the sexual rights of minors be progressively given in age-appropriate packages?

Africa in its diversities has made some inroads into laying plans toward achieving sexual rights. An important example is the African Union's 2006 Maputo Plan
of Action for universal access to comprehensive sexual and reproductive health services in Africa. The Yogyakarta Principles, adopted in 2007, are also an important
framework for articulating human rights in relation to sexual orientation and gender identity.

For contemporary scholars of African sexualities, sexual rights offer a potent
framework to rethink the pragmatics of sexualities as positive, pleasurable and
empowering human experiences. Indeed, we need 'prospects for moving from the
current focus on absence of rights toward acceptance of sexual pleasure as a component of sexual rights' (Klugman 2000: 148). We should be innovatively thinking
of strategies to achieve the realisation of sexual rights for all (especially for diverse
minority groups). This would facilitate transcending the realm of rhetoric, such as
that contained in declarations, agreements, covenants and policies.

A brief historical perspective on governing sexualities

Historically, the sexualities of Africans have been the focus of diverse, repressive
regimes. Many pre-colonial societies suffered harsh patriarchal hegemonies in
which the normative prescription for propriety of female African sexualities was
paramount. This endorsed female dependency on male 'superiors', including the
figures of grandfather, father, brother, son, uncle and even the extended relationships of clan leader, healer, spirit medium, rainmaker, warrior, chief and king. In the
era of the slave trade, African sexualities were centred on procreation and reproduction of a highly productive labour force to meet the slave masters' economic needs
and to boost the profits of slave dealers. In the colonial era, African sexualities were
the locus of control for the coloniser (McClintock 1995; Stoler 2002). African colonial subjects were perceived as inherently different, and thereby othered in order
to justify colonial subjugation and brutal 'civilising' projects. At the heart of such
projects was the image of the primitive, raw African. So, the colonial discourses of
improving, containing, controlling or even civilising African sexualities must be
appreciated in the context of whom they perceived their colonial subjects to be.

Although the control of African sexualities was important to the success of the
colonial enterprise, it was tailored differently for each of the normative genders.
Historian Megan Vaughan (1991) succinctly describes this gender differentiation,
pointing out that colonial discourse on African sexuality was not uniform, and the
extent to which it appeared male or female varied according to particular circumstances (Vaughan 1991).

Female sexuality was particularly a locus of control by local male elites, patriarchs
and colonial supremacists. Vaughan captures this complexity well:

> There was a powerful consensus of male opinion, both British and Bagandan
> [sic], around the view that the 'epidemic' could have come about only
> through the breakdown of chiefly authority occasioned by the introduction of
> Christianity and 'civilisation'. For the male Baganda elite control over women

and their sexuality was central to their control over marriage and kinship, and hence over the society as a whole. For the British, loss of control over female sexuality stood for and symbolised the problem of control over African society in general. (Vaughan 1991: 135)

Female sexuality was a danger that took centuries of 'civilisation' to tame. African female sexuality was doubly dangerous, being both African and wild and female and wild. (Vaughan 1991: 139)

So dangerous was female sexuality perceived to be, that often all problems of the colonies were subsumed under the generalised 'woman problem'. Vaughan (1991: 144) further explains that several rapid social transformations and their resultant challenges were associated with women who symbolised tradition, control and stability. These included issues as diverse as changes in property rights, labour rights, generational relations – which were described in terms of degeneration – and uncontrolled sexuality and disease.[3]

Who is having sex? Sexual stereotypes of diverse groups

Although flag independence was achieved in all of Africa, contemporary society on the continent is still plagued with diverse mechanisms that perpetuate and entrench control and regulation of sexualities. Legal instruments, social policies, religious doctrine, cultural norms of acceptability, biomedical regimes of safe sex and reproductive health and popular culture are some of the major constituencies that define and impose sanctions against unacceptable sexual conduct. Although there are areas of overlap and intersection in the realms of acceptable sexual behaviour defined by the diverse constituencies, there are also often contradictions. For example, masturbation might be constructed as sin within certain religions, but it might also be recommended as a safe sex practice in the sexual and reproductive health paradigm. Ife Amadiume argues that 'the practice of sexuality in Africa presents many difficulties to researchers and scholars due to the ambiguity of beliefs and attitudes in traditional cultures and religions. Sexuality is even more problematic in the received world religions and global popular cultures of post-colonial African modernity' (Amadiume 2006: 26).

The different discourses that establish diverse controls on sexualities in Africa create and maintain specific sexual stereotypes of particular social groups of people. The following section considers one of the social groups whose inherent diverse sexualities are often condensed into one sexual stereotype. Although the elderly are the in-depth case study, a similar analysis can apply to any of the diverse social groups explored earlier in this chapter.

The elderly as asexual

Stereotypes abound about the elderly as an asexual social group. Often these perceptions are not based on actual knowledge of the sexual preferences or behaviour of any elderly individuals. Several scholars (Ortner 2007; Thornton et al 2009) highlight the paucity of literature, research and scholarship about the interactions between old age and sexualities. Van der Geest (2001) notes that the available studies on the sexualities of the elderly are mainly focused on populations in North America and western Europe. There are scant research publications on the sexualities of the elderly in sub-Saharan Africa, among them Van der Geest's (2001) study among rural elderly individuals, Ortner's (2007) study among diverse racial groups in South Africa and Cattell's (1992) work among elderly widows in Kenya.

The limited research highlights that often the only alternative to the pervasive construct of an asexual old age are negative images about sexually active elderly people: 'The older years may be defined as the time from the mid-50s onwards. The concept of the couple having sex, let alone enjoyable sex, appears increasingly weird, even obscene, both to them and to others' (Moloney 2007: 160). Helena Thornton and colleagues refer to the 'myth that sexual interest by the elderly is a sign of illness' (Thornton et al 2009: 144). Thus there is a widespread generalisation that sexuality among the elderly has negative connotations.

However, in recent years there has developed a small but growing body of scholarship and publications about the sexualities of the elderly in diverse social geographical contexts. Against the backdrop of growing criticism of ageism, scholars and practitioners are increasingly contesting the homogenous presentation of the sexual disinterest of the elderly (see Van der Geest 2001: 1383).

This body of work has established that there are diverse sexualities, sexual behaviours and preferences among late-life couples (Van der Geest 2001; Gott and Hinchliff 2003; Ortner 2007; Thornton et al 2009). Some older people desire and continue intimate relationships (Calasanti and Kiecolt 2007). They need love, partnership and physical intimacy (Aleman 2005: 5). Sex, like love, is an important component of a close emotional relationship in old age (Gott and Hinchliff 2003; Connidis 2006). Some older people lose interest in sexual activity, particularly when they lose a partner or spouse through death, divorce or separation, for example. Scholars such as Sandra Leiblum et al (1994) and Jane Loehr et al (1997) argue that lack of sex among the elderly is often not because of lack of desire, but rather because of a lack of opportunity or of a sexual partner. However, there is also evidence that some elders exercise their agency and choose to remain single even when opportunities for remarriage are presented. For example, Maria Cattell's work in Kenya shows how especially older women 'are empowering themselves within their own homes and in their everyday lives. They do this by refusing to be "inherited" as a wife by their husband's brother or other kin, preferring widowhood to a renewed marital status' (Cattell 1992: 307).

Yet still, some other older people are inhibited because of ill health or a failing body. In a study of sexual behaviour and sexual dysfunction in later life, Alfredo Nicolosi and colleagues (2004) found that sexual desire and activity are widespread among middle-aged and elderly men and women worldwide and persist into old age. Most participants in their study had had sexual intercourse during the previous year. Their study found that the prevalence of sexual dysfunction was quite high and tended to increase with age, especially in men. The most common dysfunctions were early ejaculation and erectile difficulties among men, and a lack of sexual interest and inability to reach orgasm and lubrication difficulties among the women.

Merryn Gott and Sharron Hinchliff's study found that sexual interest among the elderly ranged from 'none' or 'little interest', particularly in conditions of widowhood, not being in a relationship or health problems, to 'very' or 'extremely important', especially for those individuals with partners (Gott and Hinchliff 2003: 1617). Thus in old age there were several sexuality possibilities, statuses and goals, including widowhood, marriage, remarriage, singleness, divorce, cohabitation, dating, companionship, intimacy and the concept of 'living apart together' (Calasanti and Kiecolt 2007). In fact for urban-based and elite elderly persons, internet dating, cybersex and pharmaceutical sexual interventions, such as the 'blue pill', might increase sexuality options.

Clearly, sexual activity during old age is informed by culture rather than biology (Kellet 1991). An example specific to Africa is Phyllis Ortner's study among older women in South Africa, which found that:

> Experiences of participants varied. Some of the respondents were completely indifferent, others experience the sexual urge sometimes, some were just a bit interested, others merely put up with sex, some said they had heightened expectations, while yet others spoke about renewed and continued enjoyment. (Ortner 2007: 174)

Ortner further reveals that responses to the question 'Do you think menopause means the end of a woman's sex life?' demonstrated the 'fluidity of women's experiences of sexuality' (Ortner 2007: 175).

Van der Geest's study includes a nuanced discussion among elderly men in rural Ghana.

> Losing interest in sex was seen as a sign of maturity and wisdom, but others saw it as one of the unfortunate consequences of old age. I asked two elderly men, Agya Kwaku Martin (M) and Mr Asare (A), who were friends, whether it was true that sexual desire diminishes when people grow older.
> M: Yes it is true, but not for everyone. Some will be old yet their organs will be strong and effective, while there are also young men whose organs are weak and ineffective. We are all human. Our organs become weak and unable to operate. When you are young, you can go two or three times per night but as it is now, if God doesn't help, you cannot go even one round.
> S: Because of what?
> M: Because of the pains and lack of interest too. We have done this thing all our life. We become fed up.
> S: Can the old man who finds it difficult to have sex with an old woman have sex with a young one?
> A: Yes, a beautiful person can generate the machine to erect and do a small job. (Van der Geest 2001: 1392)

So, evident from the literature is that, far from the stereotype of the asexual elderly, some individuals' sexuality thrives into advanced old age. Three examples confirm this. Contrasting common assumptions to lived experienced in Kenya, Michael Moloney states:

> If the couple should have sex, then it is likely to be secretive. The idea of experimentation and renewal of mutual physical love through touch and stimulation becomes unthinkable. Yet couples have been known, in the middle and later years, to enjoy not only friendship but also to rediscover the excitement and mutuality of physical closeness and the improved self image that goes with this. (Moloney 2007: 161)

Thornton and colleagues discuss an octogenarian whose sexuality was 'to be fought for': 'for this 90-year-old woman, the return of these sexual feelings was desirable and to be fought for (she did not want her "symptoms" to be cured). It shows that for Mrs. K, her experience and expression of her sexuality was part of being "fully alive"' (Thornton et al 2009: 144).

Reflexively writing as researchers, Katja Jassey and Stella Nyanzi reveal how some unknown yet apparently underlying assumptions came to the fore when, during research fieldwork in the Gambia, one of them was confronted with the reality of an elderly Muslim woman who was also infected with HIV:

> There was no silence around Mariama's diagnosis. Only fear. However, it didn't sound as if anyone suspected her of having been an immoral woman, not if her husband wanted to re-unite. It was the thought of death that drove them away. As a researcher, however, I was shamed by my initial reaction when I saw Mariama at SYSS [Santa Yalla Support Society – a local association for HIV-infected people in the Gambia]. I was bothered that one as old as her could also be infected with HIV. Later on during our debriefing sessions, my male research assistants both also reported alarm and shock when they confirmed she was indeed HIV-infected. This immediately raised the issue of stigmatisation of HIV among the elderly for me. It seemed as if having HIV in their blood stream was like a misplaced occurrence. It is as if we question their right to healthy, pleasurable and perhaps even dangerous sexuality and sexual activity. And to aggravate Mariama's situation, she was not only an elderly woman, with grey hairs that peeped out of her head, she also presented a very religious front – performing her prayers on time even if it meant excusing herself from a research activity. She also repeatedly prayed for us, as was the customary practice for elderly women in this setting. (Jassey and Nyanzi 2007: 17–18)

Furthermore, Thornton et al assert:

> Recent research tends to show that older people are interested in and can enjoy sexual activity within normal biological limitations into their eighties and nineties. Nonetheless, myths about sexuality in later life (or lack of it)

> flourish. These myths not only serve to isolate and discriminate against the elderly, but they often reflect one's own fear of ageing and discomfort with issues around mortality and sexuality. (Thornton et al 2009: 164)

For scholars of African sexualities, it is important to realise that stereotypes of an asexual old age remain pervasive, and shape not only popular images of older people but also infiltrate research, programme development and policy agendas. The danger of stereotypes influencing policy and programme development is clearly detrimental to the concerned social group. Invisibility of the elderly in available international, national and local policies and programmes means that they lack targeted interventions and services appropriate to their everyday circumstances. There is a serious gap in service provision because the range of sexual experiences of the elderly are outside the formal systems of service provision – be it public or private. And yet it is important to cater to the sexuality and sexual health needs of the elderly in Africa, particularly because HIV infection and transmission impacts directly on those elderly who are sexually active or those who are sexually assaulted. For example, based on South African data, Thornton et al report that in 2006, 4 per cent of men and 3.7 per cent of women with HIV were over the age of 60 (2009: 147).

Children as 'sexually pure and innocent'

The sexual innocence of children is an almost universal premise. Sexuality is constructed as a domain exclusive to adults, and with preconditions of physical and social maturity. Thus the notions of children's sexuality and children's sexual rights are often taboo, antithetical non-issues or even cause for moral panic (Foucault 1976: 4).

Should children be protected against their own sexuality or do children have sexual rights? Admittedly different contexts have diverse cut-off age limits at which the operational definitions of children are marked. Four common examples are considered: 1) when children access universal suffrage, 2) commencement of the age at which minors are constitutionally protected from exploitation, 3) the minimum age for criminal responsibility and 4) the definition of children provided by the United Nation's Convention on the Rights of the Child.

The age at which minors qualify for universal suffrage – when they can access the right and opportunities to vote – differs from one country to another. This age also shifts with time. The age at which minors access the right to vote is 18 years in many countries. However, it is also lower (for example 17 years in Sudan) or higher in some other countries (21 years in Tunisia). Constitutional provisions for the protection of minors from social and economic exploitation are often set at the later teenage years. In Uganda it is 16 years of age. The minimum age of criminal responsibility exemplifies a standard that has variously shifted with time in different contexts. This is the age at which children are deemed to have the abilities for discernment and judgement of right and wrong. Thus they are liable to take responsibility for criminal acts. It is the age at which children have the mental capacity to commit a criminal offence. For example, according to the 1996 Uganda children's statute, the minimum age of criminal responsibility is 12 years of age. However, this was later raised to 14 years because reviews of children's prosecutions revealed that minors mostly committed petty rather than serious crimes. Ghana also raised its minimum age of criminal responsibility to 14 years. The Convention on the Rights of the Child defines children as persons under the age of 18 years. These are individuals who are variously defined as 'minors' who must of necessity be protected by diverse institutions and structures (United Nations 1989).

So, although some constituencies assert that children need protection and cannot give consent until they are 18 years old, others counter this by highlighting that if children are deemed able to judge between right and wrong when they are much younger than 18, then they must also have the ability to decide what is right for their own lives. In relation to the sexualities of young people, the concept of the legal age of consent substantiates permission (and the lack of permission) for minors to lawfully engage in sexual activities. This bar is dependent upon reaching a chronological age – a specified quantity of years – regardless of biological, social, political, cultural, economic, structural and any other contingent factors.

Sylvia Tamale (2001: 82) critically reflects on the question, 'how old is old enough to engage in consensual sexual activity?', based on her analysis of the defilement law and age of consent in Uganda. Tamale's position is radical, particularly in contexts in which children are perceived and constructed as innocent, pure, ignorant, naive, immature minors who are neither corrupted nor corruptible by the assumed impurities of sexual stuff (Tamale 2001). Within this paradigm, the (assumed asexual) snow-white purity of minors can only be polluted by the vile scarlet-red potency of sexual activity. Basically, sex is perceived as a stain that taints the purity of childhood. The fallacy of this supposition is grounded in the fact that children are misconstrued as static and homogenous beings who neither develop nor transform. Thus children get suffocated by multiple imposed restrictions, denials and protectionisms aimed at prohibiting their sexualisation. Consequently child experts, scholars, policymakers, programme developers and implementers and societal gatekeepers formulate plans, designs, plots, policies, programmes and laws to prohibit, ban and punish the sexualisation of minors. All these actors tend to be well-meaning adults, who often exclude children from contributing to the discussions of these interventions. Often these interventions are perceived by the 'target beneficiaries' as paternalistic, patronising and presumptuous and delivered in condescending, child-hostile ways.

Is it any wonder that within this protectionist paradigm, notions of youth sexualities, childhood sexualities, adolescent sexualities or even the sexual rights of children are treated as antithetical, misnomers, subversive and violations of normative social configurations? Under this paradigm, the sexualities of minors are constructed only in negative terms, such as deviance, delinquency, degeneration, dangerous to reproductive health, sexual risk-taking, coercive or non-consensual, abusive, exploitative, sources of sexually transmitted infections including HIV and AIDS, social stigma, taboo, criminal, defilement, child abuse, child assault, paedophilia, pederasty, rape, gender-based violence and harmful traditional customs. Therefore the sexualities of minors are heavily controlled, totally prohibited and severely punished using diverse social strategies in combination with repressive or punitive state mechanisms.

Transcending this limited conceptualisation of children is a growing body of scholarship that highlights that children are sexual beings, whose sexualities evolve from conception through infancy, childhood, puberty, adolescence and the teenage years. However, the focus of this scholarship is mainly on children aged between 15 and 18 years. There is still relatively much more limited research and evidence on the sexual and reproductive knowledge and behaviour of children and younger adolescents aged between 10 and 14 years or even younger (IWHC 2001: 1). The available material highlights that children have a diverse range of sexual interests, needs and enacted sexualities. As sexual beings, children have diverse sexual rights and entitlements. Bhana (2008) stresses children's sexual rights are multiple and the need to actualise, promote and protect these rights is specially enhanced by the HIV and AIDS epidemic. The International Planned Parenthood Federation recently published its declaration of sexual rights including articles specific to the sexual rights of minors below the age of 18 years (IPPF 2009).

Given the complexities surrounding the issue of sexual rights discussed earlier, we briefly highlight some sexual rights that are critical to the well-being and optimal development of children and other young people. Children have a right to adequate sex information and sex education that is appropriate and tailored to suit their diverse age-groups and contexts. This sex education should be over and above the normative education that does not really help children and adolescents understand their struggles, for example, those who might be interested in non-heteronormative sexualities. Such sex education would not only provide an understanding of sexual risk, but also provide relevant information that would enable minors to make informed decisions as well as to give informed consent about their sexual lives. It would also develop the children's appreciation of their gendered sexual bodies and body parts, and their understanding of the maturing body and maturation processes and cycles.

Children have a right to access to knowledge about protection within diverse sexual orientations, and later to access youth-friendly sexual and reproductive health services, including voluntary counselling and testing for sexually transmitted infections including HIV and AIDS, condoms, contraceptives, antenatal care, emergency obstetric care, post-natal care, abortion and post-abortion services, treatment for sexually transmitted infections, HIV and AIDS care, treatment and support services, among others. They must be empowered with a range of skills, tools and strategies including 1) the ability to negotiate for their preferred sexual options, such as whether or not to have sex, with whom, how, when, where and why; 2) the ability to negotiate condom use, contraceptive use, whether or not to conceive, when and with whom; and 3) access to continued formal education even when they (or their female partners) conceive, carry the pregnancy to full-term, and deliver and breastfeed their babies.

Minors also have the right to meaningful, pleasurable and fulfilling sexual experiences when the time is appropriate. It is important to implement interventions that ensure a sexual debut that is free from violence, coercion or violation – be it by relatives or strangers. Children have a right to protection from sexual exploitation and violation by unscrupulous members of society. It is important to establish innovative strategies for protecting girls from diverse violations of their sexual rights by 'well-meaning' adults[4] who are often family members, cultural leaders or other people in authority over the children, such as teachers, priests, house-helps and predatory relatives. Such strategies must emphasise that children have the right to sexual autonomy, self-determination and the right to choose a sexual partner.

Recognising that the violation of children's sexual rights sometimes happens (see Daughtie's story in Chapter 11 of this volume), children have a right to access avenues of reporting, recourse and redress for sexual abuse, assault, defilement and rape, particularly by adults. It is also important to establish or enhance existing youth-friendly systems of justice and train the individuals that operate in them, such as the police, court officials, support social workers, lawyers and judges. Social, cultural and political leaders must address normative associations made between the notions of violence and masculinity, which are at the core of much sexual and gender-based violence and aggression.

Pertinent to contemporary sub-Saharan Africa, HIV-related vulnerabilities are magnified in the case of adolescents and other children involved in intergenerational sexual relationships (Edstrom and Khan 2009). When young people engage in sexual activities with adults, there are greater chances of exposure to HIV infection because these adults often have other adult sexual partners. Common cultural scenarios of cross-generational sexual interactions, such as those between adults and adolescents, include 'Sugar Daddy' or 'Sugar Mummy' relationships, early marriages of virginal brides to elderly grooms (often arranged or forced) and child prostitution, which is often associated with child trafficking or even child sex tourism.

A common feature of these age-asymmetrical sexual relationships is the motivating factor of transactional sex, in which the sexual services of the adolescent partner are exchanged for financial, material, social or other benefit. In a bid to accrue more profit from these transactional sexual connections, some adolescents engage in multiple sex partnerships in which the different partners provide for different needs including cosmetics, clothes, rent/lodging, food, entertainment, electronics (such as a mobile phone and its accessories) and sometimes tuition and transport fees for school. Often, as bodies with the capacity to exercise agency, these young people use their sexual bodies to maximise the gains they get from their sexual interactions (Nyanzi et al 2001). However, on other occasions, young people (particularly girls) are taken advantage of as passive objects trapped within the dictates of patriarchal societies. Examples include child betrothals, forced early marriages and the 'virgin cleansing myth', in which babies are raped by HIV-impacted men as a cure for HIV (see Richter 2003).

Current HIV and AIDS programming and policies in sub-Saharan Africa often fail to acknowledge children as infected with HIV but, rather, dwell on how they are affected by the virus and the syndrome. Children are infected with HIV – whether vertically (in the mother's uterus, during birth or through breast milk) or horizontally through sexual intercourse, be it consensual or non-consensual (Edstrom and Khan 2009: 45, 47).

Some final thoughts

Control of the sexualities of minority groups is a medium that powerful segments of society appropriate to maintain their hegemonic grip and position. The sexual terrain is one of the central locuses of power among human beings. Sometimes this power takes subtle forms, and at other times it presents in outbursts of virulent manic pressure. This chapter has discussed five theoretical frameworks that can be instrumental to deciphering the mentality of governing sexualities, be it in Africa or elsewhere. Rather than presenting them as 'grand man theories' from which analysts must commence their formulations, the theoretical frameworks are more potent when innovatively appropriated as analytical models to unpack diverse sexual politics.

It is important to always bear in mind the historicity, epistemological background and context-specific implications of each of the theories. Furthermore, although the five theoretical frameworks can be applied to a relatively homogenous group from one sexual culture, such as urban young homosexual men, elderly rural widows, adolescents who are living with HIV and AIDS or married university students, they should also be used to analyse the more complex heterogeneous sexual cultural scenarios, such as elderly HIV-infected disabled men and women, teenage bisexual Muslim boys or poor, black closeted lesbians.

Researchers and analysts should be encouraged to Africanise the theoretical frameworks, with an aim of proffering either confirmatory or contradictory findings of their application to local African data sets from diverse contemporary social cultural contexts.

Notes

1. I am grateful to Professor Sylvia Tamale for initiating this essay, offering mentoring during the writing and comments to the first draft. Discussions held with Professor Kopano Ratele and Professor Mansa Prah during the writers' workshop in preparation for the Reader substantially contributed to the conceptual development of the essay. Ms Sheillah Nyanzi and Mr Patrick Teko also provided input on sections of the paper.
2. In many parts of post-colonial Africa, this term refers to mistresses or unmarried spouses. Note that this phenomenon was largely unknown in traditional African societies, which were inherently polygynous.
3. For more discussions of colonial regulations of African sexualities, refer to Luise White's (1990) discussion of prostitution in colonial Nairobi, and Nakanyike Musisi's (2002) discussion of colonial doctors' production of knowledge about Baganda women's pelvises.
4. Adults may be well intentioned and want to protect what they assume to be a child's best interests, e.g. marrying off a teenage daughter to a polygynous old man to ensure security, access to land and property for the young girl. For the parent, a daughter's personal needs for pleasure or experimentation, which may be better met by her unmarried and materially poorer peer, are inconsenquential.

References

Aleman, M.W. (2005) 'Embracing and resisting romantic fantasies as the rhetorical vision on a senior net discussion board', *Journal of Communication* 55(1): 5–21

Amadiume, I. (2006) 'Sexuality, African religio-cultural traditions and modernity: expanding the lens', *CODESRIA Bulletin*, 1 and 2: 26–28

Amado, L.E. (2003) 'Sexual and bodily rights as human rights in the Middle East and North Africa', *Reproductive Health Matters* 12(23): 125–128

Bhana, D. (2008) 'Children's sexual rights in an era of HIV/AIDS', in Cornwall, A., Correa, S. and Jolly, S. (eds) *Development with a Body: Sexuality, Human Rights and Development*, London and New York, Zed Books

Bristow, J. (1997) *Sexuality*, Florence, Routledge

Buss, D. and Herman D. (2003) *Globalising Family Values: The Christian Right in International Politics*, Minneapolis and London, University of Minnesota Press

Calasanti, T. and Kiecolt K.J. (2007) 'Diversity among late-life couples', *Generations* 31(3): 10–17

Cattell, M.G. (1992) '"Praise the Lord and say no to men": older women empowering themselves in Samia, Kenya', *Journal of Cross-Cultural Gerontology* 7(4): 307–330

Connidis I. A. (2006) 'Intimate relationships: Learning from later life experience', in Calasanti, T. and Slevin, K. (eds) *Age Matters*, New York, Routledge

Dixon-Mueller, R. (1993) 'The sexuality connection in reproductive health', *Studies in Family Planning* 24(2): 269–282

Edstrom, J. and Khan, N. (2009) 'Perceptions on intergenerational vulnerability for adolescents affected by HIV: an argument for voice and visibility', *IDS Bulletin* 40(1): 41–50

Efraime, J.B. (2004) 'Armed conflict and the sexual abuse of children in Mozambique', in Richter, L., Dawes, A. and Higson-Smith, C. (eds) *Sexual Abuse of Young Children in Southern Africa*, Cape Town, Human Sciences Research Council (HSRC) Press

Epprecht, M. (2009) 'New perspectives on sexualities in Africa: introduction', *Canadian Journal of African Studies* 43(1): 1–7

Evans D.T. (1993) *Sexual Citizenship: The Material Construction of Sexualities*, London and New York, Routledge

Foucault, M. (1976) *The History of Sexuality: The Will to Knowledge*, Volume I, London, Penguin Books

—— (1991) 'Governmentality', tr. R. Braidotti, in Burchell, G., Gordon, C. and Miller P. (eds) *The Foucault Effect: Studies in Governmentality*, Chicago, University of Chicago Press

Freedman, L. (1995) 'Reflections on emerging frameworks of health and human rights', *Health and Human Rights* 1(4): 314–48

Gott, M. and Hinchliff S. (2003) 'How important is sex in later life? The views of older people', *Social Science and Medicine* 56: 1617–28

Head, B. (1974) *A Question of Power*, Oxford and Johannesburg, Heinemann Publishers

Ho, P.S.Y. (2006) 'The (charmed) circle game: reflections on sexual hierarchy through multiple sexual relationships', *Sexualities* 9(5): 547–564

International Planned Parenthood Federation (IPPF) (2009) 'Sexual rights: An IPPF declaration', http://tinyurl.com/67vzz9r, accessed 24 April 2010

International Women's Health Coalition (IWHC) (2001) 'Overlooked and uninformed: young adolescents' sexual and reproductive health and rights', New York, IWHC

Jassey, K. and Nyanzi, S. (2007) 'How to be a "proper" woman in the time of AIDS', *Current African Issues* 34, Uppsala, The Nordic Africa Institute

Kellet J. M. (1991) 'Sexuality and the elderly', *Sexual and Marital Therapy* 6: 147–55

Klugman, B. (2000) 'Sexual rights in southern Africa: a Beijing discourse or a strategic necessity?', *Health and Human Rights* 4(2): 144–73

Leiblum, S.R., Baume, R.M. and Croog, S. (1994) 'The sexual functioning of elderly hypertensive women', *Journal of Sex and Marital Therapy* 20(4): 259–270

Lemke, T. (2000) 'Foucault, governmentality and critique', paper presented at the Rethinking Marxism Conference, University of Amherst, 21–24 September, http://www.andosciasociology.net/resources/Foucault\$2C+Governmentality\$2C+and+Critique+IV-2.pdf, accessed 22 November 2009

Loehr, J., Verma, S. and Seguin, R. (1997) 'Issues of sexuality in older women', *Journal of Women's Health* 6(4): 451–457

Majiet, S. (1993) 'Disabled women and sexuality', *Agenda* 19: 43–44

—— (1996) 'Sexuality and disability', *Agenda* 28: 77–80

McClintock, A. (1995) *Imperial Leather: Race, Gender and Sexuality in the Colonial Contest*, London, Routledge

Miller, A.M. (2000) 'Sexual but not reproductive: exploring the junction and disjunction of sexual and reproductive rights', *Health and Human Rights* 4(2): 68–109

Moloney, M. (2007) 'Married couples and the expression of sexuality during and after middle age', in Maticka-Tyndale, E., Tiemoko, R. and Makinwa-Adebusoye, P. (eds) *Human Sexuality in Africa: Beyond Reproduction*, Johannesburg, Fanele, ARSC, Action Health Incorporated

Musisi, N. (2002) 'The politics of perception or perception as politics? Colonial and missionary representations of Baganda women, 1900–1945', in Allman, J., Geiger, S. and Musisi. N. (eds) *Women in African Colonial Histories*, Bloomington, Indiana University Press

Naran, J. (2005) 'More younger children are having sex – survey', *Weekend Argus on Sunday*, 10 July

Nicolosi, A., Laumann, E.O., Glasser, D.B., Moreira, E.D., Paik, A. and Gingell, C. (2004) 'Sexual behaviour and sexual dysfunction after age 40: the global study of sexual attitudes and behaviours', *Adult Urology* 64: 991–97.

Nyanzi, S., Pool, R. and Kinsman, J. (2001) 'The negotiation of sexual relationships among school pupils in south-western Uganda', *AIDS Care* 13(1): 83–98

Nyanzi, S. (2006) 'From miniscule biomedical models to sexuality's depths', *The Lancet* 368: 1851–52

Oomman, N. (1998) 'Sexuality: not just a reproductive health matter', *Reproductive Health Matters* 6(12): 10–12

Ortner, P. (2007) 'Sexuality of older women', in Maticka-Tyndale, E., Tiemoko, R. and Makinwa-Adebusoye, P. (eds) *Human Sexuality in Africa: Beyond Reproduction*, Johannesburg, Fanele, ARSC, Action Health Incorporated

Richter, L.M. (2003) 'Baby rape in South Africa', *Child Abuse Review* 12(6): 392–400

Rose, N., O'Malley, P. and Valverde, M. (2009) 'Governmentality', Legal studies research paper 09/94, Sydney, Sydney Law School

Rubin, G. (1984) 'Thinking sex: notes for a radical theory of the politics of sexuality', in Vance, C.S. (ed) *Pleasure and Danger: Exploring Female Sexuality*, London, Pandora

Richardson, D. (2000) 'Constructing sexual citizenship: theorising sexual rights', *Critical Social Policy* 20 (1): 105–35

Richter, L.M., Dawes, A. and Higson-Smith, C. (2004) 'Sexual abuse of young children in Southern Africa', Cape Town, Human Sciences Research Council Press

Schueller, M.J. (2005) 'Race – analogy and (White) feminist theory: thinking race and the colour of the cyborg body', *Signs* 31(1): 63–92

Shakespeare, T., Gillespie-Sells, K. and Davies, D. (1996) *The Sexual Politics of Disability: Untold Desires*, London, Cassell

Sheil, K. (2008) 'Sexual rights are human rights', in Cornwall, A., Correa, S. and Jolly, S. (eds) *Development With a Body: Sexuality, Human Rights and Development*, London and New York, Zed Books

Summers, C. (1991) 'Intimate colonialism: the imperial production of reproduction in Uganda, 1907–1925', *Signs* 16(4): 787–807

Stoler, A.L. (2002) *Carnal Knowledge and Imperial Power: Race and the Intimate in Colonial Rule*, Los Angeles and London, University of California Press

Tamale, S. (2001) '"How old is old enough?" Defilement law and the age of consent in Uganda', *East African Journal of Peace and Human Rights* 7(1): 82–100

Thornton, H.B., Potocnik, F.C.V. and Muller, J.E. (2009) 'Sexuality in later life', in Steyn, M. and Van Zyl, M. (eds) *The Prize and the Price: Shaping Sexualities in South Africa*, Cape Town, Human Sciences Research Council Press

United Nations (1989) Convention on the Rights of the Child, Geneva, United Nations

United Nations Fourth World Conference on Women (1995) Declaration and Platform for Action, New York, United Nations

Van der Geest, S. (2001) '"No strength": sex and old age in a rural town in Ghana', *Social Science and Medicine* 53(10): 1383–96

Vaughan, M. (1991) *Curing Their Ills: Colonial Power and African Illness*, Stanford, Stanford University Press

Wazakili, M., Mpofu, R. and Devlieger, P. (2006) 'Experiences and perceptions of sexuality and HIV/AIDS among young people with physical disabilities in a South African township: a case study', *Sexuality and Disability* 24(2): 77–88

White, L. (1990) *The Comforts of Home: Prostitution in Colonial Nairobi*, Chicago, University of Chicago Press

53

Sexuality, gender and disability in South Africa[1]

Washeila Sait, Theresa Lorenzo, Melissa Steyn and Mikki Van Zyl

Introduction

Disability and sexuality are issues that do not easily come together in the minds of most people, leading to many myths about sexuality and disability, *inter alia* that disabled people are asexual and cannot sustain sexual relationships and that they are childlike and need to be protected from harm (Deepak 2002). It is also a difficult topic to discuss, even for persons with disabilities. There are many different ways in which sexualities are shaped, but there is differentiation in the manner in which sexualities are shaped for disabled and non-disabled people and particularly in the way that sexualities are experienced. Though disabled children, like non-disabled children, grow aware of their sexuality through personal erotic experiences, peer groups, community and media, their activities are usually more closely regulated and supervised than those of non-disabled children and, more than for most children, their sexual behaviours are discouraged (Naudé 2001).

This chapter speaks to the challenges that mothers face in nurturing the sexual development of their disabled young daughters. It speaks specifically to how they deal with their parenting roles in the face of their daughters' awareness and expression of sexuality, of educating the girls about menstruation issues and the reproductive health choices made on behalf of the girls. In trying to gain some understanding of how the sexualities of disabled girls are nurtured, as well as insight into the level of awareness and information that young disabled girls have about sexuality, a small-scale study of eight households with disabled daughters was undertaken.

Introducing the participants

The study was conducted in 2005 in Kimberley, the provincial capital of the Northern Cape, the least populated of South Africa's nine provinces. The eight mothers and daughters who participated in the study came from two different population groups (coloured and African) and lived in poor townships in Kimberley. The disabled girls were between 14 and 25 years old at the time of the study, and most of them had varying degrees of intellectual disabilities; one girl had a physical disability. Five of them were attending the same special school, and one girl attended a mainstream school. Two of the girls did not attend school, one because she was over age and the other because she was a volunteer at a centre for disabled children. Two of the girls in the group were rape survivors; one of them was a young mother who became pregnant as a result of rape.

The participants in this study were identified through Disabled Children Action Group (DICAG) structures of the Northern Cape, with the support and assistance of both the national office in Cape Town and the provincial office in Kimberley. The research methodology was exploratory qualitative, and recorded the stories of the young disabled girls' lived experiences and those of their mothers as experts in rearing disabled children. Washeila Sait conducted the research and held focus group discussions and unstructured interviews with the respondents.

Living in the Northern Cape

The general living conditions in the Northern Cape are fraught with poverty and unemployment. The situation is further exacerbated by high rates of crime within communities. The 2001 Labour Force Survey (LFS) put the unemployment rate in this province at 26.1 per cent, and the rate was recorded as 33.4 per cent in the 2001 census. This is the second lowest unemployment rate in the country after the Western Cape (Stats SA 2001: 51). The unemployment rate was highest among the African and coloured populations, being about 3 per cent higher for coloured females than males, recorded as 7 per cent to 14 per cent higher for African females than males in the LFS and 2001 census respectively.

Of the eight households represented in the study, only three indicated that there were household members who were employed. The majority of the households depended on income from the social security grants of their daughters.[2] Poverty and disability are mutually reinforcing: the links between race and poverty and between disability and poverty are many, as are the links between gender and poverty. Therefore, a disabled black girl in South Africa is less likely to be able to get an education and more likely to be sexually abused than her male peers (Emmett 2006).

The Northern Cape also has almost one and a half times the murder and rape crime rate per capita (194 per 100,000 as against 119 per 100,000 countrywide) in South Africa, and the highest reported levels of child abuse and child rape in the country (Louw and Shaw 1997). At the time of the 2001 census the Northern Cape recorded the lowest rate of reported crime, at 2.9 per cent, but was still highest for rape and assault and rated second for theft and burglary. Most of the crimes at the time of the census were reported to be within the Diamond Fields jurisdiction, which includes Kimberley (Stats SA 2003).

Poverty was a major issue for the communities in which these households were located, and survival was concomitantly difficult for the households of participants in this study. Reliance on the care dependency or disability grants for the upkeep of the family meant that most of the parents were unable to provide for their daughters in the manner that they would like to. The mothers were not always able to pay school fees or buy fashionable clothing for their daughters. For some of the girls it was important to look and feel good as part of the overall expression of their identity and to be acceptable to their friends and peers. Poverty therefore further impacted the girls' capacity to express their sexualities in these aspects of their lives (Peet and Peet 2000). The societal ills born of impoverishment included alcohol abuse, drug or substance abuse and rape. The Northern Cape has some of the highest rates of crime-related alcohol abuse (Louw and Shaw 1997). The mothers indicated that they witnessed the abuse of drugs and other substances on a daily basis.

Poor socio-economic living conditions generally have a specific impact on the living conditions and nutritional needs of disabled people, and more specifically in this study on the overall development of the girls. Not only do these living conditions affect the establishment of disabled people's self-identity within the framework of psychosocial development (Hallum 1995), but they also impact on their needs for protection and participation (Max-Neef 1991). One significant impact of poverty is the manner in which disabled people's sexualities are shaped because of a lack of opportunities to gain information, ability to become aware of their sexuality or opportunities to express their sexuality through social participation and interaction. Their sexualities are stifled by living conditions framed by many limitations, including being overprotected for their safety, and silences around the discussion of healthy expressions of sexuality. This greatly impoverishes the lives of disabled people, their carers and, in this instance, their mothers.

Expressing sexuality

The experiences of disabled people in the development and expression of sexuality are revealed as perpetual struggles for acceptance as sexual beings by the self as well as others (Davies 2000; Shuttleworth et al 2002; Watermeyer 2006). Numerous authors show how society tends to dismiss sexuality as a fundamentally important factor in the lives of disabled people (Shakespeare et al 1996; Galvin 2003), to the point where any healthy expression of sexuality might be perceived as deviant (Finger 1992). The lack of recognition that sexuality is an integral part of everyone's being has resulted in silences around disabled people's sexuality, which contributes to an air of mystification or, at worst, prurience about it.

In South Africa, sexual behaviour and expression are taboo where young disabled people – especially girls – are concerned; their sexuality is deemed to be in need of regulation (to the point of being made invisible) on the basis of their being young, disabled and female. Because their sexualities are stigmatised and driven under cover, the risk of sexual abuse is increased (Marks 1999; Higson-Smith et al 2004). The lack of information available to young disabled people about issues of sexuality not only negates their right to being acknowledged as sexual beings and expressing their sexuality, it also makes them vulnerable (Fitzmaurice 2002) because they are left unable to negotiate effectively the challenges and opportunities encountered during their transition from adolescence to adulthood and through their life's journeys (Clark and Lillie 2000). In South Africa, intellectually impaired girls and women are two to three times more likely to suffer sexual abuse than their non-disabled peers (Emmett 2006: 213).

Sexual development

Loretta Haroian (2000) describes the ideal path to sexual development as starting at birth with intimate and loving care leading to the progressive development of sexuality from infancy to adulthood. The acceptance and love with which an infant is received at birth, the tenderness and love with which they are nurtured as babies and the quality of care provided during infancy lead to the child's ability to trust and to eventually display tenderness and affection to others. The progressive development of the infant from the toddler stage through to young childhood allows for the exploration of self and body, the first steps to discovering their own bodies and those of others through play, and learning and exploring the rules of the social environment through their mistakes and corrections. This process is the start of the development and building of a positive self-esteem. In this process children learn gender normative rules for social engagement – and daughters learn what it is to be a young woman in their community.

Disabled children experience the development of their sexuality very differently. From infancy the notion of disabled people being asexual is reinforced with close supervision by parents and limited interaction with peers. Throughout their lives disabled children's sexuality is negated and suppressed.

> Disabled children have sexual curiosity and sexual feelings. Despite the conspiracy of silence, they need basic sexual knowledge and information regarding how they can be sexual, given their specific limitations. As adolescents, they need opportunities to experience their sexual response cycle, to learn what their individual sexual limitations and abilities are and perhaps, more importantly, how to negotiate for sex with a partner. (Haroian 2000)

The difference between physical and mental disabilities also impacts differently on a child's sexuality. Children with the former might not conform to society's ideals of physical desirability or 'beauty', while the latter run the risk of being physically acceptable but unable to use discernment in their judgements about sexual situations. All children need clear and unambiguous information about positive sex and sexuality and how to behave with confidence.

Stigma

Throughout most of the world's cultures disability is stigmatised and giving birth to a disabled child is often seen as a disgrace. The traditions that interpret the birth of a disabled child as 'the anger of gods, or the ancestors, or the embodiment of sin in the family or of sin itself' still abound (Disabled People's International 1997). There is abundant research which shows that parents – especially mothers – feel guilt about having a disabled child, sometimes taking the blame for the impairment on themselves (Williams 2001). The stigma against disability pervades families and communities, and even service providers and medical professionals add to the feelings of guilt through their attitudes toward the child and its parents. This often results in the isolation and segregation of the disabled child (Office of the Deputy President, South Africa 1997), and can cause jealousies and tensions with other siblings in the household.

The development path for most disabled youth is very different from that of non-disabled youth. During their formative years, disabled children experience isolation from others and usually undergo clinical care and support other than being loved. As a result of sensing this 'distance' and focus on their bodies as different, the children grow up to dislike their bodies (Burkett 1996; Wendell 1996). Disabled people become unseen components of society, and this invisibility not only perpetuates and reinforces stereotypical beliefs about disability, but also determines and presets the level of their exclusion from development and social exposure (Bjarnason 2003).

Social exclusion increases as young children get older and, when seen, disabled people are pathologised into visibility (McKenzie and Müller 2006). This is the result of the continuous perceptions and emphasis of the differences between non-disabled and disabled children. Anthony Kane (2004) suggests that as many as 60 per cent of children with attention deficit disorders suffer from peer rejection and that children in general reject their disabled peers once differences between them are apparent.

Most disabled young children then seek out friends who are much younger than themselves, because younger children are less aware of the impairment and more accepting of diversity. As the cycle repeats itself, disabled children become more careful in their choices of friends and those with whom they interact, thus providing the growing disabled young child with less opportunity for developing social skills. Findings from the United Kingdom (Morris 2001) and the USA (Khan 1994) indicate that disabled children cannot further their experiences and skills as much as their non-disabled peers, and therefore disabled people remain marginalised in the arena of social development (Gay 2004). Few societies recognise the need for supportive mechanisms that could enable the realisation of disabled people's potential for full participation, self-determination and acceptance. South Africa, however, is fairly advanced on the level of policy in attempting to integrate disabled people into society.[3]

In the United Kingdom, Tom Shakespeare et al (1996) reveal the level of self-doubt and distress experienced by disabled people through exclusion and invisibility, and indicate how levels of acceptance, both by self and others, need to change to engage with debates about disability and sexuality. In South Africa, Brian Watermeyer (2006) speaks eloquently about the psychodynamics of othering when non-disabled people confront people with disabilities. Over and above the need for the recognition of their sexuality and right to sexual expression, within the African context, Adolf Ratzka (2002) indicates how important personal independence is for healthy sexual expression. He indicates that a disabled person's level of personal control over their life is of great significance for sexual liberation. Young women in particular face huge challenges of acceptance and autonomy.

Images of desirability

Part of our acceptance into society is rated by our physique, particularly if we want to 'qualify' as sexual beings (Burkett 1996). Most disabled women bear the brunt of such scrutiny in terms of sexuality: '[l]ooking towards the cultural images of disabled women for a base of positive sexual imagery is confining. In nearly all images, disabled women are presented as asexual beings' (O'Toole 2002: 3). Therefore young disabled women have a particularly tough time projecting themselves as sexual beings.

> Because we have been taught to view disability as a defect, the woman with a disability is regarded as damaged goods ... not seen as desirable or not capable of having sexual desires and lustful needs and wants ... should not indulge in sexual activity because we are not seen as 100 percent 'pure', 'normal' women who are traditionally regarded as receivers of sexual fulfilment, usually by men. (Majiet 1996: 78)

This places young disabled women in a situation in which they have to contend with multiple stereotypes: being female, being disabled and how culture regards the role of women. Merle Froschl and colleagues describe two stereotypes that young disabled girls and women have to contend with: '[t]he "passive, dependent" female and the "helpless and dependent" person with a disability. As a result, they often get a double dose of assistance that can lead to a kind of dependence called *learned helplessness*' (Froschl et al 1990: 3, original emphasis).

In the South African context, young disabled women also have to contend with issues of race and their specific cultural backgrounds. Black disabled women experience few opportunities for socio-economic participation (Office of the Deputy President, South Africa 1997). A young disabled woman might have less chance of obtaining a life partner than a young disabled man because of the cultural perceptions that she is not 'marriageable' (Disability Awareness in Action 1997). Cultural images of disabled women become the focal point in terms of their ability to establish themselves as individual sexual beings within society (O'Toole 2002). Referring to the North/South divide, Zohra Rajah (1991) indicates that for disabled women in the southern hemisphere being accepted and discovering their sexuality are particularly challenging. She further indicates that the more visible the disability, the more likely the label of asexuality. Marita Iglesias and colleagues (1998) describe clearly the discrimination that disabled women experience in terms of marriage and family in the northern context and confirm the statements made by Rajah (1991).

Childbearing

In South Africa, disabled women who used reproductive services spoke about stigmatisation and discrimination (Mgwili and Watermeyer 2006). Service providers asked rude and invasive questions about their sexual relationships, and the decision-making autonomy of women with intellectual impairments was undermined.

Yet, the experience and expression of one's sexuality is an important component for any person to experience a good quality of life.

The isolation and marginalisation that disabled women experience is reflected in popular culture in the South African context (McDougall 2006). Disabled women are perceived to have no role in society and are treated as such (Groce 2004b). Not being seen as having a role to play within society has a negative effect on the self-esteem of disabled women, causing a low level of self-confidence. A positive self-image is an integral part of identity, which in turn is an integral part of sexuality (Kupper et al 1992). Lack of self-esteem as a contributing factor to a positive sexual identity is a profound barrier to social sexual development (O'Toole 2002) and the acceptance of the self as a sexual being. The psychosocial dilemmas experienced by most disabled women demonstrate the level to which confidence and assertiveness are being undermined (Nosek et al 2003).

The physical maturation of young disabled girls into young disabled women, which is accompanied by the emergence of their sexuality, is frequently the cause for increased vigilance and protectiveness by parents, who often treat the young disabled woman as if she were asexual or still a child (Froschl et al 1990). Thus social development and opportunities for social interaction are limited. Washeila Sait's work in the disability sector revealed that because of the challenges experienced by disabled young people – in particular young girls and women – they often find themselves victims of trauma in various ways and at various stages of their lives (Policy Project 2001; Sait 2003).

Writers in the field of disability and sexuality, such as Holly Anne Wade (2002), Karin Melberg Schwier and Dave Hingsburger (2000) and Loretta Haroian (2000), address the issues of vulnerable groups, including intellectually disabled youth, the struggles that they encounter and the low self-esteem they experience in exercising their right to sexual expression (Watermeyer 2006). The more severe the disabilities that people experience, the more excluded they are from social life and the more they are 'protected' against any form or expression of sexuality. Persons with a lesser form of disability are far more likely to have opportunities to learn about sexuality through social interaction.

Disabled young girls and women are categorised as vulnerable within the disability rights movement and sectors in both developed and developing countries (Groce 2003, 2004a). The particular traumatic experiences that they encounter, such as coerced or forced sterilisation (Pfeiffer 1994; Mgwili and Watermeyer 2006), the use of birth control medications in early life (Mgwili and Watermeyer 2006), rape and sexual abuse and unwanted pregnancies attest to their vulnerability and have a direct bearing on their expression of sexuality. On the other hand, where young disabled girls and women seek to express their sexuality and to fulfil their womanhood through childbearing or engaging in relationships, these expressions are questioned or denied. From the reproductive health services system they often experience very negative attitudes in response to their requests for assistance (Pfeiffer et al 2003).

> What is striking, quite simply, is the degree to which staff members in the study, although working at a reproductive health setting, were not ready to engage with the sexuality of physically disabled women. Instead, an anxiously

fervent, denying, invalidating, critical, patronising, pitying or shaming set of responses was in evidence, underscoring an experience, within the users, of their participation in reproduction being regarded as illegitimate. (Mgwili & Watermeyer 2006: 271)

Disability as identity

A disabled person is positioned in discourse as a 'marked body'. In Western-centric cultures there is a history of erasure of difference, and humans are valued according to economies of the body. The manner in which people are 'embodied' in discourse is a simultaneous locus of power and influences how people 'marked' in a particular way are regulated (Soudien and Baxen 2006). People with 'disabled' bodies are positioned in hierarchies of marginalisation and social exclusion. Braided over and into this general position of being 'marked' is the slippage of pathologised sexualities.

Placing 'disabled' people outside the mainstream leads to misconceptions about disabled people and sexualities and influences the way the intersections between disabilities and sexualities are understood and integrated at the broader community level (Ingstad and Whyte 1995; Swartz and Watermeyer 2006). The outcomes are significantly unequal power relations that have effects on social interactions between disabled and non-disabled people (Thomas 2004). In most instances these expectations of 'disability' as other become inhibiting factors to accepting difference, and perpetuate the many forms of discrimination that disabled people experience (Taylor et al 1997). The impact of exclusion from mainstream opportunities, such as education and socialisation, undermines the confidence and assertiveness of people born with disabilities as opposed to those who become disabled in later adult life. The invisibility of disabled people that exclusion creates therefore affirms the notion that '[d]isability is a social identity and not a consequence of physical changes' (Shakespeare et al 1996: 57).

The sexuality of disabled people is a cornerstone of self-esteem (Watermeyer 2006) and consequently an important facet – both for individuals and society at large – of mainstreaming issues of disability in a country proud of its diversity. The social controls and regulation over disabled people in their social interactions and sexuality become matters of human rights. For young disabled girls it implies positive rights in access to information about their sexualities. The strong tradition of cultural silences around speaking to young people about sexuality lest they are encouraged to 'do it' has slowly been whittled away in the face of the HIV/AIDS pandemic (Swartz et al 2006). But with disabled youth, who are perceived as perpetual children and perpetually dependent, these taboos have not disappeared (Collins 2001).

A young adolescent woman with intellectual disabilities might be quite 'normal' in physical and sexual development, and be selected as a potential sex partner by a peer or an adult. Impaired mental function might, however, disallow good judgement in sexual situations. Their own sexual desire, coupled with this lack of discrimination, makes these young women easy targets for sexual exploitation. The mentally disabled young adult needs explicit sex education, reinforced, plainly stated rules about socio-sexual conduct, adequate supervision and effective birth control at the appropriate age. Disabled young women need safe places where they can have successful and safe experiences of sexuality.

The Northern Cape Office on the Status of Persons with Disabilities (OSPD 2003) argues that lack of access to sexuality education, the refusal of parents to accept sexuality as part of the growing disabled child and the isolated manner in which young disabled people live contribute to negative attitudes toward disabled people and the dismissal of their sexual identity. The dismissal of disabled people as sexual beings therefore not only relates to the impairment experienced, but also to the cultural norms and standards about issues of sexuality and disability that have been set in contemporary South African society.

The challenges of parenting

The parenting challenges for most of the biological mothers who participated in the study had their beginnings in ill health prior to and after the birth of their daughters. It was experiences such as these that influenced the manner in which the mothers would interact with their daughters in later life:

> When I was pregnant I experienced many problems with my teeth … my stomach was very small. I could not eat properly … the pain went right through my ears … when the child was born, she was very small. (Mother M1, Kimberley, June 2005)

> And they told me … when I raise the child, I need to remember to give the child water … the water would keep the child clean. The shunt will not get blocked. If the child does not drink water, the shunt will get blocked, and when the shunt gets blocked, then the child's head will grow bigger. This really scared me. (Mother C1, Kimberley, June 2005)

The foster care mothers and familial guardians could not inform on the birth history and conditions of pregnancy that the biological mothers of their daughters experienced, but they indicated the background context of the girls:

> T was born prematurely; her late mother was staying in the same house with me … her mother was drinking very much. And during pregnancy she used to fall a lot … by the time she was born, she was very small. For years she [the mother] was drinking very, very bad and my brother took her to the social worker. (Mother P, Kimberley, June 2005)

These experiences of ill health prior to birth, problems experienced after the birth and the impact of poor health management during pregnancy impacted on how the girls were received and later cared for (Melberg et al 2000). Most of the biological mothers who experienced problems with the impairment of the girls after their birth were not counselled. Only two mothers reported that they received counselling.

Reproductive health of the girls

The necessity to start teaching young disabled girls about issues of menstruation at an early age (Melberg et al 2000) is borne out in this study. Having an early start to information and training, Melberg et al argue, lessens the anxieties about menstruation that so many girls in general experience, but even more so girls with an intellectual disability. Most of the mothers in this study did not engage with their daughters about what menstruation is all about or teach them how to manage it. Instead, the mothers made decisions to use medical interventions, including medication for birth control in the form of injections, sterilisation procedures and in some cases complete hysterectomies to lessen the problems of unwanted children.

Educating the girls about menstruation

The intensity of the mothers' challenges around reproductive health came to the fore when the mothers spoke about the problems they encountered when the girls started to menstruate. Issues of communication about menstruation, its management and trying to make the girls understand what was happening were all struggles that occupied the mothers. One of the girls started to menstruate early on in her life, at the age of nine. The nature of her intellectual impairment was such that, although she had some understanding, she struggled to follow the hygiene requirements. As a result, the mother found herself in very difficult situations. She explained:

> Yes, it looks to me that she actually wants to ask me, but it look like it is difficult for her to ask me ... 'Now what is happening, what is this thing, why do I have to get this thing every time?' Now, when she is sick, no, she just keeps quiet. You will just see at times, when maybe she goes to sit, or when it starts to smell, and the menstruation is very strong. She has it twice a month. And it is a very, very lot. I wash for five days[4] ... now the little one [sibling] ... now and then I do not see that she has her period, now she plays with the little ones and they play outside. Then I hear the little one say, 'Mamma, there is blood on M's pantie.' Oh God, then I know it is that time of the month again and then I have to call her. Then she is stubborn too, because then she does not come when I call her because she knows that she will be wearing the black pantie. Then I just have to beg her, but she remains stubborn. That child gives a person stress, oh my! (Mother MK, Kimberley, June 2005)

The struggles of dealing with menstruation management in this case were very profound. The fact that some of the girls did not clearly understand what was happening to their bodies, given the level of intellectual impairment, caused a strain to most of the mothers:

> When she was menstruating, sometimes she can be so strange, and now if she menstruates, she does not tell me in the morning that she is menstruating, she

just puts her pantie on and then she goes off to school. And then, when she gets to school, then they see that she has been bleeding. (Mother J, Kimberley, June 2005)

Sometimes when she gets her period, she just takes the stuff [sanitary pads]. Then she says to her father come and help here. And then her father helps and then he tells me come and help! (Mother M2, Kimberley, June 2005)

Some of the parents said that they have initiated education about dealing with menstruation. They tried to teach the girls through examples and demonstrations. This became a strenuous task, because the mothers had to repeat it time and again. They had to give detailed explanations for each action to enable the girls to understand:

'You must wash yourself,' and I gave her one of my pads, 'here is a pad and put it on. Every time, you do not flush it through the toilet, because the toilet will block. Every time that it is dirty, just call me and I will show you.' I know that he [she] will place it in a plastic bag and I know how I am going to work with it. That is all; 'You rinse it well so that it does not show. You must not let the boys at home know by any chance that a girl inside the house is menstruating.' (Mother P, Kimberley, June 2005)

Another mother had the support and assistance of her eldest daughter:

Oh, I had a very difficult time until her eldest sister came to the rescue. So she told her, 'You must never let mamma struggle so. You must see to it that you do not do this again. When you have your periods, you need to close yourself up. You must not sit down roughly; you must not do that' ... Now he [she] knows about the pads. He [she] says, 'Hey, I am looking for my pads, I need them.' When he [she] goes to school, I must put one inside the bag and wrap it in plastic. When she comes from school, the one that is dirty, then she takes it out and he [she] will put in another one, whether it is the other way around or whether it is placed in skew as long as it is in, and then he [she] comes and tell me that it is in ... until he [she] got used to it. No, now she knows ... so it is mainly that kind of work, because now she is a bit older and it looks like she does understand a bit just so, just so. (Mother C1, Kimberley, June 2005)

Unwanted pregnancies

The mothers cited various reasons as to why they resorted to medical intervention measures to manage their girls' menstruation. These interventions were carried out with the support of the personnel (teachers) at the special school that the children attended and on the advice of social workers:

But now, there at school, they receive the injection. Yes, the girls there at school ... for the menstruation, because everything ... for family planning ... because they are not right. The others are careless you know. Now the nurses saw that they can hide it [menstruation] for three months. Now after three months then it [menstruation] comes back again and then they give them injections again, every month. They have their clinic cards, which they received, at school. (Mother MS, Kimberley, June 2005)

Another mother agreed that her daughter should have a hysterectomy.

I just felt that it is not good for things to go on like this, and lately, the day after tomorrow when I am no more, what is going to happen to her because she is the only girl that I have, and then there are the two boys. Now, my mother-in-law has died, and my own mother has died, and now there is no grandmother to take care of her. So I thought, Ag let them remove it [the womb]. Yes, because that time they were ... it looked like most of the disabled girls, they did it [hysterectomy] then ... when she was at school still, they had removed her womb ... they [teachers] said later on these children will get children and then we will not know whose child it is and then the day after tomorrow when we are no more, then we will not know what is to become of the children. (Mother J, Kimberley, June 2005)

It is evident that the motivations for using medical interventions (and some are of a drastic nature) are not strictly for the purpose of menstruation management, but primarily for the prevention of pregnancy. The reasoning here is similar to that in earlier centuries and, until recently, in the Western world, where disabled women experienced discrimination and gross violation of their reproductive health rights. Pfeiffer (1994) indicates that these enforced controls and discriminatory measures against disabled women within the US context were born of the fear of a few individuals. The measures were supported, adopted and maintained by US society at large, which feared that disabled women would give birth to more disabled children. Involuntary sterilisation was seen, as it is today within the practices that are still enforced in South Africa, to be the most effective method for preventing people with disabilities having their own children and marrying. However, the son of one of the young disabled girls in this study enjoys good health.

Therefore, in our study 'menstruation management' through medical interventions has more to do with prevention of pregnancies. For most of the mothers, it seems that sexuality is linked to sexual intercourse and childbearing. Birth control becomes uppermost in their minds as soon as their daughters start to menstruate. Washeila sensed that most of the parents believe that interventions of this nature could also reduce sexual activity (Melberg Schwier and Hingsburger 2000). The majority of these well-meaning mothers also thought that it would reduce their daughters' vulnerability to sexual abuse. Although the mothers took decisions on behalf of their girls in terms of their reproductive health rights, the girls spoke about their dreams of getting married and having children: 'I want to be a mother and have my own home and have children and be married' said one of the girls (Girl R, Kimberley, June 2005), and another stated, 'I want to get married someday because I want to have a big family and I want to be a responsible mother' (Girl V, Kimberley, June 2005).

This indicates that the girls wanted to have 'normal' gender identities. Most of these girls were not aware that they had been sterilised, or that they could not get pregnant because of contraception. This puts the nature of informed consent for medical procedures on the table.[5] On the one hand, the mothers argued that the girls were not mentally capable of understanding issues of sexuality, or what menstruation was about (having babies), yet on the other hand they asserted that the professionals concerned with the hysterectomy or birth control procedures informed the girls:

> At school they told them. Because if they remove her womb they needed to tell her what they are going to do and why they were doing it ... they [professionals] told her so that she does not menstruate any more ... 'because, if you menstruate, the possibility is there that you could have a baby, and if you have a baby, what will you do with the child?' She always says that she does not want a child because she does not know. (Mother J, Kimberley, June 2005)

When the mothers communicate with their daughters about sexuality, they limit it to information that is aimed both at preventing pregnancies and discouraging the girls from entering into relationships with the opposite sex. They do this by instilling a fear of pregnancy, in the hopes of minimising risk and harm. Although most mothers discouraged their daughters from sexual interactions when they started to menstruate, those with disabled daughters put more pressure on them to abstain. The information confused the girls and had an impact on their self-images. Instead of allowing the girls to develop a sense of dignity and pride in themselves as young women, instilling fears of pregnancy was uppermost in the minds of their mothers. The mothers translated these fears into protecting and controlling the girls inside and outside the home.

Protection

The mothers were deeply concerned about the well-being of their daughters, and put in place a variety of protective measures both inside and outside the home environment to ensure the safety of their children.

Inside the home

The strict measures the mothers implemented were a result of their own deep fears that their daughters might be harmed. The mothers were deeply distrustful of anyone they thought could possibly be dangerous to their daughters. This distrust was aimed not only at the community, but also to within the home environment. One of the main reasons for this overwhelming need for strict protection measures stemmed from the crime-ridden context in which they lived. The burden of protection placed an enormous amount of stress on the parents:

I could not go anywhere without that child. If I had to go out, to church, I could not leave her alone at home at night. My husband is at home, I have a son at home, and my son is 23 years of age … You know he is a very soft person. He will help, he talks a lot, he protects a lot, and the little ones also talk. But I do not trust him, you can't trust. I do not trust them [husband and son] at all. If I go, I have to make sure that I take them[6] to my little sister if I have to take the train, or I take them with me. I take them along; I do not leave them behind. Because they are girls … More so when it comes to my own husband, I do not trust anything, because when the man is at home, that's when the things are happening … A person cannot come off the street and then to rape the child in your home. It is the one who takes care of him [her] every day, he sees that and then he gets these devilish thoughts and then he mounts this small child. You see; look at all the babies that are being raped. Now that is the thing, I don't trust anybody with my child, with my girls. (Mother MS, Kimberley, June 2005)

The mistrust of the male members of the household was also based on the acute awareness of the mothers that their daughters had evolved into young women. The mothers felt they needed to be more vigilant and protective. This vigilance and protectiveness stemmed from the fear that the girls might attract unwanted attention and interest from the opposite sex that would cause more harm than good. This principle of keeping an ever watchful eye on their daughters was also indicative of the mothers' understanding of the threatening context of the broader community environment.

The stress of ensuring that the girls were safe and protected at all times placed a strain on the family relationships within the home. The mothers expressed a great deal of mistrust of their husbands and sons, which created a barrier to the development of interpersonal relationships between fathers and daughters, as well as between the girls and their brothers:

Sometimes, as we are going out like now, to workshops and so on, you have to tell him [her] already. It does not mean that I do not trust my children, but I cannot trust them because they are male children. Look, my child, you can trust him, but the devil is so strong, they [sons] can use that child [with intellectual impairment], such things. Now the one thing that I always do, he [she] has to be sure, he [she] must be able to take care of himself [herself] … you must always keep him [her] busy, like in the yard. And then I teach him [her] the code of the phone, and I show him [her] he [she] just needs to do so and so [use of the telephone] if he [she] feels a bit scared, you see? (Mother C1, Kimberley, June 2005)

Threat of rape

In an environment in which sexual abuse and rape occur daily, the mothers indicated that they were forced to plan for and undertake extreme measures to ensure the safety and preserve the innocence of their young daughters. They therefore made conscious decisions about the protection measures that they would apply should their daughters' safety be compromised. They indicated that they had diligently taught their daughters what steps to take in the event of being raped. One mother explained:

> There are male children that court, and there are others that hurt your child, they want to stab him [her] with the knife. Now, tell the child if he [she] gets accosted by someone like that, he [she] must just give in, he [she] must say take the condom then. If he [she] gives the condom let him get on with her with the condom, so that he does not kill her. Many of our children gets killed, they get killed and hurt because of that thing [rape]. Because they fight with the child, and he does not want to understand anything, and she does not want to understand anything. Now this one starts to kill him [her], stab him [her] with the knife, they do that with roughness. Now if he [she] sees he [she] can't, there is no chance, then he [she] just has to take out the condom and choose. Now if he uses that then it is right. You see, he will let him [her] go, and you will be happy. He will get on with your child, finish, and your child will still be alive. And then the AIDS are also not there, you see. This is the only way that you can help your girl child. (Mother MS, Kimberley, June 2005)

It was clear that the mothers found themselves in a Catch-22 situation: they needed to weigh up their options and decide which was the better of two evils: the rape or killing of their child, or the possibility that the child might survive a rape, but contract HIV. The trauma alone of having to make such decisions had a severe impact on the psychological health of the mothers. As one of the mothers put it, 'I did say ... if the sickness has not been inside your home, then you will not feel the pain. If it comes to your house at first, then you will feel that pain (Mother P, Kimberley, June 2005).

In this context, some of the mothers gave their daughters condoms and told them what to do in case of being raped.

Conclusion

Challenging living conditions among the participants introduced limitations to the young disabled women's expression of sexuality awareness. The poor socio-economic environment further impeded their access to sexuality information and expression. Such conditions limited discussions between the mothers and daughters about sex and sexuality, and the expression thereof. Lack of information and training on the part of the mothers was an additional constraint to generating these discussions and assisting the development of positive self-identities in their daughters.

That the mothers participating in this study managed thus far is admirable, but we could not imagine how they would continue to do so in the face of the growing needs of the maturing girls, and the new and daily challenges for which the mothers were clearly unprepared. In the absence of appropriate and supportive mechanisms, the shaping and nurturing of disabled girls' sexuality remains a complex issue for most mothers.

Notes

1. An earlier version of this essay was published in Steyn and van Zyl (HSRC Press, 2009). Reproduced with permission.
2. Though these grants should technically be used only for the disabled person, they support households that have no other form of income. Regarding the tensions in the social security system, see Swartz and Schneider (2006).
3. South Africa's integrated national disability strategy is the policy blueprint for addressing disability in South Africa. Mainstream structures such as the Office on the Status of Disabled Persons are charged with its implementation. See Howell et al (2006) for a history of the disability movement in South Africa.
4. This mother was clearly at a loss about how to interact and engage with her daughter. The interviewer observed that she was very tired and found it difficult to deal with her daughter's menstruation.
5. Legislation in South Africa allows for people with mental disabilities to be sterilised with the consent of their parents or guardians (Sterilisation Act 44 of 1998).
6. The mother is fostering two girls, of whom only one is disabled. She has been instructed by the social services system to ensure that the girls are protected at all times, even within the home, and she follows these instructions to the letter.

References

Barnes, C. (2001) 'Rethinking care from the perspective of disabled people: Conference report and recommendations', June, http://whqlibdoc.int/hq/2001/a78624.pdf, accessed 18 September 2003

Bjarnason, D.S. (2003) 'Students' voices: how does education in Iceland prepare young people with significant impairments for adulthood?', paper presented at the European Conference on Educational Research, Hamburg, University of Hamburg, September, http://www.leeds.ac.uk/educol/documents/00003410.htm, accessed 10 December 2004

Burkett, B. (1996) 'Believe in yourself – GET SEXY', in *Disabled People's Coalition Magazine*, http://www.leeds.ac.uk/disabilitystudies/archiveuk/burkitt/believe%20in%20yourself.pdf, accessed 24 September 2003

Clark, S.G. and Lillie, T. (2000) 'Growing up with disabilities: education, law and the transition to adulthood', *Disabilities Studies Quarterly* 20(4): 472–488

Collins, P.Y. (2001) 'Dual taboos: Sexuality and women with severe mental illness in South Africa: Perceptions of mental health care providers', *AIDS and Behaviour* 5(2): 151–161

Davies, D. (2000) 'Facilitating sex and relationships for people with disabilities: the right to be sexual – a radical proposal', paper presented at conference titled Disability, Sexuality and Culture: Societal and Experiential Perspectives on Multiple Identities, 16–18 March, http://www.bentvoices.org/culturecrash/daviessarfp.htm, accessed 26 March 2002

Deepak, S. (2002) 'Male, female or disabled: barriers to expression of sexuality', MA thesis in disability studies, Leeds, University of Leeds, Department of Sociology and Social Policy

Disability Awareness in Action (1997) 'Disabled women: Resource kit no. 6', London, in-house publication

Disabled People's International (1997) 'Right to life and development', Child Rights Information Network, 10 June, http://www.crin.org/resources/infoDetail.asp?ID=1641, accessed 24 September 2006

Emmett, T. (2006) 'Disability, poverty, gender and race', in Watermeyer, B., Swartz, L., Lorenzo, T., Schneider M. and Priestley, M. (eds) *Disability and Social Change: A South African Agenda*, Cape Town, Human Sciences Research Council Press

Finger, A. (1992) 'Forbidden fruit: Why shouldn't disabled people have sex or become parents?', *New Internationalist* 233, July, http://www.newint.org/issue233/fruit.htm, accessed 24 September 2006

Fitzmaurice, S. (2002) 'Adventures in child-rearing: The sexual life of a child growing up with Down Syndrome', *Disability Studies Quarterly* 22(4): 28–40

Froschl, M., Rubin, E. and Sprung, B. (1990) 'Having a daughter with a disability: Is it different for girls?', *National Information Centre for Children and Youth with Disabilities (NICHCY) News Digest* 14, http://www.nichcy.org/pubs/outprint/nd14.pdf, accessed 25 September 2006

Galvin, R. (2003) 'The making of the disabled identity: A linguistic analysis of marginalisation', *Disability Studies Quarterly* 23(2): 149–178

Gay, H. (2004) 'Social integration and employees with a disability: Their view', *Disability Studies Quarterly* 24(1), http://www.dsq-sds.org/_articles_pdf/2003/Spring/dsq_2003_Spring_14.pdf# search=% 22Gay%2C%20H%20disabled%20identity%22, accessed 24 September 2006

Ghai, A. (2001) 'Marginalisation and disability: experiences from the third world', in Priestly, M. (ed) *Disability and the Life Course: Global Perspectives*, Cambridge, Cambridge University Press

Groce, N.E. (2003) 'HIV/AIDS and people with disability', *The Lancet* 361(9367): 1401–03

—— (2004a) 'Adolescents and youth with disability: issues and challenges. Report to the World Bank', *Asia Pacific Disability Rehabilitation Journal* 15(2): 13–32, http://www.aifo.it/english/resources/online/apdrj/apdrj204/adolescent.pdf, accessed 26 September 2006

—— (2004b) 'People with disabilities', seminar delivered at Disabled Children Action Group (DICAG), Johannesburg, 15 March

Hallum, A. (1995) 'Disability and the transition to adulthood: issues for the disabled child, the family and the pediatrician', *Current Problems Pediatrician Review* 25(1): 12–50

Haroian, L. (2000) 'Child sexual development', *Electronic Journal of Human Sexuality* 3 (1 February), http://www.ipce.info/library_3/files/ch_sx_dev.htm, accessed 25 September 2006

Higson-Smith, C., Lamprecht, L. and Jacklin, L. (2004) 'Access to specialist services and the criminal justice system: Data from the Teddy Bear clinic', in Richter, L., Dawes, A. and Higson-Smith, C. (eds) *Sexual Abuse of Young Children in Southern Africa*, Cape Town, Human Sciences Resources Council Press

Howell C., Chalklen, S. and Alberts, T. (2006) 'A history of the disability rights movement in South Africa', in Watermeyer, B., Swartz, L., Lorenzo, T., Schneider, M. and Priestley, M. (eds) *Disability and Social Change: A South African Agenda*, Cape Town Human Sciences Research Council Press

Iglesias M., Gil, G., Joneken, A., Mickler, B. and Knudsen, J.S. (1998) 'Violence and disabled women', METIS project, European Union DAPHNE initiative, http://www.independentliving.org/docs1/iglesiasetal1998.html, accessed 24 September 2006

Ingstad B. and Whyte, S.R. (eds) (1995) *Disability and Culture*, Berkeley, University of California Press

Kane, A. (2004) 'Why other children are rejecting your child', June http://addadhdadvances.com/peerrejection.html, accessed September 2006

Khan S.R. (1994) 'Play therapy groups: Case studies of prevention, reparation, and protection through children's play', *Journal of Child and Adolescent Group Therapy* 3: 48–53

Kupper, L., Ambler, L. and Valdivieso, C. (1992) 'Sexuality education for children and youth with disabilities', *NICHCY News Digest* 1(3), http://www.nichcy.org/pubs/outprint/nd17.pdf, accessed 24 September 2006

Louw, A. and Shaw, M. (1997) 'Contextualising crime and poverty', monograph 14, *Stolen Opportunities*, July, http://www.iss.co.za/PUBS/MONOGRAPHS/No14/Part2.html, accessed 9 August 2008

Majiet, S. (1996) 'Sexuality and disability', *Agenda* 28: 77–80

Marks, D. (1999) *Disability: Controversial Debates and Psychosocial Perspectives*, London, Routledge

Max-Neef, M.A. (1991) *Human Scale Development: Conception, Application and Further Reflections*, London, Apex Press

McDougall, K. (2006) '"Ag shame" and superheroes: stereotypes and the signification of disability', in Watermeyer, B., Swartz, L., Lorenzo, T., Schneider, M. and Priestley, M. (eds) *Disability and Social Change: A South African Agenda*, Cape Town, Human Sciences Research Council Press

McKenzie, J. and Müller, B. (2006) 'Parents and therapists: Dilemmas in partnership', in Watermeyer, B., Swartz, L., Lorenzo, T., Schneider, M. and Priestley, M. (eds) *Disability and Social Change: A South African Agenda*, Cape Town, Human Sciences Research Council Press

Melberg Schwier, K. and Hingsburger, D. (2000) *Sexuality: Your Sons and Daughters with Intellectual Disabilities*, Baltimore, Paul H. Brookes Publishing

Mgwili, V.N. and Watermeyer, B. (2006) 'Physically disabled women and discrimination in reproductive health care: Psychoanalytic reflections', in Watermeyer, B., Swartz, L., Lorenzo, T., Schneider, M. and Priestley, M. (eds) *Disability and Social Change: A South African Agenda*, Cape Town, Human Sciences Research Council Press

Morris, S. (2001) 'Social exclusion and young disabled people with high levels of support needs', paper presented at the London Borough of Newham conference on social exclusion and young people, May

Naudé, J. (2001) 'Sexuality and disability – integrating the two?', *Echoes* 19: 23–26

Nosek, M.A., Hughes, R.B., Swedlund, N., Taylor, H.B. and Swank, P. (2003) 'Self-esteem and women with disabilities', *Social Sciences Medical Journal* 56(8): 1737–47

Office of the Deputy President (1997) *White Paper on an Integrated National Disability Strategy*, Pretoria, Rustica Press

Office on the Status of Persons with Disabilities (OSPD) (2003) 'Provincial programme of action on disability 2003–2007: celebrating disability in our decade of democracy', Kimberley, Office of the Premier

O'Toole, C.J. (2002) 'Sex, disability and motherhood: Access to sexuality for disabled mothers', *Disability Studies Quarterly* 22(4): 81–101, http://www.dsq-sds.org/_articles_pdf/2002/ Fall/dsq_2002_Fall_08. pdf, accessed 24 September 2006

Peet, K. and Peet, J. (2000) 'Poverties and satisfiers: a systems look at human needs: creating a new democracy', seminar delivered at the Devnet conference, Wellington, New Zealand, 17–19 November.

Pfeiffer, D. (1994) 'Eugenics and disability discrimination', *Disability and Society* 9(4): 481–99, http://www.independentliving.org/?docs1/pfeiffe1.html, accessed September 2006

Pfeiffer, D., Ah Sam, A., Guinan, M., Ratliffe, K.T., Robinson, N.B. and Stodden, N.J. (2003) 'Attitudes toward disability in the helping professions', *Disability Studies Quarterly* 23(2): 123–139

Policy Project (2001) 'Learning through practice: HIV/AIDS and disability', A final workshop report, Cape Town, Policy Project

Rajah, Z. (1991) 'Thoughts on women and disability', in Driedger, D. (ed) *Disabled People in International Development*, Winnipeg, The Coalition of Provincial Organisations of the Handicapped, http://www.independentliving.org./docs1/dispeopleintldev.pdf, accessed 26 September 2006

Ratzka, A.D. (2002) 'Sexuality and people with disabilities: What experts often are not aware of', http://www.independentliving.org/docs5/Sexuality.html, accessed 26 September 2006

Sait, W. (2003) 'Gender, sexuality and masculinity: in the context of disability', unpublished report for Soul City, Johannesburg

Shakespeare, T., Gillespie-Sells, K. and Davies, D. (1996) *The Sexual Politics of Disability: Untold Desires*, London and New York, Cassell Academic Press

Shue, K.L. and Flores, A. (2002) 'Whose sex is it anyway? Freedom of exploration and expression of sexuality of an individual living with brain injury in a supported independent living environment', *Disability Studies Quarterly* 22(4): 59–72

Shuttleworth, R.P., Roberts, E. and Mona, M. (2002) 'Disability and sexuality: towards a focus of sexual access', *Disability Studies Quarterly* 22(4): 2–9

Soudien, C. and Baxen, J. (2006) 'Disability and schooling in South Africa', in Watermeyer, B., Swartz, L., Lorenzo, T., Schneider, M. and Priestley, M. (eds) *Disability and Social Change: A South African Agenda*, Cape Town, Human Sciences Research Council Press

Stats SA (Statistics South Africa) (2001) *Census 2001: Census in Brief*, Pretoria, Statistics South Africa

Stats SA (2003) 'Provincial profile 1999: Northern Cape report, no. 00-91-03', Pretoria, Statistics South Africa

Steyn, Melissa and van Zyl, Mikki (2009) *The Prize and the Price: Shaping Sexualities in South Africa*, Cape Town, Human Sciences Research Council Press

Swartz, L. and Schneider, M. (2006) 'Tough choices: disability and social security in South Africa', in Watermeyer, B., Swartz, L., Lorenzo, T., Schneider, M. and Priestley, M. (eds) *Disability and Social Change: A South African Agenda*, Cape Town, Human Sciences Research Council Press

Swartz L., Schneider, M. and Rohleder, P. (2006) 'HIV/AIDS and disability: new challenges', in Watermeyer, B., Swartz, L., Lorenzo, T., Schneider, M. and Priestley, M. (eds) *Disability and Social Change: A South African Agenda*, Cape Town, Human Sciences Research Council Press

Swartz, L. and Watermeyer, B. (2006) 'Introduction and overview', in Watermeyer, B., Swartz, L., Lorenzo, T., Schneider M. and Priestley M. (eds) *Disability and Social Change: A South African Agenda*, Cape Town, Human Sciences Resources Council Press

Taylor, S., Rizvi, F., Lingard, B. and Henry, M. (1997) *Education Policy and the Politics of Change*, London, Routledge

Thomas, C. (2004) 'Developing the social relational in the social model of disability: A theoretical agenda', in Barnes, C. and Mercer, G. (eds) *Implementing the Social Model of Disability: Theory and Research*, Leeds, The Disability Press

Wade, H.A. (2002) 'Discrimination, sexuality and people with significant disabilities: Issues of access and the right to sexual expression in the United States', *Disability Studies Quarterly* 22(4): 9–27

Watermeyer, B. (2006) 'Disability and psychoanalysis', in Watermeyer, B., Swartz, L., Lorenzo, T., Schneider, M. and Priestley, M. (eds) *Disability and Social Change: A South African Agenda*, Cape Town, Human Sciences Research Council Press

Wendell, S. (1996) *The Rejected Body: Feminist Philosophical Reflections on Disability*, New York, Routledge

Williams, M. (2001) 'Raising a child with a disability', http://ce.byu.edu/cw/fuf/archives/2001/WilliamsMarlene.pdf, accessed 26 September 2006

54

The realities of 'choice' in Africa: implications for sexuality, vulnerability and HIV/AIDS[1]

Chi-Chi Undie

During the last couple of weeks, as I've thought about what I wanted to talk about today, I've been fixated on the term 'choice' and the ways in which this phenomenon plays out in many of our African contexts. The very word, for me, immediately invokes questions which a conference such as this one provides the space for us to consider. First question: what are the realities of 'choice' in African settings and how do these realities shape sexualities, vulnerability and the HIV/AIDS pandemic on the continent?

I was browsing through the conference agenda and I noticed that a key slogan of this conference is the following empowering phrase: *'my sexuality, my choice, my right'* – and since the phrase is italicised, I read it with an emphasis on the word *my*. Despite the liberating effect that these words undoubtedly have, in considering them, I was confronted by a series of questions: to what extent is choice an individualistic and linear phenomenon in African contexts? What do we gain by making the assumption that it is? What do we lose by addressing the possibility that it might not be?

If we talk about choice without considering how this concept is embedded in (and, thus, informed by) perceptions of culture, prescriptions by religion, economic realities, the realities of stigma and discrimination, and the legitimised censoring of sexual and reproductive health information, for instance, how much choice are we really offering to prospective rights holders? Are we merely holding forth an ephemeral concept?

I'm convinced that, in many African settings, when we employ this term, we are rarely talking about a singular choice. More often than not, we're grappling with a multiplicity of choices and players/stakeholders – some of whom (or of which) prevail today, others of which might prevail tomorrow. A key question therefore seems to be: in each instance in which choice emerges as an issue, whose choice prevails? How? And why? And what are the implications of these dynamics for sexuality/ sexualities, vulnerability and HIV/AIDS?

To explore this issue, I could introduce any number of topics that intersect with the broad topic of choice, sexuality, vulnerability and HIV/AIDS. I could talk about young people living with HIV and the ways in which their choices are constrained and their sexuality is forcibly shaped by censoring much-needed sexual and reproductive health information, or by prescribing what sexuality should mean for them. I could focus, for instance, on people living with disabilities. I could talk about coercive sex and the utter lack of choice. With the allotted time, however, it is impossible to touch on every imaginable issue. I am therefore limiting myself to just one concrete, vivid scenario to illustrate these points further.

The scenario centres on married couples. There was a time when married people were seen as being among the least interesting research subjects. Those days are gone. As we now know, marriage is no longer necessarily a sanctuary of sexual safety (Glynn et al 2003; PAI 2008). Given the reticence on the use of condoms within (as opposed to outside) marriage (Chimbiri 2007), marital sex in Africa is now increasingly acknowledged as amounting to risky sex.

In the last three months or so, I have become acquainted (either directly or indirectly) with five heterosexual women in the city that I work in, all of whom are either currently married or were once married to men who have sex with men. Most decided to dissolve the union when they became aware of this reality. One is currently in the process of deciding what to do next – whether to leave or stay. From my perspective as a qualitative researcher, an 'n' (sample size) of one is as 'significant' as an 'n' of five or 500. I was struck and intrigued by the common themes that emerged from the stories of these women. They were all initially pleased and, indeed, relieved, to observe that their partners seemed to have little interest in other women because that gave them the impression that they had 'married well', choosing committed men to spend the rest of their lives with. Secondly, they were all similarly concerned, puzzled and hurt by their husbands' lack of sexual desire, which they later came to realise was a lack of sexual desire for them as women.

Thirdly and most strikingly, most of them were proactive about employing carefully crafted strategies for enhancing their husbands' sexual desire. Their stories were strikingly similar to the extent that several of these women picked out the same exotic location, took their husbands on a trip there, armed with sexy negligées and on a mission to get their sexual needs met. The efforts of each of these women failed miserably. In one instance, the woman was shunned and accused by her spouse of being hypersexual. Ironically, she was a newly-wed and had only had sex twice in that year. In another instance, the woman's spouse was so repulsed by the idea of having sexual relations with his wife that he vomited.

The question is: who is exercising choice in a scenario such as this? Is it the men in this example, who had their sexual liaisons with other men on the side (and were therefore being 'true', in a sense, to their sexual orientation), but at the same time sought out marriage partners of the opposite sex, perhaps to fulfil societal/familial obligations? Is it the women who chose these men as life partners – women who, for the most part, chose to leave their husbands, even though a dissolved union was not what any of them really wanted? This is an example that demonstrates that our choices are often informed by many factors other than ourselves or what we truly desire.

As I'm sure we can appreciate, choice – though it has been an important buzzword for a long time – once unpacked, can be seen as a much more complex concept than its simple name suggests. As a poignant example of how choice and sexuality are intertwined with vulnerability, one of these women – the one that is yet to make up her mind about what to do about her situation – is now most likely HIV positive. Incidentally, all of the men in this true story happen to be living with HIV, although none of their wives were privy to this critical piece of information.

How much choice do we have if we can only be our authentic selves in a clandestine fashion? How much choice do any of us really have when we lack relevant information? The lack of knowledge, which translates into lack of true/informed choice, gives rise to vulnerability and plays a major role in fuelling the HIV pandemic.

I, personally, love the liberty that informed choice can afford. I'm all for choice provided it is allowed to develop in a stigma- and discrimination-free environment, and in an environment replete with comprehensive sexual and reproductive health information. I'm all for choice provided it refers to careful and considerate choices, because without care, consideration and responsibility, my choice can mean your vulnerability.

In the words of Rosalind Petchesky: 'We all share a sexuality with its capacity for erotic pleasure, fantasy, exploration, creation, and procreation, as well as danger and abuse. We all share a body, with its capacity for health and well-being as well as disease, deterioration, violation and death' (Petchesky 2005, cited in Jolly 2009). And, might I add: we all share a choice. This is why information and knowledge, openness and honesty/truth are so critical. Information and knowledge make room for true choice to exist. Openness turns shame and secrecy on their heads and makes room for honesty, thus ensuring that true choice thrives. In our presentations during this conference, therefore, I look forward to learning, to gaining information and knowledge from all of you, to being inspired by our openness and truthfulness as a group, in order to move this continent closer to the achievement of sexual health and rights.

Thank you.

Notes

1. This paper was originally presented at the 4th Africa Conference on Sexual Health and Rights, 8 February 2010, Addis Ababa, Ethiopia.

References

Chimbiri, A.M. (2007) 'The condom is an 'intruder' in marriage: Evidence from rural Malawi', *Social Science and Medicine* 64(5): 1102–15

Glynn, J.R., Carael, M., Buve, A., Musonda, R.M. and Maina, K. (2003) 'HIV risk in relation to marriage in areas with high prevalence of HIV infection', *Journal of Acquired Immune Deficiency Syndromes* 33(4): 526–35

Jolly, S. (2009) 'Sexuality and poverty: What have they got to do with each other?', in Izugbara, C.O., Undie, C. and Khamasi, J.W. (eds) *Old Wineskins, New Wine: Readings in Sexuality in Sub-Saharan Africa*, New York, Nova Science Publishers

Petchesky, R. (2005) 'Rights of the body and perversions of war: Sexual rights and wrongs ten years past Beijing', *UNESCO's International Social Science Journal*, 57: 301–18

Population Action International (PAI) (2008) 'The silent partner: HIV in marriage', Washington DC, PAI, http://www.populationaction.org/Publications/Fact_Sheets/FS37/SP_Factsheet.pdf, accessed 25 January 2010

55

Wet towel

Lombe Mwambwa

I am a soggy towel;
Heavy and sodden with dark emotion and thought,

Used to be high absorbent,
Used to be fluffy and comfy.

I am a soggy towel
Absorbed the complaints, the indifference
The cruelty and heart break,

Sucked in the insults, the ill treatment
Sucked in the lies and the fake smiles

I am a soggy towel
Heavy and sodden with sweat, blood and tears

But of what use is a wet towel?

Some one please wring me and hang me out to dry!

56

Challenges of sexuality and ageing in a barren woman: interview with Ssejja

Edith Okiria

My interview with senior citizen Ssejja was part of my exploration of women and men's perceptions of gender, sexuality and ageing in the rural Butebo sub-county of eastern Uganda. Gender relations structure the entire life cycle from birth to old age, influencing access to resources and opportunities and shaping life choices at every stage. The relevance of gender is both ongoing and cumulative; the differences that shape the lives of men and women in old age are the outcome of the many different opportunities, challenges and constraints that they have gone through in life.

My study revealed that the women were more comfortable talking about their sexuality than the men. It clearly showed that there is need for continued dialogue about sexuality for people to share their experiences. There were varying levels of understanding of sexuality and ageing. Women generally did not relate sexuality and ageing to their reproductive lives but rather to their individual feelings, health and relationships. Men, on the other hand, equated their sexuality to health status rather than age, because they believed that men stayed sexually active throughout life.

The following is my interview with Ssejja.

Q: **How old are you?**
A: I think over 80 years old but I am not sure. I know that I am very old.

Q: **Have you ever been married?**
A: Yes, I got married when I was about 15 years to a man much older than me. I stayed with him for about 10 years but we did not have any children. We used to work very hard and lacked nothing in our household. He was really a loving man.

Q: **Why did you leave your husband?**
A: He was a very loving man but very jealous at the same time. I was the last born of my mother so I visited her very often. We had a very strong bond so I would miss her a lot. My husband did not like the idea, so we had a lot of conflict over that. He was always suspicious that I had other men and that was why I claimed I wanted to visit with my mother all the time. He even confronted my mother and asked her to stop spoiling me. My mother was a very peaceful woman who was now a widow but staying with my brother.

Q: **What happened then?**

A: My husband passed on and since I did not have any children in the home, I had to leave. I could have stayed, been inherited but I felt I was not up to it. I went back to my brother's home to live with him, but if you have been used to some kind of life it is never easy. I decided to remarry since I was not very old. I think I must have been in my late thirties. The man I got remarried to had other wives, I was the third wife.

Q: **How did you cope with a polygynous marriage?**

A: It was not easy at all, because I had never been in a polygynous marriage. The other women had children and yet I was barren. They always assumed I was more loved because I had no children to make my house dirty or share my food. I was hard working so all my efforts were in ensuring that I didn't lack anything. I could afford to dress smartly, buy meat once in a while and generally treated my husband well. We had a very harmonious relationship with my husband. He always looked forward to coming to my house because he allocated each one of us three days then he would move to the next.

Q: **Some people say that women in polygynous marriages are comfortable with it. Is that true?**

A: That is not true because all the time you will be competing for the man's love. That is why you find that there is a lot of witchcraft in polygynous homes. The competition will be between women and even the children. The children are likely to follow what their mothers do. The mothers influence their children as well to behave in a certain way.

Q: **What kind of relationship did you have with your co-wives?**

A: We would have good time together sharing some of our experiences but one of them had a lot of animosity toward me. She never wanted her children to enter my house, she thought since I did not have children, I might kill her children. Such attitudes broke my heart because I did not choose to be barren. She always looked out for any faults with me to make me look like a bad person.

Q: **What made you leave that marriage also?**

A: My husband died and my co-wife immediately claimed that I had killed him. That was a serious allegation so I had to leave, after all there was no reason for me to stay on any more. I did not have any children in that home. I then decided to go back to my place of birth, to my brother. I was also ageing so there was no need to seek marriage again, so my brother agreed that I build my own house on our land.

Q: **What age were you then?**

A: I was more than 45 years because my periods had stopped. However, even then some men still wanted relationships with me. I continued having some casual relationships but from my own home and on my own terms.

Q: **What would you say about your sexual life since you are now quite old?**

A: I did enjoy my youth very much but ageing has been a pain. When you do not have children and you are ageing, there is no one to help you in any way. My brother had his own family to take care of so there is that feeling of loneliness. In fact sometimes I wished I was dead, everyone needs a companion in life. Ageing for a barren woman living on her own can be a challenge, you need someone to share with, to comfort you but all that is in vain. Even when you go out and talk to other people it is not the same as somebody with a family.

Q: **What are society's attitudes towards single ageing women?**

A: You are like a curse in society, nobody seems to respect you. Society will judge you at any given opportunity; they will think you are insensitive.

Q: **In your view, should ageing women continue to be sexually active?**

A: Yes, it is something that keeps everyone happy. We see older men marrying younger women, women also have feelings. Older women who enjoy consuming alcohol go to public drinking places where they sometimes get into sexual relationships after drinking. That means that after drinking they feel sexually aroused and end up sleeping with men. [According to the Uganda Demographic Health survey (2006) it was found that having sex under the influence of alcohol was more common among females in rural areas than urban.]

Q: **Do you think you are better off than a man of your age?**

A: I think it is easier for a woman to cope with loneliness than a man. An ageing man would need a woman to help him in the home like cooking, washing, cleaning etc. There is a higher level of independence in decision making, access and control of resources.

Q: **What advice would you give to younger women?**

A: I would advise them to enjoy themselves while they are still young. They should also behave themselves, because once men know that you are the kind of woman who is available to men all the time, they will never respect you.

Q: **How would you describe your life?**

A: My youth was good but ageing has not been easy, many times I wish I was dead. When I was stronger I used to take good care of myself but now it is a big challenge. People may even forget that you exist, I think when I die, it will take time for people to know that I am dead. I feel like I am a curse in society, I can take days without eating not because I don't want to but because I am too weak to cook. When I feel strong I go and sit with my sisters-in law, spend some time with them. On a positive note, I am lucky that I have a family, my brother's family but some old people live completely alone without any relatives. Without children you become insignificant in society, so the older you grow the more insignificant you become.

57

AIDS sting(ma)

Anonymous

Like north and south…
we were drawn to each other
by the drums of the harvest festival
ecstatic, raw, uninhibited.

In hushed tone, me ask
'What is your status?'
…'I'm clean!'
[Dwarfing pause]
Rendering me dirty
In one stinging swoop.

58

The gold rush – fiction

Isabella Matambanadzo

She was unexpected. Arrived home in the middle of the afternoon having finished a bitterly exhausting shift on the gold mine. One short phrase clamoured in her head: The Riches of the Earth. There was nothing wealthy about her life. She felt poorer than the dirt she sieved through her fingers every day in search of nuggets.

She waited for the bucket to fill. The municipal water was in a bad mood again. Only a weak trickle licked the lips of the tap and dropped, with fatigue, into the hungry plastic of the cheap battered blue bucket. There was enough for her to wash away the layer of ash that covered her skin, turning it from a rich chocolate, to some colour she could never name.

She thought about the supper she wanted to prepare for her children. Worked out how to turn the dull, green leaves into a tasty relish flavoured with the zing of ginger and garlic.

Something drew her mind away from the recipe. A cloud in her home.

Pushing back the kitchen door, she was pleased at the blob of Vaseline she was able to spare to oil the once squeaky hinges into silence.

And there he was. Buttocks exposed, trouser waist resting around the back of his knees. On top of her girl.

Questions for reflection

1.

List some of the sexual stereotypes in the public
discourse that are associated with deviance, asexuality,
immorality, inappropriate behaviour, reproduction and
victimisation. What is the basis of such stereotyping
and how can it be overcome?

2.

Think of some examples that demonstrate how
African traditional sexual morality codes were radically
transformed through the force of imported laws, policies,
religions and education.

3.

How does the state regulate our sexuality?
How do non-state actors, such as family, communities,
religion, education, media and the sex industry, influence
our sexuality? How do we exercise self-censorship in
limiting our sexual capacities? Why?

4.

How have technological advancements facilitated
'pleasure' and 'choice' in African sexualities?
How have they 'damaged' African sexualities?

5.

The common assumption that young girls do not have
sex is partly disproved by the rampant gender-based violence
that exists in our societies, including defilement and incest.
How can this pervasive problem be tackled beyond
the legal means?

Part 8
Sexuality, spirituality and the supernatural

59

Sexuality and the supernatural in Africa

Chimaraoke O. Izugbara

Introduction

Although currently a buzzword, sexuality is certainly a slippery concept, encapsulating sexual expressions, desires, fantasies and behaviour. In 2002, the World Health Organisation (WHO) rescued the concept from imprecision by providing it a working definition. It conceptualised sexuality as 'a central aspect of being human throughout life which encompasses sex, gender identities and roles, sexual orientation, eroticism, pleasure, intimacy and reproduction' (WHO 2006). It also added that:

> Sexuality is experienced and expressed in thoughts, fantasies, desires, beliefs, attitudes, values, behaviours, practices, roles and relationships. While sexuality can include all of these dimensions, not all of them are always experienced or expressed. Sexuality is influenced by the interaction of biological, psychological, social, economic, political, cultural, ethical, legal, historical, religious and spiritual factors. (WHO 2002)

In addition to acknowledging the complexity of sexuality, the above definition bears a long history of research situating sexuality beyond concerns related to health, disease and number of partners. The definition also fundamentally speaks to the legitimacy of research about the underlying social, cultural and economic factors that shape the ways that sex is sought, practised, perceived, deployed and desired and/or rejected by human beings. These include gender identities and roles; sexual orientation; eroticism; pleasure; intimacy and reproduction; sexual thoughts; fantasies; desires; beliefs; attitudes; values; behaviours; and the ways in which matters related to sex and sexuality shape perceptions, deployments and constructions of other spheres of sociocultural reality.

A perspective on sexuality that goes beyond reproductive and sexual health to acknowledge the versatility of sexuality, both as a social phenomenon and a legitimate field of research and inquiry, involves recognising the traditional links that have existed throughout recorded history between sexuality and an astonishing range of issues: politics, myths, religion, health, technology, the occult and architecture (Pearson 2005; Smyth 2006). However, in recent times and largely because of HIV and other STIs, research on sexuality in many societies, including sub-Saharan Africa, has increasingly been about its link to health, well-being and diseases (Undie et al 2009).

Clarifying the interaction between sexuality and health in Africa is critical, especially in the context of the HIV/AIDS epidemic. However, because current sexuality research in Africa continues to focus largely on matters of health, the rich tradition of scholarship on the interaction of sexuality and other social phenomena in Africa increasingly suffers. Yet, understanding the ways sexuality figures into constructions of African social and cultural processes and vice versa can reframe the ways we currently understand social and livelihood realities, furnish unique insights on the dynamics of the social forces that shape communities and people, and move sexuality research to the centre of social and political inquiry on the continent (Niehaus 2002, 2006; Izugbara 2010).

Indeed, through a focus on sexuality, various dynamics of everyday life, events, doings, anxieties, tensions and aspirations in Africa can be understood. This essay provides a basic overview of the extant literature on the nexus between sexuality and the supernatural in Africa. It is a search not only for the key themes that have dominated research on sexuality and the supernatural, but also for the lessons about social and cultural realities in Africa that emerge from this critical body of research.

Derived from two Latin root words – *super* or *supra* (above) and *natura* (nature), supernatural or supranatural refers to the department of existence further than the scientifically observable universe. Some scholars, such as William Garrett (1974) and Benson Saler (1977) suggest that religious beliefs, miracles, spells and curses, divination, the belief in an afterlife and countless others are examples of supernatural claims. Supernatural beliefs have existed throughout human history, and as Clyde Kluckhohn (1949) noted, their origin might never be known and can only be speculated upon. Supernatural phenomena are often known for their peculiarity and rarity. They are not easily replicated and often associated with the mystical and occult. In Africa, the belief in supernatural forces is omnipresent and long-standing.

Regardless of religious predilections, education levels, class and other differences, Africans generally tend to believe in the existence of a pantheon of active beings and forces operating in the realm of the supernatural. Not only are these forces unavoidable; they permeate understandings of phenomena on the continent. Indeed, supernatural forces (witchcraft, gods, spirits, ancestors, demons, Satan, magic, spells) are a common denominator in popular explanations of ill health, misfortune, success, conflict, wealth, poverty and death. Anne Fadiman's (1997) position, for instance, is that in many non-Western societies, the relationship between the supernatural realm and the sphere of the mundane, which shapes the latter's daily manifestations, is both intricate and dynamic. And Dirk Kohnert acknowledges that, although magic and witchcraft allegations have conventionally disadvantaged the poor and deprived, they also sometimes become a means used by the poor in the struggle against domination, through the establishment of 'cults of counter-violence' (Kohnert 1996). Beliefs about the paranormal are thus regularly invoked for a diversity of purposes in Africa. They not only drive a diversity of political systems, economic practices and array of sexual behaviours, but also have serious implications for development and other activities on the continent.

It is not only in the African cultural imaginary that a link exists between sexuality and the supernatural. Sexuality features prominently in anthropo-historical accounts of popular imaginations of witches in classical and contemporary Western societies (Roper 1994). One popular source acknowledges that not very long ago in many parts of Europe, certain ailments were believed to be cured by physical contact between afflicted parts and a virgin's hands (Anonymous 2002) and that this belief germinated in the context of an epidemic of sexually transmitted infections, which increased men's demand for younger prostitutes and virgin girls whom they deemed uninfected. Men's quest for untouched bed partners to safeguard themselves from contagion (which dovetails into the 'prevention' rape motivation) ultimately led to the false belief that sex with a virgin would cure an existing sexually acquired illness.

The 'virgin cure' theory resulted from the muddling of the notion that sex with a virgin would keep one from contracting general disease, with sex with a virgin would cure venereal disease. It is the obscurity about the role of the virgin in the prevention recipe that possibly prompted the belief that it was being a first-timer that cured infections. So, rather than her presumed magical properties, it was the virgin's arrival in an uninfected state in bed that really mattered (Anonymous 2002). The following description of the annual convention of medieval European witches and wizards also strongly alludes to the powerful role of sexuality in Eurocentric imaginaries of the occult:

> Then, they had to prepare for the Sabbath. Some went there simply by walk, but it was generally admitted that witches flied (sic) either on animals, companions, or demons or on their own broomstick after having rubbed their body with the Flying Ointment. Once the witches have reached the place of the Sabbaths, sometime along with new initiates, the Devil appeared, usually in the form of a black goat (He-goat) but it can also take the shape of a black cat, a raven, a crow, or a feathered toad. The attendants kissed his buttocks in greeting. Then they informed him of all the harmful spells they had done since the last Sabbath and the names of their victims.
>
> Then came the Queen of the Sabbath, a nude woman who rides a black sheep. Satan first urinates in a hole in the ground then all the audience do the same. Then they put the two fingers in the hole and make the sign of the cross reversed. Satan comes back to the Altar and gives the Queen the sacraments from hell. After the fornication, he distributes the hellish *ostie* made on the nude body of the Queen. The witches then pay homage to the Devil, renew pacts, write their names in the Black Book, and have the initiate take an oath. The baptism ceremony for the initiate consumption sometimes involved menstrual blood. The devil put its mark on the initiate and had sex with him.[1]

Turning now to Africa, we explore some of the ways in which sexuality has figured in narratives of the supernatural and vice versa. The rest of this chapter is divided into four sections. The next section addresses existing research on the relationship between sexuality and the supernatural in Africa. It is followed by an assessment of the literature on sexuality in African narratives of witchcraft and the occult. The third section deals with the theme of religion, religiosity and sexuality in Africa, and the closing section briefly reflects on key lessons from the review. The review is not exhaustive nor is it intended to be, and its focus is not to validate the claims surrounding the supernatural and sexuality in Africa. Rather, the intention is to highlight existing knowledge about the interface of sexuality and the paranormal in Africa. Like Roland Barthes (1972), I am persuaded that even if taboos, rituals, beliefs, rumours and norms are based on fables and myths, they point out and alert, they clarify issues and they enforce a direction and focus.

The supernatural and the sexual in Africa

The relationship between the supernatural and sexuality is a popular theme in ethnographies of social organisation in Africa. Extensive descriptions of such relationships are offered in studies among the Nyakyusa and Kaguru in Tanzania (Wilson 1957; Beidelman 1982), the Akan in Ghana (Appiah-Kubi 1981), the Luo and Kamba in Kenya (Hauge 1974; Ahlberg 1979) and the Igbo and Ibibio in Nigeria (Uchendu 1965a; Offiong 1991; Ekong 2001). Several African societies ascribe certain forms of coitus with sacred power. Among the Igbo, for instance, unfaithfulness of a wife is believed to cause sickness and misfortune to the husband, especially if he possesses powerful medicines (Uchendu 1965a,1965b).

In Chewa and Tumbuka cultural imaginaries, a man's sperm, ejaculated during sex with his wife and then rubbed on the body of their newborn, offers enduring supernatural defence for the child against certain ailments, including fever, cold, measles and whooping cough (Zulu 2001). Studies of the Kaguru, Bondei and Shambala sexual symbolisms also reveal close parallels (Moreau 1941; Beidelman 1963, 1966, 1972, 1982). Among the Igede of the Nigerian middle belt region, Martins Adegbola (1998) notes that sexual activity during the day is not permitted among married couples who have young children. In Igede cultural imaginary, sexual congresses held during the day can mysteriously foist suffering and disease and other misfortunes on the couple, their children and the community. Jane Chege (1993) explains that African mystical beliefs about aspects of sexuality derive from the cultural acknowledgement of sexuality as both a channel of community and individual renewal and the conduit for good and evil. She asserts that mystification is the by-product of a realisation that sexual practices, desires and orientations can foster both blessings and curses on individuals, groups and societies.

Most accounts of the sexuality–supernatural complex in African social thought have merely catalogued the different forms that these relationships assume. Where they exist, theoretical explanations of the interaction of sexuality and the supernatural in Africa have borrowed heavily from functionalism, arguing primarily that society depends on a system of sentiments, which regulate the conduct of the individual in accord with the needs of society. The framing of aspects of sexuality in supernatural terms not only mirrors the importance of the supernatural as a key social control resource in African societies, but also reflects attempts to affix definite social values to sexuality based on its social importance. The social importance of sexuality is thus not only that it satisfies sexual drives and the need for reproduction, but also that a large proportion of activities are concerned with performing, enacting and deploying sexuality, and that in these activities – with their daily instances of collaboration and mutual aid – are interrelations of interests that bind the individual men, women and children into a society (Radcliffe-Brown 1952).

Overall, functionalism holds that indigenous supernatural beliefs surrounding sexuality in traditional Africa were driven primarily by the need to minimise chaos and promote general good conduct. African indigenous societies supported sexual norms that minimised misconduct and capriciousness. Depicting sexuality in supernatural terms thus prevents deviance and excesses, unites the collective and reinforces the need for socially acceptable conducts. However, functionalist explanations focus only on the end results. They overturn the usual order of cause and outcome and account for phenomena by reference to what happens subsequently, not before (Ritzer and Goodman 2010). Furthermore, there are no plausible functionalist explanations for the construction of some aspects of the supernatural in sexualised terms.

Robert A. Levine's (1959) investigation into Gusii sexual norms in Kenya offers a good example of a functionalist analysis of the interaction of sexuality and the supernatural. Levine suggests that myths, repressive sanctions and the violent forms of punishment inflicted upon sexual offenders served to unify local moral beliefs and mobilise popular sentiment against both sexual excesses and incontinence. The Gusii accredit sexual activity with a supernatural capacity to purify, cleanse and bring blessings. Gusii norms of sexual expressions permit ritual sexual activity at certain times and prohibit it at others. Sexual activity with certain persons is also potentially critical. Two men who have slept with the same women could presage death if either visited the other while sick. Gusii key rules concerning sexual fidelity in marriage are enforced by the mystical *amasangia*, which literally translates as 'sharing', and refers to the consequences of illicit sharing of a married woman's sexual attention.

Amasangia is caused by the adulterous behaviour of a woman, but it directly affects her husband and children rather than herself. The Gusii believe that if a woman has extramarital sexual intercourse but continues to live with her husband, by her mere presence she risks provoking his death when he later falls ill. A sick Gusii husband will begin to sweat profusely when an adulterous wife approaches him. If she attempts to bandage his wounds, he will experience more bleeding instead of relief, ultimately leading to his death. Further, among the Gusii, if Mr A had sex with a woman that Mr B also had sex with, it would be fatal for a sick Mr A to be visited by Mr B, regardless of whether or not the woman was married to either of them. An adulterous Gusii wife can also inadvertently kill her child by going near the child when the child is ill. Involvement in prohibited sexual practices often results in miscarriages and secondary infertility not only for the offending women, but also for other women in the lineage (Levine and Levine 1966; Levine and Campbell 1972). Essentially, the mystical *amasangia* is a cultural strategy for minimising sexual misconduct and capriciousness and reinforcing the need for socially acceptable conducts.

The *magun* ('don't climb') is the Yoruba (southern Nigeria) equivalent of the Gusii *amasangia*. It also discourages extramarital sexual activity (Alaba 2004). The loss that sexual incontinence might bring is expressed thus among the Yoruba:

Ikun n jogede;
Ikun n redii finkin;
Ikun k mo pe hun to dun lo n pani!

The Big Squirrel is eating bananas [bait on a trap];
The Big Squirrel is savouring the sweetness;
The Big Squirrel doesn't know that it is the sweet thing that kills the eater.
(Alaba 2004)

Yoruba marital partners can secretly affix the magical *magun* on each other, and only *magun* set upon a person by his or her marital spouse works effectively. If a man or woman on whom *magun* has been affixed has sex outside marriage, they would remain glued in coitus with the unlawful sex partner until they were discovered. The fear of being caught by *magun*, similar to that of being struck by the mystical *amasangia*, minimises extramarital sexual activities among the Yoruba.

According to Isak Niehaus (2002), the Xhosa of South Africa also discourage their wives/husbands from having sex with others by doctoring them with the mysterious *likubalo*, a lethal magical potion. One popular type of *likubalo* used by Xhosa men is made by cutting a small piece of flesh from a dog's penis, drying it and grinding it into a fine powder. Once administered to a wife, her husband asks her to close a penknife, which will cause her and any other man who has sex with her to become stuck together like mating dogs. Lovers can only be released from this position if the husband himself releases the penknife. Some *likubalos* reportedly cause snakes to materialise from women's vaginas to strike their lovers; the lover to be caught by others; a husband's penis to coil up like a millipede; or the wife/husband to develop diarrhoea during coitus (Niehaus 2002).

Functionalists, such as J. Omosade Awolalu (1976) and J. Olowo-Ojoade (1983), also argue that the dangerous and supernatural polarity between sex and some human activities in most African cultures is part of a grand cultural strategy for warning against and minimising the occurrence of illegitimate sexual activity among both men and women. African beliefs about sexual bodies and how they ought to mingle also discourage forms of sexual deviance that could potentially destabilise the social order, and protect the weak and infirm from sexual exploitation and abuse. According to Peter Ezeh (2007), the Orring of south-eastern Nigeria believe that illicit sexual activity can bring mystical illness upon offenders. Sexual activity with other people's wives infects a man with leprosy, while a cheating Orring wife experiences difficult births and might die if she fails to confess her misdeeds. In several other African cultures (Zulu, Chewa, Sotho, Igbo, Ogoni), sexual misbehaviour can cause calamity (Heald 1995; Niehaus 2002).

Coitus in the bush or with certain types of beings (the handicapped, children, mentally ill people, kin and animals) or at certain times of the day, week, month or year have polluting effects and can result in disaster among the Igbo, Ibibio and

Yoruba, among others (Uchendu 1965a, 1965b; Awolalu 1976; Ekong 2001). Until recently, for instance, the Igbo associated twin births with illicit sexual activities and would kill twins at birth and sometimes sanction their mothers. Ogonna Dimgba (2000) writes that the killing of twins among the Igbo might have been connected with the traditional beliefs that only lower animals experienced multiple births and that birth of twins indicated that someone in the family, usually the husband or wife, had debased himself/herself by infracting some key social and sexual norms.

It follows then, in Ngwa-Igbo folktales, that the first woman to ever bear twins is said to have become pregnant extramaritally. Elisha Renne however notes that 'the characteristic twoness of twins contributes to their association with two opposing qualities: danger and benefit, loving kinship and traitorous competitiveness, otherworldly spirituality and earthly bestiality' (Renne 2001: 13). This continual, irreconcilable and dualistic dissonance is expressed in myths, folktales and beliefs about twins, and in turn underlines a paradoxical social structure, which encourages some African societies, such as the Yoruba, to associate twins with witches. Both twins and witches threaten the boundaries of ordinary society. Although witches might be more immoral than twins, both share a unique capacity to benefit and destroy society.[2]

Gusii community members would also abstain from sex following a death. Although this signals respect for the deceased, perhaps indicating that society is ready to suspend pleasure to honour them or is not in a hurry to replace them, it also reportedly visits upon the community and its members supernatural blessing and reprieve. Sexual activity during a period of ritual abstention pollutes the community and people. It can also result in more deaths. The Wameru of Kenya and northern Tanzania (who traditionally punish adultery by forcing deviants to lie down as if they were having sex and then pinning them to the ground with a wooden spear for several days until they die from bleeding) view involvement in prohibited sexual behaviours as a form of witchcraft. It is believed to bring calamity upon society, causing prayers and incantations not to reach their destination ancestors (Heald 1995). Among the Kaguru, the breaching of certain sexual prohibitions is equated with witchcraft (*uhai*) and ranks as a most heinous of immoral acts (Beidelman 1963). In the past, this might only be rectified by slaying the offender. Such persons were usually beaten to death in the bush, preferably by their clan.

On the other hand, some African cultures also believe in the supernatural potential of sexual activity to mystically bring favour or extirpate bad luck, contamination and contagion. Kiganda culture, for instance, recognises sexual activity as a key part of rituals used to end repetitive deaths in a home, drive away the spirits of the dead and honour ancestors (Nyanzi et al 2004). Among the Luo of Kenya and Uganda, it is believed that after losing a wife or husband a widow or widower can magically purify themselves by having sexual activity with another person (Heald 1995). Obunga (2007) argues that sexual intercourse with the living in such circumstances psychologically frees the surviving spouse from the consequent hold of the ghost of the deceased which, in Luo cosmovision and lay tales, often lurks around to take him or her with the deceased.

From a Eurocentric perspective, the dead might have no business engaging or participating actively in the mundane. But Africans generally do not see death as the end of life. The human soul is immortal and continues to exist even after death. The dead participate actively in the affairs of the living. However, when such participation becomes excessive or dangerous to the living, rituals and sacrifices of severance are deployed to keep them at bay.

The need to promote personal and collective sexual hygiene and health has been reported as a possible explanation for the several African cautionary tales about certain sexual practices or sexual and reproductive emissions (Okolo 1998). In the traditional past of many African societies, menstrual blood, semen, breast milk and other sexual and reproductive emissions and fluids were taboos for warriors, chiefs and persons going on a hunt or any kind of worship (Crawley 1895; Ahlberg 1994; Heald 1995). Among the Nyakyusa and Zulu, it is believed that beer will become too strong and even go sour if its brewer has sex.

The Ngwa (of south-eastern Nigeria) also believe that charms or treatments could lose their potency if touched by someone who just had sex or by a menstruating woman (Oriji 1972). Among the Kaguru and Bemba, it is believed that a boy's circumcision wound will not heal if someone in the homestead has engaged in sex. Contact with certain sexual fluids during certain enterprises, such as going out on a war campaign, performing a sacrifice, going out hunting, preparing treatments and carving royal or ritual objects, is considered perilous in many traditional African cultures. Eating food cooked with water used in washing a woman's genitals or containing any vaginal emissions is believed, in several African cultures, to make a man eternally loyal to the woman (Muuko 2002).

According to Elieshi Mungure (n.d.), a menstruating Kinga woman or one bleeding after childbirth is quarantined in a hut from other members of the family. She stays there until she 'dries up'. She eats from a separate plate and her food is prepared separately by other women from the community. She is considered so very supernaturally charged that contact with her can suck out life from others. The Wameru also put menstruating women under certain boundaries. For example, they are not allowed to sleep close to their husbands or any male or baby boy for the fear that the male will become impotent. They do not approach a local brewing place for fear that they will supernaturally impede the fermentation process (Mungure n.d.).

Other examples from across the continent include the Ngwa, Mende and Dogon of West Africa, who believe that a woman will transmit bad luck to or unman a male partner if they have sexual intercourse while she is menstruating. At this time even a married woman is avoided by her husband. She is often perceived as busy or as seeing the moon, implying that the she is committed to a superior supernatural task with which the husband should not compete (Ember 1978; Strassmann 1992). Within this context, Victor Turner's (1969) theory that menstruation marks a period of dangerous inbetweenness is very helpful in understanding indigenous African cultural attitudes toward menstrual blood. It is the separation and avoidance that mark the period of menstruation and link the profane and the sacred and convert the obligatory into the desirable.

The pervasive African belief about pollution arising from sexual misconduct (also negatively affecting livestock and other means of livelihood) is related to the need to unify local moral beliefs, encourage collective vigilance and mobilise popular sentiment to guarantee social stability and prevent sexual excesses and immoderation (Peters 1918; Awolalu 1976). Yields and harvests could thus fail among agriculturalists, such as the Yoruba, the Ngwa and Efik, if seedlings and plants are touched by someone who has just engaged in unacceptable sexual behaviours. Among pastoralists, such as the Zulu of southern Africa, the Maasai of Kenya and Tanzania and the Fulani of West Africa, it is believed that cattle can die en masse when a critical sexual rule is infracted. Newborns, it is believed among the Zulu and the Anaguta of Nigeria, can also die or suffer mysterious ailments if their parents engage in sex at particular periods or times. In some areas menstruating women are forbidden from going near gold mines because they reportedly bring bad luck to the task at hand (Talbot 1926).

Victor Chikezi Uchendu's (1965b) analysis of the *iko* (paramour institution) among the Ngwa of eastern Nigeria highlights the economic dimensions of the sexuality–supernatural interaction in Africa, and calls particular attention to how struggles over sexuality also engender supernatural practices. A woman who desires to contract an *iko* is required to discuss the matter with her husband, who might initially resist it but ultimately acquiesce. The Ngwa *iko* contract engenders some mystical rites during which the paramour must swear to an oath that the woman should be given no injurious medicines 'which might turn her attention and devotion away from her husband' and also that the paramour will make his time and labour available to the husband of the woman at any time they are needed.

The practice, according to Uchendu (1965b), is particularly common among elderly men married to younger women, who might require additional male farm-hands. The husband receives the services of his wife's paramour in farming and in the domestic sphere. An outright 'compensation', called *nkita asoghi anya* (dog does not respect) is paid to the husband. The compensation conveys the superiority of the husband over his wife's paramour, but unites the three parties in a binding ring of reciprocity. As a dog might well be allowed to occasionally eat with the master, so are low-ranking men allowed participation in sexual rights of their superiors. The paramour is expected to assist the husband in agricultural work when called upon and is ritually obliged to do so. A paramour who reneges on his pledge to help in the farm work of his Iko's husband does not only immediately lose his sexual rights to the *iko*, but also puts himself at risk of being mystically and fatally afflicted by the oath to which he has sworn.

African deities and their relationships with humans present important dimensions for understanding the relationship between the sexual and the supernatural on the continent. Although some of them have human or non-human sexual partners, frequently subverting gender lines and reproductive norms, others are ungendered or have more than one gender and sexuality, such as twins, the intersexed or divine pairs (Jell-Bahlsen 2008). Human priestesses (and sometimes priests), are considered the wives of the gods among the Akan, Ngwa and Yoruba. Male votaries of Yoruba *orishas* (gods) are considered their wives, and they attend ritual ceremonies costumed and dressed as women (Barber 1981). Ogbuide, the Oguta-Igbo water goddess, also has more than one husband. According to Sabine Jell-Bahlsen (2008), although Ogbuide's multiple spouses contradict Oguta-Igbo culture (which is not polyandrous), the goddess personifies the extremes that ordinary women can attain. Jell-Bahlsen writes:

> Ogbuide does not just define social norms as a role model, but also educates,
> for she informs people of alternative strategies and options available to all
> human beings, men and women alike. Ogbuide has … at least two husbands,
> the river god Urashi as well as the river god Njaba. (Jell-Bahlsen 2008)

Percy A. Talbot also observed: 'Another Ibo Water Spirit, Miri-Omumu (water the
birth giver) by name dwells with his wife, Enwenni miri, in a sacred pool near
Nkarahia … We came to a small tree round which hung several fathoms of white
cloth. This is the home of the water wife' (Talbot 1932: 87).

Priestesses among the Akan of Ghana do not marry. They belong to the gods
and therefore cannot become the property of men, as would be the case if they married. This prohibition however relates only to marriage; priestesses are not barred
from sexual activity. Emmanuel Akyeampong (1997) writes that Akan priestesses
are ordinarily very licentious. Custom allows them to gratify their passions with
any man whom they fancy. Akan priestesses often exploit this privileged position
to have sexual access to any man whom they desire.

Thus a priestess who is favourably impressed by a man sends for him and this
command the men often obey, because of fear of the supernatural consequences
should they refuse. As Akyeampong notes:

> She then tells him that the god she serves has directed her to love him, and
> the man thereupon lives with her until she grows tired of him, or a new object
> takes her fancy. Some priestesses were known to have as many as half-a-
> dozen men in train at one time, and may, on great occasions, be seen walking
> in state, followed by them. (Akyeampong 1997)

These men performed key economic functions for the priestess: tilling her farm,
tending her livestock and offering their labour freely. Usually the man swore an
oath to the priestess, obliging him to die for her, protect her and never plan, speak
or act against her.

Most sub-Saharan Africans imagine a fantasy space located at the bottom of the
sea, where money and commodities are generated in exchange for sex and sometimes blood. The beautiful, seductive and impressive Mami Wata, who occupies
and rules this space, is rich and uses her wealth and beauty to bait her adepts into
orgiastic sexual encounters, among other things (Meyer 1995, 2002). Sexual encounters with Mami Wata or her equally amorous and seductive agents and angelings
are thought to make people rich and powerful. Persons who have sex with Mami
Wata may never have sex with other humans. If they do, it is believed they could
go mad (Bastian 1997). Mary Magdalena, an Igbo Mami Wata devotee and worship-
per studied by Jell-Bahlsen (1997) had traded a mundane life as a human wife for
esoteric involvement, priesthood, water worship and marriage to Mami Wata. Even
if married, Igbo Mami Wata worshippers would normally set aside one day out of
the four-day Igbo market week to worship and serve Mami Wata and meet their
marital obligations to her.

Mami Wata theories have focused on the dual natures of good and evil, reflected
in water, which is an important means of providing communication, food, drink,

trade and transportation, a link between the dead and the living and the path through which people reincarnate, but which at the same time can drown people, flood fields or villages and provide passage to intruders. The goddess's European female features, and the fact that she is resident in African waters and active in the socio-economic and sexual lives of ordinary people, suggest she condenses both seductive eroticism and the forceful and pervasive spirit of modernity (Bastian 1997).

Jell-Bahlsen (2008) opines that Mami Wata harbours the complexities of local deities associated with both customs and changes and embodies local aspirations for a culturally guided modernity.[3] Although Mami Wata can kill, she, like many other African water deities, is also a giver of fertility, supporting the perspective that she possesses the dual natures of good and evil. Talbot, who lived and worked among different ethnic groups in the Niger delta, notes that, at the onset of foreign contact, many local water spirits in the area were attributed with fecundity and the power to grant children. Mami Wata thus personifies ambiguity, modernity, indigeneity and paradoxicality. For Ifi Amadiume (n.d.), she embodies the extremes of beauty, sensuality, compassion and eroticism, as well as jealousy, danger and pitilessness. In the more complex sexual freedoms that modernity provides, 'the goddess takes on an encroaching presence as a subversive seductive sexuality and materialistic enchantment that speak to the inhibitions of cultures and religion and at the same time the lure and illusions of capitalism itself in matters of class and race' (Amadiume n.d.: 3).

Although popularly imagined as a female, Mami Wata does not really have a familiar sexual orientation; rather, she claims human spouses indiscriminately, regardless of their gender. Defying Mami Wata's sexually related embargoes could potentially harm worshippers, as reported in the following Nigerian news article:

> It was a tragic end of a marriage ceremony, at Umunze in Aguata local government area of Anambra State, over the weekend, when a 30-year old bride-groom committed suicide, on the eve of his traditional marriage ceremony. The man from Umucheke quarters of Ururo village, Umunze, had on the fateful Saturday morning, given his elder brother some 1,500 naira being the bride price he intended paying during the ceremony. The elder brother, in expressing his happiness over the marriage, asked his deceased younger brother to keep back his money and that as he was taking a position as the father, he would pay the bride price. Arrangement concluded, the deceased went to take his bath while his friends who would accompany him to the bride's house waited. As the man stayed longer at the 'bathroom,' the people forced the door open only to find the man hanging from the top of the roof.
>
> The *Daily Star* also gathered that, at the time of this discovery, the bride's family had concluded their own arrangements to welcome the suitor and his relations. Some elders who spoke to the *Star* alleged that the deceased had been warned against the marriage because he had a wife of 'mermaid' contracted inside the water before his birth, but the man's relations did not believe. Also, his mother who owns a spiritual church in the area had allegedly assured the son of deliverance from the 'mermaid.' It was also gathered

that the man went insane when he attempted to marry some years ago. He was cured but the marriage negotiations collapsed. (*The Daily Star*, in Bastian 1997)

In Africa, homosexuality is also deeply surrounded by supernatural beliefs. Among the Dagara of Burkina Faso, gays, lesbians and transgendered people are considered key to society's psychic balance. In the indigenous background, a homosexual Dagara occupied a performance role of intermediary between this world and the otherworld, as a sort of gatekeeper. The Dagara believe that such a person:

> experiences a state of vibrational consciousness which is far higher and far different from the one the normal person would experience. So when you arrive here, you begin to vibrate in a way that Elders can detect as meaning that you are connected with a gateway somewhere. You decide that you will be a gatekeeper before you are born. (Somé 1994: 12)

Some African gods practice homosexuality, exemplified in the ancient Egyptian god, Horus, who had a sexual relationship with another god, Seth (Roscoe 1997). African homosexual men and women are also widely ascribed with supernatural powers (Greenberg 1988; Gaudio 2009). This author's (2008) study in a rural Ngwa community shows that the best and longest-living medicine man ever known to the community was a homosexual. Local folklore in the community linked his longevity and the potency of his cures to his sexual orientation.

Although functionalists suggest that the framing of homosexuality in supernatural terms works to prevent undue violence against homosexuals in traditional African societies, there were also African societies in which homosexual men and women were viewed as witches. E.E. Evans-Pritchard (1937, 1970) reports that in traditional Azande background, lesbian women were considered to be witches. They could be executed, flogged or expelled from their households. Zande women wanting to be lesbian partners would engage in a deeply supernatural ritual. Azande therefore speak of them as evil in the same way as they speak of witchcraft and cats as evil, and they say, moreover, that homosexual women are the sort who might well give birth to cats and be witches also. Evans-Pritchard (1937) notes that the framing of lesbianism as supernaturally dangerous rationalised male mistreatment of sexually agentive Zande women. However, among the Ngwa, there is also a belief that although warriors preparing for war would be weakened by having sex with women, homosexual relationships with fellow warrior men would mystically strengthen them.

Sexuality in African narratives of witchcraft and the occult

Ethnographic literature on witchcraft and the occult in Africa also regularly makes references to exotic and perverse sexual practices and to the sexualisation of the paranormal (Niehaus 2002, 2005; Izugbara 2010). Evans-Pritchard reports that Azande women witches were thought to give birth to kittens from a species of ferocious wild cat. They reportedly redirected their sexual and reproductive energies into activities that instil danger, terror and fright. Igbo cosmology and folktales make reference to witches who dance naked at night around big mystical trees or large bonfires deep in the heart of impenetrable forests while drinking or eating their and others' semen and wombs respectively, or engaging in sexual orgies among themselves or with bats, bush pigs, owls and other freakish familiars (Izugbara 2010).

Accounts of the freakish and satanic misuse of the life force of the less fortunate through shocking sexual practices still circulate widely in contemporary Africa (Comaroff and Comaroff 1999). Extant literature also highlights witchcraft as an alternative means of attaining a range of sexually related behaviours, including 'manipulating lovers, spouses, achieving violent sexual encounters, compensating for the absence of human lovers, causing male and female homosexuality, and of committing incest and inducing abortion' (Niehaus 1999).

For instance, in Zambia, witches are famed for a capacity to destroy their reproductive capacities in order not to reproduce for society (Auslander 1993), and in Cameroon they engage in homosexuality, which also denies society their reproductive potentials. In many other African societies, including among the Igbo, Ibibio, Yoruba and Efik, witches and sorcerers reportedly gain in power and strength by particularly attacking or consuming other people's sexual and reproductive parts – wombs, sexual organs, the products of conceptions and reproductive fluids. Local beliefs also posit Zulu witches as able to use a non-human being to unleash unwanted sexual intercourse.

Scholars of culture have interpreted these narratives as part of a moral system that warns about the possibility of certain sexual activities to transgress local hierarchies of domination. Given their presumed supernatural abilities, witches embody a potential for threatening the socio-sexual order. The framing of the antisocial activities of witches and other wicked persons in idioms of perverted production and reproduction, in images and tales of ungenerative sexuality, rape and deadly sexual exchanges, derives largely from the emphasis placed on fertility and reproduction in African cultures.

For instance, wealthy but wifeless/husbandless adults and childless adult men/women are thus likely to be viewed with suspicion and to trigger speculations about the possibility of exchanging natural sexuality and fertility for wealth and fame. Ethnographic data collected from Ghana by Birgit Meyer (1995, 2001) show that barren women risk suspicion of witchcraft or a devil contract, while childless men can easily inspire rumours of involvement in a sort of demonic pact, which yields them wealth in exchange for the natural use of their sexuality. She suggests that the hidden theme of satanic riches related to ritual sex is about the continuity of the human capacity to create new life and of the family relations resulting from it.

Further, in Niehaus' (2002) study among the Zulu, informants described to him a large baboon with horror-inspiring dentition and pronounced sexual features, used by Zulu male and female witches alike to rape and abuse those whom they desire sexually, cause infertility and make women abort or give birth to horribly deformed babies or even non-human creatures. The female baboon reportedly also sucks men's blood, injecting them with substances that render them impotent, and the male has an extraordinarily large penis that could stretch to virtually any size and assume any shape. According to Niehaus (2002), baboons are sufficiently human-like for it to be imagined that they could instigate sexual intercourse with humans. Further, baboons are perceived as inhibited, as displaying a childish sense of morality, as lacking the restraints that culture imposes upon their desires and ugly enough to also make them symbolically appropriate as instigators of unwanted intercourse.

In Pondo cultural imaginary, women witches hold sexual congresses with hairy little supernatural beings called *thokoloshe* and their male counterparts make love to snakelike familiars that assume the shape of beautiful, sensual girls. Niehaus (2002) has interpreted the *thokoloshe* as personifying unfulfilled and illicit sexual desires. The frequent casting of *thokoloshe* as a large baboon, description of the uses to which it was put and the duality between witches and the familiars support this interpretation. Another theory views the *thokoloshe* as a compensatory image for women whose sexual desires are repressed by rules of clan exogamy, which exclude many men resident in local areas from marriage (Wilson 1951). In Hammond-Tooke's (1974) view, the *thokoloshe* reflects men's perceptions of women's deprivation. The myth that resentful women take ape-like lovers to wreak havoc on men, he argued, provides a rationale for discriminating against some women.

In his interrogation of metaphors of consumerism, commoditised sex and sexualised commodities in Senegal and Cameroon, Francis Nyamnjoh (2005) observes that rumours of occult wealth were commonly connected to bizarre ritual sex. Nyamnjoh couches these tales within the trajectories of modernity, and holds that these claims emerge and arise as the interdependencies between contemporary economic realities, globalisation and status, pleasure, appropriation, seduction and livelihood are worked out, negotiated and performed. Accounts of occult economic activities in Africa offered by Misty L. Bastian (1997), Henry Drewal (1988), Rosalind Hackett (2003) and Stephanie Newell (2003) also contain rich references to sexual encounters and sexuality.

This author's (2010) study of the growing invocation of sexuality in lay accounts of occult economic activities in Nigeria shows that they are socially grounded idioms of the anxiety and concern of the masses with the perceived tendency of the powerful and influential to disregard the boundaries of 'responsible' and 'proper' sexuality and behaviour as they grow wealthier and more powerful. For him, these tales betray the dilemma of crisis-stricken 21st century Nigeria, in which concerns about socio-economic inequities are woven into a tapestry of legends of woes and humiliation (for the poor) and gains and triumph (for the rich). He contends that as a core and familiar site of pleasure, control, humiliation, dishonour, intimacy, production, reproduction and danger, sexuality offers a ready and veritable discursive space where the brazen and vicious disrespect for people and their privacy and the sadistic defilement of the most sensitive and sacred aspects of the lives of ordinary

Nigerians by the wealthy and powerful are currently imagined, situated and subjected to energetic lay critique.

Generally, African occult sexual rituals are about the theft of people's sexual soul, essence or force and the perverse use of human sexuality – most times exemplified in the exchange of other people's or one's own sexuality for money, power or fame (Meyer 1999; Izugbara 2010). A range of attempts has been made in the post-colonial period to reconstruct some aspects of the relationship between sexuality and the supernatural in Africa, including Nollywood (Nigeria's movie industry), which continues to dramatise these beliefs, albeit in exaggerated forms. The Nigerian urban legends collected by this author suggest that residence in Nigeria is a sufficient risk factor for occult sexual victimisation and that occult sexual rituals vary widely, from those demanding sexual activity with the mentally ill, relatives, strangers, children, albinos, virgins, very elderly people, own child(ren), own parent(s), corpses, beggars, cripples, animals and supernatural beings, such as Mami Wata or her agents, to those requiring total abstinence from sex, marriage or producing children.

In one account elicited by this author (2010), men lure unwary women home or to a hotel room (drug, hit or hypnotise them), then transform into an animal (snake, monkey, pig, dog, donkey, horse) to penetrate them vaginally. The victim of the encounter then dies, vomiting large piles of money, particularly dollars, pounds and naira. Women also pull off similar encounters. One story tells about women turning into skeletons upon sexual penetration by a man. Using its strong, bony fingers the skeleton clasps the hapless man to itself until he dies, choking and vomiting money for the woman, who soon returns to human form. Other women have evil snakes magically planted in their vaginas and stomachs by medicine men. Men who have sex with such women end up having their semen eaten or swallowed by the snakes. Such men sometimes lose their virility, which is transformed into wealth and fortune for the women.

Some women also have the powers to transform into coffins upon sexual penetration by men. Once enveloped in the coffin, such men turn into money or classy goods such as jewellery and cosmetics for the women. This author's point is that these stories depict the depraved nature of the excessive wealth and fortune of many Nigerians amid growing poverty among their fellow country people. In the current era of HIV/AIDS, there is also the particular belief, especially in eastern and southern Africa, that sex with virgins has curative potential (Leclerc-Madlala 2002; Meel 2003).

In West African lay beliefs, the sexual organs are particular targets of supernatural attacks. For instance, local views circulating in the region about genital shrinking or vanishing, which bear similarities to *koro* and *koro*-like syndrome, associate it with witchcraft and magic. Jim Goad's journalistic report holds that:

> Koro epidemics in Africa tend to add the element of mob violence. In January, 1997, 12 accused witches in Ghana were pummelled to death by crowds certain their victims had cast spells to dwindle the dicky-doos of local men. The mania spread to the Ivory Coast two months later, where superstitious phallocentric hordes murdered an additional seven suspected schlong-attenuating sorcerers. Similar bursts of violent atavistic mania erupted in Nigeria and

> Benin in 2001, when at least 24 people were slaughtered by roving packs of locals hell-bent on killing whoever was stealing all the penises. In one attack, eight travelling evangelists were simultaneously burned alive. Handshakes by a mysterious man known as 'Satan's Friend' were largely blamed for a Sudanese koro outbreak in 2003. Sudanese columnist, Ja'far Abbas warned citizens that they should neither shake the hands of strangers nor borrow combs from them. Abbas said the penis-melting comb came from 'an imperialist Zionist agent that was sent to prevent our people from procreating and multiplying'. (Goad 2005)

Charles Mather's (2005) study shows that Ghanaian people generally believe that sorcerers and witches, operating under cover, 'infect' innocent people with genital loss through body contact, especially shaking hands with their victims. When Mather asked his informants what these genital thieves aimed to achieve and where they kept these stolen wares, they told him 'that people were stealing penises to make money *juju* (also known as 'money medicine' or *sika aduro*), with no intention of returning the organs to their owners', and that there was a cult in Nigeria where people go for these supernatural powers. A vanishing or shrinking vagina or penis often appears in a shrine and vomits money and the person who causes this is rewarded financially.

Mather's content analysis of Ghanaian newspaper reports on genital shrinking or vanishing in Ghana revealed that both men and women reportedly suffer mysterious genital vanishings and shrinking. Some cases involve women who report that their breasts shrink and who claim experiencing marked changes in the size of their vulvas or both. In other instances, the vagina simply seals up or vanishes altogether. In Africa, lay explanations for genital retraction focus on sorcery because African cultures affiliate sorcery with illness and infertility. From an anthropological perspective, however, genital retraction syndromes in Africa derive from the cultural emphasis placed on sexual reproduction, which creates an extreme anxiety about the security and functioning of reproductive organs and fertility (Schroer 2005). Anxieties and beliefs surrounding genital loss and theft could therefore originate from deep-seated cultural pressures and sexual fears that women and men face in pro-natalist societies.

Religion, religiosity, spirituality and sexuality in Africa

A body of literature, situated in the HIV/AIDS era, has also focused on the relationship between sexuality or sexual behaviour and religion, religiosity and spirituality in Africa. However, it is important to note that contemporary organised religion in Africa is characterised by a plurality of doctrines, syncretism and fluidity. Commitment to foreign faiths among Africans thus remains problematic, making it common for Africans to self-identify as Christians, but to have a pantheon of active indigenous gods that they pledge allegiance to. The normative conceptualisations of religion, as well as the bounded categorisations that follow such categorisations, might thus not easily apply to Africans, suggesting caution in interpreting the interaction of sexuality and (organised) religion on the continent.

Peter Gray's (2004) review of the literature on Islam and sexual transmission of HIV in Africa showed that in 38 sub-Saharan African countries, the percentage of Muslims within countries negatively predicted HIV prevalence. His survey of published articles containing data on HIV prevalence and religious affiliation showed that six of seven such studies indicated a negative relationship between HIV prevalence and being Muslim. However, evidence also suggests that the jury is still out on the impact of religion on sexuality and sexual behaviour. In Uganda, for instance, Grey et al (2000) showed that among circumcised men, Muslims did not have significantly lower HIV rates than persons from other religions, though they were more likely to engage in post-intercourse cleansing.

Unlike Grey and colleagues, Sam Mbulaiteye et al (2000) found that Ugandan Muslims had significantly lower prevalences of HIV than non-Muslims, which they attributed to the lack of alcohol consumption, rather than to religiosity or spirituality. This finding contrasts sharply with results from a study by Emmanuel Lagarde et al (2000), which showed that although Senegalese Muslims report lower alcohol consumption, they are equally likely as Christians to report casual sex in the previous 12 months and more likely to be polygynously married.

Further, evidence from Robert C. Bailey et al (1999) shows that Ugandan Muslims are generally less likely to have had extramarital partners the previous year, more likely to have been circumcised, but more likely to be polygynously married and less likely to use condoms than Christians. But in their study of Kenyan, Ugandan and Rwandan long-distance truck drivers, Joel Rakwar et al (1999) found that Muslim drivers were less likely to be sero-positive and to have engaged in transactional sex. In a similar sample, Job Bwayo et al (1994) found that Muslims and Protestants had lower HIV rates than Catholics, an effect apparently due to circumcision status. Similar results were observed in studies by Sam Malamba et al (1994) and Andrew Nunn et al (1994).

However, Japhet Killewo et al (1994) differ markedly. Their study in Tanzania, within political units (wards), revealed that higher proportions of Muslims than Christians had a greater prevalence of HIV. And in Nigeria, Uche C. Isiugo-Abanihe (1994) found mixed results on the relationship between religion and sexual behaviour. The Muslim and Protestant men he studied were less likely than Catholics and others to report an extramarital affair the previous week. However, religious affiliation did not strongly predict sexual behaviour among the women studied, suggesting that Muslim and Christian women exhibited similar sexual behaviours. In her study of Pentecostalism and adolescent sexuality in Nigeria, Folakemi Erhabor (2004) also concluded that the conservative church doctrines that emphasise pietistic culture influence young people to refrain from sexual activity.

Jenny Trinitapoli's (2006) work shifted the focus of research on religion and sexual behaviour in sub-Saharan Africa from the implications of membership in certain religious sub-groups and regular participation in religious services for sexual behaviours among members of these groups to the ways in which religion might motivate actual change in sexual behaviour. Her analysis of the relationship between a variety of religious beliefs and practices and sexual behaviour modification among rural Malawians, for example, showed that persons from certain denominations, in particular Catholics and Muslims, were more likely to report having altered their sexual behaviour to avoid infections. She also established that 'while attendance at religious services is negatively associated with reporting sexual behaviour changes, self-identification as a born-again Christian or having made Tauba for Muslims was positively associated with reporting having made such changes' (see also Trinitapoli and Regnerus 2006).

The impact of religious involvement on sexual behaviour and practices in Africa is also an emerging theme in the literature. In one South African study, religious commitment diminished propensity to engage in sexual intercourse and delayed age for onset of sexual intercourse (Nicholas and Durrheim 1995). In another South African study, religiosity delayed first sexual intercourse, but once sexual activity began for religious persons it frequently deterred their use of effective contraceptive methods, possibly increasing the probability of infection and pregnancy. This claim is well supported by international literature on the link between religiosity and sexuality 'ignorance'. Smith's (2004) study among young Nigerian city migrants revealed that religious youth are less likely to be sexually active and might therefore feel that they are not at risk of contracting HIV.

Robert Garner's (2000) study in South Africa also found that, although the majority of South Africans are affiliated to Christian churches, the types of sexual behaviours that promote the epidemic continue. Based on research in a KwaZulu-Natal township, Garner presents evidence on the level of extra- and premarital sex among members of different churches. For him, only Pentecostal churches significantly reduce extra- and premarital sex among members. They achieve this by maintaining high levels of four crucial variables: indoctrination, religious experience, exclusion and socialisation. Clifford Odimegwu's (2005) study among university youth in Nigeria also revealed a strong relationship between religiosity and adolescent sexual attitudes and behaviour, and religious commitment was more important than religious affiliation in shaping adolescent sexual attitudes and behaviours (see also Agha 2008).

Research shows that involvement in religious institutions enhances the chances of young people making friends with peers who have restrictive attitudes towards premarital sex. Young people who are active in religion would have increased contact with adults who might be influential in leading them to delay sexual involvement. Among several others, studies in South Africa (Zantsi et al 2004) and in Ghana (Beal 2005) strongly confirm this claim. Further, according to Aisha Maulana et al (2009), although Islamic values portraying sex outside of marriage as sinful contribute to HIV transmission by encouraging people to reject safe-sex practice, and stigma associated with sinful behaviour interferes with access to care for those infected, adherence to Islamic religious can still offer a starting point for health promotion in Muslim communities. Working with Islamic leaders in Lamu, Kenya, Maulana and colleagues identified texts that apply to sexual conduct, health, stigma and the responsibilities of Islamic clerics toward their congregations. They also uncovered particular conditions under which Koranic texts justify the promotion of safer-sex methods, including condom use.

In the era of HIV, the custodial role of religion is contested as opposing parties continue to debate HIV/AIDS as God's punishment for human sexual waywardness. Denunciation of the faithful for the sinful ways that lead them to contract

HIV has contributed to extremely negative attitudes about gender, sex and sexuality, leading to unnecessary guilt and oppression among people of faith (UNAIDS 2003). Indeed, arguments continue to rage about the contribution of religion to the war of sexually transmitted diseases on the continent. A 2007 World Health Organisation report found that faith-based organisations provided 33–40 per cent of all HIV-related care and treatment services in Zambia and Lesotho and that between 30 and 70 per cent of all healthcare infrastructures across the African continent are operated by faith-based groups.

However, the response of the religious community to HIV and AIDS has not always been positive. At the international symposium Religious Health Organisations Break the Silence on HIV/AIDS, organised by the African Regional Forum of Religious Health Organisations during the 13th International AIDS Conference in July 2000 (Singh 2001), it was agreed that religious doctrines, moral and ethical positions regarding sexual behaviour, sexism and homophobia, and the denial of the realities of HIV/AIDS have helped to create the perception that those infected have sinned and deserve their 'punishment', increasing the stigma associated with HIV/AIDS. Further, the popular belief that AIDS is 'almighty intention to discipline sinners' was inspired by established religion and has stuck in many places in Africa.

Yet, there is no universality in the response of organised religion to sexuality in Africa. In some religious groups, beliefs about the paranormal are regularly invoked, especially by the leadership to obtain sexual favours from the laity, while in others strict doctrines aimed at preventing sexual expression outside monogamous marriages are emphasised. Furthermore, although some religious leaders and groups continue to stigmatise people living with HIV and sexual minorities, others have opened their arms to such people.

Sexuality has become a defining feature of some religious movements in Africa. For instance, the controversial House of Rainbow Church in Lagos prides itself as a Christian religious group that professes extravagant welcome for all persons, especially lesbians, gays, bisexuals and the transgendered. The church describes the mind of its doctrine as radical inclusivity: the belief that all persons are welcome at the table. This doctrine challenges core deep-seated beliefs, doctrines and theologies at the centre of established religion and society, which characterise people on the edges as God's foes and routinely mistreat, oppress and exclude them from the community of faith and its institutions. But the official position of the Nigerian Anglican Communion is that 'there could be no compromise over homosexuality because it is clearly outlawed by the Bible' (Ojo 2003). The Anglican communion also insists that 'homosexuals are worse than animals in the forest' (Ojo 2005).

Mainstream Islam forbids homosexuality. In some Islamic African Islamic countries, (including Mauritania and some states in Nigeria), sharia Islamic religious law prescribes the death penalty for consensual same-sex relations. Other African countries punish homosexuality with fines, jail or lashes and social stigma. The Qu'ran, writes Nicole Kligerman, is very explicit in its condemnation of homosexuality:

> In the Qu'ran, homosexuals are referred to as *qaum Lut* (Lot's people), referring
> to the prophet Lut (known as Lot in the Christian Bible) who preached against
> homosexuality in the cities of Sodom and Gomorra, which were subsequently

destroyed. In the Qu'ran, Lut questions, 'How can you lust for males, of all creatures in the world, and leave those whom God has created for you as your mates? You are really going beyond all limits' (26: 165–166) The Prophet Muhammad adds, 'Doomed by God is who does what Lot's people did [i.e. homosexuality].' The Prophet also comments that, 'No man should look at the private parts of another man, and no woman should look at the private parts of another woman, and no two men sleep [in bed] under one cover, and no two women sleep under one cover'. In his last speech, known as the 'Farewell Sermon', the Prophet added a last condemnation of homosexuality, saying, 'Whoever has intercourse with a woman and penetrates her rectum, or with a man, or with a boy, will appear on the Last Day stinking worse than a corpse; people will find him unbearable until he enters hell fire, and God will cancel all his good deeds'. (Kligerman 2007: 53)

However, Muslim community leaders from several African countries including Sudan, South Africa, Kenya and Senegal have recently begun to defy official Islamic homophobia, leading to movements in Islam that now accept and consider homosexuality as normal and natural. Some of these movements have either regarded Qu'ranic verses as obsolete in the context of modern society or dismissed prevailing interpretations of Qu'ranic verses related to homosexuality as incorrect and erroneous. One Islamic group in South Africa for instance has thus argued that the Qu'ran is against homosexual lust, but not homosexual love. The work of The Inner Circle, a human rights organisation in South Africa that focuses on gender and sexual diversity from an Islamic perspective, shows how gay Muslims are questioning the Hadith and the Qu'ran to find their place with an all-loving Allah (The Inner Circle 2009).

The immense contrasts in religious doctrines surrounding sexuality in Africa also receive amplification in Matthews A. Ojo's (2005) comparison of the Deeper Life Bible Church and College of Regeneration-all of Nigeria. Although Emmanuel Odumosu, the founder of the College of Regeneration, possessed sexual privileges over any female member or the wives of his followers as part of his divine benefits for leading them from darkness, William Kumuyi, the founder and overseer-general of the Deeper Life Bible Church, insists that any form of sexual activity occurring before and outside marriage is an unwholesome submission of one's body to sinful pleasures, which is punishable by eternal damnation. Indeed, the diversity of religious beliefs and practices with respect to sexuality in contemporary Africa suggests that there is a role for religion and faith in the struggle to promote sexual well-being and respectful human sexuality. Religious systems have core belief systems that can be harnessed positively, and research on spirituality and religion truly presents an untapped resource in the struggle for sexual health in Africa.

Conclusion

Although in no way comprehensive, this review shows that the supernatural and sexuality in Africa have historically been linked in a multiplicity of ways. Taken together, they reveal a rich tradition of research and writing focusing on both how sexuality impacts and is impacted by the supernatural. This relationship has also been theorised in many different ways. But gaps remain in knowledge about the links. For instance, very little research has carefully explored the gendered and generational nature of the sexuality and supernatural connect in Africa. And little has focused on the particular role of silence and secrecy surrounding both sexuality-related behaviours and the supernatural in contributing to the ways their relationship has been imagined and depicted.

Other issues that require urgent attention include the nature of historical changes in beliefs surrounding the relationship between the supernatural and sexuality, the drivers of these changes and their implications for social organisation in contemporary Africa. The critical role of cultural anxiety about the destabilising implications of pleasure and eroticism for political power in driving the sexuality–supernatural connect is also unexplored.

'Socio-sexual anxiety', as McFadden (2003) calls it, is based on the realisation of the potential of sexual pleasure to support new forms of self-awareness, which could disrupt power structures as well as the basis of social cohesion. In this sense, there has been a lack of in-depth theories about the ways in which the mystification of sexuality and the sexualisation of the supernatural might have been ideological tools to sustain traditional power structures by preventing certain forms of sexual exploration and experimentation, as well as behaviours that bring the supernatural into disrepute.

Notes

1. For more detail on the ritual, see http://witches.monstrous.com/sabbat_ritual.htm (n.d.) accessed 18 December 2010.
2. Consequently, there are some African societies in which twins are considered to be icons of supernatural reproduction, and feature in rituals of fertility and harvests. In some Nigerian, Beninese and Togolese cultures, it is believed that sexual intercourse with a twin can turn things around for infertile men and women.
3. An ongoing study by Chimaraoke Izugbara in Nigeria has thrown up a new concept – Papi Wata (a male sea-god) – raising the possibility of alternative, reconstituted and masculinised imaginations of the peripatetic Mami Wata.

References

Adegbola, M. (1998) 'Traditional Igede social organisation', unpublished thesis, Department of Sociology, Benue State University

Agha, P. (2008) 'Changes in the timing of sexual initiation among young Muslim and Christian women in Nigeria', *Archives of Sexual Behaviour* 10, 1007/s10508-008-9395

Ahlberg, M.B. (1979) 'Beliefs and practices concerning treatment of measles and acute diarrhoea among the Akamba', *Tropical and Geographic Medicine* 31: 139–48

Ahlberg, B. M (1994) 'Is there a distinct African sexuality? A critical response to Caldwell', *Africa: Journal of the International African Institute* 64(2): 220–42

Akyeampong, E. (1997) 'Sexuality and prostitution among the Akan of the Gold Coast c.1650–1950', *Past and Present* 156:144–73

Alaba, O. (2004) 'Understanding sexuality in the Yoruba culture', *Understanding Human Sexuality*, Series 1, Lagos, African Regional Sexuality Resource Centre

Amadiume, I. (n.d.) 'Sexuality, African religio-cultural traditions and modernity: expanding the lens', http://www.arsrc.org/downloads/features/amadiume.pdf, accessed 3 July 2010

Anonymous (2002) *Rape of Innocents*, http://www.snopes.com/inboxer/petition/babyrape.asp, accessed 12 March 2010

Appiah-Kubi, K. (1981) *Man Cures, God Heals: Religion and Medical Practice among the Akans of Ghana*, New York, Friendship Press

Auslander, M. (1993) '"Open the wombs!" The symbolic politics of modern Ngoni witchfinding', in Comaroff, J. and Comaroff, J. (eds) *Modernity and its Malcontents: Ritual and Power in Postcolonial Africa*, Chicago, University of Chicago Press

Awolalu, J.O. (1976) 'Sin and its removal in African traditional religion', *Journal of the American Academy of Religion* XLIV(2): 275–87

Bailey, R.C., Neema, S. and Othieno, R. (1999) 'Sexual behaviours and other HIV risk factors in circumcised and uncircumcised men in Uganda', *Journal of AIDS* 22(3): 213–14

Barber, Karin (1981) 'How man makes God in West Africa: Yoruba attitudes towards the Orisa', *Africa: Journal of the International African Institute* 51(3): 724–45

Barthes, R. (1972) *Mythologies*, New York, NY, Noonday Press

Bastian, M.L. (1997) 'Married in the water: spirit kin and other afflictions of modernity in southeastern Nigeria', *Journal of Religion in Africa* 22 (2)116–34

Beal, K.E. (2005) 'Religiosity and HIV risk among adolescents in Accra: a qualitative analysis (Preliminary findings from the field)', *Sexuality in Africa* 2(2): 11–14

Beidelman, T.O. (1963) 'Pig (Guluwe): an essay on Ngulu sexual symbolism and ceremony', *Southwestern Journal of Anthropology* 20(4): 359–92

—— (1966) 'Utani: some Kaguru notions of death, sexuality and affinity', *Southwestern Journal of Anthropology* 22(4) 354–80

—— (1972) 'The filth of incest: a text and comments on Kaguru notions of sexuality, alimentation and aggression', *Cahiers d'Études Africaines* 12(45) 164–173

—— (1982) *Colonial Evangelism: A Socio-historical Study of an East African Mission at the Grassroots*, Indianapolis, Indiana University Press

Bwayo, J., Plummer, F., Omari, M., Mutere, A., Moses, S. and Ndinya-Achola, J. (1994) 'Human immunodeficiency virus infection in long-distance truck drivers in East Africa', *Archives of Internal Medicine* 154(12): 1391–96

Chege, J.N. (1993) 'The politics of gender and fertility regulation in Kenya: a case study of the Igembe', PhD thesis, Lancaster, Lancaster University

Comaroff, J. and Comaroff, J. (1999) 'Occult economies and the violence of abstraction: Notes from the South African postcolony', *American Ethnologist* 26(2): 279–303

Crawley, A.E. (1895) 'Sexual taboo: a study in the relations of the sexes', *The Journal of the Anthropological Institute of Great Britain and Ireland* 24: 116–25

Dimgba, O. (2000) 'Twinship in Igbo society: a socio-historical study', Msc thesis, Department of History and Strategic Studies, University of Uyo, Nigeria

Drewal, H.J. (1988) 'Mermaids, mirrors and snake charmers: Igbo Mami Wata', *Shrines African Arts* 21(2): 38–45

Egonji, W. (2001) *Sexual Taboos of Some Ethnic Groups in Bayelsa State, Nigeria*, Department of Religious Studies, Uyo, University of Uyo

Ekong, E.E. (2001) *Sociology of the Ibibio: A Study of Social Organisation and Change*, Uyo, Modern Business Press

Ember, C.R. (1978) 'Men's fear of sex with women: a cross-cultural study', *Sex Roles* 4: 657–78

Erhabor, F. (2004) 'Pentecostal movement and adolescent sexuality in Ile-Ife, Osun State, Nigeria', unpublished MSc thesis, Department of Religious Studies, Obafemi Awolowo University

Evans-Pritchard, E.E. (1933) 'Childhood: The Zande Corporation of Witchdoctors', *The Journal of the Royal Anthropological Institute*, LXIII: 63–100

—— (1937) *Witchcraft, Oracles and Magic Among the Azande*, Oxford, The Clarendon Press

—— (1970) 'Sexual inversion among the Azande', *American Anthropologist* 72(6): 1428–34

Ezeh, P.J. (2007) 'Sex, custom, and population: a Nigerian example', paper presented at the fifth African Population Conference, Arusha, 10–14 December

Fadiman, A. (1997) *The Spirit Catches You and You Fall Down*, New York, Farrar, Straus and Giroux

Garner, R.C. (2000) 'Safe sects? Dynamic religion and AIDS in South Africa', *Journal of Modern African Studies* 38: 41–69

Garrett, W.R. (1974) 'Troublesome transcendence: the supernatural in the scientific study of religion', *Sociological Analysis* 35(3):167–80

Gaudio, R. (2009) *Allah Made Us: Sexual Outlaws in an Islamic African City*, New York, NY, Wiley and Sons

Goad, J. (2005) 'Koro, Koro, Koro: The wild, wacky, and weird phenomenon of penis panics', October, http://www.xmag.com/archives/13-04-oct05/feature2.html, accessed 13 August 2010

Gray, P.B. (2004) 'HIV and Islam: is HIV prevalence lower among Muslims?', *Social Science and Medicine* 58(9): 1751–56

Greenberg, D. (1988) *The Construction of Homosexuality*, Chicago, University of Chicago Press

Grey, R.H., Kiwanuka, N., Quinn, T.C. and Sewankambo, N.K. (2000) 'Male circumcision and HIV acquisition and transmission: cohort studies in Rakai, Uganda', *AIDS* 14: 2371–81

Hackett, R.J. (2003) 'Discourses of demonisation in Africa and beyond', *Diogenes* 50(3): 61–75

Hammond-Tooke (1974) 'The Cape Nguni witch familiar as a mediatory construct', *Man* 9(1): 128–36

Hauge, H.E. (1974) *Luo Religion and Folklore*, Oslo/Bergen/Tromsø, Universitetsforlaget

Heald, S. (1995) 'The power "African Sexuality" thesis', *Africa: Journal of the International African Institute* 65(4): 489–505

—— (1999) *Manhood and Morality. Sex, Violence and Ritual in Gisu Society*, London and New York, NY, Routledge

The Inner Circle (2009) http://www.theinnercircle.org.za/wp-content/uploads/TIC_AIR_2009_REPORT.pdf, accessed 20 July, 2010

Isiugo-Abanihe, U.C. (1994) 'Extramarital relations and perceptions of HIV/AIDS in Nigeria', *Health Transition Review* 4(2): 111–25

Izugbara, C. (2008) *Healing Traditions Among the Ngwa of Nigeria*, Aba, Mimeo Burgsey Research Centre

—— (2010) 'Nigerian tales of occult sexual economies', in Undie, C., Izugbara, C. and Khamasi, W. (eds) *Old Wineskins, New Wine: Readings in Sexuality in sub-Saharan Africa*, New York, NY, Nova Press

Jell-Bahlsen, S. (1997) 'Eze Mmiri Di Egwu: the water monarch is awesome: reconsidering the Mammy water myths', *Annals of the New York Academy of Sciences* 810: 103–34

—— (2008) *The Water Goddess in Igbo Cosmology – Ogbuide of Oguta Lake*, Trenton, Africa World Press

Killewo, J., Dahlgren, L. and Sandstrom, A. (1994) 'Socio-geographical patterns of HIV-1 transmission in Kagera region, Tanzania', *Social Science and Medicine* 38(1): 129–34

Kligerman, N. (2007) 'Homosexuality in Islam: a difficult paradox', *Macalester Islam Journal* 2(3): 52–64

Kluckhohn, C. (1949) *Mirror for Man: The Relationship of Anthropology to Modern Life*, New York, NY, Whittlesey House

Kohnert, D. (1996) 'Magic and witchcraft: implications for democratisation and poverty-alleviating aid in Africa', *World Development* 24(8): 1347–55

Lagarde, E., Enel, C., Seck, K., Gueye-Ndiaye, A., Piau, J., Pison, G., Delaunay, V., Ndoye, I., Mboup, S. and Mecora Group (2000) 'Religion and protective behaviours towards AIDS in rural Senegal', *AIDS* 14: 2027–33

Leclerc-Madlala, S. (2002) 'On the virgin cleansing myth: gendered bodies, AIDS and ethnomedicine', *African Journal of AIDS Research* 1: 87–95

Levine, R.A. (1959) 'Gusii sex offences: a study in social control', *American Anthropologist* 61: 963–90

Levine, R.A. and Campbell, D.T. (1972) *The Gusii of Kenya*, New Haven, CT, Human Relations Area File

Levine, R.A. and Levine, B. (1966) *Nyansongo: A Gusii Community*, New York, NY, Wiley

Malamba, S.S., Wagner, H.U., Maude, G., Okongo, M., Nunn, A.J. and Kengeya-Kayondo, J.F. (1994) 'Risk factors for HIV-1 infection in adults in a rural Ugandan community: a case-control study', *AIDS* 8(2): 253–7

Mather, C. (2005) 'Accusations of genital theft: a case from Northern Ghana', *Culture, Medicine, and Psychiatry* 29(10): 33–52

Maulana, A.O., Krumeich, A. and Van den Borne, B. (2009) 'Emerging discourse: Islamic teaching in HIV prevention in Kenya', *Culture, Health and Sexuality* 11 (5): 559–69

Mbulaiteye, S.M., Ruberantwaria, A., Nakiyingia, J.S., Carpenter, L.M. et al (2000) 'Alcohol and HIV: a study among sexually active adults in rural southwest Uganda', *International Journal of Epidemiology* 29: 911–15

McFadden, P. (2003) 'Sexual pleasure as feminist choice', *Feminist Africa* 2: 50–60

Meel, B.L. (2003) 'The myth of child rape as a cure for HIV/AIDS in Transkei: a case report', *Medicine Science and the Law* 43: 85–8

Meyer, B. (1995) '"Delivered from the powers of darkness": confessions of satanic riches in Christian Ghana', *Africa* 65(2): 236–55

—— (1998) 'The power of money; politics, occult forces and the Pentecostalism in Ghana', *African Studies Review* 41(3): 15–37

—— (1999) *Translating the Devil: Religion and Modernity Among the Ewe in Ghana*, IAL-Series, Trenton, NJ, Edinburgh University Press

—— (2001) 'Money, power and morality: popular Ghanaian cinema in the fourth republic', *Ghana Studies* 4: 65–84

—— (2002) 'Mami water', http://www2.fmg.uva.nl/media-religion/progress/mwmeyer.htm, accessed 14 August 2008

Moreau, R.E. (1941) 'The joking relationship *(Vbni)* in Tanganyika', *Tanganyika Notes and Records* 12: 1–10

Mungure, E. (n.d.) 'Signs of Hope: African woman's perspective in the current re-reading and re-interpreting of the bible in the Lutheran communion', unpublished

Muuko, A. (2002) *Luo Burial Rites*, Kisumu, Ouma Press

Newell, S. (2003) 'Remembering J.M. Stuart-Young of Onitsha, colonial Nigeria: memoirs, obituaries and names', *Africa* 73(4): 505–30

Nicholas, L. and Durrheim, K. (1995) 'Religiosity, AIDS, and sexuality knowledge, attitudes, beliefs and practices of black South African first-year students', *Psychological Reports* 77: 1328–30

Niehaus, I. (1998) 'The ANC's dilemma: three witch-hunts in the South African lowveld', *African Studies Review* 41(3): 15–37

—— (1999) 'Witchcraft, power and politics: exploring the occult in the South African lowfeld', unpublished PhD thesis, University of the Witwatersrand, Johannesburg

—— (2002) 'Perversion of power: witchcraft and the sexuality of evil in the South African lowveld', *Journal of Religion in Africa* 32(3): 269–99

—— (2005) 'Witches and zombies in the South African lowveld: discourse, accusations and subjective reality', *Journal of the Royal Anthropological Institute* 11(2): 191–210

—— (2006) 'Witches and zombies in the South African lowveld: discourse, accusations and subjective reality', *Journal of the Royal Anthropological Institute* 11(2): 191–210

Niehaus, I., Mohala, E. and Shokane, K. (2001) *Witchcraft, Power, and Politics. Exploring the Occult in the South African Lowveld*, London, Pluto Press

Nunn, A.J., Kengeya-Kayondo, J.F., Malamba, S.S., Seeley, J.A. and Mulder, D.W. (1994) 'Risk factors for HIV-1-infection in adults in a rural Ugandan community: a population study', *AIDS* 8(1): 81–6

Nyamnjoh, F.B. (2005) 'Fishing in troubled waters: disquettes and thiofs in Dakar', *Africa: Journal of the International African Institute* 75(3): 295–324

Nyanzi, S., Nassimbwa, J., Kayizzi-Musoke, V. and Kabanda, S. (2004) 'The impact of the HIV/AIDS epidemic on cultural ritual sex customs in southwestern Uganda', abstract no. D11089, Bangkok, International Conference on AIDS, 11–16 July

Obunga, S. (2007) *The Burial Rites of the Luo of Kenya*, Nairobi, Western Press

Odimegwu, C. (2005) 'Influence of religion on adolescent sexual attitudes and behaviour among Nigerian university students: affiliation or commitment?', *African Journal of Reproductive Health* 9(2): 125–40

Offiong, D.A. (1991) *Witchcraft, Sorcery, Magic and Social Order among the Ibibio of Nigeria*, Lagos, Fourth Dimension Press

Ojo, M.A. (1997) 'Sexuality, marriage and piety among charismatic in Nigeria', *Religion* 27: 65–79

—— (2003) 'The Anglican crackup: the view from Lagos', *Religion in the News* 6(3), http://www.trinoll.edu/depts/crspl/RINVol6No3/viewfromlagos.doc.htm, accessed 7 May 2009

—— (2005) 'Religion and sexuality: individuality, choice and sexual rights in Nigerian Christianity', *Understanding Human Sexuality*, Series 4, Lagos, African Regional Sexuality Resource Centre

Okolo, D. G. (1998) *Sexual Behavior and Hygiene in Traditional Igbo Society*, Owerri, Greenbook Press

Olowo-Ojoade, J. (1983) 'African sexual proverbs: some Yoruba examples', *Folklore* 94(2): 201–13

Oriji, N. (1972) 'A history of the Ngwa people', PhD thesis, Newark, University of New Jersey

Pearson, J. (2005) 'Inappropriate sexuality? Sex, magic, S/M, and Wicca (or whipping Harry Potter's arse)', *Theology and Sexuality*, 11(2): 31–42

Peters, I.L. (1918) 'The institutionalised sex taboo', PhD thesis, Worcester, Clark University

Radcliffe-Brown A.R. (1952) *Structure and Function in Primitive Society: Essays and Addresses*, Glencoe, IL, Free Press

Rakwar, J., Lavreys, L., Thompson, M., Jackson, D., Bwayo, J., Hassanali, S. et al (1999) 'Cofactors for the acquisition of HIV-1 among heterosexual men: Prospective cohort study of trucking company workers in Kenya', *AIDS* 13(5): 607–14

Renne E.P. (2001) 'Twinship in an Ekiti Yoruba town,' *Ethnology* 40: 63–78

Ritzer, G. and Goodman, D. (2010) *Sociological Theory*, New York, NY, McGraw-Hill

Roper, L. (1994) *Oedipus and the Devil: Witchcraft, Sexuality and Religion in Early Modern Europe*, London and New York, NY, Routledge

Roscoe, W. (1997) 'Precursors of Islamic male homosexualities', in Murray, S. and Roscoe, W. (eds) *Islamic Homosexualities*, New York, New York University Press

Saler, B. (1977) 'Supernatural as a western category', *Ethos* 5(1) 31–53

Schroer, K. (2005) 'When size matters: genital retraction syndromes in cultural perspective', *Focus Anthropology* 5, http://www.focusanthro.org/archive/2005-2006.html

Singh, B. (2001) 'Breaking the silence on HIV/AIDS: religious health organizations and reproductive health', *Conscience*, Washington DC, Catholics for a Free Choice

Smith, D.J. (2004) 'Youth, sin and sex in Nigeria: Christianity and HIV/AIDS-related beliefs and behaviour among rural-urban migrants', *Culture, Health and Sexuality* 6(5): 425–37

Smyth, L. (2006) 'The cultural politics of sexuality and reproduction in Northern Ireland', *Sociology* 40(4): 663–80

Somé, M.P. (1994) *Of Water and Spirit: Ritual, Magic and Initiation in the Life of an African Shaman*, New York, Tarcher/Putnam

Stannus, H.S. (1910) 'Notes on some tribes of British Central Africa', *The Journal of the Royal Anthropological Institute of Great Britain and Ireland* 40: 285–335

Strassmann B. (1992) 'The function of menstrual taboos among the Dogon: defense against cuckoldry?', *Human Nature* 3: 89–131

Talbot, P.A. (1926) *The Peoples of Southern Nigeria*, London, Oxford University Press

—— (1932) *Tribes of the Niger Delta: Their Religions and Customs*, London, The Sheldon Press

Trinitapoli, J. (2006) 'Religious responses to AIDS in sub-Saharan Africa: an examination of religious congregations in rural Malawi', *Review of Religious Research* 47(3): 253–70

Trinitapoli, J. and Regnerus, M. (2006) 'Religion and HIV risk behaviours among married men: initial results from a study in rural sub-Saharan Africa', *Journal for the Scientific Study of Religion* 45: 505–28

Turner V. (1969) *The Ritual Process: Structure and Anti-structure*, New Brunswick, Aldine

Transaction

Uchendu, V.C. (1965a) *The Igbo of South Eastern Nigeria*, New York, NY, Holt, Rinehart and Winston

—— (1965b) 'Concubinage among Ngwa Igbo of Southern Nigeria', *Africa* 35(2): 187–97)

—— (2007) 'Ezi Na Ulo: the extended family in Igbo civilisation', *Dialectical Anthropology* 31(1–3): 167–219

UNAIDS (2003) 'A report of the theological workshop focusing on HIV- and AIDS-related stigma', Windhoek, UNAIDS

Undie, C., Izugbara, C.O. and Khamasi, W. (2009) 'Old wineskins, new wine', in Izugbara, C.O., Undie, C. and Khamasi, W. (eds) *Readings in Sexuality in Sub-Saharan Africa*, New York, NY, NOVA Press

Wilson, M.W. (1951) *Witch Beliefs and Social Structure*, Indianapolis, IN, Bobbs-Merrill

—— (1957) *Rituals of Kinship among the Nyakusya*, London, Oxford Unversity Press

World Health Organisation (WHO) (2006) 'Defining sexual health: report of a technical consultation on sexual health, 28–31 January 2002', Geneva, WHO

Zantsi, K., Pettifor, A.E., Madikizela-Hlongwa, L., MacPhail, C. and Rees, H.V. (2004) 'Religiousness and sexual behaviour among South African youth', Bangkok, International Conference on AIDS, 11–16 July

Zulu, E.M. (2001) 'Ethnic variations in observance and rationale for postpartum sexual abstinence in Malawi', *Demography* 38(4): 467–79

60

'African sex is dangerous!' Renegotiating 'ritual sex' in contemporary Masaka district, Uganda[1]

Stella Nyanzi, Justine Nassimbwa, Vincent Kayizzi
and Strivan Kabanda

Introduction

HIV in sub-Saharan Africa is predominantly spread through unsafe heterosexual contact. For a long time, the culture of African peoples has been presented as the cause of the high prevalence and incidence of HIV/AIDS on the African continent. Examples include Caldwell et al (1989) and several Caldwellians,[2] who highlight traditional cultural practices, 'the African system of sexuality' and the values and attitudes of sub-Saharan Africans as responsible for the rampant spread of the pandemic.[3]

This article contributes to a body of criticism (including Le Blanc et al 1991; Ahlberg 1994; Heald 1995; Arnfred 2004) of the Caldwellians' positivist, deterministic, homogenising and ethnocentric view, which assumes that culture is a concept set in stone – fixed, rigid and static. Furthermore, a Caldwellian analytical framework assumes that while culture has drastic impacts on social phenomena such as health, sexuality and gender norms, these phenomena remain unchanging, dormant and stagnant. They neglect the two-way interaction between culture – in this case sexual culture[4] – and health.

Based within a Caldwellian perspective, several behavioural interventions aimed at reducing further spread of HIV/AIDS have set out to change sexual practices emanating from this 'dangerous' African traditional culture. These attempts have yielded a growing body of scholarship uncritically chronicling 'harmful traditional and cultural practices' (for example Ssengendo and Ssekatawa 1999; Packer 2002). Uganda, for example, is rife with information, education and communication messages channelled through diverse media, specifically addressing change from 'harmful' to 'safer' practices – mostly rooted within local culture. Thus Kiganda[5] sexual culture is continuously challenged.

Collins O. Airhihenbuwa (1995) criticises mimicking Western biomedical blueprint theories in different contexts without a priori contextual consideration. Based within Airhihenbuwa's paradigmatic shift away from culturalist explanations that reify and ostracise an assumed homogeneous African culture (see also Ranger 1983; Adams and Markus 2001; Winthrop 2002), this chapter describes contemporary ritual sex[6] practices among Baganda in Masaka district, Uganda. It considers the interplay between sexual culture and HIV/AIDS in a context of diverse social, political and economic transformations.

Without wishing to exoticise the sexual practices under discussion, we choose the umbrella label 'ritual sex' to define sexual activity mandated by social expectation or cultural tradition rather than individual choice. This can vary from explicit mandates to engage in sex at specific times in prescribed positions with particular partners, to cultural events and ceremonies in which the normal code of sexual exchange and negotiation is altered, making sexual partnership easier. Kiganda sexual norms of labia elongation (okusika enfuli), stylised articulation and gesticulation for sex (okusikina) and hygiene in sex (eby'ekikumbi) are excluded from this definition because they are an unmarked, standard part of ordinary life (see Tamale 2005 for details). Ritual sex is marked behaviour focalising transitions, key moments, turning points and unusual occurrences, such as the birth of twins.

When an association is made between the 'African system of sexuality' and the increasing HIV/AIDS epidemic, it is assumed that the persistence of inherent sexual practices has a direct impact on the spread of HIV. However, cultural practices by their very nature are subject to reinterpretation and change. The process of transformation might be faster in cases of ritual sex practices that have been under sociopolitical assault from institutions associated with religion, colonisation and, more recently, anti-HIV/AIDS efforts. Thus, ritual sex offers unique insights into transformations of sociocultural norms in our study setting.

The study investigated the persistence and adaptation of ritual sex practices and the institutional contexts in which they occur in contemporary Masaka district. This chapter investigates how individuals and specific groups negotiate meanings and practices of culturally prescribed sexual customs, and the diverse influences shaping local nuances within Kiganda sexual culture. It also examines the role of HIV/AIDS in re-scripting contemporary sexual behaviour.

The study setting

Fieldwork was conducted between 2001 and 2003 in rural and urban Masaka district. Masaka district was the first area[7] in Uganda to record cases of HIV/AIDS (Serwadda et al 1985; Ministry of Health 2003). Extending westwards from Lake Victoria, Masaka is predominantly a rural district whose population mainly depends upon subsistence agriculture. Historically, the area currently called Masaka district was Essaza ly'eBuddu – one of four counties comprising the Buganda kingdom.[8] Consequently, the majority of the population are Baganda – a Bantu-speaking ethnic group, who claim common ancestry and are socially organised in patrilineal clans that foster cultural identity and belonging (Kagwa 1905; Roscoe 1911).

According to Kiganda custom, marriage is both exogamous to the clan and patrilocal, although wives maintain affiliation to their paternal clan. Polygyny is acceptable. Children belong to their father's clan (Kisekka 1972, 1976; Musisi 1991). Kiganda religion revolves around the worship of ancestors, spirits and shades. Kiganda medicine and religion merge in belief and practice.

The main religion in the district is Roman Catholicism, followed by Protestantism and Islam. Uganda's colonial legacy is such that religion influences national and local politics, as well as social policy and reality. Religious affiliation determines social, political and economic outcomes at diverse levels; exclusion from and inclusion into a range of opportunities are often based on religious classification or identity. Historical legacies of religious animosities still persist in contemporary Uganda, in addition to segregation along tribal, racial, sectarian and gender lines.

Methods

Professor James Whitworth[9] seeded the idea of the study after reading Ntozi's (1997) work on remarriage and widowhood in Uganda. We initially set out to establish the prevalence of the custom of levirate marriage in Masaka district. However, in keeping with the grounded theory approach (Stewart 1998), our ethnographic study broadened in scope to explore new generic themes including ritual sex, death rituals, social policy, reconstructed tradition and institutional transformations. Data collection triangulated mainly qualitative methods, such as ethnographic participant observation, case studies, individual in-depth interviews, focus group discussions, a mini-survey of cultural ceremonies occurring in the past year and literature review.

Participants were selected using purposive, snow-ball and theoretical sampling techniques from relevant social categories including traditional healers, Kiganda herbalists, elders, *mutuba* bark-cloth makers, Luganda language instructors, clan land owners called *abataka*, clan leaders, widows, widowers, Munno Mukabi burial society members, 'twin parents',[10] religious authorities from the Roman Catholic, Anglican, Pentecostal and Islamic faiths, district administrators from the directorates of health, education and culture, and Buganda Kingdom representatives in Masaka district, such as the Pokino (a local stand-in for the Kabaka).

We attended cultural ceremonies including last funeral rites and burials in order to observe behaviour, listen to conversations and acquaint ourselves with more subtle nuances of cultural practice. Formal interviews were recorded on audio tape in the participants' language of preference, transcribed verbatim, translated from Luganda into English where necessary, and stored on a computer. Together with field notes from participant observation and debriefing sessions, this data was subjected to discourse analysis using Atlas.ti, a German scientific software.

Ethical considerations

The joint science and ethics committee of the Medical Research Council/Uganda Virus Research Institute approved the study. Clan elders were asked for permission to attend ceremonies in their clans. Written informed consent was obtained from participants before conducting formal interviews. Participants were free to refuse to participate, withdraw at any time without giving a reason or refrain from answering questions that made them uncomfortable. Names of participants and villages were changed in order to ensure anonymity.

From the special to the mundane: a continuum of sex practices

Sex appeases the spirit of death

In the data, the most frequently mentioned cultural experience associated with ritual sex was *okwabya olumbe*[11] (a literal translation is 'bursting the death'), which is a label for a series of rituals encompassed within last funeral rites. Sexual intercourse is mandated in three peculiar instances: *okumala kafiisa* (completing to be robbed by death), *okumala olumbe* (completing the death) and *eby'abakuza* (things of guardians/ widow inheritors).

Okumala kafiisa was discussed as a cultural requirement of sexual intercourse between two biological parents at the death of their offspring. Participants reported that this custom is particularly essential in cases in which the dead child had not yet produced offspring. After the burial ceremony and an ensuing period of mourning,[12] the parents are supposed to have sexual intercourse to mark or celebrate the end of their public mourning for their child. Prior to the sexual act, the parents bathe with a herbal concoction of purificative and preventive medicines obtained from traditional healers to spiritually insure their children, clan members and kin against another visit from death. This ritual culminates in sexual intercourse.

After having fulfilled their spiritual, moral, cultural and kin obligation, the couple are free to proceed with their normal life. Several elders associated the rampant rates of death in the community with contemporary neglect by parents of a responsibility enshrined in Kiganda mores and values. Some participants reported that it was so important in the past that even in cases where parents were separated by different circumstances – including divorce, war or community service to the Kabaka – they would still come together for this ritual, in order to protect the wider kin group and clan from contagion and unnecessary death. The majority of youth participants were not even aware of the existence of this ritual, although a few had heard about it:

> **Julie**: Okay. Let us imagine the man stays alone, and the woman also is somewhere else, or they have separated, and they do not meet at all. But this woman has a child by this man. Then the child dies. So what they could do in the past, they could count four days. And after those days both parents washed with some medicine. And then they have sex. So if the baby was still young – like still breast-feeding or a bit older – this means that the woman will have sex and conceive. So she will still be a member of this family again. And that is why there is sex at the weaning of babies. This is because they wanted

to conceive again. Those were tricks. And we take them to be part of the culture. (Focus group discussion with widows)

As in the above example, a few female participants were critical of the role of this
ritual because it ensured that women continued to play their reproductive role,
thereby enhancing their male benefactors' clan.

During the last funeral rites ceremony (*okwabya olumbe*), the ritual known as *okumala olumbe* is mandated for the spouses of immediate family members. The most
visible version of this ritual is the cultural prescription for widows, which was mentioned in all the focus group discussions and key informant interviews. Analysis
reveals tensions between the recipients – widows – and those who uphold its necessity. Several participants provided anecdotes about how, in the past, the widow
was required to have sex with a male agnate of her deceased husband. This was
often authenticated as enshrined in true traditional Kiganda culture. Further investigation, particularly among the widows, widowers, clan elders and the traditional
healers about actual practice reveals that no one admitted actually experiencing or
participating in a ritual involving penetrative sexual intercourse.

Instead, we collected a range of symbolic sexual intercourse practices which
different widows had undergone. Many of these widows reported that they were
instructed to sit on the floor in the doorway of their main house with legs stretched
outwards. Then a male agnate of their late spouse jumped once, twice or thrice
over their extended legs to symbolise the sexual act. Some other widows reported
that amid much debate and crying, the clan leaders instructed them to provide an
inner cloth-belt,[13] spread it on the floor in the doorway and have the male agnate
jump over it. It was important that this belt was still warm with the body heat of the
widow. A rarer version involved a young widow who was instructed to drink a lot
of tea but refrain from urination prior to the ritual of *okumala olumbe* – which was
not explained to her until the early hours of the morning, when she was instructed
to urinate in a spot directly in front of the house. Thereafter she was shoved away
and to her amazement a younger unmarried brother-in-law was also instructed to
urinate in exactly the same spot, just before her urine dissolved into the earth.

Reference was often made to the widow having to cope with imitating the sexual act with a male in-law during the last funeral rites ceremony. We often probed
participants to further examine why this form of ritual sex had varying shapes.
Many immediately referred to the fear of (re)infection with sexually transmitted
infections (STI), specifically HIV/AIDS. Some widows in the discussions were open
about their HIV-positive status and commented that even when the culture dictated
sexual intercourse with them, the minute they were suspected of carrying the virus
it was important for the family and clan elders to renegotiate how the ritual could
be conducted without necessarily having penetrative sexual intercourse. Several
participants were aware of a recently introduced practice in traditional medicine
– a prophylactic against the effect of not undertaking the ritual. In this case, a traditional healer prepared medicines to be bathed with and fetishes for carrying to
protect the wider kin group from more deaths.

However, in cases in which the cause of the spouse's death was not related
to HIV/AIDS, some widows reported approaching the ceremony with a lot of

apprehension because they were aware of the cultural expectations, but nobody had prepared or informed them about the procedures and requirements until the night of the ritual. From our data, there were no similar cultural requirements for widowers – that is, there was no requirement for sororate marriage – although two widowers had in fact produced children with their late wives' sisters.

In patrilineal societies, such as Buganda, kinship ties are established through the male parent. At marriage, a bride fetches bridewealth for her patrilineal kin when her husband's family takes over her reproductive rights and functions. Consequently, at the husband's death, the institution of levirate marriage ensures that the ownership of the widow and her progeny remains within this family. Also known as 'widow inheritance', levirate marriage in East Africa has been the focus of other scholars (Roscoe 1911; Kizekka 1972; Heald 1995; Ntozi 1997).

For the older participants, the notion of 'taking over the widow' was necessary and discussed in terms of protecting her from seeking sexual relationships outside the clan in order to support herself and the orphans. Male participants were often quick to emphasise how it was extremely challenging to provide for a widow and her progeny without expecting sexual services from her. Three male participants admitted that they had actually married their dead brothers' widows when they became the *bakuza* (levirate guardians) of the children. All were aged more than 60 years. Furthermore, even though each of these participants was interviewed separately, there was a common insistence about how the 'marriage' was a mutual agreement in which the widow was not coerced to have sexual relations with these *bakuza*. However, we were not able to obtain access to these remarried widows because one had died before the study, one lived outside the study area and the one we located declined to be identified as a remarried widow, but preferred to participate as a traditional herbalist.

Some men discussed levirate marriage in relation to HIV infection and looming poverty, describing the practice as potentially dangerous for male guardians' physical bodies and their financial pockets. Others emphasised the added social responsibility of guiding the widow and orphans – catering for their food, shelter, education, health, well-being and social character – and stressed that it was too demanding to be taken lightly. The male participants tended to be more tolerant, seeking to adjust the stereotypical image of *bakuza* portrayed by the *vox populi*, feminists, human rights advocates and empowerment lawyers, such as the Uganda Association of Women Lawyers, where the *bakuza* are always portrayed as eventually failing in their responsibility of catering for their dead brothers' families. Many male participants argued that the demands upon the *bakuza* could be overwhelming.

Although the older participants associated the opportunity to be *bakuza* with high esteem, honour and respectability, the youths in the study expressed outright rejection of the idea by arguing that there were too many deaths in the present generation for the institution to be relevant: economic hardship is more severe, and there is the risk of getting an HIV-positive widow and orphans whose upkeep is more expensive because of potentially greater need for healthcare services. Furthermore, the youth participants believed HIV-positive widows and orphans were more dependent because of the assumption that they were less able to undertake or sustain hard productive wage labour or profitable income-generating activities owing to weakness related to HIV/AIDS. There was also a general claim about breakdown in kin bonds and cultural ties that previously enhanced the value of committing to an extended family system.

For the female participants, levirate marriage was discussed as a highly ambivalent issue. On the one hand, it was presented as a sociocultural evil perpetuating female subjugation and the abuse of women's rights. At the other extreme, it was a possible solution for dealing with the problems that come with transitioning and adjusting to widowhood. Women participants tended to collectively euphoricise the past successful implementation of levirate marriage. They claimed that it was a solution in the past before poverty and economic hardship introduced phenomena such as land wrangles, inheritance rivalries, discrediting a deceased's will, the overt greed and profligacy of *bakuza*, the over-commodification of sex and the need for reciprocation. The younger widows found tales of responsible *bakuza* – those who catered for the needs of their newly inherited family (of widow and orphans) without expecting sexual services from the widow – rather incredible (see Nyanzi 2004 for details). Instead, their narratives revealed how the transition to widowhood was also a time for negotiating issues of ownership, sexuality and reproduction with their in-laws.

A much more invisible requirement of *okumala olumbe* involves the married family members of the deceased. When a wife lost family – including parents, grandparents, siblings, nieces or nephews – after returning from the last funeral rites, she was expected to sleep apart from the husband (and preferably on the floor). When he was ready to renew conjugal relations with her, the husband would have to buy his mourning wife a new traditional dress called *gomesi*. He would then present it to her and invite her to bed in order to *kumala olumbe* – also variously called *okumunaazako olumbe* – (to wash off death from her) and *okumunaazako amaziga* (to wash off tears from her).

Many of the elders and older study participants reported performing this ritual several times. Money was required to buy a new *gomesi*, and participants revealed that, when money was hard to come by, they sometimes bought or received cheaper items like a second-hand headscarf, a new handkerchief, or a half-slip, or an inner cloth-belt. The sexual act was a mark of the end of the mourning period.

Of sex and birth

The social script for ritual sex in Kiganda culture, as presented by the study participants, vividly marks out two distinct events associated with birth and necessitating specific performances of sex. These are *okumala ekizadde* (to complete a birth) and *emikolo gy'abalongo* (the ceremonies of twins). Participants revealed that after a child is born, custom demands that the parents have sexual intercourse in order to ensure that the child lives well. Varying durations between delivery and the ritual sex were frequently mentioned in the data, including 'four days', 'one week', 'when the woman has healed', 'after the bad blood stops dripping'.

Many participants reported that the ritual mandated penetrative sexual intercourse between the parents. Others described another symbolic performance, which involved simulation of the sexual act with the baby lying in between the parents. In situations where the parents had severed their sexual relationship at the time of the baby's birth, then the alternative method of jumping over the woman's legs could be appropriated in combination with bathing in herbal preventive medicines. Participants believed it was necessary to undertake at least one of these measures, otherwise the infant would suffer a culture-bound syndrome called *obusobe*[14] – characterised by deteriorating appetite, weight loss and even eventual death.

Twin ceremonies have been the focus of several discourses about sexuality in Buganda (Kagwa 1905; Roscoe 1911; Musisi 1991). This attention arose particularly because the colonial missionaries openly condemned twin ceremonies as satanic and barbaric celebrations, involving traditional ancestral worship and characterised by filthy obscenity as well as over-indulgence in promiscuity. Thus, they lured colonial anthropologists to produce ethnographic accounts. Legacies of this current prevailed in the data from twin parents, called Ssalongo and Nnalongo for 'twin father' and 'twin mother' respectively. Noteworthy in the data analysis was the thematic repetition of renouncing twin ceremonies as a prerequisite for religious affiliation to diverse Christian denominations.

> **Suuna**: I will give you the example of twins. People just say that they will treat twins in the modern way just because white people have led us astray, going away from our culture.
>
> **Moses**: But you look here, when you go to confess in church, the priest advises you not to follow the culture. So that is why I said that religions have contributed much towards undermining the culture.
>
> **Katerega**: Yes, we must confess the sin of performing twin ceremonies or even observing twin rites in the family. (Focus group discussion)

It is important to examine critically the stigma surrounding Kiganda twin ceremonies. By renouncing everything to do with cultural twin ceremonies, during the Christian ritual of confession, either to a priest or to a fellowship of brethren, what are Baganda twin parents denying themselves?

Twin ceremonies are one sociocultural space in Buganda society in which adherence to sex prohibition taboos between in-laws is lifted. In everyday reality, physical contact between in-laws separated by generation and gender is taboo. For example, it is believed that when a man touches his mother-in-law, either one or both of them could get struck by *obuko*[15] – an incurable condition in which the sufferer perpetually shakes (tremors), akin to Parkinson's syndrome. During twin ceremonies, physical contact barriers enshrined within *obuko* observances are broken. The twin parents in our study narrated the thrill of body-to-body contact with their in-laws. Amid animated ribaldry, the few twin parents who had conducted these twin ceremonies stressed the significance of the protective power of twins because none of those present had developed *obuko*.

Participants reported that after this ceremony, both Ssalongo and Nnalongo symbolically and rhetorically lose their marital status. Thus the saying, *Ssalongo tabeera mwami* (Ssalongo can never be a *mwami*). Similar to the title Mister, *mwami* is a Luganda label reserved for married men. *Mwami* also means husband. After boldly getting intimate with their in-laws, these twin parents were rhetorically elevated to an estate above marriage. Twin ceremonies were also reported as a space that provided licence to use relatively obscene language with deep sexual images and metaphors. Cultural songs for celebrating twin ceremonies are noted for their explicit employment of sexual innuendoes. In a society in which open public talk about sex and sexuality was taboo, particularly across generations (Kizekka 1976; Kinsman et al 2000; Muyinda et al 2004), the boldness of these songs is indeed a noteworthy celebration of sexuality:

> *Twakedde kumakya kuzina balongo – Be chwi*
> *Akantu kanuma kanjwi-jwiya – Be chwi*
> *Nnalongo baamuyisayo akeeyo – Be chwi*
> We woke this morning to dance/fuck twins – *be chwi*
> My little thing/sex organ is hurting me, it's aching – *be chwi*
> The twin mother had some little broom/penis swept through her – *be chwi*
> (Excerpt from a twin song)[16]

Performance of ritual sex in twin ceremonies was reported to involve more than the twin parents. At the birth of the twins, one of the necessary rituals is for the parents' families to provide a sibling to the twin parents. These (often younger siblings) are called Ssalongo *omukulu* and Nnalongo *omukulu* (translated as more significant twin father and more significant twin mother respectively). They are responsible for acting on behalf of the twins and are symbolically responsible for their well-being, lest they 'kill the whole clan'. Their role is to ensure that twin rituals and observances do occur.

In the ritual sex act specifically called *okuzina*[17] *abalongo* (dancing the twins), participants reported that amid cultural dancing and jubilation, Nnalongo lies on her back with legs spread and the young of a banana fruit (*empumumpu*) is planted on top of her genitalia. Then Ssalongo *omukulu* kneels between her legs and knocks this baby banana-fruit off her with either his penis, or another part of his body. Thereafter, the drums beat loudest, leading into another ritual which involves eating specific food ingredients cooked without salt and more violation of taboo: stepping into the food. Four nights after the twin ceremony, the twin parents must perform ritual sex called *okumala emikolo gyabalongo* (completing the ceremonies of the twins).

Therefore, when contemporary Baganda Christians renounce twin ceremonies, in essence they join in the Judaeo-Christian discourse which condemns a customary celebration of the birth of twins. They deny themselves and their kin the authentic Kiganda savour of a heightened awareness of sexuality, or cultural licence to articulate passion, lust, love, desire and desirability. They stifle the power of collective affirmation of sexual performances in this setting. Several participants indeed admitted they had not conducted the twin ceremonies in the cultural way, but instead 'tied the twins' using traditional medicines and later took the twins for baptism.

'Tying the twins' (*okusiba abalongo*) was discussed as a new variant of traditional medicine necessitated by the condemnation of twin ceremonies, which led many to publicly denounce it and yet privately seek the protection of cultural gods and ancestors against the wrath unleashed by defiance of twin observances. *Lubanga*

– the name for specialist traditional healers who work only with twins – were reported to provide new herbal concoctions and fetishes which would facilitate and protect those twin parents who declined to conduct the elaborate twin ceremonies, preferring to baptise their children. Several participants were quick to point out the hypocrisy involved in the religious acts of public confession and denial of what culture dictated.

Performances of sex to mark rites of passage

Parents have customary mandates for ritual sex to celebrate other significant rites of passage for their children, in addition to birth and death. In this regard, participants' narratives focused on *okumala amabeere*[18] (to complete breast milk), *okumala amabega* (to complete the menarche of a daughter) and *okumala obufumbo* (to complete marriage).

During the process of weaning an infant from breast milk to food supplements, and eventual termination of breastfeeding, the biological parents must have penetrative sexual intercourse. Related to the *obusobe* observances associated with birth, our study participants reported that failure of parents to perform *okumala amabeere* results in the breast milk turning sour, choking the baby, and laying it open to the ultimate possibility of death from malnutrition. Deeper interrogation about infants whose parents are separated, dead or remarried revealed that many participants believed this particular practice was one of the few occasions that necessitated a genuine attempt at reuniting for the sake of protecting the infant from harm. Some youths and urban-based discussants were totally unaware of this ritual sex practice.

In the event that the parents cannot perform *okumala amabeere* for their infant, prophylactic fetishes or charms to be worn round the baby's waist are obtained from traditional healers specialising in children. Female herbalists stressed that the sexual act was the only guaranteed protection for the infant, often recounting scenarios in which fetishes failed to protect babies who went on to develop illness at weaning. This perhaps elucidates the deep-seated belief in the preventive power of this sexual custom.

Okumenya amabega (meaning to break the buttocks) is one among several euphemisms locally employed in the vernacular to mean starting menstruation. As part of the rites surrounding menarche, participants reported that the biological parents must have ritual sex before the last day of their daughter's menstrual flow, in order to ensure her healthy menstruation, fertility and reproduction and the well-being of her children. Some female elders attributed the current increases in dysmenorrhoea, infertility and caesarean section to modern parents neglecting this duty to protect their daughters. One male shrine priest of the god Mukasa associated increases in sexual health problems, particularly HIV/AIDS and a culture-bound syndrome called *akasagazi* in which one is driven to have repetitive sexual intercourse with diverse multiple partners, to the 'present generation's shunning of this custom. Therefore women get *akasagazi* after crossing a junction[19] and the men who have sex with them also catch it.' Many participants only learned about this ritual sex practice during the study, illuminating general low levels of awareness.

Several reasons for this disparity were discussed, including separation of parents because of divorce, remarriage, migration for employment or death; the current education system whereby children are sent to boarding school where their menarche often occurs; dysfunctional extended families, in which children are raised by guardians from other tribes; and modern departures from the traditional institution in which the *ssenga* (paternal aunt) provided sexual and reproductive education to her nieces and nephews (see Muyinda et al 2000). Various participants pointed to the traditional taboo on the discussion of sexual topics between parents and children as the overriding factor: even when daughters know about the necessity of this ritual sex practice, they fear to talk about menarche with their parents, and would rather tell their friends or peers or even their teacher. Yet without knowing that menarche has occurred, they reasoned, it is unlikely that the parents will *okumala amabega*.

Parents are also mandated to have ritual sex called *okumala obufumbo* (to complete marriage) when their children marry. The bride is collected from her father's household. Prior to leaving for her husband's locale, she must undergo customary symbolic rites of farewell with different members of her clan. Customarily, on the day when the groom's family or entourage pay dowry and collect their bride, the two sets of parents must perform ritual sex before the newly married couple consummate their marriage. The father can jump over the mother's legs if they are unable to have actual penetrative sexual intercourse.

Our literature review and the *vox populi* reveal incidents where the *ssenga* instructed newly married Baganda couples in sexual intercourse (Kilbride and Kilbride 1990). Some authors claim she went to the extent of witnessing the first consummation and physically illustrating intercourse to her virgin niece by having sex with the new groom (Ssengendo and Ssekatawa 1999). Driven to link Kiganda sexual culture to HIV incidence, these authors discuss the age and assumed consequent sexual experience of the *ssenga* as a potential source of infection to the groom and eventually to the bride.

We explored occurrence of this practice among our study participants. Many of the older participants explained that the *ssenga* played a significant role in marriages in Buganda in the past. However, they also stressed that this role no longer made sense because of generational estrangement within the extended families due to migration, education, employment, poverty, intermarriages across tribes, nations or continents and the sale of clan land. Thus, *ssengas* currently play commercialised or symbolic roles in marriages (Tamale 2005), receiving material benefits of the *gomesi* as dictated by custom, without necessarily instructing the newly married couple in sexual matters or reproduction. Participants reported it was rare to find virgins at marriage. Since sexual debut was no longer simultaneous with marriage, there is the possibility that the newly married couple are more sexually experienced than the *ssenga*, and thus not in need of instruction. Because of public sexual health education, the mystery and novelty of sex have been tamed in Masaka district, further negating the *ssenga's* educational role. None of the married youths in the study had received any sexual training from their *ssenga*.

Weddings, like burials and last funeral rites, were discussed as cultural ceremonies in which the usual prohibitions against sexual interaction are loosened. Participants reported several conditions that favour sex at wedding ceremonies, including the collective presence of several relatives, friends and villagers from near and far, general merriment – drinking, feasting, laughter and dancing, and dressing up to enhance beauty and desirability – and the feelings of love and expressions of sexuality invoked by the marrying couple. Spontaneous and casual sex encounters were presented as common occurrences at weddings.

Following marriage, it was expected of a man to build a house for his wife and progeny. Customary Kiganda practice prescribed ritual sex called *okumala enju* (to complete the house) prior to occupying a new house, particularly if it was personal property, in order to ensure the benign cooperation of the ancestral shades of that lineage (*empewo z'abajajja*, or the winds of our grannies).[20] Thus, on completion of building a house, a man invited his kinsmen and friends for ancestral worship and jubilation. Later , during the first night in the house he would engage in penetrative sex with his wife (or the spouse who owned that space in cases of polygyny). This in effect symbolically stamped ownership by the ancestry over the household, property and lands, allowing the ancestral spirits access to oversee and protect members' prosperity.

The elderly men, clan leaders and most clan land owners reported that they had conducted this practice. Some urban land owners had also performed it, on the insistence of their older kinsmen. However, several other urban participants, particularly immigrants into the district, reported that they rented houses and often shifted without necessarily engaging in the ritual sex practice of *okumala enyumba*. A few others claimed that they had built their houses prior to marriage, and thus had no spouse with whom to perform this ritual. The frequent rejoinder of Kiganda tradition adherents to such arguments was to link the 'current turmoil in Buganda'[21] to this apparent neglect of tradition.

Local views of cultural change

Contrary to a homogeneous and static African sexuality, this article exposes the multilayered and shifting scripts for customary sexual practices within one district, Masaka, one of the several that comprise the Buganda kingdom. From our ethnographic data, it is meaningless to generalise patterns to a particular generation, gender, religion or location. Depending on the context, there is constantly negotiated difference and performance within the same individual, group or community. The fluidity of meaning and variations within this small setting – a tiny portion of Africa – problematises Westernised universal concepts of a bounded African other.

Documenting this change should perhaps have been a history project, because the processes of transformation and negotiation were certainly gradual and complex. Adaptation to the AIDS scare is only the latest phase in a long history of flexible reinterpretations. A limitation of the study was that, as researchers, we were unable to facilitate a scholarly recreation of this history. Our strength as ethnographers, however, was that we could focus on our participants' own sense of history, their conscious positioning in relation to tradition, true Kiganda culture and their own sense of what has changed and why, expressed in their own words.

Analysis revealed myriad forms of ritual sex practice ranging from everyday customary sexual practice in the mundane order of life to the more unusual and occasional practices designed for specific estates in the life cycles of individuals, couples and the wider kin group. Participants reported that 'proper tradition' or true Kiganda custom necessitated penetrative sexual intercourse to complete cultural rites in the past. This past was presented as a period located somewhere in the far distance and not quite specifiable. However, several influences facilitated a departure from 'pure Kiganda culture', subsequently yielding diverse forms of symbolic sex: jumping over legs, skipping over warm belts, sitting on laps, urinating in the same spot, mimicking the sex act but with clothes on – performances of sex that bypass the exchange of bodily fluids within a penis-and-vagina interaction.

Thus not all customary sex is necessarily dangerous for HIV infection. In addition, we have seen that participants discussed an innovation in Kiganda traditional medicine, in the form of prophylactic charms to 'tie' the adverse effects of not having sex – even though these parents have denounced Kiganda ethos and turned instead to other cultures for protective rituals, such as baptism. Given the likelihood of HIV infection, Kiganda custom has evolved fast enough to provide culturally accepted mechanisms for still performing the ritual, but eliminating the possibility of contagion.

The Baganda in Masaka district have varied sociocultural allegiances: to multiple religions, their ethnic group, dictates from their clan, 'modern' thinking, Westernisation, tradition and the options created by generational cleaving. Participants' narratives and experiences revealed that, as individuals, they are constantly playing out diverse notions of personhood and sexuality to the varied audiences in these social groupings. The multiple social scripts for legitimate sexual behaviour demand different (and sometimes contradictory) roles from the acting individuals. This perhaps explains the general theme of hypocrisy which permeated the discussions of Kiganda tradition diehards.

Even though we were academically conscious of the need for a departure from the reification of culture, our analysis of the narratives reveals that participants believed that the current practice of ritual sex in Masaka district is changing; shifting from the various forms of traditional sexual culture that they claim were socially scripted in the past, presumably prior to cultural contamination from outside influences. Although we have focused on transformations within ritual sex practices in this article, study participants generally discussed this change in association with – and within the context of – broader social, cultural, economic and political changes.

There are several emic explanations for the changes in Kiganda ritual sex. Departure from tradition was a recurrent theme. The older generation blamed youths for admiring other cultures, particularly a reified notion of Western culture of the *Bazungu* (white folks), and thereby looking down upon anything deemed true Kiganda culture. Several elders argued that the linear model of development had brainwashed the present generation into aspiring to be and live like the West – as a model of progressive advancement – such that Kiganda values, mores and practices were interpreted as idioms of backwardness or underdevelopment.

The youths, while acknowledging this departure, instead cast the blame on the older generation who, they claimed, were failing to transmit Kiganda heritage in its fullness. Variously, participants emphasised disintegration in the social organisation of Buganda society. In the past the lineage (*olunyiriri*) lived together in a homestead (*olujja*), in which various households (*enju*) linked through patrilineal ties cohesively provided the environment of a visible extended family structure responsible for socialising Baganda children. However, the post-modern Kiganda family in Masaka district is so removed from that pre-colonial organisation that it is a mimicry of the individualistic capitalist nuclear family of husband, wife and children. Grannies, aunts, uncles, cousins and wider kin are so busy eking out their own livings that they no longer hold the responsibility of instructing children in the extended family. In any case, many children attend boarding schools or are in employment in other locations. Migration (for education, employment, marriage, business or development) has a general impact upon the rift between observing tradition and departing from it.

Several participants also discussed the role of national politics in disrupting Kiganda cultural observances. In addition to introducing Western styles of Christianity, education, British law and rule into Buganda, the colonisers of Uganda sought to break the spirit of the tribes by homogenising different tribal political entities (kingdoms, chiefdoms and segmentary societies) into one nation with one physical geographical border. The blindness to the multiple social political boundaries and rifts within the nation sustained the calculated system of indirect rule. The colonial legacy of nation-building calls for the death of the tribe and its values in favour of nationalising philosophies and practices, which aim at uniting or homogenising the 54 Ugandan tribes into one person. Other scholars of Buganda (Mair 1934; Schiller 1990; Musisi 2002; Tamale 2005) and elsewhere (McClintock 1995; Stoler 1995; Young 1995; Cooper and Stoler 1997) discuss colonial control of the sexuality and reproductive lives of the colonised.

Perhaps this explains the contradiction between reinstalling the Buganda kingdom, together with the Kabaka, and the continued departure(s) from Kiganda traditional practices. One would expect Baganda to re-embrace Kiganda culture, because the Kabaka's exile of 1966 and the subsequent dissolution of the kingdom were seen as major political processes disrupting individual-group and private-public relations, and fostering non-compliance with Kiganda tradition. Christianity and Islam were discussed as strong deterrents to observing Kiganda sexual culture and practice: participants claimed that inner debate and conflict often tore at a religious Muganda because of contradictory requirements.

The most frequently mentioned factor responsible for changing Kiganda ritual sex in Masaka was the impact of HIV/AIDS awareness and knowledge, and the reality of the disease within the lives of the participants, either as carriers of the virus, sufferers of AIDS or carers of infected relatives, friends or wider village members. All our participants had been affected by HIV/AIDS in their immediate households. If they were not living with the virus, they claimed that they were bombarded from all fronts by awareness-raising anti-HIV/AIDS campaigns transmitted over popular FM radio stations, television, through village health educators, condom promoters, religious leaders and political administrators (Nyanzi et al 2005). Brandishing safe sex was a socio-political and economic strategy for population groups as diverse as constituent assembly contestants, flea-market vendors, burial society members, sermon preachers, disco rappers and school pupils.

Sometimes the campaign messages directly confronted aspects of ritual sex, particularly widow inheritance, polygyny, early sexual debut or sex with high-risk groups like the *ssenga*. However, the knowledge also created notions of contagion from sex and sexuality, introducing an association of danger into Kiganda sexual culture. By appealing for a reduction or termination of both concurrent and serial multiple sexual partnerships, anti-HIV/AIDS campaigns tainted customary sexual practices with potential for contamination. Several participants believed that HIV/ AIDS was responsible for the social invention of the symbolic ritual sex performances discussed above. However, literature published prior to the advent of the HIV/AIDS epidemic reveals that the symbolic custom of jumping over the legs of a spouse, or jumping over a husband's walking stick or hunting spear, were used in pre-colonial Buganda by warriors and hunters during times of collective abstinence while on duty (see Roscoe 1911).

Our submission is that HIV/AIDS has transformed the meaning of symbolic ritual sex performances such that they are now potent options for sexual rites. They are no longer simply stand-ins for penetrative sexual intercourse, which was previously only postponed until the constraining events had passed. Instead, they are viable options in and of themselves that actually complete cultural customs. Furthermore, these symbolic acts of sex are shifting from mere inferior and impotent performances to powerful media of empowerment and negotiation, such that individuals who are not agreeable to conforming to customary demands of penetrative ritual sex can now renegotiate by employing the idiom of HIV/AIDS contagion to opt for symbolic performance. Thus the fear of HIV (re)infection gives currency to otherwise redundant cultural sexual performances, and enables the agency of previously weaker social entities – women, widows, men opposed to clan dictates – to wield a measure of power.

The ambivalence of how the HIV/AIDS metaphor is used is revealed when we consider the imperialistic undertones shared by colonial, Christian missionary, colonial medical, Western educational and the current anti-HIV/AIDS discourses. The colonisers criticised Kiganda sexual culture through ethnocentric, moralising propaganda. The missionaries campaigned to displace polygyny and replace it with monogamy, and to curtail premarital and extramarital pregnancy by introducing the notion of illegitimacy. They also condemned African worship of ancestors or spirits by demonising Kiganda rites, including ritual sex.

Colonial medical discourse and practice in Buganda mistook yaws for syphilis (Vaughan 1991), demanding dehumanising medical tests and treatments for locals, and thereby heightening associations of danger of infection with Kiganda sexual culture. Western education necessitated the delay of marriage and the extension of the socially acceptable age of pregnancy and severed the sexual realm from reproduction – necessitating sexually active Baganda to obtain and maintain contraceptives, undergo illegal abortion or suffer social stigma of early parenthood. The most recent social policeman of 'illegitimate' sex in Masaka is the anti-HIV/AIDS campaign, with its messaging: 'Postpone sexual debut', 'Reduce multiple sexual partners', 'Abstain!', 'Use condoms', 'Don't remarry', 'You mess: you die!', 'Zero graze'. The social-political contexts might have changed, but policing African sexuality, as represented by the Baganda of Masaka in this case, continues to thrive through the vehicle of anti-HIV/AIDS politics.

Conclusion

Tradition is not frozen and homogeneous, but adaptive. Local people have the resources and ingenuity to modify rituals when these become unsuited to their outlook and way of life. They do not need heavy-handed health campaigners to denounce their sexual culture; they can devise their own ways of enacting ritual sex symbolically rather than performing real sex acts when the latter becomes dangerous or unacceptable. Much more than the component sexual acts, it is the meanings of the rituals that are important to individuals and society.

Ritual sex signifies completion among contemporary Baganda. It announces completion of mourning after the death of a child and the death of a wife's relative; completion of the process of childbirth, completion of suckling a baby, completion of a daughter's pre-puberty years, completion of a child's unmarried status; and completion of a husband's task of constructing a new house after marriage. To the performers, the meaning of ritual sex here is both closure on the preceding state (mourning, childhood, unmarried status and so on) and an opening of future production. It mainly occurs between husband and wife, or between the biological parents of a child even if they are no longer together. The impact upon HIV infection of this kind of ritual sex would be no different from marital sex, unless the spouses were living with other partners at the time of sex. The requirement that a widow must have sex with an agnate of her dead husband also signifies closure and reopening. This is the only form of ritual sex that carries an enhanced risk of HIV infection.

The twin ceremonies add a different dimension to the meanings of ritual sex: they are perhaps not so much about closure as they are about dealing with the extraordinary. Twins are simultaneously perceived as anomalous, dangerous and empowering. The excess, ribaldry and licence with in-laws mark and affirm this foray into the extraordinary – to acknowledge and celebrate it. The rituals signify containment of the potential danger from the twins. The flux and negotiability of these diverse forms of ritual sex among contemporary Baganda confirm the malleability and potential for transformation within customs in response to looming danger.

Notes

1. The text of this essay was originally published in 2008 in the journal *Africa*, vol. 78(4), Karin Barber (ed), Edinburgh University Press, www.euppublishing.com. Reproduced with permission. We dedicate this article to the memory of Justine Nassimbwa – our research colleague, co-author and friend, who passed on before it was published. Robert Pool discussed the research proposal. Brent Wolff was the leader of the Social Studies Department during the study. Paul Ssejjaaka, Bessie Kalina and Georgina Nabaggala attended some funeral ceremonies. Anne Mager discussed various drafts during a writing associateship funded by the African Gender Institute. We are grateful to our study participants for generously sharing their experiences.
2. This expression is adapted from Adebayo Olukoshi of the Council for the Development of Social Sciences Research in Africa (CODESRIA), who debunks ethnocentric approaches to the social science study of Africans. Because Caldwell was responsible for training many Africans studying demography at the Australian National University (ANU) and in research, he developed a corpus of scholars of sexual health who bought

into his 'African sexuality' thesis. They continue to reproduce the received knowledge, without questioning or critically engaging it (see Lauer 2006).

3. John Caldwell et al (1989) proposed the infamous thesis that there is 'a distinct and internally coherent African system embracing sexuality, marriage and much else' (1989: 187), which differs from 'a Eurasian sexual system'. This 'African system of sexuality' is characterised by some universals: ancestry, descent and the maintenance of lineage, lineal inheritance systems, female-dominated agriculture and fertility. Of significance is 'freedom of female sexuality in Africa' due to 'lack of moral and institutional limitations placed on sexual practices'. African women were reported to have 'a fair degree of permissiveness towards premarital relations', while 'surreptitious extramarital relations are not the point of sin' and therefore not punished. African women's sexual networking patterns were blamed for the rampant spread of AIDS.

4. Richard Guy Parker et al (1991) define sexual culture as the system of meaning, knowledge, beliefs and practices that structure sexuality in different social contexts. They emphasise the significance of social, cultural, political, economic and religious factors in the construction of sexuality. 'Sexual culture' is a label for the general expression of cultural behaviour and not for individual expressions of sexuality. Individuals, however, cognisant of cultural ideals of sexuality, express variations within parameters that are socially defined as normative (Parker 1991: 79–80). Implicit tensions between collective and individual expressions of sexuality can arise.

5. Emic lexicon: Buganda is the kingdom; the people are Baganda (sing. Muganda); the language is Luganda; and Kiganda is a related adjective.

6. A key word search for 'ritual sex' reveals its problematic nature (Kirby 1991) as a label for several phenomena ranging from bizarre sexual orgies involving child sacrifice, satanic worshippers indulging in sex with gendered devils, spiritual rites with symbolic phalluses, to tribal public performances of group sex. Perhaps this ambiguity originates from the historical metamorphosis of discourse surrounding ritual (see Roth 1995 for a detailed review), which is presently imbued with multiple layers of meaning associated with rites of passage, the rules and practices of co-mingling in face-to-face interactions, modern media events or even calamities, such as assassinations and mass exhumations. Furthermore, although the Western biomedical paradigm employs sex as a label for a range of practices of bodily sexual intercourse, it is our submission that there are lay translations of sex that surpass the physical terrain.

7. Before the revision of district borders, Masaka included Rakai – where HIV was first reported.

8. Pre-colonial Buganda was a relatively well-established monarchy, with a *Kabaka* (king), *lukiiko* (parliament), an army for defence against neighbouring kingdoms, such as Bunyoro-Kitara and expansionist drives. During colonialism, the Buganda kingdom was a British protectorate. Four years after independence, the kingdom was abolished by Prime Minister Obote during circumstances of civil strife, leading to the exile of the Kabaka (who earlier had been appointed ceremonial president of Uganda) and the deaths of several royalists. Things Kiganda went underground, in favour of public enactments of nationalism. The Buganda kingdom was reinstated in 1995, with the Kabaka having titular political power over Baganda, and several Baganda trying to reclaim the traditions and customs of old. (For detailed discussions of Buganda's political history, see Roscoe 1911; Mair 1934; Karlstrom 1996; Reid 2002).

9. The programme director of the Medical Research Council at the time of the study.

10. In this article 'twin parents' refers to the parents of twins.

11. *Olumbe* – the Luganda word for death – is a linguistic appropriation of a traditional legend of the origin of Baganda people, in which Walumbe – the name for death personified – is a brother to Nambi, the daughter of Gulu who owns the heavens. Nambi travels to earth to marry Kintu, the first Muganda man. Her brother Walumbe often visits the earth and carries off some of Nambi's offspring. Fatal illness is also called *olumbe*.

12. Unlike other contexts in which a specific length of time is prescribed, our data revealed no specific period of mourning required before parents conducted this ritual.

13. Baganda have adopted a colonial creation in ladies' fashion called *gomesi* or *busuuti* as their traditional dress. It involves wrapping an inner cloth to create an impression of fat, and tying it up with an inner cloth-belt. The *gomesi* is then donned over this and also held with a wide flashy belt.

14. *Obusobe* comes from the root word *kusoba*, which means 'to go wrong' or 'to fail'.

15. The word *obuko* is rooted in *omuko*, which is the Luganda word for in-law. Thus the condition is named for the belief that its cause is rooted in breaking *obuko* observances.

16. We asked elders, twin parents, clan leaders and traditional healers to sing for us the twin songs they knew. Future research will involve content analysis of the words, meanings, symbolism and power of these songs.

17. The word *okuzina* has multiple meanings, including to dance but also, vulgarly, to have sex.

18. *Amabeere* refers to breasts or breast milk.

19. The junction symbolically means a place where different things meet and is variously used as a site for disposing of polluting substances after therapeutic ministrations from traditional healers and shrine priests. When undergoing healing, patients are often forbidden to cross junctions without protective charms.

20. *Empewo*, which means wind, is the name given to spirits. Rather than being interpreted as either hot or cold wind, in the case of *empewo z'abajajja* – the winds of our grannies – it is associated with a mystical force that can either harm or protect, bless or curse, depending on the circumstance or behaviour of the individual(s). In traditional Kiganda worship, *empewo* can be called upon to intervene in bad situations, to cause harm or to vindicate, to reveal the unknown or to foretell the future. *Empewo* can also come upon diviners or healers and transform them into mediums between the physical and spiritual worlds.

21. An umbrella term used to cover the high rates of HIV/AIDS, death, poverty, lack of requisite resources, political impotence of the Kabaka, departure from Kiganda customs and inter-tribal marriages.

References

Adams, G. and R.H. Markus (2001) 'Culture as patterns: an alternative approach to the problem of reification', *Culture and Psychology* 7(3): 283–96

Ahlberg, B.M. (1994) 'Is there a distinct African sexuality? A critical response to Caldwell et al', *Africa* 64: 220–42

Airhihenbuwa, C.O. (1995) *Health and Culture: Beyond the Western Paradigm*, Thousand Oaks CA, London and New Delhi, Sage Publications

Arnfred, S. (ed) (2004) *Re-thinking Sexualities in Africa*, Uppsala, The Nordic Africa Institute

Caldwell, J., Caldwell, P. and Quiggin, P. (1989) 'The social context of AIDS in sub-Saharan Africa', *Population and Development Review* 15: 185–234

Cooper, F. and Stoler, A.L. (eds) (1997) *Tensions of Empire: Colonial Cultures in a Bourgeois World*, Berkeley, University of California Press

Heald, S. (1995) 'The power of sex: some reflections on the Caldwells' "African sexuality" thesis', *Africa* 65(4): 489–505

Kagwa, A. (1905) *Empisa za Baganda*, New York, Columbia University Press

Karlstrom, M. (1996) 'Imagining democracy: political culture and democratisation in Buganda', *Africa* 66(4): 485–505

Kilbride, P.L. and Kilbride, J.C. (1990) *Changing Family Life in East Africa: Women and Children at Risk*, University Park, PA, Pennsylvania State University Press

Kinsman, J., Nyanzi, S. and Pool, R. (2000) 'Socialising influences and the value of sex: the experience of adolescent schoolgirls in rural Masaka, Uganda', *Culture, Health and Sexuality* 2(2): 151–60

Kirby, E.T. (1991) 'Ritual sex: anarchic and absolute', *Drama Review* 25(1): 3–8

Kizekka, M.N. (1972) 'Baganda traditional beliefs and practices about love, sex and marriage', in Molnos, A. (ed) *Cultural Source Materials for Population Planning in East Africa*, Nairobi, East African Publishing House

—— (1976) 'Sexual attitudes and behaviour among students in Uganda', *Journal of Sex Research* 12(2): 104–16

Lauer, H. (2006) 'Cashing in on shame: how the popular "tradition vs modernity" dualism contributes to the HIV/AIDS crisis in Africa', *Review of Radical Political Economics* 38(1): 90–138

Le Blanc, M., Meintel, D. and Piche, V. (1991) 'The African sexual system: comment on Caldwell et al', *Population and Development Review* 17: 497–505

Mair, L. (1934) *An African People in the 20th Century*, New York, Russell and Russell

McClintock, A. (1995) *Imperial Leather: Race, Gender and Sexuality in the Colonial Contest*, New York and London, Routledge

Ministry of Health Uganda (2003) 'An overview of HIV/AIDS in Uganda', Kampala, Ministry of Health, http://www.health.go.ug/docs/HIVinUganda.pdf, accessed 28 July 2004

Mukiza-Gapere, J. and Ntozi, J.P. (1995) 'Impact of AIDS on marriage patterns, customs and practices in Uganda', *Health Transition Review* 5 (Supplement): 201–8

Musisi, N.B. (1991) 'Women, "elite polygyny" and Buganda state formation', *Signs* 16(4): 757–86

—— (2002) 'The politics of perception or perception as politics? Colonial and missionary representations of Baganda women, 1900–1945', in Allman, J., Geiger, S. and Musisi, N. (eds) *Women in African Colonial Histories*, Bloomington, IN, Indiana University Press

Muyinda, H., Kengeya, J.K., Pool R. and Whitworth J. (2000) 'The potential of traditional sex counselling in the control of HIV/STDs among female adolescents in rural Uganda', *Culture, Health and Sexuality* 3(2): 353–61

Muyinda, H., Nakuya, J., Whitworth, J. and Pool, R. (2004) 'Community sex education among adolescents in rural Uganda: utilizing indigenous institutions', *AIDS Care* 16(1): 69–79

Ntozi, J.P. (1997) 'Widowhood, remarriage and migration during the HIV/AIDS epidemic in Uganda', *Health Transition Review* 7 (Supplement): 125–44

Nyanzi, S. (2004) 'Widowhood, land wrangles and social stigma in the face of HIV/AIDS in south-western Uganda', *OSSREA Newsletter* 1(1): 18–20

Nyanzi, S., Nyanzi, B. and Kalina, B. (2005) 'Contemporary myths, sexuality misconceptions, information sources and risk perceptions of *bodabodamen* in southwest Uganda', *Sex Roles* 52(1–2): 111–19

Packer, C.A.A. (2002) *Using Human Rights to Change Tradition: traditional practices harmful to women's reproductive health in sub-Saharan Africa*, Utrecht, Intersentia

Parker, R.G., Herdt, G. and Carballo, M. (1991) 'Sexual culture, HIV transmission and AIDS research', *Journal of Sex Research* 28: 77–98

Ranger, T. (1983) 'The invention of tradition in colonial Africa', in Hobsbawm, E. and Ranger, T. (eds) *The Invention of Tradition*, Cambridge, Cambridge University Press

Reid, R. (2002) *Political Power in Pre-Colonial Buganda*, Kampala, Fountain Publishers

Roscoe, J. (1911) *The Baganda: Their Customs and Beliefs*, London, Frank Cass

Roth, A.L. (1995) '"Men wearing masks": issues of description in the analysis of ritual', *Sociological Theory* 13(30): 301–27

Schiller, L. (1990) 'The royal women of Buganda', *International Journal of African Historical Studies* 23(3): 455–73

Serwadda, D., Mugerwa, R. and Sewankambo, N. (1985) 'Slim disease: a new disease in Uganda and its association with HTZ-III infection', *Lancet* 2: 849–52

Ssengendo, J. and Ssekatawa, E.K. (1999) 'A cultural approach to HIV/AIDS prevention and care: Uganda's experience', *UNESCO/UNAIDS Research Project, Studies and Reports*, Special series 1, Cultural Policies for Development Unit, UNESCO

Stewart, A. (1998) *The Ethnographer's Method*, Thousand Oaks, London and New Delhi, Sage Publications

Stoler, A.L. (1995) *Race and the Education of Desire: Foucault's History of Sexuality and the Colonial Order of Things*, Durham, Duke University Press

—— (2002) *Carnal Knowledge and Imperial Power: Race and the Intimate in Colonial Rule*, Berkeley and Los Angeles, University of California Press

Tamale, S. (2005) 'Eroticism, sensuality and "women's secrets" among the Baganda: a critical analysis', *Feminist Africa* 5: 9–36

Uganda Bureau of Statistics (UBOS) (2002) 'Population and housing census – provisional results', http://www.ubos.org/appendix5aprov.doc, accessed 28 July 2004

Vaughan, M. (1991) *Curing Their Ills: Colonial Power and African Illness*, Cambridge, Polity Press

Winthrop, R. (2002) 'Defining a right to culture and some alternatives', *Cultural Dynamics* 14(2): 161–83

Young, R.J.C. (1995) *Colonial Desire: Hybridity in Theory, Culture and Race*, London and New York, Routledge

61

Sangoma-hood, abstinence and celibacy among *tangoma* in Swaziland

Hebron L. Ndlovu

In this chapter I describe the interface of *sangoma*-hood,[1] sexual abstinence and celibacy in the Kingdom of Swaziland. By the term '*sangoma*-hood' I refer to the indigenous African institution of divination in which exceptionally talented individuals are believed to be called by the ancestors and God to serve their respective communities as spiritual leaders, healers, social workers, counsellors and defenders of cultural heritage. Drawing on primary data[2] on Swazi *tangoma*, I contend that many *tangoma*, especially females, have used the institution of *sangoma*-hood as a vehicle to assert and maintain celibacy as their preferred sexual orientation.

Assumptions

My chapter is informed by three interrelated propositions. First, I assume that African indigenous religion is a social fact in many contemporary African societies including Swaziland (cf. Olupona 1991; Ndlovu 2006). For the purposes of this chapter, therefore, the question of the veracity and falsity of African indigenous beliefs and practices is not an issue. Rather, I view every religious tradition – including indigenous African religions – as 'culturally postulated nonfalsifiable reality' (Van Beek and Blakely 1994: 2).

The basic beliefs and practices of Swazi indigenous religion are: the belief in *Mvelinchanti* or God the Creator; the belief in universal mystical power; ancestral veneration; belief in nature spirits; belief in sacred kingship; and the practice of rites of passage (cf. Kasenene 1993).

Second, I assume that one of the major constituent features of all African indigenous religion is the belief in mystical power that may be tapped either for benevolent or malevolent means by religious specialists who include *tangoma* (diviners) and *tingedla* (herbalists) (cf. Van Binsbergen 1991; Kasenene 1994).

In Swaziland it is believed that the *sangoma* is possessed by mystical power called *emadloti* (the ancestors), who enable him or her to perform positive societal duties such as healing, spiritual counselling and witchcraft eradication (Ndlovu 2002). It is crucial to stress, however, that despite the prestige that accrues to the *sangoma*, the institution of *sangoma*-hood is hardly envied by many Swazi because it is fraught with cumbersome taboos 'on sex, food, and general behaviours that are imposed by the profession' (Kuper 1986: 66).

Third, I agree with the observation of Ioan M. Lewis that the categories of people who tend to be possessed by *emadloti* include marginalised, underprivileged and frustrated persons (Lewis 1986). In the Swaziland context, for example, Kuper and Ndlovu observe that most diviners tend to be women and men of low social standing (Kuper 1986; Ndlovu 2002).

In light of the above facts, I therefore follow Lewis's interpretation of *sangoma*-hood (or ancestral possession) as a religio-cultural practice that provides means of release or escape to disadvantaged social groups in contemporary African society. In the case of South Africa, for example, current literature suggests that there are many South African *tangoma* who have openly declared their sexual orientation and they rationalise their stance partly on the grounds that they were (and still are) directed by their ancestors to develop and stick to same-sex relationships (cf. Nkabinde 2009).

In this chapter I attempt to describe how *sangoma*-hood in Swaziland appears to offer an institutionalised avenue to women – as a disadvantaged social group – of circumventing their deprivation in a male-dominated society.

The Swazi female sangoma

The scenario pertaining to Swazi female *tangoma* is two-fold. First, most of the *tangoma* that I interviewed were married women. According to the ethical code of *sangoma*-hood, these women have the power and authority to refuse conjugal rights to their husbands if and when directed to do so by *lamadloti labangena* (the ancestors that possess them).

Second, the few unmarried female *tangoma* that I interviewed remained celibate for life following their call into the profession. When asked about the reason why they were not married as per the dictates of Swazi culture and tradition, one *sangoma* explained that all her love affairs never worked out because *bebanginukela* (my lovers nauseated me). This woman remained single for the rest of her life.

To understand this scenario in its broader context, it is necessary to be familiar with the origin, nature, and the terms and conditions of the call to *sangoma*-hood.

The call

Although many scholars describe *sangoma*-hood as 'rituals of affliction', in Swazi culture and religion *sangoma*-hood is generally viewed as a calling. The *sangoma* is called by God through his or her *emadloti* (the ancestors) to serve the people. It is believed that one does not simply become a *sangoma* through personal volition. Rather a person is selected by the ancestors – who are the deceased relatives. In the words of one diviner: *lidloti liyatikhetsela; budloti akusilo lifa* (it is the ancestor who chooses the suitable candidate; and *sangoma*-hood cannot be equated to inheritance).

The ancestor who selects the *sangoma* may have been male or female, old or young, talented or ordinary in his or her life on earth. But what is significant is that the appointed *sangoma* assumes the sex, age, personality and character of the ancestor that possesses him or her. Some *tangoma* are believed to be possessed by persons who met their death as children, warriors, Christians, national heroes and so forth. It is believed that the personality and even the character of the ancestor is frequently reflected in the personal and public life of the *sangoma*. It is said that some *tangoma*, for example, are possessed by celebrated dancers, herbalists, and even kleptomaniacs and drunks. This means that, by and large, it is believed that the ancestor shapes and regulates the life of the *sangoma*.

Despite the anthropomorphic attributes of the ancestors listed above, the *tangoma* strongly believe that the dead relatives that possess them have better eyes and ears. This means that the ancestors are not limited by space, time or physical objects. Rather *bayabona* (they have eyes that see deep, far and wide). Indeed the popularity of the *sangoma* in Swazi culture and society stems from the belief that *sangoma*-hood has a firm superhuman foundation (Ndlovu 2002).

Training to become *sangoma*: code of ethics

The *sangoma*-to-be is required to go through a long, formal period of training, ranging from six months to five years depending on the tutor's specifications and the intellectual capabilities of the trainee. The training takes place at the homestead of the *gobela* (tutor), who is ordinarily a seasoned *sangoma*.

The trainee is taught various skills, such as the art of divination, herbal medicine, psychotherapy, as well as the ability to control the ancestor that possesses him or her. With regard to latter skill, the *tangoma* believe that the mystical power that comes with *sangoma*-hood is potentially dangerous. An undisciplined or ill-disciplined ancestor, for example, can embarrass the profession itself in that a *sangoma* might go naked when in trance, speak to the wrong persons and in the wrong place, or violate the cardinal principles of *sangoma*-hood.

As noted above, *sangoma*-hood is governed by a code of ethics covering the public and private life of the *sangoma*. In terms of public morality, the *sangoma* is enjoined to refrain from murder, witchcraft and adultery. Other prohibited behaviour includes drinking alcohol in public places, especially places that are known as *emidangalazweni* (places of drinking and dance).

With regard to sexual morality, it is vital to emphasise that during the entire period of training the *sangoma*-to-be ought to abstain from sexual intercourse. Although spouses are at liberty to visit their partners during the training period, any sign of affection between husband and wife is strictly forbidden. Should one break this cardinal rule, he or she may fail the final examination. In the final examination – which is a public rite witnessed by relatives and friends – the trainee is required to drink blood from the slit throat of a goat and thereafter vomit it. If they fail to vomit the blood they are disqualified from *sangoma*-hood. All faithful trainee *tangoma* normally pass this test. It is believed that failure to pass the test is a sign that the trainee has violated some of the cardinal ethical teachings of *sangoma*-hood.

Sangoma-hood as a life-long vocation

Following his or her successful training the *sangoma* undergoes a series of rites of induction to the profession. This is not the place to describe these rites, which I observed in July 2009. For now it suffices to underline the dominant theme of these rites, namely, that the appointment to *sangoma*-hood is a life-long engagement and is irrevocable.

It is quite common, therefore, for many *tangoma* to liken *sangoma*-hood to insurmountable social problems. For example, *sangoma*-hood is commonly described as *kugula* (terminal sickness) and *kufa* (death). In addition, all my informants claimed that it was unthinkable for any *sangoma* to resign from the profession. If one ventured to do so, *angafa nekufa* (they would die instantly).

Although *sangoma*-hood is believed to be a life-long vocation, the ban on sexual intercourse between the *sangoma* and his or her spouse is lifted after graduation. But there are certain conditions accompanying the suspension of sex, namely, that the partner of the *sangoma* ought to be subservient to the wishes and demands of the ancestor that possesses the *sangoma*.

In Swaziland, all of the female *tangoma* that I interviewed claimed to be possessed by male ancestors. They explained that soon after their graduation as full-fledged *tangoma* some agreement or contract had to made between the male ancestor that possessed them and their husbands. The contract had to 'signed' through an esoteric rite in which the husband agrees to be subject to the authority of the ancestor that possesses his wife. One of the conditions of the agreement is that the husband will only have sexual intimacy with the wife if and when the possessing ancestor gives his consent. All indications pointed to the fact that sexual contact between the female *tangoma* and their spouses was minimal and in some cases non-existent.

Significantly, many of these female diviners were wives of polygynous husbands who tended to turn a blind eye to the intermittent sexual restrictions imposed by the 'jealous' male ancestor that possessed their wives. In my view, the wives of polygynous males are better placed to maintain the celibate life that is tacitly encouraged by *sangoma*-hood.

Conclusion

For many years I have been fascinated by the Swazi female *tangoma*. I admired their courage and determination to pursue a profession that earned them social esteem and the sense of self-assurance. As I have argued elsewhere, *sangoma*-hood in the Swazi context has served as one of the sources of social power in that Swazi women diviners enjoy the benefits – both material and social – of being influential figures in society (Ndlovu 2002: 23). *Sangoma*-hood provides an oblique avenue for women to affirm celibacy as their chosen sexual orientation; a sexuality that seems inimical to the cultural ideal of marital union with their husbands.

Notes

1. The word *sangoma* can be loosely translated as diviner. Its plural form is *tangoma* or diviners.
2. This material is drawn from open-ended interviews with more than 35 Swazi diviners since 1995.

References

Kasenene, P. (1993) *Swazi Traditional Religion and Society*, Mbabane, Websters

—— (1994) *Religion in Swaziland*, Johannesburg, Skotaville Press

Kuper, H. (1986) *The Swazi: A South African Kingdom*, New York, Holt, Rinehart and Winston

Lewis, I.M. (1986) *Religion in Context*, Cambridge, Cambridge University Press

Ndlovu, H.L. (2002), 'Positive images of women in Swazi traditional religion', *UNISWA Research Journal* 16: 19–25

—— (2006) 'Swaziland', in Riggs, T. (ed), *Worldmark Encyclopedia of Religious Practices Volume 3*, Detroit, Gale Publishers

Nkabinde, N.Z. (2009) *Black Bull, Ancestors and Me: My Life as a Lesbian Sangoma*, Johannesburg, Jacana Media

Olupona, J.K. (ed) (1991) *African Traditional Religions in Contemporary Society*, St Paul, Paragon House

Van Beek, E.A. and Blakely, T.D. (1994) 'Introduction', in Blakely, T.D., Van Beek, E.A. and Thomson, D.L. (eds) *Religion in Africa*, London, James Curry and Portsmouth, Heinemann

Van Binsbergen, W. (1991) 'Becoming a *sangoma*: religious anthropological fieldwork in Francistown, Botswana', *Journal of Religion in Africa*, 21(4): 309–44

Questions for reflection

1.

The phenomenon of the 'psychic' octopus oracle that predicted game outcomes during the 2010 FIFA Football World Cup tournament gripped the world and was taken very seriously globally. What does this say about the role of myths and superstition in 21st century societies? How can we explain the deepest and most enduring 'irrationalities' of supernatural influences in human affairs?

2.

To comprehend the fascinating but oft-misunderstood topics of fetishised, ritualised and spiritual traditions of African sexualities, it is important to contextualise and problematise various sexual constructs. Looking beyond the 'exotic' sex rituals and critically engaging with the why and wherefore of the issues is a must for any serious scholar. What is the context and history of each rite or practice? What are the supernatural performances doing for African societies? How are people using them? Who is getting framed? How and why? Where and when? By whom? How have they changed with time?

3.

Although most studies show how religion/religiosity influences sexuality, few examine how sexuality shapes people's religion/religiosity at both the macro and micro levels. The House of Rainbow in Nigeria, discussed in Chimaraoke Izgubara's essay (Chapter 59), is an example of such influence at the macro level. Another example, at the micro and local African woman's level, is how the need for a child drives many barren women to consult spirit mediums and witchcraft, although they might be Christians or Muslims. Why is it important to engage in a conceptual analysis of the dual interaction of sexuality and religion/spirituality at both the macro and micro levels?

4.

What are the theoretical implications of the gendered/ sexual constructions and symbolisms in African animations of supernatural powers, such as associating with fertility?

5.

What is significant about the local understandings/
interpretations of sexual-related beliefs (taboos,
prohibitions, rites, values) and how Africans make sense
of the world? In other words, what is the significance of
sexuality in the African supernatural beliefs? What does the
symbolism of sexuality represent? Life? Transformation?

6.

How are religious and spiritual planes used to organise
and shape the meanings of sex and sexuality?

7.

How did colonisation disrupt the supernatural
ritualisation of various African institutions and beliefs?
What post-colonial attempts were made (and continue to be
made) in reconstructing these indigenous traditions? Which
traditions have been transformed, which ones have survived
(with what adaptations?) and what purpose are they serving
today? Why are these legends so persistent, so popular and
widespread? What, for example, does the popularity of
Nollywood movies on the continent tell us about 21st
century African societies? What do they represent?

8.

Does morality have a place in African sexualities as they
journey along the continent's supernatural landscape?

9.

What lessons do we learn from this examination of
the materials in this part on sexuality and the supernatural in
Africa? For example:

Gender roles in Africa are not static and should not be kept
static in the name of tradition.

Although imported religions largely depict women
as subordinate ritually and spiritually, in African magic-
religious systems women are unique sources of supernatural
powers, which emanate from their sexuality and their
reproductive capacities.

Part 9
Pedagogical approaches

62

Creative methodological/pedagogical approaches to teaching sexuality in an African context[1]

Mansah Prah

Introduction

> Our culture does not permit us to talk openly about sex.
> A former student of a course on gender and sexuality, University of Cape Coast

After weeks of agonising about how to approach this paper, I eventually made an unexpected breakthrough after a chance meeting with a former student of gender and sexuality. We talked about the course, and I expressed my regrets about the reserve exhibited by her class. They had been fairly open about sex, but I thought they could have been more communicative.

'Our culture does not permit us to talk openly about sex,' she responded. 'That is very true,' I said. 'Can I use that sentence as the opening quote in a paper I am working on?'

'Certainly,' she said, beaming. Many thanks to the student, who wishes to remain anonymous.

It has been a while since I wrote the opening paragraph, during which time I have also had the opportunity to teach another group of students the same course. This group appears to have been a little more open in discussing sexuality, gender and sex than the class of 2008. Upon reflection, I think that a class's response to a gender and sexuality course depends not only on culture, but also on a number of other factors including classroom dynamics, the teacher's disposition and world view, the teacher's frame of mind, the teacher's ability to formulate and operationalise learning objectives and the ability to kindle student interest. Other important factors are the level of students' interest, their frame of mind, world views, level of rapport with the teacher, the life experiences and knowledge of both students and the teacher and the availability of suitable learning materials. Furthermore, some external factors, such as current discussions within the local, and to some extent international, environment on issues related to gender and sexuality as they appear in the media also have a bearing on the level of engagement.

Some of these factors can be influenced. Others, such as the question of the impact of culture and religion, are more difficult to change, and constitute a major challenge to teaching about sexuality in the African university setting. It is important to note that many African cultures traditionally did not exhibit reticence about issues relating to sex and sexuality, as evidenced by customs and practices around sexual initiation among the Baganda of Uganda (Tamale 2005), the Yao of Malawi (Mair 1951; Tumbo-Masabo 1998) or the Krobo of Ghana (Steenstra 2007).

The ideas discussed in this chapter are drawn mainly from my experience for at least seven years in teaching an undergraduate course in gender and sexuality. It is a subjective account, but, in the spirit of transformative learning and feminist pedagogy, the sharing of experiences is a contribution to the discourse, an aspect of the complex and shifting realities that constitute the teaching of sexualities in an African context.

I begin with a short discussion on human sexuality as it was taught in the recent past, based on a book published by the World Health Organisation (WHO) for a global audience, specifically health professionals. Next, I consider the status of teaching sexuality in contemporary Ghana, and go on to briefly sketch the theoretical influences that underlie the methodological approaches I employ. Then, I discuss ways of making inroads through the barrier of silence and other obstacles encountered in the classroom. Finally, I discuss teaching materials and strategies that can be usefully employed in teaching gender and sexuality in sensitive and creative ways.

Toward a theoretical framework

The context

Ordinarily it would have been in place to begin this section with a discussion of a history of gender and sexuality or sexuality-related courses as they were taught in African tertiary institutions in the past, in order to create a context for the discourses that follow. Where were they located, and what was their pedagogic focus? This could not be achieved because it has not been possible to access information outside medical circles on how gender and sexuality courses were taught in the past, although there is now a growing body of knowledge on contemporary gender and sexuality courses. I cite examples from an existing course, a graduate programme in gender, law and sexuality at the Women's Law Centre, University of Zimbabwe. I also draw on the African Gender Institute's Gender and Women's Studies Africa (GWS Africa) Project's website, which has a variety of feminist teaching resources including a section that features an extensive syllabus and bibliography on gender and sexualities in African contexts.

A recent study of the teaching of gender and sexualities in South African higher education (Bennett and Reddy 2007) concludes that there are a variety of courses in South African universities that take gender and sexualities seriously and argues that this is a relatively recent phenomenon, overwhelmingly found in the humanities and health sciences. However, gender and sexualities do not constitute the key curricular emphasis in those subject areas (Bennett and Reddy 2007: 59). The authors found that among several paradigms and philosophies that underpinned teaching approaches to sexuality, the biomedical/social constructivist split was the most influential. The courses did not constitute the key curricular emphasis. It would be of interest to replicate Bennett and Reddy's research in other African universities to fill in the gap.

The dearth of information on gender and sexuality or sexuality courses could be due in part to other reasons, such as poor record-keeping practices in some institutions, an issue that is fairly plausible in some African university contexts. It could also be due to the fact that the teaching of gender and sexuality is such a novelty in African tertiary institutions that information on how it was approached in the past is a non-starter.

The only volume accessed, a WHO publication about teaching human sexuality to health professionals in schools (Mace et al 1974), is of interest. The book is directed at health professionals, such as doctors, nurses, medical schools, nursing schools, schools of public health and any other schools that wish to introduce human sexuality into the curriculum or wish to improve the quality of programmes. The writers are at pains to point out the variability of the intersection of culture, cultural attitudes and human sexuality. For them, human sexuality is a proper concern of health practitioners, and the treatment of sex problems is an integral part of preventive and therapeutic healthcare (Mace et al 1974). The health practitioner's role as a sex educator is threefold:

- To give sex education as an aspect of preventive medicine
- To give advice in preparation for marriage
- To guide society to deal with the many sex-related problems that arise in community life. (Mace et al 1974: 11)

The book takes care to bring home to its readers the need to be circumspect and tactful in dealing with human sexuality. The key areas of knowledge considered necessary for a basic understanding of the subject include:

- Sexual development – biological and psychological
- The reproductive process
- The variety of sexual expression
- Sexual dysfunction and disease
- Cultural aspects of sex
- Marriage and the family. (Mace et al 1974: 21)

Taught in this way, the subject matter cannot possibly reveal that gender is not biologically given and immutable and that there are gender and power hierarchies that underpin human sexuality. The book does not throw any light on that discourse. A further critique of the nature of the subject matter and its pedagogy would be unfair, considering that the book was published in 1974, when ideas about the social constructions of gender and sexuality were still being formed. Of interest is that the book represents one discourse of human sexuality prior to the influence of feminism.

Without past curricula on human sexuality courses taught in Africa, I decided to search within my own country. A key challenge was the problem of accessing archived courses. Storage of old files appeared to be problematic (the advent of new digital technologies will hopefully help to address such issues). I then decided to investigate current courses that contain the word 'sexuality' and searched all the websites of Ghana's five state universities.[2]

Three websites yielded no results, and interestingly, one of those three was the website of the University of Cape Coast, where I teach a course in gender and sexuality. Obviously such an approach is not sufficiently thorough, because not all information about courses taught in the universities is posted on the websites. This also affects the validity of my generalisations about sexuality and sexuality-related courses taught in Ghana. More research on those courses would be necessary. Notwithstanding, one set of search findings is worth studying:

Introduction to Ethical Theories and Religious Ethical Systems
Definition of various terms, e.g., Ethics and Morality; Moral/Non-moral; Moral/Amoral; Moral/ Immoral. Examination of a variety of ethical theories; e.g. Utilitarianism; Stoicism; Kantianism; Situation Ethics. Main features of Christian Ethics, African Traditional Ethics, and Islamic Ethics. Examination of some specific ethical and moral teachings related to such things as sexuality, wealth and stewardship.[3]

Culture and Reproductive Health
Definition of basic concepts – Culture, Reproductive Health. Approaches – The Cultural Approaches; The Empowerment Approach; Development Approach; Reproductive Health Trends and Prevalence of the Components of Reproductive Health; A Focus on HIV/AIDS, Inequalities and Reproductive Health – Gender inequalities, biological differences, individual and households, societal level and Policy level inequalities. The Cultural Contexts of reproductive health – family and kinship, marriage, status of females, culture and sexuality, cultural practices, issues of vulnerability; Socio-Economic Issues – Poverty and unemployment, Education and literacy, women's equity issues; Health care situation; Cultural and Societal Diversities in Reproductive Health; Reproductive Health Services or Programmes Policy Issues.[4]

Reproductive Health
This course includes a wide range of topics related to population dynamics, human reproduction and health related issues. The population education component is intended to give the students insight into the basic principles of population dynamics and problems in order to help them appreciate the importance of family planning to national development efforts. The reproductive health component is intended to help students gain better understanding of the human reproductive process, its control and problems associated with unregulated procreation and adolescent sexuality.[5]

All the course descriptions are from the University of Ghana website. The first course in which sexuality is mentioned is located in a department of the study of religion, the second course is located within the social sciences and the final one is a course in nursing. Clearly, course descriptions do not give a comprehensive overview of what happens in the classroom, but it is clear that the place of sexuality in all three descriptions is not central to the subject matter, and the gendered nature of sexuality and its links with power cannot be inferred from them. All this suggests that critical feminist discourses are not always at the forefront in teaching that relates to sexuality in Ghana's tertiary institutions.

The second search result for the word 'sexuality' – found on the Kwame Nkrumah University of Science and Technology website – was a report on a collaborative effort between the Planned Parenthood Association of Ghana and the university to introduce sexuality education and youth-friendly services on the campus. This has become necessary in order to combat HIV/AIDS and is a fairly recent trend on Ghanaian university campuses. The University of Cape Coast, in the 2009/2010 academic year, introduced a course on HIV/AIDS which seeks to influence behaviour and inform students about the pandemic. Such programmes could eventually become spaces within which sexuality and its gender and power hierarchies could be interrogated.

In order to compare the above extracts with courses that are underpinned by feminist discourses, it might be of interest to briefly explore the objectives as stated in the syllabus on gender and sexuality in African contexts, as it appears on the GWS Africa website.[6] The objectives of the course are as follows:

- To introduce students to critical concepts: sex, gender and sexuality
- To contextualise the study of gender and sexuality in particular African contexts
- To explore the links between 'becoming gendered' and sexuality
- To explore connections between gender, sexuality and other themes.

Apart from the obvious underlying approaches of constructionism and intersectionality ('becoming gendered') that can be inferred from the course objectives, the course offers a broader understanding of sexuality than those described earlier. Further, its African orientation is clear. The description of the course gender, law and sexuality, which is offered as a graduate programme at the University of Zimbabwe, follows similar lines:

> The primary objective of this course unit is to explore the link between the human body, gender, sexuality and culture. It critically examines the social and legal construction of sexuality as it intersects with gender. The main focus is to acquire a deeper understanding of how sex, sexuality and gender are interlinked with the law, in its pluralities, and with other sites and structures of power to regulate sexual relations and control women's reproductive capacity.[7]

The comparison shows that courses that make a claim to include sexuality in their syllabuses might not present the kind of depth of understanding and analysis that a feminist lens which recognises its dynamics, links and interconnections with gender, social institutions, culture, class, power and identity can offer.

Theoretical influences

The pedagogic approach I seek to follow in teaching about sexualities is derived from 'liberatory pedagogy' (hooks 1989; Maher and Thompson Tetreault 2001) or critical pedagogy and feminist pedagogy – teaching methodologies which bring the learner to the point where s/he views previously uncritically acquired knowledge more critically.

Ngan-Ling Chow et al (2003), also following these streams, came up with the dialogic, participatory and experiential (DPE) approach, which seeks to challenge systems of domination, question social construction of knowledge and power, generate consciousness and critical thinking, and promote social change. Central themes of a general feminist pedagogy underpinning the DPE approach to teaching are: (1) an understanding that sees women as knowers; (2) concerns with equality and power among learners and teachers and between teachers and the administration; (3) the formation of community within the classroom; (4) an emphasis on consciousness raising, diversity and justice; and (5) concerns with caring and empowerment (Ngang-Ling Chow et al 2003: 260).

With the African context in mind, I would add to these five points a sixth and a seventh: (6) concerns with the influence of colonial and post-colonial discourses on our understanding of sexuality, gender and power in a globalised world; (7) an understanding of and concerns with the influence of culture and religion on the way teachers and learners view the world. The theoretical background of my course follows the spirit of these ideas.

Teaching sexuality is a political act, because sexuality is a concept of power and teaching it critically raises political consciousness. Thus the classroom can be viewed as a political arena. A lecturer might teach sexuality in a manner that has the effect of encouraging students to accept the status quo without question. Another might employ methods that produce 'Aha!' effects in students and encourage them to acquire alternative views that empower them to change their worldviews and their lives. Critical pedagogic methods, such as feminist pedagogy and transformative learning theory, offer opportunities for students and teachers to acquire knowledge that widens their consciousness.

Feminist pedagogy, which has gender as its focus and recognises that gender is a marker of identity, places value on students' personal experiences, integrating them into the teaching material. It focuses on classroom dynamics by doing away with the power divide between the teacher and students, creating a space in which all voices are heard and legitimised, and where an accommodating and cordial classroom climate is created. Feminist pedagogy rejects the concept of value neutrality and directs itself more towards subjectivities as part of a complex system of realities.[8]

The lecture format, the traditional mode of teaching in universities and a favoured teaching practice in many African universities, has been critiqued by feminists as well as radical educationists following Paulo Freire (Schniedewind 1983 in Gabriel and Smithson 1990; Maher 1985; Tisdell 1998). Isaiah Smithson, citing Maher, writes:

> The traditional mode of university teaching, that of the lecture, presumes that an expert will present to the students an objective, rationally derived and empirically proven set of information. This mode, no matter how complete, can only reflect one version (usually the one dominant in the culture). The result is that students are memorizing truths to which their own historical, cultural and personal experience gives the lie. (Smithson 1990: 15)

Smithson presents Maher's argument that traditional education, as well as the lecture format, assume that learning consists of a search for a single, objective, rationally derived 'right answer' that is separate from the historical source or producer of that answer. A cooperative and interactive pedagogy that conceptualises knowledge as a comparison of multiple perspectives leading towards a complex and evolving view of reality (Smithson 1990: 15) is suggested as an alternative to the traditional conception of knowledge and reality. According to this discourse, subjectivities are acknowledged and transcended by listening to others and drawing on their experiences and social realities.

Transformative learning is an adult learning theoretical approach, which takes the learner through a process that enables him or her to question previously acquired knowledge and gradually move away from accepting knowledge in an uncritical manner. It is a reflective discourse:

> In the context of transformative learning theory, is that specialised use of dialogue devoted to searching for a common understanding and assessment of the justification of an interpretation or belief. This is about making personal understanding of issues or beliefs, through assessing the evidence and arguments of a point of view or issue, and being open to looking at alternative points of view, or alternative beliefs, then reflecting critically on the new information and making a personal judgement based on a new assessment of the information.[9] (Mezirow et al 2000: 10)

Creating a safe classroom environment that provides opportunities for transformative learning as discussed previously is a gradual development that the lecturer consciously builds and grows, from the first introductory meetings, in which the concept of 'lecturer as facilitator' is introduced, through to the final class. In my case, I have tended to begin the course by employing interactive methods, such as the use of 'sticky notes' (presented in the next section) and small group discussions. I have found the latter to be particularly useful for occasions when the students are especially reticent.

Of course students are best engaged when the content matches with their own lived experience, and the use of the 'P's of sexuality' framework (Gupta 2000) for my undergraduate class has generally resonated well with them.[10] Students have also readily identified with some of the issues that are discussed in advice columns that appear in local newspapers. The analysis of the letters and answers to the issues relating to sexuality found in the advice columns offers students opportunities to understand ways in which sexuality is constructed and the idealised norms and values around it that they had not previously identified.

Instructional methods: some suggestions on sensitively bringing sexuality into the classroom

Teaching gender and sexuality can be both exciting and frustrating. Although we sometimes sense the novelty and excitement of treading on uncharted territory and the tensions and emotions students experience when, in class, they are confronted with ideas previously unheard of in their worlds, it can also be frustrating because culturally, sexuality is not a topic to be openly discussed and students sometimes prefer to sit in silence than to make contributions. Teaching about sexualities necessitates approaches that encourage students to relax and feel comfortable enough to open up and talk. It also presents opportunities for critical thinking and exposure of students to alternative viewpoints that they might or might not agree with. On one occasion, as we discussed the format of the final examination in class, a student asked me: 'I just want to be sure, do I have to write what I imagine you would like me to think?'

'Absolutely not!' I replied. 'As long as you are able to substantiate your argument satisfactorily, you are fine.'

However, his question unsettled me somewhat. To me, it suggested that my teaching methodology perhaps did not sit very well with all the students and was indicative of some of the challenges the approaches pose – an issue that will be discussed shortly.

Because of barriers relating to religion and culture, the teacher of sexuality is often faced with students who, despite their curiosity about a course on sexuality, seem reluctant to open up. The teacher needs to break the ice in order to proceed with the course. How can this be done? Tamale (see Chapter 63) has suggested the use of humour and appropriate icebreakers. Where all other forms of communication fail, the correct use of humour, she argues, can bridge many divides – intercultural, interfaith, interpower and intergenerational.

I often begin the course by asking all the members of the class to state why they chose it and find out if there is any topic they would like to add to the syllabus. Making room for students' interests is a way of being democratic. Then I explain the theoretical principles that constitute my methodology, stressing the 'rules': everyone has a voice, there should be no 'rubbishing' of dissenting views and the fact that I am merely playing the role of a facilitator. I make it clear that although I am a lecturer, I do not know everything, and will learn from them through our interaction. All this does not yet loosen tongues. What I have found to be decisive in breaking the ice is to assign students texts for presentation which explicitly name genitalia. When, in a presentation, students have no alternative than to articulate the words 'penis' and 'vagina' several times, a barrier is broken.

Mumbi Machera's 'Opening a can of worms: a debate on female sexuality in the lecture theatre' (2004) works well. I introduce it fairly early in the course, after we discuss sexualities, sex and the way they are linked with gender. Barriers can also be broken by introducing alternative methods, such as films. Assigning readings about practices from other countries for comparative purposes at the outset has been a success for some teachers. Sylvia Tamale,[11] for example, has recounted how her students have always expressed surprise at learning that prostitution is legal in Senegal.

BOX 62.1

Examples of instructional methods

1. Sticky note thoughts

The instructor gives all the students sticky notes and asks each of them to write what immediately comes to mind when they hear the word 'homosexual', or 'rape' or whatever concept needs to be discussed. The students must not hesitate, but put down as many words as possible. The students stick their notes on the wall and, with the teacher, they examine the answers and categorise them. Examples of categories can be 'value judgement', or 'definition' or 'myth' or 'fact' and so on. This can form the basis of a discussion.

2. Class drama

This is actually role play. The instructor and the students design a short drama sketch that presents what they think are the stereotyped characteristics of issues such as rape, homosexuality or any other topic. The class breaks into two groups. One group conceptualises and performs the sketch and the other group critiques it.

3. The question basket

Students are asked to anonymously place 'embarrassing' questions for class discussion in a specific place at an appropriate time (Tamale 2011, see chapter 63 of this volume).

4. Observational walks/field visits

The idea for this activity is based on the Transect Walk, in which a research team conducts a mobile interview by walking around a community talking with people who live there. The team seeks clarification on issues and makes observations, while discussing issues of mutual interest with community members. This method can be used for visits to women's shelters, red light districts, initiation ceremonies and other sites.

Once the initial barrier is broken, it is necessary to sustain the more open classroom environment with readings and examples taken from Africa and the immediate environment. Anecdotal evidence shows that students respond with more interest to readings based on African experiences, perhaps because of cultural similarities.

No amount of exciting instructional material will guarantee good learning outcomes if the methods of instruction are not effective. Teaching strategies modelled on workshop instruction are particularly useful, especially for courses that are meant to be empowering and interactive, such as a course on sexuality that follows transformative learning and feminist principles.

Furthermore, techniques such as brainstorming, group work and presentation in plenary or class sessions, analysis of pictures, using student's ideas to form diagrams or charts, role play and analysis are all effective means of achieving learning outcomes. Four simple activities that facilitate the discussion and deconstruction of concepts are presented in Box 62.1. The role play especially is almost always popular and encourages much interaction and discussion.

Another useful technique is journal writing, successfully utilised in a human sexuality class taught in Kenya. The authors argue that the journal writing nurtured self-expression and reflective practice, transforming what otherwise might have been an abstract course into meaningful knowledge, which was both enlightening and cathartic for the students (Khamasi and Undie 2008: 195).

The instructor assigned her students weekly journal entries in which they were asked to reflect on the content learned and their discussions in and outside the classroom. The lecturer read the journals, commented on them and returned them to the students for further writing. The students wrote quite extensively about their sexual experiences during the 12-week semester. Before the last day of class, students were asked to assess the entire course, including its content, mode of instruction and the manner in which the instructor handled the course (Khamasi and Undie 2008: 186).

Some of the tensions that this technique raised were related to honestly dialoguing about sexuality and gaining students' confidence. In this case it was achieved by the lecturer personally interrogating her own sexuality and sharing personal sexuality-related examples and incidents from her own life with the students. This also helped to construct the classroom as a safe space for dialogue around sexuality (Khamasi and Undie 2008: 193).

Cultural contexts and challenges

Cultural reticence to talk about sex is not confined to Africa. An article in *The New York Times* (Faison 1998) about the opening of a sex museum in Shanghai mentioned the 'studied reticence' of the Chinese when it comes to sex. Another article in *The Times* of London, referred to the 'Scottish reluctance to be open about sexual matters' (Bowditch 2007).

There are, however, degrees of reticence across societies and also evidence that levels of reserve about sex and sexualities change over time. Adrian Bingham (2009), for example, discusses how newspaper reports on matters about sex and sexuality changed between the period before the Second World War and the 1960s, which ushered in a period of sexual permissiveness.

Great gaps in knowledge exist regarding the nature of cultural reticence about sex in Africa. We simply do not know much about the status quo in respect of cultural reticence to communicating about sex on the continent. What is clear is that there are concrete difficulties in discussing sex and, as Ifi Amadiume has said, the ambiguity of beliefs and attitudes in African traditional cultures and religions, as well as sexuality in the received world religions and global popular cultures of post-colonial African modernity, pose challenges. Amadiume calls for discourses on sexuality in Africa that move away from prescribed sexual practices and that consider the normative and the counter-normative alternative sexuality as they relate to gender concepts and practices that address the problem of gender inequality and state patriarchy (Amadiume 2006).

Discussions about sex and sexuality in contemporary Ghana, for instance, generally occur in impersonal settings, such as on radio phone-in programmes, in sex education classroom settings, in letters to newspapers or magazines or in church-related counselling sessions. In the traditional setting, apart from the sex counselling that goes with initiation rites or preparation for marriage, the discourse on sex and sexuality is mainly found in jokes, song, dance and proverbs, and does not extend to alternative or counter-normative practices.

How does the lecturer deal with the reservation and reticence towards sex and sexuality? This is difficult to answer. Talking about sexualities is not easy, and there is no single formula that works. Following the methodologies of critical and feminist pedagogies in the classroom presents challenges. The methodologies assume that students and lecturers are free of the cultural inhibitions that might constrain their discussions about sex and desire. The lecturer has to overcome his or her own inhibitions and face the subject matter squarely.

Students' reticence on matters related to sexuality might be linked to the fact that the lecturer is not their peer. The lecturer is an adult who, according to socialisation practice, is a person to be respected and from whom they maintain a specific distance. In many African societies, younger people are accustomed to submitting to adults. Discussing private, intimate and emotional issues, such as sexualities, does not fit well with the traditional student-teacher relationship in the African context. Moreover, the lecturer is a 'stranger', someone unknown to the students before they entered the institution or enrolled for the course. And we do not generally discuss intimate matters with a stranger. The lecturer also has power, which in the eyes of students, can 'make' or 'break' them. How can a young person be open to a lecturer considering the nature of the cultural and religious inhibitions? The lecturer also has to be able to relate well with the students and, as far as possible, do away with the social barriers and work on creating a community in the classroom that is safe and comfortable. In addition to all this, the lecturer of sexualities needs to be credible to students, practising what they preach.

Institutional contexts: challenges

Challenges regarding evaluation and assessment

No classroom is an island in itself (Ngang-Ling Chow et al 2003: 272), and what happens there cannot be separated from the institutional context. The culture of the institution affects teaching to some extent. Although the lecturer enjoys the flexibility to design courses, there are administrative prescriptions to adhere to, such as mid- and end of semester examinations. At the University of Cape Coast, where I teach, the university prescribes for undergraduate courses a three-hour written examination with a specific number of questions depending on what year the student is in. This means that presentations, peer teaching and group discussions must be graded as continuous assessment. There is not much flexibility regarding the structure of the end-of-semester examination. Grading is done according to the prescriptions of the institution. The lecturer in the critical classroom can be constrained by institutional prescriptions and must be creative in order to achieve the course objectives.

In the feminist classroom, which is a friendly, non-hierarchical community, assessment should normally be a peer-based activity. This has proved to be difficult to achieve because of competition and the unwillingness of students to appear to 'mark down' their peers. I have unfortunately not been very successful in instituting this practice. What I have tried to do is to find a middle ground. Grades are discussed and awarded in the classroom, but the students and I agree that I have the final word and can use my discretion to change grades if the need arises. Evaluations should take the goals and learning objectives of the course into consideration. The format of the evaluation is often determined by the institution.

Structural challenges

Another challenge to keeping a focus on critical and feminist pedagogy in the classroom in the African context can be the seating arrangement in classrooms and lecture theatres. In my university, the majority of lecture theatres are furnished with tables and chairs that are fixed to the floor, sometimes (but not always) in ascending order from the lecturer, with the lecturer's desk located (also permanently) in front of the board. It is difficult under those circumstances to maintain an atmosphere that breaks hierarchical barriers around the authority of the lecturer, especially when one has already announced that the lecturer is in actual fact a facilitator.

But there are always solutions to challenges. When assigned classrooms of that nature, we sit on the tables, particularly during group discussions. For peer teaching and presentations I sit with the students. It is also possible to move out of the lecture hall and hold a class under a tree or in any pleasant spot outside that offers some privacy.

The classroom in Africa is changing. The younger generation are familiar and at ease with technology and this can be utilised by the lecturer. During a class recently I asked a student to search for the meaning of a concept online and then quickly stopped myself when I remembered the university's server was down. Very quickly the student pulled out his mobile phone and retrieved the information using the internet access provided by his service provider! Could such networking be used to further engage with students in other African countries taking similar courses? Structural challenges exist but, through brainstorming with students, they can be addressed.

Teaching instruments

Thus far, the actual instrument for approaching a course in gender and sexuality has not been discussed although elements of the infrastructre on which the lecturer can build have been mentioned. By infrastructure I refer to the sum total of steps and measures needed to plan and execute the teaching and assessment of the course, including a close consideration of cultural and institutional factors as well as the needs and abilities of the students and the lecturer.

A detailed discussion of curriculum development techniques is beyond the scope of this chapter, but it might be useful to sketch out some of the basic steps in planning a course of this nature. Although there are no fixed methods of creating an instrument, Posner and Rudnitsky propose a useful outline for course planning which can be adapted and is reproduced here:

1. A rationale for the course, including the overall educational goals.

2. A curriculum plan describing intended learning outcomes for the course, prioritised according to importance, to be expressed in formats that may include the following:

    a. Lists of statements and paragraphs

    b. Maps of major ideas

    c. A story or narrative expressing the course 'theme'

    d. Flowcharts of skills

3. An instructional plan describing what each unit is about, how it fits into the overall organisation of units, what learning outcomes each unit is intended to accomplish, and what general teaching strategies could be used in each unit to accomplish the intended learning outcomes.

4. An evaluation plan describing behavioural indicators for each high-priority intended learning outcome (main effects), together with a list of some unintended, undesirable learning outcomes (side effects) to be on the lookout for. (Posner and Rudnitsky 2006: 4)

Course introductions, course outlines and central questions are also instrumental by-products of this process (Posner and Rudnitsky 2006). The amount of detail expected from lecturers varies across tertiary institutions, but all of them demand course curricula.

One way of adapting Posner and Rudnitsky's suggestions for a course plan would be to include a schedule and plan for counselling students. The creation of a 'safe classroom' and discussions on sexuality invariably lead students to reflect on their own sexuality and sexual experiences, and more often than not, they confide in the teacher, within and outside the classroom.[12]

Teaching materials

It is important that teaching materials are selected based on the theoretical framework and educational goals. The theoretical framework for my gender and sexuality course, for example, is informed by critical and feminist pedagogy, but the course itself follows a feminist social-constructionist orientation. Thus, my course description reiterates that 'in this course the focus is on sexual behaviour as socially developed rather than as a biological given. It examines the way we become sexual beings and shows how this process is gendered'.

The themes chosen for my weekly lectures are selected with the aim of discovering and demonstrating through readings, discussion and peer-to-peer education sessions the social construction of sexualities and gender identities. The selection of readings and examples are as far as possible African in context. Thus, we read Julius Kaggwa's (1997) *From Juliet to Julius*[13] to illustrate issues pertaining to the acquisition of gender identity. An unintended but positive outcome was a discussion about how society treats people who do not fit into the categories of male or female, and the concept of three or more genders. At the end of the discussion and after reading Kaggwa, some students reported in class that they had found him on the social networking website, Facebook. That, for me, was an indication that the students had actually been moved by the stories. The case of the South African athlete Caster Semenya[14] was also a 'hot' topic in the media during the time we discussed gender identities in class and it engaged the attention of the students.

Since sexuality is an integral aspect of our social lives that is constantly being constructed, materials suitable for teaching sexuality are literally all around us. In addition to academic literature, there are lifestyle and fashion magazines, local and international news items, advertisements, advice columns, cartoons, online news, novels and short stories, social networking sites and popular films – all important sources for material suitable for teaching gender and sexuality.

Closing thoughts

In this essay I have attempted to synthesise the elements and features required to teach African sexualities successfully and in a creative manner. The various attributes of the feminist classroom have been described as an infrastructure that can be used and further developed. There are some difficulties, mostly related to cultural attitudinal barriers, in reaching a high level of adherence to the experiential, interactive, egalitarian and convivial qualities of a classroom dedicated to transformative learning. This should not be considered a major constraint, because the attempt to reach those standards and the gains for the lecturer and students in the learning process far outweigh the gains to be made from more traditional forms of teaching.

Apart from the theoretical pedagogic basis, the infrastructure consists of a course design that ensures that teaching objectives are met, course materials that reflect African experiences and meet the needs of students, and teaching methods that engage the students and foster interactive learning. Teachers must be prepared to step outside their traditional roles and act as facilitators. The ability to function within institutional boundaries and with flexibility is required. Assessment and evaluation of experiential, interactive learning poses a challenge and there is the need to conduct research in this area.

Although challenges, such as poorly stocked libraries and limited internet and energy access abound, Africa offers many opportunities for creative teaching of sexualities. These include the utilisation of mobile phone technology and radio for communication and networking, which can greatly facilitate comparative studies; acknowledging that the AIDS pandemic has made people more interested in sexuality issues and has created a platform from which gender and sexuality can be addressed; harnessing opportunities for inter-African research and exchange programmes and the exciting prospects for teaching about gender and sexualities and beyond that arise within a feminist classroom.

Notes

1. I am grateful to Sylvia Tamale, Kopano Ratele and Stella Nyanzi for their helpful comments and suggestions.
2. The search was conducted on 12 March 2010.
3. See http://www.ug.edu.gh/index1.php?linkid=185&sublinkid=37&subsublinkid=25&page=4&sectionid=209#204, accessed 3 December 2010.
4. See http://www.ug.edu.gh/index1.php?linkid=185&sublinkid=41&subsublinkid=42&page=4&sectionid=193, accessed 3 December 2010.
5. See http://www.ug.edu.gh/index1.php?linkid=186&sublinkid=22&subsublinkid=68&page=7&sectionid=288, accessed 3 December 2010.
6. See http://www.gwsafrica.org/teaching-resources/gender-sexuality/course-outline, accessed 29 May 2010.
7. From the course syllabus by Oliver Phillips and Sylvia Tamale (n.d.)
8. Webb et al (2002) identified six principles of feminist pedagogy: reformation of the relationship between professor and student, empowerment, building community, privileging voice, respecting the diversity of personal experience and challenging traditional pedagogical notions.
9. For a fuller discussion of transformative learning theory, see http://transformativelearningtheory.com/corePrinciples.html, accessed 21 November 2009.
10. See Prah (2009) for a detailed account of the use of this method in my undergraduate gender and sexuality course. Oliver Phillips (forthcoming, 2011) has a useful account of the employment and adaptation of Gayle Rubin's model of sexual hierarchies.
11. In personal communication.
12. A few years ago, I personally experienced a situation in the classroom during which a student openly declared that she was still a virgin. Other students began to snigger and giggle, and because I was not prepared for the situation, I failed to protect the person who had boldly revealed a personal matter. More recently, another student confided that she has a homosexual brother who is dealing with rejection from most family members. She confided that she sympathises with him and has not recoiled from him. She gives him advice but is not sure about how she can continue to have a close relationship with him and avoid rejection from the family. I had to spend time with her to reassure her that she would do well to stay as friends with him and support him. Other teachers of sexuality in Africa have confirmed that students often do need to confide in the lecturer. Revelations about rape, incest, domestic violence and abstinence have been made to lecturers of sexuality in Africa (personal communication from Sylvia Tamale).
13. Kaggwa gives an autobiographical account of a Ugandan intersexed individual who was raised as a female but identified as a male. After surgical intervention at the age of 24, Juliet's gender identity changed to Julius. His journey from female to male reveals a great deal about African culture, sexuality and gender identity. See also Chapter 21.

14. Caster Semenya is a South African athlete who attracted media attention at the 2009 World Championships in Athletics Meeting in September 2009, when she finished the 800 metres race significantly faster than all other women. She won the gold medal but subsequently questions were raised about her gender. The story unfolded just as we were discussing gender identities in class. See http://en.wikipedia.org/wiki/Caster_Semenya.

References

Amadiume, Ifi (2006) 'Sexuality, African religio-cultural traditions and modernity: expanding the lens', *CODESRIA Bulletin* 1 and 2

Bennett, Jane and Reddy, Vasu (2007) '"Feeling the disconnect": teaching sexualities and gender in South African higher education', *Feminist Africa* 9: 43–62

Bingham, A. (2009) *Family Newspapers? Sex, Private Life and the Popular British Press 1918–1978*, Oxford, Oxford University Press

Bowditch, Gillian (2007) 'Sex missionary under fire', *The Times*, 14 January, http://www.timesonline.co.uk/tol/news/uk/scotland/article1292103.ece, accessed 22 November 2009

Faison, Seth (1998) 'Shanghai journal: behind a great wall of reticence, some sex toys', *New York Times*, 5 March, http://www.nytimes.com/1998/03/05/world/shanghai-journal-behind-a-great-wall-of-reticence-some-sex-toys.html, accessed 22 November 2009

Gabriel, Susan L. and Smithson, Isaiah (eds) (1990) *Gender in the Classroom: Power and Pedagogy*, Urbana and Chicago, University of Illinois Press

Gupta, G.R. (2000) 'Gender, sexuality and HIV/AIDS: the what, the why and the how', http://www.siteresources.worldbank.org/.../Resources/durban_speech.pdf., accessed 31 August 2010

hooks, bell (1989) *Talking Back: Thinking Feminist, Thinking Black*, Cambridge, Southend Press

Khamasi, Jennifer Wanjiku and Undie, Chi-Chi (2008) 'Teaching human sexuality in higher education: a case from Western Kenya', in Dunne, M. (ed) *Gender, Sexuality and Development: Education and Society in sub-Saharan Africa*, Rotterdam, Sense Publishers

Mace, D.R., Bannerman, R.H.O. and Burton, J. (eds) (1974) *The Teaching of Human Sexuality in Schools for Health Professionals*, Geneva, World Health Organisation

Machera, Mumbi (2004) '"Opening a can of worms": a debate on female sexuality in the lecture theatre', in Arnfred, S. (ed) *Re-thinking Sexualities in Africa*, Uppsala, The Nordic Africa Institute

Maher, Frances (1985) 'Pedagogies for the gender-balanced classroom', *Journal of Thought* 20: 48–64

Maher, Frances A. and Thompson Tetreault, Mary Kay (2001) (eds) *The Feminist Classroom: Dynamics of Gender, Race and Privilege*, Lanham, MD, Rowman and Littlefield

Mair, Lucy (1951) 'A Yao girl's initiation', *Man* 98: 60–63

Mezirow, Jack et al (2000) *Learning as Transformation: Critical Perspectives on a Theory in Progress*, San Francisco, Jossey Bass

Ngan-Ling Chow, Esther, Fleck, Chadwick, Fan, Gang-Hua, Joseph, Joshua Lyter, Deanna (2003) 'Exploring critical feminist pedagogy: infusing dialogue, participation and experience into the classroom', *Teaching Sociology* 31(3): 259–75

Phillips, Oliver (2011) 'Teaching sexuality and law in southern Africa: locating historical narratives and adopting appropriate conceptual frameworks', in Tsanga, A. and Stewart, J. (eds) *Women and Law: Innovative Approaches to Teaching, Research and Analysis*, Harare, Weaver Press

Posner, George J. and Rudnitsky, Alan N. (2006) *Course Design: A Guide to Curriculum Development for Teachers*, Boston, Pearson Education

Prah, Mansah (2009) 'Advice columns as a teaching resource for gender and sexuality: experiences from the University of Cape Coast', in *East African Journal of Peace and Human Rights* 15(1): 171–85

Smithson, Isaiah (1990) 'Introduction: investigating gender, power and pedagogy, in Gabriel, S.L and Smithson, I., *Gender in the Classroom: Power and Pedagogy*, Urbana and Chicago, University of Illinois Press

Steenstra, Marijke (2007) 'Making real Krobo women: gender and the power of performance of female initiation rites (*dipo*) in Ghana', *LOVA-Tijdschrift voor Feministische Anthropologie* 28(2): 57–68

Tamale, Sylvia (2005), Eroticism, sensuality and "women's secrets" among the Baganda: a critical analysis', *Feminist Africa* 5: 9–36

—— (2011) 'Interrogating the link between gendered sexualities, power and legal mechanisms in Africa: experiences from the lecture room', in Tsanga, A. and Stewart, J. (eds) *Women and Law: Innovative Approaches to Teaching, Research and Analysis*, Harare, Weaver Press

Tisdell, Elizabeth (1998) 'Post-structural feminist pedagogies: the possibilities and limitations of feminist emancipatory adult learning theory and practice', *Adult Education Quarterly* 48: 139–56

Tumbo-Masabo, Zubeida (1998) 'Training by symbolism and imagery: the case of Wagogo and Wayao', in Rwebangira, M. and Liljeström, R. (eds) *Haraka, Haraka … Look Before You Leap: Youth at the Crossroad of Custom and Modernity*, Uppsala,The Nordic Africa Institute

Webb, L., Allen, M. and Walker, K. (2002) 'Feminist pedagogy: identifying basic principles', *Academic Exchange Quarterly*, 6: 67–72

63

Interrogating the link between gendered sexualities, power and legal mechanisms: experiences from the lecture room[1]

Sylvia Tamale

Setting the stage: 'are we really going to talk about sex?'

Talking about sex in public is taboo in most societies. Therefore when postgraduate (mostly) law students at the University of Zimbabwe's Southern and Eastern African Centre for Women's Law (SEACWL) are confronted with the choices of elective courses, most view the course on gender, law and sexuality and its underlying agenda with a certain amount of unease, curiosity, even suspicion. This is despite the fact that it is a second semester course for graduate students who have previously spent a semester being exposed to theories and perspectives in women's law.

Sexuality as an area of serious scholarship in legal academies in and outside Africa is a relatively new phenomenon. Thus, it is critical to use creative teaching methods that very early on in the course break the ice, bridge the lecturer-student divide and create a safe environment for meaningful discussions. An approach that presents fresh, relevant and critical perspectives to sexuality is always a challenge to the lecturer. In the main, students at the women's law centre come from different countries in southern and eastern Africa. Each course group presents its own dynamics, diversities and experiences. Navigating and negotiating such quandaries can sometimes prove quite sticky.

In this course we attempt to achieve two main objectives: the first is to demonstrate how sexuality is instrumentalised and deployed by culture, religion and the law, among others, as a control mechanism for maintaining unequal power relations in African societies. Here, the main focus is to acquire a deeper understanding of how sex, sexuality and gender are interlinked with the law, in its pluralities, and with other sites and structures of power to regulate sexual relations and to consolidate control.[2] Secondly, we explore sexuality as an alternative and empowering force for challenging gender and power hierarchies. Through an exploration of the linkages between the human body, gender, sexuality and culture, we critically examine the social, cultural and legal constructions of sexuality as they intersect with gender. Although the course unit focuses mainly on women, the issues traversed are not about women alone; rather, they are about the role that the law plays in maintaining particular sexual relationships and identities for both women and men, structuring and reinforcing a gendered society wherein women are largely subordinated to men.

The readings and assignments are selected to challenge students to recognise the intersecting aspects of gender, law, sexuality, culture and identity, and the ways in which individuals and groups have resisted and continue to resist oppression. The course is designed for maximum interaction and vigorous participation of students in ways that are comfortable and engaging. As much as possible, examples are drawn from everyday experiences and references to real cases from across the continent are used throughout the course. Fortunately, there is never a lack of media exposure of current stories on issues of sexuality from around the continent.

The first module of the course (taught by Oliver Phillips) introduces students to some key conceptual approaches and historical studies that are useful in considering the relationship between law and culture, as they relate to sexuality and gender. The second module of the course (taught by Sylvia Tamale) relates theory to the more specific manifestations of gendered power in the legal regulation of sexuality. It is expected that by the end of the course students will have acquired the necessary analytical skills to critically question seemingly gender-neutral, objective and universal legal concepts and sexual norms. They are supposed to leave the course wearing gendered lenses that allow them to perceive and understand the subtle ways in which the law perpetuates gender discrimination through sexuality. At the same time, students who have completed this course appreciate the positive, empowering aspects of sexuality reflected through resistance, subversion, negotiation, identity, self-desire, pleasure and silence.

My own inspiration in designing this course was rooted in the glaring gap that existed in legal training for analysing sexuality. I wished to create a space for law students to conceptualise sexuality beyond the 'funny' rape cases that they encountered in the traditional criminal law classes.[3] The African Gender Institute (AGI) at the University of Cape Town was critical in crystallising my motivation and sharpening my scholarship in this area. In 2002 I was actively involved in developing the teaching resources for lecturers in gender and women's studies on the continent.

The AGI organised several workshops with various African feminist scholars to discuss pedagogical and content issues in the area of women's studies. It was here that I honed participative feminist teaching methods, imbibed a rich array of literature and developed invaluable linkages with like-minded scholars across the continent. My close involvement in the 'Mapping African Sexualities' research project organised by the AGI and the Institute of African Studies (IAS) at the University of Ghana in 2003 was the culmination of this learning process and sealed my conviction that this area was of critical importance to emerging academic discourse on the continent.

This chapter discusses the pedagogical issues and methodological tools that I employ in the second module of the course. Although the main focus is on its instructional aspects, some non-pedagogical issues that are more conceptual and legal obviously form part of the discussion. Some of the questions that the chapter attempts to address are:

- How do we get over the initial reservations, embarrassments and reticence to engage the class in rigorous, productive and engaging analyses and reflections?
- What skills do I experiment with in trying to link theory to everyday experience as well as applying it to the professional work students engage in?
- What resources are available to demonstrate how legal mechanisms associated with sexuality hinder and/or facilitate social change or transformation?
- What tools do I employ to help students unlearn deeply embedded knowledge and relearn innovative ways of building new theories of knowledge?

Each year is a new learning process for me and for the students, facilitated by our mutual symbiotic synergies.

Following this introduction, I provide a contextual overview of the course before delving into a pedagogical discussion of some strategies that I employ to break the sexual taboos in the lecture room environment in the following section. The fourth section of the chapter discusses the unlearning and relearning processes that the course participants experience. The following section reflects on the pedagogical aspects of linking gender/sexuality theory to social, cultural and political practice.

In the penultimate section I explore the transformational potential in transgressive sexuality, illustrating how students learn to question the very categories through which society constructs, regulates and systematises the sexual. The final section of the chapter reflects on the lessons that I have so far learned from facilitating this course, the challenges encountered and its future prospects.

Contextualising African sexualities

Popular understanding of the term 'sexuality' is often limited and closely linked to the sex act.[4] In other words, the physical looms large. One of the first tasks undertaken in the course is to broaden such understanding by showing the way that sexuality is deeply embedded in almost all aspects of human life. The historical, social, cultural, political and legal meanings and interpretations attached to the human body largely translate into sexuality and systematically infuse our relationship to desire, politics, religion, identity, dress, movement, kinship structures, disease, social roles and language.

Using a historical approach to sexualities in Africa is extremely important for three reasons. First of all, it helps students appreciate the significance of various forces, such as colonialism, religion, capitalism and culture, in shaping and influencing sexuality on the continent. For example, tracing the history of rape law in common-law jurisdictions reveals that it was designed to protect the honour and the 'property' that men, such as the husband and/or father, had in the victim and not to protect the victim's bodily integrity.

It explains why the crime of rape does not fall under offences against the person, but under the offences against morality sections of most penal codes directly imported from former European colonial states. It further explains the law's narrow, restrictive approach to what constitutes rape. The historical analyses also shed light on, say, the exemptions placed on marital rape and why evidentiary rules for rape allow the accused rapist to introduce the sexual history of the victim as a mitigating factor (Coughlin 1998). The phallocentric nature of the offence is also manifest in the requirement of penile-vagina penetration as a main ingredient of the crime.[5]

The second reason for taking a historical perspective is that this approach reveals the dynamism of the phenomenon of sexuality and how it has continued to unfold over the years. Finally, a historical lens assists students in developing a broader view of contemporary sexual controversies, placing them in their proper contexts. Learning about the sexual diversities and realities that existed on the continent prior to contact with Europeans and Arabs, for example, offers perspectives that recognise the complexity and depth of African sexualities. History will likewise explain the pervasive double standards that govern men's and women's sexual morality in Africa.[6] Therein lies the answer to questions such as whose morality, what purpose do such moral codes serve and so forth.

Delving into the history of African sexualities and engaging with its political economy is a new experience for most lawyers in the class. For example, a historical discussion of the case of the Khoisan woman, Saartjie (Sarah) Baartman, the so-called Hottentot Venus, is as fascinating as it is shocking to students. The response to Baartman symbolises the racist, imperialist and sexist representations of African women's sexuality by colonial powers (see Chapter 19 in this volume). It throws light on the current attitudes toward African women's sexualities (medicalised, maternal and promiscuous, among others) that stem from colonial policies and institutions. Such stereotypes have been internalised by many Africans and are often repeated in media reports, research reports and popular culture. It also explains the nature of sexual laws in most post-colonial states that aim to suppress and regulate women's sexualities following the model of Victorian Europe.

African sexualities have long been the subject of fairly evident patterns of ethnocentric and racist constructions. A critical examination of texts from 19th century reports authored by white explorers, missionaries and anthropologists clearly demonstrates this. Either through blatant ignorance, or as part of a deliberate process of othering, they foisted gross simplifications on extremely complex realities. Colonial narratives equated black sexuality with animal primitivity. African sexuality was depicted as crude, exotic and bordering on nymphomania. Christian interpretations of the heathen practices of the African were duplicated in the arena of sexuality and depicted as immoral, bestial and lascivious. The main caricatures of Africans were to give them lustful dispositions. Such constructions of Africans as bestial and inhumane were the first essential step in masking attempts to justify and legitimise the fundamental objectives of colonialism. From such depictions it was fairly easy to make the next step in describing the imperial enterprise as a 'civilising mission' designed to enlighten and liberate the barbarian and savage natives of the 'dark continent' (Gates 1986).

Furthermore, the fact that laws that govern sexualities in Africa are sourced from various legal systems (cultural, religious and statutory) poses different and extremely complex challenges. The pluralistic legal systems found in most African countries are theoretically governed by a hierarchical paradigm, wherein 'modern' statutory law takes precedence over cultural and religious laws. In other words, applicability of the latter is subjected to the repugnancy test, meaning that only those indigenous/religious practices and values that are not repugnant to (colonial) natural justice, equity and good conscience pass the test. And yet, a critical examination of students' own experiences and knowledge about human relations (including sexuality) in Africa reveals that it is culture/religion and not statutory law that governs the day-to-day interactions of most African people. Legal tensions around social institutions such as polygyny, bigamy, bridewealth, adultery and how they relate to gender, power and sexuality are discussed. Hence, the gap between law-in-the-books and law-in-action, even when it comes to sexuality, is very apparent.

Family structures (and their evolution) present another important contextual feature of this course. Given its rich and diverse cultures, the African continent hosts a range of family arrangements and a plethora of kinship relations. Students from various countries share their cultural practices with the rest of the class. The revelations that come to students during these discussions are always astounding. They discover the range of existing family structures and authority systems – patriarchal, patrilineal/matrilineal, patrilocal/matrilocal, exogamous/endogamous, extended/nuclear, polygynous/polyandrous – and the significance of the impact of these different social systems on gender, sexuality and violence. The link is also made between various marriage arrangements and sexuality. A good example is the practice of *chimutsamapfihwa* among the Shona ethnic group of the Ndaus in eastern Zimbambwe – a type of surrogacy that links the institution of *lobola* (bridewealth), barrenness and reproductive rights. Such a traditional concept facilitates the class to understand the delinking of sexuality from reproduction in some African traditions.

Using seminal works, such as those by Ifi Amadiume, we explore the historical and ethnocentric conceptualisations of African family structures, tracing their impact on African sexuality discourses (Amadiume 1987). A deeper examination of more contemporary family arrangements that are at odds with the dominant, socially accepted ones, such as single-parenting and same-sex relations, among others, also helps to unveil the close relationship between the institution of the (heterosexual) family and the social processes of sexuality control.

For a more nuanced, critical approach we try to avoid situations that encourage what Gordon and Cornwall describe as 'the tyranny of consensus' (Gordon and Cornwall 2004), whereby no space is created for minority individuals to express different views and to explore personal feelings. A good example is our interrogation of the concepts 'culture' and 'rights'. Instead of presenting the two concepts as distinct, invariably opposed and antagonistic, we explore the emancipatory potential of culture to enhance the quality of lives in Africa.

The potential that culture holds for emancipating women in Africa is often buried, for instance, in the avalanche of literature many feminist scholars devote to the 'barbaric' cultural practice of female genital mutilation (FGM). Not only is there an acute lack of sensitivity to and recognition of grassroots and local initiatives undertaken by African groups and activists in this regard, but the missionary zeal applied to the enterprise often produces a negative backlash.[7] By taking such an approach, we surface the limitations that stem from holding culture and rights as binary opposites on our strategic interventions for transforming society (Tamale 2008).

Finally, a human rights perspective provides an excellent framework for contextualising African sexualities. Speaking the language of rights to lawyers and activists is relatively easy because it has become hegemonic in the search for equality for the marginalised. Although sexual rights as a concept has not yet been fully embraced by the international community, we explore the various rights incorporated in existing national bills of rights that relate to human sexuality. These include respect for bodily integrity; protection from violence; the right to privacy; right to decide freely the number, spacing and timing of children; right to sexuality education; equal protection of the law and non-discrimination.[8] By discussing sexuality, sexual health and reproductive health as issues of human rights, we shed new light on issues such as abortion, prostitution, homosexuality and HIV/AIDS. In particular, we attempt to demonstrate the centrality of 'bodily integrity' – the control of one's sexuality and reproductive capacities – to the emancipation of African women. Exploring the connections between sexuality and citizenship and what it means to be a sexual citizen against the backdrop of imported colonial sex laws, rising fundamentalisms (cultural, religious, economic), political dictatorship and militarisation helps unravel the challenges associated with realising such rights.

The entire discussion of sexual rights is conducted with sensitivity to the tensions inherent in the conceptualisation of sexuality within the framework of rights. Alice Miller and others have articulated the paradoxes that burden the context of rights when it comes to sexuality (Miller and Vance 2004): one cannot simultaneously use the language of sexual rights to police 'harm' (such as freedom from rape or to tackle homophobia) *and* to demand privacy (such as to defend the sexual pleasure of consenting adults). The contradictions can be seen further in claims for the right to privacy while at the same time speaking of freedom from marital rape, or the awkwardness of claiming the rights of people to sell/make images of sexual activity and simultaneously claiming that people should be protected from sexual objectification.

Transversing stigmatised boundaries, breaking with sexual taboos

As stated earlier, it is an enormous challenge for us to create a relatively free and safe space where students can shake off all inhibitions and feel comfortable enough to have a frank and meaningful intellectual discourse and engaging discussions on a range of sexuality topics (Machera 2004). Finding ways of lifting the shroud of secrecy, taboos and silences that engulfs sexuality matters and breaking through the hegemonic moral code that associates sexuality with shame and guilt requires skilful creativity and resourcefulness. Sensitive, uncomfortable subjects, such as masturbation, menstruation, orgasms, same-sex erotics, incest, abortion, wet dreams, sado-masochism, infidelity, sexually transmitted diseases, aphrodisiacs, erotic fantasies, oral sex, cyber sex, pornography and so forth are brought into public discourse. Direct reference to male and female genitals without use of sanitised

euphemisms is also encouraged. Such strategic disruptions of the social constructions of sexuality are integral to the students' unlearning and relearning curve.

Carefully thought out strategies and tools are employed to help students open
up and shift their attitudes beyond the stigmatised subject matter of sexuality. This
is extremely important in order for us to achieve our objectives and to 'spice up' the
sessions so that students get emotionally charged and engrossed in the subject matter. For example, I make use of the Question Basket technique, whereby students
anonymously deposit embarrassing questions for class discussion at an appropriate
time into a basket.[9] A candid discussion of a range of hitherto taboo topics on sexuality provides a means of empowering students on the journey toward informed
choices and better control of their lives, and with the skills to challenge hegemonic
sexuality discourse.

On of the first day of the course, it is important for the class to formulate some
basic ground rules that will govern for the duration of the course. Involving students in setting these standards means that they will own them and therefore feel
more obliged to honour them. Usually the rules are along the following lines:
respect other people's views and opinions even when you are challenging them;
tolerate differences, including diverse identities, lifestyles and sexual orientations;
respect confidentiality – private or sensitive stories shared in class should not be
broadcast outside; allow others to contribute by not interrupting and/or dominating discussions; allow individuals to pass when they are unwilling or not ready to
speak; exercise your right to ask questions, as there are no stupid questions; avoid
disparaging stereotypes that fuel racism, ageism, sexism and homophobia; and prepare for class by reading assigned materials.

As much as possible, we avoid long lecture sessions, preferring instead an interactive seminar environment in which students actively participate through large and
small group discussions, role play, visual clips, debates, poetry, personal testimonies,
case studies and peer reviewing. Participatory, interactive learning is a major tenet
of feminist pedagogical strategies (hooks 1989; Omolade 1993). I, as lecturer, take
on the role of a mere facilitator of students' learning and not the 'expert' know-it-all
who transmits information in one directional flow (Friere 1986). For example, the use
of the poem 'Moons waiting' (see Box 63.1) has offered students the opportunity to
confront the otherwise difficult topic of abortion in very useful ways.[10]

Allowing students to actively participate in their own learning holds several
advantages: first, a sense of community is built within the lecture room that allows
for free expression, trust and respect; second, students have the opportunity to be
reflexive and critical of oppressive structures and practices; third, encouraging
their participation in the various activities, allowing their voices to be heard and
developing the sense that their views are valued can be extremely empowering
for students; finally, it provides a rich learning experience for everyone (including
the lecturer) from the diverse experiences and knowledge represented in the class.
When we were discussing reproductive health and rights four years ago, for example, a professional nurse in the class enriched the conversation with her practical
experiences from the field. During a discussion of diverse sexualities, she made the
connection between the intransigent cases of yeast (*candidiasis*) infections among
her female patients and heterosexual anal sex.

BOX 63.1

Moons waiting

Many a woman knows the feeling
Of intercourse, then overdue moons
The waiting, anxiety, desperation...

Crouched on the hard bench of the lab
The acrid smells pricking my nostrils
Like a convict in a dock
I waited for the verdict

The results hit like a sledgehammer
P-o-s-i-t-i-v-e!

I had just turned nineteen
A fresher at the university
My future bright and promising
Not ready to become a mother
I had to restore my moon cycle

'Thou shalt not take the life of the unborn'
Said Mr Law
'Will you take care of it when it's born?'
I asked Mr Law
'Of Course Not'

The abortion was swift and efficient
Or so I thought

Two days later I lay in the Intensive Care Unit
They had been twins,
One remained rotting inside me.
To save my dear life,
It had to be flushed out...
Together with my womb

An eternal end to moons waiting.

However, if not handled with sensitivity, experience has also taught us that feminist pedagogical methods can have a downside. For example, sometimes the discussions can be hijacked and sidetracked, leading to petty squabbles and insecurities. This usually happens during discussions of controversial moral debates, say regarding same-sex desire. Somehow the dialogue always veers to a discussion about the sexuality of animals and statements such as: 'even animals know better than to engage in unnatural sex...'.

On such occasions, it is important to redirect the discussion and ensure that the objective of the class is realised. For instance, citing case studies that have proved homosexual pair bonds among animals and challenging the class to consider whether 'unnaturalness' equals immorality and whether homo sapiens should be looking to animals for moral standards. The brief lecture sessions at the beginning of each session are used to introduce topics and to provide a theoretical backdrop on which to hook subsequent discussions. Indeed, caution has to be applied to ensure that classroom liberalism does not become counterproductive to the learning process.

The use of humour and appropriate icebreakers is an excellent way to reduce anxieties and to create a friendly, relaxing atmosphere. If used appropriately, humour has the ability to bridge intercultural, interfaith, interpower and intergenerational divides when all other forms of communication fail. Here, we do not refer to jokes that elicit loud laughter but rather to conceptual humour that facilitates the students' learning process. For example, I often borrow Stephen Law's stimulating debate on homosexuality by having two students play the roles of God and the protagonist, Mr Jarvis (Law 2003). Another example is through a dramatisation of the famous Kenyan case of 67-year-old female activist who married a 25-year-old man (see also Kariuki 2005).[11] Through such exploration we are able to clarify some important issues regarding sexuality in family law. The use of the French phrase *la petite mort* (a little death) in reference to sexual orgasm also adds a light touch to the uneasy topic. Furthermore, sharing of personal experiences, including those of the lecturer, gives the discussions a 'human face' and helps in cultivating a sense of trust.

Once students feel comfortable enough to discuss taboo topics, reticence is replaced with excitement and enthusiasm to learn new things. They exchange knowledge about various 'exotic' practices in their different cultures, which become the subjects of intellectual discourse. Take the cultural aesthetic practice of elongating the inner folds of the labia minora among several Bantu-speaking communities of eastern and southern Africa, such as the Baganda (Uganda), the Tutsi (Rwanda), the Basotho (Lesotho), the Shona (Zimbabwe), the Nyakyusa and Karewe (Tanzania), the Khoisan of southern Africa and the Tsonga (Mozambique) (see also Tamale 2005).[12] Or the Kenyan versions of male circumcision among the Masai and Kikuyu, which involve partial circumcision, allowing the lower part of the foreskin to remain attached in a bib of atrophied flesh (Romberg 1985). Ostensibly the bib works to enhance the pleasure of sexual intercourse for both partners. The specific form of outercourse from Rwanda and parts of Uganda is another practice that always generates a lot of interest among students, especially its associations to female ejaculation.[13] The dialogue on positive sexuality usually translates into an empowering, life-changing experience for most students.

Unlearning and relearning for transformational sexuality

The introductory session of the course emphasises the importance of keeping an open mind, because minds, like the proverbial parachutes, only work when they are open. Individuals with open minds are less likely to be judgmental. A rigid, closed mind, on the other hand, limits one's intellectual potential and is less likely to lead to transformational change. But transformative learning can only be achieved through a process of unlearning and relearning. This cognitive process has proved to be a huge challenge for many students who have been educated in colonial and post-colonial education systems, which limit their instruction to rote learning and grossly neglect to hone the skill of unlearning.

Under such circumstances, it is extremely important for us to facilitate the students to wade through the layers of normative assumptions that many have never been able to question or to challenge. Unlearning requires students to leave their 'comfort zones' and to abandon deeply entrenched beliefs and practices. It calls for them to confront their prejudices and shift attitudes and mindsets. All this involves serious discomfort and disequilibrium. Relearning, on the other hand, requires the acquisition of new knowledge and/or the reorganisation of the old (Soto-Crespo 1999; Gordon and Cornwall 2004). It explains why sexual stereotypes that intersect with gender, race, religion and culture, and are deeply embedded in social and individual consciousness, become extremely difficult to overcome.

Discussions on sexuality can be extremely controversial and we often have lively, impassioned debates in class. Inevitably individuals have very strong views about divisive issues such as abortion, sex work and homosexuality. Even when students unlearn the dominant sexuality discourses, several express the huge dilemma they confront in reconciling their religious beliefs with their newly acquired sexuality discourses. These are never simple issues to tackle and we spend a lot of time discussing feminist theology, theological hermeneutics, issues of re-interpretation and contextualisation of the scriptures, drawing parallels with racist interpretations of the theological text and so forth.

On some occasions there are individuals who, in their ardent bid to voice their views, break the ground rules, crossing the line of respect and appropriate behaviour towards their colleagues. In these instances, I momentarily retreat (not physically but vocally) and let the class deal with the situation. This tactic encourages students to sharpen their critical thinking and discussion skills, drawing on the knowledge acquired from the class. It has the additional advantage of making sure that I, as lecturer, do not appear to be imposing my views on the students. Such lecture room discussions usually spill over to residential halls, where students engage colleagues who are not enrolled in this class. Sometimes we also invite guest speakers from organisations, such as Gays and Lesbians of Zimbabwe (GALZ) to have a discussion with students.

Prior to joining the programme, and this class in particular, very few students would have questioned images of femininity, masculinity, motherhood, fatherhood, family, desire, non-procreative sex, multiple sexual partners, same-sex erotics, rape, sex work, abortion, menopause, decency and sexual morality that patriarchal-capitalist societies construct for us. Neither the cultural definitions and meanings, nor the links to power and dominance that these issues raise, are often questioned. So we spend many hours in the lecture room unpacking the blocks used to construct and give meaning to these concepts, analysing the role of the law in creating, sustaining and reproducing these blocks and how individuals, groups and communities subvert hegemonic sexual norms and values.

An effective way of engaging with all these issues is to explore the various ways in which sexuality norms are institutionalised and how these are interwoven into the social fabric of students' everyday experiences, knowledge and social relationships. Theory then helps students make the connections between seemingly disparate concepts and to answer the why and how questions relating to sexuality. In their course evaluations, many students have positively rated the course using words such as 'informative', 'an eye-opener', and 'life-changing'.

Linking theory to everyday experiences

Having attempted to create a feminist lecture room environment, it is important to surface the connections between theory and practice in order for students to expand and deepen their understanding of the linkages between gender, law, inequality and sexuality. Hence, theory is the overarching contextualising factor in the course. The process of theorising sexuality begins from the simple awareness that sexuality (like race and gender) is a social construction. To a large extent, the human body enters the world as a blank slate. Thereafter, the social world promptly begins to infuse meanings and interpretations to it, turning it into a sexed body, a cultural body, a gendered body, a classed body, a religious body, a racial body, an ethnic body.

These social inscriptions – which are normalised and naturalised – are engraved on our bodies by the dominant social class (which have investments in maintaining social hierarchies) using the nibs of culture, law, politics, media, education, morality and religion. In Africa, such nibs inscribe with the bold influence of colonialism, neo-colonialism and patriarchy. Thus, the inscribed rules, images, symbols and even hierarchies that give shape and character to the bodies of African women and men become an important tool for sustaining patriarchy and capitalism.

Indeed, women's bodies constitute one of the most formidable tools for creating and maintaining gender roles and relations in African societies. Although the texts that culture inscribes on African women's bodies remain invisible to the uncritical eye, they are in fact crucial for effecting social control. The inscriptions that are encoded onto women's bodies have sexuality writ large; through the regulation and control of African women's sexualities and reproductive capacities, their subordination and continued exploitation are guaranteed. The theory of sexual scripting makes the important link between individual interactional behaviour on the micro level and the larger social forces of the macro level (Gagnon 2004).

The theoretical readings that we assign to students are interdisciplinary in nature, authored by a mix of scholars from the global North and the global South. Conceptualisations of sexuality and desire, heteronormativity, representation, sexual scripting, performance and performativity are explored using feminist jurisprudence, post-structural theory and post-colonial theory. Some of the theorists that we use in class include Sigmund Freud, Chandra Mohanty, Uma Narayan, Ifi Amadiume, Catharine MacKinnon, Gayle Rubin, Michel Foucault, John Gagnon, Judith Butler and Patricia McFadden. We are keenly aware of the dangers of uncritically using theories that are constructed from the global North to explain African societies (see Chapter 1 in this volume).

Before students leave their home countries, we request them to collect sexuality-related materials – legislation, newspaper clips, among others – and bring them for use in class. Grounding sexuality concepts in real life experiences is crucial to the process of knowledge production among students. One technique that we have found useful over the years to get students to appreciate gender/sexuality theoretical explanations is to make extensive use of analogies to racism. African students – especially males – readily appreciate theories on and comparisons with racialism and racism, more so than gender/sexuality theories. When we explain discrimination and oppression from the analogous grounds of 'racism' and 'otherness', the pieces begin to fall into place for most students. The oppressive structures that underlie racism, sexism, genocide, homophobia, transphobia, xenophobia and such doctrines are all legitimised through 'naturalised' norms that dehumanise, infantalise, disempower and disenfranchise people. Therefore, by invoking the justifications pandered by some racist theorists, students begin to appreciate analogous experiences of otherness.

Viewing inequalities through the lens of gendered sexualities facilitates students' understanding of sexual laws and policies. This in turn aids their capacities to challenge and critique institutions, laws and policies that reinforce such inequalities. For example, most students enter the course with deeply embedded prejudices about commercial sex. But a discussion of the connections between class/gender inequalities and the control of women's desire and sexual activity usually facilitates the 'light bulb' moments for students and develops their appreciation of the dynamics of sexual work and its criminalisation.

Social transformation through resistance and subversion

Talking about the positive, pleasurable aspects of sexuality is a major component of realising the objectives of the course. It goes against the prescribed cultural morality of the oppressive structures that operate in Africa. Such discussions have undoubtedly proved to be an empowering resource for students, whose incapacitated worldview is radically transformed by the end of the course. Many students have, for example, found Audre Lorde's eloquent words empowering:

> There are many kinds of power, used and unused, acknowledged or otherwise. The erotic is a resource within each of us that lies in a deeply female and spiritual plane … In order to perpetuate itself, every oppression must corrupt or distort those various sources of power within the culture of the oppressed that can provide energy for change. For women, this has meant a suppression of the erotic as a considered source of power and information within our lives. (Lorde 1984: 53)

One student told the class that Lorde's essay was such an eye-opener for her that it completely transformed her marriage and sexual life. This student had never conceived of her sexuality as a source of power.

Therefore, even though women's sexualised bodies represent powerful constraints in Africa, sexuality also holds positive, empowering possibilities for them. The body politics for African women are also possessed of empowering sub-texts, reflected through resistance, negotiation, identity, self-desire, pleasure and silence. There is a legitimate silence surrounding some African women's sexuality, a silence that cannot be engaged and is ambiguous. Here, silence is different from the Western feminist approach that often names it as a total blank while valorising voice. In many African cultures speech is necessary and empowering, but in sexuality silence can be equally powerful. For instance, silence can serve as a tool for the rejection of externally imposed projections of African women's sexuality.

Sexual initiation traditions across the continent that are espoused by erotic cultures, such as the *Ssenga* among the Baganda of Uganda, the *Tete* among the Shona of Zimbabwe, the *Alangizi* among the Yao of Malawi and the Chewa/Nyanja of Zambia, the *Mayosenge* among the Bemba of Zambia and the Lawbe women of Senegal. All carry some empowering messages for young girls and women embedded in intricate sexual practices and traditions. Most of these positive erotic cultures have survived and endured the repressive regime of foreign laws and religions that have attempted to smother them.

Analysing gendered sexualities against the backdrop of the HIV/AIDS pandemic in Africa has significant implications for subversive transformation. Not only has the epidemic opened up African women's bodies and sexualities to public scrutiny, it has also forced open a public debate on women's sexualities, vulnerabilities and power. The sheer volume of financial and scientific interest in HIV/AIDS has meant that the authors of the mainstream story have not always been African women (Caldwell 2000; Cohen 2000). However, women living with and affected by the pandemic have persisted in defining, reframing and articulating their needs and rights, and in rewriting the script (Obbo 1995; Adomako Ampofo 1999; Sisulu 2000). Although the pandemic has created new hierarchies of domination and exploitation, it has at the same time built the foundations of empowerment for African women by spurring a new kind of political consciousness and self-organisation.

Debates around the issues of sexual harassment, dress codes and gender discrimination, as well as the processes through which such oppressive structures are maintained, open up ideas for discursive techniques that can be deployed to resist them. The common stereotypes and misconceptions that students have about issues such as sexual advances, the hijab and nudity are debunked and deconstructed in transformative ways.

Lessons, challenges and future prospects

Not all students who enrol for this module have an interest in a transformatory agenda when they first join the class. As stated earlier, some enrol out of sheer curiosity, others because they see career opportunities in the subject area, and so forth. However, regardless of the initial motive, by the end of the course not only do the majority of students understand the links between sexuality and women's status but also they appreciate the intellectual place of sexuality within gender and the law. It is astounding to observe the lecture room climate transform over the days from 'giggles' to serious discussions, dialogue and interrogation.

Analysing the law through gendered lenses affords students the opportunity to critically examine the relationships between law, gender, identity and oppression. It is gratifying to hear changed voices committing to return home and become agents of transformation in their own small ways. As one criminal defence lawyer put it at the end of the 2009 course: 'I'm totally ashamed of what I've been doing to all those rape victims in court during cross-examination.'

In many ways this course is an exercise in self-discovery, personal growth, healing and empowerment. Some students have been so stimulated by the course that they have gone on to develop research proposals in the area of gender, law and sexuality. Excellent dissertations have been written on exciting topics, such as traditional marriage counselling and HIV/AIDS, sex education in schools, abortion in rape situations and sex tourism. In all these studies, we clearly see the course deeply interwoven in the analysis and conceptual understanding of the issues under discussion.

Analysing and negotiating the complex terrain of sexuality in a lecture room environment necessarily means that there are several ambiguities, contradictions and intersections that we cannot address fully in class. This is especially so given that we have a period of only four weeks to cover this subject. Just as most students are beginning to feel at ease with the subject matter, the course comes to an end and they have to prepare for examinations. It is at this 'liberated' stage, for example, that most are willing to confront the numerous contradictions between their inner desires and the social norms to which they are supposed to comply.

We face further challenges: getting students with various academic and social pressures to read and internalise the assigned materials is never guaranteed. Only a handful of them seem to take time to more than quickly browse through the readings, and the common evaluation of the readings each year is that there are too many of them. It is therefore important to think about ways of motivating students to critically read and analyse the assigned texts.

Course evaluations are extremely useful in educating us about students' expectations, interests and fears and about the effectiveness of the course. Some of the consistent feedback in this regard reveals that students appreciate that we mix lectures with other interactive methods. Not only does it provide the necessary balance in bridging the gap between theory and practice, but also it creates the informal and safe environment needed for discussing sexuality. Many students have also observed in their evaluations that this course is so central to women's law that it should cease to be an elective:

> Very essential ... This course is a must for all MWL [Masters in Women's Law] students ... It lays foundations of how the law issues impacts on gender and sexuality ... Should be part of the introductory lectures to MWL maybe soon after the Sex and Gender topic; it should not be an option.

In future we hope to expand the curriculum to lay more emphasis on topics such as sexuality and disability and sexuality and masculinities. We further plan to integrate one or two field visits into the course, allowing students to get hands-on experience with groups such as sex workers, sexual minorities and traditional sex trainers, for example. The use of films and other audio-visual materials to analyse the issues should further enrich our pedagogical repertoire. Needless to say, we are very eager to learn from colleagues elsewhere about teaching skills that have been successful in conducting similar courses.

Notes

1. This article also appears in A. Tsanga and J. Stewart (eds) (2011) *Women and Law: Innovative Approaches to Teaching, Research and Analysis*. Reproduced with permission.
2. Janet Halley (2006) expresses reservations about the efficacy of feminism in analysing sexuality and power. Until alternative theories are developed, we maintain that sex and gender currently offer the best frames for analysing sexuality and power.
3. Many criminal law lecturers are not gender sensitive and discuss the details of rape cases as though they were funny and/or blame the victim for the assault.
4. Not just any sex act but heterosexual, procreative intercourse.
5. The irony is that although the colonising countries have long jettisoned or amended these laws to reflect more equitable gender concerns, most former colonies are holding on jealously to the anachronistic and archaic laws in their bid to maintain a stranglehold over women's lives.
6. Examples of such double standards are evident in the laws governing criminal adultery, prostitution, monogamy and evidentiary rules, among others.
7. Although culturally sensitive, holistic approaches to the elimination of the practice of FGM condemn its rights violations and the health risks associated with it, they acknowledge its positive aspects, such as the celebration of the rite of passage and rite of 'being', which is crucial for people's identity and culture. Alternative rites of passage have been successfully adopted in countries such as Kenya to maintain the underlying positive social value that the practice represents.
8. This discussion is conducted in the context of 'cultural relativism' and the limitations of fitting all sexuality issues within the framework of rights claims.
9. An example of a question that keeps turning up in this basket is: 'How do lesbians have sex?'
10. I wrote this poem. It was inspired by a true story related to me by one of my students at Makerere University.
11. This case demonstrates one woman's defiance against patriarchal sexual norms that limit and oppress women.
12. A lively debate always ensues among students about whether such elongation qualifies as female genital mutilation in the definition provided by the World Health Organisation.
13. The practice is locally known as *kachabali* in Uganda (Tamale 2005) and *kunyaza* in Rwanda (Bizimana 2010).

References

Adomako Ampofo, A. (1999) 'Nice guys, condoms and other forms of STD protection: sex workers and AIDS protection in West Africa', in Becker, C., Dozon, J., Obbo, C. and Touré, M. (eds) *Vivre et Penser le Sida en Afrique / Experiencing and Understanding AIDS in Africa*, Paris, CODESRIA, IRD, Karthala, PNLS: 561–90/559–88

Amadiume, Ifi (1987) *Male Daughters, Female Husbands: Gender and Sex in an African Society*, London, Zed Books

Bizimana, Nsekuye (2010) 'Another way for lovemaking in Africa: *Kunyaza*, a traditional sexual technique for triggering female orgasm at heterosexual encounters', *Sexologies* 19(3): 157–62

Caldwell, John (2000) 'Rethinking the African AIDS epidemic', *Population and Development Review* 26(1): 117–135

Cohen, Desmond (2000) *Poverty and HIV/AIDS in Sub-Saharan Africa*, New York, UNDP/ SEPED

Coughlin, Anne (1998) 'Sex and guilt', *Virginia Law Review* 84(1): 1–46

Freire, Paulo (1986) *Pedagogy of the Oppressed*, New York, Continuum

Gagnon, J. (2004) *An Interpretation of Desire Essays in the Study of Sexuality*, Chicago, University of Chicago Press

Gates, Henry Louis Jr (ed) (1986) *'Race', Writing, and Difference*, Chicago, University of Chicago Press

Gordon, G. and Cornwall, A. (2004) 'Participation in sexual and reproductive well-being and rights', *Participatory Learning and Action* 50: 73–80

Halley, Janet (2006) *Split Decisions: How and Why to Take a Break from Feminism*, Princeton, Princeton University Press

hooks, bell (1989) *Talking Back: Thinking Feminist, Thinking Black*, London, Sheba Feminist Publishers

Kariuki, Wanjiru (2005) 'Keeping the feminist war real in contemporary Kenya: the case of Wambui Otieno', *Jenda: A Journal of Culture and African Women Studies* 7, http://www. africaresource.com/jenda/issue7/kariuki.html, accessed 14 July 2010

Law, Stephen (2003) 'What's wrong with gay sex?', 20 March, http://stephenlaw.blogspot. com/2007/03/whats-wrong-with-gay-sex.html?showComment=1174406580000, accessed 4 December 2010

Lorde, Audre (1984) 'Uses of the erotic: the erotic as power', in *Sister Outsider: Essays and Speeches*, New York, The Crossing Press

Machera, Mumbi (2004) 'Opening a can of worms: a debate on female sexuality in the lecture theatre', in Arnfred, Signe (ed) *Rethinking Sexualities in Africa*, Uppsala, The Nordic Africa Institute

Miller, A. and Vance, C. (2004) 'Sexuality, human rights and health', *Health and Human Rights* 7(2): 5–15

Obbo, Christine (1995) 'Gender, age and class: discourses on HIV transmission and control in Uganda', in Brummelhuis, H. and Herdt, G. (eds) *Culture and Sexual Risk: Anthropological Perspectives on AIDS*, Amsterdam, Gordon and Breach

Omolade, Barbara (1993) 'A black feminist pedagogy', *Women's Studies Quarterly* 15: 32–39

Romberg, Rosemary (1985) *Circumcision: The Painful Dilemma*, South Hadley MA, Bergin and Garvey

Sisulu, Elinor (2000) 'A different kind of holocaust: a personal reflection on HIV/AIDS', *African Gender Institute Newsletter* 7

Soto-Crespo, R.E. (1999) 'The bounds of hope: unlearning "Old Eyes" and a pedagogy of renewal', *Thresholds in Education*, 2 and 3: 42–46

Tamale, Sylvia (2005) 'Eroticism, sensuality and "women's secrets" among the Baganda: a critical analysis', *Feminist Africa* 5: 9–36

—— (2008) 'The right to culture and the culture of rights: a critical perspective on women's sexual rights in Africa', *Feminist Legal Studies* 16(1): 47–69

64

Through Zanele Muholi's eyes: re/imagining ways of seeing Black lesbians[1]

Pumla Dineo Gqola

Although critics of creative forms often assume that the clear labelling of the work under analysis is a necessary step to uncover meaning, some artistic production presents the challenge of resisting tidy categorisation. Zanele Muholi's photography is an instance of such resistant border-living, as Gloria Anzaldúa might say, which challenges the critical tools of our literary/filmic/visual arts and art historical training. Or perhaps it challenges what we 'instinctively' praise with our cultured eyes. Though we might immediately want to define the specific aesthetic bent of her work, fix her precise political location and conclusively identify the traditions from which she draws, Muholi's work resists precisely such endeavours to name, tame and classify.

Indeed, what is most compelling and powerful about Muholi's work is how it plays with these (im)possibilities. This conceptual difficulty is clearly discernible in some of the reviews of Muholi's *Visual Sexuality: Only Half the Picture*, the first showing of her work at the Johannesburg Art Gallery in September 2004. Gail Smith, writer, critic and cultural commentator, and Nonkululeko Godana, poet, performer and essayist, at the time both remarked at length on the jarring political project that seemed to sit at the centre of Muholi's exhibition. Although both reviewers applauded the courage and unwavering focus of Muholi's lens on the otherwise unseen Black lesbian experience in South Africa, they had an aversion to how the work resists pleasurable consumption.

Smith spoke to the aesthetic and political interventionist capacity of such a project: Muholi's work shows up the lies that heteropatriarchy sustains about who Black South African lesbians are. Her lens ensures that this space's jagged edges are seen. It requires that we do more than safely admit that Black lesbians exist. Smith's labelling of Muholi's work as 'outlaw culture', recalling as it does bell hooks, foregrounds the compelling use of the imagination in insurgent and transformative ways, even if this otherwise courageous critic flinches at the sight of some of the photographs. By her own admission she is not always convinced of their aesthetic value.

In many ways, Smith's reading resonates with the photographer's own statements about the value of her work. Witness, for example, Muholi's statements accompanying her photo-essay in the journal *Agenda*, as well as the self-narration in her short film *Enraged by a Picture*: they speak of the importance of permitting a collective lesbian coming-to-voice.

Like Desiree Lewis, however, I discern more in Muholi's work than bringing to voice, making visible and confrontation – as important as these features are within her project. Zanele Muholi's various series map out a visual vocabulary that interrogates ways of seeing. It is not only what she makes visible but *how* that fascinates me; not just whom she positions at centre stage, but the gamut of techniques and effects that she garners to such ends.

It is, of course, inaccurate to claim that Black women's bodies, and specifically Black lesbians' bodies, are invisible in South African society. The range of names given to them in various languages, along with the very unambiguous attacks on these women within South African society, suggest that they are in fact highly visible manifestations of the undesirable. The many 'curative' rapes, expulsions from the family and murderous attacks on (young) Black lesbians occur in such high numbers that Wendy Isaack, the human rights lawyer and feminist activist, has argued that they warrant the kind of high alert usually seen in a state of emergency.

Black South African lesbians are hypervisible in the media (Molobi 2005: 9; Ndlovu 2006). To point out that the print media do not carry dynamic representations of South African lesbians is not the same as saying that people do not know who in their midst is a safe target of their violence precisely because she is a (Black) lesbian. Indeed, the consistent public commentary (often on public television, which has demonstrated a far more nuanced engagement with representations of lesbian, gay, bisexual, transgender and intersex (LGBTI) communities than the print media) focused on the two most visible Black lesbians, Wendy Isaack and Bev Ditsie, both of whom retain iconic status within Black lesbian cultures, suggests otherwise. Both have repeatedly and in very different ways challenged expectations around what lesbians should embody.

Muholi's work is less about making Black lesbians visible than it is about engaging with the regimes that have used these women's hypervisibility as a way to violate them. Her photographs, some of which I will discuss in detail below, propose a queer perspective on a supposedly familiar reality.[2] It is this specific direction of the eye that prevents voyeurism that I spoke of in my interview for her short film. Muholi's photographs invite us to examine how we see Black lesbians and they chart a complicated path through which such a process of visualisation might take shape. Lewis articulates something similar when she says about Muholi's photographs:

> [I]n her oeuvre as a whole, there are many references to the way that sexuality is constructed, commoditised, and, of course, influenced by the diseases that affect real-life sexual practices and pleasure in our present age. It is implied that pleasure cannot be separated from the range of meanings and legacies that are directly and indirectly invoked in her images. (Lewis 2005: 17)

Paying attention to Muholi's images requires grappling with the competing and nuanced meanings highlighted in the represented subjects. They underline the importance of seeing the agency – life choices, decisions, failures, confusions, discoveries, rejections – of the Black lesbian in the picture. They make it hard to safely see only the victim of heteropatriarchal violence, but invite us to engage with the many layers present in the world that is Black lesbian South Africa. These images are shaped by, respond to and sometimes start off from circulating ideas about Black South African lesbians. Muholi's vision holds challenges for all of us who claim to see (Black) lesbian sexuality regardless of whether we do so in the interest of transformation or oppression. Where the challenges targeted at the foot-soldiers of heteropatriarchy are obvious, and have been discussed above, Muholi's work contains new insights for all audiences who respond to her invitation to think about lesbian lives seriously.

The lesbians photographed by Muholi are presented in ways that trouble received knowledge systems about lesbians. Bev Ditsie, in a statement to Nkululeko Masinga, expressed some of the complications present in her life – some of which can be glimpsed in many an image by Muholi:

> [I]t has taken me a long time to grow into my body ... At 19 I began to accept myself as a woman and love my body ... Society's perception of my body does impact on my self-esteem ... My sexuality as a gay woman is a part of who I am as Bev and the way that I relate to the world and other people. I can be as butch or feminine as I want, it all depends on my mood. (Masinga 2005: 59)

Ditsie articulates a complicated living-out of Black lesbian sexuality and identity, a vision that underlines choice, joy, discovery, embattlement and process. This is Muholi's visualisation of the subjects of her photographs: it is a process of imagining, circling, uncovering and implying. In other words, it is an unwaveringly nuanced representation of Black lesbian identities that gestures to the impossibility of effective containment.

When we think of creative language, after Monica Arac de Nyeko (2004), as that which gives meaning and allows us to interpret creative forms in non-literal ways, it is clear that Muholi's project of visualising Black lesbians entails more than what Godana refers to as Muholi's favouring of 'the marginalised in society' (Godana 2004). Muholi introduces a powerful idiom, what Lewis calls a documentary dialect, that allows the former to 'speak about victimisation without rendering her subject a victim and without endorsing conventions associated with familiar images of victimisation' (Lewis 2005: 14).

Indeed, because '[l]abelling articulates a gendered (and cultural) affiliation', Muholi's lens and frames guide the eye to the reckoning that even 'the designation "sexualities" begs the question of what constitutes this broad, mobile notion that represents semantic possibilities. [This is especially important because] [f]or many, the concept suggests an implied heterosexuality' (Reddy 2005: 4).

Leaking meanings and visual sentences – *Period*

In what is her most visually and conceptually provocative series, *Period*, Muholi confronts her audience with the sticky and bloody world of menstruation. In the black and white images that precede the colour series, used sanitary napkins replace what could have been an egg on a breakfast plate, flanked by recognisable condiments and cutlery. Images in the later series suggest the absence of impediment so that a messy stream of blood wends its way to a white ceramic bath tub drain and a bright red splat makes itself felt on a patch of green leaf and grass yielding to brown earth.

Here the red blood stands out amid the whites, greens, browns, blues and yellows of its various environments. The series is courageous in drawing the eye to that which patriarchy is most vehement about making invisible: menstrual blood. At the same time, because it is so provocative, the humour and sharpness of the images often escape audience responses, trained as they are to avoid the sight of menstruation and more accustomed to the blue liquid seen everywhere in the commercial products used to sanitise women's bodies.

The image of a used sanitary pad on a plate plays around with the uses to which chickens' and women's eggs are put conceptually. It interrogates notions of what kinds and forms of eggs are easily consumed, and which are codified as repulsive. In literal terms, what Muholi has on the plate is the most mundane of images, consumed every day by large numbers of humans on our planet: eggs. We are forced to rethink what it is that discomfits about human eggs on a plate. The image startles because of the meanings attached to women's sexuality and reproduction: that evidence of a woman's failure to conceive is shameful and to be hidden. A menstruating woman is a useless woman: under patriarchy she has failed to marshal her body parts to act in accordance with the rules that govern how such a society replicates. The pictures seem to ask: how much more disposable is a bleeding lesbian?

Menstruation is often central to how women learn to feel about our bodies at the onset of puberty; it is key to how we are told we matter in the world. A menstruating woman is couched in euphemisms – as Muholi shows in her naming of this series – and she is unpredictable prior to menstruation. Symbolically a (potentially) menstruating woman is out of control, a dangerous state for patriarchal order. It is against this backdrop that the visible evidence of menstruation is buried, hidden, euphemistically cast and erased transhistorically.

Muholi, however, places the visuality of menstruation centre-stage and by so doing forces it into her audience's imagination. This series is the most metaphorically fertile even if this fertility is put to unusual use. We are reminded of the stickiness, the explosions and leakings that characterise menstruation or 'periods'. The bloodied ground encompasses a conceptual pun on soil (as in 'soiled pad' meaning bloodied pad) and fertility (of women's bodies and of the earth).

In some of the photographs in the series, there is no body, only the evidence of the secretions of such a female body. Although Muholi's bleeding lesbian is sometimes physically out of the picture, the bleeder haunts us with the blood she leaves behind.

The conceptual play and provocation in this series has other aesthetic and conceptual meanings. Given Muholi's unwavering declarations that the subjects of her photographs are Black lesbians, we are forced to think about what specifically is lesbian about the *Period* series. The series normalises Black lesbians as women. It positions the most reviled women through images of the most abhorrent – albeit normal – aspect of women's lives. It shows Black lesbians bleeding uncontrollably, messily and stickily, like the rest of 'us'. Their 'periods' encompass pain and glorious explosions of colour too. Muholi's normalising of Black lesbian sexuality positions it as part of the continuum of women's sexuality at the same time that she plays with notions of what is natural and normal. Homosexuality is often demonised as abnormal because it is not 'natural', as though the natural is easily discernible and desirable. At the same time, menstruation is natural and yet hidden, which is to say abnormal to show. This series is unwavering in its critique and mocking of the routes through which knowledge is made and validated; it shows that meaning-making is a social activity, rather than self-evident.

Period plays with notions of consumption and excretion through Muholi's fruitful metaphors, which either fertilise or soil our conceptual ground, depending on the audience's vantage point. Whichever way, they are unsafe, unlike the blue liquid partner of tampons and sanitary napkins so beloved of mainstream advertising. They are from another language – Lewis's documentary dialogue – and are hard to swallow.

Visualising lesbian pleasure – *Beloved* and *Closer to My Heart*

As threatening as lesbian sexuality is to heteropatriarchy, there is an abundance of exploitative representations of lesbians which are made to function in aid of pornography. Voyeuristic imagining of lesbians' sexual intercourse permeates the spectrum of patriarchal fantasy. This is a paradox that works in the same way as the generally hypervisible Black lesbian: represented everywhere in ways that reinforce her 'safety' at precisely the same time she is under constant attack. This is one of the most central and effective features of all oppressive systems: the ability to act with unrelenting violence towards the demonised at the same time that dominant epistemic routes deny the existence of hegemony. In other words, homophobia – like patriarchy, white supremacy, xenophobia and so forth – denies its very existence through a self-representation of those valued within the respective systems of dominance – men, whites, heterosexuals, citizens – as the only ones entitled to existence as normal and natural, and the co-opting of benign images of its nemesis to prove this.

So those who belong to the valued category can periodically (tokenistically) engage with individuals from the oppressed group – or sometimes just the idea of individuals from such groups at the level of fantasy – without changing their/ our own status as privileged or interrogating the violated and reviled who they/we fashionably co-opt. Under such guise, even the most virulently homophobic heterosexuals are able to embrace homoerotic fantasy as seductive play with the forbidden. These fantasies are made safe because they are contained in the language of heterosexism, which is the dominant language of desire.

Writing about the '(im)possibility of representing lesbian desire', Natasha Distiller argues:

> [A] vocabulary to represent lesbian desire and the pleasures of their fulfil-
> ment is provided by a linguistic and representational system which has no
> space to engage with the notion of the lesbian except in relation to its own
> hetero/sexuality. One result of this situation is the difficulty lesbians have in
> speaking (of) themselves, into normativity, without invoking one or other of
> the available identity positions. (Distiller 2005: 45)

Muholi forges various avenues which address the precise quandary Distiller
bemoans. *Beloved* is a series of black and white photographs of two attractive Black
semi-naked, dreadlocked women in various poses. All the images are of the bodies leaning in towards each other, resting, gazing, kissing, embracing, with hair
and sometimes limbs interlocking. The images convey pleasure and comfort, and
although the women are both topless – one wears white-trimmed black shorts, the
second's jeans are visible in the legs that stretch to the floor and beyond the frame –
they are not the usual pictures of topless young Black women: they are neither freak-
ishly pornographically displayed nor cast in the stereotype of noble native maidens.
They lie on crumpled sheets with varying looks of distraction, contentment, pensive-
ness and pleasure. Although they are captured by a camera, and in one image one of
them looks into and past the camera, they do not pose for the camera.

Through Muholi's lens, these Black lesbians exist and relate to each other in the
midst of regimes that attempt to both violate and co-opt their lives; they are not
wholly defined by the terms of such definition. The shifting physical positions in
the images, during which they are always in touch with each other – but only briefly
and fleetingly concerned with the world represented by a/the camera – point to
the fluidity of intimacy. The images gesture toward promise and expressions of
intimacy but also to the impossibility of packaging it. In some respects the photographs announce that lesbian sexualities and relationships are open-ended and
normal rather than hypersexual as per heteropatriarchal inscription.

Another striking aspect of this series is the fact that the lesbians' faces are shown,
unlike many of Muholi's hidden faces. Here the emphasis is on the expressions on
their faces: they are thinking and feeling subjects who take on various comfortable
positions. Muholi is able to visualise intimacy's varied meanings: privacy, beauty,
pleasure, connection and exclusivity. The subjects are not useful for sexual titilla-
tion since the voyeur is not permitted access even as these women lie half-exposed.

Although visually distinct from *Beloved*, *Closer to My Heart* works on a similar
premise. The latter imagines blurry, shadowy figures against a mustard background
in an aesthetic that echoes Khoisan rock paintings. Throughout the series, the dancing bodies are connected, not just in the complimentary dance poses, but also physically joined through touch. Again, these figures are familiar, but they exist in spite
of the camera rather than for the audience's interpretation. The hand on the partner's waist, the twirling hand and kissing heads suggest a joy and intimacy enjoyed
by those in the frame and scarcely grasped by those outside of it.

In both these series, Muholi presents us with images of joyful lesbians uncon-
cerned by external dominant readings, even if such readings will continue to be
brought to bear on an array of Black lesbian sexualities. Muholi draws on an artistic idiom that gestures both toward aesthetic imagining – visualising and making

possible – and interpretative authority – the assertion of the photographer's ability to make meaning and interpret aspects of Black lesbian sexuality.

In some respects, both series play around with the notion of documentation. What meanings flow from the documentary photographer's decision to make choices about revealing and occluding? Repeatedly, she engages with the terrain of what sexuality is, can be and how it intersects with other identities. Her camera complicates categories of women and Black women by placing Black lesbian women at the centre of her enterprise and never allowing those within her frames to emerge as anything but diverse, complicated subjects.

Visualising differently

I began this essay with a declaration of how Muholi's photography resists easy categorisation. This is as true of individual series as it is of the conversations that emerge across series. The sophistry in her work stems from its ability to hold such compellingly politically subversive meanings at the same time as being aesthetically provocative.

Although I have referred to three series above, some of the analysis can be applied to other images in the collection. The specific thematic explorations differ from series to series, and the physical images and their treatment demonstrate a range of influences brought to bear upon Muholi's vision. In the final analysis, Muholi's project is one which is concerned not so much with making audiences see Black lesbians and acknowledge their very existence in the world, as with playing around with ways of seeing and looking that engender refreshing and innovative understandings of agency and subjectivity.

In the words of one of Muholi's series, the photographs collected here are a challenge to the ways we make sense of Black lesbians and engagement with the regimes that mark them as useful, 'safe' to violate and otherwise hypervisible and therefore containable. They are an exploration – sometimes joyful and mischievous as in the *Period* series, at other times gentle and self-loving as in *Beloved* and *Closer to My Heart* – of the varied range of refreshing ways of thinking through that country of the imagination titled Black lesbian South Africa. At the same time they are an assertion of what else exists and is imaginable: 'What don't you see when you look at me.'

At her most powerfully evocative and courageous, as these photographs show, Zanele Muholi ushers in a new language to articulate Black lesbian sexuality creatively and politically at the same time. She visualises it: represents it, captures it, defines it, traces its routes and imagines its worlds anew. In her pictures, Black lesbian sexualities/identities emerge as a complex myriad, with as many experiences and potentialities as exist for any human experience. The documentary and artistic dialects through which she carves such projects themselves reflect her content in their diversity and slipperiness. She is a photographer we cannot neatly classify, and one whose vision we would be foolish to ignore.

Notes

1. This chapter was originally published in *Visual Sexuality: Only Half the Picture*, edited by Zanele Muholi (Michael Stevenson and STE Publishers, 2006). Reprinted with permission.
2. Some of Zanele Muholi's photographs, including the ones analysed in this chapter, are available at: http://www.michaelstevenson.com/contemporary/artists/muholi.htm, accessed 18 January 2011.

References

Anzaldua, Gloria (1987) *Borderlands/La Frontera*, San Francisco, Aunt Lute

Arac de Nyeko, Monica (2004) 'Language, popular culture and the arts', in Gray, R., Koyana, S. and Noome, I. (eds) *Mother Tongue, Other Tongue: Proceedings of the English Academy Conference*, Pretoria, University of Pretoria Press

—— (2005) 'Ugandan monologues', *Agenda* 63: 100–103

Baderoon, G. (2005) *The Dream in the Next Body*, Cape Town, Kwela/Snailpress

Distiller, Natasha (2005) 'Another story: the (im)possibility of lesbian desire', *Agenda* 63: 44–57

Godana, Nonkululeko (2004) 'Is anybody comfortable?', *This Day*, 6 September

Gqola, Pumla Dineo (2001) 'Ufanele uqavile: Blackwomen, feminisms and postcoloniality in Africa', *Agenda* 50: 11–22

hooks, bell (1994) *Outlaw Culture: Resisting Representations*, New York, Routledge

Isaack, Wendy (2003) 'A state of emergency: hate crimes against black lesbians', http://www.equality.org.za, accessed 5 September 2005

Lewis, Desiree (2005) 'Against the grain: black women and sexuality', *Agenda* 63: 11–24

Masinga, Nkululeko (2005) 'Women of substance', *Agenda* 63: 58–59

Molobi, Timothy (2005) 'Banyana captain hits out at Ledwaba', *City Press*, 13 March

Muholi, Z. (ed) (2006) *Visual Sexuality: Only Half the Picture*, Cape Town, Michael Stevenson Gallery and STE Publishers

Ndlovu, Nosimilo (2006) 'Out in the media? Knowledge, attitudes and practices of the media towards lesbian, gay, bisexual, transgender and intersex issues and stories', Gay and Lesbian Archives of South Africa (GALA), http://www.gala.co.za/pdf/OutInTheMediaFinalReport.pdf, accessed 20 April 2009

Reddy, Vasu (2005) 'Sexuality in Africa: some trends, transgressions and tirades', *Agenda* 62: 3–11

Smith, Gail (2004) 'Outlaw culture', *Mail and Guardian*, 3–9 September

65

A radical technique to teach sexual rights

Dorothy Aken'ova

The International Centre for Sexual and Reproductive Rights (INCRESE) is based in the state of Niger, Nigeria. As part of our sexual education work to the public, we use the poster shown in Figure 65.1 to facilitate dialogue on the diverse forms of infringements of rights that women experience. We also use the poster to moderate dialogue in rural communities in Niger state.

Feelings generated by the image

Most people are disgusted by the poster on their first encounter with it. They argue that the image reduces women to being viewed as a vulva and not a whole human being. Shame, distress and anger are the most common feelings that female participants express when they first see the image and reflect upon what that means to a woman. Male participants on the other hand express anger, disgust, embarrassment and guilt.

Who is responsible?

Participants are asked to state whom they think the hands in the poster belong to. The list is long:

Politicians: for using and dumping women. They get women to campaign for them, vote for them, but never cater for women's needs once they get to power. They fail to appoint qualified women into political offices. And when they travel on campaigns or on political assignments, they use young vulnerable girls/women for entertainment, including sexually.

Policymakers: for failing to put structures in place to protect women from abuse, such as legal provisions, policies and services. They allocate meagre amounts in budgets for women's needs, and disburse even much less when it is time to implement the projects.

Tradition: founded on patriarchal values, tradition gives women lower status and prohibits them from enjoying full, equal participation in decision making at all levels, denies them equal access to resources, opportunities and rewards, and denies them control even over their own bodies.

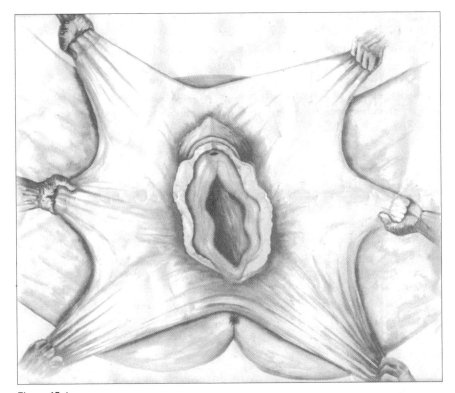

Figure 65.1

Religious institutions: like tradition, these are driven by patriarchal values and give women a much lower status than men. It denies them equal and full participation and in most cases denies them leadership positions even where they are the majority in an organisation. They are vilified and considered the source and root cause of sin. Even when men commit sin, women are blamed and punished for it.

Institutions of learning: teaching materials (until recently) passed on information that reinforced gender stereotypes. Certain aspects of education were exclusive to men, believing erroneously that women did not need education or much of it because their place was in the kitchen. Institutional policies also did little or nothing to protect women from sexual harassment and rape by teachers and other students. Despite policies in place to protect women and girls from such threats, implementation was a problem.

Men: a lot of discrimination against women is in favour of men, who enjoy many privileges and do little or nothing to change the status quo. In many instances, men blame the victims so that they can get away unpunished.

Parents: it is their responsibility to ensure that children are socialised on the basis of equality. Unfortunately, this is not the case. The parental institution is used by the powers-that-be to perpetuate the patriarchal agenda. Most families are not safe for the girl child because many abuses are perpetrated in that setting. Very often incest, molestation and exploitation take place in the home.

Health care providers: they mystify and pathologise the health of women and girls to the point of losing the sociocultural realities that impact adversely on women's health. Most providers do not educate women on what is happening to and within their bodies and do not explain even the simplest procedures to women. This denies women ownership and control of their bodies and their lives.

Media: they always portray women as sex objects, sensationalising news concerning the violation of women's rights, especially news concerning rape. Media messages further entrench patriarchy instead of challenging it.

It works!

The sessions are always wrapped up with a presentation on sexual rights and what the provisions mean to women.

Once the discussion has taken place, participants are generally more relaxed about the poster. The feedback from diverse audiences reveals that people are used to seeing posters of the vulva with a baby's head coming out during the third stage of labour, or even images of the vulva showing some sexually transmitted infections like genital warts, but are not conversant with images of the vulva depicting rights.

It only takes a few minutes of discussion for the critics of the poster to change their views.

66

Laabaan song[1]

Marame Gueye

In traditional Wolof society (Senegal), the virginity of a bride is very important. A ceremony called *laabaan* is performed the day after the couple consummates the marriage in order to celebrate the purity of the young woman and show that she remained pure until matrimony. During this ceremony women gather and perform songs that are sexually loaded and that serve as a way of welcoming the bride into womanhood and give her sexual tips. This ceremony is exclusively attended by women who are married, divorced or widowed.

This *laabaan* song was performed by two griottes, Amy Thiam and Khady, in my apartment in Dakar in 1997. The original text was in Wolof and the English translation is mine. It is often performed at the beginning of the *laabaan* ceremony. After the bride is given a ritual bath, she is brought into a room where she will lay on a bed surrounded by her paternal aunt, her cousins and friends. The griottes then start the *laabaan*, accompanied by drummers who are the only men present.

It could be said that this song is some kind of a hymn to the hymen/vagina because it represents it as something extremely valuable and pivotal to the success of marriage. The hymen is represented as capital that allows a woman to gain material wealth and respect from her in-laws and community as a whole.

The language of the song is also worthy of attention because it demonstrates that griottes are verbal artists with impressive linguistic skills.

Although *laabaan* ceremonies are rare in Senegal today, they are still performed, especially in rural areas.

1

Bissimilahi
Bassine[2]
Let me start with peace
On daughter who honoured her mother.
Ataayatulay
Zaakiyaatu
Salawaatuli lay[3]
On the hymen.

2

This hymen comes from the vagina,
A penis went to get it last night.
Gin saakin delwaar
Sa gin saak
Sa wurama jiifi jaafaa
Wassi wassi jay.[4]

3

Dear hymen,
I have not seen you for a long time,
I had missed you so much.
Going to school does not spoil the
hymen because the hymen is neither pen
nor ink
One does not write with it.

4

Virginity is a card game.
When you play and lose
Whomever you accuse, will refuse.

5

The necklace, where is the necklace?
The necklace your grandmother wore
Took off, and gave your mother,
You are wearing it today.

6

Men are not stupid.
Men's mothers are not stupid.
If a girl is serious, they will marry her
If a girl is not serious, they sleep with
her and leave her to be a burden to her
mother.

7

My daughter was born with underwear
She took it off last night. Tell me where
you bred her so she could escape men
for me to go breed there, whoever has a
daughter should entrust her with you.

8

The chicken gave me a message
And I must deliver it all.
It says that it is not worried
And none of her relatives is afraid,
It is not dead
And none of her relatives is dead.

9

There is a vagina among vaginas,
One buys it with fifty thousands CFA,
A watch and a radio
A television and a jewellery box
But there is a vagina among the vaginas
Its price is only a bottle of beer.
I prefer a silent vagina to a vagina that
honks like a car.

10

Vagina, vagina, vagina, vagina!
Its name is not vagina, it is honour
Whoever spoils it does not know it
A beautiful house
From the vagina!
A box of jewels
From the vagina!
A television
From the vagina!
Honouring your mother
From the vagina!
Honouring your paternal aunts
From the vagina!
Honouring your friends
From the vagina!
Honouring yourself
From the vagina!
Vagina, vagina, vagina, vagina!
Its name is not vagina, it is honour
Whoever spoils it does not know it.

11

The hymen is not much
If you want to live off it
And feed your mother from it
There will be nothing left of it.

12

Only a mother can dance the happiness
of her daughter since she is the one who
worked hard for it. Virginity is a
wrestling game, mothers are the
cheerleaders, daughters play it
Virginity is a wrestling game.

13

My daughter has done her laundry she is
clean. I have the leftovers of the soap
You have done your share, you are
innocent. The path your grandmother
took, your mother took,
You have taken
May adulthood bring you luck.

Notes

1. Translated from Wolof by the author.
2. Phrase from a verse of the Qu'ran recited at the start of an activity to ask God's guidance and blessing.
3. This is usually said at the end of a prayer to call upon Allah's blessings.
4. An animist incantation used to cast away bad spirits.

Questions for reflection

1.

How do factors, such as culture, religion and the way
we are brought up, affect the ways we approach sexuality?
Why is there a need to revisit and rethink our views on
sexuality? Consider what steps can be taken to break the
barriers that affect students and lecturers in talking about
sexuality in your institution and discuss them with your
lecturer in class.

2.

You live in an African country and find yourself teaching
a course on sexualities in a tertiary institution. In what ways
will you utilise available technology in your teaching?

3.

What are your thoughts about the feminist classroom
discussed in this part? How helpful is the concept for creating
a safe and comfortable climate for teaching about sexualities
in the African context?

4.

What pedagogical methods, content knowledge
and interpretive tools might be useful for teaching sexuality
effectively? Which techniques will encourage students to
question and challenge dominant sexuality discourses and
stereotypes? Are there pedagogical implications for male
and female learners?

5.

What pedagogical language(s) and literacy strategies should
we employ in teaching sexuality in Africa?

# Glossary[1]

asexual	Not experiencing sexual attraction or erotic feelings.
beastiality	The practice of humans having sex with animals.
bodily integrity	A concept that attempts to capture the complex dimensions of one's interest in one's body and the right to determine freely and responsibly what to do with it. It incorporates the principles of respect, privacy and human dignity.
bisexual	Being sexually attracted to both men and women.
butch	A term to describe a person who assumes stereotypical masculine traits, behaviour and appearance. It is usually used to describe lesbians and/or gay men.
cisgender	A person whose gender identity matches what is typically associated with their biological sex. It is the opposite of transgender.
clitoridectomy	A type of female genital mutilation that involves the partial or full removal of the clitoris.
corporeality	Relates to the notion of embodiment or the lived bodily experience. The human physical existence in the body (as opposed to the spiritual experience).
discursive	Refers to how knowledge is constructed through the spoken and written word; the imposition of meaning through discourse.
epistemology	The theory of knowledge or ways of knowing. Addresses basic (and highly political) questions, such as: what is knowledge? How do we know what we know? How do we know the 'truth'?
essentialise	Reduce people's experiences, identities, forms of domination to a fixed, generalised, essential form and ignoring the complex differences among social categories.
excision	A type of female genital mutilation that involves the removal of the clitoris and the labia minora (inner lips of the vulva).
exogamy	The customary practice that requires one to marry outside one's social group, family, clan or ethnic group.

feminist	A person who believes that women and men are of equal worth and acts to challenge and/or eliminate gender inequality.
femme	Term used to describe a person who assumes stereotypical feminine traits, behaviour and appearance. It is usually used to describe lesbians and/or gay men.
fetishisation	The process of transforming the ordinary (for example, people, things, ideas) into a fantasised and desired (usually sexual) commodity.
fistula	An injury in the birth canal that allows leakage from the bladder or rectum into the vagina leaving a woman permanently incontinent, often leading to isolation and exclusion from the family and community.
hegemony	The processes by which dominant cultures maintain their dominance, for example, through institutionalisation, the law, punishment, religion, culture, education and the media.
heterogeneity	Diversity of character or content.
heteronormativity	The sociocultural system that assumes the existence of only two sexes/genders and views human sexual relations between a man and a woman as being natural and normal, with no other possibilities.
heterosexuality	Sexual orientation or relations between individuals of the opposite sex.
homophobia	The irrational fear and hatred of homosexuals.
homosexuality	Sexual orientation or relations between individuals of the same sex.
infibulation	A type of female genital mutilation that involves the removal of the clitoris, labia minora and part of the labia majora (outer lips of the vulva), which are then stitched together, leaving a small passage for urine and menstrual flow.
intersexual	An individual who is born with ambiguous genitalia and/ or atypical chromosomal make-up, sometimes referred to derogatively as hermaphrodite.
maternal morbidity	Serious disease, disability or physical damage, such as fistula, resulting from pregnancy-related complications.
maternal mortality	The death of women while pregnant or within 42 days of termination of pregnancy, irrespective of the duration and the site of the pregnancy, from any cause related to the pregnancy or its management.

miscegenation	Sexual relations or reproduction involving persons of different races.
mysogyny	The irrational hatred of women.
ontology	Concerns the philosophical study of 'what is' or the nature of things.
othering	The political process that involves the stigmatisation and marginalisation of disempowered groups (such as people with disabilities, people of colour, the poor, women, people living with HIV/AIDS and homosexuals) by dominant social groups.
patriarchy	Social organisation and systems based on male domination at all institutional levels from the family to the state.
patrilineal	A socio-economic system in which ancestral descent and inheritance follow the paternal line.
phallocentric	Penis- or male-centred.
polyandry	The practice of a woman marrying two or more husbands.
polygamy	The practice of an individual taking on multiple spouses.
polygyny	The practice of a man marrying two or more wives.
queer	A term that captures the fluidity of sex, gender and sexuality. It is loosely used to describe non-heterosexual people and those whose gender identities do not conform to mainstream cultural models.
reification	Treating an abstract notion as if it were real and concrete.
sexual identity	The way you view yourself sexually and how you express that to others.
sexual orientation	Refers to a person's actual or perceived preference for a sexual partner(s), that is, heterosexual, homosexual or bisexual.
somatic	To do with the body; bodily experience.
subversion	The covert resistance and/or undermining of established norms, ideals, power and authority.
transformation	Qualitative change from one state to a better one.
transgender (or trans)	A person whose gender identity does not match that which is typically associated with their biological sex.

transgressive sexualities	Sexual acts that are seen to defy or violate culturally accepted norms and are described as immoral, defiling and even unnatural.
transphobia	The irrational fear and hatred of transgendered people.
valorisation	The sociopolitical enhancement of value and worth for purposes of validation.

Note

1. It is important to note that the terms and concepts in this glossary originate and have evolved from experiences outside Africa. Although they generally carry similar meanings for African sexualities, their nuanced application and relevance to the continental experiences might not necessarily mirror those of their original contexts. Indeed, sexualities are in a constant state of flux and redefinition such that symbols and meanings are themselves never constant or fixed.

Index

Information in notes is indexed as 123n4, i.e. note 4 on page 123.

Confronting Female Genital Mutilation: The Role of Youth and ICTs in Changing Africa

Marie-Hélène Mottin-Sylla and Joëlle Palmieri

2011
paperback £14.95
978-0-85749-031-5

In this age of the internet, beliefs and practices are shifting. Female genital mutilation (FGM), no longer just the private concern of women, is a social and political issue that concerns both men and women. The task of abolishing FGM in Africa and constructing a tradition worthy of being passed on must include young people – whose way of living in this world is by moving to and fro between the local and the global.

A project among girls and boys in West Africa, to explore the contribution of information and communication technologies (ICTs) to the giving up of FGM, shows how putting young people and gender at the centre of development can produce real change.

My Dream is to be Bold: Our Work to End Patriarchy

Feminist Alternatives

2011
paperback £16.95
978-1-906387-91-4

For everyone in South Africa the post-1994 period was one of hope. Women's struggles and organising efforts within and outside the anti-apartheid movement have meant that women now occupy positions of power but capitalist patriarchy is still intact and gross inequalities continue to divide and haunt women.

From differing vantage points within struggle, 19 South African activists offer a critique of women's position in South Africa today with practical examples of women and men working to eliminate a mindset that limits everyone.

This book offers a unique insight into the lives and thinking of those who bring a feminist perspective to the struggles of the organisations they work within.

African Women Writing Resistance
An Anthology of Contemporary Voices

Edited by Jennifer Browdy de Hernandez,
Pauline Dongala, Omotayo Jolaosho and Anne Serafin

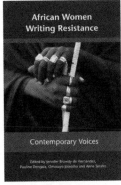

2011
paperback £16.95
978-0-85749-020-9

Confronting entrenched social inequality, women across Africa work with determination and imagination to improve conditions and to blaze a clear path for their daughters. The African-born contributors to this book, including Nobel laureate Wangari Maathai and renowned writer and activist Nawal El Saadawi, present their experiences of resistance with eloquence and strength.

They illuminate such issues as women's poverty and lack of access to education, health care, credit, and political power; female genital cutting; armed conflict and rape as a weapon of war; displacement and exile; resistant sexualities; intergenerational conflict and tensions between tradition and modernity.

'Deeply personal and accessible [this book] is a timely contribution, capturing a diverse range of responses to the struggles of African women today.'

Carol Boyce Davies, Cornell University

Order your copy from www.pambazukapress.org

Women and Security Governance in Africa

Edited by 'Funmi Olonisakin and Awino Okech

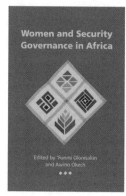

2011
paperback £16.95
978-1-906387-89-1

When the path-breaking United Nations Resolution 1325 on women, peace and security was adopted in 2000, it was the first time that the security concerns of women in situations of armed conflict and their role in peace building were placed on the agenda of the UN Security Council.

In the field of international security, discussions on women and children are often relegated to the margins. This book addresses a broader debate on security and its governance in a variety of contexts while making the argument that the single most important measure of the effectiveness of security governance is its impact on women. But this is more than a book about women. Rather it is a book about inclusive human security for Africans, which cannot ignore the central place of women.

'In the first volume of its kind, some of the best and most engaging African intellectuals and activists have gathered to expose the fallacies of the current security paradigm to show how "security for women" must entail, at least in large part, "security by women".'

Professor Eboe Hutchful, chair of the African Security Network

'We need fresh perspectives and new ways of visioning governance in Africa so that women's security becomes an intrinsic measure of development and peace. This important collection of insights from across the continent leads the way.'

Winnie Byanyima, director of UNDP Gender Team

Order your copy from www.pambazukapress.org

No Land! No House! No Vote!
Voices from Symphony Way

Written and edited by the Symphony Way
pavement dwellers

2011
paperback £16.95
978-1-906387-84-6

In 2007 hundreds of Cape Town families living in shacks were moved into houses they had been waiting for since the end of apartheid. But soon they were told that the move had been illegal and they were evicted. They built shacks by the road opposite the housing project and organised themselves into the Symphony Way Anti-Eviction Campaign, vowing to stay until the government gave them permanent housing.

Written toward the end of the struggle on the pavements, this anthology is both testimony and poetry, telling of justice miscarried, violence and xenophobia. But amid the horror is beauty. This book is a means to dignity, a way for the poor to reflect and be reflected. It is testimony that in the shacks are people who talk, think, and fight to bring about change.

'A compelling testimony.'
Issa Shivji, Mwalimu Nyerere Professor of Pan-African Studies, University of Dar es Salaam

'A magnificent and moving account … a powerful insider's view into the landscape of poverty in neoliberal South Africa.'
Michael Watts, Class of 63 professor of geography and development studies, University of California, Berkeley

'As middle-class African journalists and activists, we thought we were telling the tale of the poorest, but here we are surpassed. Their truths, spoken in their sharp vernacular tongue, fly straight to the heart of the matter.'
Michael Schmidt, journalist and author

 Order your copy from www.pambazukapress.org

SMS Uprising: Mobile Activism in Africa

Edited by Sokari Ekine

SMS Uprising brings together some of the best-known and experienced developers and users of mobile phone technologies in Africa to provide a unique insight into how activists and social change advocates are using these technologies to facilitate change and address Africa's many challenges from within. These essays examine issues of inequality in access to mobile technologies and provide an overview of lessons learned without any of the romanticism so often associated with the use of new technologies for social change.

2010
paperback £12.95
978-1-906387-35-8

'This is a handbook for the small NGO or social change activist who is daunted by technology. Help is at hand, and *SMS Uprising* will help you find it.'

The Guardian